aspects of

MODERN SWEDISH LITERATURE

Some other books from Norvik Press

P C Jersild: *A Living Soul* (translated by Rika Lesser)
Sara Lidman: *Naboth's Stone* (translated by Joan Tate)
Selma Lagerlöf: *The Löwensköld Ring* (translated by Linda Schenck)
Villy Sørensen: *Harmless Tales* (translated by Paula Hostrup-Jessen)
Camilla Collett: *The District Governor's Daughters* (translated by Kirsten Seaver)
Jens Bjørneboe: *The Sharks* (translated by Esther Greenleaf Mürer)
Jørgen-Frantz Jacobsen: *Barbara* (translated by George Johnston)
Janet Garton & Henning Sehmsdorf (eds. and trans.): *New Norwegian Plays* (by Peder W.Cappelen, Edvard Hoem, Cecilie Løveid and Bjørg Vik)
Gunilla Anderman (ed.): *New Swedish Plays* (by Ingmar Bergman, Stig Larsson, Lars Norén and Agneta Pleijel)
Kjell Askildsen: *A Sudden Liberating Thought* (translated by Sverre Lyngstad)
Svend Åge Madsen: *Days with Diam* (translated by W. Glyn Jones)
Christopher Moseley (ed.): *From Baltic Shores*
Janet Garton (ed.): *Contemporary Norwegian Women's Writing*
Fredrika Bremer: *The Colonel's Family* (translated by Sarah Death)
Hans Christian Andersen (ed.): *New Danish Plays* (by Sven Holm, Kaj Nissen, Astrid Saalbach and Jess Ørnsbo)
Suzanne Brøgger: *A Fighting Pig's Too Tough to Eat* (translated by Marina Allemano)
Kerstin Ekman: *Witches' Rings* (translated by Linda Schenck)
Gunnar Ekelöf: *Modus Vivendi* (edited and translated by Erik Thygesen)
Robin Fulton (ed. and transl.): *Five Swedish Poets*
Michael Robinson: *Strindberg and Autobiography*
James McFarlane: *Ibsen and Meaning*
Robin Young: *Time's Disinherited Children*
Knut Hamsun: *Selected Letters*, Vols. I and II (ed. and trans. by Harald Næss and James McFarlane
Michael Robinson (ed.): *Strindberg and Genre*
A Century of Swedish Narrative (ed. Sarah Death and Helena Forsås Scott)
Michael Robinson: *Studies in Strindberg*

The logo of Norvik Press is based on a drawing by Egil Bakka (University of Bergen) of a Viking ornament in gold, paper thin, with impressed figures (size 16x21mm). It was found in 1897 at Hauge, Klepp, Rogaland, and is now in the collection of the Historisk museum, University of Bergen (inv.no. 5392). It depicts a love scene, possibly (according to Magnus Olsen) between the fertility god Freyr and the maiden Gerðr; the large penannular brooch of the man's cloak dates the work as being most likely 10th century.

Cover illustration: Kathleen McFarlane

aspects of

MODERN SWEDISH LITERATURE

Second revised and augmented edition

EDITED BY IRENE SCOBBIE

Norvik Press
1999

Selection and editorial material © 1999 Irene Scobbie.
Individual chapters and sections © 1999 Ulla Callmander, Sarah Death, Inga-Stina Ewbank, Tom Geddes, Peter Graves, Brita Green, Phil Holmes, C.J.Lawton, Gavin Orton, Karin Petherick, Irene Scobbie, Neil Smith, Steven Sondrup, Birgitta Thompson, Laurie Thompson, Charlotte Whittingham.

A catalogue record for this book is available from the British Library.

ISBN 1 870041 38 0

First edition published 1988 by Norvik Press.
Second (revised and augmented) edition published 1999 by Norvik Press, University of East Anglia, Norwich NR4 7TJ, England.

Managing Editors: James McFarlane, Janet Garton and Michael Robinson.

Norvik Press was established in 1984 with financial support from the University of East Anglia, the Danish Ministry for Cultural Affairs, the Norwegian Cultural Department and the Swedish Institute.

Printed in Great Britain by Page Bros. (Norwich) Ltd, Norwich, UK.

Contents

Preface
7

Notes on Contributors
8

Chapter One
Åttitalister (Writers of the 1880s)
9

Chapter Two
August Strindberg
31

Chapter Three
Nittitalister (Writers of the 1890s)
74

Chapter Four
Swedish Fin-de-Siècle: Hjalmar Söderberg
108

Chapter Five
Tiotalister (Writers of the 1910s) and Hjalmar Bergman
137

Chapter Six
Pär Lagerkvist
162

Chapter Seven
Swedish Poetry of the Twentieth Century
187

Chapter Eight
Three Novelists of the 1930s
263

Chapter Nine
**Stig Dagerman and *fyrtiotalismen*:
Writing of the 1940s**
303

Chapter Ten
Twelve Modern Novelists
325

Notes and Bibliographies
407
Select List of Translations
457

Index
470

Preface

This volume has its origins in a Conference of University Teachers of Scandinavian Studies held over twenty years ago. We all had our own 'fields' and enthusiasms, and wanted to share some of them.

The immediate result was *Essays in Swedish Literature from 1880 to the Present Day* (Aberdeen University, 1978). These proved useful mainly to students of Swedish at English-speaking universities, but we were then asked to adapt the volume so that readers without a knowledge of Swedish could also benefit. All prose quotations were given in English translation, verse was quoted in the original but supplied with an English paraphrase, and a select list of English translations of Swedish publications was appended. The result was *Aspects of Modern Swedish Literature*, published in 1988 by Norvik Press. That edition is now out of print, and in preparing this new one we have taken the opportunity of updating much of the material, especially the chapter on Swedish poetry of the 20th century and the final chapter on the Swedish novel.

We have been careful, however, to retain the word *Aspects* in the title, for, true to its origins, each chapter reflects the contributor's(s') chosen author(s) and method of presentation. The first chapter, for example, traces the historical and social background of the 1880s, while the second deals with the quintessential Strindberg. The author of Chapter Three presents the writers of the 1890s by following important themes common to the four outstanding representatives of that period, while other contributors, as in the case of Pär Lagerkvist and Stig Dagerman, for instance, have preferred to select an author's most representative works and treat them in more detail.

Although they do not constitute an encyclopaedic history of literature, the chapters are arranged in chronological order and highlight many of the important trends or works in Swedish literature from 1880 onwards. We hope that, like its predecessor, this edition will prove useful both to students of Swedish and to the more general reader.

CORBRIDGE, 1998.   IRENE SCOBBIE

List of Contributors

Ulla Callmander was Swedish lektor in the Department of Scandinavian Studies, University of Aberdeen for three years. She now works in Adult Education in Gothenburg.

Dr Sarah Death is a freelance translator and writer, and an Honorary Research Fellow at University College, London.

Professor Inga-Stina Ewbank is Emeritus Professor of English at the University of Leeds.

Tom Geddes, formerly Head of the Scandinavian Section of the British Library, London, is now a free-lance literary translator.

Dr Brita Green taught Swedish at York University until recently.

Peter Graves is Senior Lecturer and Head of the Department of Scandinavian Studies, Edinburgh University.

Dr Phil Holmes is Reader and Director of Studies, Department of Scandinavian Studies, The University of Hull.

Dr C. J. Lawton wrote his doctoral thesis on Birger Sjöberg. He is currently a Financial Management Consultant.

Gavin Orton is a former Lecturer in Scandinavian Studies at the University of Hull.

Dr Karin Petherick was Reader in Swedish at University College, London. After retirement she is presently occupied with Strindberg, Selma Lagerlöf and Hjalmar Bergman.

Irene Scobbie was Reader and Head of Department of Scandinavian Studies, University of Edinburgh. She is currently Review Editor of the *Swedish Book Review*.

Neil Smith is a graduate of University College, London, where he studied Scandinavian Studies. He is currently a freelance translator.

Professor Steven P. Sondrup is Professor of Comparative Literature, Brigham Young University, Provo, Utah, and Editor of *Scandinavian Studies*.

Birgitta Thompson is Head of Swedish in the School of Modern Languages, St David's University College, Lampeter, Wales.

Dr Laurie Thompson was Senior Lecturer in Swedish, St David's University College, Lampeter, Wales. He is now a freelance translator and also Editor of the *Swedish Book Review*.

Dr Charlotte Whittingham is Lecturer in Scandinavian Studies at the University of Hull.

Chapter I

Åttitalister
'Writers of the 1880s'

Irene Scobbie and Birgitta Thompson

In looking for a fixed point of reference to mark the beginning of modern Swedish literature literary historians are drawn to 1871 and 1879, the year in which Georg Brandes began his lectures in Copenhagen on *Hovedstrømninger i det nittende Aarhundredes Litteratur* (Mainstreams in Nineteenth Century Literature) and the publication date of Strindberg's *Röda rummet* (The Red Room) respectively.

By European standards both dates are late, for by the 1870s intellectual life and thought in other European cultural centres had undergone great changes, already being reflected in major literary works. By the mid-nineteenth century philosophers and writers were turning away from metaphysical speculation and were beginning to emulate the more practical methods used by the natural scientists.

Developments in the biological sciences particularly affected philosophy and literature, and here one of the most far-reaching changes was brought about by Darwin's *Origin of Species by means of Natural Selection* (1859), which proved that Man has evolved from a lower species of animal and that in nature a continual struggle for existence leads to the survival of the fittest. *The Descent of Man* (1871) reinforced the argument. Darwin's work caused a great furore, proving as it did that the *Book of Genesis* could not be taken literally, but whatever attitudes were adopted towards it, it forced upon the thinking world a reappraisal of the human condition. Unlike the Romantics, writers could no longer eulogize Man's divine spark but must accept Man as one of the higher animals.

Christian dogma was under threat from other directions too, and the Bible was subjected to close analytical scrutiny. Ernest Renan in *L'Avenir de la science* (1849) found the 'real' world superior to the fantasies of the Creation. In Sweden Viktor Rydberg's *Bibelns lära om Kristus* (The Bible's Teachings on Christ) (1862) was critical of the dogma of the Church, maintaining that the Trinity and the divinity of Christ have no foundation in biblical texts and should be omitted, while in the following year Renan published a rationalistic biography of Jesus where he denied the possibility of miracles.

In philosophy Positivism was first expounded by Auguste Comte, who believed that Man would progress through theology and metaphysics on to the scientific stage of positive thought. Comte believed that all phenomena are subject to immutable natural laws and that all the efforts of the positive philosopher should be directed towards the discovery and systematization of those laws.

Once Darwinism was accepted, heredity seemed increasingly important. The French philosopher Hippolyte Taine, influenced by Comte's positivistic thesis and by Darwinism, presented in his introduction to *L'Histoire de la littérature anglaise* (1863-64) what he himself called a naturalistic theory. Given three factors, 'race' (meaning racial characteristics), 'milieu' (embracing climatic, physical and spiritual conditions) and 'moment' (a specific moment in history when 'race' and 'milieu' fuse), a cultural event becomes a problem in mechanics.

Claude Bernard meanwhile was attempting to make medicine a scientific discipline dependent on careful observation and deduction. In his *Introduction à l'étude de la médecine expérimentale* he advocated the use of scientific methods being applied in other fields.

In his work *De l'Intelligence* (1870) Taine again combined the arts with science when he tried to prove that a human character is not a unity or single element but a combination of many traits organized in such a way that one quality emerges as being more dominant than the others. According to Taine one could therefore examine a character as though under a microscope, analysing and categorizing. Strindberg's Miss Julie and Johan, his *alter ego* in *Tjänstekvinnans son* (The Son of a Servant) show Taine's influence very clearly.

In his *History of Civilization in England* (1857-61) the English historian Henry Thomas Buckle maintained that culture arises from certain geographical conditions and that its development is dictated by certain natural laws. Like Comte and Taine, Buckle saw hope for the future in the understanding of those laws, which would automatically free Man from superstitions and religious illusions. He is aware that a 'truth' will only be temporary, changing as new discoveries are made on the road to progress. (Strindberg's *Mäster Olof* owes much to Buckle's ideas on the relativity of truth).

With all its optimistic emphasis on progress there is also, nevertheless, a strain of pessimism running though the second half of the nineteenth century. The philosophies of Schopenhauer and Hartmann took the initiative from Man and posited a belief in a blind force which controls our destinies. This deterministic view did not necessarily contradict the scientific knowledge being so assiduously assembled. Man was a product of his heredity and his environment; he had no control over the former and very little over the latter. If there was no God to intercede for the individual what then could he do but accept his fate? This attitude, when assumed by the disillusioned generation whose childhood coincided with the Dano-Prussian War became the dominating trend in Scandinavia towards the end of the century. When optimists ultimately refused to accept it they were also obliged to modify their rationalistic approach to life. It was at this point that Nietzsche's belief in the *Übermensch* won adherents, for it seemed to offer an acceptable alternative to determinism.

Far-reaching changes were taking place in the social and political fields. The Industrial Revolution affected almost every aspect of life in the Western world as it gathered momentum in the second half of the nineteenth century. There was an excitement about Man's new inventive skills in harnessing sources of power in gas and electricity and in improving transport and communications through the railways, steamships, Morse telegraph, a submarine cable and the penny post. Great opportunities were there to be exploited, and in this period of energy and enterprise there seemed no limit to what human ingenuity could achieve.

It was also, however, a period when human and natural resources were ruthlessly exploited. Cheap labour was needed for new factories and mines, and the rapidly growing industrial towns had their slum districts where living and working conditions were appalling. The incredible industrial and material progress of the period was accompanied by increasing social deprivation and political unrest. In

Chapter 1

1848, the year the Communist Manifesto was completed, there was a wave of revolutions throughout Europe, and although various risings were put down with severity the motivating liberal ideas persisted. By the 1850s and 1860s increasingly strong liberal groups in Scandinavia and elsewhere included among their aims universal suffrage, reform of the legal code, freedom of the press and of religious practice.

Workers were beginning to unite. With the rise of industrialism there was now a sharp division between the capitalists and the workers, who were often living at starvation level. The latter were the people who would most obviously respond to the work of Karl Marx and the radicals. Marx's *Das Kapital* appeared in 1867; Lassalle in Germany helped form a workers' party in 1863. The following year saw the foundation of the International Working Men's Association.

John Stuart Mill's writings fuse liberal aims of the period with the positivistic approach of his contemporaries, and he attempts to form a doctrine of ethics not based on Christianity or metaphysics. In *Utilitarianism* (1863) he posits the belief that a deed is right in proportion to the happiness it spreads. Happiness of society as a whole is a pre-requisite for individual happiness, and in striving for personal happiness an individual must work for the good of society. Mill's utilitarianism implied, therefore, an altruism and a morality which extended to embrace politics and social problems. He worked for a truly democratic society which included the emancipation of women. Scandinavian suffragettes derived much support from his *Subjection of Women* (1869).

Realism in European literature increased as materialistic attitudes spread. There seemed also to be a correlation between the rise of the middle classes and the increasing popularity of the novel. The novels of Dickens, Balzac and Turgenev were read aloud in well-ordered homes all over Europe. As writers became more influenced by scientific methods Realism was superseded by Naturalism. The Naturalistic writers were more inclined to concentrate on social environment, usually stressing the flaws in human nature and society. Paradoxically, although they emphasized their role as objective observers their work tended to be subjective in its indignation at social injustices and its wish to reform society.

The brothers Goncourt in their preface to *Germinie Lacerteux* (1865) exhorted novelists to make their works a sociological inquiry *(l'enquête sociale)* and by analysis and psychological investigation to become scientists and the moral historians of the period. This Naturalistic approach was subsumed in Zola's theory of the experimental novel, for which Claude Bernard's *Introduction à l'étude de la médecine expérimentale* (1865) and Taine's emphasis on heredity and environment provided the 'scientific' background. In the preface to the second edition of *Thérèse Raquin* Zola called himself a *naturaliste* and his novel 'l'analyse scientifique'. He advocated the eradication of irrational and metaphysical elements in literature. Instead psychological cases should be studied, the subjects' emotional and moral reactions should be traced to their exact causes, understood and so guided into proper channels. Man is part of nature governed by heredity and environment, and free will is an illusion. His characters, Zola maintains, are live anatomical specimens. The soul is absent and they are 'des brutes humains' (human animals).

Zola applied his own theories in his cycle of twenty novels, *Les Rougon-Macquart* (1871-93), 'the natural and social history of a family under the Second Empire'. He became the guiding spirit of Naturalism, attracted a school of French writers, including Maupassant and Huysmans, exercised considerable influence in Germany and Austria (Sudermann, Anzengruber, Hauptmann) and indirectly affected writings by Chekhov and Tolstoy. When Strindberg was trying to launch *Fadren* (The Father), which he considered a Naturalistic play, it seemed important to have the approval of Zola, the Naturalistic accolade.

In Sweden one achievement of a liberal campaign was the Reform Bill of 1865, which abolished the four Estates and introduced a bi-cameral *Riksdag*. This proved to be the end rather than the burgeoning of liberal aspirations for many years, however, for the new electoral system was so beset with safeguards and voting restrictions that the conservative *Lantmannapartiet* (Agrarian Party) was able to gain and retain a solid majority in *Riksdagen* and prevent major social and political reform for a couple of decades. As in the rest of Scandinavia, Christianity was equated with the State Church; the universities were educational institutions providing officials who would preserve the *status quo* in the Church and in government. Society seemed to consist largely of institutions each carefully preserving its own traditions. Strindberg's play *Mäster Olof* was consistently refused for a decade by the Royal Dramatic Theatre for deviating too far in form and content from the idealism and rhetoric of a bygone age; in 1879, the year *Röda rummet* was published, the Swedish Academy welcomed two new members, Nyblom and Wirsén, who saw their duty as writers 'to solve in the light of ideals and the form of beauty those enigmas which again and again arise from the depths of the human heart'.[1] In 1884 Strindberg was indicted for 'mocking the Sacraments', and 1887 Hjalmar Branting was fined for 'denying God and an afterlife or the pure Evangelical doctrine'.

Denmark was the first Scandinavian country to lose its complacency. The Dano-Prussian War (1864) showed humiliatingly that, descended from the Vikings or not, the Danish army was no match for the trained Prussians. It also exposed the hollow rhetoric of the Pan-Scandinavian Movement. After all the junketing and speechifying, when called upon to give practical aid to Denmark the rest of Scandinavia officially offered only sympathy. Ibsen's indignation at this betrayal was expressed bitingly in *Brand* (1866), one of the landmarks in Scandinavian literature. Ibsen's clergyman sought absolute truth and was scathing about comfortable compromises within the Church and society. 'All or nothing' and 'no cowardly compromise!' sounded like a rallying battle cry to the young radicals of the 1870s and 1880s.

On November 3 1871 Georg Brandes gave his first historic lecture. He had already translated Mill's *Subjection of Women* into Danish, his doctoral thesis was on Taine, he had his finger on the European pulse and was only too well aware of the narrow-mindedness of Scandinavian society. Writing in *Illustreret Tidende* he had objected to modern writers emulating the Romantics. The spirit of the times was realistic and pragmatic and should be reflected in literature. Young writers should be indignant at the present situation. They should study not Man, but men being conditioned by the sexual and social morals imposed upon them by society.

In his lectures he launched his attack against the abstract, idealistic trend in Scandinavian literature which had become a sterile discussion on morals. Modern literature that is really alive 'sætter Problemer under Debat' (debates problems).

The 'problems' he had in mind for discussion included marriage, religion and society. Marriage had become a façade concealing vice and deceit. It led to the oppression of women and bolstered a sexual 'dubbelmoral' in society. The State Church had become a negative, even destructive, institution, while theologians had dominated Scandinavian literature for too long. As for society, it had become a conglomeration of laws and customs, mostly antiquated, which were foisted upon the individual. For the individual, society had become a complicated code of prejudices that he had to accept at an early age. What Brandes urged writers to do was to debate society and thus help to reform it.

Norwegian writers were the first to react to Brandes's call. Ibsen had already preceded it with *Brand*, but under Brandes's influence he published such plays as *Samfundets Støtter* (Pillars of Society, 1877) and *Et Dukkehjem* (A Doll's House, 1879), where he took up the question of corruption and hypocrisy in society, and of the restrictions such a society places on the individual, especially married women. Bjørnson too turned from his national romantic themes and in a series of realistic plays and novels dealt with the emancipation of women, religion, the press, commerce, education and morality in society. These issues were taken up by his contemporaries Jonas Lie, Alexander Kielland, Kristian Elster, Arne Garborg, Amalie Skram and Hans Jæger. The latter's *Fra Kristiania-Bohêmen* (From the Christiania Bohème, 1885) so openly advocated sexual and moral freedom that it was confiscated and its author imprisoned. In Denmark several gifted writers responded to Brandes's exhortation. Sophus Schandorph, J.P. Jacobsen, Holger Drachmann, Herman Bang, Karl Gjellerup and Henrik Pontoppidan were described as *Gjennembruds Mænd* (i.e. men of the Modern Breakthrough) and all helped to change the mores of the society they described.

Sweden was slower off the mark and with the exception of Strindberg and Victoria Benedictsson her writers of the period were slightly less endowed. By the 1870s the process that eventually transformed Sweden from a backward agricultural country into a highly industrialized state was underway. The timber, steel and shipbuilding industries grew rapidly, greatly assisted by a vastly improved transport system. With the building of railways and steam ships whole new areas were opened up. Banking and commerce developed to take advantage of the new openings, as did the manufacturing industries, and fortunes were rapidly made, and occasionally as rapidly lost. New industrial methods involved a more concentrated labour force and the beginning of a shift in population from rural to urban areas. Although industrial development came later in Sweden than in Britain and never created the appalling degree of social misery associated with Victorian cities, slums did grow up in the working-class districts of the larger towns, with

Chapter I

starvation, disease, ignorance and drunkenness all too common.

In Sweden as elsewhere workers formed trade unions to help gain better working conditions and a more equitable society. By 1889 the *Socialdemokratiska arbetarpartiet* (Social Democratic Labour Party) was established and in 1898 *Landsorganisationen* (i.e. Trade Union Organization) was formed, with all unions in LO to be affiliated to the Social Democratic Party.

The guardians of what was still a patriarchal society at that time were too inflexible to adapt and it was the young generation that responded to the vital changes taking place around them. A feature of Swedish *Åttital* is the way in which young people of the same generation exchanged social, political and literary views and worked together against the older generation. At Uppsala the radical student association *Verdandi* was formed in 1882 and its founder members included both writers and social reformers. A similar association was set up in 1884 at Lund, called *De unga gubbarne* (lit. The Young Old Boys). Both associations debated social as well as literary subjects.

When a number of young writers formed a literary group in 1882 they were called *Det unga Sverige* (Young Sweden) which again seems to emphasize the generation gap. Gustaf af Geijerstam, Ola Hansson, Tor Hedberg, Oscar Levertin, Axel Lundegård, Strindberg, Ernst Ahlgren (Victoria Benedictsson), and Anna Charlotte Leffler-Edgren were all associated with it. They had very few outlets, for with the exception of the liberal *Dagens Nyheter* and *Göteborgs Handels- och Sjöfarts-Tidning* the press was closed to their radical views. Branting's *Tiden*, a Social Democratic journal, was able to support them, as was the cultural journal *Ur dagens krönika* (1881-91), and Geijerstam edited the annual *1885* and *1886*, described as calendars 'i litterära och sociala frågor'. With so few openings the *åttitalister* trying to live by their pen were under constant financial threat. The lack of a regular well supported journal perhaps partly explains too why *Det unga Sverige* never was a closely integrated literary school. There were other reasons. Strindberg had the stature but was too individualistic to lead any group, Geijerstam was conscientious but lacked the personality and creative talent necessary to inspire his colleagues, while other members were literary light-weights or not committed to *Det unga Sverige*'s radical views long enough to be able to hold the group together.

Strindberg was the first Swedish author to respond to Brandes. His restless inquiring mind had led him to the works of Buckle, Darwin,

Taine and Ibsen, whilst his attempts to establish himself as an author and journalist in Stockholm after a brief, unsuccessful spell as a student at Uppsala gave him first hand experience of an Establishment which had closed its ranks against innovation.

His first important play, *Mäster Olof* (1872), completed less than a year after Brandes's introductory lecture, has an historical setting but the period is the turbulent sixteenth century when the revolutionary Olaus Petri was trying to break the hegemony of the Catholic Church in Sweden. The analogy with contemporary Sweden is obvious. The dominant theme, the relativity of truth and the differing ways in which successive generations view vital issues, owes much to Buckle while pointing to the conflict between generations which became a feature of *Åttitalet*.

The book in which Strindberg first really turned the spotlight on Oscarian society was *Röda rummet* (1879). Few aspects of society escaped Strindberg's attention: the civil service, the press and publishing world, *Riksdagen*, the world of commerce, the theatre, the incipient trade unions, the desperate living conditions and the drunkenness of Stockholm slums and the condescending attitude of those dispensing charity among the poor, those ready to exploit interest in Christian charitable associations — they were all satirized.

The book was written in a buoyant, good-humoured spirit and the characters were sufficiently caricatured not to offend the majority of its readers, and it was well received. In *Det nya riket* (The New Realm, 1882) Strindberg again attacked society, this time showing how hopes engendered by the Reform Bill of 1865 had been misplaced and underlining the deceit and sheer humbug in official life. Since his satire is much more biting than in *Röda rummet* and the real individuals behind the caricatures more easily recognisable, the book aroused much more animosity.

Ever alert to European cultural trends, Strindberg again in *Svenska öden och äventyr* (Swedish Fates and Adventures, published 1882-83) brought out current issues, despite the stories' historical settings. 'Odlad frukt', for instance, illustrates Darwin's theory on the survival of the fittest while commenting indirectly on the unsuitable educational system and on the hypocrisy of contemporary Sweden. 'Högre ändamål' and 'Beskyddare' purport to criticize the medieval attitude to celibacy and the restrictive practices of the guilds but are an effective expression of the author's view on his own moribund society and his strong

Chapter I

opposition to the clergy.

He returned to the question of sexual morals and the Church in 'Dygdens lön' ('The Wages of Virtue'), the first story in *Giftas* I (Married, 1884) and was indicted for blasphemy as if to prove his point. The book constitutes Strindberg's most important contribution to the feminist debate which had centred round Mill's *Subjection of Women*, Ibsen's *Et Dukkehjem* and Bjørnson's *En Hanske* (A Glove) and which emerged as the most important single theme in Scandinavian literature of the 1880s. To be feminist and radical had almost become synonymous by 1884, but in this as in so much else Strindberg differed. The stories in *Giftas* I illustrate the social, economic and emotional problems involved in marriage, and conclude that the causes of the problems are to be sought in the economic and educational defects of society, not in male chauvinism. Although not overtly anti-feminist at this stage, Strindberg's ideal woman is obviously a devoted wife and mother, and even in this part of *Giftas* he objects to over-indulged, under-employed upper-class women. It is perhaps ironic that the Church elected to prosecute this particular work, for at least on the question of marriage it shows Strindberg in a more conservative mood.

There is also a degree of irony in the way *Det unga Sverige* championed Strindberg during his defence and celebrated victory, for they were far from being in agreement with Strindberg's stand on the question of woman's emancipation. This was more obvious when *Giftas* II (1886) appeared, for by then Strindberg was on the way to establishing his reputation as a misogynist. The marriages depicted in the second volume of *Giftas* are mostly abnormal relationships manipulated by cunning, hypocritical wives. The fault no longer lies in society but in the deceitful nature of women who are not only social parasites but have become ambitious for power. The stories make absorbing reading but more as studies in abnormal psychology than as reasoned argument in the feminist discussion.

The views put forward in *Utopier i verkligheten* (Utopias in Reality, 1885) were more in keeping with Swedish radicals, for Strindberg declares his atheism, calls for a more just society and criticizes the present hypocritical system where 'överklassen' exploits 'underklassen' and where useless luxuries are appreciated and honest work denigrated. The work helped the debate along, but in the way Strindberg idealizes the peasant and advocates a return to self-sufficiency he seems to be pointing back towards Rousseau and the eighteenth century rather than towards Marx and collectivism.

In the four major Naturalistic plays written during the 1880s, *Kamraterna* (The Comrades, 1886), *Fadren* (1887), *Fröken Julie* (1888) and *Fordringsägare* (Creditors, 1889), the psychological struggle between man and woman takes precedence over all other issues, and again the women are emancipated and predatory. By this time, however, the feminist question was losing its central place, and the direction of Scandinavian literature was changing.

In their choice of themes and means of presentation the other writers of *Åttitalet* followed where Strindberg, Brandes and the French Naturalistic writers led. Gustaf af Geijerstam (1858-1909) had become involved in radical political and cultural movements when a student at Uppsala, and through his energetic reviews, lectures and editing as well as creative writing he worked probably harder than anyone to spread those views in Sweden. His novels *Erik Grane* (1885) and *Pastor Hallin* (1887) both take up religious and social issues and emphasize the rift between conservative parents and radical children.

Geijerstam's work is of interest to the literary historian but has less intrinsic value. His short stories are on the whole more successful as works of art. He lived with peasants in the Stockholm archipelago in order to study their way of life (the accepted Naturalistic *modus operandi*), and in *Fattigt folk* I and II (Poor People, 1884, 1889) and in the *Kronofogdens berättelser* (The District Attorney's Tales, 1890) included stories based on his observations. The meticulous study of reality with its descriptions of social environment and its effect on character, provides a good example of Naturalistic writing. There is an increasing interest in morbid psychology in Geijerstam's later novels, which gradually led him away from the social awareness of *Åttitalet*. He had also tired of financial and intellectual struggle and by the 1890s was writing popular, rather mawkish stories which assured him of a comfortable income but robbed him of literary significance.

At Uppsala Tor Hedberg (1862-1931) had been persuaded by radical views and his first published story *Högre uppgifter* (Higher Duties, 1884) was written on a familiar theme: an actress who dreams of following her true calling but is channelled into marriage with a rural clergyman which leads to her inevitable development towards intolerance and final degradation. The work contains the almost obligatory criticism of the clergy and a clergyman who becomes a rationalist. Its literary merit, however, lies in the development of the main character (which shows more than a suggestion of Jacobsen's *Marie Grubbe*), and the contrast between the individual's desire for personal freedom and society's restricting conformity. The same interest in the psychological development of the individual within the framework of society is seen in *Johannes Karr* (1885) which bears the subtitle 'En uppkomlingshistoria' (The Story of a Parvenu). As well as the conflict between generations characteristic of the period (two sections bear the title 'Far och son') the work contains an extension of the Naturalistic emphasis on heredity and environment to the point of a criminal action.

Torpa gård (Torpa Farm, 1888) resembles Victoria Benedictsson's *Fru Marianne* (see below) in that it deals with the conflict between a healthy, realistic husband and his wife who has been allowed to dwell too much on fantasy and imagination. It was preceded in 1886, however, by *Judas*, a novel in which Hedberg tries to fathom Judas's motives behind his betrayal of Christ. The theme points forward to *Nittitalet*, with its emphasis on the spiritual aspects of the character. Hedberg was never a committed *genombrottsman* and by the end of the decade had turned to different themes.

With its emphasis on portraying unadorned reality, *Åttitalet* did not offer encouragement to lyric poets. The only notable exception was Ola Hansson (1860-1925) who could be classed as an *åttitalist* strictly speaking for only a brief period. The son of a Skåne farmer, he studied at Lund and then worked on his *Slättbyhistorier* (Slättby Stories: from 1881-83, although not published until 1927) which show the influence of Pontoppidan. His first published work, *Dikter* (Poems, 1884) shows the *åttitalist* trying to free poetry from the idealized, rarefied atmosphere of latter-day romanticism. Hansson knew how hard the peasant's life could be, and in his carefully observed descriptions of rural scenes the Rousseauistic element has been removed. He portrays poverty and misery, and even the jobs on the farm that Strindberg (in *Hemsöborna*, The People of Hemsö) could show as being pleasurable are in Hansson's poems unpleasant drudgery. Hansson was alert too to the inequality of society, and in his poems contrasts effectively the well-heated comfortable home of the established middle-class with the wretched conditions of penniless families freezing in the slums.

By the next year when Hansson published his poems *Notturno* he was already going beyond the bounds of realistic description in an attempt to fuse Man and nature. With *Sensitiva amorosa* (1887), a collection of short stories, even prose poems, the process is taken further. Nature has become a mystic force but in its effect on Man Hansson describes it as being both mystical and physical, spiritual and yet erotic. In strangely disturbing, subtle prose he succeeds in both conveying the emotions evoked in Nature and analysing in almost Naturalistic fashion the sexual urges that are aroused. The moral outcry *Sensitiva amorosa* caused led to Hansson's voluntary exile, but had he remained in Sweden he would hardly have contributed further to the debate associated with *Åttitalet*, for his literary development was obviously in a different direction.

Axel Lundegård (1861-1930) could also be classed as an *åttitalist* for a very brief period only. He was attracted to the radical views debated at Lund where he was a student and he influenced Victoria Benedictsson in that direction when they worked jointly on the play *Final* (1885) and the novel *Modern* (The Mother, 1888). He also helped Strindberg revise his Naturalistic play *Marodörer*, subsequently entitled *Kamraterna* (The Comrades). For a while Lundegård could even 'be considered the epitome of the *Åttital* radical: free from humbug, bold and brutally honest'.[2] His father was a conservative clergyman and the conflict between father and son was clearly marked. The stories in his collections *I gryningen* (Dawn, 1885) often have at their centre the truthful student struggling to clear a passage through hypocrisy and outmoded conventions to an acceptance of an unsentimental world of reality. Strict, uncompromising honesty in the choice of a marriage partner is also advocated.

With the publication of *Röde prinsen* (The Red Prince, 1889), however, Lundegård marks the end of *Åttitalet*, even while following its favoured form, the *utvecklingsroman*. Max, *Röde prinsen*, the son of aristocratic, conservative parents, becomes a radical and yet there is a great deal about the young generation that he cannot accept. Max wants to write about 'the labour question: the thought of raising the poor serf who dragged out his existence in poverty and ignorance; the question of emancipation for women: through the centuries one half of humanity had been treated merely as the other half's soulless sexual counterpart; the question of morality.... There must be an escape from all this misery; and here lies the great task of modern literature.'

Brandes himself would have approved. Max finds, however, that he cannot avoid projecting himself into his fictional worker. Like the other middle-class radical *åttitalister*, he has created, however well-intentioned, 'the man with a rough exterior but tender interior,

Chapter I

Werther in rags and clogs'. Anti-democratic tendencies emerge as Max sees how the semi-educated lower classes utilize their increasing power. Lundegård's disillusion with *Åttitalism* seems complete as he describes Max's views on Ibsen and *Brand*. 'We have observed life for too long through the dark glasses of his poetic temperament; now we long for daylight, long for May air and for sunshine in life and literature'.

The new influences in Max's life are Nietzsche and Wagner. *Röde prinsen* appeared only a few days before Heidenstam's *Renässans*. Taken together they mark fairly clearly the end of the literary decade.

Prominent among the radical, avant-garde group of writers *Det unga Sverige* were three outspoken women writers who were responsible for some of the most remarkable achievements of the period, namely Alfhild Agrell, Anne Charlotte Edgren Leffler and Victoria Benedictsson (pseudonym Ernst Ahlgren). While their contemporaries have largely been forgotten, Strindberg and Benedictsson stand out as the two great talents among the writers of the early years of the Modern Breakthrough in Swedish literature. The changes and reforms in the position of women that had already been achieved in the sixties and seventies were largely due to economic pressures, as agrarian society was breaking up in the face of industrialization and urbanization, and the fact that the number of unmarried women had increased dramatically. Any reforms, such as the lowering of the age of majority from twenty-five to twenty-one in 1884 (the same as for men) concerned single women only: married women, who were assigned to the guardianship of their husbands, had to wait until 1919-21 for full civic rights and a new marriage law. Female emancipation, *kvinnofrågan*, was, however, mainly the concern of members of the middle and upper classes, i.e. what Strindberg called *kulturkvinnan*.

The early phase of the Modern Breakthrough in Swedish literature of the 1880s produced a breakthrough for women writers. More than a hundred women made their débuts as writers in this decade, twice as many as in the preceding ones. Most were contributors to journals and reviews, but even so it was a clear indication that the female perspective could no longer be ignored. Like their male colleagues, women writers focused their interest on *folklivsberättelse*r (stories of folk life), travel sketches and short novels, but above all on dramas dealing with contemporary problems and issues questioning traditional conventions, such as the relationship between man and woman, including the polarization of the sexes, and the institution of marriage. Plays by both Alfhild Agrell and Anne Charlotte Leffler were performed more often than those by Strindberg in the early eighties.[3] In 1887 Leffler wrote to a close male companion that 'Mrs Agrell, Ernst Ahlgren and Mrs Edgren are all of them more popular than any male writer'.[4] Gradually the market for tendentious protest literature began to wane, and new trends became fashionable with the approach of the next decade.

In spite of her success as a playwright in the early years of the eighties, Alfhild Agrell (1849-1923) never managed to produce a really significant piece of literature; nor did she find the great love of her life after her divorce in 1895. Although she was hailed as Stockholm's most fashionable dramatist in the mid-eighties, her fame soon faded when the public tired of the constant airing of matrimonial problems. The 'dialogue' with Ibsen that they conducted from a specific female viewpoint put both her and Leffler at the centre of public attention, not only in Scandinavia but also internationally after they had been translated into English and German and, in the case of Leffler, into Russian and Italian.

Thus, Agrell's play *Räddad* (Saved, 1882) is reminiscent of *Et Dukkehjem* and depicts how Oscarian moral hypocrisy destroys a family after a debauched, embezzling and fraudulent husband demands to be helped out by gaining access to his wife's inheritance. She finally saves her husband but humiliates him thoroughly by leaving him and asserting her independence. Yet again in *Dömd* (Condemned, 1884) the different moral codes for men and women are exposed, and the dilemma of the single mother's stigma is explored after she has been deserted by her lover, as it is in *Ensam* (Alone, 1886), and the question is put: which is more offensive, for a woman to 'love and believe' i.e. believe promises made, or for a man to 'love and betray'? Before her success as a playwright, Agrell had also written short stories, many of which were set against the background of the Norrland environment in which she grew up. However, the new aesthetic climate made her change direction, and instead of writing dramas that were no longer performed she became quite a successful humorous columnist under the pen-name Lovisa Petterkvist. Today Agrell, the literary feminist, is a rather anonymous figure; the headstone on her grave outside Härnösand is a fitting epitaph, consisting of a severed tree-trunk with sawn-off branches.

Chapter I

Although there are a number of parallels and similarities between Anne Charlotte Edgren Leffler (1849-92) and Agrell in their outlook and protest writings, Leffler is undoubtedly the greater talent, both in her language and in her capacity for objectivity and analysis. She was better educated, and all her life enjoyed much more support from her family and the social circles in which she moved, even though her first husband, Gustaf Edgren, was very much against having a writer for a wife. She was the most celebrated of the women writers in the 1880s and something of a figurehead in the Stockholm literary salons. Whereas Agrell can mainly be regarded as the writer of female defeat, Leffler is able to analyse various aspects of femininity, both positive and negative. Among her plays are *Skådespelerskan* (The Actress, 1873), *Pastorsadjunkten* (The Curate, 1876), *Sanna kvinnor* (True Women, 1883), and *Hur man gör godt* (Doing Good, 1885). Apart from the novels *En sommarsaga* in two parts (A Summer's Tale, 1886) and *Kvinnlighet och erotik* II (Femininity and Eroticism II, 1890), her most lasting contribution is her short stories, published in five volumes under the overall title *Ur lifvet* (From Life, 1882-93).

Whereas the later works display Leffler's growing maturity in expressing the need for individual liberation and fulfilment, including the right to express sexuality, the plays as well as the first couple of volumes of short stories are dominated by the subjection of women. This is the case in the story of Arla in 'En bal i societeten' (A Society Ball), in which a daughter's chances on the marriage market are ruthlessly exploited by her father. She reappears in a later story as the wife in a marriage of convenience in 'I strid med samhället' (At War with Society), loosely modelled on Strindberg's early life and marriage with Siri von Essen. Throughout her life Arla adapts herself to others, first to the same conditions as her mother, then to her husband and finally to her lover and second husband, who therefore loses all his former love and respect for her. Through her adaptability she has failed to reach her true potential and self-fulfilment, and feels that her life has been wasted. In 'Aurore Bunge', the life of a proud society ball beauty changes completely after a passionate sexual encounter with a lighthouse-keeper on a stormy night the summer before her marriage to a highly desirable suitor. Convention, however, forces her to go through with the intended marriage ceremony with her count, and thus not have 'the courage to be faithful and true'. *Sanna kvinnor* from 1883, a play to which Strindberg makes a sarcastic reference in the final story of *Giftas* II, was a timely reminder of the fight for married women's property rights and inheritance. Leffler, however, gets her message across not so much through tendentious indignation as through a keen eye for detail, wit and personal involvement. The title is an ironic reminder of how so-called 'true' womanhood is being ruthlessly exploited by patriarchal society.

Both in the early but successful and popular play *Skådespelerskan* and in the novel *En sommarsaga* Leffler deals with the difficulties that face the modern woman, and in particular the woman artist, in trying to combine talent and artistic ambition with marriage and the role of wife and mother. *En sommarsaga* provides in the end a kind of compromise solution for Ulla Rosenhane, an internationally famous painter working in Rome, and her Viking hero and future husband, a teacher at a folk high school in the North of Norway. In order to save their marriage they finally decide to meet halfway, each of them sacrificing part of their ambitions. Leffler continued to write about 'femininity and eroticism', a daring subject for a woman at the time. Her last work, the novel *Kvinnlighet och erotik* II, picks up the thread from a short story from 1883 with the same title, and traces the later development of the main character Alie. In the novel she falls deeply in love with an Italian nobleman, and in the sensuous environment of a southern country she is finally able to acknowledge her love and sexuality, shaking off the constrictions of Oscarian female moral codes. The novel parallels Leffler's own life: after divorcing her husband in 1889 she married an Italian count whom she had first met in Italy in 1888, but she died tragically a few months after the birth of their son, her only child. She claims there is not a trace of tendentiousness in the novel, but that it is a psychological study of human nature, pinpointing woman's personal liberation and right to fulfilment on the basis of inherent abilities and growing experience.

Victoria Benedictsson (1850-88) epitomizes the early phase of the Modern Breakthrough in both her life and works. Her collected works, published in 1918-20 in seven volumes, include collections of short stories, plays and three novels. Even though some of these works were published posthumously and, like the fragmentary novel *Modern* (The Mother, 1888), were completed by Axel Lundegård, Benedicts-son's friend and literary executor, her output is impressive, considering the few years she actually had as a writer. After her journal from the spring of 1882 to June 1888, the so-called *Stora boken* (The Big Book), had been published in full in three volumes by the mid-1980s, it was hailed as possibly her most central work. It provides a unique insight into the period, not least in its almost scientific investigation into the relationship between the sexes, but is also Benedictsson's continuous self-analysis and confessions to her *alter ego*. The journal reveals the complex dual personality of Ernst-Victoria who could never come to terms with her own femininity, no doubt partly due to the contempt for women that her father had instilled in his young daughter, whom he brought up as a boy instead of the son he had lost. In the posthumously published short story 'Ur mörkret' (Out of the Darkness, 1888), Benedictsson gives voice to her own deep feelings of inadequacy in being only a woman, a pariah.

Her creative work was something of a substitute for her failure to find mutual love between herself and a man, and also to find the male ideal equal to herself, something she thought she had achieved when she met Georg Brandes in October 1886. Her writing, then, was both compensation and necessity: as a writer, the woman Victoria became in her own words something of a man — Ernst. In his turn, Ernst, the writer, ruthlessly exploited Victoria's experiences, including her relationship with Georg Brandes. The reason for her suicide in July, 1888 is still a complex mystery; suffice it to say that she had made attempts before that. Her inherent inability to acknowledge herself as a woman, spiritually and physically, together with her fear that her femininity would diminish her as a writer, probably played a considerable part in the tragedy, together with persistent health problems and artistic and economic worries for her future.

The origin of this inner split is no doubt partly connected both with her early years and upbringing, and with the prevailing position of women. As the unwanted, possibly unloved child she was, she had always felt she had to earn love and recognition by exceptional achievements. She was a late afterthought in the unhappy marriage of her parents, and she married against their wishes, at the age of twenty-one, the Hörby postmaster, Christian Benedictsson, her senior by almost thirty years. This was not the kind of life that young Victoria Bruzelius had dreamt of: it had been her ambition to become a painter and to study at art college in Stockholm, like the girl heroine in her first novel. When this career was thwarted through, as she claims, parental opposition, she renewed contact with a previously rejected suitor and married Benedictsson, a widower with five children. The freedom she had been hoping for, both from an artistic and financial point of view when she escaped the constraints and oppression of her childhood home, did not come up to expectations, but she evidently managed to create a happy family life for her stepchildren, although she could never stand her only surviving daughter. She never divorced her husband, but a serious illness affecting her leg at the beginning of the eighties led to her spending long periods away from home; she then had time to study and indulge her burning ambition to write, publishing prose pieces and short stories in several journals and establishing herself as a writer. The money she earned helped to make her increasingly independent, and to spend much of her last two years in Copenhagen.

Like so many of her contemporaries, she concentrated on the realistic short story genre or 'studies', as she called them, in her first book, entitled *Från Skåne* (From Skåne, 1884). It is indeed her stories depicting everyday life of ordinary farming people in this volume that attracted most attention among critics, for their fresh and strong realism coupled with unexpected humour. Her first novel, *Pengar* (Money, 1885), won critical acclaim when it was published, not least because it was a timely and radical contribution to the prevailing discussion on the institution of marriage. It was tendentious but provided a vivid and fresh approach to the problem, which, according to Benedictsson, was taken straight from life and depicted some of her own experiences, such as her shock and revulsion when confronted with the physical realities of married life, and made more poignant because of the protagonist's young age. Sixteen-year-old Selma had dreamt of a career as a painter but was tempted by her uncle and guardian, a vicar and pillar of society, to marry a much older man, the wealthy squire Pål Kristerson. The prospect of a carefree life, a horse of her own, smart clothes and jewellery, dazzles the inexperienced little tomboy, and she agrees to marriage, i.e. 'sells' herself.

Over the next couple of years Selma learns to adapt and make the best of life with her well-meaning but completely incompatible husband who adores her in his way, but is never able to understand the child-bride he has bought. When she meets her cousin Richard again, it gives her the impetus to start educating herself in order to be the young doctor's equal. He is a radical 'new man' with modern ideas, but still strangely old-fashioned in the way he looks upon his fiancée Elvira. In frank discussions they air contemporary problems, such as the necessity of proper education for girls and young women in order to help abolish the inequality and injustice that women were still struggling with. Finally they acknowledge their love for each other, but Selma's experiences of married life force her to keep their relationship on a purely platonic and intellectual level, not entirely convincing, but probably a sign of Benedictsson's own ambivalence in this sphere, perhaps of neurotic origin. After a final show-down with her husband, Selma decides to leave him for an uncertain future with neither job nor money.

Benedictsson's second novel, *Fru Marianne* (Mistress Marianne, 1887), with its apparent defence of the institution of marriage, came as something of a shock to the radical camp, but was so much more welcome to the conservatives. Unlike Selma, Marianne decides to stay with her farmer husband, Börje Olsson, and fulfil herself as his equal partner on their Skåne estate, after the end of her platonic affair with Pål Sandell, who had tempted her with the possibility of free love, alluring decadent eroticism and aestheticism, and a taste for the kind of French literature that appealed to the avant-garde. The novel was Benedictsson's greatest venture, but its reception her greatest disappointment, especially Georg Brandes' verdict that it was too much of a ladies' novel. She called this a 'death sentence' on her writing, perhaps also on herself. Her immediate feelings of despair and failure, both as a writer and a woman, are poured out in the masterpiece 'Förbrytarblod', (Criminal Blood), first published in the collection of short stories *Folkliv och småberättelser* (Folklife and Small Tales, 1887), which was favourably received by Brandes.

Fru Marianne is one of the most remarkable and independent works of the 1880s, a bold attempt to write a female *bildungsroman* and novel of ideas in order to discuss current theories of morality, determinism and evolution; but it was caught between the two opposite poles in the morality debate. The novel emphasizes Benedictsson's belief in the possibility of lifelong love and faithfulness with no half measures, rather than free love — preferably but not necessarily within marriage. It also deals with the power and victory of free will, and depicts different extremes in Benedictsson's own temperament: in Börje, the positive characteristics — the optimism, the energy, the drive to educate oneself, but also the ability to combat hereditary weakness and be the master of one's own fate. Pål Sandell, on the other hand, is passively ruled by his temperament and moods and his inherent longing for love and beauty, and is unable even to want to try to change and to fight against either his hereditary disposition or circumstances. He is an early example of the flirtatious, decadent and pessimistic fin-de-siècle generation, and in the end takes his own life.

Benedictsson chose the same way out, but was still able to write and express her intensely-felt plight till the very end. The unfinished prose version of the surprisingly modern masterpiece 'Den bergtagna' (Spellbound) from the last few months of her life, first published in the final volume of the collected works, *Studier och brottstycken* (Studies and Fragments), summarizes in concise, symbolic form her personal development as a woman writer and the problems of artistic creativity.

Naturalism as a movement was short lived. Zola's *La Terre* (1887) offended members of his own school who were tiring of excesses, of sordid descriptions and debates on social theories. It was obvious too that science would not provide all the answers, and in reaction Paris attracted those with an interest in mysticism, the Orient and in Swedenborg. In Scandinavia Ibsen's plays from *Vildanden* (The Wild Duck) onwards were symbolic rather than socially critical. Brandes had popularized Nietzsche and was even finding some use for religion. Johannes Jørgensen, formerly a *Gjennembrudsmand*, had become a Catholic; Strindberg had taken his road to Damascus; and in the 1890s 'the new Scandinavian literature emerged to celebrate victory in the spirit of imagination, supreme joy and newly-awakened idealism. Thoughts on life, social issues and earnest literary debating of problems were ignored.'[5]

In one important sense, however, *Åttitalet* persists, for the respect for truth, the dislike of prejudice and social injustice and inequality of the sexes were features which were subsumed in some of the best Swedish literature of this century. However subdued, Hjalmar Söderberg's writing contains a social indignation and criticism inherited from *åttitalisterna*, while *tiotalisterna* ('Writers of the 1910s') and the proletarian writers of the 1930s stated their admiration for Strindberg and other writers of the Modern Breakthrough. Strindberg, Victoria Benedictsson and 'Young Sweden' collectively had cleared the way for the innovations of the twentieth century. They made it possible to introduce people from all walks of life into literature and to discuss delicate but essential issues openly. They also enriched the vocabulary of Swedish literature with their exact realistic descriptions of everyday

Chapter I

employment, while freeing the language from artificiality and pretentiousness. In that sense one can draw a clear line from *Röda rummet* to the most recent literature published in Sweden today.

Chapter II

August Strindberg (1849-1912)

Inga-Stina Ewbank

(i)

The received image of August Strindberg is that of a neurotic genius remarkable for the contributions he made to world drama at two stages in his creative career: with his 'Naturalistic' plays in the late 1880s and with his 'Expressionist' plays around the turn of the century. A controversial figure in his own life-time, Strindberg has remained something of a critics' problem child. His art is raw, immediate, relentless. He has too much personality. The story and style of his apparently self-obsessed life — his love and hatred of women, his three marriages which all ended in divorce, his devotion to experimental science which merged into a passionate pursuit of the philosopher's stone, his fascination with the occult — have a way of obtruding into any attempt to discuss his literary and dramatic achievement as such. It is with a sinking awareness of this that I propose to write in this chapter mainly on the *works* of Strindberg.

Several language barriers confront such a proposal. Some, but by no means all, are geographical, or national. Seen from outside the tradition of Swedish literature, Strindberg tends to look more like a myth than a writer; he moves upon the face of the waters of the modern theatre, or he is a metaphor for a particularly intense struggle between the sexes. The adjective 'Strindbergian' — like 'Chekhovian' or 'Pinteresque' — is often more familiar than the plays from which it has allegedly been derived. Inside the Swedish tradition, he is a far more specific *agent provocateur*. The voice of the angry young man who, though he had been writing plays since 1869, had his first popular break-through with the satirical novel *Röda rummet* (The Red Room) in 1879, could still be heard in the article against the government's method of financing armaments which was the last thing Strindberg wrote before he died in the spring of 1912. (His last play, *Stora landsvägen* (The Great Highway), had been written three years earlier). For four decades he showed what could be done to Swedish consciousness and with the Swedish language, and neither has been the same since. Even so, his own country can place him, as an innovator and a lasting force, firmly on the map. A literature given to seeing itself in terms of decades, each with its own characteristic spirit and modes of expression, does not hesitate to identify Strindberg as the leader of *Unga Sverige* ('Young Sweden') in the atheistic, socially-conscious and 'realistic' 1880s; nor as part of the new 'Romanticism' of the 1890s with its reaction against '*skomakarrealism*' (lit. 'shoemaker realism') and its fondness for religiosity, nationalism and symbolism; nor as one who, with the verse, prose and drama of his last decade, tumbled Swedish writing into 'Modernism'. Both these figures — one with, perhaps, too little local habitation, one with possibly too much — represent something real and important. The problem is how to make them speak to each other, how to surmount the barrier between them. Partly, it must be said at once, the barrier is made up of Strindberg's *corpus*, in its enormous size and variety. The Swedish reader of of his *Collected Works*[1] has available to him not only some sixty-two pieces of dramatic art but also a body of verse (narrative and lyrical), a large number of novels and short stories, autobiographies, historical studies, travelogues, nature sketches and essays on nearly every subject under the sun — let alone works which, like *En blå bok* (A Blue Book, 1908-12), defy categorization into any known genre. He can also consult the voluminous published correspondence and, if he wishes, read the unpublished writings, manuscripts and drafts in the Royal Library and the Strindberg Museum in Stockholm, and elsewhere. But availability alone is not the solution to the problem.

There is another language barrier between Strindberg's works and the student of them, one which operates regardless of geographical and linguistic boundaries. Perhaps 'gap' would be a more telling metaphor, for while the cause of the problem here is a presence: of the great bulk of directly autobiographical writing by Strindberg as well as the note of self-examination in so much else that he wrote, the effect is an absence: of a critical language and approach (the two being, as always, interrelated) which would enable us to discuss his works as we would those of Shakespeare or any other great imaginative artist. To say that 'his literary work is one long autobiography' need not be a substitute for literary and dramatic criticism, but sooner or later, in studies of Strindberg, we tend to find that we are asked to examine the art by beginning *and* ending with the man, rather than with the words on the page or the theatrical image. Even such an eloquent claim for Strindberg's dramatic powers as Robert Brustein's, in *The Theater of Revolt*, is ultimately based on the assumption that 'the roots of Strindberg's art are so clearly sexual and pathological'.[2] So no doubt were those of Blake's art, or Yeats's, but we do not in our critical endeavours stop at Blake's madness or Yeats's spiritualism; and mercifully we no longer see Shakespeare's plays as vehicles for his mythical sorrows or his sex nausea. Psychoanalytical tools may lay bare the sexual and pathological roots of Strindberg — indeed, they hardly need baring as he wore them in his cap, like Fluellen's leek. But practically every page he wrote cries out about other roots, too: in the sheer joy of writing; in observing life, creating fictions and finding forms and words to embody those fictions. It is worth remembering that the two English writers to whom he refers most frequently and admiringly throughout his career are Shakespeare and Dickens. With them, he shared a creative energy and an irrepressible interest in life in all its horror, absurdity and glory. He also shared with them the professional writer's concern for his audience.

'Diktarens kall är en självoffring' Strindberg wrote in a Postscript to the 1909 edition of his autobiography, *Tjänstekvinnans son* (Son of a Servant). This apparently simple sentence epitomizes the problem of finding a language to talk about his art. Setting aside the nightmare of the Swedish verb *dikta* and its cognate nouns *dikt* and *diktare*, which may be used to refer to any act of literary creation (or even of lying) as well as more specifically to the writing of poetry; and setting aside too the range of meanings of the Scandinavian *kall* which runs from the religious intensity of a vocation like Brand's at one end, to a non-committed task at the other; we are left with the *självoffring*. In the Swedish the stress is on the *själv*, and the multiple meanings of the verb *offra* enable Strindberg to hold in suspension the notions both of an offering forth of the self in a triumphantly sacrificial sense and of an immolation of the self as a sacrificial victim. Both the context and his whole bent throw the weight on the former alternative, but the latter remains present. At this point the lexical difficulties touch the other extreme of the problem of finding a language for Strindberg: the relation between his self and his art. The sentence quoted sounds deceptively like T.S.Eliot's *dictum* that 'the progress of an artist is a continual self-sacrifice, a continual extinction of personality',[3] but where Eliot, in 1919, at the beginning of his poetic career, is preaching the impersonality of art and the importance of a separation between 'the man who suffers and the mind which creates', Strindberg, looking back, in 1909, over most of his life's work, is describing the total *use* of his own personality, his own self, as raw material for art. At much the same time he was writing, in *En blå bok*, of Shakespeare as the outstanding example of such 'self-sacrifice' — a sacrifice not to be deplored or agonized over, as art achieved at the expense of life (as in Ibsen's last few plays), but to be celebrated as an energetic fulfilment of what both life and art are about (XLVI,72). The calling of the writer, then, is to exactly what Eliot deplores: 'the expression of personality'; but Strindberg would have seen as meaningless the dichotomy posed by Eliot: 'Poetry is not a turning loose of emotion, but an escape from emotion'. Neither a 'turning loose' of his own emotions (though this is the line of the critics who like to fail him for excessive subjectivity), nor an 'escape' from them, but an absolute commitment to them as a talent to be used, in the Biblical sense: this is how Strindberg sees the relation between 'the man who suffers and the mind which creates'. 'Is it possible,' he wrote in his diary in January 1901, 'that all the terrible things I have experienced have been staged for me so that I could be a dramatist and describe all states of mind and all situations?'[4]

Out of the context of his production, those could simply be the words of a thoroughly confused man, living on the borders of insanity. Or they might justify our concentrating on 'all the terrible things' which Strindberg experienced. The self-preoccupation of the sentence is obvious enough. But the purpose and the drive of the sentence is towards his *diktning*, his call to 'describe all states of mind and all situations'. If in Strindberg's *Poetics* life and art are totally fused, we should not be misled into devaluing his concern for the 'art' part of the product, for the process of 'describing' referred to in his diary sentence. His highly technical criticism of Shakespeare, both in *En blå bok* and in the *Öppna brev till Intima Teatern* (Open Letters to the Intimate Theatre) where he discusses details of structure and language,[5] ought to confirm what so much of his own work suggests: that he was a very conscious craftsman. Much earlier, in *Tjänstekvinnans son* (1886), he had related how Georg Brandes's essays on realism in Shakespeare burst upon him, as long ago as 1870, with the force of a revelation; and he describes it much as someone in the mid-1920s might have described I.A.Richards's *Principles of Literary Criticism*:

> He started from what was before him; examined it; pulled the work of art apart; demonstrated its anatomy and physiology without definitely saying whether it was beautiful or not. (20.287) [6]

It may be nonsense to try to apply to Strindberg the critical doctrine, upon which so many of us have been bred, of the autonomy of the work of art, insofar as his own life and feelings are what he writes about. But passages like the one I have just quoted suggest that it is equally nonsensical not to recognize his concern to make each of his works autonomous, to give it an 'anatomy' and 'physiology' which will ensure its independent life, once the umbilical cord to his own self has been cut. It is always worth paying attention to the 'vehicle' of Strindberg's metaphors, their literal, concrete element: in this case to note that 'anatomy' means 'the science of bodily structures' and that 'physiology' deals with the functioning of living things. However much Strindberg put himself into his work, however autobiographical his material, when he wrote he built structures out of it — and structures which would so live and function as to produce certain effects in readers and audiences. Sometimes, of course, he is very explicit about this, as in the famous Preface to *Fröken Julie* (Miss Julie) or the headnote to *Ett drömspel* (A Dream Play) or the discussion of his own history plays in the *Öppna brev*. Sometimes his correspondence with publishers and friends will spell out the conscious design and intention of a work. But, to avoid the intentional fallacy, we need to approach *all* Strindberg's works according to the principle that the proof of the pudding lies in the eating. If we do this, we are more likely than not to find, in most cases, that there is an extraordinary artistic control at work. Strindberg himself was scornful of the notion of 'objectivity' — 'so beloved by those who lack a subject', as he puts it in his 1889 essay 'Om modernt drama och modern teater' (On Modern Drama and Modern Theatre; XVII, 289) — but, for lack of a better word, objectivity is often just what he bestows upon his subjective content; and in the combination of the two lies an essential characteristic of his writing. Even in the outright autobiographies — *Tjänstekvinnans son, Inferno, Legender* (Legends),

Chapter II

Ensam (Alone), etc. — there is, as I hope to show presently, not just the spontaneous overflow of powerful emotion but also artistic design, carefully controlled communication with the reader. The same holds true for most of the plays. To take just one example, *Bandet* (The Bond) written in 1892 for an experimental theatre at Djursholm which never materialized, comes straight out of his own painful divorce case, and this one-act 'tragedy' (*sorgespel*) conveys, like no other play, the agonies and indignities of the dissolution of a marriage and the giving up of a child. It does so, not because all these things had 'really' been experienced by Strindberg but because he had found a form and a language to make the audience experience them: a plain surface of almost documentary exactitude to contrast with, and therefore enhance, the passions underneath; a structure which counterpoints court proceedings with intimate dialogue between the spouses so as to form a terrifying image of the public accountability and the lack of privacy in even our most private lives. It is, to return to Eliot's criteria for 'impersonal' art, 'emotion which has its life in the poem and not in the history of the poet'.

In the second half of this chapter, I wish to explore the 'anatomy' and 'physiology' of what I hope is a representative range of Strindbergian works. But before embarking on this, it is necessary to make a few more general points about what is Strindbergian, and why. To begin with, Strindberg himself would have been the last to wish to suggest a once-and-for-all definition of that adjective. Quite late in life, in one of the meditative essays in *Ensam* (1903), he writes of his admiration of Goethe, because of 'his lack of fixed views; his constant developing and rejuvenation, which made him always the youngest, always in the vanguard, before his time' (52.69-70). Clearly, in describing Goethe, he was holding a mirror up to his own nature. When T.S.Eliot re-discovered personality and claimed the hall-mark of a great poet to be that all his works are 'united by one significant, consistent, and developing personality',[7] then he had Shakespeare in mind, but we could well apply his words to Strindberg. To do so, we would stress 'developing' (hence the necessity to take, in some measure, a chronological or longitudinal approach to his works), and the 'consistency' would itself be a creative inconsistency. By this I do not just mean that Strindberg entered his Inferno as a Naturalist and came out as an Expressionist — although this crisis marked the most radical shift in his belief and his art — but that his whole corpus, like

Shakespeare's, suggests the ability to grow and change to have been fundamental to his talent. The basic consistency lies in a faithfulness to his own vision, however that vision might change; the consequent inconsistency lies in a refusal ever to cling to a form or a mode of expression for its own sake, however successful it might have proved.

Strindberg's intellectual and spiritual development could be charted as a map of the ideological history of the second half of the nineteenth century: Kierkegaard, Darwin, Buckle, Spencer, Hegel, Nietzsche, Schopenhauer, and so on, towards an increasingly eclectic vision in which Swedenborg co-existed with the elements of Buddhist thought. Similarly, his literary and dramatic development could be charted as a progress through Oehlenschläger, Shakespeare, Dickens, Balzac, Zola, Maeterlinck, and others — always remembering that, as with his non-literary reading, the progress was cumulative, and that he kept coming back to writers — to Rousseau, and to Schopenhauer; to Shakespeare and to Zola, to find new stimulus according to his own need at the moment. Scholars, notably Martin Lamm,[8] have written on the sources and influences behind Strindberg; in this chapter I must concentrate on what was made out of them. Strindberg was fond of describing his own creative processes in the image of a foundry or a crucible: not in itself an uncommon metaphor, but handled by him with a characteristic sense of the physical action involved. Thus in the third part of *Till Damaskus* (To Damascus, 1901), the central character, The Unknown, facing across the table The Lady whom he has loved *and* hated throughout the trilogy, reads in her eyes an accusation that he has 'killed' her self, her personality. He laments that what he wanted to do was give her all that was his, all that he had acquired 'during a long life's experiences and explorations through the deserts and groves of art and poetry':

THE LADY I don't deny it, but it wasn't mine!
THE UNKNOWN Yours? What is yours? Other people's!
THE LADY And yours? Other people's?
THE UNKNOWN No! What I have lived through is mine and nobody else's! What I have read has become mine, because I smashed it like glass, smelted it down and blew new glass with it into new shapes! (39.365)

It is the combination of Strindberg's receptivity with his ability to 'blow new glass' which makes him an important writer, and it is for us to take note of the 'new shapes'.

Chapter II

In doing so, we should not expect the Strindbergian 'development' to be a steady evolution. Looked at through selected plays it *is*: an evolution from apprentice works in several genres, with his own voice breaking through the conventional drama in *Mäster Olof* (Master Olof, 1872); to the plays where he finds Naturalistic forms for the struggle of men and women with each other; and — after 'Inferno' — on to the plays where man struggles against higher Powers in a world shaped like a dream or a nightmare. But looked at in terms of Strindberg's entire output, dramatic and non-dramatic, the pattern is less neat — and not simply because of occasional atavisms or anticipations. It is more like a huge experimental workshop than a map, and though the workshop has pre- and post-Inferno areas, there is a constant movement between the two.

Perhaps in the end, the single most outstanding characteristic of his workshop is its sheer prolificness. If Shakespeare never blotted a line, Strindberg worked even more rapidly — like a natural force, he liked to say. Plays like *Fadren* (The Father) *Fröken Julie* and *Dödsdansen* (The Dance of Death) were each written in a couple of weeks. Unlike Ibsen, he did not rest in wise passiveness between works but, with the exception of a few sterile years in the Inferno period, poured them out in a continuous flow. In itself this could of course mean that he was a slave to his own obsessions, and that one of these was a need to write, as a therapy. But it we look at what the flow consists of at any one time, the picture which emerges is far more that of an artist anxious to experiment in different modes. Thus, in the second half of the year 1900 he composed in succession four plays: *Midsommar*, a national-romantic play with a vast cast, in the style of traditional folk-comedy, its structure leaving room for several patriotic songs and even a whole Punch and Judy show; *Påsk* (Easter) a tightly-knit family drama of guilt and vicarious sufferings, set in a contemporary urban setting but suffused with the esoteric, so that its realism hovers on the borders of surrealism; *Dödsdansen*, a two-part drama of the power-game within marriage and between 'friends', set in a wholly Naturalistic setting but reaching through to levels of serio-comic nightmare; and, finally, *Kronbruden* (The Crown Bride), an almost operatic folk-drama of child-murder and family-hatred, observing no unities or realistic tenets. Diary entries suggest that Strindberg was working on, at least, *Påsk* and *Dödsdansen* simultaneously. Yet the plays seem, almost wilfully, to represent opposite poles. *Påsk*, its three

Acts reflecting the rhythm of the three days of the Passion and accompanied, as a *leit-motif*, by Haydn's *Sieben Worte des Erlösers*, is an attempt to write a kind of divine comedy in modern terms; like Shakespeare's Last Plays (particularly *The Winter's Tale*) it seems to suggest that suffering can redeem and miracles can happen. *Dödsdansen*, in those terms, is an infernal farce; in its intense concentration on the suffering people will inflict upon each other it seems more than any other Strindberg play (with the possible exception of *Fordringsägare* (Creditors)) to say that 'Hell is other people.' Yet only months, or weeks, before Strindberg had been creating the world of *Midsommar* where, as in the Gardener's opening speech, 'human hatred has thawed; light has returned and the night is spent' (43.13). The central action of that play shows the egoistical Student who, much like Pip in *Great Expectations*, has to (and does) learn about the moral worth of apparently insignificant other selves. But the world of the other folk-play, *Kronbruden*, is as far from that kind of concern as a medieval ballad is from a Victorian novel; its dimensions are love and hatred, family honour and revenge. *Midsommar* and *Kronbruden* represent opposite poles of the Swedish temper, too: the one embodies the joy of life of northern mid-summer, in an atmosphere familiar to admirers of Ingmar Bergman's film *Wild Strawberries*; the other the dark powers of the Swedish woods and rivers. To complete the pattern, one should also point out that the leap from the analytical *Dödsdansen* to the atmospheric *Kronbruden* is, in its way, an absolute one. It is programmatic, too: Strindberg wrote to the actress Harriet Bosse, soon to become his third wife, of how, with this play, he wanted to 'penetrate the wonderfully beautiful world of Maeterlinck, leaving aside analysis, questions and points of view, only seeking beauty in painting and mood'.[9] And in January 1901, having finished *Kronbruden*, he went on to write his most fairy-tale like play, *Svanevit* (Swanwhite), deeply under the influence of Maeterlinck.

Whatever else this variety suggests, it points again to an ability to separate what Eliot terms 'the man who suffers and the mind which creates.' For an even more remarkable example of this, and one which takes in genres other than the drama, one might briefly look at the years 1887 and 1888, dominated in his own life by crises in his first marriage and in his mind (such as fears of insanity). These crises have obviously supplied the subject matter of *Fadren*, written in February 1887, just as the technique of that play is, indirectly, described and analyzed in a series of essays he was writing during the early months of that year and which he was eventually to give the working title of *Vivisektioner*. I shall be returning to *Fadern* and to essays like 'Hjärnornas kamp' (Struggle of Brains) and 'Själamord' (Psychic Murder); here it suffices to say that all these works testify to a preoccupation with the dark recesses of the mind and with the terrible hypnotic power of one mind over another. But that summer he wrote what is probably the happiest and most extrovert of all his works, the novel *Hemsöborna* (The People of Hemsö), a kind of realistic piscatory pastoral sustained by immense forces of humour, sanity and control, and by a pervading sense of joy in the processes of life and nature. He stayed with that world — geographically the world of the Stockholm archipelago, which he loved and described like no one else — in a series of short stories, published in September 1888 as *Skärkarlsliv* (Life in the Skerries), yet also writing during much the same period that most tormented autobiography and anatomy of a marriage, composed in French, September 1887 —March 1888, as *Le plaidoyer d'un fou*, known in Swedish as *En dåres försvarstal*.[10] In the summer of 1888 he finished his tales of the skerries people and started *Fröken Julie* immediately; and August 1888 saw both the completion of that play and the entire composition of *Fordringsägare*, from which he turned at once to write a collection of descriptive and meditative essays, *Blomstermålningar och Djurstycken* (Flowers and Animals) which were published as a Christmas book. For a notion of Strindberg's range, one must put the claustrophobia of *Fordringsägare*, where three people made up entirely of brains and nerves are locked in a struggle which can only end with the destruction of the weakest, at the side of the descriptive and evocative vigour of the picture of his childhood's herbacious borders and the gentle humour and self-irony of pieces like 'Om pessimismen i den moderna trädgårdskonsten' (Pessimism in Modern Horticulture) (29.161-174) or 'Konsten att meta' (The Art of Angling) (29.180-185). Apart from the sheer Dickensian energy of output displayed, what strikes one in a survey like this is that we must allow for Strindberg the possibility of a far more multiple vision than what emerges from the standard picture of him in these years: the misogynist neurotic turning to Naturalistic drama as the form for his obsessions.

One final point must be made about the Strindbergian 'flow'. In his *dramatic* production there were stops and starts, contrasting with the metronomic regularity with which Ibsen turned out his 'contemporary' plays. The pattern here tends to reflect the way the theatres welcomed — or rejected — what Strindberg wrote; for, with the single exception of his last play, *Stora landsvägen* (The Great Highway, 1909), which he himself described as a *läsdrama*, he composed his plays very much with the live theatre, and often particular theatres, in mind. Thus there are three peaks of concentrated dramatic activity — 1887-18; 1898-1902; 1907-09 — each confirming that his internal impulsion towards the drama needed the stimulus of external theatrical conditions. He had of course had plays produced before 1887. *Dramaten* — the Stockholm headquarters of the Swedish theatrical establishment, whose conventions and practices were to be ridiculed at wicked length by Strindberg in his prose satire *Det Nya Riket* (The New Nation 1882; 12.102-114) — had briefly and unimpressively mounted two of Strindberg's earliest plays, themselves brief and uncertain of their direction, in 1870 (*I Rom*) (In Rome) and 1871 (*Den fredlöse*) (The Outlaw). But *Mäster Olof*, although (or perhaps because) it was the first play to show his mature command of strong scenes and bold characterization, was altogether too strong stuff for *Dramaten*, who rejected it. After completing the first — prose — version of the play in 1872, Strindberg spent the better part of the 1870s re-writing it. He wrote no other plays in these years, but was finding his feet as a novelist, feeling that the Norwegians (Bjørnson and Ibsen) had anticipated him writing 'the new drama' (XIX, 153). The first version of Mäster Olof (the third, in verse, rejected) was at last put on in 1881, at *Nya Teatern*, which had been established in 1875 as part of a reaction against the alleged stuffiness of *Dramaten*. By that time, Strindberg was hesitantly returning to the drama, mainly to write star parts for his first wife, the actress Siri von Essen. She appeared in his two pseudo-medieval, or Renaissance, pieces: *Gillets hemlighet* (The Secret of the Guild, 1880) at *Dramaten* and *Herr Bengts hustru* (Sir Bengt's Wife, 1882) at *Nya Teatern*. His real inclination, he confessed however, was towards the novel and other forms of prose fiction, and indeed he promptly re-wrote *Herr Bengts hustru* into a short story for *Svenska Öden* (Swedish Destinies) (14.26-40). The earliest of his realistic plays of contemporary life, *Marodörer* (Marauders) written in 1886 but revised and eventually re-titled *Kamraterna* (The Comrades) in 1887-88, is not much more than a turning into dialogue form of the kind of material Strindberg had been working into short stories in his collection of illustrations of modern marriage, *Giftas* I and II (Married, 1884 and 1885).

Chapter II

Fadren, then, in 1887, represents Strindberg's first deep commitment to drama; and its première, at the Casino Theatre in Copenhagen that same year, the first rise of the first 'peak': 1887-92. Those years saw the writing of his three great Naturalistic plays as well as a number of one-acters. He wrote (and eventually in a small measure succeeded) to conquer the Paris *Théâtre Libre* and the Berlin *Freie Bühne*, and he wrote for theatres which he himself was involved in trying to start. But the 'Scandinavian Experimental Theatre', based in Copenhagen, was shortlived, and the experimental theatre at Djursholm, outside Stockholm, never came into being at all; and by the end of 1892 Strindberg was turning his back on drama. The second peak, 1898-1902, rose from the creative impulse to turn Inferno experiences into drama and was sustained by what the Markers have called Emil Grandinson's Strindberg offensive[11] at *Dramaten*, where both *Till Damaskus I* and *Brott och brott* (Crimes and Crimes, 1899) were staged in 1900, and *Påsk* in 1901. This was also the almost incredibly fertile period of his Swedish History plays, several of which were successfully produced. But by 1902 they were being rejected, and Strindberg closed his cycle of plays on the Swedish Kings with *Gustav III*. With the Pirandellian, role-playing, hero of that play disappeared, for the time being, Strindberg's urge to write plays. It was revived under the stimulus of preparations for the first production of *Ett drömspel* (A Dream Play, written 1901) at *Svenska Teatern* (formerly *Nya Teatern*) in 1907, and above all by his first and only sustained opportunity to control a theatre of his own. For *Intima Teatern* on Norra Bantorget in Stockholm, the small experimental stage which Strindberg established together with the young actor-director August Falck, he wrote all his Chamber Plays. Many of his earlier plays were adapted for this stage, too; and the accounts of these productions,[12] together with his *Öppna brev till Intima Teatern* — an eclectic combination of practical advice to actors and dramatic criticism — form a picture of a man for whom the theory and practice of drama were unusually closely allied. The venture lasted for just over three years, dying in the end from a surfeit of Strindbergian intensity, and most immediately because Falck insisted on mounting a Maeterlinck play instead of yet another Strindberg. The final performances at *Intima Teatern* on 11 December 1910 added up to a marathon: *Kristina* at half past one in the afternoon, *Fadren* at half past four, and *Fröken Julie* at eight o'clock in the evening.

(ii)

'Diktartens kall är en självoffring'. If, then, we may turn from biography to the texts themselves in our approach to Strindberg's art, this does not mean that we have, as it were, to throw out the 'self' with the bath-water. My main theme in this second half of my essay is that Strindberg's sense of self and his sense of artistic form (which I take to include both language and structure) are intimately, not to say inextricably, related. His image of the self is also the programme for his art.

We may begin to appreciate this from the vantage point of *Tjänstekvinnans son*, which in many ways forms the iron gates through which the rest of his production was torn. It might have been the dead end of his writing career, to be followed at most by further instalments of his autobiography, for he was only thirty-seven, and had twenty-six more years to live, when he wrote it. Into its conception had gone the desire to provide a specimen of what he described as the 'literature of the future':

... this literature would consist of every citizen's autobiography at a certain age, submitted to the municipal archives anonymously and without any names cited. (XVIII, 457)

In the lively 'Interview' which he wrote for the first edition of the first part of *Tjänstekvinnans son* (and which his publisher refused to print), he points out that this notion of replacing all literature with files of autobiographical case histories was only three-quarters serious. Yet it is ominous enough, both in itself and as a parody on how we are often asked to read Strindberg. Fortunately, what he produced turns out to be, if we look at the text itself, not only an autobiography but also a work of fiction *and* a critical document which, in its awareness of the complexities of viewpoint in a work of art, is ahead of many twentieth-century theorists of fiction:

Whether the author, as he sometimes had thought, really had experimented with points of view or incarnated in different personalities, polymerized[13] himself, or whether a gracious fate had experimented with the author, the enlightened reader will deduce from the texts. (XVIII, 459)

The question of viewpoint in *Tjänstekvinnans son* is, of course, a set of Chinese boxes, for the work not only comments on his life and his writings, but it also comments on itself. Chapter 10 of the fourth part, *Författaren* (The Author), is about the writing of *Tjänstekvinnans son* and his intentions in writing it; and there are very similar arguments in the 'Interview' already mentioned, in letters, and also in the Preface and Postscript which he wrote for the edition of the whole autobiography in 1909, with a hindsight reflecting the living and writing he had done in the intervening years. By then, he points out, 'the author is...just as alien to me as to the reader — and just as unattractive' (XIX, 150). To try to disentangle these various personae of Strindberg is an enterprise labyrinthine enough to suggest that this way madness lies — or the novels of Nabokov. But, very roughly, what emerges from the text is Strindberg's ability to enter into other selves and, in the end, to stand outside even his own present self. In the early sections, there are passages rendering the young child's point of view, with vocabulary and sentence structure adapted to his vision. In the later parts, as Johan, the author's *alter ego*, grows older, the angles of vision begin to converge; but the omniscient author still keeps a saving detachment from Johan, even at the point where the lines of fact and fiction intersect. The last paragraph has Johan — who has been quoting John Stuart Mill on marriage, in what sounds like a *précis* of the plot of *Fadren* — fling open the window on a sun-lit Alpine valley, as his friend and interlocutor challenges him to write down 'all those things you have been saying':

'Yes, I'll do that,' replied Johan, 'and it will be the end of the fourth part of *The Son of a Servant*.'
'And the fifth part then, what will that deal with?'
'Ask the future!' (XIX, 297)

In an ingenious double-take, which closes the book by thrusting it right into the now of late 1886, and (as Strindbergian endings so often do) forward, and with a self-irony which is yet affirmative, Strindberg 'places' Johan. It is not that Johan's ideas or his sincerity are invalidated but that we are reminded that there is a world elsewhere, where people live joyously in touch with nature, sing rather than speechify, and where the sun shines on the mountain tops — and how differently it shines here from at the end of Ibsen's *Ghosts*. The faintly sceptical tone of the interlocutor pitches the stridency and intensity of Johan against sanity and commonsense — much as The Lady does with

The Unknown in *Till Damaskus* I in the first scene 'at the sea-shore' (39.63-71), or as Indra's Daughter does with The Poet in *Ett drömspel* — and one cannot help feeling the significance of the fact that the autobiographical narrative ends as a dramatic dialogue. The complexity of the author's attitude to his subject — himself — has forced the subject into dramatic form. Two months later he had written *Fadren*.

Strindberg wrote to his publisher, in a letter explaining what he would like a critic to tell the public about his intentions behind *Tjänstekvinnans son*

> that the author did not want to produce biography, a defence or confession but to use his life, which of all lives is the one he knew best, to seek to present the story of the origin and development of a mind (en själs uppkomst)[14] and to explore the concept of character — on which, after all, the whole of literature rests. (XVIII, 464)

The desire to trace and define the growth and development of a mind puts him in a central Romantic tradition: all the four parts of his autobiography bear virtually the same sub-title (*En själs utvecklingshistoria*) as Wordsworth's *Prelude* ('Growth of a Poet's Mind'). But the final aim — 'to explore the concept of character — on which the whole of literature rests' — has about it the ring of the naturalist's desire to penetrate to first causes and to trace general principles (and in the 'Interview' Strindberg makes no bones about having out-Zolaed Zola: XVIII, 455-458). Strindberg himself often stressed his own double nature as a 'transitional formation' with the characteristics of 'romantic and naturalist, like the slowworm, which still has the lizard's rudimentary feet inside its skin' (XIX, 140); in Johan this doubleness was 'the key to his personality and to his writing.' (*ibid*). The key fits the lock we are trying to prise open — that to his emergence as a dramatist — particularly well; for, while in the years leading up to *Tjänstekvinnans son* the Naturalist almost managed to kill not only the Romantic but also the imaginative writer,[15] in the process of writing the autobiography the two — or three — discovered a common cause and formed a union uniquely Strindbergian. The naturalist found the truths he was looking for not in the historical context or the social milieu but in the domain of the Romantic poet:

> Not Chaos, not
> The darkest pit of lowest Erebus,

> Nor aught of blinder vacancy, scooped out
> By the help of dreams — can breed such fear and awe
> As fall upon us often when we look
> Into our Minds, into the Mind of Man.
> (Wordsworth, Preface to *The Excursion* 1814)

Only, Strindberg finds even darker and deeper recesses in the Mind of Man than were dreamt of in the philosophy of Wordsworth; his clear sight and de-mythologized language make him part company, here, with other nineteenth-century writers of autobiographies, fictive or genuine, and make him what for lack of a better word we must call 'modern'. Rousseau's whole aim is to be sincere;[16] Strindberg, long before Freud, knew what a problematic concept sincerity is. The various parts of his autobiography, he says, 'are recorded quite sincerely not completely of course, for that is impossible' (XVIII, 459-60). It is not only that the author might, with the passage of time, have forgotten facts, but — far more importantly — he also recognizes the less conscious motivations:

Here confessions are made that nobody asked for, and guilt assumed where perhaps it wasn't so serious, as the author is even punishing his silent thoughts. (XVIII, 460)

Here is a blueprint, if not for 'the whole of literature', for the insight into 'character' on which all of Strindberg's subsequent plays are built. For 'author' in this sentence we could read 'The Captain' or 'The Unknown', or 'The Stranger' in the Chamber Play *Brända tomten* (After the Fire), or a number of other characters whose dramatic life depends on Strindberg's ability to engage us with their 'silent thoughts', with tensions not even recognized by themselves.

From the very beginning of his dramatic career Strindberg had, of course, relied on conflict and tension to build character and structure. But these are clearly and single-mindedly defined, and the resolution of each play leaves us (as do the Ibsen plays which Strindberg knew at this stage) with a sense of character similarly defined. Karl (*Fritänkaren*) (The Freethinker) cast off by his family goes away to America to preach Unitarianism. Master Olof commits himself first to being a Reformer, then — in the famous ending of the prose version — to being an 'Apostate' (*Avfälling*). Margit, in *Herr Bengts Hustru*, finds herself by learning exactly the lesson which Ibsen's Nora rejects: how to adjust to being a good wife. What separates these characters from Johan and these plays from the later plays, is the refusal, on the part of the author, to define character:

> If man's character finally is the role in the comedy of social life he is stuck with, then Johan at this period was most characterless; i.e. quite sincere. He sought, he found nothing and could not stick with anything. His brutal nature, which threw off all reins, would not yield, and his brain, born revolutionary, could not become automatic. A compendium of all experiences, all changing impressions, and full of warring elements.(XVIII, 127)

I have quoted Strindberg's analysis of Johan at length, as it forms a paradigm for so much of his later work. His characters there do not, indeed cannot, identify themselves with their social role — with being a Captain, or a Lady of the Manor (*Fröken Julie*) or a Lawyer (*Ett drömspel*). When they do, like the significantly-named couple in *Advent*: The Magistrate and his wife, it is usually wilful self-deception. Instead, they 'search', they 'reflect' what happens to them and those whom they encounter: and they end up not as resolved 'identities' but as 'compendia of ... warring elements'. It is this paradigm that Strindberg has in mind when he discusses 'characterlessness' as a feature of Naturalistic art in the Preface to *Fröken Julie* (27.104-106) and, much later, when in *En blå bok* and in the *Hamlet* pamphlet of his *Öppna brev till Intima Teatern* he praises Shakespeare for creating characters 'as inconsistent, self-contradictory, disintegrated ... incomprehensible as human beings really are.' (XLVII, 794). But these critical pronouncements simply underline the more important fact, epitomized by Johan, that, like few nineteenth-century writers, he knew the 'disintegrated consciousness'[17] from the inside and could re-create it, in dramatic form, from the outside. At the end of *Tjänstekvinnans son* there can be no resolution of the contradictions which make up Johan's characterless character, for

> When he is to get to know himself he finds a multi-coloured confusion which lacks substance, which changes according to the observer's point of view and which perhaps has no more reality than the rainbow which appears to be there but does not exist.(XIX, 277)

Other nineteenth-century (auto)biographies tended to lead up to epiphanic insights: Wordsworth concludes that the mind of man 'is itself / Of substance and of fabric more divine' (1805 *Prelude* XIII, 451-2),

Chapter II

and David Copperfield learns to know his own 'undisciplined heart' and writes a story with purpose. Even Stephen Dedalus, in the early twentieth century, goes off at the end 'to encounter for the millionth time the reality of experience and to forge in the smithy of my soul the uncreated conscience of my race'. As Johan goes to 'ask the future' what the fifth part of *Tjänstekvinnans son* will contain, his author commits himself to nothing but contradictions and a continued search:

Yes, there will be contradictions, for things will be viewed from opposite sides, because things aren't the same from two sides, and the author is an experimenter who in his compositions will seek to work out what the future in these given conditions might look like... And in our age of searching it is an advantage not to believe anything, since the main thing is the searching ... Search! search! (XIX, 278-279)

This quotation and the previous one add up, I hope, to an explanation of what I meant by saying that Strindberg's image of the self is also the programme for his art — at least for his most distinctive 'fictive images'. The very nature of his drama, before and after Inferno, is governed by his vision of the self as a 'multi-coloured confusion which lacks substance' and changes forms according to the viewpoint of the observer. In the Naturalistic plays such selves are tested against, and often destroyed by, strong, defined selves. In the post-Inferno plays the perception of character and reality changing 'according to the viewpoint of the observer' comes to determine the whole dramatic structure. And in both groups, the notion of art as a 'search', through suspended contradictions rather than towards reconciliation makes him an innovator who still seems strangely modern, even in *our* 'age of searching'.

It might seem absurd to apply the term 'search' to plays like *Fadren* or *Fröken Julie*, or *Fordringsägare*, which tend to strike audiences as particularly aggressive. That they do so, is an aspect of what Strindberg might have called their 'physiology' (see above): they function, in relation to an audience, so as to produce an almost hypnotic effect — 'The actor hypnotises his awake public and forces it to applaud, weep, laugh' (29.24), Strindberg writes in his essay called 'Hjärnornas kamp'. As against the measured art of Ibsen, which always seems to keep us in some detachment from his characters, evaluating their words and behaviour even as we sympathize, Strindberg's art has a terrible and wonderful immediacy. At any one moment in the play it will engage us wholly and unquestioningly with a speaker — and with his raw nerves and bared consciousness, rather than his public persona. The dramatic language of each author is, of course, to a large extent responsible for this: where Ibsen's characters tend to reveal to us no more than the tip of the ice-berg of their feelings, thus inviting us by suggestion to supply the rest from our own imagination and judgement, Strindberg's tell us all we might have been able to imagine, and more. So we tend to emerge at the end of a play bruised by traumas, shattered from having had to change viewpoints as often as we changed speakers — and without the emotional purification of a catharsis at the end. Historians of the drama are sometimes keen to call these plays 'modern tragedies', in order to legitimize Strindberg or to prove that Tragedy did not die when God did. But if we do so, we should make sure that we do not imply that, like Shakespearean tragedy, they leave us with a sense of human suffering having vindicated human existence. They simply do not. In his Preface to *Fröken Julie* Strindberg claimed for that play a Darwinian happy ending: the joy of seeing the survival of the fittest; whereas the play itself would seem finally to involve us much more with the destruction of the un-fit Miss Julie herself. He also spoke of another (no doubt Nietzschean) joy —

I find the joy of life in life's fierce cruel struggle and my enjoyment is getting to know something, learning something.(27.103)

- and this may correspond more truly with our reaction to the play, insofar as we have, willy-nilly, been involved in the fierce, cruel battle between Jean and Julie, and between one part of Julie's self and another, and as we have learned something about the powers of destruction, and self-destruction, in human beings. But we would find it difficult to say exactly *what* we have learned.

This is where we come back to the notion of the 'search' behind the dramatic form of these plays, justified — we may see now — by the fact that the author draws his audience in to participate in an experiment, an anatomy of man. With him we search into the motives and aims of his people. We are made to do so by one prominent structural feature of the plays which uncannily anticipates the modern procedure of psychoanalysis. Lionel Trilling, in his book on *Sincerity and Authenticity,* brilliantly helps the layman to see the literary and dramatic bearings of 'a science which is based upon narration, upon telling. Its principle of exploration consists in getting the story told —

Chapter II

somehow, anyhow — in order to discover how it begins' (p. 140). Just so the dialogue in these plays operates, often in defiance of the tenets of 'well-made' dramatic construction so carefully observed by Ibsen (and this is surely why early critics in England found the dramatic processes of *Fadren* to be 'naive'). Instead of Ibsen's masterly analytical structure, in which the past is gradually laid bare, its full impact coinciding (as in *Ghosts*, or *Rosmersholm*) with the final catastrophe, Strindberg constructs a no less masterly present, sufficient unto itself. It is desperately concentrated — in both *Fröken Julie* and *Fordringsägare*, let alone (by definition) the one-acters which followed, the action occupies no more time than it takes to perform it — and ineluctably heading for a catastrophe, not because of a deed done in the past, but because people are as they are, and all the characters, antagonists and protagonists (which is in any case often a useless distinction here), are driven by an urge to tell their story, 'somehow, anyhow', in order to find out why they are as they are. Julie and Jean are obvious examples. Laura, the wife in *Fadren*, shows how this need in the play's structure may override more conventional expectations of character consistency. Normally she speaks as curtly, firmly, definitely as possible: her very strength lies in her ability to state, and not analyze. But shortly before the end she has a long speech, replying to the Captain's assertion that she was his 'mortal enemy' by an analysis of her motives which, in its disclaimer of motives, raises all the problems of 'sincerity' faced by Strindberg in his autobiography:

I don't know if I have ever thought or intended what you think I have done. It may be that a hidden desire to get rid of you as an obstacle has ruled me, but if you discern a plan in my actions then possibly there was one, although I didn't see it. I have never reflected on events but they have glided along on rails you yourself laid, and before God and my conscience I feel innocent, even if I am not so. For me your existence has been a stone on my heart, pressing and pressing until my heart sought to shake off the inhibiting weight. That's how it is, and if I have unwittingly struck you I beg your pardon. (27.93-94)

One could argue that there is 'realistic' motivation for this speech in the dramatic situation: the provocation from her now strait-jacketed husband. Excitement loosens Laura's normally so firm syntax and sense of logic and drives her, though she is usually so literal in her speech, to clinch her points with metaphors. Certainly the speech has a Naturalistic level, on which it gives away far more than Laura realizes, opening shafts into unsuspected layers of her consciousness. On that level, too, it is obviously part of Laura's superior strength that she can see the irony of what is going on, and by describing it twist the knife in the wound: while she has undone her husband, he has also done her work for her, undoing himself as fast as she could push, or faster. But it is also possible to see the speech on another level, where it functions as part of an imaginative whole rather than an imitation of 'real' life. Here Laura speaks not so much her own language as that of the play as a whole; she is the voice needed to articulate the image of the play's action as a peculiarly infernal machine: an engine gliding forward as ineluctably as they all do in the railway novel Zola was about to write (*La Bête humaine*, 1889) on rails indeed laid for it by the Captain.

As Laura's speech suggests, the 'searching' part of Strindberg's structures tends, paradoxically, to show him at his most Naturalistic *and* at his most non-Naturalistic. He is, as it were, making a kind of poetic drama out of psychoanalytical techniques. The 'poetry' lies in a particularly concrete, sensuous evocation of experiences, whether painful or pleasurable: when Ibsen's characters, at least before *Hedda Gabler*, look into the past, they tell us what they did and why; Strindberg's tell us how things smelt and tasted and felt. The 'drama', to the audience, lies in the sudden juxtaposition of impressions: Jean with Miss Julie in the kitchen, and Jean as a child exploring the Turkish pavilion privy and watching a pink-and-white Julie from under a pile of weeds, 'beneath prickling thistles and wet evil-smelling earth'(27.141). Or the Captain, lying there in his strait-jacket, stirred by the soft feel of Laura's shawl against his mouth, into memories of their youth — of the smell of vanilla from her hair and the walks in the birch-woods. Strindberg knows how to use the theatre to create a complex emotional web by superimposing one scene (imagined, through significant sensory detail) on another (actual); and when the Captain concludes 'Think how beautiful life has been, and what it has become' we are torn by something far more specific than the vague nostalgia which the line out of context might suggest. He was of course to use this technique throughout the rest of his career, notably in the Chamber Plays. *Pelikanen* (The Pelican) is almost entirely built on it: the stunted Gerda of the play's present is 'explained' by the emotionally and physically starved child stealing hard bread and mustard from the side-board and slaking her thirst with the vinegar from the cruet (58.292). In the final scene of that play the technique reaches its apotheosis, as brother and sister, surrounded by the flames of the burning apartment, smell the lavender in the linen-cupboard and the spices in the kitchen, remembering Christmas and the summer holidays until they die into an imagined scene made more real to them (and momentarily to us) than the actual scene on stage.

Speeches like these — streams of consciousness in their syntax and their associative chains of images — tend towards the monologue form and could, theoretically, produce a diffuse overall dramatic structure. The brevity of the Chamber Plays is one way out: in *Brända tomten* the other characters are there simply to activate The Stranger into a series of reminiscent and analytical monologues from among the ruins of his childhood home. In the 'wander' and 'dream' plays the shifting locations thread the speeches into a string of tableaux — the whole structure becomes a search. In the Naturalistic plays a different kind of dynamism is provided by the power-struggle which they enact. The essays in *Vivisektioner* are important in relation to these plays (see above), not only because, in a general way, they show Strindberg's interest in the hypnotic power of one mind and will over another, but also because they introduce images and articulate relationships which are absolutely central to the plays. In 'Själamord' — the essay which Strindberg wrote after reading *Rosmersholm*, where he was impressed by Ibsen's creation of Rebecca West, 'an unconscious cannibal who swallowed the mind of the former wife' (29.77) — Strindberg analyzes the ways and means by which society and the family 'nowadays' annihilate the selves of individuals, in terms which could serve as a paraphrase of the action of *Fadren* (29.74-75). The battle-field of man has narrowed to the small social or even smaller domestic arena. In *Fröken Julie* class relationships determine the characters up to a point — the Count's boots hold Jean down at the end, even though he has slept with the Count's daughter and sent her to commit suicide in the barn. In *Fadren* the apparently social figures — the Pastor, the Doctor, and the ironically named adjutant Nöjd (Content) — exist only insofar as they illuminate the relationship between husband and wife. Society in the play is mainly the oppressive bevy of females which the so-called extended family gathers in: wife, mother-in-law, old nurse, daughter.

This is where we connect with the point Strindberg made in *Tjänstekvinnans son* about the undefined self which, at the mercy of 'viewpoints', is of course also desperately vulnerable. Married man (as the short stories in *Giftas* had shown, growing ever shorter, more diagrammatic and bitter as we move into the second volume) does not possess his own self. In his Second Act conversation with Laura — the centre of reasoning of the play — the Captain documents his search for a self, through 'a great action, a deed, a discovery or an honourable suicide' (27.71). Having been prevented from going to war (which one?), he had hoped to find an identity and recognition as a scientist; and then she 'chops off his arm' just as he is about to reach out for the reward of his labours. Yet, woman too is at the mercy of familial roles: the Captain and Laura knew how to meet in a mother-son relationship, but the transition from there to being mistress-lover becomes something shameful, 'like incest'. In the end, the self is at the mercy of biology: the play is called *The Father*, not *The Husband,* and the Captain is not jealous like Othello (to whom he has often been compared) but desperate for the only kind of immortality he knows: through his child. One of the cruel ironies of the play is that the role to which he is at the end reduced *is* that of a helpless child, ironically saying every good Swedish child's bedtime prayer, *Gud som haver barnen kär* (27.96). But before then we have been reminded, by the Captain himself in his surrealist prose poem on the amorphousness of the self (27.71), that at the heart of his defeat is not what Laura has done to him but the terrible practical joke of Nature in making men and women. She even denies them permanent sex identities:

When women grow old and stop being women they get hairs on their chin; I wonder what men get when they grow old and stop being men?

A reminder, too, that even this play's viewpoint extends beyond and above the sex-war to the condition of man (including woman).

In *Fordringsägare* the social world has narrowed almost as far as it is possible. Gustav's occupation, as a 'teacher of dead languages', is largely symbolic; and that of Adolf who turns from being a painter to being a sculptor, is relevant only in that it shows his very creativity at the mercy of the stronger will manipulating him. Where *Fadren* is anchored in a middle-class living-room (though in a sense this is reduced to a strait-jacket), and *Fröken Julie* among the pots and pans of the Great House kitchen, *Fordringsägare* is set, with deliberate vagueness, in a 'public room at a seaside resort'. All we know about the house is that it is where Adolf and Tekla, husband and wife, first met. Strindberg, we know, took pride in his achievement of:

Chapter II

a new Naturalistic tragedy, even better than *Miss Julie*, with three characters, a table and two chairs and no sunrise! (Letter to Bonnier, 21 August, 1888: *Letters* I.281)

He never misses a chance of a dig at Ibsen, but the target here is more general than the *Ghosts*-inspired sunrise at the end of *Fröken Julie*. As in the essay 'Om modernt drama och modern teater' written in March 1889 and so, implicitly, a record of the position which the writing of these plays had brought him to, he is turning against 'a working method elevated to an art form'. Seven years earlier, in the essay 'Om realism', he had himself thus 'elevated' realism, which then meant to him an exact reproduction of things and people as they are, and an unflinching revelation of what is 'ugly' (XVII, 192-196). Now he rejects the unselectiveness of such art and asks for a concentration on 'the points where the great battles are'. This is 'great Naturalism'

which loves to see what one can't see every day, which is delighted by the struggle of nature's powers, whether these powers be love or hate, spirit of rebellion or sociable instincts, which doesn't mind whether it is beautiful or ugly, as long as it is great (XVII, 289).

The novel may present 'the great battles' in terms of social forces (as Zola had done in *Germinal* and *La Terre*), but the drama, he clearly thinks, should direct itself to 'burrowing deeply into the human mind'. *Fordringsägare* does this in a particularly unrelieved fashion. Undistracted by the surface paraphernalia of 'realism', its real setting is in the minds of the three characters, and the real furniture is provided by the metaphors of their language, the brains and nerves and guts which they pull out of each other. Like *Fröken Julie*, it is meant to be played without an interval; but there is nothing to compare with the ballet-like interlude which conveys some sense of a world elsewhere, outside the tense relationship between Julie and Jean. Here — apart from a couple of 'travelling ladies' who happen to look in at the verandah door and point their fingers at the sight of Tekla in the arms of Gustav — there is no other world, just a relentless round of two-somes: Gustav-Adolf; Adolf-Tekla (with Gustav listening next door); Tekla-Gustav (with Adolf similarly listening).

Fordringsägare entirely follows the paradigm of 'Hjärnornas kamp', which is a fictive account by a scientist of how he demolished a young man's self, crushed his will, and planted his own thoughts to breed like parasites in his mind. The story ends with the young man breaking the hypnotic bond, as the scientist makes the mistake of 'analyzing' his victim and so rousing his consciousness of what is being done to him. In the play the process has gone too far for any such resolution. Gustav says to his divorced wife, Tekla, of her present husband, Adolf, 'then I had a desire to pull him apart — stir the pieces so that he couldn't be repaired again — and I succeeded, thanks to your meticulous preparations.' And Adolf, overhearing this and much more, is indeed irreparably in pieces. The total destruction of his self is represented by him being reduced to a thing, foaming at the mouth in a presumably fatal epileptic fit. In *Fadren* and *Fröken Julie* the hypnotic power of the stronger self is seen at work only intermittently, notably as the Nurse talks the Captain into his 'vest', and as Jean tells Julie to go and kill herself (but then it is she who wills him to will her). The Captain recounts how, when he loved her as a woman, Laura used to wield such power over him 'that I neither saw nor heard, but only obeyed; you could give me a raw potato and persuade me it was a peach' (27.71). Her power over him now, as seen in the play, is something far more ambivalent. As The Mother she is the only one who can be sure of Bertha's paternity, and as the stronger (because more unscrupulous) she can, Iago-like, break down his sanity by suspicions:

Yes, you dropped them like henbane into my ear, and the circumstances gave them growth. (27.66)

But, as this speech shows, he knows all along what she is doing to him and knows, too, that he and 'circumstances' are helping her to do it. In *Fordringsägare* Adolf has no such knowledge. It is only at the beginning of the third (and last) scene that he learns, off-stage, that Gustav was Tekla's first husband. The 'hypnotic' technique dominates throughout. Adolf is a double victim: of Tekla's sexual hypnosis in the past, which he recounts to Gustav in the first scene, and which we see a version of in the second scene; and of Gustav's manipulation of him in the present. This is shown us directly in the first scene, indirectly in the second (for Adolf now speaks to Tekla as a puppet worked by the listening Gustav), and in the third we know that the whole dialogue is a killing weapon against him. Psychological theory and dramatic technique have merged completely. We are fascinated by the characters' interactions and held by the sheer, consistent intensity of the world of mutual torment. But it is a kind of inhuman fascination, for we are

Chapter II

unable to give sympathy anywhere. In the other two plays our sympathies are moved to and fro.

That this is so, is to a large extent a matter of Strindberg's handling of the dialogue, and we must finally turn again to the dramatic language of these plays. The essays in *Vivisektioner* are insistent and explicit on language as a tool of power. In 'Hjärnornas kamp' it is the chief tool: 'I drip my thoughts into his brain in the shape of nicely stylized axioms' (29.41) the scientist says, reminding us to watch how things are said as well as what is said. In 'Själamord' Strindberg displays a more general interest in language as a 'cover' for thought: 'The wisest, or the one who could best mask his real intentions, won the battle' (29.79). And to speak spontaneously is to render oneself vulnerable:

To be true, to show oneself as one really is, to speak one's thoughts such as they are spontaneously born in one's brain, is mortally dangerous. (29.80)

Or, as Jean puts it more concretely:

You shouldn't drink, for it makes you talk. And you shouldn't talk! (27.167)

The two patterns of language suggested here — as the tool of strength and as the (often unintentional) manifestation of weakness — are also the ones which operate in the plays, though in no simple, diagrammatic manner. They overlap, intersect and perform all manner of arabesques. Even so, to keep them in sight helps us to see Strindberg the self-conscious artist at work in dialogue which is often in itself as apparently spontaneous as if he simply looked in his heart and wrote.

Fröken Julie is in this respect the most self-conscious of the plays and would seem so even if we did not have Strindberg's analysis in the Preface of his method of constructing the dialogue and of marking the interaction of minds by allowing 'the weaker to steal and repeat words from the stronger' (27.105). All three characters receive 'suggestions' from each other: it is Kristin's point about the first being the last which becomes crucial to both Jean and Julie at the end. The second half of the play is both a mirror-image of the first and an antithesis to it; visions are undone, things are unsaid, and early confidences now become devastating weapons, sometimes in stichomythic cross-bombardment:

MISS JULIE So, you are one of those...
JEAN I had to think of something to say; women always fall for pretty stories.
MISS JULIE Wretch!
JEAN *Merde!*
MISS JULIE And now you have seen the hawk's back...
JEAN Not exactly its *back*...
MISS JULIE And I was to be the first branch...
JEAN But the branch was rotten....
MISS JULIE And I was to be the signboard of the hotel...
JEAN And I the hotel... (27.155-156)

The technique can be as staccato in effect as here (and possibly a little strained), or it can be used as movingly as in Julie's self-aborting attempt to persuade Kristin to join her and Jean in a flight to Lake Como.

In *Fadren* the power wielded through language is less readily analyzable. In a sense we are made to feel that speech is weakness and strength lies in silence or in brief, brutal statements, such as Laura's declaration of her intent to have the Captain declared insane which, at the end of Act II, leaves the Captain (like Billy Budd) with no language but an act of physical violence. Speech reflects moral sensitivity: at the end of the duologue with the Pastor in Act III, in which indeed he has said far more than she, she can turn on him with a 'You talk too much, as if you had a guilty conscience! Accuse me; if you can!' (27.80). Speech also reflects the quality of intelligence and imagination: she can puncture the Captain's possibly most important speech, on life's instability, with a deflating 'You ought to have been a writer, you know!' (27.71). The Captain's speeches rely increasingly as the play proceeds on associations, metaphors, parallels, quotations; they are self-analytical and generalizing; he probes himself and the human condition. But he is ineffectual: in speaking, as in acting, all he achieves is to persuade those around him that he is mad. To be sensitive is to be fragmented; and his self is, like J. Alfred Prufrock's, made up of remembered snatches; his voice a borrowed one. Twice at least his inability to respond except through analogies is taken to self-parodic lengths: in his paraphrase of Shylock's speech in Act II and in the catalogue of cuckolds in literature, in Act III. Against the pragmatic literalness of Laura, whose strength lies in seeing only her own specific purpose, he is powerless. She has the strength of a Bolingbroke against Richard II; but as in *Richard II* neither protagonist nor antagonist

Chapter II

provokes in us a single and simple response. Though, in the Captain's words, love between man and woman is 'like race-hatred', his use of Shylock's speech (27.69) does not confer on him exclusive sympathy, as a victim. In the Naturalistic convention it is also bound to sound histrionic. Seen from her point of view — and the play forces us thus to see her at such times — Laura has something to be said for her. Ultimately, whatever we know from other sources about Strindberg's attitude to women in the year 1887, she is not all villain. Seen from his own and others' points of view, the Captain is now grotesque, now heroic, now pathetic, provoking from us in all a set of contradictory responses. The most remarkable thing about the dialogue in *Fadren* is that it achieves for the play whose action, in paraphrase, may sound so single-minded such an emotional range and such a sway of sympathies.

The power of *Fordringsägare* lies, as we have already seen, in its single-mindedness. For the first few minutes Adolf dominates the dialogue, giving himself away; then Gustav takes over (whether on stage or not), and the dialogue becomes an extended metaphor of his destructive strength. The play depends even more than the other Naturalistic ones on verbal imagery: not for exploring individual visions, but for analysing the central action, the disembowelling, taking to pieces, and so on. Imagery and action are one. If, by Strindberg's standards of Naturalism, this is the more achieved work of art, the very achievement has within it the signs of its own limitations. These become still more apparent in the one-act plays which Strindberg wrote in the same period. What I have in mind here is not so much the cranky or sensationalist side of Strindberg's interest in the powers of suggestion, which is responsible for *Samum*, in which an Arabian girl literally frightens a French soldier to death. I have in mind *Den starkare*, which is an entire embodiment of the language patterns we have been exploring, in their extreme forms.

The battle-ground in *Den starkare* is, externally, 'a corner of a café for ladies' on Christmas Eve. Throughout, only one of the two characters speaks. Miss Y's persistent silence makes Mrs X say all. Initially, Mrs X feels this as a weakness in herself and a strength in Miss Y. When the 'suspicions' and evidence add up, so that she sees Miss Y as her husband's mistress and the force who has shaped his tastes, even his passions, then she becomes imaginatively articulate about her own relationship with Miss Y:

Your soul crept into mine like a worm into an apple, it ate and ate, burrowed and burrowed, until there was nothing left but the skin with a little black dust inside. I wanted to flee from you, but I couldn't; you lay there like a snake with your dark eyes putting a spell on me — I felt how my wings, opening for flight, only dragged me down; I lay in the water with my feet bound, and the harder I tried to use my hands to swim, the deeper down they brought me, until I sank to the bottom where you were lurking, like a giant crab, to grab me in your claws — and that's where I am lying now! (33.17-18)

But then she begins to see the silence of the other woman as a limitation. It is an 'indifference' to the seasons, to the happiness or unhappiness of others and an 'inability to love or hate'. Perhaps the silence which she, Mrs X, has taken to be strength is merely because Miss Y has nothing to say; and perhaps this simply means that she has no thoughts, no imagination! So, she concludes, perhaps she herself is really the stronger?

The play's title would seem to contain an irony: who is truly the stronger self depends in the end on one's viewpoint. Undoubtedly, for all that one tends to admire the *tour de force* of the silent Miss Y's performance, Mrs X receives the stronger sympathy from the audience: not for the quantity of her speech but because of its quality. Strindberg has given this character, when under stress, that ability to think and feel in images which some Shakespearean heroes (such as Macbeth) possess; and it sets up a special bond between us and the speaker. It is not that we *approve,* necessarily, of such characters, but that we *know* them, from the inside. We follow the workings of their mind, and their images tell us of experiences — of being haunted by 'pity, like a naked newborn babe', or by giant crabs — in which they are powerless. Mrs X's speech, at points like this is 'Naturalistic' (in Strindberg's sense), rather than 'realistic'. The ex-actress who trip-traps her husband's slippers across the table would in 'real' life hardly be able to articulate her deepest fears; but the images perform what Strindberg calls a ''deep excavation' of her mind. At the same time their function belongs to poetic drama.

The overall structure of the play shows a Phyrric victory for Miss Y — and also for Strindberg. His sense of dramatic form, if we look at the rapid development from *Fadren,* via *Fordringsägare* to *Den starkare,* has narrowed to where it seems to be driving him into a *cul-de-sac.* Dramatic subject and method have fused, in a Beckett-like reduction of possibilities. Yet, inside these plays there are seeds of a kind of poetic drama of the inner life, and these were to come to fruition after his experience of 'Inferno'.

The autobiographical work *Inferno* (1897), which Strindberg composed in French, bears much the same relation to the plays which followed as *Tjänstekvinnans son* does to the Naturalistic plays. It signalled the end of a period of infertility, and in form, in structure and texture, it can be seen as the main source of the most distinctive plays of Strindberg's later career.

When Strindberg first conceived *Inferno*, he saw it as 'a poem in prose' and a response to the 'call' to become 'the Zola of the occult' (37.347). Outlining this prose poem, in which he intended to strike a 'grand high' tone, he is quite clear about its thematic structure and didactic bearings. It was to have the same theme as his Nietzschean novel *I havsbandet*:

The way an individual is destroyed when he isolates himself. Salvation through: working without thought for glory and gold, duty, family, consequently — woman — mother and child!

Resignation through the discovery that each one of us has his task allotted by Providence.(37.347)

This was written in August 1896; during the next month he feels he is 'being driven forward to the writing of Inferno'. The 'being driven' is in terms of spiritual experience: he is in fact living what was to become the Austrian and Swedenborgian parts of *Inferno* and life is continually modifying art. And so, when he finally sits down to compose the *Inferno* in the early summer of 1897, its structure becomes something very different. 'A genuine diary with digressions' (*Letters* II.610) is how he describes it in a letter, and in the last paragraph of the published volume, he warns the reader against regarding it as 'dikt'. The 'grand high tone' has been replaced by the immediacy of painful experience, as the 'I' of the book moves between Paris, Sweden and Austria, tormented in body and soul by strange persecutions. The structure follows the curve of the experience: an apparently artless chronological account of his movements, with no sign of a pattern or conclusion to produce the 'moral' envisaged in 1896. The ending deliberately casts forward, much like the ending of *Tjänstekvinnans son*, into an uncertain but immediate future: we leave him on the brink of committing himself to Roman Catholic Christianity, awaiting a reply from the Belgian monastery to which he has written to ask for a refuge.

From this time on, Strindberg's 'sense of an ending'[18] will be even further from the certainty of a resolution than it was in his earlier works. One might see it epitomized in the closing moment of *Till Damaskus I* when The Unknown follows The Lady 'towards the church door' on the one word 'Maybe!' Nearly always there will be a hovering sense of the ending as a possible new beginning. 'You see', says The Other to The Magistrate at the end of *Advent*, 'there is an end as long as there is a beginning. And you have made a beginning!' (40.125). And, like the transformation scene in an Elizabethan masque, the back of the stage changes into a Nativity scene, with a choir singing *Gloria in excelcis*. The ray of hope is rarely so literally realized and usually in more human terms (as at the end of *Påsk*). And his comedy and tragedy alike will retain the possibility that it may be a farce, at the expense of man.

It was natural for Strindberg to continue *Inferno* into a second part, and then into a third, and equally natural that these, which chart his encounter with the God of the Bible, should take the shape of an even more open-ended structure. When they were published as *Legender* in May 1898, Strindberg had added a Postscript to tell the reader about what he now saw as his failure to render his own religious struggle in 'an allegorized narrative' (XXVIII, 399). The final section, *Jakob brottas*, has, he says, 'remained a fragment and, like all religious crises, dissolved into chaos'. To a twentieth-century reader, bred on fragments, the structure is very effective, as an image of grappling with Godot and refusing (in Strindberg's words) to commit suicide on one's own self. In that sense, the fragmentary form is functional: there can be no end to this Jacob's wrestling. But there is another side to the picture, too. The autobiographical work was abandoned as a fragment, because by this time — the winter and early spring of 1898 — Strindberg was writing *Till Damaskus*, the first of a trilogy and the first of a whole rich spate of plays in which the material of *Inferno* and *Legender* — the writing as well as the living — was to be translated into drama.

For all Strindberg's stress on Inferno not being *'dikt'*, and his explicit disclaimer of having written 'a novel making claims to literary style and structure'(37.202), the work *is* also the 'prose poem' he had originally envisaged. That is, of course, a prose poem finding, under the pressure of experience, its own organic form, rather than the tendentious one of the early plan. The shaping imagination which achieved this can more easily be analyzed in parts than in the whole,

Chapter II

and a useful section to concentrate on would be the one in chapter IX which describes the author's walk through a ravine near an Austrian village. He has just encountered Swedenborg's presentation of earth as Hell; and, though he has attempted to thrust this experience 'down into the deepest recesses of the mind' (37.204-5), it not only colours but transforms all he sees and hears. Each person and animal he sees, each object, natural or man-made, all take on some mysterious significance. The miller's boys, 'as white as the false angels, tend to the wheels of the machinery like executioners' (208). In the smithy, with its black and naked smiths and their infernal instruments, the noise 'shakes the brain on its firm stem and makes the heart jump inside the ribcage' (*ibid*). At the saw-mill 'the huge saw... gnashes its teeth when it tortures the gigantic tree trunks on the rack, while the transparent blood pours onto the sticky ground' (*ibid*).

He concludes the stage-by-stage description, 'I returned the way I had come, immersed in contemplation of this combination of coincidences which together form a great whole, wonderful without being supernatural' (208). This sentence could represent the whole of *Inferno*, but also the structure of *Till Damaskus* (where, in the first part, of course, The Unknown quite literally returns the same way he came) and many of the later works: a 'wander' through scenes where people and objects are keenly perceived in their own right but also transformed by the mind which perceives them, and which follow each other *not* with logical necessity or casual connection but just because each is a station on the way. And the actions of each scene do not add up to an allegorical, 'supernatural', pattern but speak together of the 'wonderful'.

The texture of the writing in this passage, too, leads us into the later plays. Its effect is of scenery and 'actors' shifting according to the perceiver's viewpoint; objects are now innocuous, now imbued with dreadful significance. *Påsk* is a play which almost entirely depends on this effect. The characteristically Strindbergian process of perception which produces this effect is, of course, based on the Romantic refusal to separate subject and object: the mind creating what it sees. But to this Strindberg adds *both* a strong awareness of the dark recesses of that mind *and* a new sense of the possibility that the mind and external reality are jointly controlled from outside — above — by 'powers'. The typically Strindbergian quality of perception, however, which controls all the rest, and which seems to be an inalienable part of his ability to write, is the knack of keeping hold of solid, physical things even while deeply inside a mental experience. A vision of 'Dante's Hell' turns out to be a pig-sty (cf. 37.206), and a flash of solid sanity gives a saving tinge of the comic to the nightmare world of the mind. One remembers, too, the Poet in *Ett drömspel* who first appears preparing to wallow in mud. He is then given a soliloquy on the subject of clay and mud, in which 'ecstatic' and 'sceptical' lines alternate in a comically pointed epitome of human contradictoriness and of Strindberg's range of vision.

That sense of self-awareness, communicated through touches of absurd comedy, is an important strain in the later plays. It dominates whole scenes, like the infernal ball, in that wonderfully varied *Advent*; and it pervades the whole of *Spöksonaten*. It is responsible for the extraordinary emotional range of both parts of *Dödsdansen*, where the sudden shifts from despair to laughter, from hatred to love — shifts particularly important in the endings of each part, often leave an audience baffled as to how to take the play, especially if they have come expecting to see a later version of *Fadren*. It is never absent for long from *Inferno*. One moment the 'I' will see his worst fears of persecution confirmed, the next he will be released from them by an impromptu children's dance in his kitchen, to the tunes of a barrel organ — the voice of the author coming in to tell us that this 'puts an end to the dismal drama which had been threatening to develop into a farce' (37.262). Towards the end of *Inferno*, as the writer's viewpoint and that of the experiencing 'I' begin to coincide, the sense of the possibility of the whole thing being 'a gigantic joke' (37.294) grows more explicit. The comedy may be as cruel as Gloucester's vision of 'flies to wanton boys', but at least the flies are here able to share in the joke. Thus, in response to some ominous behaviour of his night candle, which he finds himself smiling at:

Smile at death! How could this be possible if life was not inherently comical? So much fuss about so little! It may even be that in the innermost recesses of the soul there is a vague awareness that everything on this earth is only a masquerade, is an illusion and a series of false images, and that the gods amuse themselves with our sufferings. (37.266)

It is this quality in the writing — the chances we are given to stand back from experiences — which prevents the horror paraphernalia of *Inferno* (the strange noises in the night, the electric shocks, etc.) from becoming horrific, and the shafts of hope (the sudden breaking through

Chapter II

of the sun, the prattle of the child) from becoming sentimental. This is why, in the end, the *Inferno* is not, despite its remarkable evocation of a hell here and now, a painful or depressing work to read. Instead, it is full of life and excitement, based on an extraordinary versatility. Every state, every object, we feel, may at any moment turn into its opposite, for good or ill. The beautiful will grow out of the morbid, only perhaps in the end to make the morbid more fearsome. Thus, quite early in the work, in the midst of his scientific experiments in Paris, his hands scorched and bleeding from heat and chemicals, he plants a walnut, the image of the human brain; and after four days

I released the embryo, which in the shape of a heart not larger than a pear seed is wedged between two cotyledons resembling a human brain. Imagine my reaction when I saw through the microscope two small hands, white as alabaster, raised and clasped as if in prayer. Is it a vision, an hallucination? Not at all! An overwhelming reality which fills me with horror. Motionless, stretched out towards me as if in supplication, I can count their five fingers, the thumb shorter than the others, women's or children's hands! . . . What is this? The first two rudimentary leaves of a walnut tree, *Juglans regia*, Jupiter's acorn. Nothing else. And yet, it was an undeniable fact that the ten fingers of human shape were clasped in the gesture of prayer: *de profundis clamavi ad te*! (37.59-60).

Scientific precision is combined with a sense of the wonderful *and* the grotesque in a way which, if I were to define it by comparison, I could only liken to those sections in Thomas Mann's *The Magic Mountain* where Hans Castorp learns what life is through a study of embryology.[19] At the same time, Strindberg's writing here is pervaded by that sense of possibilities — of the natural *and* supernatural explanations both being true — which, in English literature, we hardly find later than in Sir Thomas Browne.

Standing back from *Inferno*, one remembers it as a series of images carrying complex moods, held together into a structure by the 'I's' progression from one image to another. The 'meaning' is inseparable from that structure. To try to detach something more theoretically paraphraseable would be futile or false; and Strindberg himself confirms this when he disclaims a 'system', seeing in himself

A condition of the mind rather than a view based on theories; a motley blend of perceptions which are more or less concentrated into ideas.

If this may be said to be his epistemology in this last period of creativity, it is also a description of — a blue-print for — his dramatic art. The revolutionary discovery which Strindberg made in the first part of *Till Damaskus* and went on to develop not only in the further two parts of that play but also in, most particularly, *Ett drömspel* and the Chamber Plays, was that there was no need for an Aristotelian structure of causal connections to keep an audience under the illusion that they were watching 'real' life. After all, rather than dramatic illusion, they would be given something far truer to life: for we do not perceive our lives as neat, coherent plots; nor does the surface, which is all that can be 'realistically' depicted, tell us enough of the depths beneath. So, in giving dramatic form to his vision — performing, in his own terms, 'self-sacrifice' — Strindberg also provided the theatres of the world with what Gunnar Ollén has defined as 'the model for expressionistic drama, which depicts reality and its forms not as it seems to an outside objective observer but as it appears to the ... subject the action of the play deals with'.[20]

I have said enough about these plays already to be able now to summarize quite briefly their 'anatomy' and 'physiology'. In the Naturalistic plays, individual speeches pursued a 'search' for identity, the character exploring how he (or she) has come to be as he is now. In *Till Damaskus* and *Ett drömspel* that search has become the guiding structural principle. It breaks open all the dramatic unities. The three parts of *Till Damaskus* take The Unknown from his meeting (though not the first) with The Lady to his 'death' to the world and entry into a monastery, through a series of interwoven marital and religious conflicts. *Ett drömspel* takes Indra's Daughter to the earth to discover what man's lot is like; she lives through a cross-section of human experience, marital and social, and returns to her celestial father with the assurance that 'human beings are to be pitied'. Compared to the claustrophobic worlds of the Naturalistic plays, these are far more wide-flung and varied; yet they are also dominated by an intense inwardness which turns every external feature into an aspect of the central character's quest. This applies to locations — the geography through which The Unknown travels is ultimately a spiritual one — as well as to other characters, whose type-names alone suggest that they are not important as individuals in their own right. *Den Okände* is, by definition, The Unknown attempting to know himself through relationships with others and with his God (if there is one). As he walks

Chapter II

the long road which will transform him from a Saul to a Paul (but does it, for all the attempts at a both Hegelian and Christian resolution in the last scene of Part III?), the figures he meets may be his own doubles, like The Beggar and Caesar, the madman, or they exist in any case simply for what they bring out of his own past and present. The Lady has a name, Ingeborg, but she remains the figure of woman, provoker of an apparently never-ending cycle of love and hatred, attraction and repulsion. The Confessor, who himself splits into several manifestations, is the explicit link with the mysterious Power which drives The Unknown along his path. Analyzed like this, the play sounds rarified and allegorical. But each encounter is so sharply realized, each detail so precisely observed, that we feel in continuous contact with ordinary reality. In that sense, we are not plunged unquestioningly into the consciousness of 'the subject of the play' (Ollén) and asked to accept his or her viewpoint. Indra's daughter makes a pretty awful housewife; and we are even invited, in the depths of The Unknown's agony, to consider The Beggar's opinion that he is 'deuced funny' (39.132) — a Shakespearean touch if ever there was one.

Nor, of course, is the structure as arbitrarily composed as if to follow a random search. The first part of *Till Damaskus* is perfectly symmetrical: of its seventeen scenes, the first eight take The Unknown through eight different locations, starting 'at the street corner', to 'the Asylum', where he is cursed by men and God. From this ninth scene, which is both the low point and the pivot, he returns through the same locations, in reverse order, to end up again 'at the street corner'. Strindberg wrote in a letter about the play that 'The art lies in the composition, which symbolizes the "Repetition" Kierkegaard speaks of' (*Letters* II.624). Certainly the very obvious pattern leaves us with the sense that 'In my end is my beginning'.[21] Part I is a self-contained symbolical structure: there is no evidence that Strindberg had a trilogy in mind while he was writing this play. Nor does he try to repeat the structural pattern. The scene, each in a separate and well-defined location, remains the unit, and locations recur, with haunting echoes. When Strindberg came to write his 'Memorandum' to *Ett drömspel* he felt, in retrospect, that he had employed the same technique in *Till Damaskus*, 'his previous dreamplay':

The author has ... tried to imitate the incoherent but seemingly logical form of the dream. Anything can happen, anything is possible and probable. Time and space do not exist; on an insignificant base of reality the imagination spins and weaves new patterns: a mixture of memories, experiences, free invention, absurdities and improvisations. (46.7)

There are indeed some dream-like transitions in *Till Damaskus* but it is only in the later *Drömspel* that Strindberg fully relies on a technique of letting one scene dissolve and turn into another before our eyes, furniture and props remaining but with new significance, as when the Lawyer's office becomes the scene for an academic degree ceremony. The structure of the play indeed gives us a sense that 'anything can happen', and that our hold on reality is tenuous. The change from one scene to another needs no motivation, or no more than the Officer saying 'Let us talk about something else' (46.61), but persistent effects of echoing and repetition create strands among our perceptions which are 'more or less concentrated into ideas' (see above). The scene between Indra's Daughter and The Poet in Fingal's Cave — the shell-like cave, Indra's Ear — becomes a fulcrum for the whole play. Into it are gathered all the motifs of the sorrows and hopes of mankind which are enacted singly or in combinations, in the other scenes of the play; and out of it radiate the implications of the dialogue. The Poet tells Indra's Daughter that he has *diktat* all that she has experienced in the play, and she defines *dikt* as:

Not reality but more than reality . . . not dream but waking dreams . . . (46.91)

The wholeness of this play as a poetic drama — an extended metaphor of life as a dream — is impressive. It is also, of course, self-conscious: Indra's Daughter and The Poet also stand, as it were, at the innermost point of a nest of Chinese boxes. It is in no way to minimize the newness of Strindberg's achievement if we also remember that the principle of construction in the dream plays is very much the same as the 'polyphonous' and 'counterpointing' devices which Strindberg points to in the analysis of *A Midsummer Night's Dream* that he wrote at about the same time as the Memorandum to *Ett drömspel* and which he claims to have used, himself, as early as *Mäster Olof*. Strindberg, in one way or another, constantly reminds us of the craftsmanship which went into his art.

Strindberg's Naturalistic plays depended heavily on the spoken word. If your antagonist is an Unseen, he cannot share a dialogue; and we have seen how in *Inferno* states of mind are defined by descriptive imagery. The great challenge in translating the world and art of *Inferno*

Chapter II

into dramatic and theatrical terms was to find visual equivalents for states of mind. The ravine, for example, which the 'I' of *Inferno* experienced as a Hell on earth, is also the location of scenes six and twelve in *Till Damaskus I*, and it recurs in Part II. The features described in *Inferno* are now visually represented in Part I; in Part II the smithy and the mill have been swept away by the flood. The Smith and the Miller's Wife make brief, unspeaking appearances in the two scenes in Part I, to demonstrate human unkindness and cruelty. In Part II, when the mill itself is gone, The Beggar is allowed to expound its meaning as a 'mill of sin', but in Part I it is for The Unknown to suggest, by a reference to his fears, 'when I saw just now the blacksmith standing in the glow of his fire opposite the white miller's wife', how much the play depends on what we actually can see. The director and stage-designer have to be largely responsible for creating this particular Hell. In a similar fashion, setting (natural and domestic), social rituals (like the degree ceremony) and objects form stage images which are also projections and other ways of 'transforming the dream into visual representations without materializing it too much.'[22]

His visual imagination was running ahead of what the theatres of his day could manage: he was not, for example, to live to see a theatre and a director able to cope with the final moments of *Ett drömspel* when a castle bursts into flames, revealing 'a wall of human faces, enquiring, grieving, despairing', while at the same time the flower bud crowning the castle opens into 'a giant chrysanthemum' (46.122). The *Öppna brev till Intima Teatern* tell something of the frustrations involved in trying to find a visual language for these plays. That he persisted is an indication that some of the things he wanted to say could be said in no other language. An example of this would be the banquet scene in Part II of *Till Damaskus*, where the stage directions add up to a choreographic pattern on which rests the whole complex of emotions in the scene. Abandoning his wife in childbirth, The Unknown has come (he thinks) to be publically honoured as 'the greatest man of the century'. But the 'royal feast' turns out a hoax, and his victory turns to ashes and shame. Even as he is making a speech of thanks, the setting of the banquet is being dismantled, tin mugs replacing the golden goblets and a crew of drunkards and other wretches (ominously present at the lower tables right from the opening of the scene) sliding into the seats of honour previously occupied by gentlemen in the full regalia of tails and medals. Within minutes the banqueting-hall has become a bar and a brothel, and these eventually dissolve in 'a confusion of scenery', out of which emerges a prison cell with The Unknown sitting alone in it. If, as is no doubt the case, the subject of this scene is Strindberg's personal emotions of hope, ambition and guilt around his experiments in alchemy, he has found a superb objective correlative for them in the theatrical image. As an audience, what we see and hear is not a private confession but a kind of masque in which the antimasque overcomes the main — celebratory — masque; a *sic transit gloria mundi* enacted as a tragicomedy of man's capacity for delusion. One world is proved delusory by the invasion of another; and in the end both are equally unreal, for in the next scene the Unknown is back in 'the Rose Chamber' and his wife still in labour, and we realize that the scene took place in his dreams or imagination.

Another element of the tragi-comedy of this scene is the musical accompaniment to the celebration and the transformation: Mendelssohn's Funeral March, played 'pianissimo' as the scene opens and more emphatically at other points. Music is altogether an important part of the post-Inferno plays: as an ironic comment, or as interpreter of mood or as conveyor of a state of mind. As long ago as the Preface to *Fröken Julie* Strindberg had been interested in musical *structures* as a model for dramatic dialogue (see above); now he is preoccupied with the power of music to express and communicate emotion more immediately than words can do.

If there is a quality of 'total theatre' in Strindberg's dependence on visual and musical rather than verbal forms of expression, this does not mean that he is losing confidence in language. On the contrary, his verbal range expands in this period. *Ett drömspel* shows the extreme of that range, as we move from The Daughter's domestic disputes with The Lawyer to her lyrical interchanges with The Poet, or from the concrete idiom of the Coal-carriers to the esoteric symbolism of the Voice of Indra. The Unknown in *Till Damaskus* pushes the self-analytical monologue, or semi-monologue, almost as far as it will go; and yet his dialogues with The Lady have lost none of the Naturalistic plays' ability to show the cogs of two minds fatally failing to mesh. What is new in the dialogue of these plays is a language for togetherness (not needed in the struggles between brains in the earlier plays!), suggested in a stylized form in the dialogue between The Poet and Indra's Daughter in the Cave of Fingal and brought to full use at the beginning of the last scene of *Spöksonaten*. The sense of closeness between The Student and The Lady, amounting to an affinity, is enacted by a dialogue in which they 'interpret' the symbolism of the hyacinth and other flowers. Their speech-patterns interweave, to the point where their thoughts fuse:

THE YOUNG LADY Whose thought was that?
THE STUDENT Yours!
THE YOUNG LADY Yours!
THE STUDENT Ours! — We have given birth to something together, we are married . . . (58.213)

What is also new in the language of the post-Inferno plays is a sense of the mysteries which are beyond words. The Poet in *Ett drömspel* knows that human language is inadequate for communion with the divine; he asks The Daughter to 'translate it into the language / the Immortals best comprehend' (XXXVI, 304-305). Later The Daughter points out to him that his language isn't even adequate to his own human sorrows; it cannot stretch to match his own thoughts (325). And finally she refuses to formulate the farewell speech he asks for, because 'your words can[not] express our thoughts'. In the post-Inferno plays, the mystery is also outside the mind of man, and we have seen how characters are made to fall silent before the unspeakable. A visual or musical symbol (like the close of *Advent*) may be the best language.

Anyone reading *Inferno*, and even more *En blå bok*, must be aware that Strindberg was in these years much influenced by Swedenborg's idea of 'correspondences', of phenomena in the physical world existing as 'parallels' to those in the spiritual world. The 'chapter' entitled *Blå Bokens Historia* (XLVI, 404-415) is a good guide to life thus lived like a series of symbolical experiences. To Strindberg in this period, as Karl-Åke Kärnell shows in his study of Strindberg's imagery, the '*diktare* is an interpreter of the divine order in a universe woven through with analogies'; and a verbal metaphor is 'a concept of metaphysical dignity'.[23] Clearly his thoughts on art and its function were moving in much the same areas as the French Symbolists'. When Baudelaire says that what the poet 'asks of the world of the senses is that it give him the means of expressing the soul',[24] then he, too, is ultimately harking back to Swedenborg's correspondences. Strindberg *was* asking just that of the world of the senses; but what also characterizes him, and makes it impossible to fit him into any -ism, was his vigorous interest in that world *as such*. It is no doubt significant that he never really wrote any Symbolist poetry: the nearest he gets to it is in parts of the long poetic medley called *Trefaldighetsnatten* (The Night before Trinity Sunday). There is, for example, 'Chrysaëtos', a poem of loss and grief, with the intensity of a waking dream and with every element made part of the lyric's emotion, even the totally untranslatable sound effects:

> *Vad vänta de tråkiga kråkorna*
> *Därnere på höstlig hed?* (51.21)

But held within the loose fictional framework, of poems recited by a group of men drinking and talking together during the night before Trinity Sunday, are a vast variety of other poems, including hexameter 'idylls' of Swedish summer and a narrative-dramatic poem on marital Heaven turning to Hell at the adjusting of a shoulder strap (51.33). One cannot help feeling that it is the medley as a whole, not the rarified 'mood' lyric, which is 'Strindbergian'.

The same point applies, finally, to the Chamber Plays. When Strindberg explains what he was aiming at in writing these — 'The idea of chamber music transferred to the drama' and 'No definite form shall bind the author, for the subject determines the form'(L,12) — and when we note the centrality of music in the plays, then it would seem that Strindberg is willy nilly working to the Symbolist doctrine of form as purely functional, and of form and content coalescing, as in music. In a sense he is. Each of the five plays takes a single motif (a complex of emotions, rather than a 'plot') and explores it, exhausting it within the scope of a long one-acter; a full-length Chamber Play is as unthinkable as a long Symbolist poem. In each, ordinary logic is, as in the dream plays, more or less suspended, and the technique is suggestive. We feel that there are mysteries behind all that is said and done. And yet, even in trying to generalize as far as that, one is brought up against differences between the plays: the variety they represent and the variety which is in each one. *Oväder (The Storm), Brända tomten* and *Pelikanen* (The Pelican) all work through a kind of heightened domestic realism, probing the wounds which people living together in the family unit will inflict on each other. *Svarta handsken* (The Black Glove) — the least known and probably most uneven, but not least rewarding, of this group of plays — takes quite Baroque liberties in mixing such domestic realism with fairy-tale figures: Father Christmas (the Swedish, house-gnome variety) and the Christmas Angel. The result is not

Chapter II

altogether free from schmalz; but the half-way figures are interesting — the care-taker in his basement room, like a guardian of the block of flats; and a Casaubon-type Old Man in the attic, surrounded by sixty years' notes from which he hopes to solve the riddle of the Universe — and the Christmas gnome, in describing the 'Babel's Tower' of flats, produces some wonderful poetry of urban life. *Spöksonaten* holds elements of all the other Chamber Plays — indeed, one is tempted to say, of all that Strindberg wrote. There is a pattern of 'realistic' family relationships, for everyone in the block of flats outside and inside which the action takes place is part of an intricate network of parents, children, servants, seducers, etc. But there is also a pattern where these figures are seen — and behave — as ghosts, mummies, vampires, etc. The 'ghost supper' which brings them all together, also brings the two patterns together, into a savagely farcical version of 'psychic murder'. The Old Man, who starts as The Stronger, stripping others of their masks, has the tables turned on him by The Mummy and ends up, himself stripped, reduced to a chattering parrot in a cupboard. Indeed The Mummy acts the Jean to his Julie and provides him with both the equipment and the language for suicide (58.209). In yet another pattern, The Student is the clever youth of fairy-tale, gifted with special sight and capable of an act of heroism which helps to win him the Princess — the lovely Lady of the hyacinth room. But this pattern gets tangled in the other two: The Student's fairy god-father is The Old Man, and The Lady is part of the ghostly household and 'ill at the source of life' (58.224). She dies, annihilated as it were by words: by an enormously long speech in which The Student turns his clear sight on her, on the household and on all that appears beautiful and good. In baring his soul, he kills her.

The mode of writing in The Student's speech is an extension of one which I noted in the Naturalistic plays (see above): the semi-monologue, proceeding by the speaker's association of ideas rather than any external logic. A thought or feeling or image (and it is false to separate the three) comes up, subsides, recurs. The syntax is loose; the punctuation knows no rules outside the consciousness it is helping to imitate; full stops have practically disappeared. Strindberg did not need Joyce's Molly Bloom to teach him how to construct an internal monologue; his own expressive needs seem to have led him to the technique. It appears as a structural device in his fiction of this period (cf. *Taklagsöl)* (The Roofing Feast) and is perfected in the Chamber Plays.

Spöksonaten is, in a sense, a Symbolist poem, held together as a 'musical' structure of motifs. But I think that that sense is largely theoretical. In the theatre it lives as drama, as life concretely and tangibly realized — through moments like the fat Cook's intrusion, with all the details of domestic misery, upon the ethereal happiness of The Lady and The Student. There is no easy formula for what those moments — of beauty *and* ugliness, love *and* hatred, truth *and* illusion — add up to. Perhaps this is why Strindberg is so difficult, and seems so modern. Elements of deep pessimism, of irony, and of at least a ray of hope (at the end) are held together dramatically, in a deliberately discordant relationship, not because Strindberg was neurotic, but because he was projecting a vision of a discordant, incohesive world.

In all its tragical-comical-realistic-symbolical variety, *Spöksonaten* must stand as the finishing-post of my exploration. If I have been able to suggest that Strindberg is more robust, more versatile and more of a conscious artist than the received image indicates, then the race will have been worth its while.

Chapter III

Nittitalister
'Writers of the 1890s'

Ulla Callmander

Nittitalet (i.e. the 1890s) does not imply a clear break with the previous decade but rather grew out of it naturally, and many of the protagonists of *Åttitalet* turned to the beliefs and opinions that became prevalent during the 1890s without any difficulty. Strindberg's homage to fantasy and Romanticism was, for instance, conspicuous in *Den romantiska klockaren på Rånö* (The Romantic Sexton at Rånö, 1888). Georg Brandes, the great oracle of *Åttitalet*, was one of the few critics to acknowledge and praise the first novel by a young, unknown teacher in 1891. The novel was *Gösta Berlings saga* (The Story of Gösta Berling) and Selma Lagerlöf was to be Sweden's best known writer abroad after Strindberg. These are but two examples of the general growing opposition to Naturalism. The grey, drab, detailed realism in the novels was considered too objective, everyday life was down to earth, limited and dreary, common people were after all just common. A kind of symbiosis between reality and poetry, a Naturalism combined with fancy was desirable. Heidenstam and Levertin phrased it in *Pepitas bröllop* (Pepita's Wedding): 'A well-told ghost story where the narrator is obvious is to be preferred to the sterile, true story where the personal touch is totally lacking.'[1] Time and circumstances were on the side of statements of this kind. Strindberg had left Sweden in 1883 and remained abroad for several years, and so a pillar of the 80s was gone and most of the remaining supporters were, if not enthralled, at any rate involved in the new, romantic ideals.

What then were these new ideals? Strindberg had claimed that 'what is ugly is true' but the writers of the 90s now praised love of beauty, joy of living and imagination. A good example of this yearning for beauty is expressed by Fröding in the lines:

> Fylgia, Fylgia, fly mig ej,
> du skygga, förnäma, sky mig ej,
> du min skönhetslängtan,
> som mot dagens sorger
> är min skyddande tröst i nattens syn!
> 'Fylgia', *Nya Dikter*, 1894 p. 256[2]

(Fylgia, Fylgia do not flee from me, you shy, noble one, do not shun me, you, my longing for beauty, my protection from the day's sorrow and my comfort during the night.)

This did not mean however that *Nittitalisterna* were indifferent to philosophy or politics, which they have often been accused of. They did value aestheticism more than ethical questions and all of them were influenced by Nietzsche, but their strong belief in the artist, in individualism and their reverence for extra-ordinary people and characters did not prevent them from observing the events of the world or those of Sweden. A famous example is of course Heidenstam's views on franchise rights in Sweden:

> Det är skam, det är fläck på Sveriges baner
> att medborgarrätt heter pengar.

(It is a shame, it is a stain on Sweden's banner that the franchise is equated with money.) ('Medborgarsång'(The Citizen's Song), *Ett folk*, 1899, p. 316)[3]

The effects of World War I were obvious in Karlfeldt's *Flora och Bellona,* and Selma Lagerlöf expressed similar sentiments in *Bannlyst* (The Outcast, 1918).

Social indignation was likewise reflected in their writing, e.g. in Lagerlöf's collection of short stories *Antikrists mirakler* (The Miracles of Antichrist, 1897) about the poor people in Italy or Fröding's 'Den gamla goda tiden' (The Good Old Days) *Nya Dikter*, 1894;

> Forsen dånade, hammaren stampade
> överdundrande knotets röst,

Chapter III

> ingen hörde ett knyst från de trampade,
> skinnade, plundrade
> ännu i hundrade
> år av förtvivlan och brännvinströst. (p.217)

(The river roared, the hammer pounded thundering over the grumbling voice, no one heard a sound from the downtrodden, fleeced and still robbed through hundreds of years of despair and comfort in aquavit.)

The greatest influence on *Nittitalisterna*, however, is the upsurge of nationalism in Swedish cultural life. Painters like Carl Larsson and Anders Zorn had a great impact on the prevailing taste. They stirred the national emotions of the Swedes, e.g. Carl Larsson's 'Ett Hem' or Zorn's sensual and folkloristic paintings of dances and young girls in Dalarna. Peterson-Berger did the same for music; Stenhammar set Heidenstam's 'Sverige' to music. Hazelius' Skansen was opened in 1891 and the Stockholm exhibition of 1897 implied a national optimistic faith in the future. The foundation of the newspaper *Svenska Dagbladet* and the literary journal *Ord och Bild* was equally important as it meant that the written word could now more easily reach the reading public. Swedish history inspired *Nittitalister*. The yearning for their homeland or the part of the country where they had spent their childhood and which they had often reluctantly had to leave for ever was reflected everywhere in their writing. In this way a new, regional writing was born, especially devoted to Värmland and Dalarna.

Linked to this was the everlasting attraction of Nature which often became personified, as in Heidenstam's 'Tiveden' (*Dikter*, 1895), and in Lagerlöf's description of Lake Löven modelled on Lake Fryken in *Gösta Berlings saga*.

Rousseau's attitude to Nature had influenced *Åttitalisterna* too, as shown for instance in Strindberg's 'En ovälkommen' (The Undesired), *Svenska öden och äventyr* (1883) or, why not? the opening chapter in *Röda rummet* (The Red Room, 1879). *Nittitalisterna* were indebted to *Åttitalisterna* for their detailed descriptions, their deep analyses of characters and their freedom of style. Now *Nittitalisterna* added another literary dimension, that of lyricism and poetry. The poetic impact was very strong and even their prose indulged in images, colourful, evocative vocabulary, ornamental or highly stylized language. The new idealism needed a new language.

Nittitalet is by no means a particularly Swedish movement but it differs from the general Schopenhauer-influenced pessimism and fin-de-siècle moods in Europe at the time. However writers, painters and musicians did go to Paris for inspiration and new ideas. The new literary ideas had been preceded in England by Swinburne, in the United States by E. A. Poe and in France by Baudelaire and in the Scandinavian countries by Johannes Jørgensen and Knut Hamsun. The traditionalism and regionalism mentioned above was found in Thomas Hardy's novels from the country of Wessex. Selma Lagerlöf and Gustaf Fröding were inspired by Sir Walter Scott, Robert Burns and Lord Byron and all *Nittitalisterna* were influenced by Goethe.

Heidenstam as a spokesman for the movement called for the pleasure of the moment and a joy of living, and there were rich sensualism, exotic descriptions, new metres in the new decade. Eventually however the tone became darker, the content deeper and more mature and reflected much scepticism and despair, not only optimism. The authors hid their loneliness, their feelings of alienation behind escapist masks as Karlfeldt does in his Fridolin or Fröding in 'Ett gammalt bergtroll' (An Old Mountain Troll, *Stänk och flikar*, 1896.) Others confessed them more openly as did Heidenstam in 'Ensamhetens tankar'. Personal conflicts are mirrored everywhere in Selma Lagerlöf's writing. This brings a deep sense of understanding and pity for the outcast in society, and this feeling is mutual for all the writers in question.

This survey of *Nittitalet* in Swedish literature discusses and exemplifies the most common denominators or themes found in Heidenstam, Selma Lagerlöf, Fröding and Karlfeldt and their most important works during this literary period. They include roots; nationalism; love; outcasts and misfits; despair and resignation; reconciliation and faith.

Verner von Heidenstam (1859-1940)

Roots

Sooner or later most writers confess more or less openly what impact and influence their childhood and upbringing have had on them, and these four writers are no exception. The remembrance of their roots, the places they grew up in, the stories they listened to and the narrators of those stories were to live with them forever and they had a compelling

Chapter III

urge to write about them.

> Jag längtar hem sen åtta långa år
> I själva sömnen har jag längtan känt.
> Jag längtar hem. Jag längtar var jag går
> - men ej till människor! Jag längtar marken,
> jag längtar stenarna där barn jag lekt.
> ('Ensamhetens tankar' IV, p. 97)

(I have longed for my home for eight long years, in my very sleep I have felt the longing, I long for my home. I long wherever I go — but not for people. I long for the soil, I long for the stones where I played as a child.)

These are the famous lines on which Strindberg was to vent his spleen. They are taken from 'Ensamhetens tankar' (Thoughts in Loneliness), some short confessional poems, strangely contrasting with the other poems in Heidenstam's jubilant homage to the joy of living, to Beauty and Love i.e. the aesthetic ideals manifested in his first collection of poems *Vallfart och vandringsår* (Pilgrimage and Wanderings, 1888).

Heidenstam, the young aristocrat, had been sent abroad at an early age to convalesce and to broaden his mind by travelling. When he returned to Sweden his experiences from these far-away travels were reflected in the above-mentioned collection of poems. The reading public was thrilled. Here was a new spirit, a new kind of writing. Here were love and beauty in a sensual blending of warm colours and fragrances, sights and sounds, adventures in exotic countries and strong characters described in words whose very sounds echoed the atmosphere of the *Arabian Nights* as for example in the poem 'De tre frågorna' (The three questions).

Here was in fact an application of the literary programme which Heidenstam and his friend Levertin were to announce in *Pepitas bröllop* in 1890. But today it is not the colourful imagery or the Oriental pictures praised by his contemporaries that draw our attention. It is more likely to be the five-lined poem quoted above which is very simple in form and vocabulary and yet most evocative. It reminds the reader of Goethe's 'Wanderers Nachtlied' or Geijer's 'Nyåret 1838' (On New Year's Eve 1838) with the same confessional tone and a very distinct loneliness and longing for the homeland. The words 'jag' and 'längtar' are used repeatedly and what Heidenstam confesses is a pantheistic love for his home-country which does not mean longing for its people or his own family but for the landscape in which he grew up. He would always belong to this region of Sweden i.e. Lake Vättern, the forest of Tiveden, because it was the countryside where he spent his childhood summers. He had spent only the summers at the manor-house of Olshammar, yet this was the area he dreamed about in his poems and his novels. Here the lonely boy crowned himself King of Lajsputta, his childhood's fantasy role, and here he listened to his grandmother's stories and eagerly read all the books that kindled his imagination.

The forest of Tiveden was mentioned above and it is in the poem of the same title that he manifests his sincere urge to describe its nature in detail. It is a majestic poem, very solemn in tone, built on assonances and alliterations, a hymn to the magical, dark and mythical forces of the wild forest; the rhythm of the poem is like an incantation and the dark vowels are repeated, creating an atmosphere of gloom and ageless wilderness. Not until Söndag (Sunday), Child of Happiness, comes on stage, do we realize that Heidenstam is still praising the *carpe diem* theme. Söndag is the personification of Man living for pleasure only, but in spite of him and all the other characters that Heidenstam describes in the poem it is still the landscape that plays the leading role. It is described from experience and with spontaneity, whereas his characters often seem contrived and placed there only for effect. 'Tiveden' is the first poem in the collection of *Dikter* (Poems, 1895) which contains many poems paying homage to what home really is, as, for instance:

> ... Ett hem! Det är det fästet,
> vi rest med murar trygga
> - vår egen värld — den enda
> vi mitt i världen bygga. 'Hemmet' (The Home, p. 179)

(A home! It is the stronghold we have set up with safe walls — our own world — the only one we build in the midst of the world.)

In this collection there is also the beautiful poem about Gunnar of Lidarende, the Icelandic hero, who has been declared an outlaw. However, as he is about to leave his home for the roaring sea, the beauty of the fields and the growing grass call him back:

> ...
> Han talte sakta: — Fager blommar liden.

Chapter III

> Hon aldrig tycktes mig mer fager förr.
> Min gula åker väntar skördetiden.
> För mig finns ingen väg från hemmets dörr. (*Dikter*, pp.204-5)

(He spoke slowly: Fair is the field in flower. It never seemed fairer to me. My yellow field awaits harvest-time. For me there is no way from home.)

To Heidenstam, the cosmopolitan, who had travelled widely, home and the homeland became more and more important and the theme reappears in 'Drottning Kristinas julnatt' (Queen Christina's Christmas Night) in *Dikter,* while the dream of the homecoming appears in Heidenstam's novel *Hans Alienus* (Hans the Stranger, 1892).

Nationalism

At the end of the 19th century there was a growing nationalism in many countries in Europe, and Sweden was no exception. Very often these patriotic feelings were fostered by the printed word. The four writers discussed in this survey had a keen interest in history and Selma Lagerlöf, for instance, testified many times to the great impact the reading of Carlyle had had on her. Walter Scott's historical novels were popular, as were the Icelandic Sagas. Tegnér's *Frithiofs saga*, Runeberg's *Fänrik Ståls sägner* (The Tales of Ensign Stål) and Topelius' *Fältskärns berättelser* (The Barber-Surgeon's Tales) were important sources of inspiration, and the reading of Nietzsche contributed to confirm the aesthetic ideals through which heroic literature was much appreciated. All four writers certainly had elements of patriotism in their writing, but Heidenstam and Selma Lagerlöf probably more so than the others.

We have seen how much memories of home, his country, the actual Nature around Lake Vättern meant to Heidenstam. These feeling intensified, and an important phase in the writer's production is concentrated on patriotic writing. Heidenstam called for a revival of Swedish nationalism, and the foundation of the new *Svenska Dagbladet* in 1896 was a step in that direction. One of the aims of the newspaper was to encourage culture, and Heidenstam, a devoted supporter of this idea, contributed many articles. His collection of poems *Ett folk* (A People, 1899) was published in *Svenska Dagbladet* and contains many of Heidenstam's patriotic ideas during the nineties.

When Heidenstam published *Karolinerna* (King Charles's Men) in

1897-1898 it was evident that he had deviated from the conception of Charles XII and given an individualistic, personal interpretation much in the same way as Strindberg had done in his historical dramas. *Karolinerna* is not a novel but a collection of stories about the king, and most of all about his subjects in moments of defeat and poverty during the fall of the Swedish realm in the early eighteenth century. These humble and obedient people become heroes when they forget their fear and die for the sake of their king and country. Runeberg's *Fänrik Ståls sägner* was clearly a model to Heidenstam.

The picture of the king changes. At first Heidenstam describes the madman in him but eventually he grows more heroic in stature and finally in 'En hjältes likfärd' (A Hero's Funeral Procession) all his people mourn him wholeheartedly. Like Runeberg, Heidenstam also tried to describe the enemy and there are sections including Tsar Peter among others.

Heidenstam moved closer to the countryside of his childhood in his successive historical novels *Heliga Birgittas pilgrimsfärd* (Saint Birgitta's Pilgrimage, 1901) and *Folkungaträdet* (The Tree of the Folkungs, 1905, 1907). Both novels are characterized by the author's blend of historical facts and a subjective treatment of the main characters.

Outcasts and misfits; despair and resignation.

Sooner or later the four writers in this survey came to a stage in life when they chose to hide their own despair behind a mask and create characters who did not fit into society or whose loneliness was obvious. Because these characters had their creators' sympathy and pity their portraits became very moving and memorable. Through the state of despair the writers arrived at a kind of resignation, though they showed this in various ways.

Heidenstam had realized at a very early stage that he was an outsider. There are signs of this in the poems in *Vallfarts och vandringsår,* as in the character of Hafed, the unhappy brother who did not find the king's ring in 'Moguls kungaring' (Mogul's Ring) and it becomes even more obvious in *Hans Alienus.* Charles XII is always at a distance from his loyal subjects in *Karolinerna*, Birgitta withdraws from her nearest and dearest in *Heliga Birgittas pilgrimsfärd.*

Heidenstam certainly wanted to take an active part in Sweden's

Chapter III

political life but in his heart he never was a socialist and ultimately there remained a barrier between him and the ordinary people. Strindberg had their love, Heidenstam never did. He was at the centre of cultural life in Sweden and yet he was lonely. The once so defiant, jubilant defender of life's pleasures was more and more subdued, while his acute self-criticism thwarted his creativity. His style of writing changed, for the better, from the extravagant, somewhat contrived tone into a simple, sincere one, which to a great extent he learnt from Runeberg and Goethe.

Heidenstam did not regret that youth was behind him; he only looked forward to what was in store. Despair and disappointment gave way to resignation.

Towards reconciliation and/or faith

Heidenstam lived to be very old, accepted the thought of death and longed for it for a long time. Again and again he introduces the subject of dying and death into his writing but without fear, only reconciliation and acceptance, as in 'Vi människor' (We Human Beings, *Nya Dikter*, p. 337).

In some of his poems he comes close to confessing his belief in God. He, the former atheist, now bows his head in quiet contemplation of the miracle of the human being:

> ... prisa undret, att du föddes
> människogestaltad, gudalik,
> undret över alla under!
> 'Undret' (The Wonder), *Nya Dikter*, p. 348

(Praise the wonder that you were born in the figure of a man, godlike, wonder of wonders!)

What he witnesses in Nature also makes him affirm the wonder of creation ('Paradisets Timma', *Nya Dikter*, p. 354). Finally he stands praying humbly in the poem 'Himladrottningens bild i Heda' (The Picture of Our Heavenly Mother in Heda) in *Nya Dikter* (p.364).

Selma Lagerlöf (1858-1940)[4]

Roots

'But there she sits, Miss Lagerlöf, who is a little school ma'am, a little one, who has never been outside the boundaries of Sweden, but who has lived alone and has a whole forgotten and concealed provincial mysticism within her.'[5] These words by Levertin suggest only praise and admiration for *Gösta Berlings saga*, the first work to follow the aesthetic ideal that Heidenstam and Levertin had set up in their programme a few years earlier. But many critics found the novel too romantic and its style and content too incoherent, though they would not deny that it was different.

Selma Lagerlöf told her readers about the origin of *Gösta Berlings saga* in another tale *En Saga om en saga* (A Story about a Story) where the little girl living at Mårbacka manorhouse in Värmland listened to all the stories and legends told by the natives of Värmland in the kitchen at Mårbacka among the servants, in the toddy-room by visiting gentlemen or sitting at her grandmother's feet. All these Värmland tales were her roots, her heritage and all that she had to do was to write them down.

It took ten years before *Gösta Berlings saga* was completed and there were two circumstances which inspired its composition. The first was the tragic fact that Mårbacka, her childhood home, had to be sold. Then Selma Lagerlöf who had left her home to earn her own living as a teacher, realized that the tales of her childhood's Värmland had to be preserved, must not disappear like Mårbacka. With this resolution in mind she began to compose her novel, but her work as a teacher was too demanding, and many years elapsed before her next wave of inspiration. *Idun*, a Swedish women's magazine, announced a literary competition and then Lagerlöf wrote five more chapters and won the competition. A year later, in 1891, she finished *Gösta Berlings saga*.

The novel focuses on two different attitudes to life represented by the two main characters, Gösta Berling and the Major's wife at Ekeby manorhouse. Gösta Berling is a defrocked, drunken preacher who decides to commit suicide but is rescued back to life by the Major's wife. He becomes the leader of the Cavaliers, a band of twelve adventurers who live at Ekeby under the protection of the all-powerful Major's wife. On Christmas night however the Cavaliers conclude a pact with Sintram, a personification of Evil: they will be in charge of

Chapter III

Ekeby for one year, providing they eschew work and only lead a life of pleasure and adventure. If they break the pact they will die at the end of the year; otherwise Sintram dies. This is of course the theme of Faust, and Sintram is Lagerlöf's Mephisto. But it is not only Goethe who inspired Selma Lagerlöf but to an even greater extent Walter Scott and Carlyle, whose historical writing she had loved to read, Tegnér, Runeberg and the old Icelandic Sagas.

Gösta Berling, 'strongest and weakest of all men' develops from the young carefree hero into a man whose concern for the people who love him is stronger than his own egotistic will-power. Thus the theme of rehabilitation which Selma Lagerlöf is to use again and again appears for the first time. Gösta Berling, like the rest of the Cavaliers, is gradually convinced of the necessity of work and therefore they start the forge at Ekeby. They have not broken the pact as it happens because they are not working for their own gain. The Major's wife returns mortally ill to Ekeby and dies forgiving Gösta Berling and the Cavaliers, now that she knows that Ekeby is restored and that Order once again rules.

All the different episodes of the book are not so loosely structured as the critics originally thought. In fact the frame of the novel i.e. time (the year from one Christmas to the next) and space (all the events take place around Lake Löven) is kept throughout and almost all the interwoven stories are somehow linked to the main story. *Gösta Berlings saga* becomes an epos of a whole region and of a society. It depicts the Värmland of the 1820s, but it is tightly connected with Selma Lagerlöf's time; often events of the past are moved even further back so that the time aspect becomes quite vague.

Gösta Berlings saga is a novel of rehabilitation but it is also a novel of love. Love is a constant thread woven throughout the book but it is sacrificed for duty. All the four girls whom Gösta Berling falls in love with and who in their turn love him sacrifice their love of him for duty. Even Elisabeth Dohna, the lively and carefree countess, has to suffer humiliation, redemption and suffering before she learns what true love is and it is through her love and goodness that Gösta Berling is finally saved.

The novel was criticized by Brandes among others for its weakness in characterization but it could well be argued that characterization was not Lagerlöf's main intention when writing the book. She wanted to depict a region, her part of Sweden, and in doing so she used a style which was unique and might appear somewhat superficial. Some of her characters are admittedly sketchily drawn and quickly forgotten; others however are fully described and stay in the reader's mind; Marianne Sinclair for instance, whose development is anything but sketchy. Some minor characters appear and disappear as suddenly as the great flood at Ekeby but they belong to the great panorama of actions concerned with the regional theme. Others seem to be minor characters at first but will be remembered because, somehow, they stand out from the crowd. Lilliecrona, one of the Cavaliers, is an example of this, because Selma Lagerlöf has brought a deep, personal touch to the chapter about him. Certainly it is Mårbacka, her own home, she describes and the question remains to what extent her own parents are portrayed in the chapter.

There is in the novel a contrast between the impulsive, superficial, heroic Cavaliers and the poor, humble people whose lives have been afflicted because of the destructive living of the Cavaliers. There are romantic ball-rooms, dangerous, exciting elopements in sleighs contrasted with the misery of the girl from Nygård or the growing discontent of a starving population. There is the contrast between the defiant, jubilant young people and the wise, humble knowledge of the old, between the joy of living for pleasure and dutiful work, between spring and winter, and life and death. There are the descriptions of the young, proud, heroic Cavaliers enjoying friendship and adventures and of the Cavaliers, pictured individually, then aged, decrepit, and with individual flaws. There is the contrast between good and evil, the first personified by Captain Lennart, the latter as seen in the character of the utterly wicked Märta Dohna. There are the tales of old times and from far away brought together in the novel, myths about witches and other strange phenomena in Nature, there are fantastic tales of bears and wolves and birds of revenge but they all belong to the action. Nature is part of the novel and the moods and storms within the characters correspond to the natural element. The narrator's style varies from outbursts of true romanticism to comments of sharp, realistic insight, and her reader, as she says playfully in the last sentence, will find it hard to discern the borders between fantasy and reality. But they will know that they have been in the province of Värmland.

Chapter III

Nationalism

In 1901 Selma Lagerlöf was asked to produce a reader for nine-year-old schoolchildren about the geography of Sweden. It took her five years to write *Nils Holgerssons underbara resa* (The Wonderful Adventures of Nils, 1906-7), the book which won for her worldwide fame and all kinds of honours and which made it possible for her to buy back her beloved Mårbacka. She spent a great deal of time travelling about in Sweden and going through material for the book. She had undertaken a difficult task because all the details in the book had to be correct as it was to be used for teaching purposes. It was Kipling's character Mowgli of *The Jungle Books* that inspired Selma Lagerlöf's ingenious framework for her novel. In the story within the story there is a meeting, at Mårbacka of course, between Nils Holgersson and Selma Lagerlöf and she tells him how she got the idea of writing the book. Once she had heard a story about a goose which joined the wild geese when they passed by. So she used the flight of the wild geese as a device to describe her country from Skåne in the south of Sweden to Lappland in the north; but on this particular flight they are joined by Mårten Gåskarl (Gander) who longs for adventure and freedom. Sitting on his back is Nils Holgersson, the fourteen-year-old boy who has been transformed into a Tom Thumb as a punishment for his prank, and it is from his airborne but micro-perspective that the reader is introduced to a new, fascinating world of reality, myth, legend and adventure. *Nils Holgerssons underbara resa* is again a story of development and rehabilitation. Nils Holgersson develops from a rascal into an alert, concerned and caring youngster. He learns and experiences a great deal during his long absence from home, not only about his country and its people but also about human kindness, and a love of animals — and his teachers are the animals.

Parallel to the main theme runs the theme of the two children Åsa and Mats in search of their lost father. The two themes are linked together throughout the book and sometimes converge.

Lagerlöf's book is a patriotic hymn in prose, filled with optimistic faith in mankind and in Sweden. Many school children in Sweden have used it as a textbook and learnt a great deal about their country. Foreign translations have made it possible for young readers abroad to follow the boy on the goose's back, 'the pilot of our first airdream' as Harry Martinsson calls him.[6] Many writers have testified to how the book influenced them. 'Looking at life from above but also studying it to the smallest detail as a metaphor for the writer's mission in general' said Czeslaw Milosz, the Polish winner of the Nobel Prize in 1980.[7]

Love

The great theme in Selma Lagerlöf's writing was that of love and it appears everywhere. She has been criticized for her optimistic attitude and her strong belief in the redeeming power of love. The love theme in *Gösta Berlings saga* is the most important theme in the novel but Selma Lagerlöf was to find new variations of it in the rest of her writing. She never tired of writing about those who sacrifice their love in an unselfish way.

One example of this is the story *En herrgårdssägen* (A Tale of a Manor, 1899) in which Lagerlöf uses the famous Beauty and the Beast motif to make her point. Beauty releases the Beast from its evil spell by loving it and in this particular story Gunnar Hede is saved from his mental illness by the starry-eyed Ingrid. (Here again the loss of a home appears as a theme; the loss of Mårbacka never left Selma Lagerlöf's thoughts.) 'Amor vincit omnia' was the title of one of the chapters in *Gösta Berlings saga* and the theme reappears in this story.

Love cannot always redeem however. This seems to be the message in *Herr Arnes penningar* (Herr Arne's Hoard, 1903). A young girl, Elsalill, is the only survivor when the vicarage of Solberga is plundered of its treasure and the vicar and all his household are murdered by three Scotsmen. This was an authentic event which had taken place near Marstrand in Bohuslän on the west coast of Sweden in the late 16th century, but again Selma Lagerlöf added a love theme and she also brought in supernatural elements in the story; Elsalill's foster-sister returns from the dead as a ghost. Selma Lagerlöf believed in ghosts and thought nothing of their appearance in a story of this kind but the critics were quite condescending. Elsalill meets the murderers in Marstrand without recognizing them and falls in love with one of them, Sir Archie. When she finally realizes the truth, she is torn between her love for Sir Archie on one side and her sense of duty and justice and her love for her foster-sister on the other. She sacrifices her love for Sir Archie and when she realizes that he is unworthy she sacrifices her life too so that he will not be able to escape through her protection.

The love theme reappears in *Jerusalem* (1901-2) and *Kejsaren av*

Chapter III

Portugallien (The Emperor of Portugallia, 1914), novels which will be discussed in connection with other themes below. It also appears in *Körkarlen* (The Coachman, 1912) where again a woman gives her life to save a drunkard and wicked man.

There is a type of woman she loves to describe. These women are soft, gentle and ask little of life. They make no fuss about themselves at all, and one must often take one's time if one wants to see what they are worth, and that they are no mere pieces of fluff blown by the wind. They are madonnas but they can develop into Amazons, if the situation demands it ... They are gentle yet strong; dreamy yet practical ...[8]

Selma Lagerlöf's faith in love and the goodness of mankind was shattered when World War I broke out and in her later production the power of love does not seem as obvious as before, but it exists in *Bannlyst* (The Outcast, 1918).

In *Löwensköldska ringen* (The Ring of the Löwenskölds, 1925-1928) Selma Lagerlöf returned to the stories of Värmland and the theme of love. Again we meet a young preacher, Karl-Artur Ekenstedt, loved by women, who make sacrifices for him. But unlike Gösta Berling he is not worthy of their love. He does not know what love is, he remains an egotist, one of those whom love cannot redeem. But the two heroines Charlotte Löwensköld and Anna Svärd are strong characters and infinitely superior to the man they love. In their description Selma Lagerlöf had come a long way from her early female characters; these are mature portraits of women in many different stages of emotions.

Recently there has been a good deal of research as to what extent Selma Lagerlöf's feelings and personal experiences are reflected in her works of art. When access to letters to and from intimate female friends has been permitted, these letters reveal another aspect of Lagerlöf and most certainly one of subdued passions.[9]

Outcasts and Misfits; Despair and Resignation

Selma Lagerlöf was given more time than other children to read and absorb, to listen and ponder on what she heard. She was born with a hip deformity which left her with a limp. Because she was different from other children, she had a complex about her limp and she felt clumsy and ugly. Maybe this is one of the reasons why the young girl sought some compensation in life and turned to writing. Her own sufferings made it easy for her to pity and sympathize with the weak. This is often reflected in her writing. Gunnar Hede in *En herrgårdssägen* is an example of Lagerlöf's ability to describe and characterize someone who has fled into madness.

Kejsaren av Portugallien is another example of what happens when the pressure of reality becomes too hard to endure. The novel describes a relationship between father and daughter, Jan in Skrolycka, a poor farmer, and Klara Gulla. Jan's exceptional love for his daughter is described very movingly and also humoristically and his daughter reciprocates his love. The idyll is broken when Jan is told by his master that he will have to leave his farm if he cannot pay 200 crowns for it. Klara Gulla then offers to go to Stockholm to earn the money and Jan accepts reluctantly. The money arrives but very soon it is obvious to everyone that Klara Gulla has become a prostitute. Jan refuses to face reality and escapes into madness. He spends days and years waiting for his 'empress' to come back to him, the emperor of Portugallia. As signs of his dignity he wears a top hat, a cane and some paper stars as the imperial insignia. When Klara Gulla does return many years later she has only contempt for him. Not until Jan has died to save her, does she realize the greatness of his love for her. When her heart opens to that awareness, she finds redemption.

But there are other themes in the novel. There is the emperor's megalomania experienced possibly by Selma Lagerlöf herself when her success was crowned by the Nobel prize; and the shame she experienced at the devastating reviews of *Antikrists mirakler*. There is the father theme. The father, Jan in Skrolycka, escapes reality, as Lieutenant Lagerlöf had tried to escape, by taking to the bottle, a reality which was only too well known to the rest of the Lagerlöf family. And there is also the theme of eviction from the home which for ever haunted the author. *Kejsaren av Portugallien* becomes the novel of pretence, of make believe.

Lagerlöf wanted to call the novel a Swedish *King Lear*. Was Klara Gulla then a Swedish Cordelia and if so, was the Swedish Cordelia a description of Selma Lagerlöf?

Towards Reconciliation and/or Faith

It was important for Selma Lagerlöf to find the nucleus of a story, something that could inspire her to add themes of her own to the

Chapter III

original story. She had read about some Swedish farmers' emigration to Jerusalem to join a religious sect. When she was in Israel she visited them and stayed for quite some time with them to find out about their new life. Selma Lagerlöf decided to go back to the origin of the story, trying to trace why some people in the parish had left their country and others had remained there. She visited the parish of Nåås in Dalarna and talked to the relatives of the emigrants. Now she had the material for her documentary novel but as always in her writing the novel developed into something quite different; in fact the first part of *Jerusalem* takes place in Dalarna and the sectarians set out on their journey at the very end of that part.

In *Jerusalem* Selma Lagerlöf continues to build on contrasts and to employ the kind of descriptive devices she had used in *Gösta Berlings saga,* but her style of writing is now different. The exclamations, personifications, the impressionistic, emotional outbursts are gone and replaced by a sober, serious and simple style, reminiscent of that of the Icelandic sagas. But the descriptions of Nature are still there and more alive than ever. There was in *Gösta Berlings saga* a contrast between a life of pleasure and a life of duty and work. In *Jerusalem* work is contrasted with religious devotion, and duty becomes a key-word in the conflict between those who decide to follow God to the new country and those who feel that their love of the homeland and the soil is more important. Gertrud becomes a representative of the former and Ingmar the latter. The former live in Jerusalem in a kind of group collective, waiting for Christ's return while working for Palestine.

The latter are members of the Ingmarsson family. They are individualists, although with a strong family allegiance. They love God in their own way by doing what seems right and what their conscience tells them to do. They are stubborn, loyal, hard-working farmers who love their country, their homes and the soil they till. Selma Lagerlöf does not want to reveal any preference for either side; she weighs up the representatives and their loves.

The critics seem to be unanimous in their opinion that Selma Lagerlöf did not manage to put across the reasons for the sectarians staying in Jerusalem and that the first part of the book is the more successful. Selma Lagerlöf's view of life was basically Christian and throughout life she tried to believe in and work for mankind. She believed in development according to Herbert Spencer's evolutionary ideas and she also supported the ecumenical idea. She condemned violence, and one of her last actions was to oppose the new regime in Germany. Her feelings for the weak and unfortunate were strong. Most certainly she had, like Ingmarsönerna, arrived at a personal belief in God or Love.

Gustaf Fröding (1860-1911)

Roots

In the first two stanzas in 'Strövtåg i hembygden' (Rambles in My Homeland, *Stänk och flikar*), Fröding gives a sweeping panorama of the nature in which he grew up, at first emphasizing its brightness by using vowel harmonies like the vowels i, ö, ä, and visual impressions of the lake, the open view of shores and creeks, the green sheltering forest in the background and the soft meadows. Then, as the manor-house fails to come into focus in the third stanza because it has been ravaged by fire, the happy mood changes and is mingled with sadness. Now the auditory sense takes command of the poet's memories and focuses on the father, whose increasing weariness of life was to have a great impact on his family and on Gustaf Fröding in particular. The father's musicality is emphasized as well as his illness.

Much research has been done on the extent to which the dark family heritage i.e. mental disease, sometimes latent, sometimes in full flow, influenced Gustaf Fröding's life. He himself was acutely aware of it, as was his sister Cecilia. Both Fröding's parents suffered from serious mental depression and Fröding tried to describe his father's lack of contact in another poem 'En främmande man' (A Strange Man) in *Guitarr och dragharmonika*:

> Han var så skygg, så tyst, så ödsligt ensam,
> min själ blev vek, jag kände lust att gråta,
> som var hans gömda sorg för oss gemensam,
> ... Jag ville närma mig, jag ville bära
> den tunga tyngd, som gjort hans liv eländigt,
> men han vek undan, när jag nådde nära,
> och mellan oss låg svalget vitt som ständigt ...(p. 139)

(He was so timid, so quiet, so desolately alone, my soul weakened, I felt like crying as were his hidden sorrow common to us both ... I wanted to get closer, I wanted to take on the heavy burden which made his life miserable, but he

Chapter III

turned away, when I came close and between us was the abyss, wide as always.)

Indeed the whole poem contains no accusation, only a sincere wish to share the sufferings. Nor do the lines reveal the anguish and sorrow which Fröding's father continuously caused his family in terms of worries and financial difficulties resulting in their having to move frequently; again and again there was a new departure, a new pulling-up of roots.

The poem 'Dolores di Colobrados' is Fröding's portrait of his mother. He regrets the fact that she has changed, that she is not what she used to be, and it is on the whole a not very flattering portrait he draws in spite of her sacrifices for her family. But what he manages to catch is her estrangement and loneliness.

The lack of stability and true parental support influenced all the Fröding children. Thus it was Gustaf Fröding's sister Cecilia who acted as a substitute for the missing father and mother. She read the stories, she played the games, she became the 'Teller of Tales' in the 'Lilac-Cave' or the magician at the 'Troll-Table': 'Och gott var att luta sitt huvud mot silket och njuta var beta av sagornas bröd i vart ord ... du drottning av Saba och Bagdad och Wak-Wakland ('Sago-förtäljerskan', The Teller of Tales, *Stänk och Flikar* p.289: Lovely to lean one's head against the silk enjoying each morsel of the stories' bread in each word ... You, my queen of Sheba and Baghdad and Wak-Wak land). And it was the 'brown-eyed, frail and thin Sultana' girl, alias Cecilia, who was to sacrifice so much for her beloved brother and who at a very early stage recognized his extraordinary qualities. She was his stability and confidante, she had to support him and provide for him in all kinds of ways later in life. Fröding had other relatives but those who mattered to him were his father who would sometimes sing and compose lovely tunes, his mother whose poetry-writing inspired him, and Cecilia.

Fröding painted in poetry the province of Värmland which Selma Lagerlöf described in prose. *Guitarr och dragharmonika* (Guitar and Accordion) his first collection of poems was published in 1891 and the title is accurate because it represents not only two sides of the province of Värmland and its people but also two characteristics in the writer:- the humoristic good-hearted story-telling is the guitar, and the sad melancholy pity for the misfits and the tormented self-portraits is the accordion.

The best known of these poems is probably 'Vackert väder' (Lovely Weather) in which Fröding's description of a summer day in Värmland is heightened by images taken from various classes of society from past and present time. Thus the white church shines like a farmer's bride, the sky above the birches resembles the gossamer gauze of an aristocratic young lady's hat, the dark forests look like solemn jury members on their way to the district-court and the islands have become decorated long ships. Even the old soldier is part of the picture as are the proud, haughty, swanlike girls from the manor-houses who laugh mercilessly at the unhappy poet, always the outsider.

Another much-loved poem from the same collection is the rhythmical 'Det var dans bort i vägen' (The Saturday Night Open Air Dancing) in which the observant poet introduces the dancers with an impressionistic touch as they quickly dance by, each one by name, village and characteristic qualities. The speed is accelerated, as the dancers, free from work, enjoy themselves and the music; the rhythm and the folk-dance are perfectly blended into the poem, as is the description of the typical summer night with its people and animals. The fairy-tale of 'Titania', Fröding's version of the fog lifting is as melodious as 'Vallarelåt', the poem set in the high mountains where the croft-girl calls the cows, crying: 'Lilja-mi Lilja-mi ko'.

There is also the absolute companionship of man and beast as in 'Jonte och Brunte' (Jonte and Brunte), equally tired after work: 'Och Jonte han fumlade druligt med tömmen och Brunte han drumlade framåt i drömmen, han stötte, han stracklade — hölasset vacklade fram utmed strömmen' (p. 123) (Jonte he fumbled clumsily with the reins and Brunte tumbled along in his dream, shoving and struggling, the hay load swaying along by the stream.)

There are descriptions of the landscape with its myths and history; even the broad friendly dialect of Värmland comes alive and is caught impressionistically, as is everything aural, visual and tactile. Fröding's poetry is sensual and rhythmical, it is verse and music in perfect, natural harmony and it is a sublime symphonic homage to the province of Värmland and its people. There is nothing forced and contrived about this countryside, it seems to have grown intuitively from Fröding's roots and experience.

Chapter III

Love

'En kärleksvisa' (A Love Song, *Gralstänk*) reveals a great deal about the man who throughout his life was to long for true love, hardly experienced it but still went on praising it. Fröding's poetry deals to a great extent with the theme of love and there are various aspects of it in his writing. He often describes its objects in a narrative way and one example of this is the earlier poem, 'Det var dans bort i vägen' where the reader takes part in the village dance on a Saturday night and where young, uncomplicated love is an obvious ingredient. But the narrator himself is not part of this, he is the observer and the outsider.

Another aspect is that of fatal love i.e. love ending in tragedy. One of the protagonists is for example deserted by the other. This could be told in a slightly humorous way as in 'Farväll' (Farewell) or with great commiseration as in 'Elin i Hagen' (Elin in the Grove), both from *Guitarr och dragharmonika*. In the latter poem the once so happy young girl has a child by a stranger, drowns it and is put in prison, leaving her father in utter despair. There are other girls who die for the men they love, like Ingalill in 'Säv, Säv Susa'(Sigh, Sigh Rushes, *Nya Dikter*) and Eli-lita in 'Jägar Malms hustrur' (Hunter Malm's Wives, *Stänk och flikar*). They are poor, innocent young girls and they all belong to the same low social class and have no chance to fight an intolerant society. Only occasionally does Fröding twist the theme as in 'I valet och kvalet' (In Two Minds, *Nya Dikter*) in which a young girl in a calculating and egotistic manner hesitates between true love and a marriage based on materialism and finally settles for the latter because it means security.

Fröding was only 34 years old when his mental illness became an inescapable fact and throughout his life he had a remarkable awareness of his own illness. This meant that he was cut off from a stable relationship like that of a marriage but he often visited prostitutes and dreamed about the love he would never have. In his early poems he very often describes himself as a young, clumsy admirer, who is shy, emotional and despised by his loved one. Fröding often felt like a fish out of water at parties, he felt socially inferior and was very often too shy to do anything but dream about his beloved. One example of this is found in 'Balen' (The Ball, *Nya Dikter*) which is not only a superb satire of the bourgeoisie in a small town but also a humorous description of what happens when rejected love turns into an idealistic dream of Heaven and the young lovers, happily ever after, waltz away in the heavenly ball-rooms of the Almighty. But the smiling façade was to disappear when Fröding wrote 'Flickan i ögat' (The Girl of my Eye, *Stänk och flikar*). Here he confessed his haunting loneliness, his erotic hopelessness, his bitter despair, his drunkenness and his endless longing. Someone to dream about, to talk to, to love, the theme reappears in 'En vårfästmö' (A Spring Fiancée) and 'Ett gammalt bergtroll' (An Old Mountain-Troll) both from *Stänk och flikar*; but loneliness is all that ensues.

In some of Fröding's poems love becomes platonic and is synonymous with the poet's ideal or inspiration, as in 'Det borde varit stjärnor' (There Should Have Been Stars, *Stänk och flikar*, p.231).

Nowadays the reader would hardly be shocked by Fröding's 'En morgondröm' (A Morning Dream) in which he described two young lovers' meeting and sexual intercourse, but Fröding was prosecuted for indecency and although he was later acquitted it was a serious blow to the sensitive poet.

Dreams and reality merged however but very late in Fröding's life. Signe Trotzig who became his nurse and constant companion for the last years of his life inspired him to write 'Ghaselens makt' (The Power of the Ghasel, *Reconvalescentia*). Once again we are back in the land of fairy-tales. The angry sultan is Fröding and the Dinarsad is his enchantress who comforts him, and she is of course Signe Trotzig. The poem is an exotic hymn to human contact and also a poem of love and gratitude to the woman who could soothe the poet for a time from his horrid visions:

> Men även leken kan en sorg förjaga,
> om också för en liten stund,
> och även sorg av djup och ej alldaga
> kan leken häva för en kort sekund
> - en kort sekund av ögonblick, som ila,
> ett något litet av en liten vila.
> ('Ghaselens makt', p.648)

(Even a game can distract sorrow if only for a little while, and sorrow deep and not so common is cured in the momentary game — a fraction of moments flashing, perhaps some rest, if only a little.)

Chapter III

Outcasts and misfits; despair and resignation

At a very early age Fröding learnt to pretend that he was someone else. Because he was clumsy and shortsighted he found it easier to take on the clown role voluntarily so as to disarm his classmates, and thus August Kallsson was created. As the latter he acted the clown in front of admiring friends and subsequently used the same name as one of his pen names when working as a journalist for *Karlstad Tidningen*. Many people have praised Fröding's kindness and his engagement in and pity for other people's problems. He was a socialist at heart and many of his poems express his indignation and anger at the social injustice which he witnessed and knew about through his work as a journalist. He also objected strongly to most authorities. A gesture revealing his democratic sympathies was made by Fröding when he gave away to the franchise reform the prize money which he had been awarded by the Swedish Academy.

His pity for the outcasts and the misfits in society was often reflected in his poetry, perhaps especially in the poem 'Skalden Wennerbom' (The Poet Wennerbom, *Nya Dikter*) which describes a fellow poet who is deteriorating rapidly and escaping his sorrow by drinking, all of which Fröding could easily identify with; the poem ends rather typically with the words: 'Det är skönt för skalder att få sova' (It is nice for poets to sleep sometimes).

Again and again Fröding sides with the social outcast. Sometimes he implores the strong ones not to be so hard, as in 'En vintervisa' (A Winter Song), sometimes he just seems to relate a person's misery from an objective point of view, as in 'Lars i Kuja' (Lars in Kuja). Sometimes the tone hardens when he describes the privileged classes as in 'Bollspelet vid Trianon' (The Ball Game in Trianon, *Nya Dikter*).

The most powerful by far of Fröding's poems expressing social indignation is 'Den gamla goda tiden' (The good old days, *Nya Dikter*) which is a gloomy picture of what had happened in Värmland when industrialism took over. Fröding was inspired to write the poem when a contemporary prose description was published and his poem is a strong agitation for the defence of the outcasts in society, in this case the blacksmiths in the forges. The first three stanzas describe solemnly in powerful alliterations and vowel harmonies the working procedure in the forge but then the blacksmiths confess their sufferings in direct speech, revealing the exploitations of the owners and some horrendous conditions. The last stanza, quoted before, returns to the narrative form describing the suppressed people but also understating a possible resistance or refusal to accept further suffering. Fröding had also witnessed the tragedy which often befell the carefree landowners, unaware of the changing times, the demands for better equipment and a rationalized industry. His own father had failed as so many others, for instance Selma Lagerlöf's father, and the theme of decay and the lack of will to survive was vividly imagined by Fröding. As a result of this he wrote 'Atlantis', (*Nya Dikter*), a tale about the sunken city. The theme had earlier inspired many writers, for instance Heine and E. A. Poe, but Fröding's version had a personal imprint because he saw his own family and his own age in the tale.

Fröding's life is a long wandering towards his Golgotha, full of despair, quiet resignation and with a streak of light and hope now and then. These feelings are conveyed to the reader on a very personal, confessional level. 'En ghasel' (A Ghasel, *Guitarr och dragharmonika*) was written when Fröding was admitted for the first time to a mental hospital in Norway. Fröding used an old Persian metre (ghasel) in which one word is to be repeated at certain intervals and the word he chose was appropriately 'gallret' (the bars). In the poem the poet is standing behind a barred window looking out at life outside, its nature and its people and all that he loves and must be kept away from. Once again he is the outsider and again there is a mixture of joy of life and painful nostalgia. Again the visual and auditory senses dominate the description. The poet is tormented yet tempted by the sounds of laughter and singing and the bright colours of the trees and the water and he complains:

> jag vill, jag vill, jag skall, jag måste ut
> och dricka liv om blott för en minut ...

(I will, I will, I will, I must go out drinking life, if only for a minute ...)

but then he resigns, realizing his own weakness and convinced of the uselessness of despair.

> ... i mig själv är smitt och nitat gallret
> och först när själv jag krossas, krossas gallret (p.137)

Chapter III

(...within myself the bars are forged and riveted and only when I am crushed will the bars be smashed.)

Fröding knew that there was no escape. When he urgently needed help he sent for his sister but otherwise he wanted to be left in peace.

Nature was always present in his writing and in many poems he uses pathetic fallacy as a device to reveal his feelings. One example of this is 'Viken' (The Creek, *Guitarr och dragharmonika*) in which his own depression becomes the devastated creek of his childhood. Fröding was a master of lyric form and he took a delight in pastiche writing. 'En fattig munk från Skara' (A Poor Friar of Skara), the last poem in *Guitarr och dragharmonika,* is written in doggerel verse, a form well-chosen to fit the content: a friar has committed all kinds of sins and has now become an outcast and is balancing the books of his life and himself. Behind the mask is of course Fröding himself struggling with the problem of guilt, and Fröding's message is that despite all evil there is a streak of hope. Nature brings hope to the outcast friar and the poem conveys Fröding's hope that love and goodness will prevail.

The tone is harsher and the loneliness more tangible in 'Fredlös' (An Outlaw, *Stänk och flikar*) and the indifference is pretended. But Fröding was to reach the stage where not even his beloved Nature could intrude in his dark world as a comfort any more. In 'En majvisa' (A May Song, *Nytt och gammalt*) the poet who had praised uniquely the beauty of Swedish nature is again the observer, standing inside, looking out:

> ... all världen är ung, all världen är ny
> och ändå så ville jag snyfta.
> Ty morgonen kommer för klar, för snar
> för friska dess daggdroppar dugga,
> den lyser för ljust på den, som var
> för nyss i dödens skugga. (p. 359)

(... all the world is young, all the world is new and still I feel like crying. For morning is too bright, too soon, too fresh its dew-drops fall, it shines too bright on someone who was too near the shadows of death.)

Towards reconciliation and/or faith

Fröding spent much of his time reading and studying the history of religion while he was at various mental institutions. The kind of faith that he had experienced in his childhood home meant nothing to him and in his studies he turned to other worlds. He continuously brooded on the questions of good and evil and the universe. This was illustrated in his various poems about the Holy Grail. Fröding took up the old legend but recreated it to symbolize what is beyond our knowledge and beyond good and evil but what the human beings are aspiring to all the time. He dismissed thoughts of death in many poems as in 'Livets värde' (The Value of Life) 'Längta jag orkar ej/till det jag ej känner och önskar' (I cannot long for what I do not know nor wish) p. 407. This is expressed even more strongly in the poem 'Giv liv och grönska' (Give Life and Verdure).

Fröding was haunted by hallucinations and voices from the past and tormented by anguish. In a collection of poems called 'Mattoidens sånger' (*The Songs of the Mattoid*) he used a new style of writing, an approach towards modern verse, to illustrate his subject. The songs are a homage to lower creatures in nature, again a sign of Fröding's pantheistic mind and his pity for the small outcast, as in 'Snigelns visa' (The Snail's Song).

Whether Fröding ever reached a kind of reconciliation is very doubtful, but maybe he did get a glimpse of love at long last, as suggested earlier. What is certain however is that he tried to find a personal faith in the midst of his personal tragedy.

> Jag tror icke mycket, jag själv, på Gud,...
> Dock är det väl sant att ibland jag tror
> mig höra en röst från min far och mor,
> av andar som tala,
> förskräcka, hugsvala,
> ibland är ock rösten en gudastor.
> Men det kan ju vara
> en hallucination,
> ett föremål bara
> för tron. (p. 616)
> 'Symptom' (Symptom, *Efterskörd*)

(I myself do not have great faith in God,... But it's true that sometimes I seem to hear a voice of my father or mother, of spirits speaking, frightening,

Chapter III

comforting. Sometimes the voice is Godlike too. But for all I know it might be a hallucination, only an object of faith.)

Erik Axel Karlfeldt (1864-1931)[10]

Roots

> Mina fäder, jag ser er i drömmarnas stund,
> och min själ blir beklämd och vek,
> Jag är ryckt som en ört ur sin groningsgrund
> halvt nödd, halvt villig er sak jag svek.
> 'Fäderna' (My forefathers, *Vildmarks och kärleksvisor* p. 8)

(My fathers I see you in my dreams and my soul becomes soft and depressed, I was pulled up like a sprouting plant half forced, half willingly I failed you.)

These four lines illustrate the anguish and sorrow that afflicted Karlfeldt for the rest of his life when his childhood's happy days were cruelly devastated. He grew up on a farm in southern Dalarna but when he went away to school, his father was imprisoned for embezzlement, the house was auctioned and the family was left in great poverty. This was a blow from which Karlfeldt never quite recovered, and from then on he always strove for justice and honesty. He felt discriminated against and socially inferior and he suffered from fears of financial dependence. Not until he became a permanent secretary of the Swedish Academy was he finally reconciled with his past.

But he dreamed of his origins, of the province of Dalarna, its traditions and its people, devoted to the care of the soil and the mines. The old agrarian culture was a privilege, something to be proud of; just as the farmer had been in Geijer's 'Odalbonden' (The Yeoman). 'Fäderna' becomes a homage to his forefathers and the rhythm of the poem contributes to the pregnant note of gravity that it evokes. At first Karlfeldt honours his ancestors' devotion to work, their faithfulness in love, their loyalty to the king and their sincere faith in God. Then he proceeds to compare himself to them. Although weak and torn between futile needs and materialistic temptations, he is filled with gratitude for what they have taught him, yet he realizes that he has failed by deserting them and therefore pledges to honour their toil by writing about them in their spirit.

Karlfeldt easily adopted Langbehn's theories about the peasant proprietor. 'He became a poet on peasantry grounds and made use of the individualistic farmer for this artistic originality.'[11] In the eighteenth century the poet Bellman had introduced Fredman to serve as his spokesman. Fredman, a former watchmaker in Stockholm, became a leader of a group of carefree dissolute vagabonds and his songs and epistles were much appreciated. Now Karlfeldt uses a similar device. He created Fridolin who, like Fredman, has two collections of poetry named after him, *Fridolins visor* (Fridolin's Songs, 1901) and *Fridolins lustgård* (Fridolin's Pleasure-Garden, 1901).

Fridolin is introduced to the readers in a foreword. There are many similarities between him and his creator but he is not quite Karlfeldt's alter ego. He is a bachelor who, having returned from his studies to farming, quite naturally becomes a central figure in the small village life among his friends and eventually marries and becomes a member of Parliament. In his spare time he takes up writing and through him Karlfeldt now tells his readers that his poetry must be of two kinds, the folkloristic one and a more refined, scholarly verse. Fridolin is the answer to Karlfeldt's aspirations and dreams of compensation. He is stable, yet adventurous, dignified yet popular with all and sundry, firm and decisive yet a man of weaknesses. Just as the painter Anders Zorn depicted Dalarna in his paintings capturing traditions, joy of living and moments of intense happiness and lightheartedness, so his friend Karlfeldt painted in words and rhythms the same people and nature. This was the aesthetic programme of *Nittitalet* in a rustic setting and Fridolin was a born leader representing also individualistic thoughts of freedom, as in 'Sång efter skördeanden' (Song after Harvest, *Fridolins visor*) p. 173.

In *Dalmålningar på rim* (Wall-paintings from Dalarna in Rhyme, 1901) Karlfeldt successfully put into verse the mural painters' attempts to illustrate Biblical motifs and tales and he caught the humoristic mode with perfect accuracy. One fine example is 'Elie himmelsfärd' (The Assumption of Elijah) where Elijah bids all of Dalarna farewell from his chariot. Karlfeldt varies between realistic descriptions and slight irony, but the reader's lasting impression is that of fine humour. The same is true of 'Jone havsfärd' (The Voyage of Jonah), a luxuriant and comical description of the prophet, who, after being found too fat and thereby hindering the ships's passage, is thrown overboard and devoured by a whale from which he narrowly escapes, after which he appears in the local pub ordering a dram. His fellow sailors originate of course from

Chapter III

Dalarna and the clash of styles is most intentional.

Everywhere in Karlfeldt's poems Nature is present and becomes a necessary good or evil. There are no borders between Man and Nature and Karlfeldt makes frequent use of pathetic fallacy to describe feelings or passions. Nature is always described in detail and knowledgeably, be it flora or fauna. The senses dominate the descriptions and they are always based on facts. To accompany Karlfeldt in the Dalarna countryside is a genuine lecture in zoology or botany. Nature is sometimes very intricate and mystic and rooted in old medicine and popular belief and sometimes it is quite practical and based on the *Farmer's Almanac*.

There is almost always a wind blowing in Karlfeldt's poems, often used for a symbolic purpose to denote a person's feelings. In 'Fäderna' he speaks of the sweep of the storm echoing in his poetry, young love is always accompanied by wind or a soft breeze, the outcast looks back on a stormy life, the wind roars all the way from Åland in 'Svarta Rudolf', it forebodes war and death in Karlfeldt's later poems and it is absolutely central in 'Första minnet' (The First Memory, *Hösthorn*) where the same words reappear at the end of every verse: 'it's a wind, a strong wind'.

The moon has a mythical role, reminiscent of D. H. Lawrence's *Women in Love*. A new moon shines on young, innocent love, the moon is cold as deceitful love, Fridolin lifts his girl towards the autumn moon's red saucepan, a symbol for red, hot love; harvest moon sometimes symbolizes tradition, sometimes war, and the moon is always present in descriptions of sensual tormented love.

Karlfeldt's poetry is concentrated on the province of Dalarna and the scene of action very rarely moves outside the boundaries of that province which he loved so much.

Love

> Vänd dig till mig, vänd dig från mig! Jag vill brinna, jag vill svalna
> Jag är lust och jag är längtan, gränsbo mellan höst och vår.
> 'Dina ögon äro eldar'
> ('Your eyes are fires', *Fridolins lustgård* p. 293.)

(Turn to me, turn from me! I will burn, I will grow cool. I am desire and longing, bordering between autumn and spring.)

The most important vein in Karlfeldt's work is his love poetry. Love takes on many different roles and the objects of love are as varied. In the poem 'Sång efter skördeanden', *(Fridolins visor)*, Fridolin is the dancing hero, a symbol of manliness in the midst of friends and the girl clings to him 'lik vallmon på slikande skaft' (like a drooping poppy). There are many men of his kind in Karlfeldt's poetry on the verge of being male chauvinists; a good example is 'Svarte Rudolf' (Black Rudolph, *Flora och Bellona*). The young women are like wax and suffer long hours' waiting for them. In *Vildmarks- och kärlesksvisor* Karlfeldt often describes young, wild, primitive, lighthearted love in close harmony with nature.

Karlfeldt was a man of many masks and inaccessible to most people. Only a few friends knew a little about the storms that raged in his heart and the passions that were tormenting him. The women in his poems range between two extremes.[12] One is the virgin, representing young, innocent, pure, platonic love. She exists from his first collection of poetry and is noticeable in e.g. the poems to 'Cecilia Böllja'. She is depicted in a sublime way in 'Jungfru Maria' (Virgin Mary), one of the *Dalmålningar på rim* which becomes Karlfeldt's Song of Songs. The young girl wandering alone in the landscape around Sjugareby after sunset is the very symbol of innocence and purity and she is described throughout by images taken from Nature. There is a remarkable peacefulness and stillness in the poem, the wind is here but a cool summer-breeze and the moon reflects only tranquillity and an atmosphere of quiet wonder.

Yet in other poems the demons are there. It is obvious that Karlfeldt's attitude to love changed in his later years and this is reflected in his poems. Love is no longer innocent; it is dangerous, deceitful and wicked, and woman is often a demon, as in 'Häxorna' (The Witches, *Flora och Pomona*). The Nature imagery, particularly that of flowers, makes Karlfeldt's love poems sensuous and erotic. He consciously uses old names of flowers and herbs to reveal old magic and colloquial beliefs and customs. Impressionistic colours are mingled with fragrances, the rhythm is strong and skilfully built up in the poem 'Nattyxne' (Butterfly Orchid, *Flora och Pomona*). Eventually the note of resignation becomes stronger. In 'Änklingen' (The Widower) there is most certainly a confession of personal conflict, never resolved.

Chapter III

Outcasts, misfits; despair and resignation

Karlfeldt was an uprooted soul, nostalgically remembering his safe childhood but also looking into the future for possible peace. His rootlessness was expressed in many poems like the following:

> Jag är ett drivande blad i höstens vida rike,
> min levnad är en lek vid alla vindars kör.
> Om jag stannar på ett berg eller drunknar i ett dike,
> det vet jag ej, det bryr mig ej, det rår jag icke för.
> 'Jag är en sjungandes röst' (I am a singing voice, *Fridolins visor*, p.233).

(I am a drifting leaf in the wide realm of autumn, my life is a game to the choir of all winds. Should I stop on a mountain or drown in a ditch, I don't know, I don't care, I cannot be blamed.)

There is a piercing note of despair in the lines above, echoing much of the same deterministic attitude that was to be characteristic of the fin-de-siècle writing. Karlfeldt again chose a mask, this time called 'En löskerkarl' (A Vagrant) in *Fridolins visor* and he is Fridolin's counterpart. He has no home, no family, no heritage; but there is in spite of suffering a glimpse of optimism and of gratitude. Infinitely sadder though is the poem 'Längtan heter min arvedel' (Longing is my heritage, *Fridolins lustgård*) where loneliness and sad memories haunt the fortress i.e. the poet's soul. Even Fridolin despairs:

> Min längtan vill flyga, men vingen är tung
> min mun vill sjunga men tonen är glömd
> och vårgigan sprucken och gömd. p. 194
> 'Jag lever allena' (I live alone, *Fridolins visor*).

(My longing wants to fly but heavy is the wing, my mouth wants to sing but forgotten is the tune and the spring-fiddle cracked and hidden.)

World War I broke out and Karlfeldt symbolically called his new collection of poetry *Flora och Bellona* (Flora and Bellona). A new bitter reality became obvious to Karlfeldt which he could not avoid by turning to his old themes:

> Ett dårhus och ett bårhus

är människornas krigande värld.
Det spelar i minnenas vårhus
och lockar min själ till färd.
'Poeten till sångmön' (The poet to his muse)

(A madhouse and a mortuary is the human warring world. The spring-house of my memory plays a tune calling my soul away.)

Youth, love and spring, all is *vanitas vanitatum* and what is left is a slow decay, loneliness and autumn.

Karlfeldt was accused of not being involved in the problems of his time but in this collection his indignation at the war appeared in many poems like 'Svart jul' (Black Christmas), 'En pesthymn' (A Pest Hymn), and 'Det röda korset' (The Red Cross). There were also a few poems in which Karlfeldt expressed his social indignation and pity for the poor, e.g. 'Statarvisa' (The Farm-Labourer's Song). 'Till en jordförvärvare'(To a Soil Acquisitioner) is a strong defence of the farmers who own their strip of soil and a fierce attack on industrialism.

Thus the overall lingering theme in Karlfeldt's writing running parallel with his love poetry is the theme of everything's vanity. This is a common characteristic trait in literature of the time and Karlfeldt was probably influenced by Levertin and Heidenstam. The same feature appears abroad, for example in Matthew Arnold's poetry.

Towards reconciliation and/or faith

In a speech in 1919 to the Swedish Academy Karlfeldt said 'A man's life goes through much suffering on its way towards personality and harmony. The poet must take the same road. The more a man, the more a poet.'[13] No words could more truly describe Karlfeldt's own development. He more than anyone had fought against despair and he had very reluctantly resigned. In the poem 'Sjukdom' (Illness) he describes how, when he was nearly dying, he learned to look upon death as a friend. To accept mortality meant a kind of reconciliation but there were still echoes of despair in his poetry and a refusal to give up the joy of living.

In Karlfeldt's last collection of poetry *Hösthorn* (Autumn Horn) it is obvious however that he is closing the books on himself. He now knows what is in store, he can look back on his life and remember his passions. He does not envy young people their future life any more but

Chapter III

he can share the memories of being young with them:

> Jag är en höstpoet, men tro ej, vårtid,
> din tjusta oro är mig fjärn och forn.
> Tag mina bruna blad, o vårtid, sång- och sårtid,
> Sjung i min själ och dallra i mitt horn.
> 'Ungdom' (Youth, p. 802).

(I am an autumn poet, but do not think, o Spring, your charming worry is past and far away from me. Take my brown leaves, o, time of spring, and song and sore. Sing to my soul and make my horn tremble.)

The last collection probably embodies Karlfeldt's richest poetry in both style and content. There is the powerful 'Kornknarr, sänghalm' (The Corncrake and the Bedstraw) which is a delightful symbiosis of all the important ingredients in Karlfeldt's poetry: growing up close to Nature, the specific knowledge about this very Nature, the hidden farmer's soul within, and of course passionate love. 'Sub luna', the poem of incantation, is Karlfeldt's retrospection on his life and also a variation on the themes mentioned above. Linked to them also is the theme of vagrant despair 'fladdrande som min längtan/fladdrar mot månklara loft' (fluttering as my longing flutters towards moonlit skies) p. 712.

Karlfeldt believed in a power beyond and it is obvious that what he confesses is his belief in God in his last collection of poems. He is the only one of *Nittitalisterna* who has openly given evidence of it.[14] 'Höstpsalm' (Autumn Hymn) illustrates the crisis that Karlfeldt went through before achieving a confirmation of his faith. The deep anguish followed by the question 'quo vadis?' is replaced by a quiet confidence and a humble gratitude.

Heidenstam, Selma Lagerlöf and Karlfeldt lived to be quite old. They experienced World War I and the outbreak of World War II. People no longer found any comfort in the voices of *Nittitalet*. There was only widespread despair and cruel reality, the ideals were shattered and the joy of living was considered a myth. A new literature was born, based on Angst and realism, poetry found new forms and a new language.

However, almost a hundred years after *Nittitalisterna* first began to publish there seems to be a kind of renaissance for them. A new regional writing is well established in Sweden, represented by Sara

Lidman, Sven Delblanc, Kerstin Ekman, Göran Tunström, Torgny Lindgren and others, writing about their childhood years in various parts of Sweden. At the same time Selma Lagerlöf's stories are being refilmed and her books reprinted. Is there possibly a need for a new kind of imagination? Perhaps Fröding would have answered:

'rosor i ett sprucket krus är ändå alltid rosor.'
'Idealism och realism' (Idealism and Realism, *Nya Dikter*)

(roses in a cracked vase are always still roses).

Chapter IV

Swedish fin-de-siècle: Hjalmar Söderberg (1869-1941)

Tom Geddes

Fin-de-siècle is the term used to define a literary trend, which, in common with most periods or movements in literature, is not such a homogeneous tendency that it can be precisely defined or exactly delimited in time. The general use of the French expression points to the fact that the trend it attempts to designate is broader than any particular national literature. Both *fin-de-siècle* and the equivalent Swedish terms *sekelslutet* or *sekelslutspessimismen* suggest a period of limited duration at the end of the nineteenth century. But the beginnings of the pessimistic mood which characterizes *fin-de-siècle* can be clearly seen as early as 1857, when Baudelaire published his collection of poems *Les Fleurs du Mal*. Hjalmar Söderberg started contributing short stories to journals and the press in 1888, and Swedish *fin-de-siècle* is largely confined to the last decade of the outgoing century and the first decade of the new. As late as 1914, however, Sigfrid Siwertz published his novel *En flanör* (An Idler), which, although it embodies a rejection of the *fin-de-siècle* philosophy, nevertheless provides evidence of the continuing preoccupations of the period.

The last few decades of the nineteenth century marked the beginning of a profound transformation in man's view of himself. Shared beliefs and an acceptance of tradition gradually gave way to a questioning of all values and a sense of radical reappraisal of the human condition. The new critical awareness expressed itself in one direction in demands for social reform, in a desire to improve the external conditions of life. But at the same time such a fundamental rejection of the past brought with it a malaise going beyond the social or the psychological into the realms of philosophical enquiry. Lack of certainty and accepted beliefs led to an inner search, to a need to find ultimate truths which society and religion could no longer provide. In simplified terms, the *fin-de-siècle* period in European literature could be seen to stand historically as a transitional phase between the more external, social concerns of Naturalism, and the more subjective analysis of existence found in Expressionist literature, perhaps best epitomized by the existential uncertainty displayed in the works of Franz Kafka.

To postulate such a simple historical development is, of course, to distort the facts. No one literary period can be totally isolated from the preceding, and indeed at any one time different tendencies exist side by side. An investigation of the progression of prevailing trends reveals a process of interdependence and of gradual merging which does not allow any absolute divisions. For example, most writers categorized as *fin-de-siècle* share with their Naturalist predecessors a critical view of society, and state or imply in their writings the need for social change. But in general they display a scepticism and cynicism moving away from social commitment to apathy and resignation. One basic tenet of Naturalism, a view of man as a product of his heredity and environment, leads *fin-de-siècle* writers to the pessimistic portrayal of the individual as a helpless victim of deterministic factors beyond his control. Active steps for reform frequently give way to purely intellectual preoccupation with social, psychological and existential problems. At the same time the break with past traditions is often expressed in the depiction of behaviour which represents a rejection of the socially accepted norm, a tendency which led to the concept of Decadence as a literary label synonymous with *fin-de-siècle*.

Decadence is a term which often proves more misleading than helpful to literary history or analysis. A Decadent character, as a literary phenomenon, implies one in whom intellectual activity predominates over the practical ability or desire to cope with everyday life, and who expresses this proclivity either in passive withdrawal or in an active rejection of accepted conventions. In other words, Decadence denotes an individualism which can lead either into the world of the imagination or to the deliberate pursuit of experience for its own sake. The latter development can involve a way of life or a philosophy which could be regarded as morally reprehensible, and it is the application of the word 'decadent' in this popular sense which obscures its meaning as a literary term.

The trend which came to be designated *fin-de-siècle* can be discerned in most European literatures. While Baudelaire's poetry, with its themes of degeneration and decay, its interest in eroticism and evil, and its tone of boredom and disgust with life, is a precursor of later developments, it is his fellow-countryman J.-K. Huysmans who is usually cited as one of the primary representatives of the *fin-de-siècle* period itself. His novel *À Rebours* (Against Nature, 1884) depicts a totally amoral hedonist who believes in uninhibited sensuality and the gratification of all personal desires. In English literature the most central work of the period is undoubtedly Oscar Wilde's *The Picture of Dorian Gray*, 1891, where Decadence is depicted as a kind of extreme aestheticism. Wilde traces the gradual corruption of a young man who pursues 'aesthetic' experience as an end in itself; the aesthetic includes both sensual indulgence and moral indifference. In the works of the Austrian writer, Arthur Schnitzler, social criticism, eroticism, the dissolute life of the 'flaneur', or indolent man-about-town, are all combined with a world-weary cynicism.

For Scandinavian literature the term *fin-de-siècle* by no means implies any frivolous or degenerate amorality. Most works portray characters who incline far more to melancholy, pessimism, and a general existential weariness; they lack will, are inactive, and without hope. They also show a marked tendency to philosophize about their outlook on life. The title of Herman Bang's *Haabløse Slægter* (Generations Without Hope, 1880) alludes to a process of degeneration in one family which is symptomatic of the hopelessness and decline of the whole epoch. The dreamy, melancholy nature of the central character, William Høg, is manifested in an inability to cope with reality which culminates in suicide. His *alter ego*, Hoff, though in many ways more adapted to society, leads a dissolute life which embodies a defiance of social conventions. Jens Peter Jacobsen's novel *Niels Lyhne*, 1880, is also set in the framework of hereditary determinism. The propensity towards the world of the imagination which Niels inherits from his mother imbues him with a heightened sensitivity which prevents him taking an active and successful part in life.

Herman Bang's novel was impounded and its author accused of immorality. Similar charges were laid against several members of the bohemian circle of writers and artists in Oslo, where such works as *Fra*

Swedish fin-de-siècle

Kristiania-Bohêmen (From the Christiania Bohemia, 1885) by Hans Jæger, and *Albertine*, 1886, by Christian Krohg, were confiscated and their authors prosecuted. Both writers concerned themselves with the need for radical social reform, especially in respect of public attitudes to sexual morality. But their characters are also endowed with a pessimistic lack of will and regard life as ultimately meaningless. Arne Garborg's *Trætte Mænd* (Weary Men, 1891) gives expression to a critical view of society, but marks a much stronger and romantic withdrawal into subjectivity. Gabriel Gram suffers from a nihilistic weariness which prevents all action. He avoids the conflict between reality and the ideal by insisting on his subjective illusions precisely because he sees life as meaningless. The tendencies apparent in the literatures of Denmark and Norway are also to be seen in Sweden.[1] It must be remembered, however, that the literary mood subsumed under the term *fin-de-siècle* was only one aspect of the period under review. The major movement of the 1890s in Sweden was the neo-romanticism represented by Selma Lagerlöf, Karlfeldt, Heidenstam and Fröding; and Strindberg's play *Till Damaskus* (To Damascus) appeared in 1898, marking the advent of the Expressionist movement in European literature.

Of the Swedish authors closest to the *fin-de-siècle* trend, the two most outstanding are Bo Bergman and Hjalmar Söderberg. There are other writers in whom *fin-de-siècle* tendencies can be discerned, among them Oscar Levertin, Emil Kléen and Sigfrid Siwertz.[2] Much of Levertin's early poetry inclines to an aestheticism closer in mood to the French Decadents than to the more affirmative romanticism of such Swedish contemporaries as Heidenstam. Kléen was an exponent of Decadence in the Baudelaire tradition, deliberately cultivating an air of decadence in his personal behaviour and appearance as well as in his literary works. The title of Siwertz' first poems, *Gatans drömmar* (Street Dreams, 1905) characterizes the mood of the collection. The later novel, *En flanör* (A Flaneur, 1914), is a portrait of a melancholy romantic. But the central character's rejection of his inactive life for a return to study, work and self-respect is in a totally different spirit, as are most of Siwertz' other works.

Bo Bergman remained for only a comparatively short period truly under the influence of *fin-de-siècle* pessimism, although an air of melancholy permeates all his works. He published his first poems, *Marionetterna* (The Marionettes), in 1903. The title poem continues to be quoted in almost every history of Swedish literature as an image of the prevailing mood of pessimistic determinism: human beings are mere puppets who can only react to the pulling of the strings that control them. Other poems in the same collection express a melancholy verging on desperation or disillusion and resignation. 'Drömmen' (The Dream), the story which lends its name to his first volume of short stories (1904), concerns an ageing bachelor who avoids taking any action for fear of the possible consequences, and has withdrawn into a totally empty and isolated life. When finally he decides to act, the negative result of a very generous deed confirms his already pessimistic view of life. The theme of the story is determinism and the inability of any apparent act of free will to change the course of life. But the depiction of this man seems also to imply that his outlook stems largely from a psychologically motivated fear of life. The events of the story do not in themselves constitute any philosophical basis for his previous or subsequent lack of action.

This of course does not totally invalidate the deterministic view presented, and there is no doubt that Bo Bergman, like Söderberg, himself subscribed to the disillusioned cynicism he portrays in his writing. But while both authors feel obvious sympathy with their literary characters, each preserves also a certain critical distance. For Söderberg in particular, narrative irony plays a large part in the overall picture he creates. It soon becomes apparent that he is not only Sweden's foremost representative of the melancholy disillusion of the *fin-de-siècle*, but that he is also very much aware of the dangers inherent in the attitudes he himself describes and in some of the excesses of his predecessors and contemporaries.

Söderberg began writing stories and reviews in 1888, but his first book was the novel *Förvillelser* (Aberrations), published in 1895. The work was attacked for its immorality as soon as it appeared.[3] It depicts a period of a few months in the life of an aimless young man, Tomas Weber, and his relationships with two girls. Tomas is a melancholy but superficial hedonist, living his life with no real sense of purpose; he is a student, but never studies. Of all Söderberg's characters, he is nearest to the flaneur; in his way of life he is representative of a whole literary type, spending much of his time as a leisured man-about-town. But he can by no means be labelled a Decadent in the same category as, for instance, Wilde's Dorian Gray. He is something of a dandy: in the opening scene of the book he has just bought a pair of new red gloves;

but his appearance and attire are not exaggeratedly ostentatious. His way of life, despite his lack of occupation and his sexual relationships, is not deliberately amoral, although of course sexual affairs outside marriage (especially, as here, without even the mitigating factor of love) represented an immorality which was enough to offend contemporary society.

All of Söderberg's works state or imply a criticism of society. In this respect he continues the rational and socially committed tradition of the 1880s. In *Förvillelser* the prevailing double standards of the time are implicitly attacked: Tomas makes use of one girl, Ellen, a shop assistant, as a safety-valve which can help him to maintain his relationship with Märta, a girl of higher social standing, on a platonic level. Ellen's later marriage to an older man to preserve her reputation alludes negatively to marriage as an institution which has little to do with love. It is society's intolerance which separates Märta and Tomas when her eventual pregnancy causes her mother to take her to Norway to avoid scandal.

Söderberg's primary concern, however, is not with social attitudes but with personal relationships. In this very first novel he shows his pessimistic attitude towards the possibility of happiness and a lasting, satisfactory partnership between the sexes. When they are reunited, after a self-imposed separation caused by their guilt at having consummated their relationship, Tomas and Märta do not find happiness, but only a melancholy emptiness. And the same feeling of emptiness occurs simultaneously for Tomas in his affair with Ellen. Söderberg is depicting here what he saw as the transience of love, a theme which was to concern him again and again. For nearly all his characters, sexual involvement separates rather than joins two people. Tomas Weber has nothing from his experiences but 'a wasteland of grey indifference' (119).[4]

The other characters in the novel confirm this concept of love. Mortimer cynically recommends that love should be totally avoided, because it is so meaningless. Johannes Hall begins a relationship with Tomas Weber's sister at the very moment when Tomas' two affairs have come to an end. The inevitable waning of this love is thus suggested by the juxtaposition. It is also more explicitly commented upon in Tomas Weber's thoughts: 'Now it was the others' turn. For himself and Märta the game was over' (122). The metaphor of a game anticipates the title of Söderberg's later novel *Den allvarsamma leken*

Chapter IV

(The Serious Game): an indication that he was to continue to be preoccupied with the same problems.

Despite this pessimism, love is nevertheless depicted as the only experience that can give any significance to life. Johannes Hall is described as 'the most destitute man in the world' (107) because he loves nobody and is loved by nobody; and Tomas Weber sees in his relationships with Ellen and Märta the only meaning in his short, unhappy life as he prepares himself for suicide.

It is in Söderberg's portrayal of Tomas Weber's suicide attempt that his attitude towards his hero is most clearly expressed. Suicide, which for many Decadent authors gave conclusive expression to a disgust with life or a lack of will to live, becomes for Söderberg a motif which laconically embodies his own ironical distance from his creation. Tomas shoots himself in order to escape the financial embarrassment engendered by his way of life, but the bullet merely grazes him, so that he falls first into unconsciousness and then into sleep.

To say that Tomas finally decides to live would be to use too strong a term; rather, he resigns himself to living — not with a positive affirmation of life, but in deterministic passivity. He does not have the energy to resist the course expected of him. The 'zest for life' (155) which is attributed to him on the final page of the novel suggests a kind of superficial re-adaptation rather than the new philosophy of life which he feels might one day come to him.

This first novel, like almost all of Söderberg's work, is set in Stockholm. Even after marital difficulties caused him to live in self-imposed exile in Copenhagen, no other city could ever replace Stockholm in his affections. The city is an essential part of the life he depicts: his characters can hardly exist without the streets, cafés and restaurants of the Swedish capital. The topographical references which provide so realistic a background consist usually of a selection of details, an economical, impressionistic technique in the presentation of setting matched by a tendency to a laconic understatement of the most important events and emotions affecting his characters. This is his most typical stylistic feature, imbuing his stories with both a hint of light-hearted irony and at the same time a deep sense of tragedy.

Much of the background description in his works has a symbolic function. He frequently uses the weather and seasons as a device to evoke mood. The course of events described in *Förvillelser* runs from April to December, from the youthful hopes of spring to the melancholy bleakness of winter. When Tomas and Märta go out to Drottningholm, the rushing storm clouds offer a symbolic parallel to the rapidly approaching end of their relationship; on the day of his suicide attempt Tomas' state of mind is rendered through the description of the buildings around him: 'The ringing of the bells caused the earth to quake and the air to sing and the houses to totter like drunkards' (127). Söderberg's Naturalistic impressionism here gives way to the distortion more usually associated with Expressionism.

His second novel, *Martin Bircks ungdom* (Martin Birck's Youth, 1901), is a much deeper, more philosophical work than *Förvillelser*. Whereas Tomas Weber has only a superficial awareness of himself and of life's problems, Martin Birck is a thinker. Where Tomas acts without regard for the consequences, Martin thinks to such an extent that he finds it difficult to act.

The first section of the novel concerns Martin's childhood, a subject which might seem to have little in common with life-weary pessimism. But there are three very pronounced themes in the description of his childhood which place the book firmly in the *fin-de-siècle* mould: melancholy, eroticism, and determinism.

A mood of melancholy is created, as in *Förvillelser*, by frequent reference to season and weather: the setting is one of dark, overcast days when 'autumn advanced over the earth, and in the city...the houses were grey and black with rain and smoke' (18). Martin himself, even as a very young child, displays a melancholy temperament that seems to be predetermined: 'he had suddenly become melancholy without knowing why' (23).

Eroticism forms the theme of the very first page of the book. Martin's dream of picking a red, poisonous flower instead of the blue flower he had grasped, and of simultaneously losing his mother, implies not only a loss of childhood innocence in a general sense, but suggests too the attractions of the erotic sphere with its attendant dangers. (The symbolism may well include an allusion to the forbidden fruit, man's fall from innocence and expulsion from Paradise.)[5] The implicit suggestion that the results of one's actions are outside one's own control also foreshadows the theme of determinism which is later announced more clearly. Erotic motifs pervade the early pages, even though, of course, they are not understood as such by Martin: a sexually suggestive song from a drunken caretaker; the temptation of a pear which assumes almost sexual overtones; the beauty of Ida, a girl of his own age, with whom he falls asleep. There is an unmistakably Decadent trait in the dual nature of woman implied in this scene of the two children playing together: the Catholic religious symbols to which Ida introduces Martin present an image of woman as the Madonna; while in his mother's warning that Ida has fleas there is a hint of a lower, dangerous aspect to the female sex.

The theme of determinism is also found in an image immediately intelligible to the reader if not to the consciousness of the child Martin. Söderberg uses the symbol of a puppet (the symbol later to be used by Bo Bergman in his poem 'Marionetterna'), which believes that its own free will is causing the movements which are dependent on the pulling of the strings from above.

Martin Bircks ungdom is the story, recounted in pertinent episodes, of the development of the hero from small child to thirty-year-old man, a melancholy outsider, critical of society, constantly searching for the truth but going through a gradual process of disillusionment. The conflict between dreams and reality which occurs in many works of the period is central to this novel. Martin has the aspirations of the young romantic to be a poet, to find love, to find a meaning to life. But the unattainability of the ideal (prefigured in the opening dream by the disappearance of the blue flower, the symbol of the Romantics) leads only to disillusion. Martin's failure is partly determined by his own lack of will to action, which he shares with the flaneur type. He dreams of being a poet, but remains unproductive. His literary aims are connected with an idealistic pursuit of truth.

His critical awareness begins with a rejection of religion; but far from setting him on the path towards a new rational philosophy of life, his idealism develops into a melancholy nihilism. In this he is typical of his times. In a world bereft of meaning he can find no answers to his questioning, and he becomes more introspective and his attitude to life more apathetic. Unlike Tomas Weber, his aimless wandering on the streets of Stockholm is directly attributable to his insight into the meaninglessness of existence and the vanity of a more active search for truth or fight for social improvements.

As in several novels of the period, disillusionment brings thoughts of suicide as a possible way out of life's emptiness. But here again Söderberg distances himself from his Decadent predecessors. Martin entertains the idea not in reality, but in a mentally conceived projection of his possible path as a poet, envisaging himself failing in his search for truth and progressing through self-contempt to desperation and ending as a typical Decadent: 'No vice would be unfamiliar to him, and he would pass the night with gaming and drinking. Until one dreary October evening he would tire of his crazy and empty life...'(55). But he has enough self-irony at this stage to see such a solution as banal. Nevertheless, suicide still represents a possible response to life's meaninglessness. The death of another character is portrayed in precisely those terms: 'And old Abraham, who had given him the puppet and who had hanged himself from a rope one rainy day when he found it not worth the bother of living any longer, was soon forgotten...'(49). The information comes in part of a subordinate clause, as if in parenthesis and thus of little note. It is a good example of the understatement that Söderberg reserves for important matters.

In Martin's own thoughts on suicide and in a later depiction of a Decadent poet Söderberg implicitly criticizes some of the excesses of the Decadent tendency in literature. The poet (a figure modelled on the poet Emil Kléen) characterizes himself:

He confided to Martin that he was decadent. He adored everything that was in a state of decomposition and decay....He hated the sun and the light...he loved the night and sin and all alcoholic spirits....He had the majority of known venereal diseases, and agoraphobia too....This illness gave him particular joy, since he regarded it as a precursor of *paralysie générale*...that was the great sleep, that was Nirvana. (83-84).

Martin is impressed; but Söderberg's attitude is obvious in the caricature.

Söderberg's treatment of the themes of love and sexuality shares many features with other Scandinavian literary works of the turn of the century. Martin attacks the double standards of the time, which encouraged the use of prostitutes and what he calls two sorts of love: the pure and the sensual. He criticizes the social hypocrisy inherent in this attitude and shows an awareness of the problems involved for both sexes. In condemning society's attitudes he is clearly acting as the mouthpiece of his author.

But Martin's own unfulfilled desires stem largely from his lack of action. He is in many ways an aesthete, in that he shows a marked propensity to retreat from real life into the world of the imagination. He writes a letter to a young lady, for example, but decides not to send it. Not only does he thus draw back from a possible relationship, but he

Chapter IV

also goes one stage further: he keeps the letter for inclusion in a story he may write. An aesthetic response to life indeed!

Although *Martin Bircks ungdom* is a lyrical novel which concentrates on the moods and thoughts of its very introspective central character, the attitudes and opinions attributed to him do not necessarily, of course, accord fully with those of the author. The inclusion of other characters allows Söderberg to present alternatives. Dr Markel's humorously cynical recommendation of pantheism as the ideal belief presents a contrast to Martin's deeply troubled religious speculations. Henrik Rissler is equally cynical about society and life in general, but unlike Martin he is not an idealist. What Markel and Rissler have in common, and what Martin lacks (except in the one instance mentioned above) is self-irony. Rissler in fact is writing a thesis on romantic irony. The juxtaposition of these two characters to Martin implies that an alternative attitude is necessary to cope with life. Rissler's more ironical detachment enables him to lead a more active life than Martin, even though in many respects they share the same philosophy. Rissler refers to melancholy as a deliberately cultivated mood: 'a new stimulant invented by the upper classes. But it only remains melancholy while it concerns moods and music and ideas....I have been thinking of women and love. When you get into that sphere, it's not just melancholy any longer....' (96). Despite his pessimistic view of the inevitable transience of love, he goes on to ask rhetorically, 'How can there be anything tragic in a man being deceived in love? If he takes it as a tragedy, he just becomes comical' (97). The portrayal of Rissler's more detached attitude does not suggest that such an outlook would be possible for Martin. His tragedy lies in the fact that it is not. The cynicism of Rissler and Markel is clearly not intended to be seen entirely in a positive light, but they do function to some extent as critics of Martin Birck.

Rissler also criticizes Martin when he comments on the static nature of his life: 'Time has stood still here' (94); and it seems that Söderberg may be indicating the dangers of surrendering to the apathy to which a nihilistic view of life can lead. Martin dwells on Rissler's remark, and develops the idea into an image of a clock with no hands, with its connotations of timeless eternity. He displays here an increasing alienation from reality itself, which amounts almost to a death wish.

The final scene can be interpreted as just such an experience of eternity, of death, of self-annihilation. In the passionate kiss on which the novel ends, Martin feels himself 'dissolving' (131), 'painlessly burning up' (132). He imagines himself finally rising out of his cold and empty life, not into the warmth, but into a heat much more all-consuming. It is a subjective moment in which all life's contradictions are resolved. The strength of the experience for Martin points to the redeeming power of love; but it also represents a retreat from life's problems which emphasizes his resignation. And even in this moment of passion his head is full of mental images of transience: summer butterflies become autumn leaves, and Hamlet's words 'I loved Ophelia!' (131) echo in his mind. Not only does the reference to Hamlet's love suggest that Martin's too can provide no solution; it also alludes to the fatal flaw shared by both characters: a tragic lack of action caused by a melancholy and introspective nature.

Doktor Glas (Doctor Glas, 1905) demonstrates an equally pessimistic resignation. But here, even more than in *Martin Bircks ungdom*, a distinction must be made between the subject-matter of the book and the narrative perspective. The themes and motifs of the novel have much in common with the tendencies of the turn of the century, and for that reason the book was regarded by its contemporaries as yet another expression of Decadence. But while the author clearly feels sympathy for his fictional character, such sympathy does not necessarily imply complete advocacy of the ideas or actions attributed to him. Because Söderberg based much of the story of Martin Birck on his own life, it was assumed that both that work and *Doktor Glas* were part of an autobiographical confession. Dr Glas was regarded by many as an older Martin Birck, despite the fact that Söderberg gave different names to his two eponymous heroes and even introduces Birck as a distinct character in the later novel. At the most, one could perhaps see in Dr Glas an exaggerated development of one side of the personality of Martin Birck, a withdrawal into passive isolation; but he is given his own psychological development totally independent of his literary predecessor.

Glas is a lonely Stockholm doctor who murders a clergyman, pastor Gregorius, to whose wife he is attracted. His motivation is partly psychological, and partly stems from a conscious application of his philosophy to a concrete situation. He has already formulated his view of life when the story begins. He embodies an attitude of pessimism, resignation and lack of will to act which marks a culmination in the development of the passive resigned outsider in Scandinavian *fin-de-siècle* literature. There is no trace at all of the hedonist; all that remains is the habit of the flaneur to sit in cafés or to walk the streets pondering the meaninglessness of life.

Dr Glas has reconciled himself to being an observer. The novel's diary form stresses his non-participation even more than the same narrative framework in Garborg's *Trætte Mænd*. The climax of the book is his desperate attempt to commit one act, in this case a murder, a motif which continues the amorality of earlier Decadent literature. But here the act is conceived not as a subjective indulgence in experience for its own sake, but as an extension of Dr Glas's argument on the problem of free will and determinism. He attempts to present his actions and motives in a philosophical perspective. The conflict between free will and determinism plays a more central part here than in *Martin Bircks ungdom*, and the discussion of free will is extended to a consideration of the power of the will and the right of one individual to impose his will on another. But the concept of free will remains for Dr Glas firmly in the realm of the subjectivity which is the hallmark of Decadence.

In this novel Söderberg distances himself far more unambiguously than before from his literary creation. He illustrates one possible course of action, which is dependent not only on a certain philosophical conviction, but also on a particular individual psychology. He seeks to explain Dr Glas's character, in particular the passivity which culminates in the need for action, by reference to his past experiences, especially in the erotic sphere, thus attributing his attitudes not so much to the *Zeitgeist* as to individual psychology.

One of the reasons for the murder is Dr Glas's attraction to fru Gregorius. She belongs to the category of women to whom he is attracted because they appear to be already in love. Such a desire for the unattainable acts as a rationalization of his fear of participation in life, and also expresses a longing for the ideal which he shares with the other melancholy romantics of the turn of the century. Although he ascribes his motivation for the murder in part to his need for involvement with his fellow human beings: 'One's heart shudders at the emptiness and seeks contact at any price' (55), he does not seek to involve himself with fru Gregorius after her husband's death and her abandonment by her lover. He even ignores a clear offer of affection from another woman whom he finds not unattractive.

The narrative provides an explanation of this passivity in

psychological terms. Dr Glas reveals several aspects of his past which have an obvious bearing on his development and present predicament. His attraction to women beyond his reach is closely connected with his abhorrence of the physical aspects of sexuality. By separating the physical and the spiritual he is able to maintain the division between reality and the ideal which he seems to find so necessary. What we learn of his past suggests a fear of physical sexuality which may have stemmed from his early relationship with his parents. In any case he has subjected himself to a continuing process of repression, attempting to ignore the physical side of life which he finds so disgusting. It seems that Söderberg is portraying here an individual psychological background which could lead to the kind of romanticized idealism that Dr Glas professes. The result is a romanticism that borders on an intellectual and emotional sterility with its parallel in the physical sterility which his attitude to sexuality implies.

The profound emptiness and tiredness of life which Dr Glas feels at the end of the book is thus not simply an expression of pessimistic disillusion based on a rational enquiry into the human condition. After the murder he inclines more to a belief in determinism, whereas before it he had wanted to believe in free will. But nothing has in fact changed. His actions and their results prove nothing. His final situation is the result of his own psychology, not of the workings of fate. The book could be regarded as a portrayal of the kind of individual psychological determinism which can lead to the philosophical outlook so typical of the *fin-de-siècle*. While, therefore, Dr Glas's view of life seems more negative than that of either Tomas Weber or Martin Birck, and his propensity to philosophize gives a spurious credibility to his attitudes, it is evident that in creating this figure Söderberg was in fact dissociating himself further from the direction in which such a melancholy, pessimistic and disillusioned view of life could lead.

Seven years passed before the appearance of Söderberg's next novel *Den allvarsamma leken* (The Serious Game, 1912), during which time his chief publications were the plays *Gertrud* (1906) and *Aftonstjärnan* (The Evening Star, 1912), the collection of stories *Det mörknar över vägen* (Darkness Falls, 1907) and the aphoristic *Hjärtats oro* (The Heart's Unrest, 1909). He had begun *Den allvarsamma leken* in 1908 and published the introductory section in 1910, but did not resume work on it again until 1912.

It is immediately apparent that this novel differs from the previous three in scope. Its greater length is a sign of Söderberg's use, for the first time, of the full discursive potential of the novel form. Where *Martin Bircks ungdom* and *Doktor Glas* were so economically composed that every passage had a relevance to the major themes of the book, *Den allvarsamma leken* functions as a chronicle of its times, over and above the strict requirement of its plot or subject. The references to world events and to the political and social scene in Sweden are so frequent that at times they almost become part of the subject of the book, acting as a counterpoint to the main plot. Towards the end of the novel, for instance, the sinking of the Titanic and Strindberg's impending death provide an atmosphere of gloom which underlines the emptiness and sense of loss experienced by the central character. But most of the references, such as to the Dreyfus affair, or to the Swedish-Norwegian union question, appear for their own sake, and the choice of a newspaper office as a setting for many of the episodes provides the only motivation for their inclusion. The realism of the contemporary Stockholm milieu, so prominent in all Söderberg's novels, is further strengthened by allusions to actual names: *Nationalbladet* and *Dagens Post* clearly refer to the Swedish national dailies *Svenska Dagbladet* and *Dagens Nyheter*; and it is not hard to discern the names of the poet and critic Levertin, or Böök, the literary critic, in their fictional counterparts Levini and Löök.

The hero of this book, Arvid Stjärnblom, is much more integrated into society than Söderberg's previous protagonists. He is still a thinker, with ideals, but spends less time pondering on life. Nor does personal behaviour present so much of a conflict with public morality as before. Arvid regards prostitution, for instance, as a useful service, and remembers with gratitude the woman who initiated him in sexual matters. Marriage is again portrayed negatively as a social institution in which love plays little part. Sexual relationships are presented as a more natural feature of life than in the previous novels, although here too they embody a vain search for love rather than happiness and fulfilment. Arvid's comments on the morality of such relationships seem to stand for the author's viewpoint: '...both women and men are at times impelled by instincts and desires which are not easy to accommodate within any kind of rational or moral framework' (84).

The title of the book refers, of course, to love. There are differences between Tomas Weber's rather melancholy irresponsibility, Martin Birck's resignation and Dr Glas' empty sterility, but the theme of love remains the central concept in Söderberg's novels. It is only love which can imbue life with meaning, but it remains an elusive prize, constantly sought, occasionally glimpsed, never retained. The analogy of a game, and a very serious one, provides a suitable metaphor for man's constant striving for a goal which never provides lasting fulfilment: Arvid Stjärnblom, after his marriage to a woman he does not love, meets Lydia, who was his first love and is herself now unhappily married. The plot centres on the relationship between Arvid and Lydia. Their affair gives them only a very fleeting happiness. Lydia is twice unfaithful to Arvid, and when she finally deserts him he simultaneously leaves his wife, recognizing the emptiness of his life. Further disappointment and repetition for Lydia are inevitable, since for her current lover she represents only an enjoyable interlude.

In the figure of Lydia, Söderberg gives concrete expression to the constant pursuit of love which is bound to be disappointed. It is as if her demands on love are such that continued renewal is required as soon as her feelings begin to wane from the first passion of a relationship. Arvid reprimands her for playing with the feelings of others, but for her it seems in fact to be no less serious a game than for him: they share the same basic search for love. Only at one point does it seem that Lydia is behaving somewhat capriciously. She tells Arvid she had taken another lover while he was away; she is not fully aware herself of her motivation, but feels it may have been partly a need to escape her loneliness, and partly 'a desire to know whether I could influence a person's fate' (169). Such an attempt to exert her will on another person is parallel to Dr Glas's act of will. But where for Dr Glas it was preceded by a theoretical examination of the nature of will, for Lydia it is apparently a more instinctive act: she makes no attempt to intellectualize her actions. In both cases the attempt to play the role of Fate fails to bring any positive reward. In Lydia's case it results in the suicide of the young man she had encouraged and then rejected.

Den allvarsamma leken gives a central place to the conflict between the emotional demands of love and the claims of the intellect. Arvid cannot think of marrying Lydia when they are first in love because he does not have the necessary financial resources and because he feels too young to tie himself so permanently. But when the time comes for him to make a decision about marrying his eventual wife, Dagmar, these considerations take second place. 'I have such a strong and imperative need to be alone,' he explains to Dagmar, '... I want the right to begin and above all to end my day alone. To think alone, to sleep alone' (79). He cannot reconcile the contradictory impulses of the emotional and the cerebral. But whereas Martin Birck's intellectual activity involved an introspection which could only inhibit a love relationship, and where Dr Glas allowed a sterile intellectualism to exclude totally any true emotional experience, Arvid Stjärnblom successfully combines his work, for some years at least, with a fairly satisfactory marriage. 'Oh, to be alone! Oh, to be free!' he exclaims to himself; but the narrative continues: 'But generally speaking they lived very happily together' (97).

In all respects Arvid is a more balanced character than his predecessors. He retains certain features of *fin-de-siècle* passivity, but these are given a secondary role. The attitude expressed in the thought 'let chance take its course' (21) is not that of a man who feels himself to be at the mercy of fate. It represents his realization that he should let his life take its course without encumbrance for a while longer. His marriage to Dagmar, which happens more or less against his will, is put in a deterministic perspective, not least by the words attributed to his friend Markel (which are also selected as the motto to the second section of the book): 'One does not choose one's fate. And equally one does not choose one's wife or one's lover or one's children. One acquires them, and one has them, and it can happen that one loses them. But one does not choose!' (63). Despite the air of determinism and the pessimistic view of love which this book shares with Söderberg's earlier works, however, Arvid does not succumb entirely to cynical disillusion.

From the beginning he is a more positive and practical character. He stands as a rejection of the more unviable side of Martin Birck. Looking at the only poem he ever finished, Arvid thinks about himself: 'No — he was not a poet. He saw the world too plainly and soberly for that. He did not have the happy gift of self-deception and self-intoxication needed for it' (33). Where Martin believed in an idealized search for ultimate truth, Arvid is more realistic. He had a similar ideal, but he is aware that it is purely an ideal. He explains to Lydia that he had wanted to be 'something that probably does not exist...the world soul...the one who knows and understands everything' (94). In fact his more practical ambition, expressed as a desire to make his name in Swedish history, is something he in some measure attains. He is a journalist who progresses from music critic to foreign affairs editor, and also publishes several books, including one on Sweden's foreign policy.

Arvid retains his critical awareness while at the same time adapting to life. His advice to an aspiring young playwright is an obvious condemnation of Martin Birck: 'My dear friend, you seem to be suffering the usual curse of youth, which by the way Henrik Rissler has depicted in one of his books: the belief that one dare not reveal one's real face....' (200). By thus alluding to one of his own books, Söderberg clearly distances himself from the attitudes of Martin Birck. This represents a development in the author himself, but it may also be evidence of a detachment intended even at the time of composition of the earlier work.

The more stable character of Arvid Stjärnblom suggests that of all the novel heroes he is the one with whom the author most identifies. Despite his cynicism and a certain tendency to romanticism he comes closest of all Söderberg's figures to achieving a reconciliation of life's contradictions. Nevertheless, at the end of the novel his life is emotionally empty: he has been deserted by his mistress, and has left his unhappy marriage. Söderberg presents further confirmation of his pessimistic message: love cannot last, and yet it provides life's meaning. The conclusion is not entirely bleak, however. Arvid travels abroad, not into emptiness, but as his paper's foreign correspondent. Marking a break with the introverted nature of Söderberg's previous characters, Arvid is saved from total dejection and disillusion by his commitment to socio-political realities. It is an attitude which reflects the increasing commitment which Söderberg displayed in his own life and his non-literary writings.

Of Söderberg's three plays, the first, *Gertrud* (1906), is by far the most successful. It had its stage première simultaneously in Stockholm and Copenhagen in 1907, and has been performed much more often than either *Aftonstjärnan* (1912) or *Ödestimmen* (Hour of Destiny, 1922). The subject of *Gertrud* is closely linked to a major theme in *Den allvarsamma leken* : the conflict between intellect and emotion, between on the one hand dedication to work, ambition, success, and on the other a total commitment to love for another person.

Gertrud is presented in relation to three men: her husband Gustaf Kanning, her lover Erland Jansson, and her lover from many years before, Gabriel Lidman. The three are characterized as representing three different attitudes to love. Kanning is a man for whom work is more important than love; he has neglected the emotional side of life for his political ambition. Ironically he is at the height of his career — he

Chapter IV

has just been appointed to ministerial office — when Gertrud decides to leave him. Jansson is a superficial philanderer, who wants merely a casual and uncommitted affair. Both men present an antithesis to Gertrud, a woman for whom love is everything.

Gabriel Lidman, from whom Gertrud had parted years before when she recognized that love was only of secondary importance for him, has come to feel the emotional vacuum in his life and has returned in the hope that Gertrud will respond to his continuing love for her. Like Kanning, he too is at a pinnacle of public success. He has achieved fame as a poet, but only at the expense of love. He tells Gertrud he realizes now that 'love is everything'. But she cannot accept the possibility of such a radical change in a man who had once written aphoristically: 'Woman's love and man's work — the two have been antagonists from the beginning' (150), and who all his life has been satisfied with mere physical lust and has rejected love.

Gertrud's experience has led her to the cynical view originally expressed by Lidman: 'I believe in the lusts of the flesh and the incurable loneliness of the soul' (145). She leaves all three men, because none can offer the absolute love that she demands. Her tragedy lies in the impossibility of finding such total love. She is a similar figure to Lydia in *Den allvarsamma leken*, but is more sympathetically portrayed. In Lydia's case the problem is presented more from the man's point of view, and her motivation is not clearly explored. Her behaviour thus seems more self-centred.[6] It has been suggested that Gertrud's concept of love, too, is self-orientated; that despite her insistence that she has loved more, hers is a selfish love that is transferable from person to person, whereas Lidman has a deeper love which he has retained over the years solely for her.[7] There is some truth in this; and Lidman is certainly portrayed sympathetically as an embodiment of the problem of the conflicting claims of intellect and emotion. But Gertrud's quest is not in principle self-seeking even though in practice it may appear selfish; it is a search for the ideal, and as such it is doomed to failure. She is yet another of Söderberg's characters whose unattainable ideals lead inevitably to emptiness. Such idealism of course, involves in every case a dissociation of the self from the real world and from other people, and the negative results Söderberg portrays implicitly criticize the inviability of this approach to life.

Despite a slightly forced exposition, *Gertrud* is a well-constructed play which skilfully presents the problem of love in terms of a dramatic conflict. What is lacking in Söderberg's next play, *Aftonstjärnan*, is precisely the conflict of ideas which constitutes good drama. This short one-act play is set in a café which gives its name to the title. Vivan, a waitress, converses in turn with three customers: a doctor, her boy-friend, and an elderly man who is trying to buy her affection. Attention focuses alternately on Vivan and on a totally unrelated group of four men who are engaged in a discussion of premonition. The constant switching of attention from one group to the other fails as a dramatic device; it soon becomes tedious and serves only to highlight the lack of coherence in the play. The sketch of Stockholm café life which it attempts to provide might have found a more suitable medium in the short story.

Many of Söderberg's usual themes recur, but they remain allusions without any real function within the play. The doctor, for instance, has come to the café to read because he is married; the elderly man describes the course of life as hell, a pessimistic view for which the action and dialogue do not provide enough evidence. The doctor, prompted by the subject of the book he is reading, comments on the notion of free will as self-deception, a concept which is only tenuously linked to the motif of will which occurs again at the end. Vivan's elderly admirer finally persuades her to agree to go home with him, but then rejects her. He admits that his one intention was to enforce his will, in order to retaliate for the humiliation he had felt when she originally refused him.

In the person of Vivan, Söderberg portrays woman as a pawn in man's game. Her situation also illustrates a deterministic view of life: she is a victim of her circumstances, someone who does not fit into her environment but who has little alternative. The conversation of the four customers running parallel to the events which centre on Vivan seems at first to be an argument about superstition and rationality. But the subject of premonition is another aspect of determinism, and it seems that this, if anything, is intended as the theme which should have moulded the play into an integral whole. Whatever his intentions, however, Söderberg did not succeed in creating a satisfactory drama in *Aftonstjärnan*.

His third attempt in this genre is the much later play *Ödestimmen*, which although technically more competent, fails to provide the audience or reader with enough interest in its characters or their

Chapter IV

problems. Unusual (but not unique) for Söderberg is the location of events in an imaginary setting, here a country he calls Taurien. Without his customary Stockholm milieu it all seems rather artificial. The subject centres on politics and political decisions, thus developing the sphere of which Gustaf Kanning, in *Gertrud*, provided a foretaste, and at first sight marking an apparent break with the themes of his earlier works. The title, although alluding to fate, in fact introduces a rather different concept of man's relationship to events. Cassius, acting as adviser to the Emperor, puts forward the following view of history: 'The business of the ruler is to *create* history .... There is no such thing as chance in history!' (91,93). Man is seen here then not as a passive victim of fate, but as a creator of events. The conflict of the play centres on the need for a decision for or against war. After listening to this counsel the Emperor decides on war.

But Söderberg is not here subscribing positively to a view of man as a creator of his own fate, and of his own history. The decision for war is shown as a victory for irrational forces, whose arguments are based on notions of expansionist nationalism and racial superiority reminiscent of the mood which took Germany into the First World War, and prefiguring some of the arguments of the Nazis after 1933.

Against these forces stands the lone figure of Rikard Anker, the chancellor, supported only by his wife and maintaining his humanitarian beliefs against his fellow politicians and the popular mood in the country as a whole. The play ends with his death after injury at the hands of a mob. While the subject-matter is on one level quite different from most of Söderberg's works, and represents a shift towards the political arena, the play in fact portrays an individual at the mercy of events he is powerless to control. Anker embodies an idealism which fails to survive against the harsh realities of life. Söderberg's pessimism remains.

Söderberg has never enjoyed a high reputation as a dramatist. He has, however, always been regarded as a master of the shorter form of narrative: the anecdote and the short story. Most of these shorter items were first published separately in newspapers or journals, and are by no means all of equal literary merit. They range from philosophical speculations on life's meaning to humorous and sometimes fairly trivial anecdotes. The short literary form spans the longest period in his production: he first began writing short stories as a schoolboy, and his last book of a purely literary nature was the collection of stories *Resan till Rom* (Journey to Rome, 1929). There is, however, no clear line of development from the earlier to the later stories, and it is the novels which remain both the best expression of his development as a writer and the most serious treatment of his themes.

The themes apparent in his novels and plays recur repeatedly in the five collections of short stories. Söderberg displays the same deep pessimism about life, and presents individual tragedies with a superb economy of form. But he also gives freer rein to his less serious side, revealing a humour which is occasionally present in the novels, usually in the form of irony, but which is there restrained by the serious nature of his subject.

Historietter (Stories, 1898) begins and ends on the theme of life's meaninglessness. In 'Tuschritningen' (The Drawing, 1897) a drawing not only provides a symbol for the aesthetic self-sufficiency of a work of art, but also alludes to the vanity of man's search for meaning in a wider context. Both the introduction and conclusion of the story mention the narrator's long-since-abandoned search for a meaning to life. Söderberg returns to a similar theme in the final story, thus providing a framework structure for the collection as a whole which is also a frequent device in the individual stories.[8] 'En herrelös hund' (Dog without a Master, 1894) is an allegory in which a dog without a master symbolizes man's situation in a world where God is dead. The existential *Angst* of this story also forms a subsidiary part of many of the others, and is one of the first expressions in Swedish literature of the *Angst* which was later to pervade the works of Pär Lagerkvist. Indeed Söderberg's *Historietter* have been compared to Lagerkvist's *Onda sagor* (Evil Tales).[9]

In 'Drömmen om evigheten' (Dream of Eternity, 1897) life is referred to as 'a dark and confused dream' (9) and its meaning described as a gradual approach to truth through a succession of dreams. The narrator then relates a dream in which he climbs an apparently endless staircase into the realm of the dead, a vision of death which contradicts the belief in the immortality of the soul which was mentioned ironically at the beginning of the story. Here too life is presented as ultimately meaningless.

Although death does not have such a morbid fascination for Söderberg as it did for many of the Decadents, it nevertheless occurs as a fairly frequent motif. In another dream, under the title 'Mardröm' (Nightmare, 1892), the narrator witnesses his own death and finds

Chapter IV

himself surrounded by a laughing crowd. The story seems to encapsulate both a fear of death and a sense of individual isolation in the midst of antagonism. A fear of death also introduces 'Skuggan' (The Shadow, 1898): the narrator's prefatory remarks describe his unwillingness to die and his attachment to life despite its vicissitudes. Again a dream follows, this time presenting the theme of love in a very negative perspective. The symbol of a red rose alludes to the consummation of the relationship between the narrator and the girl he loves; and the force that prevents their continuing union is embodied in his shadow, described as an image that seems to represent both the financial poverty that causes their separation and the emotional poverty resulting from it. The dream compresses the time scale to present the melancholy resignation of a whole wasted lifetime. The symbolic flower occurs again in *Martin Bircks ungdom* and *Dr Glas*.

Frustrated love is also the subject of 'Syndens lön' (The Wages of Sin, 1897), a story of unrequited desire, and in a different guise in 'Pälsen' (The Fur Coat), from the same year, an ironical but sympathetic portrayal of a husband's discovery of his wife's infidelity. A doctor who has been living in a state of poor health, financial difficulties and marital unhappiness acquires new self-confidence from a fur coat borrowed from a friend, and comes home to his wife full of hope that his life will change. His realization from his wife's affectionate embrace that the friend is her lover is a moment of tragic irony that makes this scene one of the most poignant of anything Söderberg wrote.

But not all the tales in the collection are so serious. 'Nattvardens sakrament' (Holy Communion) and 'Kyrkofadern Papinianus' (Father Papinianus), both written in 1897, satirize the clergy. There is a trace of blasphemy in the humorous exchange between God and the Devil in 'Duggregnet' (Drizzle, 1897), where the motif of autumnal weather which contributes so much to the melancholy mood in Söderberg's works forms the basis of God's punishment of mankind. The misery caused by the perpetual grey clouds and drizzling rain results in a suicide epidemic that destroys the human race.

Social criticism is also presented in a humorous vein. In 'Vox populi' the public's moralizing condemnation of art is likened to the unthinking barking of dogs who join in the chorus with no understanding of the object of their displeasure. 'Kronärtskockan' (The Artichoke), is a lighthearted attack on individual hypocrisy. 'En kopp te' (A Cup of Tea) is a comic satire on social convention. All three stories are from 1897. The scene of indignation caused by the narrator's late evening visit to a café for a cup of tea has more serious undertones, however. It points to the discrimination against the individual who diverges, however slightly, from the norm.

The isolated individual is the subject of the three stories 'Historieläraren' (The History Teacher, 1894), 'Registratorn' (The Clerk, 1897) and 'Gycklaren' (The Clown, 1898), all of which depict people who try to compensate for some weakness or abnormality by becoming clowns. Söderberg's sympathy for the misfit or the weak is also apparent in 'Sotarfrun' (The Chimney-Sweep's Wife, 1895), a story of a very different type totally devoid of the humour which prevails in most of the others. It is a little tragedy in which evil triumphs over innocence. There is no redeeming hope: the weak are overcome by the strong. The chimney-sweep's wife's lack of remorse for the deaths she causes enables her to continue her life in self-righteous unconcern.

The narrator distances himself from this tale by presenting it as one he heard as a child. The same stylistic device occurs in many of the stories; usually it forms part of Söderberg's ironical attitude to his subject. Almost all the stories are presented in some kind of framework which preserves a narrative distance. A similar irony is achieved by contrast, as for example in the combination of such incongruous motifs as life's meaning and the purchase of a cigar ('Tuschritningen'), or in the contrasts on which a whole story is constructed ('Pälsen'). Understatement, and particularly the use of detailed descriptions of relatively trivial events with only allusions to important or tragic moments, is also part of his irony. The narrative attitude occasionally implies some criticism of a character; more usually, however, sympathy. It is a technique which lessens the impact of life's tragedies and allows the world to be viewed with a wry humour that makes it bearable.

The themes and stylistic features present in *Historietter* recur in Söderberg's other collections, with little obvious development either in his treatment of these themes or in the literary quality of his writing. All the volumes contain stories that are clearly weaker than his best. Some remain mere anecdotes, often based on actual events from his own experience which show too little adaptation into successful literary form.

Främlingarna (Strangers, 1903) contains three early stories from

Chapter IV

1892-1893, of which the most accomplished is 'Fröken Hall' (Miss Hall, 1893), a story which well reveals the understatement of dramatic tensions and dilemmas which was to form such a prominent feature of his style. Only by a gradual process of allusion is the reader made aware of what actually took place many years before. 'Fröken Hall' is a story of a life tragically wasted because of social prejudice and morality.

Also from a relatively early period is 'Med strömmen' (With the Current), written in 1895 during the composition of *Förvillelser*. It offers an interesting parallel to his first novel. Its seriousness is a clear indication that Söderberg did not share the superficiality he depicted in Tomas Weber. The title of the short story refers to the inability of Mortimer, the central character, to fight against his fate. Again, many of the usual themes are present: Mortimer's marriage conflicts with his intellectual needs, yet it does not fulfil his need for love. He eventually falls into a fever which is an external manifestation of his lack of will to live. After his recovery he decides to exert his free will and no longer let himself be a victim of chance. His failure is expressed first symbolically in his inability to row a boat against the current, and then in his defiant attempt to commit suicide by jumping from a train. In the final ironical twist he is robbed even of that act of free will — at the last instant he changes his mind, but loses consciousness and falls to his death.

In 'Det blå ankaret' (The Blue Anchor, 1902) the motif of social class, which runs as an undercurrent through most of Söderberg's works, is linked to the theme of marital infidelity. 'Kyrkoherdens kor' (The Vicar's Cows, 1901) is a jocular anecdote at the expense of the clergy, and shows his ability to mock without malice, and to turn away from the tragic and problematic side of life to its purely humorous aspects. The title story, 'Främlingarna', written for the collection, has little to commend it and is one of his weakest.

Söderberg's humour, which is the attitude that most distances him from the *fin-de-siècle* mood, is also apparent in the four stories written between 1900 and 1903 to which he gave the collective title 'Generalkonsulns middagar' (The Consul-General's Dinners).[10] They are light-hearted social satires poking fun at social snobbery, at individual types in whom he discerned hypocrisy, or commenting on topical issues of the day, such as the church's attitude to suicide, or the problems of Sweden's military defence.

In *Det mörknar över vägen* (The Road Grows Dark, 1907) there are several depictions of childhood experience, from the perceptive portrayal of the limited imagination of a four-year-old in 'Den brinnande staden' (The Burning City, 1905) to the adolescent experience of the cathartic effect of poetry after disgrace at school, 'Oskicket' (Misbehaviour, 1906). These stories show his continuing interest in the world of childhood which played such a large part in *Martin Bircks ungdom*.

This collection reveals considerable contrasts between the individual stories. Following directly after 'Den brinnande staden' comes 'Drömmen om ålderdomen' (Dream of Old Age, 1904), a dream in which the narrator suddenly finds that time has rushed by and that those he knew are all dead. The feeling of *Angst* is presented in a realistic yet nightmarish atmosphere. 'Blom' (1903), in which a released convict meets a previous lover who robs him while he sleeps, shows a cynical view of human behaviour. At the other extreme is 'Kyssen' (The Kiss, 1903), a delicate psychological portrait of the thoughts of a boy and a girl leading up to their first kiss. As omniscient narrator, Söderberg for once bridges the gap that separates the sexes.

Social satire is still present, in for example the satirical depiction of both poets and businessmen in 'Skalder ock folk' (Poets and People, 1906) or in the portrayal of the dinner party in 'Sibyllans grotta' (The Sibyl's Cave, 1907). But the central point of the latter story is the prophecy of an old lady that a young couple's love will not last equally; that the feelings of one will fade when the other's are strongest. In a typical example of Söderberg's irony, the advice is given less prominence than the kiss of the young lovers at the end of the story, and their certainty of the eternal nature of their love. The scene offers an interesting parallel to the final kiss in *Martin Bircks ungdom*.

The title story 'Det mörknar over vägen' is a vehicle for many *fin-de-siècle* themes: a grey autumnal mood, tiredness, melancholy, isolation. Not only does it represent no advance in Söderberg's outlook, it seems almost emphatically retrogressive. A typically humorous and ironical motif is the juxtaposition of the search for truth and wisdom with the life of a flaneur and erotic experience with a prostitute.

Den talangfulla draken (The Talented Dragon, 1913) contains some stories that are little more than autobiographical sketches. They nevertheless show Söderberg's undoubted ability as an anecdotal humorist, and also mark a development away from the melancholy

Chapter IV

introspection of much of his work. As early as 1904, however, he seems to take delight in humour at his own expense. The story 'Halv rakning' (Half a Shave) from that year is obviously an ironical portrait of the weaker side of himself. A shy, nervous and indecisive man who finds himself in a barber's shop being shaved by a woman allows his discomfort to build up into imaginary fears so strong that he rushes from the shop half shaved. This is a much more direct humour than the dry irony with which he was presenting his own beliefs in some of the very early stories.

The title story, written for the collection in 1913, is a pastiche of the fairy-tale genre. The tale of a ballad-singer who makes love to a princess by flying to her room on a dragon in the guise of a war-god, it is a fable about social ambition, and also portrays the inability of the artist to cope with the harsh political realities of life. The singer's laughter and deliberate betrayal of his identity bring him simultaneous honour and execution in a scene parodying political compromise and expediency.

Despite what appears to be a different tone in *Den talangfulla draken*, Söderberg's last collection of stories, *Resan till Rom* (Journey to Rome, 1929), shows his continuing concern with previous themes. 'Aprilviolerna' (April Violets, 1922) is a reworking of the marital infidelity motif. Jerneld's compensatory affair with a waitress when he is unable to have the woman he wants repeats a minor motif in *Den allvarsamma leken*. Where Arvid Stjärnblom provided financial support for the illegitimate child resulting from what remained a casual encounter, here the affair leads to a marriage which eventually founders. Jerneld loses his wife to the very man whose own wife he had earlier desired. The circularity of the plot, the repetition of the same events with changing characters, re-introduces the idea of love as a game.

Söderberg's repeated return to the same basic patterns in so much of his writing points to the autobiographical provenance of his works to which almost all critics refer. His books obviously reflect his own experiences and beliefs even where — perhaps especially where — his ironical distance is most clearly expressed. The attitude to love, in particular, which his books display, has its basis in his own life. The experiences which had the most lasting influence on his writing seem to have been his unhappy first marriage and a simultaneous extra-marital relationship, both of which came to an abrupt end in 1906. The final sentence in 'Aprilviolerna' refers humorously, in a more than usually explicit allusion, to his own flight to Copenhagen to escape from his marriage. Söderberg himself recognized the value of literary expression as an objectivization of the writer's own problems: Arvid Stjärnblom, referring to Goethe and Strindberg, rejects the possibility that real poets could succumb to despair: 'They have other resources. They have the ability to express their suffering in a cycle of poems, a novel or a play' (193). Ultimately, however, a work of art must be judged in its own right, not as a biographical confession, and it is beyond the scope of the present chapter to investigate parallels between Söderberg's life and his works.

In all four of these collections in which an individual tale, written specifically for the volume, also provides a name for the whole, the title story proves somewhat disappointing. 'Resan till Rom' (1929) is no exception. Like *Doktor Glas*, it tells of an unfulfilled youthful love which came to nothing because of the girl's death. But here the reported death turns out to be untrue, and the narrator, who had taken up the priesthood after hearing of her 'death', meets his former love years later when she is unhappily married (a motif common to several of Söderberg's works). Her suicide, caused apparently by the arrest of her present lover for forgery, prevents any possibility of a relationship between them and decides the priest to withdraw entirely from the world. The sequence of events appears rather contrived, not least in the number of chance meetings on which the plot depends and which give a central place to the role of chance itself. The work is also laden with criticism of religion and the church, expressed through the priest but scarcely integrated into the story as a whole. Söderberg allows extraneous concerns to destroy the economy of style which contributes so much to the success of the best of his short stories.

Söderberg had long realized that he could not satisfactorily formulate all his concerns in purely fictional works. *Hjärtats oro*, published in 1909, gave expression in a more direct form to his thoughts on topical political and social issues, on his own philosophy of life, and on religious questions. His three later works — *Jahves eld* (Yahweh's Fire, 1918), *Jesus Barabbas*, 1928, and *Den förvandlade Messias* (The Transformed Messiah, 1932) — were all devoted to a critical historical investigation of Christianity. He also wrote some poetry, without any great success, and was active as a translator and critic.

Chapter IV

It is for his novels and short stories that Söderberg is most remembered. He is a realist whose works are firmly based in a Swedish society in transition, combining with his realism the philosophical questioning of an increasingly secular age and the melancholy romanticism so typical of the European *fin-de-siècle*. His obvious sympathy with the disillusion of the period is tempered by his ironical detachment, presenting a dual perspective which persists throughout his work. His irony developed over the years to a more overt criticism of the passive and life-weary attitude, and his interest shifted to include characters more adapted to society than his earlier melancholy outsiders. The clearest expression of his development is his eventual move away from imaginative literature. In the fictional works he did continue to produce — the later short stories — he reveals an increasing tendency to satire and to humour for its own sake, to a view of life often more whimsical than tragic. Nevertheless, a sense of the tragic is still present, and he continues to be absorbed by earlier themes. His most profound and lasting theme is mankind's unending search for love and for a philosophy of life which can impart meaning to an otherwise pointless existence. His view of the human condition remains deeply pessimistic. The *fin-de-siècle* mood found in Söderberg one of its leading exponents and one of its most perceptive critics.

Chapter V

Tiotalister ('Writers of the 1910s') and Hjalmar Bergman (1883-1931)

Karin Petherick

Tiotalisterna ('Writers of the 1910s')

Åttital and *nittital* — very roughly speaking, socially committed realism versus romantic imagination — were a part of the social and cultural climate in which Hjalmar Bergman and his literary contemporaries grew up. When they in their turn began writing, they came to be called *tiotalister*, a term originating in C. D. Marcus' survey *Den nya litteraturen* (1911), with the straightforward meaning: writers who published their first works after the turn of the century and were established authors by the beginning of its second decade. The designation *tiotalismen* gradually became synonymous with the broadly realistic narratives of the half dozen or so writers from middle-class backgrounds who produced works of quality early in the twentieth century, and the designation *tiotalister* has become interchangeable with the term *borgerliga realister* ('Middle-class realists'). On the other hand their contemporaries Martin Koch and Gustav Hedenvind-Ericsson, autodidacts concerned with proletarian reality, can in the perspective of hindsight more fruitfully be considered as the first generation of the remarkable literary phenomenon *proletärförfattarna* ('The Proletarian writers'), while the second generation is represented by the massed talents of Artur Lundkvist, Harry Martinson, Eyvind Johnson and Ivar Lo-Johansson.

Chapter V

The middle-class realists who epitomize the *tiotalister* are Ludvig Nordström, Gustaf Hellström, Elin Wägner, Sigfrid Siwertz, Sven Lidman and — in a category of his own — Hjalmar Bergman. Nordström, Hellström and Wägner had worked as journalists and their lively interest in describing the processes of political and economic change in contemporary Sweden is well served by the skills their trade had taught them (see histories of literature for more on individual *tiotalister,* and for the feminist Elin Wägner in particular,[1] see Select bibliography p.423 below). Bergman's determinism as opposed to the belief in positive social change held by his contemporaries sets him apart from them, and his outstanding creative imagination makes him one of Sweden's great twentieth century writers.

Hjalmar Bergman (1883-1931)

Introductory Remarks

Bergman was born in Örebro in 1883 as the only son (with two older sisters) of Claes Bergman, the dynamic and temperamental manager of Örebro Sparbank, and his wife Frederique, daughter of a wealthy Örebro business-man. Thus by birth and upbringing Hjalmar was firmly ensconced in a prosperous middle-class environment, but his relationship with his father was fraught with fear and his constitution so vulnerable that the sense of insecurity originating in his childhood only deepened with the passage of time. He had material security but emotionally he was gravely handicapped. The child Hjalmar's predicament is highlighted in a letter Bergman wrote to his wife, describing how he as a child in imagination ruled over seven worlds:

And *what* was I in reality? A small, awkward, abnormally fat and clumsy child. Adults laughed at me, kids persecuted me. Have you any idea how many humiliations I swallowed during my first decade? My heart had no shield. A glance and a laugh pierced me to the quick. That's when I had to learn my art: that of parrying. Parry, parry, parry. Never to meet anyone, child or adult, without thinking of defence.[2]

Linder writes that 'his father could not abide him for many years. He despised his little fatty for his slowness and timidity, he could not understand how he could have had such a son'.[3] It is not hard to imagine what this must have felt like to the hyper-sensitive Hjalmar, and by the time his father discovered that his son, then in his teens, was highly gifted, the damage had been done. One of the writer Bergman's most striking characteristics is his propensity to camouflage deeply personal and painful themes. In a letter to Ellen Key, contemporary of Strindberg and authoress to whom Bergman sent a number of his books, he wrote 'Maybe one day I shall step out of my house and talk to my fellow humans ... What I have communicated so far has been symbols. ... I believe it must be a well-nigh insurmountable shyness vis-a-vis myself which has constantly forced me to disguise my thoughts.'[4] Here we undoubtedly have an explanation for Bergman's virtuoso use of parody and pastiche, both of which function as disguises.[5]

Bergman's existential anguish was to continue and deepen throughout his life. In 1908 he married Stina Lindberg, daughter of actor-manager August Lindberg, and became intensely dependent upon her. The marriage survived for many years and it was not until 1926 that Hjalmar and Stina were separated for more than a few hours or days. By now he was a very sick man, drinking heavily and emotionally plagued by the homosexuality he for a long time had repressed. It is all the more remarkable that he went on working right up to the end. His creative drive was immense and he published thirty-nine volumes during his life-time, comprising novels, plays and short stories, before he died in Berlin at the age of forty-seven.

It is a difficult task to present briefly the work of so complex a writer. I shall first provide a short chronological survey of his works, then comment on certain aspects of his art, and finally examine in some detail three major novels which represent his creative powers at their height.

Works[6]

Bergman's first published work was the play *Maria, Jesu moder* (Mary, Mother of Jesus, 1905). Mary is the precursor of many dominant and dynamic women in Bergman's production, whose strong wills come into conflict with the realities of their respective situations, while Jesus, with his unworldly gentleness and love represents an ideal close to Bergman's heart: 'For me the dearest character in fiction and history was, is, and remains Jesus of Nazareth', he wrote to Ellen Key.[7] His subsequent plays will be dealt with at the end of this account which will continue with a listing of his novels and short-story collections. Next followed the novel *Solivro* (1906), a symbolic fantasy about a young prince who experiences love, aggression, jealousy and disillusionment

Chapter V

— all recurrent themes in Bergman's work. The stylized, dream-like character of the work has affinities both with the dramas of Maeterlinck and the exoticism of Swedish *nittitalism*. His next novel, *Blå blommor* (Blue Flowers, 1907), provides a striking mixture of realistic dialogue and symbolic treatment of forbidden passion; the middle-aged Bengt is in love with his foster-daughter Ingrid, and his feelings are projected as a dream of reaching out for the blue flowers of longing, while the white flowers of death conclude the book. This early novel contains themes which were to occupy Bergman throughout his life: forbidden love, guilt, the visiting of the sins of the fathers upon their children, the destruction of illusions and dreams of love, and the peace of death.

The young author had to rely on his father's financial help to get these first works published. During the same period he wrote three more plays, and then in 1909 he published the ambitious historical novel *Savonarola*. This is a remarkable study of the Florentine monk and martyr, presented through the eyes of his contemporary Guidantonio Vespucci, and Bergman handles the historical material with great skill. *Amourer* (Amours, 1910), a collection of short stories, also had Italy as a background, a country which Bergman loved dearly. He started visiting it in his late teens and subsequently lived there with his wife Stina from 1909 to 1911. In 1910 he published *Hans nåds testamente* (His Lordship's Last Will and Testament), which makes a good starting point for readers embarking on a study of his works. It is a comedy under whose humorous-fantastic surface can be detected themes which constantly preoccupied Bergman — young love disillusioned, the irrationality of human behaviour and the inevitability of death. The characters are engaging caricatures, with the exception of the two youngsters around whom the plot revolves. Their presentation is typical of the melancholy tenderness Bergman felt for young lovers, who by his reckoning will at best become saddened, at worst cynical, with the passing of time. The novel has a geographical location in the Bergslagen area of central Sweden, which was to become the setting for his most famous works.

Vi Bookar, Krokar och Rothar (We Books, Kroks and Roths, 1912) shows us a glimpse of the young heroine of *Hans nåds testamente* grown into an unfaithful and restless married woman, and his lordship's butler Vickberg plays a small but poignant part in the novel. The re-emergence of characters in work upon work is, of course, familiar from Balzac's *Comédie humaine*, and has the advantage of making the reader feel at home in the wider context of the author's production as a whole. *Vi Bookar* is a chronicle of a fictive town which in later novels is given the name of Wadköping — a town clearly based on Örebro. It is peopled by eccentrics and respectable worthies, by a prosperous middle-class and workers struggling to survive in slum conditions. Bergman exposes the greed of the slum landlord while yet showing him as a pitiable creature, he shows us heartbreak and sudden economic deliverance. He had a predilection for what he himself called 'Oriental' outcomes, by which he meant the workings of Fate, which so effortlessly and unexpectedly upset painstaking human calculations. The words *slump* (chance) and *nyck* (caprice) have a noticeable frequency in his works, and in *Vi Bookar* it is the unexpected *whim* of the rich Blenda which in fact saves the working-class community of the town from financial ruin.

1913 saw the publication of two books — *Loewenhistorier* (Loewen Stories), three stories about the artist-cum-antihero Leonard Loewen, and *Fru Gunhild på Hviskingeholm* (Mistress Gunhild of Hviskingeholm), a study of repressed love and mental illness. It will be seen that Bergman was extremely productive in spite of the fact that he was passing through a period of personal crisis and illness. In 1914-16 three parts of a work collectively entitled *Komedier i Bergslagen* were published: they comprised *Två släkter* (Two Families), a chronicle of the rivalry between two Bergslagen families over two centuries, *Dansen på Frötjärn* (The Dance at Frötjärn), a tale of tragic love and death in a setting reminiscent of Selma Lagerlöf's *Gösta Berlings saga*, and finally *Knutsmässo marknad* (Knutsmässo Market), a riotously funny account of the annual January fair which marked the end of the Christmas season in the Bergslagen town with which readers are now familiar. For those who have ears to hear, this mid-nineteenth century tale has tragic undertones. *Mor i Sutre* (Mother at Sutre, 1917) tells the fateful story of the love a forceful innkeeper's widow feels for her favourite and youngest child, Daniel — and of his death at the hands of destitute, itinerant labourers. Flashbacks indicate that her dreams of love were disappointed in her youth, and subconsciously Daniel became for her the precious symbol of these dreams, which has led her to deal unfairly with her other children. Daniel's death can be seen as Nemesis. *En döds memoarer* (A Deceased's Memoirs, 1918) followed. Here Bergman explores the notion that the sins of fathers are visited upon their children even unto the third or fourth generation of those who hate

Chapter V

God. His narrator Jan Arnberg finally succeeds in freeing himself from the curse of his heredity by metaphysical means. He 'dies' by renouncing his own will and placing it instead in the hands of the Almighty.[8]

Now followed three major novels in as many years — *Markurells i Wadköping* (God's Orchid, 1919), *Herr von Hancken* (1920), and *Farmor och Vår Herre* (Thy Rod and Thy Staff, 1921). Bergman himself spoke of them as 'farewells' and they occupy so central a role in his authorship that they will be dealt with separately at the end of the chapter. *Eros begraving* (Eros's Burial, 1922) is a thematic short-story collection, *Jag, Ljung och Medardus* (I, Ljung and Medardus, 1923) a semi-autobiographical novel of childhood and youth remarkable for its interesting Freudian study of the child-parent relationship.

Bergman set out for Hollywood in 1923. He had become fascinated by the new art of the cinema and had high hopes of a fresh start in life. His stint as a scenario writer for Sam Goldwyn proved a bitter disappointment and he returned to Europe after only three (unhappy) months. He now wrote *Chefen fru Ingeborg* (The Head of the Firm, 1924), an account of a middle-aged woman's vain efforts to repress her love for her son-in-law. Ingeborg finally chooses death rather than dissimulation. The charming trifle *Flickan i frack* (The Girl in White Tie and Tails, 1925) followed, and then *Jonas och Helen* (1926) and *Kerrmans i Paradiset* (1927). In the latter two books Bergman follows the fortunes of a young couple who fall in love, their engagement, marriage and middle-age. In many ways the most moving part of *Jonas och Helen* does not concern these two but Jonas' unhappy, vain-glorious father, who in common with many Bergman characters has to pass through the needle's eye of self-knowledge and learn to renounce personal ambition and dreams of happiness. It might equally be said of *Kerrmans* that the most moving passages refer to the loneliness of the dissolute and ill-starred Mikael Arnfelt, an old acquaintance from *En döds memoarer*. Amongst the rewards of reading Bergman's works, that of getting to know unforgettable characters is not the least. It comes as no surprise to learn that Bergman was an admirer of Dostoevsky — he shares the latter's concern for spiritual regeneration and his sympathy for bizarre and colourful personalities.

Lotten Brenners ferier (Lotten Brenner's Vacation, 1928) is worth taking seriously in spite of its burlesque incidents and jocular narrative tone, for it deals with the problem of being lonely, unlovely and unloved. Bergman's state of health was by now very precarious; anxiety and stress had led him to consume growing quantities of alcohol and to rely on drugs. He felt that the end could not be far off. *Kärlek genom ett fönster* (Love through a Window, 1929), a short-story collection, was followed in 1930 by what can accurately be described as Bergman's testament, the novel *Clownen Jac* (Jac the Clown), commissioned by Swedish Radio as a serial. Although failing rapidly, he managed to finish this work and participate in its broadcasting before dying alone in Berlin on 1 January 1931. The novel shows us an unhappy and vulnerable artist, who needs the stimulus of fear in order to be creative. The climax of the novel, which is set in Hollywood, comes when the Clown dares to challenge his public and tell them that they are living vicariously off his suffering. There are splendidly satirical portraits of show-business tycoons and financial backers. The Clown appeared earlier in *Farmor och Vår Herre*, where his relationship to his grandmother forms the central core of the book. The problem of heredity and transmitted suffering much occupied Bergman, and the Clown's illegitimate daughter, unbalanced and unhappy, proved to be her father's Cross or Nemesis.

Bergman regarded himself as equally dramatist and novelist. Since the bulk of his plays (which cannot all be mentioned here) are seldom performed, his dramatic works are of subordinate interest to the average reader. *Maria, Jesu moder* (1905) has already been mentioned. It was followed by some early Ibsen-inspired dramas. Then in 1915 came the historical play *Parisina*, and in 1917 three plays under the title *Marionettspel* (Marionette Plays). These are of considerable symptomatic interest since their stylized presentation of puppet-like human beings clearly demonstrates Bergman's deterministic view of life. Of these three, *Herr Sleeman kommer* (Mr Sleeman is coming) is occasionally revived. Three more plays, *Spelhuset* (The Gaming House), *Vävaren i Bagdad* (The Weaver of Bagdad) and *Porten* (The Gateway) were published in 1923. *Porten* is arresting for its treatment of reasoned self-restraint (*besinning*) and death. Bergman's most popular play, a perennial box-office success, is *Swedenhielms* (1925). This story of an aspiring Nobel prize winner and inventor and his carefree family lacks the pathos which underlies Bergman's great 'comic' works, but the intrigue is skilfully constructed. *Patrasket* (Riff-raff, 1928), another stage success, was written for the celebrated actor Gösta Ekman, and is a both funny and moving account of a Jewish family and its rich, imaginative life. The play *Sagan* (The Fairy Tale) was written in 1923 but consigned by Bergman to his writing-table drawer. It was adapted by his wife Stina after his death and has been frequently performed. It is a sad, romantic piece, half-legend, half-reality, and mirrors de Musset's theme 'on ne badine pas avec l'amour'. It is worth noting that Bergman's dramatizations of his novels *Hans nåds testamente*, *Markurells i Wadköping* and *Farmor och Vår Herre* were extremely successful. They lent themselves readily to adaptation for the stage since they have a basic unity of time and place and contain many magnificent 'scenes'.

Some Aspects of Bergman's Art

Caricature

In a lecture entitled 'Karikatyr och kliché', Hjalmar Bergman addressed an audience in Uppsala in 1929 on the subject of his preference for what he called 'caricature' as opposed to 'cliché' (the latter term not pejoratively intended).[9] By caricature he meant a simplification, a powerful underlining of essential characteristics at the expense of detailed realism. He pointed out the central role which memory plays for human beings and emphasized that the good artist has a well-stored memory from which he is free to choose the essentials required for his caricature. The artist remembers far more than his simplified presentation would have us suppose. It is his technique to seize upon and highlight certain chosen aspects of his subject only, and Bergman cites Michelangelo, Dostoevsky and Balzac as artists who represent this form of communication. The opposite technique, that of 'cliché' or detailed completeness of presentation, has outstanding exponents — for instance Benozzo Gozzoli and Goethe — but it does not lie close to his heart.

Bergman's own work abounds in caricatures — in his sense of the word — in examples of 'an exceeding emphasis on characteristic elements'. The characteristics which he stresses and the reader recalls are idiosyncrasies of behaviour, striking aspects of appearance and personality. Who can forget that in *Markurells* Colonel Edeblad always gallops astride a drawing-room stool at family councils of war or that his niece, the beautiful Elsa de Lorche, has graceful legs? Or, to take *Knutsmässo marknad*, that the formidable battle-axe, the Headmaster's wife, always carries a bag of ginger-nuts, that Abraham Lilja is so mean that every other human attribute he might have pales into insignificance by comparison, and that the travelling player Pretorius is for ever repeating that he has had the honour of performing 'before the highest and most exalted circles'? Sometimes the distinctive and unforgettable characteristic is a physical trait, sometimes it is a mode of speech. Bergman is skilled at literary pastiche or the art of approximating to a given linguistic model. He can imitate the affected speech of nineteenth-century gentry, the cant and sentimentality of a dishonest Free Church preacher, biblical rhetoric and American advertising jargon. His ability to conceive and project vivid characters must be related to his double role as novelist and dramatist.

Symbolism

There are famous passages in Bergman's letters which shed light on the role of symbolism in his works. He wrote to Ellen Key that all his mental activity from childhood onwards had been through the medium of symbols. And he makes the following interesting statement: 'Everything human has been and is mine — but I've experienced it as a glance, an inclination of the head, a movement of the hand, a bodily posture, a sigh, a tone of voice; in short, as a corporeal symbol of something spiritual.'[10]

In a letter to Hans Larsson, for a short while his Philosophy tutor at Uppsala, Bergman mentions the crucial importance to him of the concept of 'rustning' (armour). Larsson had referred to Heidenstam's image of a much-admired and feared knight-at-arms, who in reality was a puny individual, as was discovered after his death when his armour was removed. In his reply Bergman explains that the most important task for human beings is to learn to live without 'armour', to know themselves and to be themselves — a demanding moral task involving the pruning and discarding of everything extraneous and dispensable. He writes: 'As I've said, the problem of "defensive armour" has probably been the most constant and central element of my world picture.'[11] We immediately perceive a dilemma: the writer who self-confessedly was unable to speak except by means of symbols, was deeply conscious of the need for openness. In the 'farewell' novels we shall shortly be looking at, the need to lay down the trappings of power and to stand naked before the world, plays a central part.

Chapter V

Themes

There is in Bergman's major novels a core of Quietism, a belief that action and outward achievement are but wind and that the one thing needful is to find stillness of the soul and humility in the face of death and eternity.

Fate and providence

Throughout his novels there are numerous references to Fate, chance and fortuity. In *Hans nåds testamente* the manor house of Rogershus is described as a place 'Where caprice alone smiled ... Where capriciousness was a passion, and passion a caprice' (72). Human beings are impelled by irrational motives and are the playthings of chance. Wisdom resides in accepting this fact. And wisdom is a form of resignation. When Baron Roger Bernhusen de Sars has to abandon his whim of playing Providence and making out his will in favour of his housekeeper's son Jakob (with the proviso that he marry the Baron's daughter Blenda), we are told that he smiled to himself, 'smiled as only an old, weary person does, calmly and without joy, free from hope and free from fear' (228f.).

Fate is a key concept for Bergman. He did not believe that man is a free agent except in the sense of being responsible for his attitude to the determined or arbitrary events and circumstances of his life. In *Knutsmässo marknad* the theme of pre-ordained Fate is treated playfully. The local gentry give a performance of Voltaire's play *Zaïre*, a tragedy in which ill-starred lovers meet a tragic end. The humorous trivialities of the actors and the invited audience are seemingly in total contrast to the sombre theme of the play. But in fact Anders Ekmarck, the leading player, is himself fated to lose his sweetheart who plays Zaïre, and who will deny her love and instead marry a rich old man. In a striking passage we read that he suddenly realized that: 'here, as in *Zaïre*, all the parts and gestures and lines were determined in advance. Indeed, in a sudden flash he thought he saw the whole of life as a comedy already completed and written out, in which sorrow and joy, success and failure, poverty and riches, were pre-determined roles, gestures, lines' (51).

Bergman had a very personal theory about the will, which he regarded not as an integral part of the individual's personality but as being an external force which affects and directs the individual and his actions. The will — and the actions it leads to — is to be seen as an instrument of The Unknown ('Den okände eller kanske Det okända').[12] For our purposes it is enough to note that these ideas provide a speculative base for Bergman's determinism and that their major artistic expression comes in *En döds memoarer*. In it he unfolds the fate of two related families and shows individual members reacting to the external will to which they are all subject. The novel can also be read as a critique of a consumer society in which Bergman exposes advertising slogans (which he cleverly parodies) and sales techniques as devices for exploiting the human need to believe that tangible goods and goals can transform life. In fact we are powerless, no actions of ours can alter our dependent condition, and in the words of Fader Johannes, 'our power, and our sense of security reside in the very fact that we are powerless' (408). When the hero Jan Arnberg reaches this point of insight he is no longer 'of this world', he is 'dead', not biologically but dead to vain illusions — hence the title *En döds memoarer*.

Memory

Bergman regarded the human memory as of vital importance for the individual's spiritual development. This is not so strange, for our whole existence as thinking beings with cognitive powers is dependent upon the functioning of our memories. The virtue which many of his characters strive for or are painfully forced to acquire is thoughtful self-restraint which can only be achieved through self knowledge, in its turn based on the memory of what we have done (or failed to do) in our lives. Memory can uncover repressed motives and disregarded consequences. In *Chefen fru Ingeborg*, as Gunnar Axberger has pointed out, three-quarters of the novel shows us the repression of unwelcome facts by fru Ingeborg, while the final quarter shows us what happens when she allows the true significance of memories and scenes from the past to become apparent to her.[13] In *Farmor och Vår Herre* the divergent memories of identical events held by the old lady on the one hand and other members of her family on the other, constitute the major theme of the book. In *Clownen Jac*, the Clown and Lillemor Längsell, who had a brief affair some twenty years earlier, are forced to open *'gömsel- och glömsellådan'*, i.e. the metaphorical drawer into which we stuff our unwanted memories and rejected experiences. The shame and disgust which Lillemor experiences upon opening it make painful reading, and Jac himself has to learn to take responsibility for their illegitimate daughter.

Chapter V

Self-awareness and Death

Increasingly as the years passed, Bergman came to regard life as a preparation for death. He wrote to Hans Larsson: 'For me life is one long, generally subdued but occasionally vociferous and angry, exchange with death'.[14] He propounded to Larsson his theory that no one dies before deciding to do so (albeit it is sometimes a last-minute decision). And in a letter to Algot Ruhe he speaks of 'my little private theory: every death is self-elected, voluntary. Every death is a *convinced* death'.[15]

Death is a final leave-taking, and we prepare ourselves for it by learning the art of *besinning*, the art of self-awareness and self-mastery. It was with this conviction that Bergman had embarked on three literary leave-takings: 'In *Markurells* from love and family life, in *Herr von Hancken* from ambition and all manner of day dreams, in *Farmor* from the middle class environment from which I come.' He continues this letter to Hans Larsson with the following interesting observation: 'The fact that I have a grin on my face means nothing. That's just a weakness in shy awkward people. And in cowardly ones!'[16] This remark leads us straight to the heart of his narrative method. For the more urgent and painful a theme, the more likely he is to present it in a humorous guise. This is precisely his method in these three novels, which are representative of him at the height of his creative powers.

Markurells i Wadköping

This is a story of overweening pride and a subsequent agonized awakening. The central character and innkeeper, Harald Hilding Markurell, loves his son Johan above everything else on earth. His devotion to the boy amounts to idolatry, and when his business associate Carl-Magnus de Lorche coldly indicates to Johan that his visits to the de Lorche home no longer are desirable, the enraged and doting Markurell determines to ruin de Lorche and expose him as the financial swindler he undoubtedly is. He sets about doing this with characteristic ruthlessness and energy, not one whit deterred by the fact that the down-fall of de Lorche will inevitably involve the ruin of countless innocent Wadköping families whose savings are invested in de Lorche's company. Mrs Markurell tries vainly to persuade her husband to let de Lorche off and not pursue vengeance in this way, and tante Ruttenschöld, de Lorche's aged relative and a moral and social pillar of Wadköping, also intercedes with Markurell on de Lorche's behalf, but to no avail. He is relentless.

The main action of the novel, led up to by a series of flashbacks, takes place on June 6, 1913, the day on which Johan Markurell and his friend Louis de Lorche, son of Carl-Magnus, have their decisive matriculation orals. When Markurell gets a message that the orals are going badly for Johan, he decides in a flash a) to offer the Board of Examiners lunch and b) to donate money for the endowment of a prize 'in memory of Johan Markurell's successful matriculation 6.6.1913'. His reaction is in other words primitive and urgent and his motives cannot be misunderstood. Markurell and two waitresses set off for the school laden with food and drink. After some natural hesitation, the examiners allow themselves to be persuaded to eat the delicacies offered to them. Markurell rejoices inwardly and imagines that he has achieved his aim. But then he hears an examiner refer to one of the candidates as the illegitimate son of Carl-Magnus de Lorche, and slowly it dawns on him that this boy can be no other than his own adored Johan.

Let me at this point observe that what I have given above is the merest outline of one particular strand of the story. This is an immensely rich and complex narrative in which several things are always happening simultaneously.[17] Two parallel developments are under way in the novel; one of them is the rise, the short spell of ruthless pride and the subsequent fall and humiliation of Markurell. The other is the career of Carl-Magnus de Lorche and his beautiful wife Elsa. This handsome couple have had a secret understanding for twenty years that spiritually they are entirely independent of the Wadköping society of which they are leading members. Carl-Magnus has felt a compulsion to break the law and speculate with charity funds for the sense of excitement and danger it gives him. Together the couple exult in their special relationship while yet outwardly seeming to conform. A sorry awakening befalls them. The beautiful Elsa discovers that Carl-Magnus is prepared to betray her and make his get-away to South America alone, while Carl-Magnus is subjected to the humiliation of having his treachery exposed.

When Markurell has learnt the truth about Johan's parentage, he is accompanied home by his friends the baker and the wig-maker. These do their best to comfort and admonish him when he gives way to grief. The wig-maker believes that God, by showing Markurell that in reality he is alone and without an heir, has punished him for his meanness, heartlessness and thirst for power. When Markurell's grief becomes

Chapter V

dangerously uncontrollable his friend Barfoth takes the place of the other two who have fled the scene, and he attempts to explain the ways of God to man by means of a parable, as follows. Just as a certain Dutch botanist had built a whole Botanical garden in order to cultivate a single unattractive but unique plant specimen, so, Barfoth suggests, the Almighty let Wadköping be founded and grow and flourish all in order that Markurell might be born seven hundred years later. We do not live for our own sakes but we fulfil the designs of the Almighty. Or as Barfoth puts it: 'The idea that people are cultivated for their own sakes is simple fraud and illusion. They are cultivated for the cultivator's sake' (234). The moral of Barfoth's tale is clear: it behoves man to accept the state to which God has called him, and not to puff himself up with pride and implacability as Markurell had done. When the latter declares that he will go away and avoid seeing Johan again, Barfoth is able to awaken the genuine love Markurell bears his son by suggesting that the boy may already be dead, not having been able to stand the strain of the day's revelations. The howl of pain and anguish with which Markurell greets this entirely unfounded remark proves beyond all doubt that Barfoth has been successful in his aim. Markurell realizes that his own suffering and his own desires are of no significance. In a passage of sublime and moving simplicity he voices this new insight:

You needn't say anything, Barfoth. I realize you were lying. The boy doesn't know anything, nothing terrible has befallen him. You wanted to tell me the truth and went on to lie. But you told the truth all the same. Of course I don't want to get out of seeing him. And even if I did, what do my wishes matter? ... Am I not trapped? Who can release me? Who can redeem me? No one. What's to be gained by howling? Nothing's to be gained. (238f.)

It is a miracle of Hjalmar Bergman's art that he was able to create one of the funniest books in the Swedish language out of this situation and theme. The satirical presentation of Wadköping society, the many caricatures and burlesque scenes, are the very stuff of comedy. The lonely suffering of Markurell at the close of the novel is high tragedy.

Herr von Hancken

The fictional basis of this novel from 1920 is that its first-person narrator wrote it around 1836 as a memoir of events and experiences which took place at a small Swedish spa in 1806. Bergman has clearly not striven to produce a convincing early nineteenth-century text, but he has zestfully caricatured some of the salient features of vocabulary and syntax of the period in question. These archaisms are reinforced by his humorous use of setting and action strongly recalling the picaresque novels of Fredrik Cederborgh (1784-1835).[18] In Cederborgh's *Uno von Thrazenberg* (1809-1810) and *Ottar Trallings lefnadsmålning* (Ottar Tralling's memoirs, 1810-1818), written with great good humour and containing many slap-stick situations, a young, inexperienced hero travels by stage-coach, puts up at inns, meets a beautiful but false siren, is robbed, falls in temporarily with bad company, meets people of varying social degrees, and so on. All these ingredients are present in *Herr von Hancken*, but in addition Bergman's novel has a serious purpose quite lacking in Cederborgh's entertaining works.

The narrator in *Herr von Hancken* is one B. B. Carlander, who looks back from the comfortable security of his rectory and middle age to the year 1806 when he was engaged by the von Hancken family as tutor to their dim-witted son Adolphen, and accompanied them on their expedition to Iglinge spa in an attempt to improve the failing health of Captain von Hancken, the head of the family. On their journey they spend the night at an inn where they meet a mysterious French doctor and his beautiful travelling companion, Countess d'Aiguille di Rocca Antica, as well as an unmarried lady of ample proportions — mamsell Arrenander — with her three inebriated admirers, and Tomson, a well-meaning youth of comfortable means. During the night von Hancken's purse is stolen and circumstantial evidence points to Tomson as being the guilty party (although the reader rightly suspects that he has been framed). The entire company now proceed to Iglinge spa. Here the von Hanckens are looked down upon by socially prominent guests due to their poverty and von Hancken's eternal misfortunes and dissatisfaction, although Carlander's situation is enlivened by the mutual affection which develops between him and young Nora von Hancken, Adolphen's sister. Two crucial events now occur. Von Hancken is informed by the physician in charge that he has only six weeks to live, and Lesage, the French doctor first encountered at the overnight inn, mysteriously visits von Hancken by night and asks him to take the Countess di Rocca Antica under his protection during Lesage's enforced absence from Iglinge. Von Hancken not only undertakes the task but becomes completely infatuated by the lovely lady, although it presently emerges that she by birth is plain Anna-Lisa Carlsdotter and that her virtue is not

Chapter V

of the stable variety. Faced with imminent death von Hancken loses all sense of reality. In Bergman's words: 'Death's sudden approach had at a stroke swept away all self-restraint.'(183) He sees himself as a romantic knight paying court to his mistress, he squeezes money out of the luckless Tomson and spends it like water on clothes, carriages and other extravagances, he informs his wife that the beautiful countess has at last taught him what it is to love. And he is seized by the entirely unfounded notion, which he succeeds in imparting to the other guests, that the King will be paying a visit to Iglinge. Great preparations for the royal visit are now set afoot by von Hancken, and when it presently becomes clear that the monarch, although passing through the province, has no intention of visiting Iglinge, von Hancken exclaims: 'The King has deceived us!' (179). The words are treasonable in the unstable political climate of 1806, and they are aggravated by the fact that von Hancken has provided the local peasantry with a sectarian preacher, which is an offence against the law forbidding conventicles. From having been an ardent royalist, von Hancken finds himself a Jacobin. Finally, when the beautiful countess has departed with an admirer and von Hancken's followers have all dispersed, he is faced with the reality of his situation. At the eleventh hour he achieves the *besinning* he so sorely has lacked throughout his life. At this point Dr Lesage urges upon him an abdication ceremony whereby von Hancken, illegitimate son of a Count, renounces his coveted title. This is the central symbolic gesture in the book, for throughout his life, which has been beset by all manner of tribulations, von Hancken has clung obstinately to the belief that *if only things had been otherwise*, he would have been a count and a man of consequence. He now solemnly lifts an imaginary coronet from his head and affirms that:

All that I have longed to be and become, everything for which I have cherished a passionate desire and noble ambition but not the ability, I lay down before the Almighty. May he create thereof a new and perfect being, should it so please him. Empty as wind I came into the world, and I wrote my name in water (235f.).

This is the climax of von Hancken's development; what remains is the humorous parallel ordeal and development of the narrator B.B. Carlander. Von Hancken's conviction that if only things had been different, then everything would have been different, is expressed repeatedly in antithetical terms, e.g. 'you, too, might have become a great man, if only you hadn't been such a wretched specimen' (85), 'I assure you, Carlander, that I would have been a knight of purest crystal, if circumstances hadn't turned me into an oaf' (87), 'That man's a genius. But I would have done it better, if only I'd had the ability' (165).

Carlander shares his employer's belief in a grand personal destiny, and believes that he is intended for something great, but that circumstances so far have conspired against him. Like von Hancken he is an illegitimate child, and his youthful imagination is full of fantasies of his hypothetical noble birth and impressive future. In fact his fantasies of greatness are so powerful that he is finally persuaded to break with his sweetheart Nora for the sake of receiving from Dr Lesage a document purporting to enlighten him on his true character and station in life. As it turns out the document is a mockery, for it is the frontispiece of a handwritten theodicy with which Carlander had incurred his uncle the Bishop's displeasure some months earlier. The splendid title of the work is *A New Theodicy or An Attempt at a Universal Explanation by B. B. Carlander Natural Philosopher* (274). Lesage has underlined the words Natural Philosopher in red, thereby highlighting Carlander's propensity to seek whatever prestige and glory he can, just as von Hancken (before his abdication) always stressed his own status as 'natural' count. Carlander now has the sense to abandon his foolish notions of grandeur after a miserable night spent out of doors in the rain — and it proves to be his salvation. For the very collapse of his dreams leads him to the ample bosom and appetizing table of mamsell Arrenander. This determined lady offers to finance his theological studies in return for the prospect of becoming a vicar's wife — a proposition to which Carlander soon agrees. And narrating these events years later, he exclaims:

I no longer have any grandiose ideas and inflated notions about my own person, God have mercy upon me! And haven't had these past thirty years... Thank the Lord that I didn't return from Iglinge as a natural philosopher but as a healthy ecclesiastical seedling, which now rejoices in both root and stem and foliage!(273 f.)

Carlander's theodicy provides the book with a central image of great importance — that of God having the planet Earth as a plaything with which he benevolently amuses himself as a form of relaxation after his arduous task of ruling the vast universe. Carlander compares the

Chapter V

Almighty's pastime with the way in which his lordship the Bishop relaxes with a game of patience after a day's work. When God plays with his creation and the Bishop lays his patience, all is well with the world, from both the divine and the diocesan perspective. But how then, asks Carlander, are we to explain the occurrence of revolutions, pestilence, sin and catastrophe on this globe of ours? They arise, he argues, because God's servant the Devil, normally a hard-working and dependable employee, in a mischievous mood has mixed up the good Lord's playing-cards, whereupon trouble and chaos ensue. When the Almighty discovers what has happened, however, he scolds his servant and puts his cards in order again. The image of God playing patience is derived by Carlander from childhood memories of his uncle the Bishop engaged in the same pursuit, and he sees a parallel between unrest on earth on the one hand and on the other the consternation and flurry arising at the Bishop's card-table when his lordship's wayward eldest son had egged the infant Carlander on to mix up his uncle's playing-cards. In neither case does the mischievous interference have any long-lasting effect on the Divine Will or the Bishop's habits — as indeed we would expect from a theodicy, which by definition sets out to explain the occurrence of calamity and suffering within a divine providential frame-work. What is so clever in Bergman's use of the motif is not primarily the good-natured parody of Luther's Catechism in the actual wording of the theodicy, but the fact that it enables him to cast Dr Lesage as the Devil or mischief-maker in a double sense and that it so perfectly expresses his own deterministic view of life. For lo and behold! The doctor who sows disruption at Iglinge, turns out to be no other than the Bishop's black sheep of a son, the same who as a lad impudently contrived to play a trick upon his father's game of patience, while it is his machinations and intrigues with regard to von Hancken which lead to the severing of marital bonds, heresy, treason, rebellion and sudden death at Iglinge spa. Now these latter events are indeed of a kind which a theodicy is normally called upon to explain and reconcile, but the comic power of the novel resides in the fact that their occurrence at Iglinge is so undeniably parochial and trivial. Iglinge is a microcosm in the likeness of a duck-pond. The fact of the novel being humorously absurd makes it all too easy for the reader to miss its deeper implications. These are that there is a Providence or a metaphysical World Order, which Bergman here chooses to personify in the figure of God, and that human beings are objects of his Divine Will, not sovereign and independent. Whether life proceeds smoothly or is suddenly disrupted by cataclysms, uprisings and revolutions, individuals are exactly as God created them, neither more nor less. This does not mean, however, that we should abandon ourselves to the deepest fatalism, for as Carlander points out:

In a game of patience the suits and values of the cards are paramount, and if they become jumbled, then everything breaks down. It is therefore incumbent upon us to consider our own suit and number carefully and humbly to adapt ourselves to it, so that a Two does not usurp the position of a Ten or a Jack that of a King. Each one of us has his own predetermined value to retain and demonstrate, and false pretensions are the major cause of mankind's misfortunes. (28)

The notion of a fixed and given personal destiny is of course in one sense the determinism of the naturalists, but what distinguishes Bergman's treatment of the situation are the moral consequences he draws. In figurative terms we must accept our suit and number. Von Hancken's misfortunes and endless complaints have their basis in his unwillingness to accept that he *is* a small man. The fundamental ethical imperative of this book is: Know Thyself.

B. B. Carlander's spiritual development describes a parallel curve to that of von Hancken's in much the same way as the fate of Elsa and Carl-Magnus de Lorche echoes that of Markurell. But Carlander not only reinforces the theme of the necessity of abandoning vainglorious ambitions, he also provides the book with a comic diction. He is an amiable, rather vain person, one of whose literary progenitors undoubtedly is the very much vainer and naiver hero of August Bondesson's immortal work *Skollärare John Chronschough's memoarer* (Schoolteacher John Chronschough's Memoirs, 1897-1904). Chronschough's artlessly pompous literary style has passed into Swedish folklore as the prototype of naive self-satisfaction and semi-educated verbosity. The period flavour and historical setting of *Herr von Hancken* is achieved by borrowing some stock situations and characters from the early nineteenth-century picaresque novels of Cederborgh, by clever reference to authentic historical events, and by language sprinkled with humorous archaisms laced with comic-elevated Chronschoughian diction.

Herr von Hancken is a book which needs to be read philosophically. It requires of the reader the ability to abstract a moral from

Chapter V

an absurd action. We can only guess at the personal suffering which Bergman masked by choosing as his narrator a naively loquacious parson and as his hero a querulous nonentity.

Farmor och Vår Herre

Farmor och Vår Herre[19] is the story of Agnes, a simple country girl who marries into the well-established Borck family in Wadköping. She gives ample proof of her resourcefulness and strength of will already at the age of sixteen, when she reports her father to the local policeman for having appropriated her savings. She wins her point (although at the cost of having to leave home), and throughout her long life she thinks back to the episode with pleasure, for it was the first big victory gained by virtue of her sharp wits. She finds employment with Grundholm, builder-turned-architect, and thanks to her cool head she manages to keep Grundholm at bay when he is feeling amorous, to become engaged to Axelsson, youngest and most amenable of his workmen, and to break off the engagement without compunction when young Jonathan Borck proposes to her, for, as the text repeatedly illustrates for us, she has 'a clear head and is quick in the uptake'. Her husband Jonathan is delicate and frail, and Agnes rapidly takes over the family business and the running of their home. Over the years she helps to build up the fortune of her immediate family — at the expense of the rest of the Borck clan, who discover to their cost that Agnes can be entirely ruthless when she deems it necessary.

After the death of her favourite son Gabriel and her husband Jonathan, she is left alone with Gabriel's illegitimate son Nathan in the house. He is a highly-strung, insecure child, the complete opposite of his powerful and self-confident grandmother. Nevertheless a friendship develops between the two, in spite of Nathan's unfortunate nervous propensity for telling tall stories. Of this latter failing Farmor says, '"You'll grow out of it. But promise me you'll always come to me if you get into trouble." "Yes," he promised, and kissed and hugged her' (142). Yet when the teenage Nathan does come to her after he has broken into a neighbouring jeweller's shop and stolen ornaments (which he doles out to schoolfriends) for no apparent reason and with no attempt to cover his tracks, her reaction is one of disgust. Agnes with the quick wits feels some pity but mostly contempt for his weakness — he must be a fool! — just as she did when her husband Jonathan had epileptic fits. She demonstrates her feelings unequivocally, and Nathan runs away to America.

The action of the novel, enlarged though it is by numerous memories and flashbacks, takes place on Farmor's seventy-eighth birthday. During every single day of the ten intervening years since Nathan's flight to America, she has longed for him and for his return. Naturally, being who she is, she expects him to return contrite, destitute and needing her, and she has planned her birthday so as to coincide with the sale of her large house and the handing over of a large portion of the proceeds to her children. It is evident that she is sure Nathan will turn up, although she never speaks of him: 'she never spoke of Nathan, not even to the Lord'. (148) Or as the housemaid puts it when Farmor has Nathan's dog put to sleep just before the great day (having cherished it since Nathan's departure): 'It mustn't show that we'd been thinking of Nathan ... Can Madam admit that she's been pining for ten years? No. All she can do is to have a poor old dog killed, so that no one'll suspect that she's been pining.'(199)

Nathan does turn up, but not in the manner she had envisaged — he is enormously rich and had in fact been hoping to buy the house secretly in order that Farmor can both have the proceeds and go on living there, but the house has already been sold. His arrival at the family gathering precipitates a host of memories on the part of the assembled company. And his status as millionaire so excites Farmor's children that they dare to voice their critical views on her past behaviour. The picture that emerges is very different to the one she has of the past: 'they confused her by their handling of her memories' (210). They side with their father against her, they present her as domineering and hard. Yet she rallies, she recounts for the umpteenth time the story of how she outwitted her father with the arm of the law, and she asserts proudly: 'Strip me of what you like, but you'll always have to grant I've a clear head'(220).

But this is to be a day of discovery for Farmor, in the spiritual sense. Finding that Nathan no longer needs her help, she decides to beg his forgiveness, to beg for mercy, impelled by the sense of inner poverty and failure the day has entailed. But instead of apologizing she loses her temper — an easier way of masking her pain — and she orders Nathan with his millions to leave the house. Whereupon she discovers that her children have planned to have her certified in order that the sale of the house can be declared invalid and they be enabled to benefit from Nathan's more generous offer.

Chapter V

The climax of the novel is reached when Farmor climbs up to the attic, bearing an armful of fire-wood with which to set the house on fire. The higher she climbs the more her anger evaporates and is replaced by tears: 'She sat there crying. Above her she had the copper roof and the sky, and beneath her she had the stonebuilt house and the earth' (255). This is an image of central importance — the copper roof and stone house juxtaposed against the sky and earth. For it is a fact that all her life Farmor has responded to the twin urges of power and material security. On her seventy-eighth birthday she discovers how utterly destitute she is, for she has nothing to give Nathan, whom she loves more than anyone else on earth. As God puts it to her: 'We're both old [...] and we don't need to put on an act for each other. You know that you've nothing to give him. Otherwise you'd never have thrown him out' (258).

The only thing Farmor can give is her *klara förstånd*, the calculating intelligence with which she has built up and ruled over a prosperous, bourgeois home and copper-roofed mansion for over sixty years. Copper and stone stand for material security, as against earth and sky which represent natural affection and freedom. She has gained material security at a heavy cost, for Agnes' instinct for the practical and profitable has allowed her no scope to develop her emotional life. In fact on only two previous occasions has she been moved by an emotion at variance with the shrewd practicality that characterized her choice of a husband and the running of her home. Many years ago she was momentarily filled by an irresistible tenderness towards a handsome young relative, and some years later she fell in love with her own eldest son Gabriel. The girl who had never been in love before, felt intoxicated by happiness and reacted like 'a foal in a green pasture'. She lost her head, for as Bergman points out 'Her shrewd intelligence could cope with everything, excepting joy' (110). Where real love and happiness are concerned, calculation and shrewdness have no place. So for a short while she moved in what Bergman calls God's *other* world, the one he created for lovers, in which material objects become transparent and lose their significance and in which only the flame of love has existence and meaning. But as soon as the flame of love died out — as it did in both cases — Farmor's relentless sense of practical advantage impelled her to deal the young men ruthless blows. The third time her emotions are involved the case proceeds very differently. The powerful old lady, whose authority over her family had never before been questioned, loves Nathan more deeply than she has ever loved anyone. Yet so ingrained is her craving to command and own, that as God says to her: 'You wanted him to eat out of your hand like a dog. Because that's the queer thing about you, the person you care for has to be your dog. Otherwise you aren't satisfied' (257). But Nathan, returned, has no need to eat out of her hand, and the only thing she can find to give him — at the Almighty's suggestion — is the sharp intelligence with which she has constantly scored off her fellow-humans. She lays down this weapon and is thereby enabled to meet Nathan in love and trust.

It is typical of Bergman that he scatters hermeneutic clues (pointers to interpretation) in his text, whilst abstaining from explicit authorial comment. There are, for instance, clues indicating that Farmor is in reality struggling with her conscience in the big, final dialogue with God in the attic. She reproaches him for not answering her prayers and he refutes her arguments point by point. She complains that Nathan did not come as she wished him to: 'He didn't come the way I wanted him to, said Farmor. He ought to have come so that I could have helped him. He didn't need me' (256). God answers by laughing: 'Ho, ho, ho — loud and deep like a cow bellowing' (257). But Farmor's children, anxiously listening outside, think it is their mother laughing in her madness (which it clearly is). A few lines later Bergman repeats the indication: 'The Lord ... laughed as loudly again. Or else it was Farmor laughing.'

Why, we may ask ourselves, the ambiguity? Well, given that Farmor has a vital lesson to learn in her old age, and given that Bergman wishes to demonstrate the process for us in narrative terms, it is a reasonable conjecture that he has chosen to externalize the process of the old lady's deepening insight by giving it the dialectical form of a dialogue with God. It works with great effectiveness. Bergman tells us, in diction which is entirely expressive of Farmor's personality, that God is always handy. He sits at her bedside and listens to her and remembers what happened half a century ago and more. Above all, he has the great virtue of not raising objections; for 'Farmor dislikes objections' (14). The attentive reader who is informed that God 'knows that he who works and saves grows rich, and he who squanders and idles grows poor. It's as simple as that, but you have to have the sense to understand it and the wits to grasp it', realizes that Agnes is justifying her own ruthless energy by imputing her values of hard work

Chapter V

and thrift to the Almighty, couched in phraseology which, like the smugly sententious conclusion 'but you have to have the sense to grasp it' is entirely her own.

There is a beautiful consistency in the development of Farmor's relationship to God if we accept the premise that it represents an internal dialectic between her go-getting ego and her conscience. For Farmor no longer speaks to God after the climactic scene in which she sacrifices her sharp wits for the sake of entering the world of love. The next time we see her in bed, her normal trysting place with the Almighty, we read that 'She was not talking to the Lord. She was just lying staring at the nightlight and fingering her ears. And then one, two, three, there he came, tiptoeing in and sitting down on the side of her bed. Not the Lord, but Nathan' (264). Nathan comes and sits on her bed and puts his hand trustingly in hers. She no longer frightens him, she no longer judges him, she no longer exercises power over him, neither over him nor over her children and grandchildren.

As we have already noted, Bergman wrote to Hans Larsson that *Farmor och Vår Herre* represented a farewell to 'the middle class environment from which I come'. In friendship ('i godo') as I hope, he adds. Nathan, later to figure as Bergman's mouthpiece in his last novel *Clownen Jac*, is Farmor's opposite in every respect; weak and vulnerable all his life, his creativity is triggered by acute fear, its well-spring is insecurity. He does not belong within the solid Wadköping framework. Were it not for the fact that he has earned a fortune in America, his relations (apart from Farmor) would not wish to meet him. He is beyond the pale of the society in which he was brought up. The interesting thing is that not only had Nathan left Wadköping — his return visit there is only a fleeting one — but finally Farmor also does so in the figurative sense. She leaves the world of stone houses and copper roofs, and crosses the boundary into the world of unconditional love. She listens, nods and understands. 'This is her art, and she's alone in performing it. It's a big turn, a star turn, it's unique' (269).

And how did Farmor achieve this *art* or *konststycke*? She did so by *getting to know herself* as the unscrupulous pragmatist she had been for close on three-quarters of a century, just as Captain von Hancken *got to know himself* as an undistinguished man puffed up by illusions of grandeur, and Markurell had to *face the truth* of his childlessness and essential loneliness.

Let us give Bergman the last word on Agnes Borck, for it represents the creed which he expressed so often and so unforgettably:

It's a good thing to have a clear head and a good memory. The time comes when you have to recall everything, your whole life; you have to see — and judge — yourself. But after that it's best to forget (269).

Chapter VI

Pär Lagerkvist (1891-1974)

Irene Scobbie

Pär Lagerkvist's reluctance to divulge during his lifetime personal details about himself or his approach to his work made his autobiographical prose work *Gäst hos verkligheten* (Guest of Reality, 1925) a useful point of departure for anyone studying his writing. In 1974 it was revealed, however, that Lagerkvist had deposited a great deal of material at Kungliga Biblioteket in Stockholm, to be made available after his death. This material, comprising many of Lagerkvist's manuscripts from original sketches through to typescript form, note books, diaries and correspondence, throws a great deal of light on Lagerkvist's method of composition and on more personal aspects of his life.

Even so, *Gäst hos verkligheten* retains its central position, for it contains not just practical biographical details only slightly disguised but an evocation of the young Lagerkvist's emotional responses to his family environment which adumbrate key passages in many Lagerkvistian works.

Lagerkvist was born in Växjö, a Småland town more immune than most to the social, economic and cultural changes wrought in Sweden at the turn of the century. The leaders of the community were still the bishop, senior ecclesiastical and local administrative officers and a few conservative business men, the two local newspapers were both conservative and were quick to condemn any attempts to change the social order, whilst many Växjö inhabitants were only first generation town dwellers more inclined to preserve old rural traditions than to assimilate new urban, progressive ideas.

Even Växjö made some concessions to the age, however. A branch of the railway reached Växjö as early as 1865 and trade unions were established, though poorly supported. The Lutheran church was being challenged on a modest scale by free church movements, including the so-called *läsare* (pietists) and the Salvation Army, and by the publication of Darwin's *Origin of the Species* in Swedish translation. The latter first appeared in 1872, and by the time Lagerkvist reached the Sixth Form (1907-10) was recommended vacation reading. Strindberg's attacks on the clergy and society were also known to Lagerkvist's generation, and in his last two years at school Lagerkvist and his companions followed with great interest the controversies in which Strindberg was involved.

Lagerkvist himself was firmly rooted in the Växjö tradition. Both his parents were of Småland peasant stock and although they set up house in town, they identified themselves with the farming communities where their respective parents lived. They were pious, God-fearing people and like their parents before them they believed implicitly in the Bible. Lagerkvist's father was employed on the railway, but his life was focused on the old rather than the new.

Lagerkvist, however, was caught between two worlds. He was deeply affected by the religious atmosphere in his home and by his love for his family, but at an early age he was also acutely aware of the world of change so pervasively evident in the bustling station yard and restaurant which could be seen and heard from the Lagerkvist living room. By the time he reached the Sixth Form he had also absorbed socialist ideas sufficiently to form a radical group at school.

In *Gäst hos verkligheten* Anders, Lagerkvist's *alter ego*, can no longer accept his parents' religious beliefs; he has, however, preserved the temperament of a religious believer, and so begins the search for a substitute faith to fill the awful and seemingly unendurable void. We see the young Anders's *ångest* caused by an exaggerated fear of death and of a life without a religious aim. In his futile attempts to find an anodyne he considers 'the new doctrine', a reference to Darwin's theories on evolution, which perhaps gives a scientific basis to his rejection of the Book of Genesis, but provides no spiritual solace.

Lagerkvist's strong reaction to a life without any discernible pattern is conveyed through Anders. So too is his enjoyment of the beauty of nature. Anders' elation as he speeds through the beautiful

Chapter VI

Småland countryside is as intense as his fear of darkness and death on other occasions. Thus we have here in essence both the *livsångest* and the *livstro* (Life Angst and faith in Life) which become successively associated with Lagerkvist's work.

Being caught between two worlds gave rise to another of the themes running through Lagerkvist's works: that of identity. 'Vem är jag?' (Who am I?) is closely allied to 'vad är meningen?' (what is the purpose of life?) and to the wanderer featured so often in Lagerkvist's works.

However alienated Lagerkvist may have become, he retained throughout his life an affection for the genuinely devout, unsophisticated people he had known from childhood. Not infrequently simple, hard-working people appear to have found an answer to the meaning of life, not through reasoning but through humble acceptance. As his metaphysical searching led him to consider good and evil in Man it is not surprising that his representatives of evil are so often tortured, *Angst*-ridden souls, whilst goodness is reflected in simple unquestioning people.

Apart from some derivative poems revealing an admiration for *nittitalisterna* (Writers of the 1890s) Lagerkvist's early work is obviously that of a young man in revolt. In *Människor* (People, 1912) the passionate, daemonic Gustav Mörk tries desperately to assert himself. His defiance, however, is not against society but against his home background. He maintains that he has never been understood, and that even as a child he was lonely and afraid of death. Mörk is a tormented soul, for he still loves his home, and although he goads himself into hating his family, it is the violent kind of hatred which is the warping of a passionate love, and in his sentimental moods he reveals a desire to return to the security of the family.

In this excessively sentimental expression of an unbearable tension between the harsh but alluring outside world and the secure but stifling home, contrasts are employed crudely — the dark, daemonic Gustav Mörk is off-set by his fair-haired, honourable brother; a turbulent chapter depicting Mörk dashing through the stormy forest is followed immediately by a pastoral scene suffused with idyllic sabbatical peace, etc. The surge of Lagerkvist's writing is unmistakable, but the violent emotions hover between the frightening and the ludicrous.

In Paris in 1913 Lagerkvist met the Swedish cubist painter John Sten and through him several other avantgarde artists. Lagerkvist had been groping his way to a new kind of literature based on simplicity and contrasts but early works like *Människor* were marred by uncontrolled emotions. It is easy to understand his immediate enthusiasm for Cubist painters who could subordinate strong personal emotions to a rigorous, intellectual pattern.

In a series of articles and tracts on literature and art written between 1913 and 1918, notably *Ordkonst och bildkonst* (Literary Art and Visual Art, 1913) and *Modern Teater* (1918), Lagerkvist explains how new trends in the visual arts could be adapted to literature. There should be conscious simplicity in psychological presentation; the author must strive for 'simple lines ... with a tendency to stylization ...; simple people who compel our interest not so much through human (or rather personally characteristic) traits but through the severely unified, gathered strength of their composition.' A work of art must be constructed, should be mathematical in its proportions, thus appealing to the intellect as well as to the emotions. Modern art had found a source of inspiration in the art of primitive people, art which brought one back to simplicity, not only of form but of content. Their framework consists of 'simply considered, uncomplicated feelings in the face of life's eternal forces, joy and sorrow, reverence, love and hatred, expressions of the universal rising above the particular'.[1]

Två sagor om livet (Two Stories of Life, 1913), *Motiv* (1914) and *Järn och människor* (Iron and Humans, 1915) show Lagerkvist striving to submit to this artistic discipline. He had also maintained that literature must reflect the period in which it is composed, and Europe was now caught up in a singularly bloody war. Each of the five *noveller* comprising *Järn och människor* is focused on war, but even such a potentially overwhelming theme is governed by a strict form. The contrasts between hard, grey iron (armaments, shrapnel) and human beings (soft, red flesh and blood) and between hatred and love are consistently worked out, and no anguished comment outside the framework of the stories intrudes.

However, as the war — and, one supposes, Lagerkvist's inner conflict — intensified it proved impossible for him to keep his emotions under such rigorous control. The outburst came with his cycle of verse and prose poems entitled *Ångest* (Angst, 1916). The desperation of *Människor* has even been exacerbated by the madness and pointless killing of war on a world scale but his control of form and means of expression now makes it possible for him to project his personal

Chapter VI

problem in such a way as to give it universal application. However alien to his essential temperament, the artistic discipline of the intervening years had been necessary.

Ångest proved to be an important landmark in modern Swedish literature, being the first Expressionistic work to be published in Sweden. Lagerkvist found the traditional forms of poetry in Sweden inadequate to express the world as he experienced it, but he also broke with the strict Cubist ideas on art and aestheticism at this point. His own personal dilemma is the driving force in *Ångest*, and the autobiographical element is easy to trace. He describes the feeling in his youth when he was singled out to experience the *Ångest* which we recognize from *Gäst hos verkligheten*:

I have never forgotten you, Life, since the night you seized me by the throat! I was young, my body pimply and raw. You seized me so firmly by the throat![2]

He has lost his childhood religion and found no substitute to give his life meaning: 'No hand is as empty as mine/no heart so desolate.'(9). 'The new doctrine' offers no solace and he is irritated by 'the thought of all those lower, more or less unsuccessful animal forms that have preceded man in his unsteady development upwards ... But the most horrible thing of all is that the animals' souls are also mine...'(12).

The realization that he is simply part of an evolutionary system does not still the longing for eternity which is symbolized in the stars. The poet knows that this longing can never be fulfilled, but he cannot endure the thought of the complete void which awaits him after death. As the violent world closes in on him he is caught in a desperate situation which gives rise to *Angst*. But this is the situation which involves the whole of Mankind, and the poet becomes the representative of twentieth-century Man.

In both content and form Lagerkvist has again worked in contrasts. *Angst,* the dominating emotion, is immediately thrown into prominence in the introductory poem, 'Ångest, ångest är min arvedel' (Angst, Angst is My Heritage). E. Hörnström suggests that Lagerkvist has consciously parodied Karlfeldt's 'Längtan heter min arvedel' (Longing is My Heritage).[3] Karlfeldt experiences a not unpleasant melancholy longing whilst dreaming in his romantic castle among roses. For longing Lagerkvist substitutes the much more intense *ångest*; instead of the fragrant, gentle night which soothes away the poet's troubles we now have night's coarse hand, whilst the Swedish sky and forests have frozen and clamped down on the poet. Active pain and desperation supersede melancholy longing:

I grope around in this dark room, I feel the sharp edge of the cliff against my fingers, I tear my upstretched hands on frozen rags of clouds until they bleed.

Man in this setting assumes giant proportions, large enough to reach the skies. He is helpless in his suffering, and he stretches his hands upwards, as though in supplication, a modern Prometheus, but this Promethean figure shrinks as the poet considers how futile his gesture is: 'Mine is a meagre soul'.

Here Lagerkvist has plotted the two extremes. Man is a wretched being, an insignificant animal incapable of fathoming the mysteries of life, but he bears within him a longing to strive upwards, to free himself from the earth. The heights to which faith can raise Man are shown in 'På frälsningsarmén' (Salvation Army Meeting)(19). A wretchedly dressed individual has found God and rises 'high towards the eternal stars'. But in the following prose poem:

The whole thing is ludicrous! Here is this round earth wallowing in the outer space, and sticking out of it in all directions like rough nails, like spikes on an angry hedgehog, are weeping, pining, howling human beings!

Love is a strong force in Lagerkvist's work generally, and there is a momentary suggestion that it could prevail as in the poem 'Dina läppar äro som skogar efter regn/ så tunga och friska./ Hur jag törstar, törstar efter dig!(23)' (Your lips are like a forest after rain so heavy and fresh. How I thirst, thirst for you!) but there is no room for either physical or spiritual love in this world and in the next poem, as if to stamp out any emotion that could detract from his total absorption in his suffering the poet declares that 'Love is nothing. Angst is all'(24).

There is an attempt at defiance — 'I spit at the filthy arches of the firmament/and the stars' pale snouts'(15)[4], but then the poet is over-awed by the vastness of the cosmos and the insignificance of Man:

Insignificant, I creep out of my musty cave listen, hunched, look around with jaundiced eye. The silent stars of eternity are shining. (32)[5]

Only at the end of the work is there a note of resignation. Man has

Chapter VI

tried feverishly to free himself from his situation but failed. In the last poem, 'Under stjärnorna' (Under the Stars) he now stands silent 'with bowed head. Sacred spheres. No human words are true.'(35) The poem perhaps suggests Man's humility in the presence of the symbol for the vast universe, but he has been brought here by exhaustion, not conviction, and he has found no solution to this problem.

Lagerkvist lived in Denmark for part of World War I where he turned his attention to modern drama. His first play, *Sista mänskan* (The Last Man, 1917) modelled on post-Inferno Strindberg, and medieval and Indian drama, endeavours to express the period and to show Man's situation in a chaotic world. His main character is Man *in extremis* and he projects on to the stage the last of mankind. The setting takes us back to the first poem in *Ångest*: the earth is frozen and laid waste and the sun is on the point of extinction. He has dispensed with the conventions as understood by Naturalistic playwrights. There is no plot, no development, very little inter-play, of characters; the time is the end of the world, the setting is the dying world.

In effect Lagerkvist has given dramatic form to the world he conjured up in *Ångest*. Post-Darwin Man strives towards heaven, but he knows he is only a higher animal, evolved over millions of years, dominated by basic instincts and propelled by an instinct for self-preservation. He is powerless either to change or to accept his condition and is caught in an unbearable tension. His desire for life is countered by his certainty of death; his fear of death by his *Angst* in the face of a meaningless life; he shows both humility and defiance, love and hatred, sympathy and indifference, humanity and cruelty.

A play in which a character rails impotently against his fate and shouts his *Angst* is bound to become tedious during the course of three acts without a plot to sustain our interest. Its excesses too in the end detract from the overall impact. Lagerkvist himself no doubt realized just how far he had strayed from his own *desiderata*. *Sista mänskan* was followed by three one-act plays with the common title *Den svåra stunden* (The Difficult Hour, 1918) where, although he again evokes the horror experienced by Man as death approaches, he has constructed three compact and much more effective plays. The one outside influence which remains is that of the post-Inferno Strindberg, who, like Lagerkvist, was dealing with the indefinable boundary between dream and reality. The three plays are so arranged that everything contributes to the mood, which is no longer static as in *Sista mänskan* but is carefully built up until finally reaching an almost unbearable and yet inevitable climax.

In 1919 Lagerkvist published a one-act play *Himlens hemlighet* (The Secret of Heaven), a collection of prose passages, *Den fordringsfulle gästen* (The Demanding Guest) and of poems, *I stället för tro* (Instead of Faith) under the general title *Kaos* (Chaos). The setting of the play is not unlike that of *Sista mänskan*, but the mood is slightly less despairing. The central figure, the Youth, is not concerned with warding off death so much as finding a meaning to life and establishing contact with another human being. For a while as he talks of beauty to the young girl it seems possible that love may transform his callous indifferent world. The girl's madness reasserts itself however, she falls again under the influence of the philistine dwarf, and the Lagerkvistian god and executioner, both supremely indifferent to Man, resume their sawing of wood and beheading of puppets respectively. The Youth is overwhelmed by the pointlessness of life and leaves the earth.

In *Den fordringsfulle gästen* the search for life's meaning continues, but the feeling of urgency is intensified and there is a note of irritation and often indignation. The traveller is only on a very short visit, he has a great deal to fathom in such a short time and so 'it irritates me.... that everything here is in such damned disorder'(19).[6] The hotel symbolizes the chaotic world Lagerkvist experienced at the end of a major war.

In this extreme situation the guest on the one hand is prone to self-assertion, using strident language. The implication is that the guest has a right, as an individual, to certain conditions. Conversely, he is also the victim of doubt and humility. He wants an explanation, but daren't go to the manager, and even admits to himself that he has no right to be staying at the hotel at all. Finally he is made to realize the individual's complete insignificance in the vast universe. Having found the courage to ask the manager why he has lived he receives the reply 'You personally? ... Well, the devil knows!'(28). Like the Youth in *Himlens hemlighet* he leaves the chaotic world and wanders into the darkness, an action viewed with brutal indifference by the other figures.

Self assertion is weighed against Man's insignificance in the remaining prose passages. In one passage there is a spontaneous outburst of *Angst* as Lagerkvist experiences the full significance of Darwin's evolutionary theory. Mankind will go on, but the individual has only one short life and after that nothing. In another the chaotic world is a broken pitcher which has borne a pleasing picture of human figures but is now in pieces. The narrator is trying to fit the pieces into some form of pattern, but always distortion and ugliness displace grace and beauty. In this passage too he abandons his attempt, exclaiming querulantly 'Oh, go to hell, the lot of you. Go to hell!'(34).

The mood of irritation changes abruptly in the final passage, where the chaotic world is now a circus performance; men have performed incredible feats, but when the narrator considers how a puff of wind could destroy the circus tent, i.e. how transient Man's life is, and compares this with the eternal stars in a silent sky he admits 'I feel man's humility in the face of eternity'(37). As in the last poem of *Ångest*, the poet now stands with bowed head under the eternal stars exhausted after battering himself against cosmic forces, but now he goes further and experiences an almost mystical feeling in the presence of eternal elements in Nature, and he questions his own right even to doubt or deny. The outburst of temper was apparently the last desperate attempt at self-assertion, for the prose section ends on this resigned note, only vaguely hinted at in *Himlens hemlighet*.

I stället för tro goes one step further. The world first presented is dark, cold and indifferent to Man. The emphasis, however, is considerably changed. The universe has become a mother's breast which affords comfort. As so often with Lagerkvist, the change of attitude is emotional rather than logical. In the first poem, 'jag lutar mig trygg' (I Rest Securely), the philosophical question posed earlier is still in the poet's mind, here called heaven's 'tanke' (thought) but it is silenced by the new feeling of security he derives from the maternal cosmos.

The transition from despair to resignation is best illustrated in 'Lyft dig på blodiga vingar' (Rise up on Bloody Wings) which in form recalls an old Protestant hymn, but in content is wholly modern. Man has again attempted to solve the secret of heaven, but the poet now admits that this 'thought' was God's province and far beyond Man's comprehension. Only Man's longing for a solution, his driving force, is of superhuman stature.

The poet's attitude is ambivalent. He seems to imply that since Man was given a superhuman longing but only human intelligence to satisfy it, he was doomed from the outset. And yet he calls his God 'rättfärdig' (just). Even more enigmatic, however, is the fact that he presumably does not believe in the God he is invoking. The poet is sincere, but his sincerity lies in a profound longing for a just God to come to Man's assistance, not in a belief in his existence. In other words his religious beliefs have progressed little, but his attitude has changed in that he has ceased to ask why we are here. We cannot possibly understand the point of our existence and, perhaps more important, we are wrong even to try.

From a point of humility and resignation, Lagerkvist can afford to view life in a positive spirit, and he finds a vast mystical world full of splendours. He moves into a world bathed in sunshine. Man is allowed to enjoy this beauty only on sufferance, and afterwards comes the void, 'Jag skall vandra — ensam, utan spår' (I shall wander — alone, without trace). ('Det är vackrast ...') The enjoyment is so intense, however, that the poet seems able to contemplate annihilation with no more than subdued melancholy.

Perhaps this can partly be explained by the birth of his daughter. Previously Lagerkvist had interpreted Darwinism as meaning the removal of all traces of the individual after death but in the three poems addressed to his child he shows how the child helps to foster a feeling of continuity. The child is born into a bright harmonious era after the dark chaotic struggle of the previous generation, but the father will remain without balance and harmony. This approach certainly explains the paradox in the last passage in the work 'Uppståndelsens morgon' (Resurrection Morn) where Lagerkvist believes and yet does not believe. A beautiful new world has dawned, but only the child's generation can see it. It sums up his attitude in *I stället för tro*, for he is both pessimistic about his own soul and optimistic about the future; unconvinced of his own chances of salvation and yet strangely resigned to the fact, since those coming after him will achieve a great peace of mind.

The work also reflects Lagerkvist's hard-won appreciation of the beauty of life itself, now that he is able to keep his fear of death at bay. It is a short step from the final passages of *Kaos* to Lagerkvist's period of *livstro*, a belief in life that has almost religious connotations. Sven Linnér says that '"life" is a religious keyword, to be mentioned rather like the Christian mentioning God'.[7]

There are three works in this 'livstro' period, *Det eviga leendet* (The Eternal Smile, 1920), *Morgonen* (Morning, 1920) and *Den lyckliges väg* (The Path of the Happy Man, 1921). If we look more closely at the first we can see something of the nature of Lagerkvist's

Chapter VI

belief and also how he constructs a fullscale prose work.

It falls into four parts: a series of anecdotes related by dead people; the rebellion of these people and their journey to God; their encounter with God; and finally their return to their original positions. The anecdotes in the first part are carefully selected, offering us a composite picture of Man. The child, the lover, the aged, the Christian, the sceptic, the criminal, the aesthete, the passionate, the phlegmatic, the sensuous, the ascetic, the primitive, the simple and the sophisticated are all represented.

Lagerkvist begins by stating through the medium of three different characters three basic attitudes to life. The first denies life utterly, his first word is 'No', he is 'as if created to die' (44)[8] and his argument against life goes so far that it leads him to the paradoxical conclusion that only the dead are really alive. The second has led a full, brilliant life and loved everything living. He is 'as if created to live'. (45) The third, Pettersson, states the neutral theme between these two extremes. 'I was like everybody else ... I thank God that I was allowed to live.' (47) Using these three views as a ground base Lagerkvist proceeds to embellish them, presenting a picture of life in all its profusion and richness and attempting to establish Man's position in the world.

As in *Kaos* Lagerkvist alludes to the evolutionary process, in this case by including among his characters an ape man who 'remembered only the scent of another human, of something warm like himself ... He remembered only the scent. Then his widened nostrils quivered in the darkness and he bellowed like a weeping animal'.(82) There is compassion in the primeval man's longing, but Lagerkvist no longer rails against the universe for causing Man to be part of the evolutionary system.

Perhaps as a corollary to this acceptance of Darwin's theory Lagerkvist also demonstrates that he has abandoned any lingering faith in Christianity. He includes a dignified, sad man who had been convinced in his lifetime that he was God's son but found after a martyr's death that he was mortal. Like the first character in the work this 'saviour' had been more concerned with death than life and brought to the same paradoxical point where life denied is indeed death.

Four of the life stories are recounted in some detail. The first forms a symbolic variation on the denial-of-life theme. The choice of a locksmith as the *raconteur* is an effective one. 'Der Schlüssel, sonst ein magisches Symbol, das den Zugang zu den Geheimnissen des Daseins erschliesst, wird hier im Gegenteil zum Symbol der Lebensfremdheit, die den Einzelnen unweigerlich auf sich selbst zurückwirft.'[9] Those who deny life are people apart, with no contact with the community. This is epitomized in the locksmith, who is not only a recluse but uses his considerable skill to keep other individuals locked up within themselves.

The locksmith ignores the natural beauty which surrounds his workshop and works incessantly in his dark smithy. The contrast between the light, vital world outside and the dim sterile smithy is heightened by the appearance on a bright summer's day of a happy, blond young girl who looks around her as she walks. She symbolizes the happiness and human friendship the locksmith has literally locked out of his life. Although he is in love for the first time he denies the emotion and returns to his work. When death approaches and he feels compelled to seek human company it is too late, and he dies alone, barren in every sense. Lagerkvist has chosen to show the reverse side of his *livstro* first.

The obverse is displayed with some brilliance in several anecdotes, above all in the rider to the mill. His story, the longest, presents in a high-spirited humorous fashion the acceptance-of-life theme. It is replete with symbols, the mill hidden away in the forest being a symbol of life itself. Lagerkvist thinks in pictures, and this rider's approach to the mill in early sunshine through dewy grass to the sound of birdsongs, might well have been entitled 'Primavera'.

Two opposing aspects of life are symbolized here. On the one hand there is the sensuous aspect, shown in numerous details: when first introduced the miller's wife is standing with her legs apart, smiling, while the miller stands with his legs together. The entrance to the mill, we are told immediately afterwards, is a fairly high hole in the wall with no steps leading to it. The floor is covered with soft white flour which deadens sound and, together with the distant drone of the machinery driving the wheels in the background, has a relaxing, soporific effect. The similes used to describe the corpulent wife all lead our thoughts to sensual pleasures — her breasts are like large loaves and she has 'well-fattened arms'. She smiles contentedly, appears to wear nothing under her dress and has a seductive walk. Under her influence the guest forgets the outside world and becomes wholly engrossed in material pleasures.[10] In this happy condition he 'understands a great deal he had never understood before ... everything is calm and secure and healthy'(66). Here is a typically Lagerkvistian use of the word

Chapter VI

'understand' which doesn't mean that one has logically grasped a point but has emotionally responded to an atmosphere and has ceased to ask questions.

The other aspect of life is symbolized by the miller, a small, swarthy, tense man, and his engine-room. The water flowing below is turbulent and frightening, and yet it fascinates the guest. After spending 'many years' (so the dream-like anecdote tells us) in bed with the miller's wife, the guest is awoken by the roaring stream, is torn to pieces by the mill-wheels and 'gives up the ghost in ecstasy'(79). Interpretations of the work diverge at this point, but it would seem that the guest, lulled into indolence by sensuous pleasures, had been denying part of life. When he shook off this animal influence and also accepted the more spiritual aspects of life he was then able to appreciate life in all its profusion — hence the ecstasy, but also, it would appear, his death. Erik Blomberg makes the point that 'it is a strange intoxication with life. It results in the ecstasy of death'.[11]

This strange kinship between intoxication with life and ecstasy of death is also found in the story of Giuditta, a tale replete with fertility symbols associated with early Mediterranean civilization. Here too we are presented with two aspects of life. On the one hand, villagers in a fertile valley tend their vineyards and olive trees as their forefathers had done, living happily and 'understanding' the meaning of life. Giuditta goes barefooted and is close to the earth; she is unquestioning and happy.

The other aspect of life in introduced when she and her lover ascend a mountain, entering a supernatural realm. There a sibyl-like woman predicts that when Giuditta bears a child she will die. Giuditta was wise for her years, for she realized that restricting her enjoyment of life's pleasure would be to deny life itself. She therefore enjoys her brief life, bears a child and dies in childbirth. Her death coincides with a festival celebrating fertility rites, and when the young father holding the new-born child in his arms sees the procession, his parents, all the villagers and

the whole of life ... Then I thought I understood the meaning of everything ... Then I knew that life simply wants itself. It wants the trees, the people ... the flowers; but not one of them. Life has no love for you, tree, for you, individual man ... for you, flower ...(93)

The passage is not only an acceptance of Darwinism but a paean to the life force which these primitive people so accept that they continue to chant their joyful hymn even as a volcano erupts and the lava engulfs them all.

We come then to the unassuming Pettersson. The best variation on his theme is found in the underground lavatory attendant, a diffident, conscientious figure drawn with obvious affection. In his way, however, he is one of the most important figures in the work, for, 'seen in isolation' he 'can be seen as a symbol for the basic intention of the whole book: a humble acceptance of life'.[12] He had learnt to know and understand humanity, to accept his own insignificance and so he remains happy.

From a consideration of all four of these stories, that of the locksmith, the rider to the mill, Giuditta and the lavatory attendant, it would appear that Lagerkvist believes in a life force beyond our understanding. It we deny it our life becomes sterile and pointless; if we strive consciously towards it, or even stray too far in the direction of the centre of this force we shall experience a moment of intoxication, even ecstasy, but we shall meet a violent death. However, if we can accept with equanimity or resignation the portion of existence meted out to us we shall find happiness and, in a rather tortuous Lagerkvistian sense 'understand' life, even though this 'understanding' is rather disconcertingly synonymous with the peace of mind that passes all understanding.

When the dead are incited to journey to God to ask him about life's purpose they are filled with a spirit of companionship, which for a while creates such peace of mind that it seems to be an end in itself. The masses soon realize however that they have 'nothing to fight for, nothing to suffer ... it is gloomy and empty'. (108) Lagerkvist may well be asserting here that Socialism is not sufficient to satisfy Man's spiritual needs.

The God they eventually confront is the wood-sawing figure we recognize from *Himlens hemlighet* and *Gäst hos verkligheten*. The representatives of the life-denying and life-embracing groups put forward their opposing demands which are then fused into:

We must demand full clarity about everything and moreover the confusion which exists in everything. We must demand certainty of radiant happiness, our right to happiness and light; moreover certainty that no such happiness exists. We must demand the deepest abysses of *Angst*, our suffering that no one can fathom, our *Angst*, our darkness where we pine away and die, and moreover the certainty

Chapter VI

that no cause for *Angst* exists. We must demand a cohesion in everything, peace for our thoughts, for our tortured, struggling hearts and moreover demand that there is no cohesion, no peace, no tranquillity. We must demand everything. (117)

Lagerkvist summarizes here the demands he has made in his literary production, and is obviously aware of how impossibly contradictory they are. Only a God capable of miracles could respond, and in a sense this is what Lagerkvist tries to present in the emotional appeal of the humble, simple God who has done his best to keep Mankind going. It is the wholly pervasive goodness of the wood-sawer that provides a satisfactory answer. The crowd 'experienced secretly and profoundly their inner communion with God. They understood that He was like them, only greater and more profound.'(119). We are dealing again with the peculiar use of the word 'understand' for it is when they cease their quest for knowledge and respond emotionally to God's goodness that they 'understand' him. In the final pages of the book as the crowd return whence they came they have abandoned their attempts to reason intellectually and, being still under the influence of the god's goodness, they achieve true harmony.

This is emphasized when a sorrowing man nevertheless manages to smile at a family group. He smiles not just because they are amusing but also 'for their sake, so that they would understand that he thought they were happy'.(126). This smile comes back to him even when he is plunged once more into his own suffering and helps him. Goodness, it seems, comes from within us. God is the epitome of goodness in Man, and like him (i.e. the wood-sawing god) we should work for each other.

In a series of epigrammatic utterances contained in the last pages of the book Lagerkvist attempts to convey the wonder of life felt by the people who met the god. 'The richness of life is boundless ... as great as we can comprehend. Can we demand more? When all the same we do demand more then there is also all the incomprehensible, everything we can't fathom.'(124). This dawning realization of the vast riches of life fills the crowd with gladness and leads them to the conclusion that it is Man's duty to be happy, but it must be the happiness of a man 'busy living his life'.(125).

Det eviga leendet shows Lagerkvist's strength and weakness as an author. When conveying philosophical ideas through characters his creative genius and storytelling technique carry his reader along enthralled. When he tries to state something profound without recourse to this creative process, however, he risks producing quasi-philosophical utterances which spread heat rather than light. The powerful impression left by this book is derived not from the final aphorisms but from the feeling of a tremendous life force conveyed by the stories of the rider to the mill and of Giuditta.

There is an element of determinism running through Lagerkvist's work, and this is connected with his treatment of good and evil in Man. There is in *Det eviga leendet* a murderer whose brothers were 'happy and good, I was evil and without peace, there'd been none left for me'. (54). Evil exists as a force and the characters embodying it are tormented, destructive but also dynamic beings. Goodness as portrayed by Lagerkvist is more static, constant and unchanging.

As the political situation in Europe worsened in the 1920s Lagerkvist was increasingly aware of the forces of evil. In 1933, the year Hitler came to power, he published *Bödeln* (The Executioner), at once reflecting the times and attempting to state a timeless, universal truth about evil in Man. The medieval section of the work focuses on Man's superstitions and fascination with dark forces which are nevertheless suppressed. The patrons of the tavern can still believe in the superiority of Christ and the saints. The modern section shows that the dark forces have been allowed to break out and take over. With all their sophistication representatives of modern Man have returned to the jungle. Throughout the entire work the Executioner sits, feared and revered through the ages as a scapegoat for Man's evil deeds. God had created him when he still had power over Man and evil forces could be governed, but now evil has gained the upper hand and Man has no need of God, or rather the representative of evil has become their exclusive god. However, Lagerkvist cannot wholly accept that goodness is dead and evil unchecked. Throughout the work the Executioner has by his side a fair, serene woman who remains faithful to him in all adversity. Here is an embodiment of goodness which appears to be as eternal as evil's representative, even though fulfilling a very passive role.

The most consistent symbol of evil is found in *Dvärgen* (The Dwarf, 1944), where in the figure of the Dwarf Lagerkvist projects the dark forces within us. The Dwarf frightens 'normal' people but 'what people are afraid of is themselves ... They are generally scared when something surfaces from their inner selves, from one of the muddy pools in their souls'.(21).[13]

The Dwarf is isolated and sterile, he has no spiritual aspirations

Chapter VI

and his strongest emotions are hatred and a daemonic pleasure in destruction. His greatest adversaries are Bernardo, who symbolizes all that is best in Humanism, and Angelica, whose sweet temperament and pure innocent love drive the Dwarf to fury. The character he most admires is the Condottieri, an unscrupulous mercenary whose life is devoted to the destruction of war.

The Dwarf's master, Prince Leone, represents Man, both good and evil. As the work progresses it would seem that evil is gaining the upper hand, for the Prince first invades a neighbouring territory without warning and then has his enemies treacherously poisoned at a conciliatory banquet. As the Prince watches his Dwarf dispensing poisoned wine he realizes with horror what he has unleashed, whilst the Dwarf has reached the zenith of his power.

Lagerkvist now takes the role of evil a step further than in *Bödeln*. The Dwarf is as eternal, certainly, as the Executioner, and if unchecked is capable of unleashing frightening forces, but his energies can also lead to Man's spiritual improvement, provided they are controlled in time. The Dwarf is used to arrange Princess Teodora's assignations with Don Riccardo, but he is also paradoxically the means of arousing her sense of guilt which leads her to accept responsibility for the suffering of the people and to die a saint. Similarly, the poisonings lead to a siege which brings down on the people starvation and plague, and turns their thoughts again to God. They confess their guilt and penitently recommence work on the abandoned campanile. Indirectly even the dark forces of evil can turn Man's thoughts heavenwards.[14]

From 1950 until his death Lagerkvist was concerned most closely in his works with the existence and nature of God, and the relation between God and Man.

In *Aftonland* (Evening Land, 1953), a collection of poems which form a good introduction to his last six novels, often 'explaining' the setting and mood and the symbols found in the prose works, the 'Aftonland' of the title is the land which prepares Man for death.

Some of the poems take us back to *Gäst hos verkligheten* and to *Ångest*, referring to the child's traumatic spiritual awakening 'Vem gick förbi min barndoms fönster' (Who Went Past My Childhood Window, 46)[15] and introducing symbols we recognize from the earlier works. In 'Vad upplevde jag den kvällen' the poet asks

What did I experience that evening, the autumn evening when I went to get mother some firewood? I remember it so well,... It was then that I saw the stars for the first time ... When I came in again to mother ... there was nothing special about me to be seen but when I went and sat on my stool a long way from the others I was no longer a child.(50)

Others express Lagerkvist's religious quandary: he can neither believe in a god nor yet accept that God does not exist. Nor can he ignore the enigma and live his life in indifference. In poem after poem he poses simple but paradoxical questions which underline this dilemma. 'Who are you who fill my heart with your absence?'(59); 'What fills the heart like emptiness. / What fills the soul like longing for something that doesn't exist ...' (60); 'If you believe in God and there is no God / your faith is an even greater miracle.'(63).

The symbol of Man becoming aware of God's power is a spear. It is first linked to his well-known star symbol in the poem 'Säg mig du eviga stjärna':

Tell me, eternal star why you stare down on me. Your gaze is sharp and bores down deep into my soul. Spear point from eternity, you do not intend me any good.

Then it re-appears in 'Spjutet är kastat och vänder aldrig tillbaka' (The Spear is Cast and Will Never Return) where he asks 'Whose hand was it who hurled the spear / who the spear thrower? ... I who have been pierced ask.'

Once the spear has pierced Man, he is doomed to become a lonely wanderer, a 'desert' man. The poem 'Öppna ditt hus för mig', in which God addresses Man, makes the point strongly:

Open your house to me. Open all the doors, all the gates to me who come like a whirlwind. When I enter your house there shall no longer be room for you, you shall live in the desert like an outcast. I shall drive you into the desert, you shall lie naked in the desert under the stars.

As one reaches the final section of *Aftonland* it becomes clear that no matter how 'absent' the God may be, Lagerkvist believes that he exists at least as some form of power. In 'Från mitt väsens yta' (73) he says:

From the surface of my being he blows away the grey film and makes me alive like a dark well ... In my dark well he reflects the depth of his light.

Chapter VI

The dark well reflecting God's light remains enigmatic, but recurs in Lagerkvist's last novels.

In 1950 Lagerkvist published his novel *Barabbas*, a work which was largely responsible for his being awarded the Nobel Prize for literature the following year. The central figure is the robber who had been sentenced to death but then released instead of Christ. One might say that as a condemned man Barabbas had entered a kind of Evening Land, and throughout the work he stands out as a figure of darkness. God, through the agency of Christ, has entered Barabbas's life, and now Barabbas both metaphorically and often literally has to 'live in the desert like an outcast'. Barabbas had lived the life of a criminal without any apparent thought of God or his soul, but after having seen Christ on his way to Golgotha he is held, against his will, in the power of a God whose existence he cannot accept. The novel shows his fevered attempts either to accept or to reject.

Barabbas's struggle is centred round three crucifixions, events on the threshold to death, or 'Aftonland'. The first is that of Christ himself, which Barabbas witnesses reluctantly for it was Christ 'who had forced him to come, who had such a strange power over him'(8).[16] Barabbas remains in Jerusalem for some time trying unsuccessfully to find out what the Christian doctrine implies. The confused muttering of 'Love thy neighbour' are wholly alien to his nature and background, and it is hardly surprising that he gains no insight or satisfaction from Christ's followers. He is also afraid of the thought of death and can derive little solace from a religion that seems to place so much emphasis on it. When he visits the man raised from the dead his only question is 'The Kingdom of the Dead — what is it like there?' (47) and far from interpreting the story as evidence of Christ's vanquishing death he is only aware of 'the taste of corpse' (48) when breaking bread with the resurrected man.

If, however, Barabbas cannot accept Christ, neither can he return to his previous mode of life. The fat woman offers him sexual pleasure, but Barabbas derives no satisfaction from her company, and turning from one Lagerkvistian symbol, he spends much of the night gazing in the direction of another: the stars(20).

He sees what faith can do for the humblest of beings, for both the hare-lipped woman and Sahak radiate a spiritual happiness which even the threat of execution cannot shake. It is the kind of faith Lagerkvist recognized throughout his life and caught so well for instance in his poem 'På frälsningsarmén'. Barabbas, like his author, is moved by it and wants to be convinced by it, asking Sahak to inscribe Christ's name on his slave disc. It is futile, however, and Barabbas is telling no more than the truth when he states before the Roman governor that 'I wanted to believe' but that 'I have no god'.(104).

The last section of the novel shows him making another attempt, this time in Rome. He loses his way in the catacombs ('the Kingdom of the Dead') and is as *Angst*-ridden as any character dating from Lagerkvist's *Ångest*-period, but again he can derive no comfort from the thought of Christ. In fact the only occasion on which he does fully identify himself with the Christians can only be classed as a case of mistaken identity. As Rome burns he believes the rumour that the Christians are to blame and helps to spread the conflagration with a great sense of relief at finally being able to perform a task for Christ. In the dungeon it is brought home to him that the strange God he had been persuaded to serve would never countenance destruction, and Barabbas again has to reject the existence of a God. The final crucifixion is his own, and as he hangs on the cross, about to leave 'Aftonland' and step over the boundary into death he abandons his struggle. '"To you I deliver up my soul"' he cries 'into the darkness as if speaking to it'. (129). Some readers have interpreted this as a last minute conversion, but on both internal evidence and from the more or less contemporary poems in *Aftonland* it is difficult to accept such a reading.

The structure of the novel too points to Barabbas's final words being an acknowledgement that he belongs to the darkness. He is contrasted to Christ in a clearly defined pattern. He is called 'the released man' as opposed to Christ, 'the crucified'. He is 'powerfully built' (7) while Christ is 'thin and spindly'(8). He first emerges from 'the dungeon' (6) whereas Christ is 'surrounded by a blinding light'(6). Christ restores life to Lazarus, but Barabbas can only register 'the taste of corpse'. The hare-lipped woman's life was filled with a belief in an afterlife through meeting Christ, but all Barabbas could do for her was force her to conceive a still-born child and then carry her corpse to its final resting place. Christ was God's beloved son and was loved by his mother, but Barabbas was loathed by his father and was cursed by his mother who bore him in hatred. Christ is surrounded by loved ones at his death whereas Barabbas dies completely alone. With such a carefully-planned system of contrasts it seems most probable that since Christ addressed God as he died, Barabbas using the same words would

Chapter VI

be addressing darkness.[17]

Few works illustrate so well Lagerkvist's method of construction. The pattern of parallels and contrasts embraces all the main characters: Barabbas versus the hare-lipped woman and Sahak; Barabbas versus Simon Peter; the fat woman versus the hare-lipped woman, etc. It also is a superlative example of Lagerkvist's ability to introduce simple symbols which are part of the story and yet carry the reader's thoughts into more subtle channels. Treating the question of God's relation to Man, Lagerkvist has chosen an immediate route: Christ's crucifixion and the man who was literally 'saved' by Christ. Barabbas's fear of death is linked to a man raised from the dead and then the catacombs. He inhabits the shores of the Dead Sea. His attempt at accepting Christ is conveyed by having Christ's name carved on his disc. His spiritual loneliness is reflected by his being physically alone most of the time. It would be difficult to find a more consistently wrought illustration of Lagerkvist's views on construction expressed in *Ordkonst och bildkonst* than his novel *Barabbas*.

In *Sibyllan* (The Sibyl, 1956) the relationship between God and Man is again examined and although the findings are more varied and the mood more optimistic the conclusion takes us again to *Aftonland*. Barabbas had been visited by God against his will, but the Sibyl looked forward to her initiation and sought him out.

Her description of her years as pythia reveal two classical aspects of the god, the wisdom of Apollo symbolized by the temple bathed in light, and the dark, erotic and chaotic forces of Dionysus which overpower the Sibyl in the subterranean crypt. Other characters she describes in her narrative embody other ways of approaching God. Her simple, diffident parents worship a pantheistic god found in streams, trees and sacred groves. Like the temple servant they accept without question and so can enjoy a harmonious life.

The Sibyl has a probing temperament. She veers as far in one direction as Barabbas does in the other. Whereas he tried repeatedly to free himself from 'the thought of god' she not only accepts God's existence but desires happiness in her dealings with him. Her summing up at the end of the novel shows, however, that her life, although richer, has been as troubled as Barabbas's and she has suffered as intensely as he.

More than any other Lagerkvist character she embodies the sentiments expressed in *Aftonland*. An old woman, she sits on her mountain overlooking the temple where she formerly served and looks back on her life. ('Med gamla ögon ser jag mig tillbaka' ('With old eyes I look back') (51)) Her face is 'severe and lined, dark-skinned as if it had been in contact with fire; her eyes had the look of having once seen God' (8)[18] which takes us again to the poem 'The god who does not exist/it is he who ignites my soul/who makes my soul a desert/a smouldering plot of land, burnbeaten land smouldering after the fire.' (61). Whether one accepts or rejects God, once one is made aware one can never again know peace of mind, harmony or happiness. When the Sibyl tries to live normally with the one-armed man she finds that her 'passion was like a wild schism which would swallow him up'(135). Her desires, after knowing the god in the crypt, are of almost supernatural proportions and like Barabbas she is caught between two worlds. The embrace of the mortal was 'security ... but I was not intended for security. I grew to be a stranger in it'.(136). On her way back to the temple after this attempt at normal love-making she 'was freezing under all the cold stars', she was 'completely alone' and when she was visited by the god 'he seized me by the throat as if to strangle me ...'(138). Whether one goes willingly to God or he seeks one out, the result would seem to be the same.

Ahasverus, also one of the 'desert' people singled out by God, hopes the Sibyl can give him some advice, but she can only emphasize that 'human beings ... can never escape the curse and the blessing which come to them from God. Whatever they think or do, whatever they believe or don't believe their fate will always be bound by God'. (220).

Ahasverus had simply not recognized God when he entered his life, and had tried to refuse Christ permission to lean against his house. The result leads us back to two poems in *Aftonland*: 'Who went past my childhood window ... Left me deserted for ever' (46) and 'Open your house to me'. Having tried to deny God, Ahasverus is doomed to an eternity of sterile isolation. He has to abandon his home and his family and live in the desert like an outcast.(66).

On his long pilgrimage Ahasverus observes many different approaches to God, but in *Ahasverus död* (1960) it is the behaviour of Tobias and Diana, that helps him ultimately to die. Tobias found an emaciated woman bearing the stigmata of the crucifixion who had died entirely alone and is prepared to undertake the pilgrimage for unselfish reasons, a break in the isolation of Lagerkvistian wanderers. Diana

Chapter VI

seeks the Holy Land because she loves Tobias, and when God visits them, symbolized by the arrow ('Spjutet är kastat' (The spear is cast)), she willingly sacrifices herself to save Tobias. These two unselfish actions help to penetrate the wall of isolation and sterility around Ahasverus. He can see that the crucifixion is imposed upon us by a cruel vindictive force which he now recognizes as a false god. Beyond this force 'there must be something which for us is inaccessible'.(89).[19] The 'inaccessible' is a well where he will quench his 'raging thirst for what I cannot comprehend but know exists'. We have come full circle, for Ahasverus has acknowledged he cannot fathom the mystery, has ceased to search for an explanation of the god, and 'understands'. His peace of mind is restored and he is able to die.

Tobias continues his pilgrimage in *Pilgrim på havet* (Pilgrim at Sea, 1962) and *Det heliga landet* (The Holy Land, 1962). In the former Giovanni tempts him to abandon himself to the sea, 'and not to worry about anything at all, justice or injustice, sin and guilt, truth and falsehood and evil salvation and grace and eternal damnation, the devil and God and their silly disputes with each other' (19)[20] — in other words without the thought of God. Giovanni accepts this kind of existence, having found his earlier life void of true love, a fact symbolized by an empty medallion. Tobias cannot accept Giovanni's attitude to either symbol. Having been visited by the thought of God he must continue his wanderings, while the medallion symbolizes its previous owner's great longing for love and so carries the power of love, even if empty.

In *Det heliga landet* Tobias and Giovanni arrive in a barren land free from the doctrines and observances of religion, yet even here Tobias digs up 'a god who lay with his scornful smile turned down towards the earth' (41)[21]; here too the simple shepherds worship a child and in times of trouble sacrifice a lamb and examine the entrails of birds. Man has, apparently, an atavistic tendency to search for God, even though God is scornful and indifferent.

In the final part of the Pilgrim cycle, however, the God is assuaged by the power of love. As Tobias wanders through 'Aftonland' he encounters the woman he had loved and betrayed. In a dream-like sequence she is identified with the madonna, with human suffering and forbearance. In her Tobias finds forgiveness, gentleness and perfect human love. When she hangs the empty locket on her own breast 'it began to beam like a most splendid jewel'.(99). For simple, unquestioning souls the thought of God can be happily endured by humble acceptance, as we see throughout Lagerkvist's works (Pettersson, the W.C. attendant, the Sibyl's parents, etc.). The people who want to fathom 'the point of life' are likely to die as burnt out cases unless like Tobias they can find and acknowledge perfect love.

Lagerkvist's final work, *Mariamne* (1967) presents in Herod yet another 'desert' man, a man of primitive urges who finds no peace of mind. Mariamne represents human goodness and bears a divine quality. She influences Herod and for a time he becomes milder, but even she cannot penetrate permanently his wall of isolation and selfishness. The conflict between good and evil seems unresolved, for although Herod causes Mariamne's death and reverts to his primitive life he can never free himself from her memory or his desire for her.

An examination of the symbols in the novel points, however, to a resolution not unrelated to *Det heliga landet*. Mariamne fills the role of *mater dolorosa* through whose suffering goodness is born into the world. After her death three wise men from the desert land follow a star (recognisable Lagerkvist symbols!), reach Herod and announce the birth of 'a royal child ... who shall become lord of the whole world'.(108).[22] They bear three gifts, a pebble, a thistle shaped like a royal sceptre and a jar containing water from a miraculous spring in the desert. The pebble is explained in *Den befriade människan* (Liberated man, 1939), where man imprisoned within his own egocentricity, gazes on a pebble which is a symbol of the great life outside the prison walls. The gift is thus an aid to help Man escape from his own selfishness. The thistle has sprung up through the desert sand, a sign of the great potential even in 'desert' man, The miraculous spring is the well Ahasverus referred to on his death bed. Thanks, perhaps, to the goodness of Mariamne the time is ripe for the symbol of human love to be born while Herod's race, whose souls are deserts 'shall be obliterated from the earth'. *Mariamne* is in many ways a desolate work, for a strong air of evil emanates from the powerful figure of Herod. And yet, if one interprets the symbols, it would seem that ultimately Lagerkvist believed in the future of Man.[23]

In 1945 Lagerkvist prepared a draft of a 'conversation on his conception of Man, his view of things in these disturbed times':

The writer's message? The writer's faith? The meaning of my works? I am what I was in our youth. My messages are the same and my faith. But one book answers another. I carry on a constant dialogue with myself ...[24]

Chapter VI

At an early stage Lagerkvist indicated the poles at the extreme limits of his world: a total acceptance and a total rejection of life; an assertion that there is no point to our existence and a humanistic belief in Man's progress towards a divine existence; a projection of Man as an insignificant mortal and Man the possessor of a divine spark; Man eternally bearing within him elements of evil and of pure goodness. Throughout his long career he adopted a position now at one, now at the other extreme. He was able moreover to take his reader with him, for his theme is always some aspect of Man's situation, of the human condition, a universal theme that concerns us all.

Like all great authors he has created his own recognisable fictional world. By means of his compulsive story-telling gifts he has led his readers into that world and forced them to ponder over essential human issues. His greatest strength lies in his ability to embody his ideas in palpable, almost sculptural figures who remain in our minds and take us back repeatedly to the question of good and evil, life and death, the material and the spiritual world. Long after the details, and admittedly the inconsistencies, of his metaphysical arguments have faded, we remember clearly such characters as the Executioner, moving in his superhuman suffering; the Dwarf, frightening in the intensity of his hatred and destructive urges; the Sibyl, a human who has known God; and Barabbas, perhaps the most successful of all as a symbol of modern Man searching for a faith in an alien world.

Chapter VII

Swedish Poetry of the Twentieth Century

Peter Graves, Brita Green, Phil Holmes, C.J.Lawton, Gavin Orton, Karin Petherick, Steven P. Sondrup and Laurie Thompson.

Introduction
by Gavin Orton

One comprehensive anthology of twentieth-century Swedish and Finland-Swedish poetry, Tom Hedlund's *Den svenska lyriken från Ekelund till Sonnevi* (The Swedish Lyric from Ekelund to Sonnevi, 1978), contains the works of 194 poets. In the face of such overwhelming material, this chapter concentrates on a mere handful of the more interesting poets in Sweden this century: Birger Sjöberg, Hjalmar Gullberg, Karin Boye, Harry Martinson, Gunnar Ekelöf, Erik Lindegren, Karl Vennberg, and Tomas Tranströmer. Two sections look at poetry since the 1960s. Some other poets are considered briefly in this introduction, while Bo Bergman and Pär Lagerkvist are discussed in other chapters.

The development of twentieth-century poetry in Sweden can be followed through a number of 'isms', of which the most important are Symbolism, Expressionism, and Surrealism. All three can be summed up as aspects of Modernism — a desire to experiment with a whole range of new literary techniques in an attempt to reflect an increasingly complex and confused view of man's mind and soul.

Symbolism originated in France, owing a considerable debt to the works of Baudelaire. Writers in the Symbolist tradition are interested primarily in the subtleties of human emotions and sensations (often of a

Chapter VII

decadent nature) and seek poetic symbols and images to project these states of mind. Often they use landscape as symbol: sometimes the landscape exists both as landscape and 'soulscape', while sometimes the landscape is purely a projection of the soul and lacks geographical reality.[1] Perhaps the most successful Swedish Symbolist is Vilhelm Ekelund (1880-1949), who published his first collection of poetry in 1900. Ekelund came from Skåne, and his poetry contains beautiful descriptions of Skåne landscapes that at the same time reflect his melancholy temperament and sense of alienation in the world. For example, in the poem 'Då var bokarna ljusa' (The Beech Trees were Light Then) — in the collection *Melodier i skymning* (Melodies at Twilight, 1902) — the light beech trees stand for the happiness of the poet's lost childhood while now a different and gloomier landscape expresses his aimless adulthood:

> Tyst det regnar. Himlen hänger lågt på
> glesa kronor. En vissling: tåget sätter
> åter i gång. Mot sakta mörknande kväll jag
> färdas vänlös.

(Silently it rains. The sky hangs low on sparse treetops. A whistle; the train sets off again. I journey friendless towards a slowly darkening evening).

A more recent poet using Symbolist techniques is Tomas Tranströmer, discussed below.

The rather dreamy emotional states of Symbolism were shortly overtaken by the more violent visions of Expressionism. Expressionism, originating in Germany, is a form of literature that gives direct and immediate expression to man's emotions, generally in highly dynamic and energetic language. Expressionism occurred as a conscious revolt against Naturalism: the Expressionist sees the world not realistically and scientifically, but emotionally and irrationally. Instead of analysing human experiences in terms of inheritance, environment and circumstance, the Expressionist portrays timeless universal emotion. His characters are not individuals but representatives, often without personal names. The most celebrated exponent of Expressionism in Sweden is Pär Lagerkvist: in his famous poem 'Ångest' (Anguish) he expresses violent anguish in a thoroughly stylized and unrealistic landscape. Another notable poet, Birger Sjöberg (discussed below), moved from idyllic scenes of small-town life in his early works to apocalyptic visions in an Expressionist style in his collection *Kriser och kransar* (Crises and Wreaths, 1926). His use of a seascape in 'Vid mörka stränder' (By Dark Shores) provides a good example:

> Hav, som slår i kalla styrkan
> dånar mer än psalm i kyrkan,
> klämtar lik en klocka i brand eller nöd.
> Går till svarta nattkravaller,
> spränges, splittras, sönderfaller,
> stormar fram som hop vid ett anskri om bröd.

(Sea, which beats in cold strength, thunders more than a hymn in church, tolls like a bell for fire or distress. Goes to black night-riots, is burst, is split, falls apart, storms forward like a mob crying out for bread).

Most influential of the 'isms' in Sweden was Surrealism, a movement that is generally considered to have begun with the French author André Breton in 1924. The Surrealist writer, influenced by the theories of psychoanalysis, tries to penetrate into the deeper reality of the subconscious, beneath the logic of everyday thought and language. He seeks this deeper reality in dreams, in visions, in the flow of images not obviously connected with one another — in the most extreme cases in 'automatic writing', material written down on the page exactly as it springs from the subconscious, without any logical or aesthetic control. The nature of Surrealism is probably best observed in the visual arts; for example in the works of Salvador Dali, where a multitude of disparate images are presented on one canvas. Surrealism had the effect of liberating the imaginations of poets and providing them with a greater freedom of expression, but its disadvantage was that the unorganized flow of ideas held together only by the poet's private world of associations and allusions could be completely incomprehensible to anyone else — perhaps, in the case of automatic writing, even to the poet himself. Consequently, accusations of incomprehensibility against Surrealist poets are frequent, Lindegren's *mannen utan väg* (the man without a way), discussed below, being a case in point.

The two pioneers of Surrealism in Sweden were Gunnar Ekelöf (discussed below) and Artur Lundkvist (1906-1991). Artur Lundkvist was a writer and critic of extraordinary energy, whose name occurs in several important contexts. His first notable achievement was to focus attention on Harry Martinson when he produced his anthology of young poets *Fem unga* (Five Young Men) in 1929. Later he encouraged Erik Lindegren with *mannen utan väg*, and as a critic he was responsible for introducing many foreign writers, particularly from the Americas, to the Swedish public. Lundkvist saw life as a process of continuous movement and change, and his poems and novels reflect this restless vitality. Surrealism was one of the many stages on his literary way and is most developed in his collections *Nattens broar* (The Bridges of Night, 1936) and *Sirénsång* (Siren Song, 1937).

Swedish Modernism came into its own in the 1940s: from being a process of experimentation by a few *avant-garde* figures, the Modernist style became the norm. No doubt this process was assisted by the Second World War, which led in Sweden to a sense of pessimism and failure and to apocalyptic visions best expressed in fragmented and violent forms. The two leaders of *40-talet* (The 40s) in Sweden were Erik Lindegren and Karl Vennberg (both discussed in more detail below). Although they were two different types, their greater age (they were about ten years older than most of the *40-talister*) and their superior achievements made them into natural authorities, commanding the respect and admiration of the younger generation. Among the most significant of their many disciples and imitators, who emerged as fine poets in their own right, are Werner Aspenström (1919-97), Ragnar Thoursie (born 1919) and Sven Alfons (born 1918).

Some older poets, more traditional in their styles, were encouraged by the success of the younger generation to attempt more Modernist methods — to some extent Hjalmar Gullberg (discussed below), and even more so Johannes Edfelt (1904-97) and Bertil Malmberg (1889-1958). The typical features of Modernist verse as it predominated in the 1940s have been summarized as follows:

(1) A lack of formal structure, such as rhyme, metre, or division into stanzas, and its replacement by other unifying devices, such as repetition of key words or phrases, or a musical structure, or even a typographical structure;

(2) compression, which might be by omission of words (ellipsis), or short-cuts in syntax, or, in a different sense, by making words carry a great weight of meaning and associations;

(3) free associations of images, as in Surrealism.[2]

The Modernist movement continues in the 1950s with writers like Östen Sjöstrand (born 1925) and Lars Forssell (born 1928). Sjöstrand's first volume of poetry, *Unio*, appeared in 1949 and was followed by a number of books in the 1950s, but his best work came later, with such collections as *I vattumannens tecken* (In the Sign of Aquarius, 1967) and *På återvägen från Jasna Góra* (On the Return from Jasna Góra, 1984). His deeply felt religious commitment (he is a convert to Roman Catholicism) is coupled with an awareness of the problems of language — full of ironies and ambiguities, and yet a meeting place where human beings transcend their personal limitations and their isolation and can create a more human, less materialistic world. Sjöstrand's sophisticated poetry has received international recognition, though his readership is probably not large.[3] Lars Forssell is a much more accessible poet, with a wide range of styles, from popular songs to thoroughly intellectual poems about the dancer Nijinsky.

A reaction to Modernism occurs in the politically conscious 1960s, when writers like Göran Palm attack Modernism for being too exclusive and inaccessible to the reading masses. Palm is associated with a style called 'nyenkel' (neo-simple), as in his famous poem 'Havet' (The Sea): 'Jag står framför havet./ Där är det./ Det är havet./ Jag tittar på det./ Havet. Jaha./ Det är som på Louvren.' (I stand in front of the sea. There it is. There's the sea. I look at it. The sea. Well. It's like in the Louvre). On the other hand, other writers of the 60s went in for ultra-Modernist effects, with their Concrete poetry and their Happenings. Poetry since the 1970s sees no startling stylistic innovations, but an interesting sociological change is the number of women poets who make their mark.

The small Swedish-speaking community in Finland saw the establishment of a strong Modernist movement relatively early — perhaps because of the unstable political climate in Finland generally and the anomalous position of the Swedish-speaking community in particular.[4] The two pioneering poets of the movement were Edith Södergran and Elmer Diktonius. They were followed by Gunnar Björling and Rabbe Enckell, and the movement's domination of Finland-Swedish poetry was not seriously challenged until the 1960s.[5]

Edith Södergran (1892-1923) was brought up partly in the cosmopolitan atmosphere of the Russian capital, St Petersburg, and partly in the Finnish countryside of southern Karelia. She contracted tuberculosis in 1908, and her short life was lived in the shadow of death, a shadow darkened further by the disasters of the Bolshevik takeover in Russia and the Civil War in Finland. Her first collection of poetry, *Dikter* (Poems, 1916), was partly in the Symbolist style: it seemed daringly modern to the conservative literary world of Swedish-speaking Finland. Her following collections, such as *Septemberlyran* (September Lyre, 1918), are wilder and more ecstatic in the style of Expressionism. The poet feels herself to be a stranger and prisoner in the world and can only realize her full potential in a cosmic setting. Her last poetry, however, published posthumously in *Landet som icke är* (The Land Which Is Not, 1925), is in a quieter vein, as in the celebrated title poem where she dreams of the non-existent country where we cool our harrowed brow in the dew of the moon.

Elmer Diktonius (1896-1961) was ultra-radical in both politics and literature. In *Min dikt* (My Poem, 1921) and *Hårda sånger* (Hard Songs, 1922), he shows himself to be a Modernist in his use of free verse, free syntax, and dramatic imagery. He is more violent and explosive than Edith Södergran, though the emotion is often contained in a very compressed form. His poem 'Jaguaren' (The Jaguar) from *Hårda sånger* is a well-known example of his style:

> Ur gröna blad sticker fram
> röd nos
> ögon med
> trekantiga blickar
> spräckligt;
> morrhår vågrörelse
> klotass — du flyger ju! mitt hjärtas jaguar —
> så flyg och bit och riv och söndersarga!
> Din — min moral: att slå.

(From green leaves a red snout sticks forth eyes with triangular glances speckled: whiskers wave-movement claw-paw — you fly — my heart's jaguar — so fly and bite and tear and lacerate! Your — my morality: to strike).

There is, though, a quieter side to Diktonius, and he uses his Modernist style to equal effect in idyllic nature poems. Gunnar Björling (1887-1960) is also a master of the brief creation of scenes and impressions from nature, but he is more revolutionary in style than Diktonius, and his complete disregard for syntax can make his poetry difficult to understand. The early poetry of Rabbe Enckell (1903-74) — for example in *Flöjtblåsarlycka* (Fluteplayer's Happiness, 1925) — consists of delicate nature lyrics in a free-verse form, while in his later poems he is much occupied with themes from Classical mythology, and with Classical attitudes.

Not all poets in Sweden in the twentieth century write in a Modernist way. Of particular interest is the strong continuance of the old tradition of the troubadour, associated with such writers as Lasse Lucidor in the seventeenth century and Bellman in the eighteenth. In some cases the troubadour writes both lyrics and music and performs his own songs, like Birger Sjöberg and the immensely popular Evert Taube (1890-1976), with his songs about seamen and exotic ports of call or the more native delights of Bohuslän and Roslagen. In other cases authors' poems are set to music and performed by singers drawn by the inherent musicality of the verse, as with Fröding and Karlfeldt of the *90-talister*, or more recently with Dan Andersson (1888-1920) and Nils Ferlin (1898-1961). Dan Andersson writes about charcoal-burners in the wilds of western Sweden in *Kolvaktarens visor* (The Charcoal-Burner's Songs, 1915) or the poor and oppressed in general in *Svarta ballader* (Black Ballads, 1917). Ferlin also takes the side of the underprivileged, in such collections as *Barfotabarn* (Barefooted Child, 1933) and *Goggles* (1938). Ferlin's traditionally composed verse is musical and playful but his message is of the loneliness and meaninglessness of life.

Birger Sjöberg (1885-1929)

by C. J. Lawton

Birger Sjöberg was born in Vänersborg, where his father had set up a small hardware business. Sjöberg's formal education ended abruptly at the age of 14, when he left school with a wretched set of reports, in which the main complaints were of inattention and lack of application. His failure as a scholar was to haunt him deeply throughout his life, as is revealed in frequent academic allusions in his works. Already in his early teens, Sjöberg was developing his natural talents for verse, mimicry and humour, to entertain his friends. There is no doubt that he deliberately cultivated this role of buffoon and jester to compensate for his own feelings of social and academic inadequacy.

The years up to his final departure from Vänersborg in 1906 provided the background and basis for the best known and most extensive of Sjöberg's writings, the Frida songs. During these years, his occupation of shop assistant gave him ample opportunity to study the

Chapter VII

figures and conventions of the small town. And during these years, too, grew his shy love for the dark-eyed Karin Lustine, which, unrequited, was transferred to the manuscript page as the romance between the unnamed shop assistant of the songs and his Frida.

Through his elder brother, Gösta, Birger Sjöberg gained a position with *Stockholms Dagblad*, where, despite his lack of qualifications, his observant, witty articles on the daily life of Stockholm caught the eye of a newspaper magnate from Skåne, John Christensén; in 1907 Sjöberg became a sub-editor of his *Helsingborgs-posten* in Hälsingborg, where he was to spend the remainder of his career as a journalist. In Hälsingborg, he acquired a reputation as an entertainer in his circle of friends, one of whom in particular, the author Ernst Norlind, recognized the literary merit of the lyrics and persuaded Sjöberg to consider publication.

His first book, *Fridas bok* (Frida's Book, 1922), was met with an initially hesitant, although favourable critical response, which gradually swelled to a roar of public acclaim. His first public performance of the songs, when he accompanied himself — as always — on the guitar, was at Lund University in February 1923. There followed two exhausting tours of Sweden performing *Fridas visor* (Frida's Songs), which took their toll of Sjöberg's nerves and caused him to examine the nature of his success, which he increasingly felt to be undeserved in that he had used his artistic ability to create a false front, concealing his real nature and beliefs. During 1923 and 1924, he worked feverishly at a continuation to *Fridas bok*, moving closer to the contemporary time, and including the First World War and the economic depression, in which the idyll of Lilla Paris (Vänersborg) is first cracked and finally destroyed. The plan was never completed, although much of the anecdotal material was used in the novel *Kvartetten som sprängdes* (The Quartet That Split Up), published in 1924.

The success of the novel brought him financial independence, but the solitude of an author's life increased his introspection and caused him to react bitterly to what he now regarded as the cheap fame of his literary success. For two years he struggled with deeply personal thoughts about the nature of life and death, of the integrity of the artist and the meaning of life, but made progress only when economic exigency forced him to produce a manuscript for Bonniers in November 1926. This slim volume of poems, *Kriser och kransar* (Crises and Wreaths), was met with incomprehension by many critics, who then covered their confusion with accusations that the poems were ill-constructed, garbled, even containing signs of insanity. This reception destroyed Sjöberg's confidence almost totally, and the last years of his life were filled with half-finished plans for novels and poetry collections written amidst increasing isolation, poverty and illness. The only completed manuscript during this time, *Vidundrets röst* (The Voice of the Monster), a bitter, symbolic examination of his own authorship, was rightly rejected as unsuitable by Bonniers in November 1928. He died just five months later, on 30 April 1929, in a hotel room in Växjö.

Apart from his newspaper articles and a number of separate poems and stories, Sjöberg published three works during his life: *Fridas bok, Kvartetten som sprängdes*, and *Kriser och kranser* (1926). In addition, the following posthumous collections have been published: *Fridas andra bok* (Frida's Second Book, 1929), (edited by Gösta Sjöberg); *Minnen från jorden* (Memories from Earth, 1940), (edited by August Peterson); *Syntaxupproret* (Syntax Rebellion, 2nd ed., 1965), (edited by Staffan Larsson); *Fridas tredje bok* (Frida's Third Book, 2nd ed. 1971), (edited by Staffan Larsson).[6]

Fridas bok is one of the best known collections of poetry in the Swedish language. The songs Sjöberg performed (but regrettably never recorded) from *Fridas bok* and *Fridas andra bok*, are as widely performed and recorded as those of Bellman, Taube and Ferlin, and still very popular. The music and words are closely connected and best studied as an entity; in many cases it is clear from Sjöberg's manuscripts that the tune grew with the poem, for even early sketches clearly display the verbal rhythm of the final product.

Sjöberg composed thousands of poems and plans about his idealized heroine, Frida, and her milieu, between 1910 and 1925. His unsuccessful proposal to Karin Lustine caused him to channel his erotic energy into the creation of a dream figure in a world unsullied by personal rejection. The perfection of this fiction took years of refinement into a style characterized by the naivistic portrayal of nature, the slightly ridiculous, down-to-earth tone and formal mode of address of Frida's friends, the mixture of colloquial, poetic and academic language, at once comic and endearing, and the ironic distancing of subject from author. These general features of the Frida songs, described more thoroughly by Gunvor Edstam,[7] can be seen well in the first three songs, 'Den första gång' (The First Time), 'Lilla Paris' (Little Paris) and 'Samtal om Universum' (Conversation about the

Chapter VII

Universe). Particular features worthy of note are the frequency of adjectives and nouns describing light, the conversational tone — which prevails in all Sjöberg's writing — and the use of wind, water and light changes to give movement even to descriptive scenes.

Yet for those who seek it, the turmoil and doubts of Sjöberg's later poetry are already discernible in *Fridas bok*. The Parisian visions of revenge and revolution in the last two stanzas of 'Lilla Paris' are a little too vivid to be entirely humorous. Cosmic thoughts sometimes threaten to break the everyday tone, while twice, in 'Svartsjukans demon' (The Demon of Jealousy) and 'Beskrivning över Näckens rosor och vattnet' (Description of the Sprite's Roses and the Water), water is used as a symbol of a calm exterior concealing frightening depths.

Nevertheless, overall the atmosphere persists of a town in which the most dramatic events are trivial, and nature is kindly. Most of the scenes are set in holiday or free time — further evidence of the distancing with which Sjöberg protected himself from reality.

Fridas andra bok consists mainly of songs performed by Sjöberg but not published in the first collection, while *Fridas tredje bok* is a much later collection from the archives in which a number of poems are from the planned continuations to the Lilla Paris fiction.

In the novel *Kvartetten som sprängdes*, sheer quantity of anecdotal material and characters threatens to break apart the careful structure. The unity of the novel is provided by the milieu — a Swedish town of the 1920s which owes not a little to Hälsingborg — in which the pursuit of wealth and happiness is threatened by the greed of speculation and the spectre of economic collapse. Close inter-relationships of character, and plots intricately interwoven with sub-plots hold the various threads together, while the whole structure is reinforced with leitmotifs, starting with the very first words of the book: 'The A-string on the cello broke'. The broken string forebodes much: the splitting up of the quartet, the abandonment of the pursuit of art in favour of the pursuit of wealth, the lost fortunes when the stock market crashes. Especially important are the roles of 'Blamageguden' (The God of Disgrace) or 'Kontrollanten' (The Controller), the other selves which expose poor Cello mercilessly to himself, and of Stoltz and Backlund, the social parasites who are present at every disaster. Apart from lack of structure, *Kvartetten* is most often criticized for lack of social insight. It is present, but in a form compatible with the tone and subject of the novel. Sjöberg was an artist, not a politician, and as such confines his social comment to exposure of those vices and evils which reveal themselves in the course of the narrative: the cold pragmatism of Planertz, the snobbery of Fru Åvik, the sloth of Stoltz and Backlund, and the foolish pursuit of cheap gain by speculation which nearly ruins many central characters.

More important than the social content of the novel is the development of Sjöberg's ideas on love, life and death. Cello's friend, Pensionatskurken, concludes that life is its own reward, as does Karl Ludwig: 'The earth is a good place to be on' (122, Delfin ed). Thus concludes also the retired Grosshandlare Borg, who seeks knowledge of all kinds, but most of all whether he will ever rejoin his beloved dead wife Elisabet. 'No, I shall never meet her again' (507), he decides, but in a final scene full of sunshine and the colours of autumn, his little granddaughter of the same name comes to him, fulfilling nature's circle and promising a form of eternity.

Kriser och kransar is Sjöberg's slimmest, yet most complex and rewarding work. The poems reflect the intensely personal war he had been waging since the publication of *Kvartetten* with his own artistic integrity, with the contradictory faces of deceit and exploitation on one side, but on the other hope and growth, which life presents. The book is best studied in the three sections into which it is divided. In the first the poet realizes that popularity is not the yard-stick of artistic integrity. In 'Orons eldmetoder' (Anxiety's Fiery Methods) artistic creation is portrayed as an intensely painful process, like birth itself, but:

> Lidit har hon gruvligt.
> Se dock vilket ljuvligt
> blomstrande barn!

(She has suffered dreadfully. Yet see what a sweet and blossoming child!).

In 'Statyernas samkväm' (The Statues' Meeting), Sjöberg then lampoons the stifling effect of social convention on individuality, and at the end of this section, in 'I ditt allvars famn' (In the Embrace of Your Earnestness), overcomes his fear of solitude, abandoning social existence for a more spiritual life:

> Svarta gruvan, alstrar, skyddar, gömmer
> sällsam sten med klar och ädel hy.
> Mullen, tung och mörk, om blomman drömmer.
> Dröm blir blod och blod blir blomstersky.

Chapter VII

(The black mine begets, protects, hides strange stone of clear and noble hue. The soil, heavy and dark, dreams of the flower. Dream becomes blood and blood becomes a cloud of flowers).

The central section of *Kriser och kransar* moves from the earthly to the cosmic, starting with a review of social problems coloured by Sjöberg's journalistic experience. The themes are of corruption and speculation, old age and insanity but the underlying concern is with the incompatibility between the structure of society and the desires and needs of the individual. The central poem, 'Konferensman' (Conference Man), is one of the major poems of Swedish literature. The background is the World Ecumenical Congress of August 1925 in Stockholm, and as Tideström points out, many of the opening stanzas can be traced to the news columns of that month.[8] The concerns of the delegates function increasingly as a satirical contrast to the problems of the Conference Man who, during an inner crisis, reviews most of the metaphysical problems with which Sjöberg was grappling. The conclusion seems to be that it is the *yearning* for transcendental life which brings inner, spiritual freedom, not its *achievement*. The same conclusion is reached in a series of poems in which the poet faces the bonds placed by earthly life upon his spirit, the fear of infinity and of death itself. Death is accepted as an ally, not as a threat, to the soul.

In the final part of *Kriser och kransar*, the theme 'School of life' dominates, reflecting the importance of Sjöberg's educational failures as a boy. The young man, full of hopes and illusions, approaches the town of life and in the following poems is roughly robbed of innocence by life, but at the same time enriched and strengthened by experience, until a state of spiritual bliss is attained in 'Avresa' (Departure).

The language and structure of *Kriser och kransar* is always difficult. Sjöberg had found the courage to abandon all pretence and convention and use the whole range of vocabulary and experience available to him, to give the greatest possible intensity and expressiveness to his work. The result is unusual juxtapositions of the trivial and the sublime, the romantic and the technical. A consistent pattern of imagery — especially of colours — and richness of allusion binds the poems into a complete work.

Sjöberg left a vast quantity of unpublished writing which is largely collected in the archives of Gothenburg University Library. Two collections of 'non-Frida' poems have been published from these archives, *Minnen från jorden,* and Staffan Larsson's controversial

Syntaxupproret. For an understanding of Sjöberg's poetic method, the second section of *Syntaxupproret* should be read in conjunction with Barbro Ohlson's fine essay 'Rörelse och samtalston' (Movement and Conversational Tone),[9] while many of the poems of the fourth section are of the simpler, more lyrical style adopted by Sjöberg in the last months of his life.

Hjalmar Gullberg (1898-1961)

by Karin Petherick

Gullberg was born the illegitimate child of a couple who, although they subsequently married, placed him with foster-parents and never themselves gave him a home or acknowledged his parentage. Their son's resultant sense of rejection and incomplete identity would seem to provide a key to the poet's early preoccupation with belonging to an invisible fellowship and with having an unseen mentor and principal (God). His foster-parents were kindly but could not prevent the boy's awareness of his anomalous position — he was an occasional guest in his real parents' home, but was treated as a stranger there. This was the difficult beginning of a life which was to bring him success as a poet, membership of the Swedish Academy, distinction as a translator of verse, and directorship of Swedish Radio Drama for some years. The last decade of his life brought him a woman to love and trust, but also appalling suffering in the form of a creeping paralysis which attacked his lungs and limbs. During the final years of his life he spent long periods in a respirator, paralysed, tracheotomied, unable to speak. It is one of the most astonishing and moving examples of the human spirit triumphant that the mortally sick Gullberg yet managed laboriously to write poems on scraps of paper, poems which were then copied out and read back to him by his constant companion for further re-working. He rallied on three occasions and was allowed out of hospital. When it became clear that he was doomed to a slow death by choking, he took farewell by driving his wheelchair down into a nearby lake.

Gullberg's work falls into two parts, chronologically and stylistically speaking. The first period goes up to the early 1940s and is then followed by several years of silence. The second period, marked by a switch to more complex language and imagery, begins in 1952. His first six collections were entitled *I en främmande stad* (In a Strange

City, 1927), *Sonat* (Sonata, 1929), *Andliga övningar* (Spiritual Exercises, 1932), *Kärlek i tjugonde seklet* (Love in the Twentieth Century, 1933), *Ensamstående bildad herre* (Gentleman, Single, Refined, 1935), and *Att övervinna världen* (To Overcome the World, 1937). He published a selection from them under the title *Hundra dikter* (A Hundred Poems, 1939), which still provides the best introduction to his work.[10] In *Fem kornbröd och två fiskar* (Five Loaves and Two Fishes, 1942), his concern was to encourage and strengthen resistance to the powers of tyranny during the darkest hours of the war. His prewar poems show a pre-occupation with the poet's *vocation*, with the vicariously suffering Christ, with the mystical experience of union with the divine, and with bitter-sweet human love, expressed in varying proportions of wit, sincerity, scepticism and irony. Gullberg's presentation of spiritual matters is often juxtaposed with the highly profane and enlivened by agile rhymes. (It cannot be over-emphasized that Gullberg wrote predominantly rhymed and always strictly metered verse, and that these formal properties are essentially characteristic of him. Only a translator of exceptional gifts can convey the flavour of the original, and I have the good fortune occasionally to be able to quote Gullberg translations by Judy Moffett;[11] failing this resource, a literal translation is offered, but the reader is begged to bear in mind that the character of the original has thereby been lost). Gullberg lets Christ in 'Drömd visit' (A Dreamed Visit) drop in on the poet and hang his crown of thorns on the hat-rack:

> Du hänger din törnekrona
> i kapprummet på en spik.
> I fjärran hörs ekot förtona
> av dagens bråda trafik. (100:22)[12]

(You hang your crown of thorns on a nail in the hall. The echo dies away in the distance of the day's bustling traffic).

The poem ends with Christ taking his host's burdens upon him.

In 'Kallelsen' (The Calling) the poet is summoned by an unseen but omnipotent principal just as summarily and unequivocally as ever the disciples were directed to abandon their nets:

> Jag svänger de klockor du hör i din själ.
> Så lämna ditt hus. Gör avskedet kort!

> Jag tar över dig för all framtid befäl.
> Jag kallar dig bort. (100:7)

(I swing the bells you hear in your soul. So leave your house. Cut short your farewell! I am taking command of you for all time. I call you away.)

Gullberg's non-confessional relationship with the divine found nourishment in sources as diverse as the Spanish mystic St John of the Cross (whom he translated), the Indian religious poems Bhagavad-ghita and Thomas a Kempis's *De imitatione Christi*. He repeatedly expresses a mystical sense of oneness with God, the dissolution of opposites and the union of disparate elements.[13] In 'Den utvalda' (The Chosen One) it is hard to tell if the beloved is divine or mortal in the poem's Indian setting:

> motsatsers enhet, skepp och ankargrund,
> orkan i skog och stjärna över hav —
> o Evighet som skiftar var sekund
> du är min vagga och du är min grav! (100:77)

(union of opposites, vessel and anchorage, gale in the forest and star over sea — O Eternity which changes every second you are my cradle and you are my grave!)

The poem 'Kärleksroman' (Love Story) opens with modern diction and fashionably simplistic mores:

> Att gifta sig! Man är väl inte dum.
> Vi ämnar ha vår frihet i behåll.
> Du stannar hos din man. Jag har mitt rum.
> Vår enda lag är födelsekontroll. (100:84)

(Get married! One's not such a fool. We mean to keep our freedom all intact. Stay with your husband while I keep my room. Our only law is: birth control.)

Yet the final verse apostrophizes the sea, birthplace of Venus, and sings of love of a very different order:

> Eviga källa, ur vars bottenflöden
> gudinnan lyftes på en snäckas skal,
> du sjöng för mig om kärlek intill döden!

Chapter VII

> Än brusar i min själ din blå koral.(100:88)

(Eternal spring from out whose nether waters raised was the goddess on an aqueous shell, you sang for me of loving unto death! Still echoes in my soul your blue chorale.)

Gullberg grew up in Malmö and studied in Lund as both undergraduate and postgraduate. His virtuosity at rhyming and word-play was encouraged in an academic environment with a long-standing tradition of poetic and musical parodies and travesties (so-called *studentspex*). He was a witty and urbane classical scholar, deeply concerned with eternal verities. The poem 'Bedragaren' (The Impostor) shows us a gentleman at a dinner party, adept at the social graces, who suddenly hears a violin in his heart and absents himself from the company's midst, although still corporeally present. It is all over in a minute:

> Han, en sällskapslivets mannekäng,
> återfår sin röst, men tiger stolt
> om en gömd fiol, där sträng vid sträng
> svänger mellan andakt och revolt. (100:56)

(He, a mannequin of social life, regains his voice, but proudly says nothing of a hidden violin, which string by string ranges from devotion to revolt.)

The antithetical attitudes devotion and revolt are both characteristic of Gullberg: his deep respect for spiritual values was spiced by a sharp, sceptical intelligence.

Gullberg — like Birger Sjöberg — often uses linguistic stereotypes from a non-poetic sphere; typical examples are found in 'Efterlyses' (Wanted) based on a standard Wanted Person's description but in essence being the poet advertising the loss of his own childhood faith, and in 'Kontrakt' (Contract), a purported binding agreement between eternity and the poet as its terrestrial representative, is couched in a skilful pastiche of legal terminology.

A particularly famous Gullberg poem is 'Hänryckning' (word-play on ecstasy and the term *ryckas hän*, literally to be snatched hence). Its metaphor for death is the lady and gentleman being relieved by the cloakroom attendant not of their hats and coats as they arrive for the dance, but of their five senses:

> Medan i fem fack han lägger undan
> ögon, öron, tunga, näsa, hud,
> står vår själ i andakt och begrundan.
> Stjärnor brinner i den blå rotundan,
> där vi äntligen skall möta Gud. (100:78)

(While he puts away in five compartments eyes, ears, tongue, nose, skin, our soul stands in devotion and reflection. Stars are burning in the blue rotunda, where at last we shall be meeting God.)

Swedish readers smiled in recognition at the apotheosis of the blue starspangled dome of the Academic Union building in Lund.

Ironic humour against a Lund background gives the collection *Ensamstående bildad herre* its appeal.[14] The title is a familiar signature in the Personal Columns of the press, but is here used to characterize the unheroic schoolmaster Örtstedt, Gullberg's tragi-comic alter ego, idealistic, and unworldly. Örtstedt falls asleep while reading Kant, and dreams that a parcel is delivered to him from Königsberg. On examination the sender proves to be no less a person than Professor K. himself, and the contents DAS DING AN SICH!

> Vem törs dock rycka undan slöjan kring
> den rena verkligheten, tingens ting?
>
> Adjunkten Örtstedt ryggar bort bestört
> från det som ingen sett och ingen rört.
>
> Om gåvan i hans grova händer sprack!
> - Han returnerar den med tusen tack! (100:126)

(Who'd dare to rip the giftwrap and the strings / off pure Reality, the Thing of things?/ Professor Örtstedt backs away unnerved/ from what no hand has touched nor eye observed./ Think if his clumsy fingers let it crack!/ With many thanks he mails the parcel back.) (JM: 9)

Gullberg fell silent in the late 1940s. He felt that he had exhausted the poetic form he had used up to that point. When he returned with *Dödsmask och lustgård* (Deathmask and Eden) in 1952 it was with a new Modernist diction characterized by paradox and ellipsis and compressed, allusive imagery. He declared that it had become necessary for him to revise a number of his basic assumptions: 'It is this revision with its stamp of stripping and unmasking, which provides the spiritual background to my new poems'.[15] God's existence was no longer real to him. Instead, it is the demi-gods (among them the semi-mortal Hercules and Christ) who remain to us, 'de outhärdliga/ hjälparna i vår nöd' (the unbearable helpers in our need), intolerable because they are so close to us in their humanity, and because their suffering and their goodness are more than we can bear:

> — dessa ögon,
> dessa ord och händer! Man stod inte ut! (50:25)

(— those eyes, those words and hands! People couldn't stand that!) (JM:39).

Gullberg had moved from theism to a humanism expressed in terms of religious and classical myths.[16] In the poem 'Sjungande huvud' (Singing Head) the image of Orpheus, god of poetry, who was torn to pieces by the raging Bacchae, an Orpheus now blind, mutilated, tossed by the waves, replaces the image of the poet at his writing desk awaiting dictation from his divine principal. We recollect the simplicity of the soul's meeting with God in the star-spangled dome ('Hänryckning'), but now, in the breathtakingly beautiful 'Det finns en sjö och sedan aldrig mer' (A Lake There Is and Ever Nothing Then) the travellers shed their human attributes as they pass across the Styx, until the waters no longer reflect Narcissus, the symbol of self:

> Och floden vaggar oss mot spegeldjupet
> som i gestaltlös vila återger
> Narkissos död och sedan aldrig mer. (50:3)

(And the stream/ cradles us toward the mirrordeeps agleam/ which reproduce in formless rest therein/Narcissus dead, and ever nothing then.) (JM:43)

Gullberg's next collection, *Terziner i okonstens tid* (Terzinas, 1958), is largely written in Dante's terza rima, three-line stanzas rhyming aba, bcb, cdc, etc., whose formal stringency provided a taut framework for his deepening pessimism. The accessibility of his early poetry is replaced by a structure at once severe yet enlivened by bold enjambement and ellipses which stimulate the reader to interpretative effort. The simplicity of his earlier poems on poetic vocation is succeeded by metapoetry (poetry about poetry).

Gullberg was ill by now. In *Ögon, läppar* (Eyes, Lips, 1959) the tone of suffering is unmistakeable and the invalid's stoicism profoundly moving. He was uncompromisingly set against idealization. In the poem 'Död i dyn eller Han som fann Ofelia' (Dead in the Sludge or He Who Found Ophelia), he juxtaposes the polite courtly version of Ophelia found floating among the water-lilies with the sight of swollen, putrid flesh:

> Vad gjorde jag väl först när i all stassen
> jag fann en hovdam i den blöta mullen?
>
> Såg jag vad jag såg. Så kräktes jag i vassen. (ÖL:18)

(What I did first when there in all that splendour I found a girl-in-waiting in the mire? Saw what I saw. Then threw up in the reeds.)

In 'Leksaksballongerna' (The Toy Balloons) the child who thought the moon was a yellow balloon belonging to baby Jesus and determined to offer his own balloon as a twin gift, found his present ignored by the heavens:

> ingen tog emot min skänk.
> Och det fanns ingen måne utom månen. (50:97)

(no one received my gift. There was no moon but the moon.)

In keeping with this bleak bedrock of unbelief, death no longer promises a mystical union with God, but finally in 'Bara en önskan' (One Sole Desire) it becomes the martyred invalid's one and only desire:

> Djupare in, genom märg och ben,
> dagar och nätter långa:
> bara en önskan, bara en.
> Somliga har så många. (50:101)

(Ever deeper through marrow and bones, days and nights unending: one sole desire, one wish alone. Some people have so many.)

Speaking as one 'som av det slappa och porösa/ fått nog' (as one fed up with flab and sponginess), his hope lies in 'en hög geometri, en

Chapter VII

hemlig stadga' (a high geometry, a secret strength) which is found in the stars of the astronomical universe and in terzinas which eternally link triad to triad, 'och Linjen löper ut i evigheten' (and Line runs out and out for evermore).[17] In 'Du plattfisk måne med den blanka buken' (You Flat-fish Moon With Shiny Belly) the poet addresses the moon, traditional companion of poets, in provocatively unromantic diction and imagery, held strictly together by the terza rima. He begs the moon (subsequently characterized as an electric ray):

> giv också mig ett lösenord att viska
>
> till dem som diktar i din tjänst och målar!
> Lär mig att skapa bilder och slå sönder,
> försvunne, du som lämnat rom i skålar
>
> efter dig: stjärnor, kaviar för bönder...(50:73)

(give to me too a password I might whisper to those who in your honour write and paint! Teach me to create pictures and destroy. O vanished one, who have left roe in bowls behind you: stars, caviare to the general...)

This cry for a new art form has much in common with Birger Sjöberg's transition from *Fridas visor* to *Kriser och kransar*. The flat-fish moon turns into a proxy for the vanished God who has left roe (a fertile source of life and poetry) behind him in the shape of stars, but this is — in Hamlet's words — caviare to the general, too exclusive for ordinary tastes.

'Terziner med passare' (Terzinas with Compasses) and 'Terziner till hopplösheten' (Terzinas to Hopelessness) open and close the collection from 1958. The metaphor of the first is the pair of compasses which have circumscribed the outer limits of our life. Yet it happens that our minds, while the rainbow forms an arch over us, transcend our confinement by a Homeric journey away from ourselves. Our dream of freedom triumphs for a while. But the closing poem presents a world in which the gods have died, in which no messenger or angel escorts us after death to blessed regions. The poet is faced with the inescapable return to human limitations which gods and myths have lost the power to relieve.

Karin Boye (1900-41)

by Karin Petherick

Karin Boye trained as a teacher on leaving school and subsequently studied at the universities of Uppsala and Stockholm. She joined Clarté, a group of young radical intellectuals, and in 1931 was co-founder with two friends of the journal *Spektrum*, which specialized in *avant-garde* literature, art and contemporary issues such as psychoanalysis. Her translation of T. S. Eliot's *The Waste Land* (together with Erik Mesterton) was published there. She taught for brief spells, but mainly lived by her writing.

In attempting a presentation of Karin Boye's work, it seems natural to refer to C. J. L. Almqvist's fable *Ormus and Ariman*, in which the traditional concepts of good and evil are reversed, for the spirit of life, freedom and creativity proves to be linked to the lawless and mysteriously demonic Ariman, while the law-abiding and conscientious deity Ormus ends up by stifling human nature and endeavour. Karin Boye felt compelled to break with the high ideal of Christian obedience and choose her own truth, although in some senses the notion of choice is inaccurate, for as she wrote: 'There's something called necessity. My necessity. My will'.[18] But in Existentialist terms there is always a choice, for an ethical imperative can in fact be stifled or dodged or undertaken in bad faith. It was characteristic of Karin Boye to face the issue head on. And it was a painful one, for she battled against the accusations of a powerful super ego which advanced the claims of obedience and the abandonment of self. It is highly significant that she gave the title 'Inåt' (Inwards) to a poem in which she speaks of *her* God (nothing *external* for her), and when she speaks of drinking her cup of truth in anguish, she chooses imagery unequivocally linked to Christ's agony in Gethsemane, a measure of the extremity of her situation. (I must again stress that most of the translations of her poems are purely literal).

> *Min* Gud och *min* sanning
> såg jag
> i en sällsam stund.
> Mänskors ord
> och bud tego.
> Gott och ont

Chapter VII

> min själ glömde.
> *Min* Gud
> och *min* sanning drack jag
> i min ängslans stund. (27, *M*)

(*My* God and *my* truth I saw at a singular moment. Human words and commandments fell silent. My soul forgot good and evil. I drank *my* God and *my* truth in my moment of anguish.)

The element of necessity is beautifully brought out in a late poem with the image of a divining rod inexorably drawn to the well-spring:

> Där slagrutan sänker sig
> går källådern fram:
> ... Fly inte bort i drömmar om rikare jord.
> Här är din grund, och makterna
> har sagt sitt ord. (282, *DSD*.)

(Where the divining rod dips the well-spring runs up: ... Don't escape into dreams of richer soil. Here's where your ground is, and the powers have spoken their word.)

Conflict was inevitable when the passionate and idealistic Karin Boye, who had taken her commitment to the student Christian movement very seriously, discovered at the age of twenty that she was drawn to women. Falling in love was for her experiencing Eros, being drawn body and soul through beauty to truth. In her autobiographical novel *Kris* (Crisis, 1934), the headmistress's pet, who is expected to read Divinity and fulfil all the ambitions entertained on her behalf, has to fight for her freedom. It is clear that she adores a fellow girl student, but the sexual problem is only hinted at and the dynamics of the novel arise out of the conflict between authority and liberty. Karin Boye admittedly belonged to a generation of young radicals who found release and even licence through the teachings of Freud, but she found it impossible to speak openly of her sexual pain in her prose works, where her problems are transposed into heterosexual terms. She does, however, open her finest collection, *För trädets skull* (For the Tree's Sake, 1935) with the words:

> Jag är sjuk av gift. Jag är sjuk av en törst,
> till vilken naturen icke skapade någon dryck. (169, *FTS*)

(I am sick from a poison. I am sick with a thirst for which nature created no drink.)

The power of poetry lies in its ambiguity as well as its inclusiveness. Words of pain wrung from her Existential predicament speak by means of images and symbols to readers who can transpose them into their own particular contexts.

In *Kris* the object of adoration is beautiful and serene. There were to come times when Karin Boye fell under the spell of demonic attractions which she followed compulsively in the belief that ultimately, when all things stand revealed, they too would be seen to be a part of the divine, as in the poem 'Fördärvaren' (The Destroyer):

> Vem gav ormen hans frukansvärdaskönhet,
> avgrundendragning,
> döden sötma?
> Vem gav fasan den ödesdigra ljuvlighet,
> som lockar lik en mörkare lycka?
> Kanske där bortom, vid de eviga källorna,
> där slöjorna faller,
> möter mig Fördärvareni annan gestalt.
> Är du Guds skugga, du onde?
> Guds nattlige tvillingbroder? (160, *H*)

(Who gave the serpent his terrible beauty, the abyss attraction, death sweetness? Who gave horror its fateful delight, beckoning like a darker joy? Maybe in the beyond, by the eternal springs, where the veils fall, I shall meet the Destroyer in another guise. Are you God's shadow, you evil one? God's nocturnal twin brother?)

Karin Boye was a fighter. It is no accident that Gullberg called his memorial poem to her 'Död amazon' (Dead Amazon). Her own poem 'Sköldmön' (The Valkyrie, 1924) speaks of blood, fire, roses and death in battle. It is immediately apparent that this imagery is a mixture of the erotic and the martial; the male and female sides of her personality were both strong. On the other hand she was femininely intuitive and vegetative, something strikingly brought out in the poem 'Kunskap' (Knowledge) in *För trädets skull*, in which seekers on a beach with long-handled fishing nets are laughed at by the sea because knowledge can never be caught or owned, whereas if you fall into the sea as a drop of water ready to be transformed:

Chapter VII

då skall du vakna med pärlemorhud
och gröna ögon
på ängar där havets hästar betar
och vara kunskap. (200, *FTS*)

(then you'll wake with mother of pearl skin and green eyes in meadows where sea horses graze and be knowledge.)

In other respects her life was one long battle. But even if struggle is inescapable, there is a choice of ways in which to conduct it. The need for openness was crucial to Karin Boye, and in 'Jag vill möta ...' (135, *H*) (I Want To Meet ...) she speaks of being encased in an armour moulded of shame and fear, and of wanting to cast it and her weapons aside, for she has seen the power of life over iron, the power of tender grass shoots emerging defenceless through heavy soil. And she concludes: 'Jag vill möta livets makter/ vapenlös.' (I want to meet life's forces weaponless.)

The longing to be known and revealed as the real people we are lies at the heart of Karin Boye's remarkable novel *Kallocain* (1940). It is a vision of a totalitarian state in which the individual counts for nothing and only the organization which rules the collective is of any consequence. The narrator Leo Kall, loyal citizen and inventor of the truth-drug Kallocain, has always seen life as a staircase with each successive landing representing a further stage in his career; but his drug reveals that fellow-citizens, although outwardly and of necessity conformists, inwardly are full of passionately held (albeit repressed) hopes and fears and dreams. In particular, there is a group of people who make up a brotherhood whose members meet for human fellowship and the singing of strange songs (in fact poetry, which the State has dispensed with), the clasping of hands in greeting (discontinued by the State as unhygienic), and the placing of a ritual unsheathed knife beside themselves as they lie down defenceless beside it, as a sign of trust. Although Kall fiercely denies to himself that he envies them, he dreams of the brotherhood's deserted city and of being beckoned into the ruins of a cellar open to the sky, with tendrils of greenery and grass growing between the stones under a clear sky, where he is greeted and embraced by a woman. Leo discovers clear water, the well-spring of life, running across the earthen floor and is filled with indescribable gratitude. The contrast between the staircase leading up into a sterile block on the one hand, and the open cellar on the other is unmistakable: arid enclosure versus open foundations. The cellar image prompts associations both to the notion of building upon rock (the Sermon on the Mount), while at the same time this foundation is peacefully mingled with nature (the greenery and living water). The State is built of dead matter, while the brotherhood grows from inside, like trees, in the words of a member. The one is a sterile organization, the other a living organism. The image of the tree is central to Karin Boye's vision. It is linked to the female element in life, that of birth and organic growth. Leo Kall's wife, once she has the courage to speak openly, asks if a new world of mothers could not become a reality, irrespective of whether they were men or women, and whether or not they had given birth to children.

A 'police eye' monitors every move made by citizens of the State, but Leo is far more distressed by his wife's eyes. For whereas the State is predictable in its mechanical repression and familiar in its soullessness, he senses that his wife's eyes are the windows of a soul with which he has no communication. The mystery of the human being eludes and frightens him. His growing inkling of the existence of an inner life is brought out in his confrontation with his colleague Rissen, whom he hates precisely because Rissen in his vulnerability and openness represents what Kall both fears and longs for. The State wants conformity and pressures its citizens into it, but as Leo's wife has learnt from her children, every human being is essentially unique. So despite vividly conveying a nightmare regime, the message of *Kallocain* is hopeful and exhortative: the human spirit can be driven under ground, but it can never be destroyed.

In her essay *Språket bortom logiken* (The Language beyond Logic) Karin Boye stresses the role of the irrational and unconscious in life and art, speaking of the 'subterranean world of meaning in a work of literature, the secret and personal language within the logical utterance'.[19] Her poetic diction came increasingly to make use of images derived from the subconscious and dreams; a good example is found in 'Min hud är full of fjärilar', (185, *FTS*) (My Skin is Full of Butterflies), in which the butterflies provide an image of superficial sensations while eagles captive within the poet's veins and marrow illustrate her repressions. Probably her best-loved poem with the general public is 'Ja visst gör det ont', (175, *FTS)* (Yes Indeed it Hurts) which with crystalline and accessible imagery speaks of the fear of growing, the fear of the new and unknown — transposed into the pain felt by buds before they burst, the trembling fear of glittering drops of rain on a twig before they fall. The essence of this poem could be summed up in some lines from Eliot's *The Waste Land*, lines which Karin Boye chose as a motto for Kallocain: 'The awful daring of a moment's surrender/ Which an age of prudence can never retract./ By this, and this only, we have existed'.

Karin Boye's personal life was fraught with problems. Margit Abenius, who knew her and her circle, has written a sensitive and scholarly biography which is indispensable for any serious study of her work (see bibliography). Karin Boye took her own life in April 1941, leaving behind an unfinished cantata entitled *De sju dödssynderna* (The Seven Deadly Sins). Before God's throne stand the Prosecutor and the mortal sins Sloth, Lust and Pride. The Prosecutor urges the ultimate penalty and choirs alternate the cries 'Förinta oss!' (Destroy us!) and 'Förbarma dig!' (Have mercy!). The sacred tone of these invocations is matched by the beauty of the defence pleas. Lust speaks of a primal creative experience before the advent of law and order:

> Här, i den enda och yttersta handlingen
> kastar vi jagets nio hudar,
> stiger med slutna ögon i källan,
> nakna som foster och gudar...(230, *DSD*)

(Here, in the only and ultimate act we shed the nine skins of the self, step with closed eyes into the well-spring, naked as embryos and gods.

Once more we come close to Almqvist's paradoxical view of good and evil, and even closer to Nietzsche's vision of an order beyond these concepts.

Harry Martinson (1904-78)

by Brita Green and Philip Holmes

Harry Martinson's childhood in Blekinge in southern Sweden was spent in particularly harsh circumstances. His father died when he was only six and, soon after, his mother emigrated to America, abandoning her children to the care of the parish. Harry ran away from foster-parents several times. School was a refuge for him, a place where he could assert himself. 'They [the other school children] went home from school in the afternoons. He went *away* from school' (*Nässlorna blomma*)

Poetry of the Twentieth Century

(Flowering Nettle, 1935). After a spell with the Sea Cadets at Karlskrona — he ran away from there too — he finally got a berth on a motor schooner in Gothenburg in 1920 when he was sixteen. During the next six years he saw many different parts of the world, working as a stoker and deckhand on fourteen different vessels. He also spent long periods ashore, wandering as a tramp both in Scandinavia and in India and South America, before finally returning to Sweden in 1926.

The year 1929 was a turning point in Martinson's life. He married Moa (née Helga Maria Swartz). It was a stimulating partnership, and they both made their names as writers during the decade the marriage lasted. Martinson's début was a collection of poetry, *Spökskepp* (Ghost Ship, 1929), and the same year he also contributed to a Modernist anthology, *Fem unga* (Five Young Men). The contributors to this work have been called 'primitivists', because they celebrated the natural and instinctive forces in life and regarded the morality and habits of modern western civilization as inhibiting.

Martinson's breakthrough as a poet came with the collection *Nomad* (1931), which exhibits many of the themes and stylistic features which were to become characteristic of his work. Among several pictures of childhood is 'Lyssnare' (Listener), which contains the often quoted line 'Jag frös vid min barndoms härd' (I was cold by my childhood hearth). The sea pictures prefigure the travelogues in their wealth of associations and sheer exuberance of sound. 'Sjöman talar till kapduvor' (Seaman Talks to Cape Doves) begins:

> Duva. Columba — columba kap!
> duvor i vita skyar;
> stoft av monsuner från Saipang och Yap
> segla kring kaffrernas byar.
> Kapduvor två, kapduvor tre,
> kapduvor för och akter;
> komna att slutas till Goda hopps
> ändlösa albatrossjakter.

(Dove. Columba — columba cape! doves fly in clouds of whiteness; dust from monsoon storms from Saipang and Yap sail around kaffirs' enclosures. Cape doves two, cape doves three, cape doves afore and abaft; come to join up with the Good Hope's endless albatross chasing.)

The sea poems in the collection are among the best known of

Chapter VII

Martinson's work, poems like 'Kol' (Coal), 'På Kongo' (On the Congo) and 'Efter' (Afterwards). He is often able to conjure up a picture, an action, even suggest a whole world of nature or a social context with great economy and simplicity. 'Ute på havet' (Out on the Ocean) has the deftness of a Japanese landscape painting:

Ute på havet känner man en vår eller en sommar bara som ett vinddrag.
Den drivande Floridatången blommar ibland om sommaren,
och en vårkväll flyger en skedstork in mot Holland.

(Out on the ocean a spring or a summer is just felt as a breath of wind. The drifting Florida seaweed blooms sometimes in summer, and on a spring evening a spoonbill flies in towards Holland.)

The themes and style of *Nomad* are largely continued in *Natur* (Nature, 1934), although his approach here is more Expressionistic. Its reception was cool. Many of the poems were felt to be contrived and the language overloaded. Martinson — always sensitive to criticism — followed the advice of one critic and fellow poet (Elmer Diktonius) 'to abandon poetry for a few years'.

However, his position as a leading writer was ensured by the prose books he published during the Thirties, starting with two idiosyncratic travel books, written in poetic prose, *Resor utan mål* (Journeys with No Goals, 1932) and *Kap Farväl* (Cape Farewell, 1933). The opening pages of *Resor utan mål* outline Martinson's utopian 'nomadic theory', whose ultimate aim is to produce the 'World Nomad': by travelling we will learn to ignore national and racial differences, create tolerance and understanding and break down prejudice and bigotry. Martinson's own travels had been neither those of a tourist nor of the writer seeking inspiration. He had travelled without a thought of describing what he saw, working his passage in a burning hot stokehold, and his viewpoint is therefore an entirely fresh one. A comparison may be made with Ivar Lo-Johansson's portrayal of working-class life in Britain and France from this period, though the approach and style of writing are different.

During his life as a seaman, Martinson had collected picture postcards from all over the world, but his collection was stolen. In order to preserve his memories he put the images down on paper. Despite their being written some years after the events depicted, they have the freshness and immediacy of diary entries. Martinson provides a myriad of impressions of the harsh working conditions at sea, of storms and calms, of distant places like Rio, Bombay, Santa Fe, and of the more familiar North Sea and Dover. The style is impulsive and spontaneous. The prose is full of unexpected associations and daring images, and many scenes stand out in picture-postcard clarity: the Brazilian jungle and the waterfall in 'En tid i Santa Catarina' (A Time in Santa Catarina), the tiny dancing girl plagued by a tyrannical master in Bombay — 'If only I could do something for you, you dear little creature, little living child. But me, I am just a stoker from Western Europe where the icy-hearted technicians live.' (*Kap Farväl*).

After the travel books Martinson returned to the world of his childhood with the autobiographical novels *Nässlorna blomma* (Flowering Nettle, 1935) and *Vägen ut* (The Road Out, 1936).[20] Time had healed some of the bitter memories, and now at a distance he began to analyse his development and his character. The result is one of the finest insights into childhood in Swedish letters. The mature writer calls his youth to account. He has been censured for being too hard on himself, for reproaching his young alter ego, Martin, too severely for childish weakness and exaggerated self-pity.

Nässlorna blomma begins with the disintegration of the Tomasson family. Martin's father's business fails, and the family moves from the magical Trollvik to 'Gula faran', the house near the quarry which is both a dangerous playground and an image of impending catastrophe. When father dies of TB and mother runs off to America, sister Inez attempts to keep the large family together, until she too succumbs to TB and the children are dispersed to different foster-homes. Martin is at first taken in by Hanna and Sven at Vilnäs, a poor couple, unable to give him any affection, and when they have a child of their own, Martin has to move on. At Tollene, a model farm, his physical circumstances are much improved: it is 'a well-run farm with no less than six diplomas', and the young master is honourable and correct:

It would not have been surprising if it had turned out that he had exactly an acre of honour and precisely six and a half acres of faith. He had a metre rule with which he measured his father, a foot rule with which he measured his sisters, a centimetre rule with which he measured farm labourers, an inch rule with which he measured maids, and a millimetre rule with which he measured children of the parish.

As a reaction to the chilly correctness, Martin lashes out in frustrated rage at a neighbour's calf and kills it (an invention with no

Chapter VII

basis in Martinson's own life), and the guilt he feels for this deed haunts his childhood. At his next home, Norda, the nettles which flower in summer bear witness to sloth and decay. Here he encounters coarseness and brutality, but he is near to life. The large women at the farm partly compensate for his missing mother, but also stimulate his sexual fantasies. The 37-year-old daughter Karla is, like her mother, 'siren-like, enormous and shapely, fantastic to behold, a gigantic sexual animal flung to and fro on the breakers of her instincts'. After a beating he runs away again and, now eleven years old, he is placed in the care of the Old People's Home. Here, in a grey world of senility and poverty, he finds some of the tenderness he needs in the person of fröken Tyra, the matron. The novel ends in a cry of anguish when Tyra dies suddenly from typhoid fever.

In *Vägen ut* we follow Martin to Ekevik and the Ahlrots. It is wartime and he cuts peat at Varpinge, then works on a beet-farm in Skåne. He makes his way to Gothenburg, but is taken to a Children's Home. He joins the Sea Cadets but is discharged. Finally he signs on the M/S Willy and goes to sea. The main theme running through Martinson's autobiographical works is a search for tenderness and affection. He regards the lack of love as a tragedy almost as bad as evil itself, yet the tone of the novels is not bitter. Least of all does he blame society for his predicament, and the works are intended as a search for personal understanding. The style is impressionistic — rapid revelatory glimpses, flashes of insight and observation. Martin's naive viewpoint and the narrator's own provide a double perspective, a child's-eye view interpreted by the grown man, often with self-irony. Martin's imagination is triggered by nature, as he walks through the forest to Vilnäs or sits by Grotte Spring, but it can also be stimulated by wall posters such as the one for the White Star Line: 'The mighty steamship *Teutonic* sailed on the poster into Nevjårk, just as if it wanted to creep under the skirts of the *Liberty Maid* who stood waiting with a pitch-torch to light him up the Indian River.' The language is highly concentrated and the imagery reveals a richness seldom equalled in prose. It is very original but, as Peter Hallberg has pointed out, never unintelligibly personal.[21]

At the end of the Thirties, Martinson published three collections of philosophical nature studies or essays, *Svärmare och harkrank* (Sphinx-Moth and Cranefly, 1937), *Midsommardalen* (Midsummer Valley, 1938) and *Det enkla och det svåra* (The Simple and the

Difficult, 1939). At the Soviet Writers' Congress in Moscow in the summer of 1934, which both Harry and Moa Martinson attended, he was appalled by what he experienced of Stalinist culture. The motto of the Congress was 'The writer is the engineer of the human soul', and Martinson saw his contemporaries and his country as being under threat from the 'world engineer ethos'. Engineers had produced aeroplanes used to bomb civilians in Guernica and radios used to broadcast Goebbels's propaganda. Martinson pondered what in Sweden he wished to preserve: not the big towns, but rural Sweden, the unspoiled ageless Sweden of forests and lakes and folktale. It was in that spirit that Martinson took part as a volunteer in the Finnish Winter War. In *Verklighet till döds* (Reality Unto Death, 1940), he describes the 'unequivocal idiot-howling concrete grenade reality' of war.

In the early Forties, he was divorced from Moa, and he married Ingrid Lindcrantz. With *Passad* (Trade Wind, 1945) Martinson returned to poetry. The familiar themes are presented here with greater clarity and force, but there is a new emphasis. Instead of being concerned with travel in the external, physical sense, *Passad* maps out the conquest of inner space:

> Jag har planlagt en färd,
> jag har inrett ett hus
> på nomadiska kuster inåt.
>
> Sjustjärnans brödfruktsgren lockade evigt.
> Oåtkomligt i vintergatornas trädgård
> var den en gren av skådebrödsfrukter.
>
> Men nya visa upptäcktsmän jag mött
> ha pekat inåt
> mot det nya Gondwanas kuster.
> Och de ha sagt mig
> att gömda vågor alltid vandra där,
> att hav av gåtor alltid strömma där
> kring inre resors obeskrivna öar
>
> och jag har lyssnat till dem
> och anat
> en ny passad — ett nytt Gondwanaland.

(I have planned out a journey, I have furnished a house on nomadic coasts

Chapter VII

inwards. The Pleiades' breadfruit branch tempted always. Inaccessible in the garden of galaxies it was a branch of showbread fruits. But wise new explorers I have met have pointed inwards towards the coasts of a new Gondwana. And they have told me that hidden waves for ever wander there, that seas of riddles for ever flow there round uncharted islands of an inner journey and I have listened silently and sensed a new Trade Wind — a new Gondwanaland.)

The image of the trade winds is a deeply personal one, which stays with him all his life. They had already appeared in *Kap Farväl*: 'Our ideal should not be calm, which can turn the ocean itself into a mire, and not gales, but the great strong trade winds, mighty, full of vigour, fresh and alive; an eternal airing.' They represent a harmony of different aspects of existence. He contrasts Odysseus and Robinson Crusoe: a classical cultural ideal and an empirical scientific view, and he laments that they are 'grasped as one and the same by only a few'. As usual, the sea and nature figure largely in this collection, the titles alone revealing the poet's preoccupations: 'Öppen kust' (Open Coast), 'Brev från en oljare' (Letter from a Greaser), 'Daggmasken' (The Earth Worm), 'Blad' (Leaves), and the well-known 'Enbusken' (The Juniper Bush):

> Tyst står han vid stenen,
> enig med ljungen.
> Bland stickbarren
> sitta bären svärmvis
> som uppfångade hagelskott ....
>
> Åt gravar och golv gav han ris
> och ett gott öl bryggde han
> där han stod, stark och vänlig,
> klämd mellan gråa stenar i Thule.

(Silent he stands by the rock, at one with the heather. Among the prickly needles sit the berries in swarms like captured buckshot.... To graves and floors he gave branches, and a good ale he brewed standing there, strong and friendly, wedged between grey rocks in Thule.)

The novel *Vägen till Klockrike* (The Road, 1948), about tramps and life on the open road at the end of the last century, has no plot and little development of character. Klockrike is a parish in Östergötland surrounded by police districts patrolled by mounted police, the enemies of the vagabond. It represents the unattainable. The book consists of a series of independent lyrical-philosophical tales held together by a central idea. Unused Klockrike material was published posthumously in the short-story collection *Bollesagor* (Bolle Tales, 1982).

It is the story of Bolle, cigar-maker and craftsman, whose livelihood disappears on the advent of machine-made cigarettes. Having saved with a friend enough money for one passage to the USA, he loses on the throw of a dice and joins the army of vagabonds on the highways of Sweden. Like Martin, Bolle seeks refuge from the harsh realities of life in the countryside. He develops his own philosophy to be able to deal with the people he meets. He survives by his mildness. He can even forgive the cruelty of people like 'hedersknölen' (the honourable swine) who first lectures him on how inadequate he is and then gives him a thrashing, or the girls who give him a packet of sandwiches that actually contains two boards spread with shoe polish and a dead rat. But old women, eccentrics and the sick welcome Bolle and show him compassion and kindness. Many chapters read like independent short stories, depicting strange incidents or providing sketches of Bolle's fellow tramps. One of the most interesting is Sandemar,[22] a globe-trotting tramp who gathers a sect around him at a brickworks. Sandemar preaches that 'sloth and indolence were God's protest through Man, directed at the meddlesome idolization of frenzy and toil' and he castigates 'this new achievement-sickness'. The message of strength through passivity and mildness has affinities with Buddhism. The age of the professional tramp coincides with Bolle's lifetime. The great wave of unemployment in the 1920s brings an influx of 'amateurs' on to the roads and vagabonds of the old school are submerged. Bolle dies in a sanatorium but, in a rather surprising ending, his soul transmigrates and he is reborn into a primitive Indian tribe in the Brazilian jungle.

Lars Ulvenstam holds that there are echoes of John Steinbeck's California tales in this work,[23] but there is also much that is pure Martinson: man's enemies are superficiality and the extremes of exaggerated efficiency. Man's allies are nature and the middle way, a path of reconciliation and wholeness. The way to Klockrike is a variation on the dream of the World Nomad.

In the collection *Cikada* (1953), which contains some of his finest nature vignettes, Martinson also included a cycle of 29 poems entitled 'Sången om Doris och Mima', which he had written in a fortnight in October 'whilst the typesetters were waiting.'[24] The cycle grew to 103

Chapter VII

'songs' and was published in 1956 as *Aniara. En revy om människan i tid och rum* (Aniara. A Review of Man in Time and Space). Superficially, Aniara is a science fiction story: the time is the future and the Earth is suffering from acute radiation damage and must be evacuated. The giant spaceship Aniara takes off for Mars, but is soon forced off course by an asteroid, and finds herself on an unalterable course out of our galaxy. The refugees on board seek consolation from the Mima, a supercomputer which can show pictures from Earth (Doris), to which their thoughts increasingly turn. As the situation grows more desperate, sects and cults flourish. After it has shown the holocaust when a 'phototurb' destroys the city of Dorisburg, the Mima collapses and ceases to function. After 24 years in space the last passengers die, and Aniara becomes a giant sarcophagus heading for the constellation of the Lyre.

Aniara is spaceship Earth and modern man is moving away from nature. The characters and groups aboard represent different aspects of modern life. Here as elsewhere Martinson sees feminine values as a sign of hope for the world, and women figure prominently and significantly. There is the opening scene with the blond Doris, who later lends her name to Earth itself. Both the blind poetess from Rind and Mima represent creative forces and art, and Isagel, pilot and mathematician, is a seeker after truth: logical clarity and exact science but also spirituality. In a sense, they are all mythological beings, representing the forces (instincts, emotions, intellect) which in different ways shape our life and give meaning to it.[25]

Martinson saw *Aniara* as his most important work. Johan Wrede characterizes it as 'the richest work in Martinson's lifelong project to show us — often in the guise of a journey across the seas, a voyage of discovery, or just a stroll in the countryside — man's attempts to see himself and his role in creation'.[26] The subheading, 'A Revue of Man in Time and Space', is important, as Wrede points out, with its use of the ambiguous word 'revue'. *Aniara* is a survey, a critical assessment, of man's situation, but it is also presented as something of a revue in the entertainment sense of the word, consisting of 'sketches' loosely linked to each other and a sometimes frivolous style that contrasts strongly with the serious message. Martinson tries to show us that we are lost if we rely on rationalism, on an uncompromisingly scientific view of the world, and appeals to us to temper it with humane values and a respect for nature, to feel responsible for each other and for the Earth. We must strive to achieve a balance between our instincts, our feelings and our intellect. This philosophy of life — which owes much to Taoism — is one that the Aniara passengers have not achieved.

Whilst Aniara is thus a part of Martinson's lifelong message, some specific events, which made a deep impression on him, formed the immediate impetus for writing it, and for writing it as a space epic. One was the use of the atomic bomb against Japanese cities, another the news in August 1953 that the Soviet Union had exploded a hydrogen bomb in Siberia. There was also great tension in international politics in the early 1950s. Martinson had taken a great interest in mathematics, physics and astronomy, and in August 1953 he gained a view through his telescope of the Andromeda galaxy, one and a half million light years away.[27]

The poetic technique and style of *Aniara* are remarkable. Almost all the songs are written in iambic lines, usually pentameters, and often partly rhymed. 'The Song of Karelia' (song 72), one of the most beautiful memories of Earth, stands out with its trochaic metre, echoing Finland's national epic the *Kalevala*. That is only one of many literary allusions. The opening line 'Mitt första möte med min Doris lyser' brings to mind Birger Sjöberg's 'Den första gång jag såg dig'. In song 8 the spaceship's measurements are specified rather like those of another refugee vessel, Noah's Ark, and in song 73 the strains of the old popular song 'Daisy, Daisy' (On a bicycle made for two) are distinctly recognizable. There are also fragments that reflect the general style of popular science, instruction leaflets, pornography, etc.

The vocabulary is inventive: new plausible-sounding technical terms are formed based on Latin or Greek stems, and a rich associative technique underlies the names. Isagel, for example, may have been formed from Isis, the Egyptian goddess of navigation and 'gasell', a graceful antelope, while Chefone, Aniara's dictator figure, may be a blend of 'chef' (boss) and Al Capone. Aniara itself was freely invented by Martinson as a nonsense word as early as 1938, but has been subject to several analyses and interpretations after the event. A different kind of linguistic innovation is Daisi's Dorisburg slang (song 12).[28]

Aniara was immediately a great critical and popular success. Streets, ships, hotels have been named after it, and the word has entered the language in the sense of approximately 'our troubled times' (e.g. 'aniarabarn' — 'Aniara child'). The book has been translated twice into English. It has inspired an opera by Karl-Birger Blomdahl with libretto by Erik Lindegren, which had its premiere in 1959. A new edition of *Aniara*, with a very perceptive and comprehensive postscript by Johan Wrede, appeared in 1997. His final verdict is that in the long run, it will 'stand out in Scandinavian literature as the work that in an incomparable way revealed the ethical problems of this technological century.'[29]

In *Gräsen i Thule* (The Grasses of Thule, 1958) and *Vagnen* (The Wagon, 1960), Martinson occasionally returned to Aniara themes, in poems like 'Den yedisögda berättar (skärva)' (The Tale of the Yedis-Eyed (Fragment)) and 'Till Isagel' (For Isagel), but most of the poems in these collections are of a type closer to that of *Passad*, sometimes with direct links: 'Li Kan tar avsked under trädet' (Li Kan Bids Farewell Under the Tree). *Vagnen* finishes with the cycle of 17 poems that gave the whole collection its name, in which Martinson continues his criticism of modern civilization. It was not well received. In the few years since *Aniara*, the cultural climate in Sweden had changed, and the younger generation now began to see Martinson as a negative reactionary.

In *Dikter om ljus och mörker* (Poems about Light and Darkness, 1971), Li Kan again returns but now with a sad, disillusioned voice:

> Att tala för världen är att tala i vinden.
> Det finns en världsblåst i allt. Den tar
> alla ord. Allt måste ropas om och om
> igen — av alla.

(Speaking for the world is speaking in the wind. There is a world wind in every thing. It takes all words. Everything must be shouted again and again — by all.)

It is in this collection, and in the posthumous *Doriderna* (The Doridians, 1980), which was intended as a continuation of *Aniara*, that Martinson takes us on yet another kind of journey, a journey into the smallest possible spaces 'in the nature of things / in the hall of miracle / in the interior of the atoms'. In one poem he goes even further, not only into the atom, but into the 'innermost nuclei of the innermost nuclei'. He attempts to describe a world which cannot be perceived with the senses, an abstract world of energy and movement: 'den verkligheten som genombrusar alla verkligheter, / och spinner själva tråden i de tyg / som drömmar vävas av' (the reality which resounds through all realities, and spins the very thread in stuff that dreams are made of).

The last book published in Martinson's lifetime was a short collection of nature poems, *Tuvor* (Tussocks, 1973), which bears his usual trade-mark of humbly entering into nature on its own terms. As Kjell Espmark has pointed out,[30] he does not use nature as a medium for his own moods or feelings but, armed with his magnifying glass, he reverently attempts to read its own secrets. The language is no less fresh and inventive than in his more youthful poetry.

> Gran står tätt invid gran.
> De schalar sig samman
> håller ett barrbrätte över linneornas klockor.
> Lågt fladdrar gräsmottet framåt
> med ohörda vingslag.
> Här viskar skogen i Norden
> sin minsta visa.

(Spruce stands close to spruce, shawling themselves together holding a needle brim over the bells of the twin-flower. Deep down a grass-moth is fluttering with unheard wing-beats. This is where the forest of the North is whispering its smallest tune.)

In 1974, the year Martinson was awarded the Nobel Prize, another collection of mainly nature poetry had reached the proof stage, but he decided not to go ahead with publication. His health was failing, and he was increasingly pessimistic about world events. The announcement of the prize gave rise to a bitter debate in the Swedish press, and he was deeply disillusioned and upset. The planned collection appeared four years later, shortly after his death, under the title *Längs ekots stigar* (Along the Paths of the Echo, 1978). It contains poems on familiar themes, and some fresh glimpses of nature observation, but there is also evidence of an increasing feeling of frustration towards the end of his life, and of thoughts of death:

> Till att avveckla sig skall man alltid vara beredd.
> Att tackla av sin rigg, att packa in seglen.
> Vara inställd på vågornas sömnsång och på att huggas upp av havet.
> Skeppets själ skall en gång lämna skeppet i en liten båt i passaden.
> Då skall matrosen vara med,
> skrämd och blottställd, men beredd
> för en längre och mörkare färd.

Chapter VII

> Ingenting har sagts och ingen har vågat fråga.
> Kompassen en annan.
> Havet ovisshet.
> Kanske finnes en okänd ö.

(One must always be prepared to wind down. To dismantle the rigging and furl the sails. Be prepared for the sleep-song of the waves and ready to be broken up by the sea. The ship's soul will one day leave the ship in a small boat in the trade-wind. The seaman will be there, frightened and exposed, but ready for a longer and darker journey. Nothing has been said and no-one has dared to ask. The compass is different. The sea a mystery. Perhaps there is an unknown island.)

One of the first poems in *Doriderna* sums up Harry Martinson's view of the world and his own role in it. Nature is indifferent, there is no divine purpose, but our personal, individual purpose must be to defend and preserve our beautiful planet.

> Över gravarna fortplantar den likgiltiga vinden
> de odödliga gudarnas viskning
> om att ingen förlust är förhanden i stort.
> Men vad vet väl gudarna
> — dessa himlarnas slösande miljardärer —
> om den sköna och underbara Doris
> hur hon varit värd att evigt sparas
> och att den som älskat henne
> aldrig kan tröstas av gudarnas fortsatta slöseri.
> Om henne sjunger en fågel nu ensam i gravens träd.
> Om henne sådan hon var, den härliga, om ingen annan
> sjunger doridernas trast.

(Over the gravestones blows the wind, indifferent, passing on the whispers of undying gods about there not being any loss involved, really, taken overall. But what do they know — the gods, the careless milliardaires of heaven — what do they know about the wonders of the lovely Earth? About the way she should have been saved for ever and how to someone who has loved her there is no solace in an endless Olympian extravagance? It is of Earth the bird sings in the tree there on the grave. Of Earth, the way she was, the beautiful. Of no-one else the Earth's thrush sings.)

Harry Martinson won popular acclaim very early in his career. He was elected to the Swedish Academy in 1949, was made an honorary doctor at Gothenburg in 1954, and was awarded the Nobel Prize in 1974 (shared with Eyvind Johnson). His innovative and rich language makes him unique in Swedish literature. He talks disdainfully about his own 'velvet tongue', and about the delicate balance between the simple, recognizable, but fresh and 'dewy', and the banal, worn-out and 'dusty' language. In his best poetry he is one of the most powerful of Sweden's writers. And his poetry is by no means restricted to his poems: it pervades his whole output, which was very extensive. In addition to poetry, novels and essays, he wrote radio plays, and he contributed widely to magazines and newspapers. He left behind a large number of unpublished poems, some of which were printed in *Ur de tusen dikternas bok* (From the Book of a Thousand Poems, 1986).

In his perception of the risks connected with technological progress Martinson was before his time. He began to see the danger signals long before anti-pollution, the green movement and environmentalism took hold. We have only just begun to catch up with him.

Gunnar Ekelöf (1907-68)

by Laurie Thompson

Gunnar Ekelöf is widely regarded as one of Sweden's greatest twentieth-century poets. Always a passionate individualist, he defies categorization — his stance as an outsider is not only the inevitable result of his being an innovator, perpetually extending the limits of poetic expression and plumbing the depths of man's being in search of the nature of reality: his isolation is intentionally sought, he refuses to conform, resists being organized or classified, insists on going his own way even though it may not be the obvious or easy one. Paradoxes and contrasts run through his works — indeed it is a common-place of Ekelöf criticism to refer to him as 'motsatsernas man' (the man full of contradictions), but all his books have a theme: as Erik Lindegren put it: 'He doesn't really write poems, he composes collections of poems'.[31] *Helheten* (the whole) is a key word for Ekelöf who, true to his life-long interest in music and Eastern philosophy, probes beneath and beyond the superficial in an attempt to find the link between all things, between

Chapter VII

past, present and future, life and death, body and soul. Most of his poetry is far from easy to understand; moreover, he is one of Sweden's most learned poets and incorporates into many poems references to and quotations from other literature in the allusive style usually associated with T.S. Eliot. However, few poets are so rewarding of detailed study.

Bengt Gunnar Ekelöf was born in 1907 in Stockholm. His childhood was disturbed and unhappy; several of the trends in Ekelöf's work can be traced back to his feelings of rejection and isolation in his early years. His well-to-do father contracted syphilis and died in 1916 after a lengthy period of insanity; even before this tragedy his mother had seemed incapable of giving him normal, tender love and the coolness of their relationship continued after Gunnar had left home on passing his school-leaving examination in 1926. He became increasingly interested in Oriental mysticism and even considered emigrating to India; he studied at the School of Oriental Studies in London, and read Persian and Sanskrit in Uppsala, although illness and restlessness made him give up without taking any degree examinations. Ekelöf's interest then turned to music and he studied in Paris at the end of the 1920s, intending to become a musician. 'For me, music has been the most frequent and most fruitful source of inspiration,' he wrote many years later;[32] but instead of becoming a musician, he grew fascinated by French painting and poetry, especially Surrealist writers such as Desnos and Breton. Ekelöf had written some poetry a few years earlier, mainly poetic prose, which had never been published until he included them as 'Skärvor av en diktsamling' (Fragments of a Poetry Collection) in his *Dikter 1-3* (1949). As a result of his experiences in France, however, the poet's taste became more Modernistic: his first published collection of poetry, entitled *sent på jorden* (late arrival upon earth, 1932), was advertised as Sweden's first Surrealistic poetry. Reluctant as ever to be categorized, Ekelöf declined to accept the label 'Surrealist'; nevertheless, in spite of his claim that 'I never set to work in accordance with Surrealistic doctrine',[33] the description seems accurate to most readers. Images are linked in striking but unexpected combinations and create a dream-like atmosphere reminiscent of paintings by Salvador Dali; it is as if the poet's subconscious were addressing the reader direct, missing out the normal, conventional logic of speech:

hjälp mig att söka min egen snäcka som försvunnit i oändlighetens hav och det stora obestämda som jag älskar blint som ett barn för hoppet om livets pärla

(Help me to look for my own shell which has disappeared in the sea of eternity and the vast vagueness that I love blind as a child in the hope of finding the pearl of life)

Ekelöf indicated that *sent på jorden* was influenced greatly by Stravinsky — he would play records of *The Rite of Spring* repeatedly while writing — and called the collection 'en självmordsbok' (a suicide book).[34] The final poem, 'apoteos' (apotheosis), opens with the much-quoted line 'ge mig gift att dö eller drömmar att leva' (give me poison to die or dreams to live) and ends with a wish to dissolve into the absolute, the last line 'till intet' (to nothing) being followed by the symbol for infinity. The suicide reference seems to hark back to the Nirvana wish of Oriental mysticism, although there are also illustrations in the book of the Surrealistic trend of wishing to destroy violently all established conventions. One of the best examples is 'sonatform denaturerad prosa' (sonata form denatured prose) in which Ekelöf vents his desire to smash the conventions of language:

krossa bokstävlarna mellan tänderna gäspa vokaler, elden brinner i helvete kräkas och spotta nu eller aldrig jag och svindel du eller aldrig svindel nu eller aldrig. vi börjar om

(Crush the alphablast between your teeth yawn vowels, the fire is burning in hell vomit and spit now or never I and dizziness you or never dizziness now or never. let's start again)

As the title suggests, the poem is constructed in accordance with the rules of sonata form in music although individual 'notes' are disjointed and linked polyphonically, even discordantly, rather than harmoniously; the rhythms also create a persistent, drumming effect which tends to benumb the senses and combines with the words to eradicate the distinction between 'I' and 'he she it'.

Dedikation (Dedication, 1934), is prefaced by a quotation from the visionary French poet Rimbaud: 'Jag säger: man måste vara siare, man måste göra sig till siare' (I say: you must be a prophet, you must turn yourself into a prophet). The desire to annihilate reality in the previous book is now replaced by a positive hope for the future: 'En lång, regnig afton kände jag inom mig hur den nya människan längtade att födas' (One long, rainy evening I felt the new man inside me, longing to be born) ('Betraktelse') (Meditation). The links with Swedish Romanticism

Chapter VII

are affirmed in a series of elegies dedicated to and in the spirit of Stagnelius, and a favourite theme of Ekelöf's is frequently sounded, the continuing connection between past and present. *Dedikation* was followed two years later by *Sorgen och stjärnan* (Sorrow and the Star), in which the Romantic trends are even more pronounced (cf. 'Sommarnatten') (Summer's Night). Many of the poems are descriptions of nature in calm and controlled verse, the mood generally being wistful, even melancholic. The poet is isolated, lonely and contemplative.

Ekelöf continued with his 'outsider' stance in the title poem of his next book, *Köp den blindes sång* (Buy the Blind Man's Song, 1938). The poet symbolically adopts the yellow and black arm band worn on the Continent by blind persons, thus renouncing the political insignia of the activists preparing for the imminent World War II: 'De seende, som svindlas / och svindlar och luras och litar,/ må pryda sin arm med vita,/ svarta och bruna bindlar... / Köp den blindes sång!' (Those who can see, who are swindled and swindle and fool and rely, may adorn their arms with white, black and brown armbands... Buy the blind man's song!). The trend towards simpler language and simpler poetic style is continued and there are several nature poems that could easily have appeared in the previous book. However, the theme of blindness and darkness running through *Köp den blindes sång* refers to the gloomy state of world events. 'Här ar det mörkt och tomt / I framtidens land' (It's dark and empty here in the land of the future), he writes in 'Elegier I' (Elegies I); but the opening of the final poem, 'Coda', indicates Ekelöf's faith in the future: 'Allt har sin tid, så även detta mörker' (The day dawns for everything, even for this darkness). He may not be sure about the nature of reality, but he can assert that 'den allena / som tjänar livets sak, skall överleva' (only those fighting on the side of life will survive).

Färjesång (Ferry Song, 1941), is a powerful book, full of animated argument culminating in what appears to be the attainment of a philosophical standpoint which satisfies the poet: 'allt som var outsägligt och fjärran är outsägligt och nära' (Everything ineffable and distant is ineffable and near) ('Eufori') (Euphoria). A succession of paradoxes runs through the poems, a key motif being variations on the dialectic theme of thesis-antithesis-synthesis. Ekelöf's answer to the question 'what is reality, what is truth?' is the individualistic outsider's solution:

> Liv är konstrasternas möte,
> liv är ingendera parten.
> Liv är varken dag eller natt
> men gryning och skymning.
> Liv är varken ett ont eller ett gott,
> det är mälden mellan stenarna.
> Liv är inte drakens och riddarens kamp,
> det är jungfrun.

(Life is the meeting place of contrasts, life never takes sides. Life is neither day nor night but dawn and dusk. Life is neither good nor evil, it is the grist between the stones. Life is not a battle for dragons and knights, it is the virgin.) ('Tag och skriv—4', (Set About Writing).)[35]

It is also the solution of a poet steeped in Oriental mysticism: 'En människa är aldrig homogen:/ Hon är sitt första och sitt andra,/ på en gång! Inte i tur och ordning'. (A man is never homogeneous: he is his first and his second, at the same time! Not in order.)

Ekelöf considered *Färjesång* to be a break-through as far as his own attitudes and achievements were concerned, but his break-through with the reading public and critics came with his next work, *Non serviam* (1945). The title echoes Satan's refusal to serve and hence his expulsion from heaven, also the attitude of James Joyce's Stephen Dedalus (first referred to specifically in Chapter 3 of *Portrait of the Artist as a Young Man*): it is an affirmation of Ekelöf's individualistic, anarchistic stance. His impatience with the paternalistic, over-organized side of modern Swedish society is expressed in the title poem: 'Jag är en främling i detta land / ... / Här, i de långa, välfödda stundernas / trånga ombonade Sverige / där allting är stängt för drag ... är det mig kallt' (I am a stranger in this country ... Here, in boring but high-born, cramped and snug Sweden where all draughts are excluded ... I feel cold), and he demonstrates his cynicism at the expense of 'Folkhemmet' (The People's Home, i.e. the Swedish welfare state created by the Social Democrats) in the satirical poem 'Till de folkhemske' (To the Horrible People in their Horrible Home). The horrors of war are evocatively expressed in 'Jarrama' and were also the starting point for the deeply disturbing poem 'Samothrake',[36] a haunting vision concerning death and the meaning of human life. The finest poem in the book is probably 'Absentia animi' in which Ekelöf continues the metaphysical and mystical meditations characteristic of his previous

Chapter VII

work. In his search for Abraxas (or Abrasax), an ancient name for the highest being, the poet delves into his own self to find something beyond time and space that is the essence of all existence which, in line with mystical tradition, he calls simply 'någonting annat' (something else):

> O långt långt bort
> i det som är bortom
> finns någonting nära!
> O djupt nere i mig
> i det som är nära
> finns någonting bortom
> någonting bortomnära
> i det som är hitom fjärran
> någonting varken eller
> i det som är antingen eller

(O far far away in the beyond there is something near! o deep down in me in the nearness there is something beyond something beyondnear in the nearfar something neither nor in the either or)

The plays on words and rhythmical repetitions create a trance-like atmosphere suggesting parallels with Indian music, until the words fall into an apparently meaningless jumble; and the poem ends by returning to its beginning, closing with the words 'om hösten' (in autumn). Ekelöf took that line as the title of his next book, *Om hösten* (1951), which contains poems written over a number of years, including sketches of earlier poems and preliminary workings of themes to be treated again later. The collection begins and ends with poems about dreams called 'En verklighet (drömd)' and 'En dröm (verklig)' (Reality Dreamt and Dream Real) to stress the motif of contrasts and paradoxes that run through the book. In 'Röster under jorden' (Voices Under Ground) the poet investigates the nature of life and death, of individual existence and the passage of time, using as a key image the fossilized remains of prehistoric birds.

Strountes (Trifles, 1955), refers to an Almqvist quotation stressing the almost insuperable difficulty of writing whimsical trifles (*strunt*). The poems abound in wit, plays on words and cross-references to other literature: as the poet declares in 'När man kommit så långt': 'När man kommit så långt som jag i meningslöshet / är vart ord åter intressant' (When you've got as far into nonsense as I have every word becomes interesting again.) Frequently the playfulness is not as nonsensical as it seems, as is hinted in 'Ex Ponto': 'Det är inte konstverket man gör / Det är sig själv / Och man måste alltid börja från grunden / åter och åter börja från grunden' (It's not the work of art you're making it's yourself and you must always start from the beginning over and over again from the beginning). *Opus incertum* (1957) and *En natt i Otočac* (A Night in Otočac, 1961), are similar in kind to *Strountes* — in the afterword to *En natt I Otočac* Ekelöf commented: 'Jag skulle ha kunnat kalla denna bok *Opus incertum II* (eller rent av *Strountes n:r 2*) eftersom den tillhör samma antiestetiska, bitvis antipoetiska linje' (I could have called this book *Opus incertum II* (or even *Strountes No. 2*) since it belongs to the same anti-æsthetic, and at times anti-poetic line). In 'Poetik' (Poetics) he claims that formal perfection is:

> ... sökandet efter ett meningslöst
> i det meningsfulla
> och omvänt
> och allt vad jag så konstfullt söker dikta
> är kontrastvis någonting konstlöst
> och hela fyllnaden tom.
> Vad jag har skrivit
> är skrivet mellan raderna.

(... looking for something meaningless in what is meaningful and vice versa and everything I try to create so artistically is on the contrary artless and all the filling is empty. What I have written is written between the lines.)

Otočac is a town in Croatia, but in the afterword referred to above Ekelöf indicated that it can be interpreted as Hell; in the paradoxical fashion typical of him, he seeks Heaven and Hell. What he has written is 'written between the lines'; similarly, the elusive *helheten* (whole) he is searching for may be found among disparate, chaotic things. He is too much of an anarchist ever to believe he will find it, but it is essential to conduct the search even so. 'De som lever för *en* stor sak är lyckliga / Den som söker denna enda stora sak i ett otal saker / i mångfalden / han blir utnött och trött som jag' (People who live for *one* great thing are happy He who looks for this one great thing among a host of things in multiplicity will be as worn out and tired as I am.) ('Poesi i sak') (The Essence of Poetry).

In 1960 Ekelöf had published a remarkable long poem on which he had been working for more than twenty years: *En Mölna-Elegi* (A Mölna Elegy). Several excerpts of the Elegy had been published previously, notably the first third of the finished poem in *BLM* in 1946: a note explained that it was 'a poem about the relationship between time and our experience of time, perhaps also an attempt to capture the "essence of life"'. A figure is standing on Mölna jetty (a place on Lidingö near Stockholm) in late September or early October, watching the sun set over the water. An apple and a drop of water fall to the ground and the lake respectively, and the poem refers to the noise they make: the sounds are heard both near the beginning and near the end of the poem, and it is stressed that they are the same sounds we hear; in other words, the whole work takes place in a very short space of time. By employing a complicated technique of allusion and quotation, however, Ekelöf is able to compress into that very short space of time the cultural experience of centuries.

Nevertheless, the starting point of the poems is personal. The figure on the jetty is Ekelöf himself, and the chain of memories which flash through his consciousness includes several of the poet's relatives and ancestors. A key quotation is a line of Edith Södergran, one of Ekelöf's favourite poets: 'Ett flyktigt ögonblick stal min framtid' (A fleeting moment stole my future) (Södergran actually wrote 'ett nyckfullt ögonblick' (a capricious moment)), and many other quotations illustrate Ekelöf's preferences — James Joyce, for instance, Rimbaud, Swedenborg, Ibn el-Arabi, and a number of references to Bellman (Ekelöf was particularly fond of the eighteenth century). Most startling, however, is the middle section of the poem where the left-hand page is taken up by vulgar Latin and Greek quotations, most of them authentic graffiti from the walls of ancient Italy and many of them unashamedly obscene. The right-hand page is in Swedish and, broadly speaking, the verse echoes the spirit of the Latin with a 'dirty ditty' and descriptions of rape and abortion. Some authentic drawings, chosen by Ekelöf himself, illustrate the text, which is sometimes in dramatic form and has marginal comments, usually a key-word setting the tone of the section.

By stressing the parallels and connections, Ekelöf is trying to show the essential similarity of people and events at different periods of time as well as pursuing his mystical search for the unifying factor of life, the familiar theme from earlier works. The stress on sex in *En Mölna-Elegi* seems to be an acknowledgement of Freud's psychoanalytical theories and the poet's assessment of his own nature. Another motif is that of the four elements, earth, air, fire and water, especially the last two; many memories are triggered off by a section marked 'Böljesång' (Song of the Billows) which some critics see as a high-point of lyricism in Ekelöf's poetry:

> Vindsus och vågstänk
> Vågsus och vindstänk
> Vågor och dessa skiftande klockklangsviftande vindar — närmare, fjärmare ...

(Windswish and wavespray waveswish and windspray Waves and these shifting bellpealwafting winds — nearer, more distant ...)

In the last section of the poem, after the sexual violence, the water-poetry is echoed in terms of fire before reverting back to water to signify the return of the poem to its starting point.

Generally speaking, critics were impressed by *En Mölna-Elegi* although there was a feeling of disappointment with the final section which, it was considered, did not measure up to the promise of the earlier parts. Moreover, it was felt that the Latin and Greek graffiti did not merge with the Swedish poem as easily and naturally as they might: they tend to be adornments rather than constituent parts of the poems as a whole. Understandably, there was complete agreement about the difficulty of interpreting the work: no doubt it will be many years before light is thrown on all its obscurities and the full extent of its treasures revealed.[37]

In 1962 Ekelöf published a revised edition of *sent på jorden* (late arrival upon earth) in a volume which also contained *En natt på horisonten* (A Night on the Horizon) — the latter collection having the explanatory parenthesis '1930-1932'. In both cases, the poet was returning to his beginnings, wrestling once more with the problems that had concerned him in the early 1930s and solving them with the wisdom acquired in thirty years of writing poetry. There were some alterations and additions, but many of the poems were left in their original — and hence definitive — state.

Having completed that circle, Ekelöf was ready to proceed to his last and what is generally considered to be his greatest work, a trilogy consisting of *Dīwān över Fursten av Emgión* (1965), *Sagan om Fatumeh* (1966) and *Vägvisare till underjorden* (1967) (Diwan on the Prince of Emgión, The Saga of Fatumeh and Guide to the Underworld). Like all

Ekelöf's works the Diwan trilogy is carefully composed as a whole. In his notes to *Vägvisare till underjorden*, the poet explains that although this part was published last, it was conceived as what he calls *mittvalvet* (the central arch) of the trilogy — his choice of words stresses the architectural construction and a drawing at the end of *Vägvisaren* shows how that book itself was planned architecturally. The middle work is symmetrically balanced, and the first and third parts of the trilogy can be seen as counterbalancing each other: the basic components of the 'outer' books are two series of 29 poems, and in connection with *Sagan om Fatumeh* Ekelöf explained that they correspond to a 'naẓm', a string of beads, and a 'tesiḥ, a rosary. Ekelöf's preoccupation with Oriental mysticism is clear in the form as well as the content of his Diwan trilogy.

The material for each of the three books is based on authentic myths and historical happenings pertaining to the Byzantine Empire in the Middle Ages: *Dīwān över Fursten av Emgión* refers to an eleventh-century epic romance describing the capture and sufferings of Digenis Acritas, *Sagan om Fatumeh* tells the tale of an Arab girl in the fourteenth century who deteriorates from a position as a courtesan and the beloved of a prince to a wretched existence as a whore, while *Vägvisaren till underjorden* contains a less unified selection of thoughts and dreams and features a meeting between a novice nun and Satan in a palace situated in Croatia. It will be obvious that to understand the trilogy properly, the average reader needs a battery of notes and explanations; Ekelöf provides some at the end of each volume, but in addition to the historical, mythological and linguistic complications there is also the fact that the poet refers to or quotes from a large number of other literary works — indeed, he frequently quotes from his own earlier poems.

Nevertheless, one can read the Diwan trilogy in ignorance of many of the subtleties and be fascinated by the love poems, the sufferings and erotic adventures of Fatumeh (whose name incorporates the Latin word for Fate), the torture and religious search of the Prince. Familiar Ekelöf themes and symbols recur, notably the *jungfru* (virgin) (cf. the quotation from 'Tag och skriv' above), whose symbolic significance hovers between an erotic ideal, the Virgin Mary, a cosmic mother-figure and the mystical 'någonting annat' (something else), which formed the core of Ekelöf's creed. The other great theme is that of time which, as was shown by *En Mölna-Elegi*, the poet did not see as a mere linear process. The symmetrical form of the trilogy and the network of references to different epochs illustrate the concept; some of its implications are perhaps best expressed in the concluding poems of *Vägvisare till underjorden*, the last part of the trilogy to be written:

> Ensam i tysta natten trivs jag bäst
> Ensam med vägguret, denna maskin för icke-tid
> Vad vet väl en metronom om musik, om takt
> om det den är konstruerad att mäta. Dess ansikte
> är blankt och uttryckslöst som en främmande gudabilds
> Det gör mig medveten om relativiteternas oförenlighet
> Liv kan inte mätas med död, musik inte med taktslag

(Alone in the silent night is when I feel best Alone with the wall-clock, this machine for non-time What does a metronome know about music, about tempo, about what it is constructed to measure. Its face is blank and expressionless like that of a strange idol It makes me aware of the incompatibility of relativities Life cannot be measured by death, nor music by down-beats.)[38]

Gunnar Ekelöf received many prizes and honorary awards in the last ten years of his life, and was elected a member of the Swedish Academy in 1958. He died in 1968 after a long and painful illness, suffering from cancer of the throat: *Partitur. Efterlämnade dikter* (Musical Score. Posthumous Poems, 1969), contains some moving poems from this last period. Perhaps the most appropriate epitaph for Ekelöf, however, is a quotation from *Strountes*:

> Mot helheten, ständigt mot helheten
> går min väg
> O mina kringkastade lemmar!
> Hur längtar ni inte till era fästen
> till helheten, till en annan helhet!

(Towards the whole, always towards the whole that is my way Oh, my far-flung limbs! How you long for firm ground for the whole, for a different whole!)

Chapter VII

Erik Lindegren (1910-68)

by Laurie Thompson

Johan Erik Lindegren was born in Luleå and spent most of his youth in Norrland. At school he was a noted sportsman and jazz pianist. He moved to Stockholm in 1931 and began studies in literature and philosophy at the university there; always the individualist, he soon found it more appropriate and useful to read independently and so gave up his formal studies. Besides acquainting himself with the major works of European literature, notably Eliot's *The Waste Land*, he intensified his interest in music both as a listener and a performer.

Increasingly, Lindegren's energies were directed towards writing poetry. His first book of poems, *Posthum ungdom* (Posthumous Youth), was completed by the spring of 1934 and published the following year. According to his own statement, it was planned as 'a confrontation with Romantic clichés which catch on so easily (I am especially partial to them)'.[39] In later years Lindegren distanced himself from *Posthum ungdom* and did not include poems from it in his collected editions.

During the next five years Lindegren concentrated on translating and published Swedish versions of works by Faulkner, Eliot, Greene, O'Casey and Valéry. Signs of his increasingly Modernistic outlook in poetry were his visit to Finland in 1937 and discussions with Gunnar Björling, Elmer Diktonius and Rabbe Enckell, also his close association with Artur Lundkvist, one of the most knowledgeable of Swedish advocates of Modernism.

From the autumn of 1939 onwards Lindegren began collecting poems for his next book. Entitled *mannen utan väg* (the man without a way), it consists of forty sonnets — the poet used the term 'söndersprängd sonett' (exploded sonnet) — each of which is unrhymed and virtually unpunctuated, and divided into seven couplets. At first sight the poems seem obscure in the extreme, although closer examination reveals that the syntax is logical and that apparently irregular rhythms and sounds are in fact highly organized in musical fashion (the poet acknowledged the influence of Bach and Stravinsky). There are references to world events, also to other literature, for a parallel was being drawn between the political situation and the crisis facing contemporary art, the problems of disorientation in all branches of culture. Confusion is central to *mannen utan väg*; the form is inseparable from the content and demonstrates how traditional conventions (the sonnet) must be radically revised (exploded) in order to cope with the possibilities and abuses now within the scope of mid-twentieth-century man. Logical thought has proved inadequate to solve the dilemma, and Lindegren gives central importance to imagery, the progression of which is achieved by associations. There is no clear, linear development of ideas; instead, the reader is placed in a labyrinth and must work out for himself how best to pick his way through the multiplicity of possible meanings.

The scene is set in the first two poems, whose introductory nature is indicated by their being placed in parenthesis. The real world is depicted as a hall of mirrors creating seemingly endless reflections which make it impossible to distinguish fact from illusion — an appropriate image for the way in which the symbols suggest seemingly endless possibilities of interpretation.

In *mannen utan väg* the poet, who one must assume is the disorientated man of the title and also Lindegren himself, acknowledges that truth is unknowable. Nevertheless, man continues to search: 'vem kastar ej sin enda sanning åt sidan / för att finna en större och grönare fångenskap' (III) (who does not cast aside his only truth in order to find a greater and greener captivity). Similarly, from the point of view of civilized man the war appeared to be lost in 1940, but the only acceptable reaction was to fight back and hope for a victory of sorts eventually. Various possibilities are explored — 'det milda klimatet av fullständig glömska' (IV) (the mild climate of complete oblivion), a mystical union with nature (XI), resignation (XV), love (XXII) — but none is acceptable for long. Man is faced with an apparently insoluble dilemma: the impossibility of avoiding defeat, but the impossibility of accepting it.

The cycle ends on a defiant note with the poet dedicated to his memory of past hope ('jag drömmer om minnet av hindens klöv i labyrinten' (XXXVIII)) (I dream of the hoof of the hind in the labyrinth) and the prospects of a hopeful future ('framtidens dröm' (XL)). Disorientated man acquires even in apparent defeat a defiant desire to reconcile opposites, to fight back, to continue the search for a direction and to assert the superiority of life over death. This aim is indicated in poem XXI, where a series of *att*-clauses suggests the hypothetical nature of the hope tentatively expressed and the difficulty of achieving it. It is a central poem not merely because of its position at

Chapter VII

the half-way point in the cycle:

> att minnas allt som gjort ont med ett leendes
> slöja och kasta en sten långt in i evigheten
>
> att kunna sätta ihop allt man plockat sönder
> och åter höra syrsor som tidens eggande småljud
> att känna smärtan brusa i lågande glorior
> att ha savens utsikt högst upp i trädets krona
>
> att skjuta sin önskan framför sig som en vårens mur
> och veta att det värsta och det bästa återstår

(to remember everything that hurt, with the veil of a smile and throw a stone far out into eternity to fit together everything one has taken to pieces and once more to hear crickets like the stimulating small sounds of our time to feel pain roaring in flaming haloes to have the view of sap high up in the crown of a tree to push one's wishes out in front like a wall of spring and to know that the worst and the best is still in store).

In the concluding poems the disorientated man is reconciled to a future in which he awaits 'den lycka som förestavas av allt och ingenting' (XXXIX) (the happiness induced by everything and nothing).

Lindegren's *mannen utan väg* was soon recognized as a breakthrough in the establishment of the Modernistic style among Swedish poets, and was widely imitated. It was at the centre of the controversy about incomprehensibility in modern literature which raged in 1946,[40] and it is undeniable that parts of Lindegren's poetry are obscure, some of the symbols too private to permit general understanding. Nevertheless Lindegren's defence of the Modernistic style and its widespread acceptance among poets were more convincing than the criticisms.

In the mid-1940s Lindegren worked as a critic for several newspapers and journals, and published a new collection of poems, *Sviter* (Suites), in 1947. After the pessimistic introductory poem 'Hamlets himmelsfärd' (The Ascension of Hamlet) — which was actually written before *mannen utan väg* — the book is divided into nine sections, each of which contains variations on a theme, as might be expected from the musical allusion in the title. Indeed, several of the headings continue the musical parallel, e.g. 'Scherzando' (VI), 'Abstrakta variationer' (VIII), 'Pastoral-svit' (IX) (Scherzando, Abstract

Variations, Pastoral Suite). The connection between the various suites, and also the poems within each suite, is looser than in the preceding work and allows Lindegren to indulge in a wider range of moods. The love poems in the suite 'Amoroso' (VII) are particularly appealing and display a sensuousness typical of the poet. 'De fem sinnenas dans' (The Dance of the Five Senses) is justly admired for its beautiful and sensuous imagery:

> O att få dricka dig sanslös och byta vingar
> medan pärlfiskaren sjunker i sitt bländblå djup
> medan hjärtat flyter mot sin gröna katarakt
> att smaka en djupare glömska att glömma

(Oh, to drink oneself senseless and change wings while the pearl fisher sinks down into his dazzling blue depths while one's heart floats to its green cataract to taste a deeper oblivion to forget).

The style in *Sviter* is generally more relaxed than in *mannen utan väg*, the collisions between images less violent. Some poems maintain the harsh attitude towards contemporary events so typical of *fyrtiotalismen* (the style of the 1940s) e.g. 'Stupad soldat' (Dead Soldier), 'Döende gladiator' (Dying Gladiator) — but the overall tone of the book is more romantic.

Sviter was widely acclaimed and enhanced Lindegren's stature as the leading poet of the 1940s. In 1948 Lindegren became editor of *Prisma*. Typically, he encouraged contributors to write articles on all branches of art, including music, ballet and architecture, and to explore the inter-relationships between them.

Lindegren's final poetry collection, *Vinteroffer* (The Rite of Winter), was published in 1954. The title contains an ironic reference to Stravinsky's *Rite of Spring*, and the poems abound in many references to the tiredness and numbness one associates with winter, the feeling of growing old and closer to death. Lindegren appears to have become increasingly aware of the inevitable isolation suffered by a poet who is constantly trying to transcend reality and express the inexpressible. The introductory poem, 'Ikaros', is based on the Greek legend and depicts the poet soaring heavenwards towards what Keats called Beauty and Truth. The opening line refers back to *mannen utan väg*; 'Bort domnar nu hans minnen från labyrinten' (Now his memories from the labyrinth die away); the poet grows increasingly remote from the real world he has left behind — but unlike the Greek hero, Lindegren's Ikaros does not crash back to earth as his wings are melted by the sun: instead he triumphs and is reborn into a world of higher reality. Isolation and death need not be reasons for despair.

Nevertheless, the dominant impression gained by the reader is one of melancholy. The imagery is intense and sensuous, but the form of the poems in *Vinteroffer* is disciplined in a way best described as Classical.

Lindegren continued to be active as a critic and translator (of Eliot, Dylan Thomas, Spender, Saint-John Perse, Claudel, Anouilh, Rilke, Sachs), but he became increasingly interested in the combination of branches of art to form a *Gesamtkunstwerk*. He wrote several ballet and opera libretti in the 1950s and 1960s, notably an opera based on Martinson's *Aniara* (1959) and another based on Hjalmar Bergman's *Herr von Hancken* (1963), both with music by Karl-Birger Blomdahl.

Erik Lindegren was elected a member of the Swedish Academy in 1962. He died in 1968.

Karl Vennberg (1910-95)

by Laurie Thompson

Karl Gunnar Vennberg was born in Småland. After working on his parents' smallholding and taking correspondence courses, he attended secondary school in Lund and became associated with left-wing socialism. Subjected at an early age to the influence of his parents' pietism, Vennberg oscillated between rejection and acceptance of religion throughout his life, and in Lund described himself as a 'religious communist'.

Vennberg's first collection of poetry, *Hymn och hunger* (Hymn and Hunger, 1937), was not particularly well received. The disappointment stimulated Vennberg, who began to develop a new Modernistic style which was to become recognised as *fyrtiotalistisk* (of the 40s) and his critical writings won recognition among the new generation of poets. Vennberg began to assume the rôle of leader, along with Erik Lindegren. (Vennberg had married Lindegren's sister in 1938, making cooperation between them natural.)

Vennberg's breakthrough came in 1944 with the publication of *Halmfackla* (Straw Torch). The book was complete by early 1943, and several of the poems date from as early as 1938. As was the case with Lindegren's *mannen utan väg*, the impact of *Halmfackla* was all the greater for its having been delayed for several years. The bleak pessimism of the period is captured in the famous poem 'Om det fanns telefon' (If Only We Had a Telephone): in unpunctuated, unrhymed lines in free rhythms, Vennberg uses stiff official language, some of it lifted straight out of military first-aid manuals, to describe the many ways in which 'we' could assist a badly wounded patient. Unfortunately none of them is possible because of a lack of equipment, and in any case the dying man is beyond help. The final quatrain reveals the key to the whole poem:

> Om liket ska vi emellertid slåss
> om rätten att begrava
> den västerlandska kulturens
> stympade lemmar

(However, we shall fight over the right to bury the stunted limbs of Western culture)

'Klassisk prolog' (Classical Prologue), written in 1938 but revised, is typical of Vennberg's new style, pregnant with intellectual irony and disillusioned pessimism. In a luxuriant, summery park the poet expounds his gloomy philosophy to his uncomprehending baby, explaining that 'ingen enda gåta nånsin låtit / sig lösas eller nånsin ämnar låta / sig lösas' (not a single riddle has ever allowed itself to be solved nor does it ever intend to allow itself to be solved).

The following year Vennberg published *Tideräkning* (Chronology). In 'Att leva' (Living) Vennberg suggests that living is a choice between 'det likgiltiga / och det omöjliga' (the indifferent and the impossible), and in the title poem comments that 'Överhuvud förefaller det / som om de ben / som världshistorien slänger till oss / skulle vara rätt magra och avknaprade' (All in all it seems as if the bones thrown to us by world history are pretty lean and well chewed).

Not surprisingly, Vennberg was at the centre of the debate on pessimism which was conducted in the journals and on the cultural pages of newspapers in the mid-1940s. Pessimism was a central trait of the *fyrtiotalistisk* style, and the debate was initiated by Vennberg's article in *40-tal* at the beginning of 1946, 'Den moderna pessimismen och dess vedersakare' (Modern Pessimism and Its Opponents).[41]

Chapter VII

Vennberg played a leading rôle in almost all the important cultural debates in the 1940s, and was also chiefly responsible for acquainting Swedish readers with Kafka, whose Expressionistic style, laden with guilt and Angst, seemed ideally suited to the times.[42]

Fiskefärd (Fishing Trip, 1949), is an altogether more benign and relaxed work. The rejection of isolation and bitterness is perhaps most forcefully expressed in 'Blott icke samma ensamhet' (But please not the same loneliness):

> Vad som helst blott icke samma ensamhet på nytt
> ensamheten
> djupare än havet
> beskare än ökentörsten
> vassare än kniven mot ett öppet öga.
> Vad som helst blott icke samma ensamhet på nytt.

(Anything you like but please not the same loneliness again the loneliness deeper than the ocean more bitter than a desert thirst sharper than a knife at an open eye. Anything you like but please not the same loneliness again.)

However, the apparent relaxation of Vennberg's bitterly ironic, critical and pessimistic stance soon proved to be a temporary phenomenon. Four new collections of poetry were published in rapid succession at the beginning of the 1950s in which the poet reverts to his attitude of some ten years previously: *Gatukorsning* (1952), *Vårövning* (1953), *Synfält* (1954), *Vid det röda trädet* (1955) (Crossroads, Spring Manoeuvre, Field of Vision, At the Red Tree). The 'loneliness' Vennberg had dreaded is now accepted as unavoidable, and the poet acknowledges in 'Oktober' that 'Några av oss måste förbli ensamma; / alla kan vi inte bäddas ner i familjegravar' (Some of us must remain lonely; we can't all be bedded down in family graves). Although some poems depict summery landscapes, the dominant tone is autumnal, if not wintry. The gloomy attitude seemed justified by world events as the Cold War dominated politics; Vennberg was the leader of a group of Swedish writers who advocated *Tredje ståndpunkten* (The Third Point of View), a neutral position independent of the two superpowers, albeit inclined left of centre.[43] The poetry is characterized by ironic withdrawal and resignation, as if to acknowledge that an individual poet cannot influence events and should retreat to a realm of intellectual speculation. He wonders about his usefulness as a poet and critic —

perhaps he might as well have become a clog maker, and his epitaph would have read: 'här vilar vår siste träskomakare./ Lika överflödig i detta livet / som i det tillkommande' (here lies our last clog-maker. Just as superfluous in this life as in the next) ('Träskomakare')(Clog-Maker).

After the publication of *Vid det röda trädet* in 1955 Vennberg concentrated on journalism, mainly as cultural editor of *Aftonbladet*, and for the next twenty years produced only two collections of poetry: *Tillskrift* (Attribution, 1960), and *Sju ord på tunnelbanan* (Seven Words on the Underground, 1971). He claimed later the political commitment so characteristic of the 1960s and early 1970s stimulated his journalistic instincts but frustrated his poetic aspirations. 'Leva vidare, i brist på bättre' (Go on living your life, for want of anything better), he comments wryly in 'Program' from his 1971 collection.

Vennberg published several new collections of poetry in the 70s and 80s, and even the early 90s, and was highly regarded by later generations. Possibly his best from this period were *Dikter kring noll* (Poems Around Zero, 1983), *Längtan till Egypten* (Longing for Egypt, 1987), and *I väntan på pendeltåget* (Waiting for the Commuter Train, 1990). All the typical Vennberg characteristics of scepticism, irony and resignation are very much to the fore, but an interesting development was his emergence as an outstanding writer of love poetry. He wrote love poems as a younger man, of course; but the quality of his later ones made readers look back to the earlier volumes and rediscover a side of Vennberg that had been overshadowed by his dry pessimism. In 1990, to celebrate Vennberg's eightieth birthday, Agneta Pleijel and Birgitta Trotzig edited a special anthology of Vennberg's love poetry, *Du är min landsflykt* (You Are My Refuge); it was very well received, and deservedly so.

Karl Vennberg was a highly competent poet; but it may well be that his most significant contribution to Swedish literary history is his ability to pick on controversial topics for debate, pointing opinion and trends in certain directions. His heyday as an innovative poet was the 1940s and 1950s, but his influence as an opinion-former lasted for another forty years, and its full extent has yet to be properly appreciated.

Chapter VII

Tomas Tranströmer (born 1931)

by Gavin Orton

Tomas Tranströmer was born in Stockholm and graduated from the university there in 1956. He has worked as a psychologist, including some years in a prison for young offenders. Of the poets starting their careers in the 1950s, Tranströmer is the one whose reputation has remained surest and whose poetry has been least influenced by the fads and fashions of Swedish literary life, dealing as it does with the ultimate mysteries of existence. In an interview Tranströmer has explained: 'One can easily say that my experience of reality is, at heart, that I consider existence as a great mystery and that sometimes, at certain moments, this mystery has an enormous charge so that it has a religious character, and it is in these contexts that I write.'[44]

Tranströmer's published work is small in quantity and shows no dramatic development over the years. It consists of the collections *17 dikter* (17 Poems, 1954), *Hemligheter på vägen* (Secrets on the Way, 1958), *Den halvfärdiga himlen* (The Half-Finished Heaven, 1962), *Klanger och spår* (Bells and Tracks, 1966), *Mörkerseende* (Seeing in the Dark, 1970), *Stigar* (Paths, 1973) (half of which consists of translations of the American poet Robert Bly and the Hungarian Janos Pilinszky), *Östersjöar* (Baltics, 1974), *Sanningsbarriären* (The Truth-Barrier, 1978), *Det vilda torget* (The Wild Market-Square, 1983), *För levande och döda* (For Living and Dead, 1989), and *Sorgegondolen* (The Sad Gondola, 1998). Tranströmer has a considerable international reputation. A number of English translations of his works have appeared, including a half-share in a volume of the Penguin Modern European Poets (1974), and an edition of his collected poems.[45]

Tranströmer's work has attracted attention for its style as much as for its content. His verse is full of striking and unexpected imagery. The Russian writer Gogol, for example, is described in *17 dikter* as follows: 'Kavajen luggsliten som en vargflock./ Ansiktet som en marmorflisa' (The jacket threadbare as a wolf-pack./ The face like a marble slab) (F, 23), while a giant oak in the poem 'Storm' is 'lik en förstenad älg' (like a petrified elk) (F, 21). Sweden in December in the poem 'Epilog' is 'ett uppdraget,/ avtacklat skepp' (a beached/unrigged ship) (F, 34). Like the Surrealists, Tranströmer uses imagery in a suggestive rather than a precise way, and it is often up to the reader to supply his own interpretations. The liveliness of the imagery is restrained by highly disciplined verse, with laconic, low-key language, and this creates a tension in the style which matches a similar tension in Tranströmer's universe. One of the most noticeable features of this tension in his poetry is the struggle between movement and rest. The title of one of the poems of *17 dikter* is 'I den forsande stäven är vila' (There is Peace in the Surging Prow) (F, 27). Another example in the same collection is provided by the opening lines of 'Ostinato': 'Under vråkens kretsande punkt av stillhet / rullar havet dånande fram i ljuset' (Under the buzzard's circling point of stillness / ocean rolls resoundingly on in daylight) (F,22). This sense of restrained power and drive is expressed on a cosmic scale when in 'Svenska hus ensligt belägna' (Solitary Swedish Houses) in *Hemligheter på vägen* the poet talks about 'Guds energi / hoprullad i mörkret' (God's energy / coiled up in the dark) (F,40).

Tranströmer's main preoccupation is with man's spiritual and mental experiences, and when in his later collections he shows some awareness of the social and political aspects of life, he generally distances himself from them. He seems to be trying to grasp some vision beyond ordinary reality and he explores states of mind in which insights into the mysteries of the human soul, or of the universe itself, may be attained. In the poem 'Preludium' in *17 dikter* he describes the comprehensive vision of the world he obtains at the moment of waking up: 'I dagens första timmar kan medvetandet omfatta världen / som handen griper en solvarm sten' (In day's first hours consciousness can grasp the world / as the hand grips a sun-warmed stone) (F, 21). He appears to be waiting for some kind of religious revelation, though what this revelation is and whether or not it ever arrives is unclear.

Another of Tranströmer's preoccupations is history. He sees the historical past as living on in the present. In the poem 'Elegi' in *17 dikter* he describes civilization as a whaling-station, where the inhabitants are always aware of the dead whale's presence by its stench: in other words, the past — particularly its crimes — is very much part of the present. He describes how all ages coexist in the present in another image in the same poem:

>   Det finns korsväg i ett ögonblick.
>   Distansernas musik har sammanströmmat.
>   Allt sammanvuxet till ett yvigt träd.
>   Försvunna städer glittrar i dess grenverk

Chapter VII

(There's a crossroads in a moment. Music of the distances converges. All grown together in a leafy tree. Vanished cities glitter in its branches.) (F, 32).

The past also repeats itself in the present — there is a sense of *déjà vu* about things. For example, in the poem 'Om Historien' (About History) in *Klanger och spår* Tranströmer sees Gide as a latter-day Goethe: 'Goethe reste i Afrika 1926 förklädd till Gide och såg allt' (Goethe travelled in Africa in '26 disguised as Gide and saw everything) (F,76). And when Tranströmer hears the news with reports of French army atrocities in Algeria, he sees the face of Dreyfus, an earlier victim of French militarism. The individual too is made up of layers of history, of inherited instincts. Visiting an iron-age fort in the poem 'Skyfall över inlandet' (Downpour over the Interior) in *Klanger och spår*, the poet hears 'En lång hes trumpet ur järnåldern. / Kanske från inne i honom själv' (A long hoarse trumpet from the iron age./ Perhaps from inside himself) (F, 82). Man changes but remains much the same through the ages. In the final poem of *17 dikter*, 'Epilog', Tranströmer describes this procession of mankind through the ages — 'en sjöresa, en vandring / som inte är ett jagande men trygghet' (a voyage, a journey / which is no wild rush but gives security) (F, 35) — and behind it he sees God, also changing and unchanging:

> Och slutligen:
> Guds ande är som Nilen: översvämmar
> och sjunker i en rytm som har beräknats
> i texterna från skilda tidevarv.
>
> Men Han är också oföränderlig
> och därför sällan observerad här.
> Han korsar processionens väg från sidan.
>
> Som fartyget passerar genom dimman,
> utan att dimman märker något. Tystnad.
> Lanternans svaga ljussken är signalen.

(And finally: God's spirit, like the Nile: flooding and sinking in a rhythm calculated in texts from many epochs. But he is also immutable and thus observed here seldom. It's from the side He crosses the procession's path. As when the steamer passes through the mist, the mist that does not notice. Silence. Faint glimmer of the lantern is the signal.) (F, 36)

While Tranströmer's earlier works are preoccupied with such attempts to catch glimpses of God through the mist, his later poems touch on the more tangible world. Tranströmer's relationship to his fellow men is ambivalent: he sees the need for social contact and indicates that without a social context man can lose his identity, but at the same time he feels the need for solitude. This is expressed in a two-part poem called 'Ensamhet' (Alone) in *Klanger och spår*. In the first part he describes a skid in his car which takes him into the path of oncoming traffic. In a sudden moment of fear he seems to be thrown out of society and to lose his identity. In the second part of the poem, however, he shows his pleasure at living in such a sparsely populated country as Sweden where he can be himself, not surrounded by a swarm of eyes.

Tranströmer views social and political problems in a detached way, seeing them against an enormous time-scale or a divine plan. In a poem about the conflict between nature and technology ('Trafik' in *Mörkerseende*) he does not seem unduly worried about the growth of urban development: 'Byggnaderna sjunker två millimeter / om året — marken slukar dem sakta' (the buildings sink two millimetres / each year — the ground is eating them slowly)(F, 91). As for pollution, the cycle of nature may be interrupted, but only temporarily: 'Och ingen vet hur det ska gå, bara att kedjan / bryts och fogas ihop igen ständigt' (And no one knows what will happen, only that the chain / perpetually breaks, perpetually joins together again) (F, 91). The same Olympian view prevails in the poem 'I Nildeltat' (In the Nile Delta) in *Den halvfärdiga himlen*, where after seeing the appalling poverty in Egypt the poet hears a voice in a dream saying: 'Det finns en som är god./ Det finns en som kan se allt utan att hata.' ('There is one who is good. / There is one who can see all without hating.') (F,62). Yet there is evidence that this detachment is hard-won. In the poem 'Allegro' in *Den halvfärdiga himlen* he indicates how after a hard day he finds solace in playing Haydn:

> Klangen säger att friheten finns
> och att någon inte ger kejsaren skatt.
>
> Jag kör ner händerna i mina haydnfickor
> och härmar en som ser lugnt på världen.
>
> Jag hissar haydnflaggan — det betyder:

Chapter VII

'Vi ger oss inte. Men vill fred.'

(The music says freedom exists and someone doesn't pay the emperor tax. I push down my hands in my Haydnpockets and imitate a person looking on the world calmly. I hoist the Haydnflag — it signifies: 'We don't give in. But want peace.' (F, 64)

Östersjöar, a poem in six parts, can be read as an anthology of Tranströmer's main themes, expressed in the symbol of the Baltic — or rather several Baltics, for the sea symbolizes several different things. Firstly, the Baltic is a symbol of how many ages coexist in the present, with its monuments and activities from many different periods of time. (And several historical Baltics live within the poet, since his ancestors come from the archipelago.) The Baltic also has a political significance, washing the shores of free countries like Sweden with its open frontiers, but also the Soviet Union — 'platser där medborgarna är under kontroll' (places where citizens are under control) (F, 107). And as is usual in Tranströmer's verse, the landscape is also a picture of abstract concepts. The poet's grandfather, a pilot charting vessels in the mist through the labyrinth of the archipelago and talking in half-understood languages to foreign sea-captains, becomes a symbol of the poet seeking in the unknown and invisible and achieving: 'Samtal på felstavad engelska, samförstånd och missförstånd men mycket lite av medveten lögn' (Conversations in misspelt English, understanding and misunderstanding but very little conscious falsehood) (F, 106). Similarly, the open (or closed) frontiers become symbols of Tranströmer's search or visions beyond everyday reality: 'Man går länge och lyssnar och når då en punkt där gränserna öppnas / eller snarare / där allting blir gräns.' (You go on, listening, and then reach a point where the frontiers open / or rather / where everything becomes a frontier) (F, 107).

Life, like the Baltic, is full of risks, but there are moments of peace, and Tranströmer expresses this in the image of a Gotland font, with its sides covered in images of men in struggle, while inside is the still water. Or in a modern and typically drastic image: 'Och friden kan komma droppvis, kanske om natten / när vi ingenting vet,/ eller som när man ligger på dropp i en sal på sjukhuset.' (And peace can come drop by drop, perhaps at night / when we know nothing / or when you are lying in a hospital ward on a drip)(F, 109).

It is the expectation of this sudden and unheralded revelation — of peace, of God — that is at the heart of Tranströmer's poetry.

Three Poets of the 1960s

by Peter Graves

Although in retrospect the 1960s appears as the decade when the most important feature of Swedish poetry was its politicization it was not in fact until the second half of the decade that such a development took place. In the earlier years of the period the interests of poets centred on experimentation with form and language, the aims of which were to break out of what was felt to be the all-constricting, inward-looking stranglehold of Modernism and to make poetry a means of speaking to a wider public on a wider range of themes.

Göran Palm (born 1931) in 'Megafoner i poesiparken' (Megaphones in the Poetry Park) from his first collection *Hundens besök* (The Dog's Visit, 1961) gives an ironic expression to this sense of constriction:

Och meningen? Ni frågar efter meningen? / Men dikten själv är diktens mål, förstod ni inte det? / Det gäller att bli ett med poesin, naturligtvis, / att själv bli megafon... / Men jag vill ingenting av detta! / Vad säger ni? Hur kom ni in egentligen? / Ni måste ha gått fel, det här är diktens park. Ge er iväg! [46] (55-56)

(And the meaning? You're asking for the meaning? But poetry itself is poetry's aim, don't you understand? It's a matter of becoming a megaphone oneself. But I don't want any of that! What did you say? How did you get in anyway? You must be lost, this is the Poetry Park. Go away!)

Palm, one of the most prominent literary critics of the 1950s and innovators of the 1960s, argued that the way forward lay through a return to simplicity rather than through the ever-increasing complexity of Modernism: 'In order to count as an experimenter a modern poet does not need today to work with compound fragmented and disharmonic forms of language. In fact, it is not just a small band of rebels who work in that way but the majority. If he wants to count as an experimenter he would seem to have a lot more to gain by trying out simple, direct and comprehensible forms of language'.[47] Much of his early poetry thus concentrates on language, and on his desire to de-mythologize poetry. It is not an easy task and in this first collection much of the writing concerns his sense of isolation, both social and linguistic: the isolation is underlined by the Spanish setting of a series of poems. There he is the complete outsider, uncomprehended and incapable of influencing what he sees:

Jag packade min resväska och gick. / Solen lyste vit. Och ingenting / som låg på vägen rörde sig / för mina steg. / Jag återlämnar allt i orört skick.(75)

(I packed my case and left. The sun shone white. And nothing that lay on the road moved before my feet. I leave everything in an untouched state.)

Palm's second volume, *Världen ser dig* (The World is Looking at You, 1963), shows him moving out of isolation towards community and communication through political involvement. It contains the long and complex poem 'Själens furir', in which the successful middle-class literary figure confesses to the many threads in his soul that hold him back on his new road. The poems begins by referring to this 'Sergeant in the Soul' who is an internal voice, perhaps conscience, perhaps false conscience, sometimes rebellious, sometimes ingratiating.[48] The messages it sends are contradictory and usually reactionary. They represent the reverse side of the political idealist, the urge to individual aggrandizement at the expense of collective principle. In the dialogue between the poet and 'furiren' it is the poet — the idealist — who has the final word: 'I go with bold calm steps'.

'Själens furir' is a central poem not merely within Palm's production but for the poetic development of the decade as a whole — so much so that Björn Håkanson wrote in his preface to the important anthology of poetry of the 1960s, *Nya linjer* (New Lines, 1966), that it was essential reading for anyone desiring a complete picture of the new trends in poetry.[49] What Håkansson is suggesting is that the poem signals the approaching radicalization of poetry in Sweden, its almost total political engagement, its discovery of an audience and of the language to reach that audience. Like Palm, other poets were ransacking their souls and discovering an isolation that they attributed partly to their middle-class backgrounds and partly to being Swedish. The solution lay in socialist internationalism. In 'Själens furir' Palm had stated: 'There are two ways of going astray: conformism and isolation'. The process had its dangers, however, and some argued that the new poetry was artistically inferior to that produced in the 1950s.[50] Much of the 'engaged' poetry ignored or rejected any concept of structure and thus degenerated into little more than sloganeering or advertisement listing where the high-mindedness of its aims finally proved incapable of concealing the developmental limitations.

In the case of Göran Palm radical involvement led him to write poetry only sparingly in the following years. Instead, he produced a number of books of political argument and investigative journalism in which he used the conscious simplicity of style and argument that he had proposed for poetry. Most discussed of these was *Indoktrineringen i Sverige* (Indoctrination in Sweden, 1968) in which he revealed from a socialist standpoint the all-pervading nature of capitalist propaganda in Sweden. That led to his next book *Vad kan man göra?* (What Can We Do, 1969) — a practical handbook in political thought and action which also contains poems illustrative of his theme. Among them are those which deal with his own past and present the road from a bourgeois stance to socialism. His literary aims are now 'to waken and deepen in as many people as possible the consciousness that stimulates collective action, and to bring about this with the help of all conceivable artistic methods'.[51] Among his chosen methods was to become an anonymous industrial worker and to describe his experiences in 'report' books such as *Ett år på LM* (A Year at LM's, 1972).

Palm's return to poetry in 1984 with *Sverige — en vintersaga* (Sweden — A Winter's Tale) provides the reader with both surprise and familiarity. The surprise lies in the form — 280 pages of blank verse, a metre not common in Swedish poetry and, indeed, one that does not easily fit in with the structure of the language. The book, moreover, concludes with five pages of end-notes in which Palm details his sources. The familiarity lies in the ideology: *Sverige — en vintersaga* consists of stories, anecdotes and vignettes from both past and present-day Sweden with the spotlight focused mainly on class conflict and oppression. Thus, for example, the story of the lynching of Axel von Fersen by the Stockholm mob in 1810 is told, the regulations concerning the industrial disease silicosis are discussed critically, the situation of the Sami is presented and so on. And a long satirical section is devoted to the state of poetry today, which Palm sees as too fragmented, too inward-looking, too narrow in terms of theme, too exclusive and too private: he calls instead for a thematic broadening, for the acceptance into the canon of popular song and lyrics, and for a return to tied forms. *Sverige — en vintersaga* and the volumes that Palm has produced since, voices in the wilderness though they seem to be, are among the most interesting and hopeful omens in the Swedish poetry of recent decades.

Chapter VII

Göran Palm's striving for linguistic simplicity — 'nyenkelhet' as it was rapidly christened — formed only one of the experimental lines that attempted to break with the immediate past in the 1960s. A second line of development is what has been termed 'welfare state realism'. Its prime exponent is Sonja Åkesson (1926-77), a poet whose work was both immediately accessible and linguistically and thematically innovative. The central poem in her production is 'Självbiografi' from her collection *Husfrid* (Domestic Peace, 1963). The poem is subtitled 'reply to Ferlinghetti' and a comparison with Laurence Ferlinghetti's 'Autobiography' is revealing. What Sonja Åkesson has done is to write an almost line-by-line critique of the view of life expressed by the American poet — a critique summarized in the lines:

Jag lever ett lugnt / liv läsande hyllningar till tillvaron / av någon som inte led tillräckligt. (20)[52]

(I am leading a quiet life reading paeans to existence by someone who didn't suffer enough.)

Ferlinghetti writes from the point of view of the Beat generation: trivia and the passing moment are snapped up and somehow dignified into cosmic experience without further analysis. The poem is a hymn to life, or at least to that sort of life dependent on continuous motion and wide open spaces. It is very Beat, very American and very male. Sonja Åkesson's reply reveals a life based on wholly different experiences and interpreted with different values. She writes as a Swede and uses 'Swedish' almost as a synonym for small and claustrophobic: not dreams of 'Tom Sawyer catching crayfish in the Bronx river' but the enclosed world of the Junior Baptist Union were the formative memories of her childhood. Like Ferlinghetti, Åkesson deals with the everyday, but she refuses to imbue it with grandiosity. Instead the trivia fix the poem in a concrete milieu of the popular singer Alice Babs, 'sewing circles' and 'sober supermarkets'. It is a world in which trivia form the bars of a prison, not the wings of escape. Characteristic of the poem are words of enclosure: 'double-buttoned', 'snowed in'. The society she presents is repressed, its facade of respectability conceals hypocrisy, isolation and a threat of violence:

Och jag har sett slaktarn i min hemby / spela orgel med feta saliga fingrar / på ett f.d. järnvägshotell / medan hans fästmö virrade utanför / besatt av en annan sorts ande. (12)

(And I have seen the butcher in my village play the organ with fat and blessed fingers at a one-time railway hotel while his fiancée wandered confused outside possessed by a different sort of spirit.)

The confinement Sonja Åkesson gives voice to is aggravated by her role as woman and mother. She sees women as the sufferers in the world, in childbirth, in abortion, in rape, and not least in marriage. Escape towards the limitless horizons pointed at by Ferlinghetti is not a possibility; at most it can be a question of flight into materialism or the escapism of the popular television programme 'Hylands hörna'. Higher flights are rapidly grounded:

Jag sprang ut i den tidiga skymningen / och ville sträcka handen genom himlen / men skyndade tillbaka hem / för att inte bränna potatisen. (16)

(I ran out into the early dusk and wanted to stretch my hand through the sky but hurried back home so as not to burn the potatoes.)

The themes in 'Självbiografi' recur throughout Sonja Åkesson's poetry, often within a similar confessional context. But she can also be sharply satirical as in the Pidgin poem 'Äktenskapsfrågan' (The Marriage Question), also from *Husfrid*. Or she may resort — rather too often later in the decade — to lists of advertising slogans and the clichés and personality cults of pulp magazines to achieve the same effect. Sonja Åkesson's strengths lie in a sharp and bilious eye for the everyday detail, particularly where it affects women. She is firmly anchored in time and space, sometimes hysterical, often satirical, but always a humane and sympathetic reporter.

Without doubt the single most discussed poem of the decade was 'Om kriget i Vietnam' (On the War in Vietnam) by Göran Sonnevi (born 1939). It appeared in *BLM* in March 1965 and marked the discovery of the Vietnam war by Swedish intellectuals: it has been described as 'the event which more than any other contributed to the obvious radicalization among young intellectuals...'[53] The poem is in fact more humanitarian than directly political. Sitting in front of a television on a snowy night the poet watches news reports from Vietnam and compares the peace and safety of his life in Sweden with the situation there:

Chapter VII

Den svenska / ekonomin dödar numera / inte många, i varje / fall inte här i landet. Ingen för / krig i vårt land för att skydda / sina egna intressen. Ingen / bränner oss med napalm / för en feodal frihets skull. (88)[54]

(The Swedish economy doesn't kill many these days, at least not in this country. Nobody wages war in our country to protect his own interests. Nobody burns us with napalm for the sake of a feudal freedom.)

Much of the impact of the poem derives from the quiet, everyday tone of the sympathy and from the simplicity with which the poet articulates his sense of impotent, excluded helplessness in a series of uncomplicated statements. In later Vietnam poems Sonnevi comes to his subject from a more intellectualized Marxist position but, whatever the theoretical stance, the driving force behind his political poems remains his humanitarian instinct allied to a stubborn optimism that few of his contemporaries express:

Det är svårt att reparera / men det måste gå / annars kunde vi lika gärna gå och dö / allesammans. (127)

(It is difficult to repair but it has to work or we might as well go and die the whole lot of us.)

In his best work Sonnevi shows a rare ability to synthesize the abstract and the concrete. In his early collections — he made his début in 1961 — abstraction dominates even though many of the poems are concerned with nature. That he himself is aware of the dangers of abstraction in his work is made clear in the poem 'Det abstrakta' (The Abstract) in *Det måste gå* (It Has To Work, 1970). There he writes of two sorts of abstraction: 'abstraction / as illusion / deformation...the other sort / is that which gives necessary knowledge / about the world' (165). In a poem such as 'Vad förmår kärlekens strukturer' (What Can the Structures of Love Do) the synthesis is complete: his universal human sympathy comes together with his specific wonder at procreation, his concepts of language with his political viewpoint. It is noteworthy that the poem is dedicated to Noam Chomsky and in *Dikter 1959-1973* (Poems 1959-1973, 1974) Sonnevi adds that his starting point was Chomsky's ideas on the deep and surface structures of language. In these poems we become familiar with the typical Sonnevi tone: there is a purity and coolness about the surface of the poems, an almost disinfectant quality which leaves little room for rhetorical posturing, self-consciousness and generalization. And there is an immense consciousness of language itself because that and that alone will enable us to establish contact between man and man, man and idea, man and reality. In the collection of fifty-one sonnets, *Små klanger, en röst* (Small Sounds, One Voice, 1981), it seems sometimes that the poet despairs of achieving such contact. The tone changes and expresses, in a language now pervaded by tension rather than coolness, a pessimism that contrasts with his earlier stubborn 'it has to work': 'there is nothing here other than / the attempt, despairing, stupid, / repetitive, throwing itself / against the wall, bloody, raging, / building itself Now it is/ time The angels of peace sink / in the blood-red, transparent war / War lives now in the cry for peace'.

The apocalyptic imagery used here reminds us that Sonnevi might fittingly be viewed as a visionary poet, a mystic. It has often been pointed out that his image world connects 'with traditional systems of symbols — Jewish mysticism, the cabbala, alchemy'.[55] There is a dichotomy at the heart of his work and it lies in the fact that through language he attempts to reach what lies beyond language, through the self he tries to reach the universal, through time he reaches for the infinite. Not surprisingly, then, for all his emphasis on language, the literal meaning of much of his work is obscure, illuminated by flashes of clarity and brilliant insights. It is symptomatic that he frequently makes reference to music, particularly Mozart, for reading Sonnevi is an experience akin to listening to music, an experience that is simultaneously meaningful and beyond ratiocination:[56]

> Mozart i den första hjärnan, i den klingande andra, musiken
> Vi är i den uteslutna tredje, motstycket, omöjligt,
> i dess ständiga förändring, som alla andra hjärnor
> Vi är en liten del av den
> Så rör vid oss musiken,
> hela den förflutna, hela den kommande (234)[57]

(Mozart in the first brain, in the ringing second, music We are the excluded third, the counterpart, impossible, in its perpetual change, like all other brains We are a small part of it Thus music affects us, the whole of the past, the whole of what is to come)

Chapter VII

Swedish Poetry since 1970

by Steven P. Sondrup

Swedish poetry since 1970 is particularly interesting in terms of what it preserves, what it adapts, and what it rejects from the highly innovative and more volatile preceding decades. The fifteen-year period following World War II saw the full blossoming of the high Modernist mode in Swedish poetry in terms of the major accomplishments of Gunnar Ekelöf and Erik Lindegren, for example, while the late 1960s and the 1970s witnessed a growing concern with a variety of political issues ranging from the war in Vietnam and the coup with its subsequent military dictatorship in Chile to the ever changing but always disquieting tensions between Western Europe and the United States on the one hand and the Soviet block on the other. The acute awareness that Sweden was positioned both geographically and ideologically between two hostile camps with terrifying arsenals of conventional as well as nuclear weapons found expressions in both direct and indirect ways. The question of the inherent political status of poetry itself was explored in thoughtful reflection as well as often shrill debate. The most extreme positions maintained that all poetry is necessarily political and should, therefore, in good faith be deployed to conscious political ends rather than ultimately becoming escapist fantasy.[58]

The often unspoken but implied motto of many strands of political commitment focused on securing a more humane existence for all of the world's inhabitants rather than tolerating the cultural and economic exploitation of a large majority of the people by the wealthy elite.[59] Much of the poetry as well as the theorizing was oriented toward the political left, but even those voices that could be identified as clearly Marxist tended to mix in a complex polyphony of orientations, emphases, and agendas rather than articulating a consensus or a univocal position. The generally egalitarian *Ord och Bild,* the more intellectually oriented *BLM,* as well as *Lyrikvännen* were seen as and occasionally criticized for having become excessively politicized and polemic. While Stig Carlson, for example, was outspoken in his defence of politically engaged poetry, arguing variously that poetry that failed to confront contemporary political issues was of little merit, Artur Lundkvist, on the other hand, spoke with a degree of cynicism of his distrust of the Maoists who appeared to have commandeered Bonnier's typesetting operation.

The lyric evolution of Tobias Berggren (born 1940) began with poetry that criticized contemporary social conventions from within a generally Marxist framework (*Det nödvändiga är inte klart* (What is Necessary is Unclear, 1973)) but is particularly interesting in terms of the subsequent development of his thought concerning the complexities of language and its relationship to any conception of reality. Berggren is an unabashedly cerebral yet highly fluid poet who draws on often complex mythic patterns as interpretive matrices and models of contemporary experience (*Bergsmusik* (Mountain Music, 1978)). The vexing relationship of the empirical world's phenomenological reality to its ephemeral and nearly inaccessible fundamental essence forms the conceptual core of *Resor i din tystnad* (Travels in Your Silence, 1976) and *Thernos* (1981). Berggren is also the master of short, lyrically intense poems that succeed remarkably in evoking richly diverse and subtly modulated moods even while exploring complex questions as *24 romantiska etyder* (24 Romantic Etudes, 1987) well attests. Music in general, an important aspect of Berggren's lyric consciousness, and specifically Chopin's twenty-four preludes (opus 28) here not only provide a structural framework for the collection but also an interpretive context. In this volume, a poem is devoted to each of the preludes and thus to each of the twenty-four musical keys. The first poem, 'Etyd nr 1, som i C-dur' (Study no.1, in C major), begins by proposing challenging images for the nature of language that are suggestively open to affective elaboration or resolution.

> Landet där språket är mitt
> börjar med sovande sten. Dröm och vaka
> växer där språket bryter ljuset. Som en mörk,
> graviterande kropp sitt ljus drar växandet åt sig
> sina tidsformer. Som det oupphörligen
> rinnande vattnet sitt läckande
> drar drömlöst sovande människokroppar åt sig
> historiens enslighet. (7)

(The country where the language is mine begins with sleeping stone. Dream and wakefulness grow where language refracts the light. Like a dark gravitating body attracting its light growing attracts its temporal forms. Like the unceasingly running water attracting leaking, dreamlessly sleeping human bodies attract history's loneliness).

Chapter VII

After following the musical cycles of modulation full circle with corresponding verbal and imagistic modalities, the series of poems ends, just as the cycle of musical tonalities, so near yet so far from where it began.

> Jag retirerar
> in i fläcken av skugga, den dansande, dansande
> skuggfläcken
> där språket omintetgörs; där
> den ohyggliga fasan är
> i det morrande och vrålande suddet,
> där djuret är
> för vilket språket
> saknar alla betydelser
> utom förgörelsens.
> Där språket är rendrömt. (76)

(I retire into the spot of shadow, the dancing, dancing shadow-spot where language is destroyed; where dreadful horror is in the growling and bellowing smudge where the animal is for which language lacks all meaning except that of destruction. Where language is dreamt pure.)

Although the political intensity of the preceding decade nearly vanished during the mid-1970s and 1980s, poetry nonetheless was not completely without social engagement. Much of what earlier may have been understood as nature poetry assumed an ecological orientation in advocating greater attention for the protection of the environment. Lennart Sjögren (born 1930) with *Dikter ur landet* (Poems From the Country, 1969), *Havet* (The Sea, 1974, a response to Göran Palm), *1452 och Dikter för vår tid* (1452 and Poems For Our Time, 1977), *Men också denna skog* (But Also This Forest, 1980), and *Bilden: Tankar om poesi och miljö* (The Picture: Thoughts of Poetry and Environment, 1981) is especially forthright in his expression of his concerns about environmental issues.[60]

Paralleling similar social concerns around the world and accompanied by the introduction of the work of Sylvia Plath and Anne Sexton into the Swedish literary dialogue, the question of women's poetry came to the fore. In 1975 *BLM* published a special issue on women's literature that engaged with the question, but in general the lyric was not the genre most amenable to promoting women's concerns *qua* ideology in a politically engaged and consistent manner. Paralleling but also transcending this specific attention to women's poetry as social agenda, three women who in subsequent years have become enormously important figures in Swedish cultural affairs made their début: Eva Ström (born 1947), Kristina Lugn (born 1948), and Katarina Frostenson (born 1953).

Of these Eva Ström has, perhaps, captured the broadest attention outside Sweden in the form of translations and anthologies of contemporary poetry. Although passing biographical observations suggest poetic inclinations and sensitivities extending well back into her childhood, her professional training was in medicine which she practised from 1974 until 1988. She first came to the attention of the public as a poet of stature in the late 1970s and early 1980s with the publication of *Den brinnande zeppelinaren* (The Burning Zeppelin, 1977), *Steinkind (1979), Det mörka alfabetet* (The Dark Alphabet, 1982), and *Akra* (1983). These generally slim volumes are characterized by an economy of means, emotional intensity, and cogent dialectical juxtapositions. Ström communicates a continuing awareness of working in the medium of language and the simultaneous realization of the degree to which it is incommensurate with experience. The only recourse is to oneiric dissonances or archetypal imagery arising somewhere near the threshold of consciousness being expressed before conventional syntax and grammar can shape them according to the dictates of conventional logic and ideology. Her most recent publications, *Kärleken till matematiken* (Love of Mathematics, 1989), *Brandenburg* (1993), and *Poesi och musik* (Poetry and Music, 1997 with Ákos Rózmann, 10 pages and a CD), reveal, perhaps, an even greater visceral intensity and raw immediacy.

Kristina Lugn's poetry is by contrast more personal, perhaps more explicitly confessional in tone, and more absorbed with the isolation and challenges facing women in contemporary society. Although by the mid 1980s she had become an extremely popular and widely discussed poet, her début in 1972 was notably inauspicious. Her first volume of poetry, *Om jag inte* (If I Didn't), did not sell well and attracted no critical attention. Subsequent volumes, *Till min man, om han kunde läsa* (To My Husband, If He Could Read, 1976), *Döda honom!* (Kill Him!, 1978), *Om ni hör ett skott* (If You Hear a Shot, 1979; also released as cassette recording of Lugn reading aloud), *Percy Wennerfors* (1982) and especially *Bekantskap önskas med äldre bildad herre* (Acquaintance Wanted With Older Refined Gentleman, 1983), sounded chords that attracted broad sympathetic response. By 1984, Lugn had become such a widely acclaimed lyric voice that a volume of her collected works, *Lugn bara Lugn: Samlade dikter*[61] — with a now justly famous afterword by Karl Vennberg, was published and has been reprinted several times since, most recently in 1992. These poems are not formalistically innovative and many have a familiar or even old-fashioned style, but it is used so deftly and with such cunning irony that the poems invite readings on many levels that often subvert and parody one another. Much of their power derives from an intense narrative drive that moves unrelentingly and with disarming concision. Without sentimentality or self-indulgence, the dangers, suffering, anxiety, and vacuity implicit for women in everyday bourgeois life are stripped of their deceptive patina; the despair of self-contempt and desperate solitude of empty marriage are portrayed as hideous afflictions from which suicide is the only escape. *Hundstunden* (Dog Hour, 1989) is, perhaps, Lugn's most personal and intimate collection as the subtitle, *Kvinnlig bekännelselyrik* (Feminine Confessional Lyrics), suggests. Tragic farce, black humour, grotesque absurdities, and liberal doses of self-irony throughout, however, keep the reader at the requisite critical distance and deflect superficial attempts to construe the poetry as narrowly or neurotically autobiographical. Lugn has also written plays for radio: *Svenska radiopjäser* (Swedish Radio Plays, 1985) and the theatre: *Tant Blooma,* (Aunt Blooma, 1993) and *Idlaflickorna,* (The Idla Girls, 1993). In 1997, her works were once again published in a collected edition, *Samlat Lugn.*[62]

Katarina Frostenson achieved a good deal of fame and recognition when she was elected to the Swedish Academy in 1991 as the youngest member in nearly seventy-five years. Although she has written prose sketches and monodramas, she is most highly respected for her poetry, but all her writing, whatever the formal generic designation, seems to have been cut from the same fabric. The disjunctive and fragmentary nature of her poetry offers formidable challenges to her readers. Rarely are thoughts developed by means of logical sequences, any kind of readily accessible emplotment, or traditional metaphoric elaboration. Indeed Lars Ellerström entitled an essay on her poetry appearing in *BLM,* 'Att försöka förstå en dikt som inte vill bli förstådd'.[63] Though challenging, Frostenson's poetry is by no means incomprehensible or impenetrable. One of the underlying principles upon which her poetry is based is an awareness of the lack of nuanced flexibility of language, particularly language that endeavours to codify or systematize human experience. *Imellan* (Between, 1978), *Rena land* (Pure Country, 1980), and *Den andra* (The Other, 1982) are based on misgivings about the rigidity and the seeming taxonomic imperative of much public discourse. They and subsequent collections, for example *Stränderna* (The Beaches, 1989) and *Joner* (Ions, 1991), draw much from an innovative and revealing exploitation of the paradigmatic as opposed to the syntagmatic axis of linguistic communication. The subtleties, shades of meaning, and indistinct boundaries of similar words which diverge, converge, or run asymptotically are teased out and expanded. Registers, modes of expression, and discourse communities collide and clash, but the poetry arises from the bewildering juxtapositions as well as the shifting fluctuations.

The early 1970s also saw broadly popular efforts to involve much larger segments of the population with poetry. This popularization of the lyric attracted considerable attention but will be best remembered in sociological rather than literary critical or broadly aesthetic terms.[64] Almost as a counterpoise, other poets during the middle of the decade stressed the importance of private and personal inward experience in various encomia on the individual ego.

Something of an enigma among contemporary Swedish poets, Kjell Espmark (born 1930) is a scholar internationally recognized as a specialist on poetic Modernism having published important studies on Artur Lundkvist and Swedish as well as European Modernism.[65] Yet as a poet, he wears his erudition lightly and with considerable grace and has occasionally had to remind his readers and critics that his scholarship is not a key to hidden dimensions of his poetry. The lyric purview of the trilogy *Sent i Sverige* (Late in Sweden, 1969-75) is relatively modest, and each volume in its own particular way is animated by a disarmingly colloquial and familiar texture, punctuated on occasion by the gently ironic scholarly allusions. In a manner if not derived from T.S. Eliot at least reminiscent of the Modernist master, Espmark's poetry is impersonal and unsentimental. Although his ethical stance is not noticeably grounded in the political engagement of the 1960s, it bespeaks a responsive and compassionate indignation at unmerited suffering and misery. In subsequent volumes, *Försök till liv* (Attempt at Life, 1979), *Tecken till Europa* (Signs to Europe, 1982), and *Den hemliga måltiden* (The Secret Meal, 1984), the compass of his moral concern is considerably broader. Beginning with something of an

Chapter VII

autobiographical note, his sphere of concern is gradually enlarged both spatially and temporally giving voice to those who have endured suffering as a result of circumstances and conditions beyond their control. These poems have little in common with the rhetorical posturing of the various cults of victimization that arose in the early 1990s but rather are animated by a regard and care grounded in a broadly comprehensive view of human history.

Chapter VIII

Three Novelists of the 1930s: Vilhelm Moberg, Ivar Lo-Johansson and Eyvind Johnson

Peter Graves and Phil Holmes

The most remarkable feature of the 1930s is the rise to prominence of a large number of working-class writers who in retrospect seem to dominate the decade. In terms of background they have much in common. Most of them came from the agricultural rather than the industrial working class, most of them worked in manual occupations for some years, most of them experienced lengthy periods of unemployment, and they were all self-educated as regards formal education beyond the compulsory elementary school. Indeed, the struggle to gain an education which was not provided for them by the state — and which was often disapproved of by their parents and by those around them — provides a theme common to many of their books. They were fortunate in that, whatever the lack of formal education, a great many informal opportunities did exist thanks to a wide variety of popular movements which ranged from temperance lodges to political parties.[1] Numerous working-class writers have acknowledged the debt they owe to the libraries and study circles set up by such movements, just as they have acknowledged their debt to the Folk High Schools whose courses so many of them attended.[2] This chapter will look at three of these writers — Vilhelm Moberg, Ivar Lo-Johansson and Eyvind Johnson. Harry Martinson is discussed elsewhere in this volume.

They were not the first generation of working-class writers. In the years around 1910 writers such as Martin Koch, Gustav Hedenvind-Eriksson, Leon Larsson, Alfred Kämpe, Maria Sandel and many others had begun to publish their work. With few exceptions most of what they produced has been forgotten as literature, however valuable it may be as social and literary history. It is a propagandist literature with immediate aims — the forwarding of the demands of the working-class for political and social equality. Consequently the class struggle and bitter social criticism dominate while individual psychology, fantasy, topography are pushed to the side.[3] By the 1930s the emphasis of working-class writing was firmly back on the individual and this is reflected in the genre that many of the generation favoured. One after another they produced autobiographical novels in which they described their early lives and struggles and attempted to come to terms with their backgrounds. To an extent this change in emphasis may be explained by changed social conditions — many of the things that the earlier generation had been demanding had been achieved, and with the existence of the beginnings of social democracy much of the rest could be expected. There was, of course, nothing new about the autobiographical novel and one can point to such distinguished forerunners as Strindberg's *Tjänstekvinnans son* (Son of a Servant Woman, 1886-1909) or much later Lagerkvist's *Gäst hos verkligheten* (Guest of Reality, 1925). What was unusual, however, was the sheer number of such novels and the background of their authors. Moreover, the realism of these novels — whether it be psychological realism or external realism — goes much further than anything produced earlier.

It is clear that several of the working-class writers felt the individualist bias of their works to be a limitation and attempted to broaden the scope of the autobiographical form by giving almost as much prominence to the class background as to the development of the main figure. This is true of Eyvind Johnson's *Romanen om Olof* (The Novel about Olof, 1934-37) and Ivar Lo-Johansson's *Godnatt, jord* (Goodnight, Earth, 1933). The same feeling led to the attempts at writing collective novels — novels in which the individual main character is replaced by a group bound together usually by ties of class and work.[4] The form proved to be a difficult one and few successful collective novels were produced. Josef Kjellgren's *Människor kring en bro* (People Around a Bridge, 1935) and *Smaragden* (The Emerald, 1939) come closest to satisfying the collectivist programme.

Another area of tension within the working-class writing of the period is the tension between town and country. The majority of these writers had grown up in rural areas and at least initially they viewed the urban environment as a desirable opposite to the narrowness they had experienced in the countryside. A reaction set in and novels such as Lo-Johansson's *Kungsgatan* (King Street, 1935) draw attention to the countryman's problems of adaptation to town life. In the case of Moberg and Martinson the tension is even more marked and one can speak of a back-to-the-countryside movement which decries modern technological development and urban civilization and extols old peasant values. There is more than just a personal reaction to urbanization in this; there is the influence of the literary Primitivism that flourished in the 1930s.[5] Although Primitivism influenced the poets more obviously than the prose writers we can see its effects in the attitudes towards the soil, fertility and the peasant, and in the depiction of women as Earth-Mother figures. It is in this area that the most interesting and fruitful recent critical approaches to the 1930s have occurred. Ebba Witt-Brattström's 1988 book *Moa Martinson. Skrift och drift i trettiotalet* set out to re-evaluate the writings of Moa Martinson, the main woman writer among the working-class authors and a writer whom traditional critical opinion had dismissed as interesting, popular, but lacking any serious literary merit.[6] Witt-Brattström argues that Moa Martinson was in fact a conscious woman Modernist and a renewer of Swedish prose writing. At the same time, Witt-Brattström studies the Primitivist ideas of the male writers of the period (including the three subjects of this chapter) and finds that the acclaimed class radicalism of their works actually cloaks a deep-seated reactionary view of woman — what she summarizes as 'sexual politics disguised as the class struggle'.[7]

Unlike the earlier generation of working-class writers, the novelists of the 1930s rarely wrote about immediately current problems: they preferred to return to a period some twenty years earlier and chart the problems of their youth. As the decade progressed, however, they — along with many other literary figures in Sweden — reacted to the increasingly dark international scene of totalitarianism of the Right and of the Left by coming to the defence of democracy. Before and during the war they added some of the finest contributions to the body of literature that has become known as *beredskapslitteratur* ('literature of preparedness'): Moberg's *Rid i natt!* (Ride This Night!, 1941), Martinson's *Verklighet till döds* (Reality unto Death, 1940) and Johnson's *Krilon* (Krilon, 1941-43) series fall into this category. They were active in other ways, too: Martinson as a volunteer in the Finnish Winter War, Johnson as a propagandist journalist for the Finns and later for the Norwegians and Danes, Moberg as one of the scourges of the Swedish government over its policies on censorship and appeasement.

It is a mistake to consider the working-class writers who achieved recognition in the 1930s as some sort of 'school'. The initial similarities of background, choice of autobiographical form and sympathy for the social underdog are marked enough. From there they moved out in widely different directions and many of their most important works were produced long afterwards. Ultimately the differences become more important than the resemblances.

Vilhelm Moberg (1898-1973)

Vilhelm Moberg was born in the parish of Algutsboda in S. E. Småland in a soldier's cottage.[8] His father was a soldier-crofter under the old militia system whereby each parish furnished a man for the ranks and provided him with a small croft on which to support his family. In return these part-time soldiers had to attend manoeuvres for a month each autumn. Vilhelm was the fourth of seven children, and he was brought up in a poor family and poor province; this part of Småland is rocky upland with thin infertile soils and many tiny farms, and was during the last century an area of mass emigration to the USA.

Moberg's was a working childhood, on his parents' farm and then, from the age of eleven, at the local glassworks. Yet his childhood was a happy one, and he returns to it repeatedly in his works, to the summers spent wandering the forests and fishing the streams. In the essay 'Brodd' (Germination) from 1932 he stresses the significance of the local people for his life and work:

They belong indissolubly to one phase of my life. They are my people ... Conversely I am in large measure theirs. They have given me lasting impressions. To a certain extent I still see things with their eyes. My childhood environment proves increasingly to dominate my attitude to social and human problems.(*Berättelser ur min levnad*, 16 (Stories from my life, 1968).

Moberg's formal education was very brief, and he has described the 'läshunger' (hunger for reading) of his childhood and youth and his desperate search for reading matter. His family was devout and he encountered the Bible at home and at school; despite an early loss of faith, the Bible remained a lasting influence on his work. Gradually he succeeded in breaking out of the conservative world of the peasant community and was influenced by his reading — he joined a temperance lodge largely to gain access to the library — and by contact with his workmates at glassworks and peat diggings. Socialism was a formative influence upon the young Moberg: he joined the radical Young Socialists before the Great War at a time of political ferment, and later left to join the more moderate Social Democrats, but his socialism remained always a distinctly personal belief. At the age of 18 he went to Folk High School and also embarked upon a traditional career for working-class writers, that of journalism, working on a number of local newspapers in Southern Sweden. Moberg's apprenticeship as a writer was a lengthy one. In his youth he had published *bygdehistorier*, short stories often after E. A. Poe with local settings, in newspapers he worked on, but his breakthrough came with a series of comic plays. One such comedy, *Kassabrist* (Embezzlement, 1926) was a financial success and allowed him time to write his first important novel, *Raskens. En soldat-familjs historia* (Rasken's. The Story of a Soldier's Family, 1927). *Raskens* depicts the life of a Småland soldier-crofter and his large family in the last half of the nineteenth century, and much of the material for it derives from Moberg's personal background.[9]

It is a generation novel, a picture of a man's adult life, work and growing family. The young farm-worker Gustav becomes a soldier and is given a croft and the soldier-name Rask. After some false starts he marries the faithful Ida, who bears him many sons and endures with fortitude his occasional drunkenness and womanizing. The two women in Rask's life represent two aspects of Woman: his wife is hard-working, pious and a good mother, but ages quickly and loses her physical attractions for him, whilst his mistress Anna is lazy, amoral and deceitful, but also sensual. Rask himself is Moberg's archetypal Swede, a powerful tiller of the soil and rugged individualist, often at odds with his neighbours, a man who believes God only helps those willing to help themselves. Ida is more spiritual, with a simple fatalistic belief, but also tries to put Jesus' teachings into practice in her everyday life.

The setting of the story is limited to the farm and village, largely isolated from the outside world, but gradually changes make themselves felt: the railway brings industry to this rural area and this deals a death blow to the old social order. Moberg documents the end of a rural culture unchanged for centuries.

The chronicle in *Raskens*, Moberg's recreation of the area and its people, is painstakingly thorough, reflecting a didactic aim, his desire to record this disappearing world for posterity. The difference between Moberg's work and earlier depictions of folk life in Swedish writing, such as Strindberg's *Hemsöborna* (The People of Hemsö, 1888) is that Moberg is able to present an inside view of this world — it is after all his own world. Furthermore Moberg's characters are often crofters rather than the well-to-do farm-owners who figure in earlier rural novels. Moberg writes:

When in 1927 I published *Raskens* it was my intention with this novel to make a little room in our literature for the people in the small cottages, the rural proletariat — at that time I had not been able to find them there. (*Avsikter*, 157f.) (Intentions, 1945)

A deep and abiding fascination for the details of rural life and work characterizes Moberg's work. Here are all the different tasks of the farmer's year, the preparations for a wedding, setting up house and reviving a run-down croft on which to support a family. But there is no folksy romanticism — at times the tone is harshly naturalistic — only the fittest survive in this testing physical environment. To provide comic relief Moberg inserts a storyteller, another feature characteristic of his work, who entertains with his ribald tales. The drama of the novel lies partly in the complex interaction of the fates of Rask and Ida with those of Klangen and Anna, their antithetical counterparts, and partly in the longstanding feud between Rask and Oskar which simmers through the story, erupting irregularly and ending in tragedy for both men. There is a great deal of dramatic incident to counterbalance the steady rhythm of an existence close to nature. But it is the chronicle which completes the circle and provides the novel with a firmer structure than the more independent central sections would seem to indicate. The two novels *Långt från landsvägen* (Far from the Highway, 1929) and *De knutna händerna* (The Clenched Hands, 1930) continue the depiction of rural life whilst introducing an element of social criticism. *De knutna händerna* has leaner, more classical lines and the focus of interest lies in the personal tragedy of the ageing Adolf at Ulvaskog, a man increasingly out of step with the modern world. The growing migration of young people to the cities, the change to a cash economy, mechanization on the land and the arrival of the railway and rural industry are all regarded by Adolf as a threat to a system of values which operate to the benefit of the whole community.

This sceptical attitude to the supposed benefits of modern life is also found in the trilogy about Knut Toring from the late 1930s. The classical dramatic line of *De knutna händerna* is continued in *Mans kvinna* (Man's Woman, 1933) which is set in a remote community in the 1790s. The novel has few characters, a restricted setting and follows the seasons of one year from spring to autumn.[10] The action is the eternal love-triangle with the main character, the young wife Marit, torn between husband and lover. She must decide whether to stay within a dull marriage, but in the security of a flourishing farm, or risk all by running off to outlawry in the forest with her lover. Marit is one of Moberg's finest creations; he combines in her the attributes of both her menfolk: a desire for freedom and roots deep in the community. She must choose between these, and her dilemma is a compelling one. Despite the historical setting the moral problems explored are familiarly modern, and the novel was a contribution to the debate on sexual freedom conducted in the 1930s. *Mans kvinna* also possesses stylistic strengths of a new kind for Moberg. Its unusual lyricism sets it apart, particularly in scenes evoking the harmony of Man and Nature, such as this one in which the lovers meet in the open air:

They were close to the earth, in a world of procreation which was untroubled by thoughts of life and death. A natural freedom from care prevailed. Birth and extinction belonged together and caused no anguish. Above them glistened the fresh leaves of spring; beneath them decayed the fallen leaves of the previous year. One depended on the other. And they themselves were two newly opened leaves suspended from their branch, from the firmament of life, while the summer passed. And they were small and trembling in the eternal wind that would one day tear them from their firmament. (111)[11]

The marked unity of tone is also unusual, and the book has been made into a successful drama. The three novels about Knut Toring, *Sänkt sedebetyg* (Memories of Youth, 1935), *Sömnlös* (Sleepless Nights, 1937) and *Giv oss jorden!* (The Earth is Ours!, 1939), though popular at the time, now seem dated and of uneven quality. The first is the most effective, with its semi-autobiographical account of Knut's childhood, schooling, religious doubts, and sexual awakening. The last two volumes in which Moberg develops his ideas for rejuvenating the rural community lack force and become purely polemical. Increasingly in the novels the threat of a European war looms over the events in Sweden, beside which these parochial concerns pale into insignificance.

The historical novel *Rid i natt!* (Ride This Night!, 1941) forms Moberg's main contribution to *beredskapslitteratur*, showing his defiant stand against Nazi tyranny, but it is only one manifestation of his determined opposition: he also lectured and wrote on the Nazi menace throughout the war. *Rid i natt!* was his greatest popular success to date and undoubtedly the most outstanding literary reaction to the wartime political discussion in Sweden.

The setting is Värend (S. Småland) in the 1650s during the reign of Queen Christina, and the main motif the granting by the Queen of virtually feudal rights to the German aristocrats who had aided Sweden in the Thirty Years War. The little village of Brändebol thus comes within the domain of the local manor, and when the villagers are unable to pay their taxes the German lord demands that the free men of the village work on his estate like the thralls of old.

The villagers meet and debate whether to resist or appease the baron, who, when they do oppose him, resorts to threats of violence. Eventually the men succumb to terror and become his serfs. One man alone resists the loss of his age-old freedoms: Ragnar Svedje escapes into the forest to become an outlaw rather than submit, and becomes the living symbol of resistance and hope. Meanwhile a *budkavle* arrives secretly in Brändebol. This ancient wooden token sent from village to village was used to summon men to meetings but also as a call to armed revolt against authority. It is received by the village alderman with the time-honoured formula 'The token is passing! Ride this night!' but the faint-hearted alderman buries the token, and takes no action. Tragedy ensues for Svedje: he is captured in the forest by the public executioner and his posse and buried alive. But the *budkavle* with its message of resistance mysteriously re-appears and travels onwards 'through nights and days, through years and centuries' (297).

Rid i natt! contains a number of allusions to Sweden's situation at the outset of the Second World War, and may be read both as an adventure story and a powerful allegory. The differing attitudes of the villagers towards the totalitarian regime typify contemporary Swedish reactions to the threat of Nazism. The alderman and some others are intimidated into unwilling collaboration with their new overlord; one villager openly aids the enemy, whilst another gathers trustworthy men into an underground resistance movement. Contemporary criticism of the novel underplayed its forceful, if oblique attack on the government of the day and its leader Per Albin Hansson for appeasing the Germans. Amazingly in the dark days of 1941 Moberg states the conviction that one day justice and freedom will be re-established.

The strength of the novel as a timeless work of literature lies in the powerful evocation of historical atmosphere, achieved by the use of archaic language and carefully researched historical detail. The character drawing is less successful though some of the minor characters attain a real presence. The novel was a best-seller at the time and was adapted for the stage in 1942 and made into a film in the same year.

Moberg spent five years writing the massive novel *Soldat med brutet gevär* (Soldier with a Broken Rifle, 1944) as he was interrupted by urgent war work.[12] It is his second Bildungsroman, and tells the story of Valter Sträng from his birth in 1897 through a number of trials and discoveries to 1921 when he finally finds his calling in life, to write about the people he comes from. In outline Valter's life corresponds closely to Vilhelm's: both worked at glass factories, felled timber and dug peat, both were influenced by the Temperance Movement and Socialism, attended Folk High Schools and entered journalism. They both considered emigrating to America and nearly died from Spanish influenza. But there are considerable shifts of emphasis for thematic reasons — Moberg stresses how emigration decimates the Sträng family and emphasizes Valter's political involvement (not important facets of Moberg's own youth) and — to avoid repeating ideas already explored in the Knut Toring novels — Valter's religious life, hunger for reading material and experience of school are not dealt with in depth here.

Valter comes from a poorer home than his creator but his father is also a soldier, and as he spends his last years invalided out of service he becomes Valter's *kamrat*, a term of great significance to the lad. Soon, when he starts work his ideas come into conflict with the conservative and pious patriotism of his parents. Valter joins the radical Young Socialists whose banner reads 'DOWN WITH THE THRONE, THE SWORD, THE ALTAR AND THE MONEY BAG!', and his rifle, unlike his father's, is a broken rifle on his pacifist lapel badge. Valter is an idealist who strives constantly beyond the temporal, 'a striving beyond the brief and inadequate life of the body' in the words of the motto of the novel. His life consists of a series of discoveries which are later abandoned; thus he progresses through beliefs in Christianity,

Chapter VIII

teetotalism, radical socialism, education, Schopenhauer's nihilistic philosophy and finally a pragmatic democratic socialism, but none of these live up to his high expectations, and eventually he returns to his roots, determined to write a great novel about his own people (just as Moberg wrote *Raskens*).

In the course of his search for truth Valter passes through a series of stations portrayed in a sequence of brilliant interiors — the glassworks, temperance lodge, conservative Folk High School, newspaper offices — which together paint a panorama of Swedish society at a time of ferment. But it is in the depiction of Valter's involvement in politics that the atmosphere of the period is most clearly evoked, in a fascinating account of the rise to power of the Social Democrats and the arguments and schisms within the labour movement. All the time the atmosphere of the period is underpinned by the use of documents, both real and fictitious.

Soldat med brutet gevär was written between 1939 and 1944 when Social Democracy had been a reality in Sweden for a decade, but Valter's goals had not been achieved by 1944, and the novel is an attack born of disillusion: the Throne was not overturned, the power of the military not broken, the church not disestablished, the means of production not nationalized. Moberg's hero of twenty years before, Per Albin Hansson, now Prime Minister, seemed to have forgotten his fine words about freedom of the press and introduced wartime censorship. The last part of the novel is heavy with dramatic irony, for events are presented through Valter's eyes and he is unaware of what the future holds, while the reader sees a different dimension in the broken socialist promises of the 1920s. Moberg particularly stresses the socialist attacks on censorship and compromises made to neutrality in the First World War. The parallels are clear to readers during the Second World War.

Migration from the countryside to the towns is a major theme in Moberg's early work and emigration is a minor theme in *Soldat med brutet gevär*. Both are part of Moberg's personal and social background; when he grew up nearly all of his cousins lived in the USA. Yet in *Den okända släkten* (The Unknown Relations, 1950), a collection of factual articles on emigration, he writes that he could not find in either historical or literary works an adequate account of the million Swedes who left their homeland in the years 1850-1920. In 1916 he had intended to emigrate but thought better of it; now in 1948 he did go to America in search of material for a major work. It was to take eleven years before the emigrant tetralogy of 2,000 pages was complete.

The first part of 'The Novel about the Emigrants', simply called *Utvandrarna* (The Emigrants, 1949), begins with a documentary account of the parish of Ljuder in Småland in the 1840s.[13] The emigrants-to-be are visited in turn and their several reasons for leaving Sweden are demonstrated in a series of dramatic scenes. Karl Oskar and Kristina Nilsson can never hope to make a decent living on their tiny rock-strewn croft, and the death of their daughter during a famine helps them to decide. Karl Oskar seeks to realize a vision: in a newspaper he has seen a picture of an enormous wheatfield in North America. His wife is more dubious about the risks of taking a family on a dangerous ocean voyage to an unknown continent. The antithesis between the personalities of these two provides much of the psychological interest in the work: he is a rugged individualist, willing to risk all to improve his lot, while she is more deeply rooted in a conservative tradition and pious in a simple fatalistic way. Karl Oskar's brother Robert is an intelligent lad with a rich fantasy life who seeks freedom from masters in the New World, and a brutal beating at the hands of his employer sets him planning his escape. Arvid, Robert's dull-witted but kindly friend, also seeks escape — from a malicious rumour about himself, and Jonas Petter flees a shrewish wife. Danjel Andreasson's primitive Christian lifestyle brings him into conflict with the local priest and the authorities who regard his teachings as heresy and are determined to suppress them. Danjel sees the New World as a haven of religious tolerance where men may worship God freely in their own way, a Promised Land to which he, like an Old Testament prophet, will lead his little band of persecuted dissenters.

The farmers all sell their property, pack their most vital belongings in old clothes chests and in 1850 a group of sixteen take the ship at Karlshamn for New York. The ten-week journey in the brig *Charlotta* is fraught with dangers: many are seasick and several passengers die from scurvy. The account of the journey is largely used to explore the minds of the characters and their backgrounds. In *Invandrarna* (Unto a Good Land, 1954) the long journey continues, after a brief stay in New York, by boat and train to Minnesota Territory. Moberg concentrates on the reaction of the Ljuder peasants to this new and at times terrifying world, and the use of the character's own viewpoint, the depiction of novelties in terms of their own limited experience, reflects both upon the Old World and the New. For the first time the emigrants encounter

Chapter VIII

a railway train, Red Indians and the awful bleakness of the prairie, but at last feel at home in the forests of Minnesota. In contrast to the often harsh realism of *Utvandrarna*, there is often a marked lyricism in *Invandrarna*, as, for example, when the emigrants gather beneath a giant oak to give thanks to the Lord for a safe crossing, or when Kristina gives birth in a scene reminiscent of the Nativity. The novel which has hitherto had a collective structure now centres on Karl Oskar and Kristina, showing how with ingenuity and grit they manage to survive their first harsh winter in a log cabin by Lake Ki-Chi-Saga. Karl Oskar has realized his dream, but Robert is not content with his lot, and sets off with Arvid to seek gold in California.

Nybyggarna (The Settlers, 1956) takes up the story after three years. The Nilssons have established themselves on their farmstead; other settlers arrive and a small community grows up, complete with church and minister, school and schoolteacher. The central section of this novel depicts in a series of flashbacks the nightmarish experiences of Robert and Arvid on the California Trail. On his return Robert dies from a mysterious illness, and attention is focused on Kristina, her homesickness, the strain of her repeated pregnancies and her religious doubts. Kristina's spiritual development leads to a kind of resignation as she places her fate in God's hands.

In *Sista brevet till Sverige* (The Last Letter Home, 1959) outside events crowd in upon this quiet corner of rural America. The Civil War breaks out, and then an Indian uprising occurs in Minnesota. During this emergency Kristina lies dying, having risked a final pregnancy. Karl Oskar, embittered by his loss, is later struck by a falling oak, and spends the rest of his life as a invalid, tracing out the paths of his childhood on a map of Ljuder. His sons become Americanized and when he dies none of them remembers enough Swedish to write the letter to Småland informing his relatives.

The emigrant cycle is Moberg's masterwork: the theme of emigration struck a deep chord in him and the presentation of this theme marks the culmination of his narrative and stylistic talents, as well as his growing devotion to historical research and documentation. This is the key to the work: the blend of documentary and story, fact and fiction. The novel is regarded as an important contribution to the history of emigration, and critics have paid close attention to the documentary sources for the work and the way he uses these.[14]

The characters are drawn in part from earlier novels: Karl Oskar is descended from a long line of self-sufficient peasants from Rask to Ragnar Svedje, whilst Robert shares the characteristics of the dreamer with Håkan (in *Mans Kvinna*), Knut Toring and Valter Sträng. Kristina's piety is to be found in *Mans kvinna* as freedom from the rigid constraints of society and in *Rid i natt!* as freedom from oppression.

Above all there is Moberg's compelling fascination with the tangible details of an emigrant's life: he lists what they pack in their America chests and shows how they solve a hundred problems of living in the wilderness.

The series has been an enormous best-seller and won critical acclaim. It was filmed in two parts by Jan Troell in the 1970s. *Din stund på jorden* (A Time on Earth, 1963) is in some ways a sequel to the emigrant novels. An ageing emigrant, Albert Carlson, has settled in a small town on the California coast and reminisces about his past, about the failure of his emigration, against the backdrop of the 1962 Cuban Crisis when the world seems on the brink of nuclear war. The narrative centres on a different crisis, the death of Albert's brother Sigfrid in Småland some 50 years before. Moberg's tale is an attack on militarism, but also one of his most personal and thoughtful works, a premature leave-taking.

Moberg's last fictional work, *Förrädarland* (Land of Traitors, 1967) returns to a historical setting, the Värend of the 1520s caught between the ambitions of Gustav Vasa and Kristian II of Denmark and trying to remain neutral. The novel may be read as an allegory of other divided peoples of our time; the Vietnamese must have been in Moberg's thoughts.

After *Förrädarland* Moberg turned his attention full-time to a lifelong interest in history, and before his death had published two volumes of *Min svenska historia berättad för folket* (A History of the Swedish People, 1970-71) which covers the period up to the Dacke revolt in 1542. Moberg's is a personal narrative and its main aim was to trace the history of all the people — not just kings and nobles but peasants and soldiers and not forgetting the women of history. But the great figures of mediaeval Sweden are all present, and some are viewed in a more critical light than previously.

Moberg's admitted weaknesses as a novelist of ideas are more than compensated for by his strengths as a storyteller and his marvellous use of the Swedish language. His vocabulary is deliberately pure and his prose style, rooted in the Småland dialect and in the archaic language of the Reformation Bible, is one of the most positive features of his writing. The marked rhythms especially, resulting from the use of word-pairs, antithesis and parallelism, help support the epic tone.

Moberg was always something of an outsider, an uncompromising idealist and an irascible scourge of the Establishment, who often fought lonely battles against injustice, hypocrisy and bigotry, but who through his personal qualities and his writing eventually endeared himself to a great number of his fellow countrymen.

Ivar Lo-Johansson (1901-91)

Ivar Lo-Johansson was born in Ösmo in Sörmland in 1901. For most of their lives his parents had been *statare*, a group of deprived farm workers whose wages were mainly paid in kind.[15] When he was twelve they realized the dream of owning their own land as small-holders. Lo-Johansson has often described his early awareness of the narrowness of his environment. Among other things it took the form of a hunger for books. On leaving school Lo-Johansson remained at home for some years working on the land; and he was already dreaming of becoming a writer. In fact his break with home was a gradual one. In 1917-18 he attended a course at Västerhaninge Folk High School and another at the same school in 1920-21. Between these courses he had moved to Stockholm and begun his first tentative attempts at journalism. During his years in Stockholm he had many jobs — postman, labourer and mason among them — as well as being politically active in Social Democrat youth organizations.

The real beginning of his career may be dated to 1925. He began a series of journeys around Europe that were to last on and off until 1929. On these travels he supported himself by taking any job available and by sending home newspaper articles. From his experiences he wrote five travel books: *Vagabondliv i Frankrike* (Vagabond Life in France, 1927), *Kolet i våld* (In the Power of Coal, 1928), *Nederstigen i dödsriket* (Down into the Kingdom of Death, 1929), *Zigenare* (Gipsies, 1929), and *Mina städers ansikten* (The Faces of my Cities, 1930). Lo-Johansson, whatever his own working-class background, is very much the innocent abroad and it is this that gives the books their lasting freshness. Always comparing things with conditions he knew in Sweden, he is surprised by the easy-going attitudes of the French workers, overwhelmed by the poverty of the East End of London, shocked by the sheer toil of the miners. *Vagabondliv i Frankrike* is the weakest of the books. It is marred by a tendency to speculation and generalization whether it be about national character, the nature of the peasant or the purpose of travelling. And there is a certain coyness about the author's over-consciousness of himself in the role of traveller. *Kolet i våld*, the best of the books, avoids these faults. It is a factual account of the Northumberland and Durham coalfield where Lo-Johansson spent the autumn and early winter of 1927. The self-conscious traveller is replaced by the good reporter: he describes the scene, gives the background and asks the right questions. The result is a nuanced and objective portrait of a depressed community.

Lo-Johansson's travel books point forward to much that is present in his later production. The scale of the ambition itself — to describe all the workers of the world — reminds one that Lo-Johansson prefers to write in massive more or less connected series. There is the desire to portray the lives of whole communities and classes; the logical conclusion of this was his collectivist programme of the 1930s. There is the belief that literature should deal with social problems and there is the strong documentary element. But the travel books do more than foreshadow later work. Lars Furuland has written:

He made himself master of a genre which has since become common in the literature of social description but which he was almost unique in practising in Sweden in the 20s: social reportage on the borderline between non-fiction and fictional prose with its created characters.[16]

It is this that led to the resurgence of interest in his early work among the Swedish documentarists of the 1960s and 1970s.

Alongside his main fiction production Lo-Johansson continued to cultivate this genre right through until the 1950s though now his interest was concentrated on conditions in Sweden rather than those abroad. *Jag tvivlar på idrotten* (I Have No Faith in Sport, 1931) reveals Lo-Johansson's skills as a polemicist. He pushes every argument to its extreme, sets up a viewpoint and knocks it down or allows it to reveal its own weaknesses as the case may be — all with a degree of humour which he has rarely received credit for. Most of his works in this genre run parallel with the novels he was writing at the same period: *Statarklassen i Sverige* (The Statare Class in Sweden, 1939) was produced while he was involved with his *statare* novels of the 1930s, *Monism* (Monism, 1948) treats the sexual theory he advanced in his

Chapter VIII

novel about puberty *Geniet* (The Genius, 1947), and *Ålderdoms-Sverige* (Old People in Sweden, 1952) takes up problems he approached in the autobiographical novel *Analfabeten* (The Illiterate, 1951). Lo-Johansson, in his belief that literature should deal with social problems, carried his belief to its conclusion and made no distinction between fictional literature, reportage and polemics. The problem is primary, the means of making it the subject of attention many. So he was prepared to use journalism, broadcasting and public debate to the same ends and even, in the case of agricultural workers, to take an active part in union activities from the 1930s to the 1950s, partly by acting as unpaid cultural editor of their paper *Lantarbetaren* (The Agriculture Worker), partly by travelling out with the union organizers on their campaigns.

Lo-Johansson's first novel *Måna är död* (Måna is Dead) was published in 1932. It tells of the love affair between a young working-class writer Bo Propst and an upper-class woman Måna. From a state of passion the two gradually move to positions of hate during a summer spent alone at a shieling in Norrland. It ends tragically with the drowning of Måna but for Bo Propst her death means freedom to follow his own road. The theme of the novel is that of the writer at the crossroads: he must choose between his work and ambition on the one hand and woman and love on the other. As an analysis of the stages of alienation between two people initially bound by erotic attraction but ultimately incompatible *Måna är död* is a very fine book. The tension created by the isolation of the pair is overwhelming. The reader's sympathies remain with Måna, the loser, whereas the ambitions of Bo Propst become uncomfortable in their unquestioning single-mindedness.

Godnatt, jord (1933) marks the start of Lo-Johansson's ten year literary involvement with the *statare*. It is the first of the great working-class autobiographical novels of the 1930s as well as being one of his finest books. We follow the central character of the novel, the author's alter ego, Mikael Bister, from his first perceptions of life in his *statare* home to his escape from his environment at the age of fifteen. Right from the beginning Mikael manifests a love of freedom which contrasts with his terror of being swallowed by the anonymity of *statare* existence, and which is expressed throughout in a series of superb symbols: one of Mikael's earliest memories is of the two heifers that escape and go wild in the woods — they are hunted and shot because their freedom is an insult to the Baron who owns the estate. On another occasion Mikael watches an ant-hill: 'Lying on his stomach on the ground he brooded consciously for the first time about closed chances and the poverty of submission and weakness.' (73).[17] Step by step he distances himself from the attitudes of his class and becomes ever more conscious of his need to escape — a need which cannot be understood by his parents or by the *statare*. A contrast to Mikael is his friend Ture i Dundret. Ture, too, is a gifted child with a longing to escape but he lacks Mikael's stubbornness and is unable to survive the pressure of his environment. For him there can be no freedom; instead he is sucked down and ends in a worse condition than if he had never had talents and dreams.

Godnatt, jord is a novel of vast scope, for, although the two boys and their opposite lines of development provide the central theme, behind them the whole of *statare* life unfolds. Lo-Johansson's point of view is that of the children of the community and by adopting this stance he is able to observe the *statare* from within and without at the same time.[18] We follow the children as they learn about life and death, work and sex; we watch their growing awareness of their parents' poverty and slavishness and their blaming them for them; and we see them gradually accepting the same prejudices as their parents — losing their freedom and becoming the next generation of *statare*.

Lo-Johansson concentrates on the psychological poverty of the *statare* rather than on their material poverty. Generations of subservience have conditioned them to an embittered acceptance of their lot and turned their frustration inwards against members of their own group. As a consequence they are puritanically narrow-minded at the same time as they are scandalmongers, they are envious of the gentry and obsequious to them in turn; they are grimly jealous of their internal social hierarchy in which the coachman ranks higher than the cattleman; worse — they have lost the ability to make decisions or to act either as individuals or as a group. Thus the efforts of the union agitator Bronténare doomed to failure and he himself is treated as an outsider, a man dangerous to know.

Fittingly, *Godnatt, jord* is a slow-moving novel. The story is told in chronological order across the whole width of the stage at the same time: incidents occur, slide into the background, and return into the spotlight when they have matured. The prose style is sober and factual — Lo-Johansson avoids dialect, for instance, as he feels that it could have a romanticizing effect on his material. The result is a rounded picture of a whole social class at a particular historical stage — a

Chapter VIII

picture in which the poetic element is provided by the symbols of freedom.

In *Kungsgatan* (1935) Lo-Johansson turns to the problems of adaptation faced by country children who have moved into the city. The novel, though not a direct continuation of *Godnatt, jord*, is largely autobiographical and the main character Adrian, a farmer's son, passes through many of the same experiences as Lo-Johansson himself had done. He takes a Folk High School course, works as a postman and building worker, is politically active and struggles to educate himself. Just as Ture i Dundret was a contrasting character to Mikael Bister in *Godnatt, jord*, Märta the *statare* girl who becomes a prostitute functions as a contrast to Adrian in *Kungsgatan*. The city destroys Märta morally and physically whereas Adrian survives the stresses of adaptation by surrendering part of his individuality and becoming a unionized worker who shares the security provided by the working-class collective.

In spite of its realism — the depiction of prostitution and sexual disease were considered particularly objectionable at the time — and the relevance of its theme, *Kungsgatan* is an unconvincing novel: the characters are too obviously contrasts; the propagandist element is too near the surface.

Lo-Johansson has claimed that *Bara en mor* (Only a Mother, 1939) was one of his greatest disappointments.[19] What was planned as a collective novel about *statare* women became the moving story of one *statare* woman from her youth to her early death. At the age of eighteen Rya-Rya brings shame upon herself by bathing naked in the lake on a hot summer's day. From then on the *statare* consider her to be a woman from whom any kind of sexual immorality may be expected and as a consequence she loses the man she is to marry. She marries another, Henrik, a *statare* full of boasting. In terms of intelligence and sensitivity he is obviously his wife's inferior yet Lo-Johansson is careful not to make him a wholly negative character. Henrik is in no sense a bad man, merely a typical product of his class and age. Inevitably, however, the marriage lacks warmth and communication and Rya-Rya's path can only be downward until worn out by work and childbearing she dies at just over forty.

Rya-Rya is one of the outstanding woman characters in Swedish literature. She is not, however, portrayed as an unusual woman: just as much as any of the other *statare* women she is capable of pettiness, narrow-mindedness and the desire to be better than her fellows. And as with them motherhood becomes the dominant aspect of her life. The warmth that she cannot give or receive in her relationship with her husband is found instead in her relationship with her children, and mother and children form a closed circle from which Henrik is excluded. Motherhood may, in fact, be seen as both the triumph and the tragedy of Rya-Rya.

During the 1930s and 1940s Lo-Johansson became the main Swedish proponent of two literary forms in particular: the collective novel and the short story with a social tendency. On the subject of the collective novel he wrote 'Given the entry into literature of the collective, of the masses, the form of the novel must also undergo a change. Somehow or other it must become a collective novel'.[20] Both *Godnatt, jord* and *Bara en mor* offer broad pictures of the life of the whole *statare* group but neither may be considered collective novels for in both an individual main character remains at the centre of the action. The massive novel *Traktorn* (The Tractor, 1943) is, in fact, Lo-Johansson's only collective novel in anything like the purist sense of the programme he argued for.[21] It sets out to depict the history of an agricultural estate in the years between 1938 and 1940, years in which the estate was changing from traditional farming to modern mechanized agriculture. *Traktorn* is also the most strongly documentary of Lo-Johansson's novels: unfortunately much of the documentation is only peripherally relevant to the action.

Lo-Johansson's collective programme came closer to fulfilment in his volumes of short stories than in his novels. *Statarna I* and *Statarna II* (The Statare I and II, 1936-37) contain eighty-six stories. A further twenty-five stories appeared in *Jordproletärerna* (The Agricultural Proletarians, 1941). For the most part the stories are very short — some hardly more than sketches a page or two in length — but taken as a whole they cover all aspects of *statare* life, attitudes, history and legend from the origin of the class in the eighteenth century to the activities of the Agricultural Workers' Union in the twentieth. Individual stories stand out with a wide variety of mood: there is the haunting brutality of 'En hästs historia' (The Story of a Horse) in which a drunken crofter brings his horse into his cottage and stabs it to death; or the humour of 'Efter legostadgan' (After the Law Changed) in which a farm-worker loses his personal freedom to a woman on the very day that the abolition of the last vestiges of the medieval agricultural employment law finally gives full freedom to his class. Stylistically, too, there is a wide range. Many of the stories that spotlight incidents in the growth of the union are narrated almost as newspaper reports. Others, particularly those set in earlier centuries, share some of the qualities of the folk-tale. With full justification these stories are rated along with Strindberg's *Svenska öden och äventyr* (Swedish Fates and Adventures) and Heidenstam's *Karolinerna* (The Soldiers of Charles XII).

As one author's campaign against a specific social evil the years Lo-Johansson spent involved on behalf of the *statare* must be unique. The abolition of the system in 1945 was, without doubt, at least hastened by the attention brought to bear on it by Lo-Johansson and by others such as Jan Fridegård and Moa Martinson. But, at the same time, the abolition left him in the position of an author without an immediately obvious subject and the next few years saw him casting around until he settled on his autobiographical books of the 1950s.

In *Geniet* (1947) Lo-Johansson approaches the problems of puberty through the fate of a *statare* child Kristian Dahl. The estate owner recognizes that Kristian is an unusually gifted child and pays for his education to continue at a high school. But the onset of puberty destroys Kristian's work. He becomes more and more self-centred until at last he is disgraced when caught simulating sexual intercourse with a statue. He returns home and finally castrates himself and commits suicide. *Geniet* is an attack on the puritanical sexual morality that places adolescents in an inescapable trap: heterosexual experimentation is forbidden and consequently the adolescent is forced into the lonely situation of masturbation. But that too is surrounded by a wall of taboos. In such a situation sexual guilt is inevitable, loneliness and inability to form relationships with the opposite sex the result. As a novel *Geniet* fails to convince. Nevertheless, together with the purely polemical volume *Monism* that followed it, it created widespread debate around a field that had largely been ignored — it thus fits logically into the literary programme that Lo-Johansson had set himself.

Analfabeten (1951) is the first of a long series of eight autobiographical books. Taken together these volumes trace Lo-Johansson's life from childhood right up to around 1950. The books differ in terms of style, mood, theme and weight of autobiographical content — the quality, too, varies a great deal; the first two volumes, however, are among the highpoints in Lo-Johansson's production. In *Analfabeten* the autobiographical figure plays only a secondary role for much of the time; in the foreground are his parents, above all his father, 'the illiterate' of the title. The father is the former *statare* who by years of sweat has gained first the partial independence of the crofter and then the total liberty of the self-owning smallholder — a liberty which, however, is limited by his debts to a finance company and to a relation who has lent him money. He is a man who understands nothing but the land and his greatest joy is to be now working his own land, to be breaking new ground and harvesting it. He is not a romanticized character; he is a simple man with limited horizons but in his taciturn and toiling pride in the achievements of his own labour and in his hard-won independence he becomes an unforgettable figure. There is a contrast between the father and the mother. In her the *statare* mentality is so deeply ingrained that she finds it difficult to adapt to independence and longs to fall back on the security provided by the estate. The son contrasts with both. He shares his father's stubbornness and independence but turns them in a new direction. The land, self-owned or not, still represents a prison to him. He dreams of escape to books, to studying, to the city — things which are inevitably meaningless to his illiterate father; thus throughout the book there is a tension created by mutual incomprehension, a tension which is all the more moving because of the elements of love and admiration it hides.

Analfabeten is in every sense a rich book. As with Lo-Johansson's *statare* novels of the 1930s the background presents a whole picture of a class and age. In this case it is the smallholders' movement of the 1910s and he portrays a variety of the human types involved — they vary from the idealistic but incompetent back-to-the-land brigade to farm-labourers who have succeeded in buying a small plot. What most of them have in common is an over-developed sense of independence that prevents them from working cooperatively. It is one of the ironies of the situation that the qualities that enabled them to get land of their own act as a limitation on them thereafter. Above all, *Analfabeten* has humour. There is a character humour in the eccentricities of individual smallholders, satire aimed at those in authority, much self-irony in the treatment of the 'I' figure but most of all the gentle smile of affection and admiration (sometimes compounded with embarrassment and exasperation) for the father.

Gårdfarihandlaren (The Travelling Pedlar, 1953) takes up the story at the point where the narrator makes his first attempt to leave home. With a case of trinkets he sets off northwards on his bicycle to make his fortune as a pedlar spurred by the suggestion that the only purpose in life is to be on the move. Throughout the summer he cycles from his native Sörmland right up to Norrland and back. As a businessman he is a failure: he is too romantic, too inexperienced and all too conscious that it is rubbish that he is selling. He is in search of 'The Poem and the Woman' on his trip — and discovers neither. Instead he discovers the Swedish countryside in summer and depicts it with an idyllic delight that contrasts totally with the dark toiling picture of the land his earlier books have offered. He also discovers the Swedish character — or rather characters — for the book is full of the most splendid series of eccentrics.

The three novels Lo-Johansson produced during the 1960s are not among his most impressive works — to an extent one might suggest that, just as *Geniet* had marked a pause following the decade that he had devoted to *statare*, these novels mark the pause before his discovery of his next major area of interest. *Lyckan* (Happiness, 1962) bears the subtitle 'A Novel about Love on Earth' and tells in the first person of a love affair between two middle-aged people. *Astronomens hus* (The Astronomer's House, 1966) is a continuation of *Måna är död*. It revisits Bo Propst to discover how his existence had taken shape after his decision to dedicate his life to work and ambition rather than to love. *Elektra. Kvinna år 2070* (Elektra. Woman A.D.2070, 1967) is a utopian novel in which a writer, Peter Bly, is put to sleep for a hundred years and wakes in a Sweden in which technology rules supreme.

In 1968 Lo-Johansson returned with undiminished vigour to the short story and produced no fewer than eleven volumes. Seven of these belong to the series known collectively as *The Passion Series*. They are *Passionerna* (The Passions, 1968), *Martyrerna* (The Martyrs, 1968), *Girigbukarna* (The Gluttons, 1969), *Karriäristerna* (The Careerists, 1969), *Vällustingar* (The Voluptuaries, 1970), *Lögnhalsarna* (The Liars, 1971) and *Vishetslärarna* (The Teachers of Wisdom, 1972). As the titles suggest, each volume concentrates on a general area of human passion though Lo-Johansson does not adhere too strictly to the title theme of each book. There are a hundred stories in all — many of them at least based on historical or pseudo-historical characters and incidents — and they range widely in time and place from the Israel of Solomon to twentieth-century Sweden.

Lo-Johansson uses the term passion to cover all the urges that drive an individual to act the way he does, whether the urge be towards self-fulfilment or towards self-annihilation. But in whichever direction the passion leads — and in these stories the destructive aspect dominates — Lo-Johansson sees man as its victim rather than its master. For passion in his sense is something that exists outside the rational sphere and consists often of self-delusion. Thus the circus dwarf in 'Dvärgen och primadonnan' (The Dwarf and the Prima Donna) risks his life by taking over the almost impossible act of the trapeze artist he loves when he has an intimation that her farewell performance will end in death. When he has performed successfully he weeps. ' — He won a triumph, said one of the clowns. And now he is weeping. — Forgive him, said the other. He did not understand that what he was doing was impossible.'(68)[22] The impossibility was not that of performing the act, however dangerous, but of winning the woman by doing so.

There is a strongly deterministic element in Lo-Johansson's view of the passions. In each case the passion fixates the character to the extent that all freedom of decision and action are removed. Here again self-delusion is a central theme: those gripped by the passion continue to believe themselves capable of influencing their own fate and convince themselves of the rational basis of their actions. And the stories in the series are disturbing not least because, in many of them, Lo-Johansson's chosen narrative position is that of the cold observer apparently uninvolved in what he is describing. He refuses throughout to act as a moral adviser to his readers and this can sometimes leave us with the sensation of having been morbid onlookers of suffering too coolly observed. But it compels us to clarify our own standpoint, to try to deepen our own understanding of the motives of the individuals and the nature of the passions, with an urgency that a more obviously partisan stance on the part of the author would have weakened.

After the completion of the Passion stories Lo-Johansson remained with the genre and produced four further collections. Taken together these eleven volumes, containing as they do no fewer than one hundred and forty-five stories, constitute one of the greatest bodies of literature to have been produced in this genre in Sweden. They also widen our view on an author who has perhaps been stamped all too readily as a purely social writer. At the same time, the earlier lines of his work are not forsaken. The painstaking documentarist remains, as demonstrated in the story 'Konsten att skriva en novell' (The Art of Writing a Short Story) which is just as much about how he goes about the long process of gathering his material as it is the story of the eighteenth-century plantation owner Jonas Filéen. The social pathos remains as strong as

Chapter VIII

ever as we see in the story 'Gruvponnyn' (The Pit Pony) where he returns to the material he gathered in Northumberland in the 1920s. He can be the same direct polemicist in the cause of those pushed aside by social changes, as he shows in the masterly though horrifying story 'På åldersdomshemmet' (At the Old People's Home). But beyond these things the stories emphasize aspects too often overlooked in his earlier work. It is easy to forget that Lo-Johansson is a master of the language and an incomparable weaver of symbols, that even his earlier work has a massive historical perspective, and that the individual psyche as well as society had been his field of operation.

It is the individual psyche that holds centre stage in these stories, reminding us that in Lo-Johansson's work there has always been an unresolved clash between the collective and the individual. For all the social commitment of his work, for all the programmatic emphasis on class, community and solidarity, Lo-Johansson's main characters (including the semi-autobiographical figures) are and remain outsiders who stand at the window and look in longingly; that is the tragedy of so many of those depicted in The Passion Series. More than anything else, these stories concern attempts to overcome the isolation of the individual whether it be by means of love, duty, political persuasion or whatever. But what stays with us are the bleak images of the failure to do so. Nowhere are they bleaker than in 'Den ensamma ålen' (The Lonely Eel), the story with which the whole series opens, as if to set the tone of the coming volumes. The main character (a nameless 'he') has been a lifelong womanizer until age gradually reduces his successes to nil. He is alone, with meaningless memories. He is, like the eel the fisherman has told him of, colourless, blinded, undeveloped, swimming in the dark isolation of a well. Nor can the reader draw comfort from the fact that 'he' has taken the wrong road in his search for community. The same story relates the anecdote of the fisherman's old mother who sits and waits for the return of her sons from the sea: 'He saw so clearly the features of her face as though engraved in the glass; melancholy and expectation, some anxiety, but mostly love without anyone to lavish itself on.'[23] She, too, is isolated. The pessimism is unremitting despite Lo-Johansson's statements to the contrary and despite the humour, grotesqueness and irony of many of the stories. As a reviewer of the final volume pointed out: 'The result more often than not is *Vanitas Vanitatis Vanitas*; human wisdom is patchwork or illusion, wilfulness or madness.'[24]

In 1978, the grand scale of his plans undiminished by age, Ivar Lo-Johansson began the publication of his memoirs of a long life. He had time to produce four volumes: *Pubertet* (Puberty, 1978), *Asfalt* (Asphalt, 1979) and *Tröskeln* (The Threshold, 1982) and *Frihet* (Freedom, 1985). They bring us up to the 1950s. Obviously, much of the material is familiar from his many earlier autobiographical works but the real fascination of the books lies in their unrepentant revelation of the extreme individualist who lay behind the collective programmist that Ivar Lo was during the 1930s and 1940s. Personal fame and honour were the spurs: 'Honour for me was mainly an ascetic ideal related to the existence of the solitary hermit in the desert. Only intelligence, the ability to do the impossible, the feeling of absolute superiority mattered. Honour as I saw it could not be bought for money or won dishonestly. It was irreproachable and without defect or blemish. It could only fall to the most highly deserving of all. And I tried to imagine I was that person.'(319)[25]

Eyvind Johnson (1900-76)

Eyvind Johnson was born in Sweden's northernmost province, Norrbotten, where his father had remained after moving north as a railway navvy. Johnson's childhood was isolated and unhappy. Owing to his father's ill-health Johnson lived with foster-parents from the age of four and although they were relations and treated him kindly, he suffered from homesickness. At the age of fourteen he left home to earn his own living and for the next five years he worked in a series of mainly manual jobs in various parts of the north. During the same period he became active as a trade unionist, joined the anarchist-inclined *ungsocialister* (Young Socialists) and wrote regularly for their newspaper.

In 1919 Johnson moved south to Stockholm and began moving in left-wing literary circles. Unable to find work he went abroad in 1921, first to Berlin and then to Paris, and for most of the 1920s he lived out of Sweden making for much of the time a very precarious living from writing. These were formative years. From childhood on Johnson had always been a voracious reader; now his reading widened to include the most radical European writers of the period, in particular Proust, Gide and Joyce.[26] Their influence on him was profound and lasting; he was to become a pioneer of Modernism as far as the Swedish novel is concerned as well as one of the most internationally oriented of Swedish writers.

Eyvind Johnson's first book was a volume of short stories with the title *De fyra främlingarna* (The Four Strangers, 1924) and it was followed a year later by his first novel *Timans och rättfärdigheten* (Timans and Justice, 1925). Stig Timan is the son of a rich industrialist but his sense of guilt at his own privilege leads him to take the part of the workers. Stig, however, is one of Eyvind Johnson's many Hamlet figures and he lacks the decisive quality to become fully involved on either side of the fence — instead he remains an outsider. *Stad i mörker* (Town in Darkness, 1927) although written in Paris is set in winter in Eyvind Johnson's northern Swedish home-town. This novel, too, has an outsider as its central figure — the schoolteacher Andersson who views everything about the town with a cynically superior smile. He is compared with the watchmaker Hammar who has made his own way in the world, finally becoming a town-councillor. By the end of the novel the positions of the two men have drawn together: Hammar has lost much of his security, Andersson has achieved a less pessimistic outlook: 'We ought to think about those who cannot smile. We ought to curse the world because it is evil and unjust to the majority of people, but we ought to smile at spring when it comes and speak words of the future' (255).[27]

Stad i ljus (Town in Light, 1928) leaves the north once again for Paris and was, in fact, first published in French. One is inevitably reminded of Knut Hamsun's *Sult* (Hunger, 1890) when one reads this study of the Swedish writer Torsten who drifts through Paris starving because of the non-arrival of a registered letter with money from Sweden. The focus of the novel lies in the contrast between the hungry writer and the joyful city celebrating Bastille Day with fervour — it is a contrast that allows Eyvind Johnson much scope for gallows humour: 'I am because I eat, sings the town. I am everyone, I am everyone, we bite, we chew, we swallow, we have a good time, and our only desire is a desire for music to go with it'(92).[28]

Eyvind Johnson's last two novels of the 1920s, *Minnas* (Remembering, 1928) and *Kommentar till ett stjärnfall* (Commentary on a Falling Star, 1929), are at the same time among his most experimental novels and among his most despairing. Tragedy in Johnson's personal life in the form of the death of his younger brother seems to have destroyed the glimmer of optimism that shows in *Stad i mörker* and the reconciling humour, however black, of *Stad i ljus*. In *Minnas* all memories are bleak memories, with a deterministic power that the characters cannot escape or come to terms with. The characters in *Kommentar till ett stjärnfall* fare only marginally better. The central character, Stormdal, a man who has worked his way from a working-class background to wealth and a socially acceptable marriage, suffers a breakdown from which he only recovers in the last moments of his life by remembering and accepting at last his roots. His son Magnus is reminiscent of Stig Timan in his Hamlet-like ambivalence to his partially working-class origins: he attempts to show solidarity with the workers but like Stig he remains an observer rather than a participant. In terms of its technique the novel is advanced: Johnson uses both Gide's method of breadthwise cutting in order to tell a number of stories at the same time as well as Joyce's stream of consciousness to follow the course of Stormdal's breakdown.

The very title of *Avsked till Hamlet* (Farewell to Hamlet, 1930) is suggestive of the position to which Eyvind Johnson has moved. Its central figure, Mårten Torpare, appears in no less then five of Johnson's works from the 1930s and it has been remarked that 'books in which Mårten Torpare appears may be regarded as polemical works on contemporary issues'.[29] Unlike the characters in Johnson's earlier novels, Torpare, a man who has been brought up outside his own class, overcomes the split within himself by returning to his class background with pride: 'The most important element in civilization at present is the workers' movement because it has the will without which everything is dead' (188).[30] Mårten Torpare's role is less central in the two novels that follow — *Bobinack* (Bobinack, 1932) and *Regn i gryningen* (Rain at Dawn, 1933) — though he continues to function as Eyvind Johnson's mouthpiece. The first of these novels contains much satire aimed at the capitalist system while at the same time putting forward the then current Primitivist ideas of a society that can be freed from its repressions by a return to nature. In the second, the same ideas are taken up in a more practical form in that the main character, Henrik Fax, actually does give up his successful position and go back to nature. Typically, the Hamlet-side of Eyvind Johnson's own character leads him to question Fax' behaviour almost as much as he approves of it.

Eyvind Johnson returned to Sweden from his self-imposed exile in 1930. With the tetralogy *Romanen om Olof* (The Novel about Olof, 1934-37) one might say that he marked his spiritual return. Set in his

Chapter VIII

home province of Norrbotten, it is his contribution to the autobiographical form so common in the 1930s. In *Nu var det 1914* (Now It Was 1914, 1934) we meet the young Olof leaving his fosterparents and beginning a series of adult jobs. His childhood has been lonely and unhappy but his road to adulthood is no easier as he faces first the dangers of timber working, then the dirt of the brickworks and discomfort of potato picking. He is a child forced into an adult world, a child forced to forget play and face toil, though his childishness repeatedly shows through, as when he catches himself swinging on the supports of a jetty, dreams of leading a band of robbers or is ashamed of himself for playing football instead of working. Work is toil, and Olof notes its effects on those he works with. Of the lumberjack August it is said:

He carries his back like a burden, someone has thought. He carries life's toil — a tough rucksack of many years and half-starvation. He is not hunch-backed, you can see that his back was once straight but has been bent year by year, however much he struggled against it (49).[31]

And Olof is determined that though he must work he will not become like his fellows: 'He knew that his life would not become theirs — that was a certainty'(46).

Not only toil but also fear must be faced on Olof's road out of childhood: above all a fear of death and a fear of darkness. Death is ever present at the log-jams on the river, is always on the minds of the men working: 'It was as if they wanted to but could not fight against the crushing force and seriousness of the jam. Their voices became less sure, their gait more uncertain, the dying day more mysterious' (41). A less rational but for Olof more paralysing fear is that of darkness. Alone in the brickworks at night when the other workers have left he tries to fight off his fears by thinking rationalist thoughts: 'There is no God and we descend from apes. But it didn't help' (124). Only at the end when he meets an old woman on a dark road and recognizes that she too is afraid — afraid of him moreover — is his fear defeated and 'when he came home to the barracks and groped his way up the dark staircase, it was as if he was armoured in joy and hope'(152).

Nu var det 1914 ends with the words: 'And so his childhood was over' (153).This final statement of the ending of Olof's childhood is preceded by his sensation of 'a wild desire' for a girl he has met in a shop. These intimations of sexuality are only occasionally taken up in the second volume *Här har du ditt liv* (Here You Have Your Life, 1935) which concentrates instead on the development of Olof's intellectual curiosity. Throughout the novel Olof is employed at a sawmill where he is surrounded by workers fettered by a slave mentality:

At the sawmill it happened that people set to work and toiled like slaves if no more than a fourth grade factor or eighth grade boss approached, even if there was no more than the scent of something boss-like in the air (203).

Against such a mentality Olof sets two different ideals: the spirit of the independent *rallare* (navvy) who considered himself the equal of any boss, and the world of the imagination which he meets in fairy tales and books, borrowed and begged, anything from Homer to Nietzsche and not excluding pulp fiction. In one way Olof's reading represents 'a flight, a rushing, blind flight from reality' (241), but in a more profound sense it represents his refusal to fall in with the apathy of his fellow-workers: 'You should never be satisfied: to be satisfied is to be dead and no longer want things' (309). Books and Olof's learning of German inevitably create a distance between him and those around him. He senses in his fellow-workers a fear of himself and a fear that he is acquiring something that they have become too weary to bother with, but the independence he retains against the slave mentality stands him in good stead at the end of the novel when he has the courage to refuse to follow unreasonable orders from his boss. Instead, he leaves the job (to the incomprehension of his fellow workers) and moves on with the thought: 'You are you. It is you who is you. You must try to stand on your own feet and eat your own food' (327).

Se dig inte om (Don't Look Back, 1936) introduces us to the now sixteen-year-old Olof working in a cinema and dreaming of becoming an impresario himself. The mood is more optimistic than in the earlier volumes, partly because the emphasis is less on physical toil, partly because of the humour with which side characters such as the cinema director are viewed, but mainly because the isolation in which most of Olof's childhood and youth has been spent is now replaced by friendships. With his friend Fredrik Olof discusses everything from films to anarchism, and from Fredrik, a lovable boaster trusted neither by the reader nor by Olof, he hears tales of worldly experience: 'At that time he drank. Now he neither drank nor smoked ... The only things I actually use are just coffee and women, he explained' (55). Olof's own

Chapter VIII

experience of women takes a step forward when he falls in love with Maria, who leaves him only to remain in his mind throughout the novel however much he tries to 'erase' her. It is with incidents from these two friendships that the novel draws to a close. Fredrik, in need of cash, asks Olof to steal oil and Olof refuses. But then he agrees because: 'He has a friend. The friend was called Fredrik' (186). The theft comes to nothing for on the night of the planned crime Olof is again afflicted by his old paralysis in the face of darkness, by memories of his father buried close to the scene, and above all by the sense of responsibility for himself and his own actions. Now, too, he can at last 'erase' Maria.

In the final scene of *Se dig inte om* Olof puts a film into the projector at the cinema, locks the door and begins to read Homer's *Odyssey*. He has already earlier in the volume dreamt, thought about and played with his own first tale. In *Slutspel i ungdomen* (Finale in Youth, 1937) literature comes to the fore; indeed one might say that Olof's mind has been so affected by his reading that he is only capable of seeing 'life through literature' (39), through a series of stylistic pastiches that mask rather than express his own activities, thoughts, feelings and perceptions whether they be as revolutionary union organizer or as muddled lover of Queen Olivia, owner of the fairground shooting-gallery. Olof's survival, as in the earlier volumes, is dependent on his stubborn insistence on his own individuality, though now it is tempered by a recognition of the collective humanity within which that individuality exists: 'Everything depends on yourself because only you can be you — but you can't live alone in the world and you must believe in other people's value and dignity ...' (259). What remains for him, however, is to find a means of expressing what he has learned about himself and the world: 'to find words for what you actually knew. There were no instructions you could follow' (293).

In purely external terms *Romanen om Olof* follows essentially the same pattern as the other autobiographical novels described elsewhere in this chapter: meetings with work, with friends, with literature, with politics and with women are linked chronologically, and the point of view of the narrative is almost exclusively that of Olof. It is only into his mind that we enter and it is through his eyes that we perceive the events he is part of and the personalities he meets. But however much the central interest in these novels concentrates on the development of Olof, the province of Norrland itself plays a role as more than mere setting. In perhaps the most original of the 1930s' efforts to portray the collective as well as the individual Eyvind Johnson incorporates what he calls a saga into each volume. Each saga takes a different form but what they have in common is that they move away from more-or-less realistic narrative and use the techniques of the folk-tale and folk-ballad in order to universalize the harsh fates of the people of this most exploited of provinces. In 'The Saga of Mist and TB' the scourge of tuberculosis carries off all the children of an isolated family until the mist (symbol both of the disease and of the souls of the dead children) finally takes the mother too. It is an unforgettably moving picture not just of the disease but also of the poverty, the simplicity — ultimately a holy simplicity — and the limited horizons of these people. 'The Saga about Johanna' is narrated half as a sentimental broadsheet ballad, half in narrative prose that fills the gaps and comments on the ballad. The story tells of the fate of Johanna, a peasant girl seduced and abandoned by a young navvy. In cold prose she wanders from navvy camp to navvy camp descending to being little more than an alcoholic camp whore; in the ballad, however, her wandering is portrayed as a romantic search for a lost lover. So reality and myth join in yet another aspect of Norrland: 'And she was the Poem, the song — everything. She carried a part of mighty Norrbotten within herself and out with her into the world' (298). The third of the sagas, 'The Saga of the Country of Brazil', treats the emigration of a group from Norrland to Brazil, their land of dreams and plenty. Reality is very different and few survive hunger and disease to return.

'The Saga of the Land of the Pleasures of the Soul and Spiritual Vanity' subtitled 'A Meeting with the Spanish Woman' differs in that it centres on Olof himself. In a dream induced by influenza he sees himself and Olivia of the shooting gallery in a series of roles that reflect his reading, everything from Xenophon to Dumas. To most readers it is perhaps the least successful of the sagas yet Eyvind Johnson himself described it as 'an attempt to depict the preconditions for the novel itself' (296). As one critic has expanded on it: 'Literature colors Olof's interpretation of his experiences while his experiences in turn are expressed through literature.'[32]

Of the many autobiographical novels of the 1930s *Romanen om Olof* is undoubtedly the most subtle in terms of tracing an individual's development and simultaneously the most skilful and imaginative in its creation of background. Many years later, in the 1950s, Eyvind Johnson returned to the autobiographical form less successfully with *Romantisk berättelse* (Romantic Tale, 1953) and *Tidens gång* (The Course of Time, 1955). These follow his life abroad through the 1920s.

With the approach and arrival of World War II Eyvind Johnson's attention, like that of many other Swedish writers, turned to more immediate questions. Although a pacifist he reached the conclusion that against the evils of Fascism only force could provide an answer, and he campaigned vigorously for Sweden to shift from its neutral stance and become actively involved in support of its neighbours whether it was a case of Finland against invasion by the Soviet Union or Denmark and Norway against the German occupation. As with Vilhelm Moberg, his activities included journalism, public debate and the production of a number of novels that are classed as *beredskapslitteratur*. In the first two such novels the figure of Mårten Torpare returns. *Nattövning* (Night Manoeuvres, 1938) depicts the motives of a group of Swedish Nazis and finds them to be 'rootless, scorned, unhappy, vengeful' (93). Reluctantly, Mårten Torpare comes to the view that the Primitivist ideas he has subscribed to in *Regn i gryningen* are no longer tenable and that now one must not accept but actively resist: 'Violence for peace, violence for justice, violence in order to kill violence. It is conceivable that that is the right way now' (194). In *Soldatens återkomst* (The Soldier's Return, 1940) Sten, who has fought as a volunteer in Spain, Finland and Norway, returns to his home village only to be murdered by a rival in love — a man he recognizes to be of the type he has fought against in his campaigns. Once again the message is put into the mouth of Mårten Torpare: 'One should prevent others from killing. If necessary one should prevent them by force' (22).

It is, however, the immense trilogy of novels *Grupp Krilon* (The Krilon Group, 1941*), Krilons resa* (Krilon's Journey, 1942) and *Krilon själv* (Krilon Himself, 1943) that is Eyvind Johnson's most enduring contribution to *beredskapslitteratur*. Johannes Krilon is a Stockholm estate agent who has gathered around himself a group of six friends who meet for weekly discussions. Misfortune strikes them one after another and the group disintegrates, most of its members falling into the economic power of Krilon's crooked business rival Staph. Gradually they reach a recognition of the error of having allowed Staph's machinations to destroy their former freedom and solidarity but feel themselves powerless to resist. Krilon, however, does not succumb. Although close to defeat he fights back, the group re-forms around him and finally between them they defeat Staph.

Krilon is an allegorical work on a huge scale and on many levels. Most obviously there is the direct wartime parallel between Krilon's struggle against Staph and Britain's struggle against Germany: like Britain Krilon — a Churchill-like figure — stands alone until his group joins forces again. His main enemy is G. Staph (Gestapo) whose supporters are Görén (Goering), Góbén (Goebbels) and Höllén (Himmler). Many other such direct parallels may be found. And there are, of course, open references to the wartime situation, particularly that of the Scandinavian countries, for the story of Krilon and his associates not only parallels the war but is acted out against the background of the war. On a more universal level of allegory *Krilon* treats the struggle between Christ and the Devil, between Good and Evil whether they be seen as two external forces or as forces in competition within the individual. *Krilon*, then, is a complex novel of ideas, often obscure and often difficult to disentangle. It is narrated with a wide variety of styles and techniques and it shifts backwards and forwards between realistic narrative, allegory, fairy-tale and propaganda. Ultimately, however, it is on its characters and their fates that it stands, especially on that of its title figure — a man who through personal suffering has become 'sceptical or in any case non-enthusiastic while his aim, as everyone now understands, was to order the world or to contribute to its ordering along reasonable lines' (19).[33]

From the time of *Strändernas svall* (The Swell on the Beaches, 1946) the majority of Eyvind Johnson's novels are given historical settings and deal with historical events. *Strändernas svall*, however, is also given the sub-title 'A Novel About the Present' and that sub-title could without impropriety be applied to his other historical novels. Johnson was fascinated by the problems of time and history, particularly by the ideas of simultaneity and reiteration. In his study of Johnson's historical novels Stig Bäckman has written:

The idea of simultaneity has a psychological origin, is based on an analysis of the human consciousness and involves the notion that, as regards the individual experience of time, no clear boundaries can be drawn between different times and events: present and past merge together in the consciousness and different moments exist side-by-side ... The idea of reiteration involves the notion that the same situation and trains of events constantly recur in history and that mankind and the fundamental situation of mankind have not changed in the course of the centuries.[34]

Chapter VIII

Johnson, as an experimenter with the novel, tackles these problems in various ways.

In *Strändernas svall* Eyvind Johnson retells the story of Homer's *Odyssey* in modern realistic terms. When the novel opens Odysseus is on his return journey to Ithaca from the Trojan War. For seven years he has been delayed with the nymph Calypso on an isolated island until Hermes, messenger of the gods, visits him and commands him to return home to his wife Penelope who is being courted by suitors who believe her to be a royal widow. Reluctantly and dressed as a beggar Odysseus obeys and returns to Ithaca, meets his former swineherd Eumaeus and between them they plan and execute the slaughter of Penelope's suitors and of their slave concubines.

The bare bones of these bloodthirsty events fail to reveal that the Odysseus that we are presented with in *Strändernas svall* is a far more complex figure than a merely vengeful slaughterer. Warrior he may be, but he bears on his conscience the acts that he has committed as a warrior, and at each stage of decision he doubts, questions and feels indecision. Nowhere is this more clear than in the chapter (pointedly titled 'The Man in Doubt') in which Odysseus discusses with his swineherd Eumaeus whether there exists any other option than the slaughter of Penelope's suitors. Eumaeus thinks not:

I have heard of other peoples far beyond great seas and lands, peoples that have a choice. There it is considered a great shame, a defilement and a crime against the gods to kill people. But now we are in reality — traveller — we are in the present! We are in the civilized world! There is no choice (338).[35]

And, indeed, Eumaeus would help Odysseus:

I would do it because his struggle is just — or less unjust than theirs against him. He would diminish their growing power. He would create order again and that could be the basis for something better. I would help him to reach a starting point (341).

But Eumaeus adds: 'Don't think afterwards that it is a holy act and that your war is a blessing for anyone affected by it. It is a way to a possibility, no more than that!' (342).

'The way to a possibility' is as far as Eyvind Johnson will lead us; the reader can never be certain (any more than Odysseus himself can) of the motivations of Odysseus for his decision nor of its results but it is a decision that must be taken because 'reality' and 'the present' demand it. His years with Calypso are years outside time and reality — are escapism — as he himself half recognized and which he half desires to be released from. He is, nevertheless, reluctant to leave and does so only at the direct command of the gods: 'I know what it is, said the one to whom the call had come. I'm supposed to go to war again now. I know that it's an order. But I feel no joy' (47). So the moral problem faced by Odysseus is ultimately the same as that which Mårten Torpare or Johannes Krilon have been faced with in a more modern context: in what circumstances can violence be justified?

Drömmar om rosor och eld (Dreams About Roses and Fire, 1949) is set in a different historical period, the seventeenth-century France of Cardinal Richelieu. It is based quite closely on genuine historical events, the same events as were used by Aldous Huxley for his novel *The Devils of Loudun* (1952). In 1617 Urbain Grainier, a priest, comes to the town of Loudun. Grainier is handsome, charming but utterly arrogant and very soon his behaviour, especially towards women, has angered many of the citizens. Worse than that, he makes an enemy of Cardinal Richelieu who as part of his anti-Huguenot campaign wishes to tear down the fortified walls of Loudun. It is Grainier who leads the opposition to the Cardinal's plans. Grainier's enemies are given their chance to move against him when the nuns at the convent in Loudun show signs of possession by devils — devils that conveniently admit to being under Grainier's control. Grainier is accused and tried for witchcraft, a crime which he denies even when tortured to the limit. Brutally mutilated but still capable of stating his innocence he is taken to the town square and burned at the stake.

The immediate contemporary relevance of Johnson's novel is quite obvious: Grainier's trial is as much a show trial brought on trumped-up charges by his totalitarian opponents for their own political purposes as were the Stalinist trials of the 1930s and the Czech trials of the 1940s. They all demonstrate the same mixture of political persecution and personal paranoia on the part of a leader who feels himself to be identical with the state. Of Cardinal Richelieu Eyvind Johnson writes:

...He is supposed to have answered that he had no enemies and had never felt enmity except against the enemies of the State. Throughout his whole life he retained his childhood belief, that is to say: he believed in demons. Alongside this belief, as a subordinate part of it, there was his insight as to how superstition and even true faith can be used and exploited in the service of the public — for

Chapter VIII

example, to strengthen policies which in spite of their strength always needed and need support of all sorts and by all means: those policies which rest on the security and protection of a single person or of a small group of people (250).[36]

Johnson underlines this contemporary relevance by repeated reference to the judgements that posterity will make of men and events. As Grainier puts it to Minet, one of his interrogators:

Every judge who judges is also pronouncing a judgment on himself — and that will go down to posterity. We are frightened of posterity whatever we say about it and however we pretend to express our indifference, indeed, our scorn for what it will think (216).

In the figure of Grainier Eyvind Johnson has created a complex psychological figure: he is at one and the same time a priest and a lover of women, a seeker for the truth yet capable of unprincipled behaviour. Perhaps above all, it is power that motivates him, and it is a motivation that he recognizes himself and admits to his mistress Madeleine: 'I defend myself. And I must win. If I don't win — time after time — then I am lost. There is no middle way, no compromise for me' (22). With the same clarity he recognizes that even his approaching martyrdom is a means to power: 'I am now the most powerful man in the town I once called mine and it gives me a joy that I cannot deny' (294).

Lägg undan solen (Put Away the Sun, 1951) returns to the present and deals with the stories of a group of refugees hiding together in a mountain hut. Even here, however, history is drawn in, rather unsuccessfully for once, in that the characters recognize that their contemporary situation parallels that of rebelling Roman slaves two millennia earlier.

A much more impressive, though still not wholly convincing, mixing of past and present is to be seen in *Molnen över Metapontion* (The Clouds Over Metapontion, 1957).

Johnson's intention in *Strändernas svall* was to cause the picture of the present to emerge gradually from the picture of the past ... In *Molnen över Metapontion*, he tackled the opposite problem: how to get two initially separate pictures to fuse into one.[37]

In the modern story we meet a Swede, Klemens Decorbie, who during the war fought for France as a volunteer, was taken prisoner and spent the rest of the war in various camps. In one of these he meets the Jewish archaeologist Lévy who tells a classical story from Xenophon's *Anabasis*. After the war, Decorbie, by now a writer, travels to Metapontion in Italy to visit the setting of the story he has been told. In the historical story the main character is the Greek, Themistogenes, who is taken prisoner during the invasion of Sicily and sent to labour in the quarries. After his release his wife and children are murdered and he joins Xenophon's army on its ill-fated expedition to Persia. The Greeks fight their way home and Themistogenes returns to the Greek colony in Metapontion in Italy.

There are obvious parallels between the two stories: both Decorbie and Themistogenes are soldiers who are captured, both lose their families, both finally are on the victor's side at least in the sense that they survive, and both at last come to Metapontion. There, the clouds of the title of the novel symbolize future dangers for them and their contemporaries; in the case of the modern story, the danger of nuclear war. It would seem, then, that Eyvind Johnson is arguing pessimistically that mankind and its sufferings have not and cannot change. But:

It might seem (whispered Professor Lévy), it might appear sometimes, when one is tired, it might appear that everything has happened before in all the places where people have been. It might appear as if every event has already happened. It might appear that everything is completed. But that is not how it is, dear friends. Every event is a completely new event. That is why life still exists. And that is why we can all hope (309).[38]

In other words, events do not repeat themselves though parallel events may later occur. This is what gives mankind the possibility to learn from the past and so develop.

The motto with which Eyvind Johnson introduces *Hans nådes tid* (The Days of His Grace, 1960) leads us straight to the central theme of the novel:

Living on an aspen leaf — No one can live in safety on an aspen leaf. Yet there are tiny creatures living there who do not know that their land is an aspen leaf. For them it is a home, a homeland in a world, the aspen leaf world.

The novel tells the story of some sixty years in the life of Johannes Lupigis, a Lombard living through the genuine historical events of the age of Charlemagne in the period around AD 800. At the opening of the

Chapter VIII

novel the Kingdom of Lombardy has just lost its independence and been incorporated into the Frankish Empire. Two strands dominate the life of Johannes — two strands that are inextricably entwined. Firstly, at the age of sixteen he falls in love with Angila but is soon separated from her by the tide of events when she is forcibly married off to the Frankish Baron Gunderic. Decades later they are re-united when Johannes frees her from her captivity. Sick and weakened, however, by her years of misery Angila dies. Secondly, there are the political events: Johannes takes part in a uprising against Charlemagne and when the uprising is crushed he survives and escapes, swearing an oath that he will one day kill Charlemagne. Under suspicion of plotting he is imprisoned for three and a half years in darkness. At first his mental strength enables him to resist, but at last a vision of the devil, of earthly temptations and a recognition of the futility of rotting in a dungeon weakens his resolve. He is released and in time becomes the private secretary of the Emperor he had sworn to kill.

Johannes Lupigis and Angila and their nation, then, are 'living on an aspen leaf', a world in which small creatures and small nations are shaken by forces too powerful for them to control. Physical resistance, as the failed Lombard revolt demonstrates, leads only to increased oppression and is thus pointless. But there is another way of survival, a way that demands resignation on the part of the individual and an understanding of the historical process. Johannes begins to see this while in hiding after the uprising: 'That which has the possibility of surviving is probably the spirit we possess, which some possess. It can develop knowledge about life and learning from writings' (235). In other words, Johannes is beginning to understand and achieve the wisdom propounded by his uncle Anselm early in the novel — the wisdom that teaches that the present can only be comprehended and accepted in the context both of the past and of the future:

Our people's past is piling itself up in front of us, he said. In front of us, precisely... We must go through it once again although it ought to lie behind us. We have certainly lived through it and made our mark on it and had marks made on us by it; indeed, our people has lived through everything. Now the time has come when we must take in everything we have lived through, swallow it however it tastes, in order to be free from past things that can still hurt us (72).

The message of the novel is one of resignation, its tone melancholy and weary, but ultimately there is no pessimism for memory makes it possible for the spirit to survive against all the odds. *Hans nådes tid* is arguably the greatest of Eyvind Johnson's historical novels: in it the shifting narrative styles, the ideas, the characters, the tone and the atmosphere of the period come together in a rare way.

Johnson's twin historical ideas of reiteration and simultaneity are most clearly seen in *Livsdagen lång* (Life's Long Day, 1964). It is a love story, but a love story in which the lovers, Donatus and Astalda, are brought together only for short periods over a time span of a thousand years. In each episode Donatus loses Astalda only to seek her again in future centuries; each time they know each other and remember the past. Finally, it emerges that the past reaches into the present when the Narrator sees Donatus and Astalda in a vision and understands that he himself is Donatus, Astalda a woman he lost: 'I saw myself as if in a trembling mirror, not a reflection from the surface of the water but a mirror with convex, dusty-steamy glass' (325).

In *Favel ensam* (Favel Alone, 1968) Eyvind Johnson returns to the modern day and an English setting. The characters have all in some way been victims of Nazism and the central theme is a discussion of the motivation of idealists and, indeed, of the desirability of idealism at all. This rather weak novel reaches the conclusion that 'we probably can't manage without a Utopia ... an absolutely essential island for a humanity that does not want to perish' (24). Johnson's last novel *Några steg mot tystnaden* (Some Steps towards Silence, 1973) resembles *Livsdagen lång* in that it consists of a number of separate stories ranging from the 15th century to the present.

Of the writers treated in this chapter Eyvind Johnson was undoubtedly the one least bound by his proletarian background. Although class-conflict figures as a theme in a number of his novels, it is really only with the autobiographical *Romanen om Olof* that his career coincides with those of his contemporaries from the working-class. Even in that novel the differences are greater than the superficial similarities. Whereas Moberg and Lo-Johansson work within the mainstream tradition of the realistic novel, Eyvind Johnson experiments and innovates whether it be in terms of narrative technique or characterization or theme. His literary models are to be found outside Sweden rather than at home, and he is in every respect their equal. But he is much more than merely a literary experimenter for he has tackled the great universal theme of mankind's situation in the world, of how it is possible for us 'to live on an aspen leaf'.

Chapter VIII

In 1957 Eyvind Johnson became a member of the Swedish Academy, and in 1974 he was awarded the Nobel Prize together with Harry Martinson.

Chapter IX

Stig Dagerman and *fyrtiotalismen*

Laurie Thompson

Stig Dagerman is now widely recognized as one of Sweden's leading twentieth-century prose writers (as well as being a notable dramatist and an accomplished writer of verses). His novels and short stories have attracted international attention, and have been translated into many languages. Although Dagerman is not as well-known in the English-speaking world as he is in France, most of his main works are available in English.

While it is clear to us at the end of the twentieth century that Stig Dagerman's works have a timeless appeal, it was felt in Sweden during his lifetime (his dates are 1923-54) and for a couple of decades afterwards that his main claim to fame was as the most typical of the *fyrtiotalister*, the young writers who set the tone in Swedish literature of the 1940s. His writing appeals especially to those who generally feel ill at ease in the world, who often feel powerless in the face of overwhelming and sometimes frightening forces, social as well as psychological, but who would like to think nevertheless that earthly bliss is a possibility in spite of everything, who place ideals on a higher level than the disappointing realities of a world that sometimes appears bent on self-destruction, whose instinct is for comradeship and solidarity even though real life seems so often to suggest they are ultimately unattainable. In order to understand Stig Dagerman, however, it is first necessary to place him in the context of the time when he was writing, and to attempt a definition of the *fyriotalismen* of which he was so typical.

Chapter IX

The meaning of the term 'fyrtiotalismen'

The term *fyrtiotalismen* as applied to the literary style of the 1940s can be misleading. In 1962, a version appeared in *Folket i bild* of a conversation between Karl Vennberg and Pär Rådström in which they discussed the literature of the 1940s and agreed that what is termed *fyrtiotalistisk litteratur* was restricted to the years 1944-47;[1] even a more liberal definition than theirs would probably place the limits at about 1943-48, while some would argue for 1945-1946.

Moreover, there was no school as such, and indeed, if one were to name the most important Swedish novels of the 1940s, one would probably have to mention Eyvind Johnson's *Krilon* series and his *Strändernas svall*, also Pär Lagerkvist's *Dvärgen* and Vilhelm Moberg's *Utvandrarna*: yet none of these writers had any connection with the *fyrtiotalister*. Central to the creed of the *fyrtiotalister* was disillusionment with dogmas, shared ideas, organized groups — instead, they believed fervently in a critical and individual approach; how could they form a school?

And yet, despite such facts, there is a recognizable *fyrtiotalistisk* style. It is most obvious in those writers who published their work in the journal *40-tal*, which never attempted to be the organ of a uniform movement but nevertheless became a forum for like-minded individuals. Karl Vennberg refers to an 'inner group' of writers who would meet regularly for cultural evenings at the homes of Axel Liffner and Sonja Bergwall, including (in addition to the hosts) Lars Ahlin, Werner Aspenström, Olov Jonason, Erik Lindegren, Lennart Göthberg, Ragnar Thoursie, Sven Alfons, occasionally Stig Dagerman, and of course Vennberg himself. It was all very informal, even casual, and there were as many disagreements as agreements in the course of discussions — and certainly no attempt to formulate a programme.

In order to understand the *fyrtiotalister* and to appreciate how they came to write as they did, one has to consider a number of features of the 1940s in Sweden — political, social and cultural. These conditions dictated the style and subject matter of the younger generation of Swedish authors to an even greater extent than is usual.

The Second World War dominated the 1940s throughout Europe. Sweden was neutral and escaped the ravages of bombing raids, battles on her territory, and the many tragedies that inevitably occur when a country's citizens are involved in active fighting. The position of the young intellectual and artist in Sweden, however, was an agonizing one. His sympathies were on the Allied side and against Nazism, but he was frustrated in that not only did he have to stand helplessly on the sidelines and watch the devastating fighting take place, he was not even allowed to express his preferences because of the strict Swedish censorship laws designed to prevent Hitler being given an excuse to invade Sweden. The brutality and destruction caused by the Second World War were shattering, and the Swedish observer was deeply depressed by what seemed to be the collapse of civilized values, even the wanton destruction of Western culture. His optimism when the tide of the war turned and it became clear that Hitler must lose was tempered by what seemed to be the illiberal attitude of the Western powers: Swedes had hoped German Fascism would be replaced by some liberal system of benevolent socialism, but instead they saw how the Western powers hardened their attitude towards the Soviet Union and took up what many Swedes regarded as a reactionary stance not far removed from the Fascism that had just been defeated. Revelations regarding the incredible brutality of the extermination camps were depressing indeed, but so was the saturation bombing of German cities such as Dresden by the Allies, and even more so the atomic bombs dropped by the USA on Japan in 1945 to bring the war to an end. How could anyone be anything but pessimistic about the future of Western civilization?

This lack of faith in political solutions, and disillusionment with the kind of society which led to the war, also that which was establishing itself as the war came to an end, resulted in a widespread feeling of scepticism and insecurity. A Third World War was widely expected, and the incomprehensible destructive powers of the atomic bomb — and later the hydrogen bomb — resulted in an atmosphere of European Angst.

This was the key concept of the dominant philosophy of the 1940s, Existentialism. Sartre and Camus had propounded Existentialist doctrines in the occupied France of the early 1940s, and although their works were known to a few Swedish specialists and their ideas discussed in some literary circles, it was not until the end of the war that they were translated into Swedish and the full extent of their influence felt.[2] Swedish was ripe for this pessimistic creed which concentrates on the meaningless nature of life, the fundamental loneliness of the individual when he is placed in a position where he has

Chapter IX

to make a moral choice, and in spite of his awareness of his isolation and hopelessness, he attempts to choose 'den rätta handlingen' — the right action (a phrase which was widely used by several Swedish writers of the 1940s without their needing to make the reference clear).

Another strong influence on the *fyrtiotalister* was Franz Kafka. Although Kafka died in 1924, it was not until the mid-1940s that his works became widely known in Sweden.[3] Extravagant claims were made for Kafka, who was thought by some to have anticipated the totalitarian dictatorships of the 1940s (both Nazi and Communist), also the inhuman treatment of the Jews in concentration camps. More relevant was the all-pervading atmosphere of Angst in his novels and stories — *Der Prozess* (The Trial) and *Das Schloss* (The Castle) were translated into Swedish soon after the end of the war, as were several short stories — and the Expressionistic style which starts from some absurd premise, e.g. that a man might wake up one morning and find that he has turned into a beetle overnight (*Die Verwandlung*) (The Metamorphosis), but having once accepted that absurdity, treats all subsequent developments with strict realism and occasional grotesque humour. The result is a strange dream-like atmosphere which manages to capture the sense of hopeless inevitability felt by so many writers of the 1940s to be characteristic of the age. Kafka's style was widely imitated, although it is probably truer to say that as far as the most celebrated 'Kafka disciple', Stig Dagerman, is concerned, it was a case of kindred spirits rather than a young Swede being unduly influenced by a mentor.

Although the philosophical and literary influence of Kafka and the French Existentialists did not make itself fully felt until the latter half of the 1940s, so that it is doubtful whether critics are justified in thinking in terms of a formative influence on the Swedish *fyrtiotalister*, the impact of American literature was felt much earlier. Artur Lundkvist had written extensively about all the leading American writers during the 1930s, and his introductions were added to in the early 1940s by Thorsten Jonsson, who was *Dagens Nyheter*'s correspondent in the USA for several years. His *Sex amerikaner* (1942) dealt with Hemingway, Faulkner, Steinbeck, Caldwell, Farrell and Saroyan, while his own short stories *Som det brukar vara* (As It Usually Is, 1939), *Fly till vatten och morgon* (Flee to Water and Tomorrow, 1942), obviously owe a considerable debt to American models, especially Hemingway. The tough, uncompromising style of Hemingway in his bull-fighting stories or novels such as *A Farewell to Arms* (and represented in the cinema by the Humphrey Bogart films) became fashionable in Sweden in the early 1940s. The *'hårdkokta'* writers (i.e. from the American expression 'hard-boiled') used short, simple sentences to describe often violent and squalid events: violence, crudity, sex, immorality — *'de hårdkokta'* were accused of exploiting an excess of all these features and severely censured by conservative critics.

Peter Nisser's novel *Blod och snö* (Blood and Snow, 1941) caused much discussion concerning the raw violence it contained, and the starkly realistic description of scenes from the so-called Winter War between Finland and Russia in 1940 were considered shocking by some readers.

Conservative critics were particularly concerned about the 'hard-boiled' authors' preoccupation with squalid perversions and sexual excesses. They reserved their severest strictures for the New Vitalists *(nyvitalister)*, who had attempted to form a genuine school based on 'hard-boiled' principles and went so far as to publish a manifesto in *Dagens Nyheter* (17 December 1943). At the centre of the movement were Sven Forsell, Bertil Lagerström, Mårten Edlund and Gustaf Rune Eriks, and one of the most representative works from those writers (because of its extremes with regard to violence and perversion) is Edlund's novel, *Tag vad du vill ha* (Take What You Want, 1944). A leading conservative critic, Martin Rogberg, called it a 'repugnant product', commenting that its 'moral negativism is just as concentrated as the piling on of nastiness is unprecedented' (*Svenska Dagbladet*, 23 October 1944). Åke Runnquist's summary of the perverse features of the novel give some idea of why it was attacked by traditionalists:

Within the space of 280 pages and in a single family (including in-laws), Edlund depicts two alcoholics with the DTs, a homosexual schoolteacher, a murderer and sex maniac to boot, and a more or less nymphomaniac mother. A suicide and a murder vie for the reader's attention, as does the fact that in one case mother and daughter share the same lover.[4]

The up-and-coming generation of authors that was to form the core of the *fyrtiotalister* approved of the willingness to deal frankly with what had been considered to be taboo subjects, and the realistic language used by the 'hard-boiled' writers. They objected, however, to the tendency to indulge in sex and violence for their own sakes, and to preach a kind of sensuous romanticism that lacked an intellectual

Chapter IX

foundation, avoiding rather than facing up to fundamental problems in contemporary society. Reviewing books by *nyvitalister* Nisser, Bergström and Edlund in the Christmas issue of *40-tal*, 1944, Lennart Göthberg summarized their approach as follows: 'Common to all of them is their anti-intellectualism, a romantic exaggeration of sexual ecstasy, and a hard-boiled style mixed with a large portion of sentimental self-pity.'

As its name implies, the journal *40-tal* had pretensions to being a rallying point for like-minded writers attempting to create literature genuinely appropriate to the 1940s. Published by Bonniers, it first appeared in the autumn of 1944, 24 pages of A5 size, modest — not to say spartan — in design and layout. Its policy was declared on the front page:

40-tal aims to be a vehicle for polemical articles by young authors and new voices. We are not in the business of promulgating a literary programme. We intend to provide a free forum where diverse views and opinions can be expressed ... We hope to attract readers interested in following literary trends, in Sweden and elsewhere.

40-tal was greeted with reserve, even scepticism. It was clear the war would not last much longer, but there were still serious shortages, not least of paper and print: for a new journal to be launched at all was remarkable, and for a journal edited by three 'unknowns' — Werner Aspenström, Lennart Göthberg and Claes Hoogland — to claim representative status by calling itself *40-tal* was presumptuous in the extreme. Karl Vennberg, then cultural editor of the newspaper *Arbetaren*, attacked the first issue with vicious sarcasm aimed particularly at Göthberg and Aspenström; no doubt the sarcasm derived to some extent from the fact that, together with Axel Liffner, Stig Carlson, Olov Jonason and Artur Lundkvist, he had recently been thwarted in his attempts to produce a new journal himself...[5]

Bonniers were disturbed by the negative reception afforded to their new journal, and tried to reconcile Vennberg and other critics with the editors of *40-tal*; in fact, a reconciliation soon took place.[6] *40-tal* rapidly became what it had set out to be: the forum where views central to the literature of the 1940s were aired and debated. There is no better way of acquainting oneself with the spirit of the 1940s in Swedish literature than reading *40-tal*, which was published from October 1944 to Autumn 1947. A whole book would be needed to do justice to the issues raised in the journal during the three years or more of its existence. Some of the most important ones ought to be examined briefly here, however, since they are central to an understanding of the creative literature written during the period. They are inter-connected, in fact, but can be regarded under three headings: radicalism, obscurity and pessimism.

The theme of radicalism was expounded in the very first issue of *40-tal* by Werner Aspenström, in his article 'Radikalitetens problem'. Vennberg was right to criticize the article as being rather superficial, but the tone was set for a succession of articles claiming that the modern artist must be committed — by which the authors meant committed to a socialistic view of life. Gunnar Gunnarson frequently preached the Communist line in *40-tal*, but he was regularly attacked by objectors who preferred the more Social-Democratic outlook as propounded by writers like Lars Ahlin, Sivar Arnér, and indeed Aspenström. Anarchistic beliefs, surprisingly widely held in Sweden at the time, were expressed by Erik Lindegren and, especially, Stig Dagerman. Dagerman's article 'Diktaren och samvetet' (The Writer and His Conscience, *40-tal*, No. 6, 1945) is one of the clearest statements of the typical *fyrtiotalistisk* outlook on political commitment, also on the *obegriplighet* (obscurity) of which he and his contemporaries (especially the poets) were so frequently accused. The radical aspect of a writer's commitment is taken for granted:

How should a writer be committed? It seems simple enough. He must write, of course, and no doubt he will do so. He might compose resolutions, or publish social criticism, give tendentious replies to questions asked by literary magazines, or write poems for May 1st. All this is important. You could call it his military service as a human being. But even so, sooner or later the conflict must come to a head. If he is at all serious about his commitment, should he not then devote his writing to the downtrodden in society?

Dagerman goes on to attack those who insist that in order for a work of art to be 'socialistic' or 'radical', it must be easily comprehensible to all and sundry. Immediate comprehensibility is the prerogative of advertising slogans, claims Dagerman, and if a writer has that as a priority, he is reducing his art to drawing-room entertainment instead of using it as a means of passing on a vital message from man to man. People who demand instant comprehensibility

Chapter IX

...have never understood that creative writing is the product of compulsive forces: it is not some kind of rhythmical rhyming to be dabbled in when passé revolutionaries who have never taken poetry seriously can think of nothing better to do. If such people come across a poem which cannot be learnt by heart within five minutes or does not reveal its meaning instantaneously, and shout out 'Reactionary rubbish!', they themselves are being reactionary, partly because they are denying the poet's compulsion to write and partly because they are questioning whether poetry concerns people — not as a drawing-room entertainment but as a test of one's honesty when confronted with life.

The biggest cultural debate of the 1940s concerned pessimism, and was started by Karl Vennberg. He had lectured on the subject in the autumn of 1945, and his talk was eventually published in the first issue of *40-tal* for 1946, under the title: 'Den moderna pessimismen och dess vedersakare' (Modern pessimism and its adversaries). In many ways, this article amounted to an attack on conventional Marxist views of literature as represented in Sweden by Gunnar Gunnarson. Marxists believed that literature should fall within the limits imposed by Socialist Realism, and should be optimistic in that it pointed forward to a better society. Vennberg maintained it was no longer possible to believe in any '-ism' as a panacea for all problems: 'We have put behind us, unsolved or only partially settled, all the big crises of ideas: the crisis of Socialism, the crisis of Christianity, the crisis of Humanism, the crisis of psychology, the crisis of politics.' The article comments briefly on pessimists currently at the centre of cultural debates in Sweden, such as Kafka, Sartre, Koestler and William Sansom, and concludes that pessimistic writers are after all truth-seekers, not mere defeatists. The pessimists, too, are looking for 'the right action':

...some significant action lies behind the very analysis of cowardice, terror and impotence. Indeed, one may well ask whether this analysis, which discloses the blindness we all suffer from and, irrespective of creeds, returns the ball firmly into the court of human nature and the way we are all made — it may well be that, in the position we now find ourselves, this analysis is itself 'the right action.'

Vennberg's article aroused widespread response, both attacking and defending his views, and the debate dominated the cultural pages of most newspapers and journals for months — Lennart Göthberg summarized what seemed to him the main trends of the argument in issue No. 5 of *40-tal*, 1946, under the title 'Marginalanteckningar till en debatt' (Marginal Notes on a Debate). It seemed that a whole generation of Swedish writers had found themselves in agreement on the question of pessimism, however much they might disagree on other matters: although it is incorrect to think in terms of a *fyrtiotalistisk* school, their unity in the pessimism debate was the nearest the writers of the 1940s came to forming a coherent movement.

By 1947 many Swedish writers of the younger generation had begun to go their separate ways: travel was once more a practical possibility, and they were keen to make the most of their new-found freedom. The journal *40-tal* was unable to survive beyond the autumn of 1947, and only four issues appeared during that year instead of the expected ten. Two new journals were launched: *Utsikt*, edited by Axel Liffner, set out with the intention of continuing the role played by *40-tal*, but although it carried some interesting and important articles, it never achieved the central significance of its predecessor. It was a forum for writers fumbling to find a style appropriate to the 1950s, and lacked the sense of identity which made *40-tal* so impressive. The other journal was *Prisma*, published by Norstedts and edited by Erik Lindegren: it is generally accepted that *Prisma* achieved a higher standard of presentation than any other journal of the period, but its aim was very different from that of *40-tal*. It was more lavish in form, more cosmopolitan in outlook, and it covered all aspects of the arts, including music, sculpture and architecture. The journal was never intended exclusively, or even mainly, as a forum for new writers and for ideas and debates current in Sweden. Both *Prisma* and *Utsikt* ceased publication in 1950.

The obvious lack of a focal point, and the diffusion of interest among writers of which this lack was symptomatic, was the main reason for the demise of *fyrtiotalismen*. Its decline was accelerated, however, by the dispute which split the Swedish Writers' Union in late 1947 and early 1948 — a dispute which left several *fyrtiotalister*, including two of the leading figures, Stig Dagerman and Erik Lindegren, isolated from most of their contemporaries of the younger generation. In November 1947, the Soviet Union celebrated the thirtieth anniversary of the Communist Revolution: a group of thirty-one Swedish writers, including seven committee members of *Svenska författarföreningen*, sent a telegram congratulating the Russians on the enormous cultural progress that had been made in the meantime. Many other Swedish writers objected to this telegram, which was used for propaganda purposes in the Soviet Union: they feared it would be taken as representative of the views of all Swedish writers and imply that Sweden was indifferent to the lack of freedom of speech in the USSR and the persecution of writers who held views unacceptable to the regime. Signatories to the telegram included some of the most prominent *fyrtiotalister*: Lars Ahlin, Werner Aspenström, Stig Carlson, Gustav Rune Eriks and Karl Vennberg.

The crisis came to a head in February 1948, when Russia annexed Czechoslovakia: writers who objected to the November telegram waited in vain for a similar telegram from *Författarföreningen* protesting against Russia's action and declaring solidarity with the Czech writers. Eyvind Johnson (who was in Switzerland at the time) wrote what amounted to a challenge to the leaders of the Writers' Union to produce such a protest, and his firm but measured article, 'Förslag till opinionsyttring' (Proposal for an Expression of Opinion — *Dagens Nyheter* 9 March 1948) was soon followed by a much more colourfully outspoken tirade from Vilhelm Moberg, 'Var står Sveriges författare?' (Where Do Swedish Authors Stand? — *Dagens Nyheter* 13 March 1948). The dispute raged, and on 19 March, a protest telegram was sent to the USSR, signed by 122 Swedish authors: a further forty-five or so added their names soon afterwards, but the thirty-one who had signed the congratulatory telegram the previous November were not allowed to sign the protest. At the general meeting of the Writers' Union held a few days later, all the thirty-one authors were censured, and those who had been committee members either resigned or were voted off. Among those who replaced them were Lindegren and Dagerman (although the former resigned before attending any meetings).

The confusion and rancour lasted for some considerable time, and enmities were caused among *fyrtiotalister* which were never really overcome. The thirty-one writers were labelled 'crypto-communists'; although some were in fact Communists, others objected to the designation and in turn accused their opponents of being too naively benevolent towards the USA. Eventually, they became advocates of *Tredje ståndpunkten* (The Third Point of View), which was claimed to be a neutral position favouring neither East or West, but distinctly socialistic in outlook. It is no exaggeration to say that nowadays, current attitudes in Swedish literature can be traced back to the *Tredje ståndpunktsdebatt*.[7] However, to all intents and purposes, *fyrtiotalismen* was dead.

Stig Dagerman (1923-1954)

Stig Dagerman was born in 1923 in Älvkarleby, a small village some thirty miles north of Uppsala. His (unmarried) mother left him only a few weeks after his birth, and he spent most of his childhood on his grandparents' farm. Memories of this period in his life served to provide the background of several of Dagerman's short stories, and also his last novel, *Bröllopsbesvär* (Wedding Worries, 1949). In the early 1930s, young Stig moved to Stockholm and lived with his father in a cramped flat in a working-class district — an environment depicted in the novel *Bränt barn* (A Burnt Child, 1948). At his father's instigation, he soon became deeply involved in Anarcho-Syndicalist politics, and after leaving school became a journalist on the syndicalist daily newspaper *Arbetaren* (The Worker), being promoted to cultural editor — one of the youngest ever in Sweden in 1944. Stig Dagerman had been called up for military service in 1943, but he was soon discovered to have a weak heart and transferred to an office, where he managed to combine military clerking with civilian journalism) and began to write a novel based on his army experiences. Entitled *Ormen* (The Snake, English transl. 1995), it was published in November 1945 and was immediately hailed as one of the most significant novels of *fyrtiotalet*. It contains so much that is typical of the period that it demands to be examined in some detail.

Ormen is divided into two sections. The first, headed 'Irène', is a short novel of some 120 pages and deals with a day in the life of Irène. The style is intense and packed with images, and the network of imagery is used cleverly by the author to help in his psychoanalysis of the heroine. The Angst which permeates the whole novel is symbolized by a snake which Irène's boy-friend Bill captures and conceals in his rucksack; he releases the snake during an orgy that is the climax of the section, and it crawls across a table towards Irène, seemingly accusing her. The Angst she has been suppressing within her combines with the threat from outside, symbolized by the snake, and Irène is forced to face the facts of her situation.

The second half of *Ormen* entitled 'Vi kan inte sova' (We Can't Sleep), has an entirely different set of characters. The link is provided by Bill's snake, which has escaped: some conscripts are terrified by the fact that the snake is loose, possibly somewhere in their barrack-room. They are unable to sleep, and their terror pursues them even when they

Chapter IX

are in town on a late night pass. The half-dozen stories that make up the second part of *Ormen* are allegorical and give Dagerman the chance to examine contemporary Swedish society and culture in symbolic form.

Dagerman gave *Ormen* a motto which seems enigmatic, indeed obscure at first sight:

If literature is a drawing-room entertainment, I will venture out into the twilight with blackened foot, and make friends with the snakes and the little grey desert rat. If poetry is an essential part of life, make sure you don't forget your sandals, and watch out for mounds of stones! Now the snakes are after my heels, and the desert rat disgusts me. (My friend Scriver) [8]

Scriver is the name of a key figure in the second part of the novel, an author doing his military service. That he is an *alter ego* of the author becomes clear when one realizes the motto is a quotation from the end of Dagerman's article 'The Poet and His Conscience', referred to above. The theme of the article was that a true poet must write, not for mere entertainment, but from a sense of inner compulsion: he must tell the truth as he sees it, be radical in his political outlook, and express his message in symbolical form as best he can, even if the meaning is not immediately obvious. Bearing this in mind, it becomes clear that the motto can be read as a plea for the abandonment of comfortable illusions and for the facing of facts, however unpleasant or unpalatable they may be.

All the characters in 'Irène' shrink from accepting the truth about themselves: the title character goes to considerable lengths to avoid acknowledging her true personality and the facts of her situation. Dagerman's portrayal of Irène owes much to Freudian psychology, with its analysis of different layers of consciousness, repression of unpalatable truths and the subconsciously known but consciously unacknowledged erection of an elaborate system of defences designed to prevent a truth rising from the subconscious into the conscious.

A key image is that of knives, or similar sharp-pointed instruments, e.g. bayonets, daggers, teeth, fish-hooks. There are sections in 'Irène' where the mental battle between the two sides of the heroine's character are depicted in argument, and her conscious self holds a knife at the throat of her unconscious self in an attempt to prevent subconsciously acknowledged facts from rising into the conscious. Freud claimed that in dreams, knives are symbolic of both violence and sex (he produced evidence of many dreams in which a knife or similar objects stood for the male organ). Dagerman endows his symbolic knives with both these significances in Chapter 2, where Irène greets Bill through the window of her ground-floor dormitory. As he persuades her to meet him later in the day and discuss details of the projected party, he asserts both his superior strength and his sexual domination of Irène, and this is symbolized by his sticking of his bayonet in the window-ledge between them: Irène drops the sheet that has been protecting her nakedness, and leans over the bayonet to kiss Bill: 'and he bit her mouth like a man possessed and as they were kissing the bayonet fell over on the window ledge and she cut herself on its edge and it was like two bites. One in her mouth and one there.' (13/20) The web of imagery is closely interwoven, and every mention of sharp-pointed instruments refers back to the bayonet incident, reminding the reader of the sexual motivation and the desire to be dominated physically that lie behind many of Irène's actions.

The high density of imagery in Dagerman's prose in the 'Irène' section of *Ormen* is obvious from even a cursory glance at the opening chapter. The intense richness of the language itself creates an atmosphere that echoes the benumbing sultriness of the day being described, and the unwillingness of the characters to think clearly and truthfully about the facts of their situation. However, the interlinking of motifs and symbols is subtly and relentlessly consistent, and plays a major role in the psychological analyses the author is conducting.

The most important symbol in the 'Irène' section, and indeed of the whole novel, is the snake. Dagerman had a predilection for animal imagery, and the snake symbol, representing Angst, appears in one form or another in most of his books. The author is hardly unique in his dislike of snakes, which is generally agreed to be one of the commonest of human phobias. Apart from the flesh-creeping fear that many people have of them, snakes are connected through the Bible with the fall of man and original sin; and Freud's reasons for designating them a major sexual symbol need no elaboration. Sergeant Bohman's terror when confronted by the snake is understandable; when Bill captures the snake and puts it in his haversack, it symbolizes the fear he seems to instil in others as a result of the power he exerts over them (through his violent strength and his sexual domination). However, the traditional significance of snakes suggests a deeper and more universal Angst.

Irène is afraid of Bill, but much of her Angst stems from her refusal to face facts — the facts of her own character, of her

Chapter IX

relationship with Bill, of the apparent killing of her mother. This Angst is symbolized by a mysterious animal which gnaws away at her innards: psychologically speaking, Irène represses unpleasant thoughts, and the symbolic equivalent is for her to place a cardboard carton over the animal. But the animal soon gnaws through its prison (i.e. the subconscious thoughts threaten to emerge into the conscious) and she has to place another, larger carton over it, then another, and so on in a continuous process. The animal is never identified, but its description makes it appear to be a cross between a snake and a rat (the author was also terrified of rats), accounts of its swishing tail being very reminiscent of snakes.

The climax of the first part of the novel comes when, at the height of the orgy, Bill releases the snake from his haversack; it crawls towards Irène, and we are told that the animal within her bursts out of its prison as she emits a terrible scream. The external source of fear and her internal Angst seem to coalesce, she can no longer maintain her illusions, and she is forced to face facts — in the first place, the alleged fact that she has killed her own mother, but she must also acknowledge all the rest of her hypocrisy.

Stig Carlson was probably right to suggest in his review of *Ormen* that the 'Irène' section is, to some extent at least, a deliberate attempt by Dagerman to parody the 'hard-boiled' style.[9] A list of the violent or sexually outspoken scenes makes grim reading and is not completely out-classed by the similar list made above in connection with *Tag vad du vill ha* — a naked embrace over a bayonet, a mother apparently murdered by her daughter, a violent fight, an attempted rape by a blood-stained butcher's boy, a drunken orgy in which a girl dances naked, an attempted murder when a girl is thrown into a well and the lid replaced. Everything is slightly exaggerated, the intense style slightly overdone: one of the messages in the first part of the novel seems to be that violence and sex do not in fact provide a solution to, or even a refuge from, the problems of life, as the *nyvitalister* would have us believe. Indulgence in such things merely postpones the moment when reality must be faced, and accepted.

The atmosphere and intense style of 'Irène' is reminiscent of the novels of William Faulkner, and Dagerman admitted to being influenced by him. The second part of the novel, however, shows distinct traces of Kafka in several places. The atmosphere in the barrack-room, for instance, is Kafkaesque — the snake does not appear until it is found dead very late in the novel but the Angst represented by its unseen presence permeates the whole barracks and, as with Kafka, every move made by the characters is overshadowed by its mysterious power.

Dagerman satirizes the army, taking the opportunity to depict the squalid nature of everyday reality in a typical camp in contrast with the glorious splendour and heroism that conventional attitudes usually ascribe to the military. He captures the mood of the Swedish army in particular, and by implication equates this with the mood of the country as a whole, in that he portrays his characters loitering impotently, being unable to take part actively in the war, but very afraid of the outcome. The Angst that was described in personal terms in 'Irène' is now given a more universal significance in 'We Can't Sleep'. Formally, the second part of *Ormen* is a collection of short stories: the first one deals with the whole group of General Duties conscripts who share a barrack-room in an army camp in Stockholm, and it contains within itself three more short stories told by the soldiers as a means of passing the time during their sleepless nights and of sharing out the terror that afflicts them all — and by so doing, making it bearable. (Several reviewers pointed out a similarity with Boccaccio's *Decameron*). The soldiers then go out on a late pass, and the remaining five chapters of the novel follow individuals or groups during the course of the afternoon and evening. The stories are allegorical, and together amount to a statement on various aspects of life in Sweden in the 1940s. There are two types of story, in fact: 'Järnbandet' (The Iron Band), 'Ormen' (The Snake) and 'Flykten som inte blev av' (The Flight that Didn't Come Off) contain undisguised theorizing about politics, society and culture in Sweden in an attempt to explain the contemporary situation and to suggest how life could best be improved; the other two, 'Spegeln' (The Mirror) and 'Tygdockan' (The Rag Doll), are less theoretical, more Kafkaesque in style, and illustrate aspects of Dagerman's thesis that people must stop wandering aimlessly through life in the unthinking, unseeing fashion to which they are accustomed. Instead, they must look into themselves, decide what is the 'right action' demanded of them in any particular set of circumstances, and try hard to bring themselves to perform that action irrespective of the various difficulties and obstacles that will doubtless stand in their way.

The titles of the chapters refer to significant symbols contained in them. The mirror image of 'Spegeln' has to do with the idea of 'know thyself', and Laxen's disgust at his failure to realize the truth of his

Chapter IX

situation and the squalid nature of his behaviour is symbolized by his smashing the hall mirror at the end of the chapter. In 'Tygdockan', Sörenson has every opportunity to intervene and prevent a small boy being seduced by a homosexual sailor, but he fails to do so, thus condemning himself to suffer from pangs of conscience for the rest of his life. He knows what was 'the right action', but was too cowardly to take it. His punishment is just and deserved.

The allegorical aspects of the other three chapters are obvious. In 'Ormen', there is a long and detailed account of Gideon's home background, of his father's business career, the conventional attitudes of his family and the circles in which they moved, also the way in which experience of the army had affected Gideon. The hypocrisy of typical middle-class life is exposed, and the ease with which not only individuals but even whole classes of people can be manipulated. The importance of that chapter is indicated by the fact that it is given the title of the whole novel: nevertheless, it is an understandable fact that the two remaining chapters have received more critical attention.

In 'Järnbandet', it is clear that Dagerman is criticizing the political system in the Sweden of the 1940s, and by implication suggesting that radicals should be working towards an improvement on Anarcho-Syndicalist lines — the political views of the author himself. The iron band quite obviously represents the restrictive powers of the state: despite the security and welfare the state can provide, all centralized systems fail in that they impinge on the freedom of the individual and fill him with Angst as a result of the feeling of helplessness that possesses him as soon as he realizes how little control he has over his own fate:

'I feel pressurized,' said Edmund, 'I feel as if there's an iron band pressing into my skull when I find there are laws nobody's asked me if I will accept that make me practically defenceless ... All this means ... that I feel threatened, I feel bloody well threatened by my security supplier.' (160/186)

Of course, Edmund continues, one can get used to the iron band, just as one can be satisfied with the benefits bestowed by a paternalistic state: to do so, however, is to betray fundamental principles. It may be that, in realistic terms, the individual is powerless to combat the system; not to continue fighting, however, even on a symbolic level, is immoral.

In the final chapter, 'Flykten som inte blev av', Dagerman comments on contemporary culture, especially literature, but draws clear parallels with society as a whole. The central character is Scriver, who has already been established as an *alter ego* of the author himself. Echoing typical radical criticism of the New Vitalists, Scriver attacks them for being excessively sensual and insufficiently intellectual — although Scriver's criticism is basically literary, he extends it, significantly enough, to include all aspects of life. Modern man no longer dares to be afraid, he claims; instead, people nowadays shun an intellectual approach to life's problems and resort to what he calls 'blodsmystik å sköteskult' (blood mysticism and sex cult) (203/236). Scriver goes on to argue against what he calls 'the philosophy of harmony', i.e. the attitude to life that insists one should be happy at all costs, and that the job of society is to shield its citizens from any kind of threat or unpleasantness — the unmistakable implication is that this is the aim of conventional socialism. No, one must not be afraid, for facing up to reality and living an honest life is more important than mere happiness:

the solution, or maybe not the solution, because there could well not be any solution as such, but the possible way forward, is a new epoch of intellectualism which can give people at least some courage to look their Angst in the eye instead of creeping away into the infantile caves and bedrooms crawling with mysticism. Perhaps it is necessary to run away, but certainly not in the naive way advocated by the hard-boiled school (206/240)

The novel ends with a question-mark as Scriver attempts to demonstrate his arguments by symbolic action: the 'hard-boiled' procedure, he maintains, is like leaving a room by climbing out of a window but then returning by climbing back into the same room through another window. (In other words, the method and philosophy of life of the New Vitalists do not solve the problems they set out to deal with since their advocacy of sensual indulgence fails to tackle the root cause, which is the social and political system in which they live). Scriver climbs out of the upstairs window and intends to work his way along a ledge and climb into a different room but he loses his grip and falls to his death. The implication seems to be that solutions are not easy to achieve: the writer can indicate what he thinks is the answer in symbolic fashion, but that is the limit of his powers. It is up to society to try it out and see if it works. It is not impossible that in the real world, the solution indicated by the writer is impracticable: no matter. By pointing it out, the author has performed 'the right action'. Dagerman's position is

Chapter IX

summed up nicely by the concluding paragraph in his article 'My Views on Anarchism':

As an anarchist (and a pessimist in so far as he is aware his contribution can probably be no more than symbolic), a writer can for the moment retain his good conscience and take on the modest role of an earth-worm at a level of culture which would otherwise grow stiff in the dried-out atmosphere of convention. Being a politician of the impossible in a world where all too many restrict themselves to the possible is, when all is said and done, a role which can satisfy me personally as a social being, an individual and the author of *The Snake*.[10]

Ormen was greeted as a remarkable first novel, and was so typical of *fyrtiotal* trends as to be almost a paradigm of the style — intense, radical, pessimistic, outspoken, symbolic yet also naturalistic, influenced by Faulkner and Kafka and reminiscent of French Existentialists, dominated by Angst. The form of the novel was criticized — the division into two such different parts was thought by some to make *Ormen* broken-backed, and a few reviewers actually referred to it as a collection of short stories. Predictably, some critics thought the dominant mood of Angst was too intense and monotonous. Almost everyone agreed, however, that Stig Dagerman was an exceptional writer with such masterly control of a variety of styles even in his first novel that his potential was almost unlimited.

The following year, 1946, Dagerman published his second novel, *De dömdas ö* (Island of the Doomed, English transl. 1991). Some competent judges regard this novel as Dagerman's greatest achievement, but it was hardly a popular success. It is a strange novel with marked Expressionistic tendencies; the atmosphere is even more intense than in *Ormen*, the imagery even denser, the ruthless process of intellectual analysis even more uncompromising.

Following on some catastrophe — possibly a nuclear explosion — six passengers and one crewman are shipwrecked and cast away on a remote island in a tropical ocean. The island has only two types of living creatures: horny-skinned lizards of various sizes which are capable of being vicious when provoked to attack, and mysteriously ominous blind seagulls. The seven castaways are clearly identified as rounded characters, but each one also represents certain aspects of life or attitudes to it. Lucas Egmont is an Anarcho-Syndicalist (his name refers to a sixteenth-century Dutch freedom-fighter), while Captain Wilson seems to be a Fascist (Dagerman originally intended to give him the German name Besserwiss, and Hans Sandberg has shown how his character owes much to Nazi philosophy).[11] Boy Larus represents the average man of weak character, so easily dominated by a totalitarian regime, while Tim Solider is representative of the working class — his servile inferiority is compensated for by the sense of solidarity implied by his name. Jimmy Baaz is a boxing champion unable to cope with the demands made on him by his public for constant success, while both the women characters represent attitudes to sexuality (and the deceit so often connected with it).

Many of the qualities personified by the castaways in *De dömdas ö* are traits of Dagerman's own character, giving the book an element of self-analysis. The main significance of the novel, however, is as an analysis of contemporary society, the chief didactic element being concentrated in the symbolic struggle that forms the core of the last part of the book. The castaways find a white rock, and decide to scratch onto it an emblem symbolizing the meaning of life as they see it. Captain Wilson wants to copy a trademark imprinted, significantly, on his jackboot: a lion sitting on the body of a man it has just killed, symbolizing the victory of the 'master' over the 'slave' and implying merit in the willing acceptance of a solitary death or a lonely existence as the sole survivor. The Nietzschean conception of the superman, developed by Nazis into that of the master race, is clearly implied, as is the patronizing praise of the subordinates — be they individuals or countries — who submit themselves willingly to a position of inferiority.

Lucas Egmont refuses to accept this symbol. He would prefer a snake, he says, the reference back to Dagerman's first novel being obvious, as is the suggestion that Angst is the key feature of life. If there must be a lion, then it must be a lone lion, with no victim:

I won't go so far as to suggest it represents togetherness, but it does demonstrate calm strength, the whole personality, the harmony which might be rent asunder at any moment by the roar of a wild beast. Terror and harmony in the same character, you see, that is my lion. (214/316)[12]

As in *Ormen*, Dagerman is pleading for a facing up to the facts of life. Happiness and harmony are not compatible with uncompromising adherence to one's ideals, no '-ism' can provide a satisfactory solution. Each individual must realize his own nature and that of life, and having done so must proceed to cooperate voluntarily with his fellows to

Chapter IX

improve the lot of everyone on Earth — there must be no superior isolation, no violent subjugation. Egmont is clearly advocating Anarcho-Syndicalism as against Wilson's Fascism, and he wins the ensuing battle before committing suicide.

The political level is only one of the levels on which the novel operates, however. It is also about the nature of human beings, about sex, about art. *De dömdas ö* might not be the kind of novel one would read for pleasure and relaxation, but it is one of the few Swedish novels which can rank alongside the works of Kafka, Sartre and Camus as an aesthetically and intellectually stimulating statement on the human condition, unmistakably a product of *fyrtiotalet* but timeless in the universality of its message. In recent years, however, it has been suggested that *De dömdas ö* is *too* contrived, *too* symbolic, *too* artificial, and hence short on genuine feelings and the human characteristics necessary for a truly great novel.

Dagerman rocketed to popular fame and success in April 1947, with his play *Den dödsdömde* (The Man Condemned to Death); his first popular success as a writer of fiction came with his collection of short stories, *Nattens lekar* (The Games of Night), published in the autumn of 1947. The familiar themes run through almost all the stories: face the facts of life, learn to live with Angst, accept that life is made up of pain as well as pleasure. The book contains an astonishing range of styles, however; the first five of the seventeen stories are autobiographical and basically realistic, while others later in the collection are Expressionistic in the extreme. Dagerman exhibits considerable skill in his use of a variety of narrators, and achieves a *tour de force* in 'Var är min islandströja' (Where Is My Icelandic Sweater), a virtuoso display of mastery over stream-of-consciousness techniques.

Dagerman's two other novels, *Bränt barn* (1948, English transl. A Burnt Child, 1950) and *Bröllopsbesvär* (Wedding Worries, 1949) confirm his mastery of narrative techniques. Both novels — especially the former — achieved greater popular success than any of his earlier works; they also mark a significant change in the author's approach to his art. He had been having difficulty in writing, and had failed to complete several projects; the sterility lifted long enough for him to write the two novels, but they are noticeably more autobiographical than his earlier works, with less effort to marry the personal side of his work with a didactic message concerning the reform of society.

Bränt Barn concerns the struggles of a young man, Bengt, to achieve *renhet* (purity), and demonstrates his inability to stop deceiving others and also himself. When Bengt's mother dies, he tries to convince himself he hates the mature woman who is his father's mistress and, eventually, his stepmother; in fact, Bengt loves her. The novel deals with Bengt's complicated emotions, his guilt, his attempted suicide, his continual refusal to face facts. Although it is more realistic than the earlier novels, *Bränt barn* makes considerable demands on the reader in that the narrative point of view is generally that of Bengt, and his self-deceptions result in frequent inconsistencies which are left to the reader to resolve. Conventional third-person narrative alternates with letters written by Bengt to other characters or to himself, and the style is much less intense than in *Ormen* or *De dömdas ö*, being reminiscent of Hemingway in its short sentences and precise vocabulary.

Bränt barn was turned into a successful stage play, *Ingen går fri* (No-One Goes Free). It is instructive to compare the two versions of the same plot, partly in order to see how the writer coped with aspects of the novel which were impossible to reproduce in the theatre, and partly also to note some subtle changes in the characters, probably due to the real-life circumstances on which the story is based. The autobiographical nature of the plot has become clearer in recent years, not least as a result of revelations made by Björn Ranelid in his novel *Mitt namn skall vara Stig Dagerman* (My Name shall Be Stig Dagerman, 1993) and the publicity surrounding it.[13]

It is not possible to summarize the plot of *Bröllopsbesvär*, which is written in Uppland dialect and varies between bucolic naturalism and rhapsodic poetic prose. The usual Dagerman themes are present, and the most striking feature of the novel is the atmosphere the author creates as he recounts the grotesque happenings (often delightfully humorous) surrounding a country wedding between a conceited butcher and a wistful and pregnant young farmer's daughter. The search for love is perhaps the outstanding motif, but the threat of death is constantly present in the background as the multiplicity of characters, each one Angst-ridden in his or her particular way, blunders through a single day on a farm recognizable as the one where Dagerman spent his childhood. If one were to suggest a comparable selection of simple characters whose motives and actions vacillated between the noble and the squalid, one would have to select Fredman and his cronies in the poems of Carl Michael Bellman. An early working-title for the novel was *Svanesång* (Swan-Song); perhaps it was an ominous choice, for not

Chapter IX

only do several characters sing a kind of swan-song, it was also the last novel the author was able to write. The stock of *Bröllopsbesvär* has risen significantly in recent years, critics suggesting it is more genuine, more heart-felt than a novel of ideas such as *De dömdas ö*. It is a very humorous book, but also a very sad one: a keyword is 'resignation', and with hindsight we can see that it may well be the most fitting epitaph for a novelist of genius who was destined to take his own life.

Dagerman's personal life became increasingly chaotic, and he was able to complete only one more full-length work — the radio play *Den yttersta dagen* (The Day of Judgement, 1952). Even that had been conceived in 1949. After a number of unsuccessful attempts, Stig Dagerman finally committed suicide in his gas-filled garage in November, 1954. As critics were not slow to realize, the most typical of the *fyrtiotalister* had been unable to write anything once the 1940s had passed.

Nevertheless, much of Dagerman's work has withstood the test of time. His novels and stories appeal to successive new generations, indicating that his message is as relevant today as it was in the 1940s. Scholars occasionally suggest Dagerman was a better dramatist than he was given credit for at the time, but it is hard to argue that he was in the same class as a dramatist as he was as a prose-writer. He certainly had poetical aspirations, and it is not impossible that a genius with words of his calibre might have developed as a serious poet, had he lived longer than his thirty-two years. Those who find Dagerman too unworldly a writer with too depressing a view of life would do well to take a look at his occasional verses (*dagsverser*),[14] which have justly enjoyed a renaissance since his death. Many have been set to music and are frequently performed (and broadcast) in Sweden. Mainly satirical verses aimed at the absurdity and injustice of society, some are dated, but many are as relevant today as they ever were, and are worth the attention of any twentieth and twenty-first century readers with a social conscience and a sense of humour.

Chapter X

Twelve Modern Novelists

Sarah Death, Tom Geddes, Phil Holmes, Gavin Orton, Karin Petherick, Neil Smith and Charlotte Whittingham.

Introduction
by Gavin Orton

It is too early to write a definitive account of the Swedish novel since 1950. Active writers who now seem important may in time fade into obscurity, while the presently obscure may rise to prominence. This chapter gives an account of a number of novelists who have won general approval: Lars Gyllensten (born 1921), Lars Ahlin (born 1915), Sara Lidman (born 1923), Per Olof Sundman (1922-92), Sven Delblanc (1931-92), P. C. Jersild (born 1935), Per Olov Enquist (born 1934), Torgny Lindgren (born 1938), Kerstin Ekman (born 1933), and Göran Tunström (born 1937). A couple of younger authors are presented as an example of the latest developments: Carina Burman (born 1960) and Jonas Gardell (born 1963). Older writers omitted, principally for lack of space, include Birgitta Trotzig (born 1929), and Per Gunnar Evander (born 1933); younger writers who have their advocates include Agneta Pleijel (born 1940), Jacques Werup (born 1945), Lars Andersson (born 1954), Klas Östergren (born 1955), and Mare Kandre (born 1962).[1]

The authors described here do not belong to literary groups and do not try to form groups; they are individualists. But even individualists work in a common political and economic world and receive common literary impulses. A brief attempt is made here to sketch the common background before the writers are analysed individually.

The period from 1950 to the early 1970s is characterized by the peaceful development within Sweden of a welfare state in a mixed (largely private) economy under, for the most part, a minority Social

Chapter X

Democrat government. Faced with consensus and prosperity at home, Swedes took a much greater interest in the rest of the world. The interest in Europe that was a major feature of Eyvind Johnson's postwar work became an interest in more distant continents in the works of a younger generation. This internationalism was expressed politically through Sweden's lively involvement in the United Nations, most notably in the work of the Swedish Secretary-General of the United Nations, Dag Hammarskjöld (1905-61).

In literature this internationalism changed radically the work of two writers, Sara Lidman and Per Wästberg (born 1933), who were converted on the road to Africa. Sara Lidman went to South Africa in 1960 and was expelled for infringing the race laws; the result was two African novels and a passionate indignation at the evils of colonialism and imperialism that widened from Africa to other underdeveloped areas. A similar awakening struck Per Wästberg when he went to Rhodesia and South Africa in 1959; his trilogy *Vattenslottet* (The Water Castle, 1968), *Luftburen* (The Air Cage, 1969), and *Jordmånen* (The Soil, 1972) is an account of the lives and love affairs of privileged people in a privileged Sweden, but also shows how this idyll is set against a quite different backcloth — in this case represented by Botswana. Two other writers came to the problems of underdeveloped countries via Asia. Jan Myrdal (born 1927) is the chief spokesman of the radical Left. He reached this position through travels in Afghanistan (described in *Kulturers korsväg* (The Crossroad of Culture, 1960)) and revolutionary China (described in *Rapport från kinesisk by* (Report from a Chinese Village, 1963)). Sven Lindqvist (born 1932), after a number of rather literary meditations, spent some time in Beijing, which he first described in *Kina inifrån* (Inside China, 1963), but more importantly and influentially in *Myten om Wu Tao-tzu* (The Myth of Wu Tao-tzu, 1967), where he agonizes over the conflict between his earlier philosophizing and the massive poverty of China and more hopeless wretchedness of India. China and Chairman Mao became something of a cult among the Left in the late 1960s. China was seen as the proof that Communism might work, where it had so obviously failed in the previously idolized Soviet Union, disgraced by Stalin and scarcely redeemed by his successors.

The anti-colonial and anti-imperialist sentiments prompted by these writers' experiences of Africa and Asia came to a head in the campaign in Sweden against the American involvement in the Vietnam War. The

FNL-movement in support of North Vietnam led to a thorough radicalizing of many Swedish writers' attitudes, and to great pressure on non-political creative Swedish writers to become involved — *engagerad* became a key word. This in turn rubbed off on home affairs and was compounded by the effects of the student riots in Paris and Berlin and the appearance of a more democratic Communism in Prague, all in 1968. Sara Lidman, deeply involved in the fate of the Vietnamese, also turned her attention to the iron-ore mines of northern Sweden, and in her book *Gruva* (Mine, 1968), showed how the miners there were exploited and oppressed by the economic and class system. When the miners went on strike in the winter of 1969-70 they were eagerly supported by the radicals in Stockholm: the strike was the most serious industrial conflict in Sweden since the engineering workers' strike of 1944 (itself described by Delblanc in *Stadsporten* (The Town Gate, 1976)). It might seem that the Revolution was at hand, but the established order reasserted itself: De Gaulle won a sweeping victory over the students in the French elections in 1968; Brezhnev crushed 'Socialism with a human face' by invading Czechoslovakia; and Swedish administrators recovered their control over Swedish society by the sort of democratic manipulations described in Jersild's *Vi ses i Song My* (See You in My Lai, 1970). The result was for some radicals serious disillusion, expressed by Enquist in his *Sekonden* (The Second, 1971) and in the title of his pessimistic *Berättelser från de inställda upprorens tid* (Stories From the Age of Cancelled Revolutions, 1974).

From the mid-1970s Sweden began to lose confidence in itself. The post-war boom came to an end and Sweden started to slip down the economic league tables. The Social Democrats' long hegemony was broken by short-lived Centre-Right coalitions. There was retrenchment in the welfare state. Much soul-searching was caused by the assassination of the prime minister, Olof Palme, in 1986, which was seen as a sign of a loss of innocence. Sweden, the Scandinavian utopia detached from the world's alarms, became more like other countries, a condition confirmed when a Social Democrat government announced unexpectedly, perhaps desperately, that Sweden would abandon its traditional policy of non-alignment and apply to join the European Union, in 1995.

One way in which Sweden changed was through immigration. The economic boom attracted large numbers of economic migrants, mainly from Europe. After economic migration was halted, Sweden became a haven for refugees from more exotic parts of the world, which led to a backlash in the form of tiny but vicious neo-Nazi groups. A previously remarkably homogeneous population now has to cope with cultural diversity and racism. One Greek immigrant, Theodor Kallifatides (born 1938), has made a name for himself as a novelist writing in Swedish, about both Greece and Sweden. Other international phenomena that have profoundly influenced modern Swedish society are environmentalism and feminism. A grassroots protest that won considerable support was the anti-nuclear power movement, which culminated in a referendum in 1980 on the phasing-out of nuclear power. Grand hydroelectric schemes, of the sort described in Sundman's *Undersökningen* (The Investigation, 1958), have also been abandoned. The most obvious impact on the relatively unspoilt Swedish environment is made by the forest industries, and both Sara Lidman and Kerstin Ekman have been active in attacking them. The re-emergence of feminism as an important political and social issue was partly due to the financial independence of women, as 'the housewife' became an obsolete concept. Kerstin Ekman and, more recently, Carina Burman, are among those who devote novels specifically to women's issues. Other disadvantaged groups have also make their voices heard, for example the gay movement in Jonas Gardell's novels.

The administration of Sweden has long been highly centralized, but the opposite is true of its culture. Sweden has a lively regional press, and many of the novels described in this chapter place strong emphasis on regional character. This does not mean that they are 'provincial' in a pejorative sense. Probably no country is more aware of international literary developments than Sweden, partly because — unlike England or France — it cannot pretend to be self-sufficient in literature, partly because as awarder of the Nobel Prize for Literature it sees it as its duty to be informed of the state of the world's literature. There is nothing rustic about the techniques of the novelists described in this chapter, as the range of styles shows. While Sweden has its share of 'magic realism' (Tunström, for example), many of the major works described here are closer to reality. A genre that has aroused particular interest is the documentary novel, which documents events that actually occurred, but in an artistic way, as in Enquist's *Legionärerna* (The Legionnaires, 1968) and Sundman's *Ingenjör Andrée's luftfärd* (1967, translated as The Flight of the Eagle). One step removed from this is the novel that documents historical processes using fictional characters. Vilhelm Moberg's novels about American emigration have been followed with novels of social history from Lidman, Enquist, Ekman, and Delblanc. Another factor common to many of the novelists presented here is the use of Biblical allusions, despite the thorough-going secularization of Sweden. Perhaps Biblical myths are seem as the only myths Swedes have in common in what is so often portrayed by these novelists as a superficial, rootless consumer society.

In connection with the modern Swedish novel it is worth mentioning two other fields in which Swedish authors have made international reputations: the detective novel and children's literature. Maj Sjöwall (born 1935) and Per Wahlöö (1926-75) wrote ten best-selling novels about the work of the Swedish police, starting with *Roseanna* (1965) and ending with *Terroristerna* (The Terrorists, 1975). The novels have a documentary element: an attempt to describe police work as it really is and not as it appears to amateur detectives in the English detective-story tradition. As the series progressed the authors used the novels increasingly as vehicles for radical social criticism, something that may be argued to be incompatible with the genre.[2] The other field in which Swedish writers have excelled is in books for children. A major figure here is Astrid Lindgren (born 1907), with her books about Pippi Långstrump (Longstocking, 1945-48), *Lillebror och Karlsson på taket* (Little Brother and Karlsson on the Roof, 1955), and *Emil i Lönneberga* (1963). A more serious note is struck in *Bröderna Lejonhjärta* (The Lionheart Brothers, 1973), about children and their attitude to death. Equally celebrated is the Swedish-Finnish writer Tove Jansson (born 1914), creator of Mumintrollet, who has extended her range beyond the Mumin family books to a charming autobiography, *Bildhuggarens dotter* (The Sculptor's Daughter, 1968), and some short stories and novels.

Lars Gyllensten (born 1921)

by Gavin Orton

Lars Gyllensten was born in Stockholm in 1921. For some years he pursued both a literary and medical career, qualifying as a doctor in 1948 and later teaching and researching at the medical school in Stockholm, before devoting himself entirely to literature.

Chapter X

By date-of-birth Gyllensten belongs to the generation associated with *40-talet*, and his work springs like so much of theirs from a violent reaction to ideological fanaticism and to the war. Like the writers of *40-talet* Gyllensten sees the world as evil and meaningless, but he views it as a scientist, and this is important both for his philosophy and his way of writing. As a scientist he approaches 'reality' in a wary fashion. He regards all ways of describing the world as provisional, in the way that scientific theories are. Scientific theories are merely attempts to describe the behaviour of natural phenomena in a comprehensible and usable form, just as a map describes the countryside in a convenient way. But neither theories nor maps are the real things: they are only representations of reality, and if they conflict with reality, they must be scrapped. Gyllensten argues that we should adopt the same attitude to religions and ideologies. They are only provisional guides to the world we live in; they help us to find our way in existence, but if we take them too seriously and assume our images and maps of existence *are* reality, then we become fanatical in defending them against doubters. Gyllensten calls people who cling to impractical or harmful beliefs *desperados* — the title of a collection of short stories from 1962. He sees the lack of ideologies and religions in *40-talet* as a positive thing. It is better not to believe too dogmatically in anything, and to remain sceptical and 'trolös' (faithless) towards beliefs. 'Trolöshet' becomes one of the popular ideas of the early 1960s in Swedish literature.

Gyllensten works as an author in the way he works as a scientist — by experiment. He tries out various attitudes to life in his books and sees what the consequences of each attitude are. Consequently, he adopts different roles as an author in each book, and uses different styles. As a scientist he argues that the instruments and operations we use to explore reality often determine the results we achieve — we tend only to see the things that interest us or that we are equipped to see or that we want to see. By adopting different roles Gyllensten hopes to overcome the limitations of a single author-viewpoint.

Gyllensten's first important work is *Moderna myter* (Modern Myths, 1949), a book in which he considers the problem of living in a world without creeds and ideologies. *Moderna myter* is a collection of aphorisms, poems, and sketches in many different styles — sometimes parodies of other authors. Gyllensten explains the background to the book in a postscript: 'The book derives from the concept of something which for want of anything better could be called the bankruptcy of naivety. With this definition I mean the decline of immediate involvement in something — a faith, a reality, call it what you will.'(175).[3] Where there are no gods we can blindly believe in, whether they be set by the Church, Stalin, or Hitler, then we have to create our own goals, working towards them as though we believe in them, but never forgetting that they are man-made artefacts. An example of this is described in a poem about the Pharaoh Cheops, who decrees the building of a pyramid. The goal itself — the pyramid — is arbitrary and meaningless, but the building of it gives a meaning to the builders' lives. To emphasize the artificial nature of his solution to the meaninglessness of life, Gyllensten deliberately makes his 'myths' as bizarre and grotesque as possible. An example is the story 'Kvinnotornet' (The Women's Tower), about a man who has built a tower containing six women, one on each storey. From Monday to Saturday he lives with a different woman each day, in a different style, all styles equally valid but all equally arbitrary and artificial. On Sunday he steps back from his wives to demonstrate his detachment from them.

In a world without love, the hero of 'Kvinnotornet' chooses marriages of convenience. In *Det blå skeppet* (The Blue Ship, 1950), Gyllensten considers the alternative: to dare to believe in the possibility of a love match, with love coming from outside like 'a miracle' (180). In the much praised *Barnabok* (Children's Book, 1952), Gyllensten presents both alternatives in the form of an erotic conflict. The hero, Karl-Erik, is torn between two women, Klem and Lucy. Klem, an unexciting but faithful girl, stands for a way of life that must be created by the participants, as an artefact, while Lucy, passionate but dangerous, offers Karl-Erik a faith that will sweep him off his feet. To begin with, Karl-Erik tries a 'marriage of convenience' with Klem, but he does not have the strength of will to carry it through. Instead he wagers his happiness on the miracle happening with Lucy, but she deceives him. Unable to bear the collapse of love, Karl-Erik becomes a 'desperado' and murders Lucy's baby. *Barnabok* is especially notable for its expressionistic language. With great virtuosity Gyllensten destroys syntax and mixes styles to create an immediate expression of the characters' moods: childish gibberish, teenage jargon, colloquial inanities, and a general disgust at the human situation.

In *Barnabok* Karl-Erik is constantly surprised and thrown off balance by the misfortunes that befall him: he has a child's naivety. In the novel *Senilia* (1956) Gyllensten adopts the opposite point-of-view, of a man who tries to protect himself against shocks and surprises by acting as an old man, someone who has already experienced everything before. This dialectic between Gyllensten's books is a feature of his work — a reply to *Senilia* occurs in *Juvenilia* (1965). The novel *Senatorn* (The Senator, 1958), is also about a man who has clothed himself in a protective armour, in this case ideological. The story concerns Senator Bhör, an official in a Communist state. In his youth he adopted Communism as a religion, but when the novel begins his faith is crumbling. The state he works for is not the state he dreamed of building. He is sent off to recuperate by his boss, but he deviates from the official rest-cure and becomes involved with a nymphomaniac, Elisa. After a brief but hectic affair with her he returns to his boss and an uncertain future. The central conflict of ideas in the novel is the clash between Bhör and Elisa. Bhör argues that the individual must be moulded by society and can only fulfil himself as a member of that society. Bhör has lost one faith that had given him shape — Communism — and he is in search of another shell to crawl into. In the meanwhile he feels himself adrift and drawn towards his own destruction. Elisa, however, is constantly striving to keep a shell from forming round her, maintaining an open attitude to experience and a willingness to destroy her past. The conflict, between Bhör who stands for shape and order (expressed in his Communism) and Elisa who stands for chaos and anarchy (expressed in her nymphomania) is fundamental to Gyllensten's work, both — he claims — as an author and as a scientist. In an interview between himself as scientist and himself as artist, he writes of the relationship between 'order' and 'provocation'.[4] The scientist wants to bring order into the universe by formulating theories, but he also wants to provoke nature into revealing new secrets that will mean destroying and revising the old theories; the author wants to find a meaning and pattern in life and the mass of suffering and cruelty around him, yet at the same time he feels boredom and weariness in an established life and so destroys old patterns of behaviour and seeks new experiences in his works.

Sokrates död (The Death of Socrates, 1960), is also concerned with the problems of order and the provocation of disorder, but where *Senatorn* is written in a highly rhetorical style and is subtitled 'a melodrama', *Sokrates död* is told in a light-hearted, facetious manner that reduces Socrates' heroic death to everyday proportions. Socrates himself does not appear in the novel. It is his family's and his friends' view of his self-chosen execution that is presented, and their arguments are with Socrates and with each other. Socrates, in Gyllensten's version, is a philosopher who has spent his time destroying people's certainties and instilling scepticism and 'faithlessness'. Yet paradoxically he chooses to die to prove that his scepticism was deadly serious. His family and friends reject this fanaticism: his wife Xanthippa wants her husband and lover, not a philosopher seeking immortality, while his daughter Aspasia approves of his scepticism but rejects 'the demon of love' (117) that drives him to commit suicide. The family slave has no illusions: 'To live is to prepare oneself to go on living' (161). The weight of the arguments is on the side of these lesser mortals.

In *Kains memoarer* (The Memoirs of Cain, 1963) and *Juvenilia* (1965) Gyllensten operates with the Biblical myth of Cain, who slew his brother Abel. Cain becomes for Gyllensten the symbol of the iconoclast, the destroyer of accepted belief and behaviour, the man who provokes disorder. *Kains memoarer* is a witty account of the life and works of the Cainites, a sect of the early Christian period who argue that if there is a God over this world of suffering and misery, then he must be evil. They venerate people who have revolted against God, like Cain. In fact, the author argues, there is no God. The world is not basically concerned with man at all and if men smash the masks of the gods they themselves have created they will find only meaninglessness.

In *Kains memoarer* Cain must destroy man-made gods to reveal the world as it really is. In *Juvenilia* the problem is the destruction and rejuvenation of a petrified personality. *Juvenilia* is a fragmentary novel, revealing by its form its message of dismemberment and reassembly. The author calls it 'a kind of *collage* novel'. There are three main characters in *Juvenilia*, each more active then the last in trying to destroy the mask of his personality and its egoistic limitations: 'It is my *image* that must be destroyed. The image of myself hovering between myself and the others, between myself and reality' (185). Another major problem raised in *Juvenilia* is that of 'compassion' — the reaction of the major characters to the suffering of others and the general wretchedness of the world. 'Oh, liberate me from love of men!' (228) is their cry, and they seek escape from impotent compassion by turning away from other people and from communication with the world.

Gyllensten pursues the theme of Cainism in *Diarium spirituale* (1968), which is a collection of an author's notes that show his progress from a state of chaos, where all models and shapes are destroyed, through a period of spiritual poverty and humiliation, to the creating of new models and a new productivity — a post-Cainite period. *Palatset i parken* (The Palace in the Park, 1970), returns to the theme of compassion, using the myth of Orpheus as a base. The novel is the account in the bewildering form of a dream-sequence of a man who returns to his childhood town and tries to conjure up the spirits of the past. The memories he recreates are a definition of his personality, for he can only create a world that corresponds to himself; he is composed of his memories, just as they are stamped with his image. The meeting between the subjective world of the individual and the objective world about him is explored through the main — and in a sense, only — character's meeting with the suffering of others. The palace in the park is a lunatic asylum, and the main character is involved in a number of relationships with the mentally ill. 'Compassion' is seen as a selfish reaction to suffering, and the palatial asylum is an expression of men's desire to display an emotion that satisfies the giver more than the receiver, whose needs may be more practical. Sickened by the sentimentality and empty gestures of compassion, the main character is driven to the opposite extreme of contempt for others but in a final vision he sees freedom from the claims that their suffering makes on him as lying in 'delaktighet' — 'participation' (214).

The title of *Grottan i öknen* (The Cave in the Desert, 1973), indicates, by contrast, that the characters are concerned not so much to establish contact with their fellow men as to withdraw from the world altogether. The first of its three parts, 'Eremiten', is a witty and tongue-in-cheek account of the hermit St. Antony, who turns away from a life of pointless endeavour in a crumbling Roman Empire and devotes himself to asceticism. The central section of the book, 'Andarna' (The Spirits) is the story of St. Antony's biographer, Bishop Athanasius. The story is interfoliated with a number of passages that match the Athanasian episodes in theme but involve different characters. Athanasius, a politically active bishop and scourge of the Arian heresy, is driven in old age into exile. Like Antony, Athanasius is plagued in his retreat by ridiculous spirits, such as the ducks quacking down by the river. They seem to mock all he has achieved in life: it was all dust and ashes, and death will shortly disperse it. Athanasius's driving force in life has been his anger — anger at the sufferings of mankind, and anger at man's total inability to do anything about his situation. Now in his exile he is tempted to relapse into apathy and give in to death, whose chill he feels in his bones. But there is a third possibility, between the heat of anger and the coldness of death. He can refuse to accept the conditions of human life and live in the world as in a kind of exile, but at the same time he can work to the best of man's limited ability to improve conditions in this place of exile.

The third section of *Grottan i öknen*, 'Eremitaget', is in a modern setting, though as decayed as the Roman Empire. The narrator returns to the house where he boarded as a schoolboy to write the life of its owner, Johannes Elfberg. In a cold, factual style that matches his subject, the narrator describes Elfberg's ascetic existence. He knows nothing of Elfberg's inner thoughts but lets his actions and the environment he created round him speak for themselves. Devoid of visible emotions — compassion, tenderness, or aggression — Elfberg gave up a secure existence to found an unprofitable home for incurables and worked in its service with no apparent regard for what the world thought of him. In his denial of the material world and his contempt for its manifestations, Elfberg both worked in the world and yet withdrew from it, a modern realization of Athanasius's ideals.

Grottan i öknen is much preoccupied with early Christian theology, not because Gyllensten has become a Christian but because he sees the ideas of the Church Fathers as fruitful ways of exploring existentialist questions. He talks of the 'mysticism' in *Palatset i parken* and *Grottan i öknen*, 'mysticism' being interpreted as a process of coming into contact with the objective world outside us ('God').[5]

A couple of novels explore the myth of Don Juan. In *I skuggan av Don Juan* (In the Shadow of Don Juan, 1975), Gyllensten presents Don Juan as a symbol of the arrogant exercise of human power (expressed as seduction) and shows this power to be hollow. In the more interesting sequel, *Skuggans återkomst eller Don Juan går igen* (The Shadow's Return or Don Juan Walks Again, 1986), the theme is the opposite one, that of self-abasement — which is an equally arrogant expression of human will. Men cannot create their own destinies, but can only serve humbly in the world and hope that some meaning may be revealed to them through sudden insight ('Grace' in Christian terms). The narrator of the novel builds up his story by interpreting a number of prints he has bought in Seville. The pictures are for him 'icons'; not representations of scenes, but a medium for encouraging the non-human world (God) to reveal itself.

The seven short stories of *Sju vise mästare om kärlek* (Seven Wise

Masters on Love, 1986) employ a Buddhist framework, where the pupils learn from their masters (bodhisattvas) in a series of reincarnations. One of Gyllensten's most accessible books, it presents existentialist themes in the form of love stories. The pupils here must learn to destroy their own self-absorption and their attempts to create love in their own feelings. They must avoid the opposite temptation to disparage their own feelings. They must open themselves to what is different from them. In the final story, 'Silverräv och rödräv' (Silver Fox and Red Fox), the bodhisattva is a silver fox and the pupil a red fox who loves his master's silver daughter. The red fox learns that he and his differently coloured partner have been lovers in certain previous incarnations and enemies in others. There is a danger and tension in their relationship that makes their love a creative and stimulating encounter. Much the same themes are repeated in the novel *Det himmelska gästabudet* (The Heavenly Banquet, 1991), a collection of tales told at a feast. Here too the final tale deals with a man's love for a woman who causes him both pain and pleasure — and whose innermost being remains a mystery. That is how human beings face the world: in love for its beauty and richness, in pain at its betrayals, and in a never-ending exploration of its essence.

Lars Gyllensten is a difficult writer. His works are not concerned with psychology but with philosophy. He is an existentialist author who tries out various ways of living in his books. His arguments are sharply defined, but his novels can be confusing in construction: the broken syntax of *Barnabok*, the collage of *Juvenilia*, the jumbled time sequences of *Palatset i parken*. His language is rich, with a large number of foreign words, but also an element of archaic or rare Swedish. His work achieves its greatest effect when viewed as a whole, where the different books argue with or elaborate each other. It is a corpus that bears comparison with one of his mentors — Søren Kierkegaard.

Lars Ahlin (1915-1997)

by Gavin Orton

Lars Ahlin, who was born in 1915, has a certain amount in common with Lars Gyllensten. Like Gyllensten he is an opponent of desperadoes who attempt to change the world (or themselves) to fit their dogmatic philosophies. Like Gyllensten he rejects the realistic or psychological novel, and his characters are often bizarre and implausible if looked at as people of flesh and blood. But where Gyllensten's overall attitude is that of the sceptical scientist, Ahlin's is that of the visionary. His vision is religious: all men live in sin and can only be saved by God's grace; equal in sin, they should not set up ideologies or moral codes to judge one another by. Ahlin's distaste for desperadoes is evident in his novels of the 1940s. In *Tåbb med manifestet* (Tåbb with the Manifesto, 1943), the unemployed young hero Tåbb is rejected by his own dogma (the Communist Manifesto), because he is taught by Marx that a working man without work is useless; indeed, his very existence is unjustifiable. Tåbb finally comes to the conclusion that it makes more sense for him to reject the uncompromising Manifesto and follow the more pragmatic Social Democrats in this imperfect world. *Min död är min* (My Death is Mine, 1945), is a rich scrap-book of a novel, portraying everything from repulsive perversion to tender love. The hero, Sylvan, is a symbol of utter failure, who contemplates suicide as a means of reasserting his dignity, 'out of pure respect for oneself'. But he comes to accept his failure and finds salvation in love with an equally wretched woman, Engla Kjäll. Her name has connotations of 'angel' and 'spring', and their love is granted them as a Grace, 'without cause'. Ahlin's rejection of the well-made novel is even more marked in *Om* (If, 1946), written in a convoluted style that emphasizes the book is an artefact and rather obscures the story about a father-son relationship.

Ahlin's post-1940s production is concentrated in the ten years from *Fromma mord* (Pious Murders, 1952), to *Bark och löv* (Bark and Leaves, 1961). Between these two difficult and obscure works he published five more accessible novels: *Kanelbiten* (Cinnamon Girl, 1953), *Stora glömskan* (The Great Amnesia, 1954), *Kvinna, kvinna* (Woman, Woman, 1955), *Natt i marknadstältet* (Night in the Market Tent, 1957) — generally regarded as his masterpiece — and *Gilla gång* (Normal Course, 1958). Ahlin published no fiction between 1961 and 1982. His recent novels and short stories have aroused less interest than his early work. An examination of *Fromma mord* and *Natt i marknadstältet* may give some idea of Ahlin's idiosyncratic world.

Fromma mord is the story of Aron, who returns to his native town (as usual, based on Ahlin's home town of Sundsvall) to come to terms with his past by placing a stone on his father's grave and by marrying his childhood sweetheart Evangeline. Distracted by old friends and their demands, he fails in his task and finally sinks in a bog (apparently voluntarily), tied to his gravestone. These external events are only symbols of deeper happenings, and the mystery is compounded by Ahlin's use of a special vocabulary. Aron's hope after placing the stone on the grave is that he will be able to 'svara på (respond to) tilltal' (27);[6] in other words, he is isolated and lonely, unable to respond to others' advances ('tilltal'). He claims that he and others live in 'viljans tankar' (thoughts of the will) and not, as they should, in 'förnuftets tankar' (thoughts of reason): living in 'förnuftets tankar' is accepting the world as God has created it, as it really is, while living in 'viljans tankar' means exercising human will in revolt against God's will. An example of this is provided by the people who built the tower of Babel: 'They built (it) to make a name for themselves. Why, do you suppose? They...were afraid of nature. Then you try to cut yourself off...The main thing was to have God just for themselves. But God isn't God for individuals...In his creation he shows solidarity with everyone. The builders' plans therefore came to nought' (99-100).

In God's sight all are equal, but some human beings try to be more equal than others, set themselves up as judges of others, claiming they have a monopoly of God, and then judge others by what they do rather than by what they are as people. This is called 'fromheten': 'Fromhet gör saken större och bäraren mindre' (Piety makes the matter greater and the bearer smaller, 265). For example, a murderer is condemned for his murder ('saken'), while his total personality ('bäraren'), of which being a murderer is only a part, is overlooked.

In *Fromma mord* Ahlin demonstrates a number of human solutions to life's problems, through 'viljans tankar', and shows how they fail. Brinkman, for example, is a business man who manipulates men for his own profit. But there is one thing he cannot manipulate — death. He expends frantic efforts trying to get himself killed at a moment of his own choosing, and preferably killed unjustly, so as to wipe out his own considerable burden of guilt. He fails, and is apparently drowned by accident. Another character, Berglund, a staunch Socialist but failed politician, is unable to cope with his disappointments in life because he will only view them in political and social terms. He collapses after a mock parliament proves that his sufferings must be imaginary since they are neither political nor social. Aron himself seeks salvation not through money or politics but through love. Unfortunately, for most people love is made up of emotional attachment and sexual desire and tends to fall apart into its two components. In *Fromma mord* Aron is loved (but not desired) by Agnes and desired (but not loved) by Lilly. Aron sees a third possibility, a heavenly love. He has previously experienced this love with Evangeline, in a mystical union, but they cannot find a way to realize this love in a world of flesh, blood, and work — something made clear when Aron lyrically talks of this love in the functional corridors of the hospital where Evangeline works. Evangeline, however, despairs of the possibility of finding 'a path from Eros to our bodies' (189) and commits suicide. Man cannot, the novel indicates, create his own happiness, by 'viljans tankar': his powers are insufficient, and his attempts to exercise his powers lead to harm to others, 'fromma mord'.

Natt i marknadstältet is set in the 1920s in the period up to and during the autumn fair, in a town like Sundsvall. Like most of Ahlin's novels it is loosely constructed, with several main stories and a number of separate tales inserted into them. The central story concerns a middle-aged couple, Leopold and Paulina Dahl. Leopold is an unhappy man who has been passed over for the job he wants and therefore feels humiliated and unworthy of Paulina's love. He periodically disappears from home to try to make his fortune and thus prove himself worthy of Paulina. Paulina, however, is not worried about her husband's lack of social success. She loves him and is therefore prepared to put up with his absences. This love is the core of her being; but another vital part of her ability to survive is her sense of humour. Ahlin uses the concept of 'humour' in a very special sense: it is the ability to reconcile the opposites of life, to accept both grief and joy, to be able to laugh and cry at one and the same time. Paulina says to her husband: 'Don't say we can do without humour — which is : being faithful to death when at one's most vital, and to life when most distant from it; constantly, always, Leopold, we seem to need the readiness of humour to make the world's contradictions equal, so that none dominates us' (389). Yet the novel ends with Paulina murdering Leopold. This may be psychologically unlikely, but Ahlin's novels must be read as novels of ideas. Leopold represents a harmful principle — a refusal to accept life as it is, a preoccupation with dreams, 'det fantastiska' (fantasy). This leads him to crime and a readiness finally to destroy others in his own desperation. Paulina kills him to prevent him killing others, and she takes on his guilt in her love.

The conflict between reality and 'det fantastiska', between Paulina and Leopold, is reflected in a number of minor characters. One is Frans

Chapter X

Ledin, who has been unsuccessful in love and relapses into 'det fantastiska'. But while Leopold tries to make himself better than others to prove his worth, Frans Ledin adopts the ridiculous and humiliating disguise of a clown — Glada-Frasse. For as Paulina notes: 'He brags that comparisons are comparable both upwards and downwards. One can find superlatives in the depths as well as the heights' (406). This is a repetition of Ahlin's theme that men are equal in God's sight and should not indulge in comparisons or condemn one another on grounds of piety or social standing.

Another character, Paulina's nephew Zacharias, is a young boy who for much of the novel is a lively but basically uninvolved observer of events. The tragedy of Leopold's murder, however, provokes a crisis in him. After helping Paulina carry the body home, he goes to Glada-Frasse's tent and tries to hide from the world in the clown's doll-mask. Crying inside the doll he compares his tears with Paulina's tears of love and humour: 'Were his tears like Paulina's — or was it worry or weakness or wretched despair?... Was it acceptance and love for moving, changing, enigmatic life, the unbroken stream which constantly gives and takes, creates and smashes, gives life and death? And could he smile with these tears in his eyes? Here is night, he whispered and struck the doll's monstrous forehead. It is night in the world's market tent' (459-60). As in *Fromma mord* the world is presented as an unsatisfactory place — a circus of darkness and colour, sorrow and joy. Zacharias, however, seems to resist the temptation to retire like Glada-Frasse into the image of a clown. He has a 'humorous' approach to life, and is ready like Paulina to accept new experiences, good and bad; and in the last words of the novel he is crying with a smile on his lips. Yet he also feels himself an outsider: 'I can only play. I can't be serious' (461). The reason is that he lacks, as yet, love. It is only the combination of love and humour that can save man in the night of the world's circus tent.

Gyllensten attacks ideologies on the grounds that they are unscientific; Ahlin objects to them because they are against God. In adopting ideologies men distance themselves from their fellows by condemning others' beliefs as wrong — but in God's sight we are all equal. Gyllensten's work was compared above to Kierkegaard's. Ahlin's, in its mixture of exalted religion and low burlesque, is equally comparable to Dostoyevsky's.

Sara Lidman (born 1923)

by Phil Holmes

Sara Lidman was born in 1923 in Missenträsk in Västerbotten, and her first four novels from the 1950s are all set in this remote part of northern Norrland, as are the six novels in the Jernbanan (Railway) suite, published between 1977 and 1996. She attended university and in the early 1960s she visited South Africa and Kenya and wrote two novels based on her experiences of colonialism. She was in fact imprisoned in South Africa for infringing the Immorality Act which prohibited relations between blacks and whites. After a visit to North Vietnam in 1965 she became increasingly involved in the Vietnam protest movement as a spokesman and author of books and articles. Sara Lidman's progress is, therefore, representative of the growing political radicalism among post-war writers as well as the tendency to express this radicalism in more direct forms than that of the mainstream novel. Her first novel, *Tjärdalen* (The Tar Still, 1953), centres around the complex structure of turf and wood which it has taken Nils a year to build, and which is intended to provide tar and a valuable income. In brilliant sunshine and high hopes Nils sets off to light the still, but discovers that it has collapsed, and that the vandal responsible, Jonas — called Räven (The Fox) — is trapped beneath it. Nils has a fit from the shock, while the injured Räven is carried off and placed in the care of the half-witted Vela. The villagers of Eckstäsk, who have long been plagued by Räven, leave him without any medical attention, and he dies slowly of gangrene. The novel is the depiction of a collective, here an isolated village, and the action is limited to one week round Midsummer. One character stands out from the rest, a poor crofter called Petrus, who discovers too late what has happened to Räven, and reproaches his neighbours for their lack of Christian charity. They claim that they have enough troubles of their own without worrying about such a reprobate, but this is not good enough for Petrus, as he believes we have a duty to our neighbour. He explains to the priest after Räven's death: 'He was a penance for the entire village, we won't argue about that. But he was still a human being.'(157)[7] We see Räven's viewpoint in a scene in which he asks Vela for a baby bird:

'Vendla: — What do you want the little bird for? Then he half raised himself up and shouted: — Poke his eye out for him, break his legs, tear off his wings, give him my hell' (54).

Petrus, like his Biblical namesake, fails in his duty and suffers bitter remorse. The tar-still is sold off at a ridiculously low price, and Petrus does not intervene because he is in debt to the purchaser. Morality, it is stressed, can never be completely divorced from the material world. Petrus is guilty of inaction in this instance, but on one occasion he does act. Alone on his farm he discovers his children's cat torturing a mouse. Unable to bear the thought that his children might witness such cruelty, he kills the cat with an axe, but the deed haunts him afterwards. The oppressor — the cat, Räven, Petrus himself — becomes the victim, and Sara Lidman displays compassion for both.

The style of *Tjärdalen* is terse and characterized by the considerable use of Biblical motifs and allusions from the lips of the god-fearing farmers and by the use of Västerbotten dialect. The dialect helps evoke a particular remote provincial scene but also considerably enriches Sara Lidman's language.[8] Another feature of the style is the way the author is concerned to represent the character of the words themselves.[9] When, for example, Nils has his epileptic fit, Petrus suggests he be put to bed 'in a voice as knotted and uneven as a badly spun thread' (60).

Hjortronlandet (Cloudberry Land, 1955), is also a collective depiction, and relationships within the collective provide the main focus of interest. The village of Ön is 'a streak of firmer ground in a sheet of swampy mire, an island of solidarity in an ocean of loneliness' (5). This community of poor crofters is distant geographically and socially from the farm-owning Ecksträsk, and the author paints a vivid picture of life here in the 1920s and the way people faced up to these harsh conditions. Claudette links together the events of the novel: her christening begins the story and her departure from Ön ends the story, and she serves as our guide to the farms — 'There were evenings when she wandered between the farms like a pendulum, incapable of staying in one place' (84). She introduces us to the warm, squalid home of 'Skrattars' — Jani, Stina and family — and to the hapless Nordmarks, who live one day at a time, who dream of eating as much sausage as possible at one sitting and sit all day playing 'klums', a guessing game with buttons on a string. Jani has a daughter called Märit who stands out from the rest: she is beautiful, vivacious and intelligent, the very antithesis of Claudette. The schoolmistress encourages Märit to continue her education, but this would mean leaving home. She stays, sleeps with the local lads, marries one of the Nordmarks out of pity and dies of consumption. Märit is an amoral child of nature, a beauty as rare in the village as the cloudberries of the title. The finest character-portrait in the book is of Claudette's grandmother Anna, a dominant Earth Mother who is rumoured to possess extraordinary powers. After being raped as a girl and losing her child, Anna makes it her life's work to help women give birth. When Stina asks for Anna's help as midwife she at first refuses it because Stina did not heed her warnings about the pregnancy and indulged in an extra-marital affair. When Anna has to intervene it is too late and she is forced to kill the child to save the mother. Being right gives her no satisfaction, and she wanders off after a white ptarmigan to die alone in the forest.

As Sara Lidman has indicated, *Hjortronlandet* is hardly a work of social criticism,[10] yet one passage has a definite tendency: the villagers all farm free government land as part of a pioneering settlement scheme, and the government inspectors' visit, presented partly in the form of a set of responses between 'De ansvarskännande' (Those conscious of their responsibilities) and 'De odugliga' (The incompetents) (74f) reveals the administrators' total lack of understanding for and empathy with ordinary rural people. The novel may also be regarded as a farewell to childhood and Claudette as the author's alter ego. When she finally leaves Ön we read: 'But Ön sighed and whispered at the back of her mind: I shall always be with you' (194).

Regnspiran (The Rainbird, 1958), is set in Ecksträsk and traces the life of Linda Ståhl from her birth until the time she bears an illegitimate son. The setting is somewhat earlier than that of *Hjortronlandet*, the story ending before the First World War. 'Regnspiran' is the name given in Norrland to a bird of ill-omen, and comes to represent Linda herself. As a child her strong will soon comes into conflict with that of her father Egron, a pious puritan and a truly unloved figure. In retaliation for her misdeeds Egron burns Linda's favourite doll and the six-year-old refuses to forgive him. Then, after he has beaten her, she threatens to kill him. Egron goes off to fell timber, and that evening Linda has a vision in which she sees how his axe slips, gashing his leg, and how he bleeds to death. When Egron is found dead, Linda acquires a reputation as a witch and the villagers hold her in awe. She wields power mercilessly, seemingly compelled by unseen forces to hurt and destroy. Among those she ruins is the orphan Simon, one of a number

Chapter X

of Christ-figures in the novel; like Judas she betrays him. As an 18-year-old she seduces the fiancé of her best friend, who later kills herself when she hears the news. Linking together the fates of the different characters is a ring that passes between them.

The story of Linda continues in *Bära mistel* (Carry Mistletoe, 1960). Now in her thirties she is a well-to-do guest-house owner whose settled life is disturbed by the arrival of Björn Ceder, an itinerant violist. Linda soon abandons her home, security and respectability to follow Ceder about the north of Sweden, accompanying his performances on her accordion. Ceder is homosexual, and Linda is blindly, hopelessly in love with him, believing that the impossible will happen and that one day he will return her love. He treats her very badly, and through this long penance she is allowed to atone for her past misdeeds. Ceder has pretentions as a serious composer, and the title of the book alludes to a ballet he composes which is based on the Norse myth of Balder who is killed by a shaft of mistletoe. Superimposed on the study in erotic psychology is the theme of the frustrated artist.

The narrator in *Jag och min son* (I and My Son, 1961, revised 1963), is a nameless Swede living in Johannesburg with his young son Igor. He aims to make a lot of money in South Africa and return to his farm in Jämtland, and he is willing to do anything to protect his son and provide for his future, including theft and selling out his friends to the police. The Judas motif is once again in evidence. The narrator is a rootless individual who flits from job to job, and through him a picture of South African society emerges: the shanty towns, the political unrest, the iniquity of apartheid and the pass laws. The novel is one fevered monologue, the confessions of a man torn between his compassion for the exploited Africans and the love of his son. He builds a shell around himself, denying to himself that he is part of the exploitation he sees around him. As the novel ends he drives frantically towards Durban to try to take his sick son home.

Much more satisfying as a novel is *Med fem diamanter* (With Five Diamonds, 1964), which is set in Kenya. The viewpoint here is entirely African and the Whites are presented as caricatures, yet despite this and the criticism of the conditions under which urban Blacks live, the author remains more concerned with human relationships than with political ideologies. There are three main characters: Wachira, his brother Thiongo, and Wambura, the girl Wachira hopes to marry and who has borne his child. The major themes are the love of Wachira for Wambura, his increasingly desperate attempts to purchase the traditional bridal goats, and the relationship between the brothers which comes to resemble that of Cain and Abel. The five diamonds are set in a ring which Wachira is suspected of stealing from a guest at a hotel where he works. He loses his job and gets another as a houseboy in far-off Nairobi, separated from Wambura. Thiongo is an intellectual who represents the new African elite, and he sets Wachira up in business as a tobacco grower. Wachira finally realises that it is Thiongo who stole the ring and caused him so much suffering, and kills his brother. As in *Regnspiran* a repeated motif — the ring — helps to weave the narrative together, and as in several other of Sara Lidman's works there is an inserted tale, a parable, similar to the tales found in Eyvind Johnson's *Romanen om Olof*.[11]

Sara Lidman now leaves conventional fiction behind. *Samtal i Hanoi* (Conversations in Hanoi, 1965), is her report on a visit to battle-torn North Vietnam, yet the book is also a very personal document. The material — depictions, reflections, interviews, quotations — is arranged in an effective pattern. Nor does the narrator seek to present an objective, that is dispassionate, report; rather as in the African novels she tries to get inside the skin of the people. There are some passages that at the time were shocking, particularly the testimony of an FNL-guerrilla about torture in South Vietnam. But there is a general spirit of hope too: even amid the ruins of a bombed-out hospital the author finds the flowers still blooming in the patients' little gardens.

Sara Lidman next turns her attention to conditions nearer to home. In *Gruva* (Mine, 1968), she presents transcripts of tape-recorded interviews with workers in the iron mines of Kiruna and Svappavaara. In contrast to *Samtal i Hanoi* the narrator herself withdraws entirely from the work and the voices of the workers alone are heard. The miners talk of the gas, the noise, the silicosis, the bosses and the union. The author has described the technique employed:

There are subjects that are too great for an author to get on top of with her own interpretations... one has to allow the subject matter itself to speak... There are turns of phrase the miners would use that were so precise, brilliant and true that I was taken aback. As a writer, who after all, has been going a few years, I often find myself standing corrected.[12]

In *Gruva* we find perhaps the ultimate example of documentarism: a technique which is at the same time contemporary and de-personalized and renders the exact words of the subject, and yet arranges these so as to achieve maximum effect.

In the 1960s and early 1970s Sara Lidman's political activities almost entirely replaced her literary production, but she has since made an astonishing come-back with a series of novels which may come to be regarded as her major work, and certainly makes an attempt to produce the great Västerbotten novel to rank alongside Moberg's Småland epics and Delblanc's Sörmland series.

In the six parts published so far, *Din tjänare hör* (Thy Servant Heareth, 1977), *Vredens barn* (Child of Wrath, 1979), *Nabots sten* (Naboth's Stone, 1981), *Den underbare mannen* (The Wonderful Man, 1983), *Järnkronan* (The Iron Crown, 1985), and *Lifsens rot* (The Root of Life, 1996), she writes about 'what it cost to populate the interior of Norrland', about the period 1878 to 1920 and the attempts to link Västerbotten to king, capital and 'Schwärje' by rail. The bringing of the railway to remote Västerbotten is the dream of one man, Didrik Mårtensson, and by the end of the series it is close to realization, but at great cost to Didrik himself and many of his neighbours. In *Din tjänare hör* we are introduced to some of the many characters of the suite in the year 1878, but the action reaches back to 'Storsvagåren' (the famine years) in the late 1860s and to the Russian invasion of the Västerbotten coast in 1809. Many independent tales extend the main themes of the work. In 1878 Didrik is 21, in the full vigour of young manhood, one of seven children of Mårten and Lena at Månliden in Lillvattnet parish. His speech at a parish meeting draws attention to him as a possible future leader. On Mårten's land lives Nicke the hunter with Nora and his family who live off the forest, and have an almost supernatural relationship with animals and trees. Nicke's son Nabot, the son of a servant, is a rival of Didrik's who soon runs off to America, but his presence continues to haunt the narrative in the form of Didrik's guilt at having driven him out. Among their neighbours is Spadar-Abdon, who has twice walked all the way to Stockholm to seek justice in a boundary dispute and been defrauded by 'den underbare mannen' (the wonderful man).

Didrik attracts the attention of two mentors: the drunken doctor Ström and the larger-than-life *länsman* (policeman) Holmgren who teaches him to speak and write officialese and grooms him to be a future Chairman of the Council, 'Olförarn' (Ordföranden). Didrik falls in love with Anna-Stava from Basnäs, but it is to be some time before they marry.

In *Vredens barn* Didrik begins to learn something of parish affairs by assisting länsman Holmgren. The long central section of the novel details a fateful journey to 'Skjellet' (Skellefteå) for the trial of Nicke for illegally killing an elk. There Didrik encounters the businessman konsul Lidstedt who enlists his aid as a go-between and organizer of teams of foresters in order to exploit the riches of Lillvattnet's forests. At the same time Lidstedt establishes Didrik with goods and credit as a storekeeper at Månliden. During the dangerous return journey in a thaw, carter Abdon's overloaded sleigh results in the death of his horse, causing him once again to feel a sense of injustice and exploitation. Didrik then marries the almost saintly Anna-Stava.

At the opening of *Nabots sten* ten years have passed. Didrik is on business in Skjellet when, after a series of girls, Anna-Stava gives birth to Storsonen and nearly dies. On his return Didrik is asked to bring a mysterious passenger and her child: the servant woman Hagar (a female equivalent to Nabot) is miraculously able to wetnurse Storsonen Isak Mårten when Anna-Stava is unable to feed him. With her mystery, her enticing fragrance and amazing culinary skills, Hagar torments Didrik's dreams before leaving as suddenly as she has come. During her stay Didrik's horse Hästn is cruelly maimed and has to be put down. When Didrik begins felling the forest on his land Nicke is driven out, his livelihood ruined.

In *Den underbare mannen* the railway approaches but turns out to have many disadvantages: Didrik is now 'Olförarn', but his sister Tilda runs off with Goliat, the boss of a gang of railway navvies, and there are constant disputes with local farmers over compensation for land, sleepers and infill for the many bogs which compromise Didrik's reputation. As the middle-man he is partly responsible for the exploitation of the small farmers by the big business magnates on the coast. He overlooks the many small injustices in order to provide the railway he is convinced will improve everyone's lot. But his position becomes untenable: he is over-generous in allowing credit to farmers who provide raw materials and labour for the railway building. He is also obsessed by Hagar. Meanwhile Anna-Stava is haunted by a skull found in a local bog that she associates with a dream she once had of a man drowning while trying to save Hästn. The crisis comes when Didrik must borrow to stave off bankruptcy, and he comes close to

Chapter X

murdering a former rival for Anna-Stava. Discovering the skull saves him from this crime, but as the novel ends he remains on the brink of financial disaster.

Järnkronan narrates with bitter irony how, just as his all-consuming dream is realized, and the railway finally reaches Lillvattnet, Didrik is taken off by train to Långholmen prison in far-off Stockholm to begin a prison sentence for embezzlement of emergency poor relief. His nightmare has always been that he will end his days in Ecksträsk at Spadar-Abdon's cottage, digging ditches, the antithetical image to the triumph of modernity represented by the coming of the railway, but this backward move is indeed to be his tragic fate.

In *Lifsens rot*, a free-standing continuation of the epic, Lidman takes the story on to the time around the First World War, a period she has described in her first works, thus closing a circle. The tale follows Rönnog Martinson, a god-fearing dairy maid with training, a career and a wage, who dreams of an unmarried life with a room of her own. Rönnog is, however, pursued by suitors, and, when nearly thirty, she succumbs to the charms of the much younger Isak Mårten, Didrik Mårtenson's son. She marries him and moves to Ecksträsk with its large, extended family, its poverty and its enormous debts, and she keeps her father-in-law's creditors at bay by sacrificing her savings. The very focussed Rönnog tries in vain to introduce some order into the chaos of Ecksträsk, where modern inventions are beginning to appear — the telephone and electricity — how else will the young people be able to read and educate themselves during the winter darkness?, asks the dreamer Didrik. Finally realizing the hopelessness of her self-imposed task, the heroic Rönnog flies into a rage and in an ending from Greek tragedy, assaults Didrik. In the struggle Didrik dies and Rönnog bears a still-born son.

The novels deal with an unrealistic idealism (Didrik's) perverted by ruthless and cynical exploitation (by big business interests). As go-between Didrik tries to help the little man while gaining a measure of power himself in order to secure the line through Lillvattnet. But both Didrik and Anna-Stava are consumed by shame and guilt at sins of omission and commission. They apply a frightfully strict Christian morality most harshly to themselves.

The works are perhaps most remarkable for their style and technique. Sara Lidman produces a very subtle and satisfying weave, the threads of which run through the whole garment. One example must suffice of the kind of multi-faceted motif she uses. When Didrik first gets the idea of the railway he feels a pain in his neck, and he later damages a vertebra in his neck when lifting a vast stone out of a ditch in order to show up the ditchdigger Nabot. He knows his limitations after this, the burdens he cannot lift, the situations he cannot face. These are seen in his attack of fear when faced by the big businessmen in Skjellet, his refusal to help Abdon lighten his load on the fateful journey home, his powerlessness to deal with the rapacious Goliat or with Hagar who causes him new pain in his spine when she resists his advances. He nearly kills Hagar's (and Nabot's) son Otto by lifting him by his head like a stone. Ultimately he cannot lift the whole parish out of its poverty.

The author strives to create and explain a forgotten world in precise ethnographical detail and (as in her early works) dialect and Biblicisms pervade the narrative. The extensive use of dialect words, phrases and outmoded concepts necessitates the provision of translations, and explanatory word lists, and the use of dialect extends beyond the dialogue to author narrative. But the subtle linguistic features are, as ever, important — modes of address, the differences between parish and town speech, the officialese used in speech and writing by local officials and mastered by Didrik — and are given close attention by the author. Many of the protagonists are very pious (they mostly have Old Testament names) and their thinking is formed by Bible-learning (something a contemporary secular readership must find difficult to follow). Biblical allusions are frequently used to illuminate and give depth to the action. But there is also a fruitful tension between the characters' Christian piety and the primitive superstition that abounds in these remote forests, as well as with the sudden decline in morality brought by the railway.

Per Olof Sundman (1922-92)

by Phil Holmes

P.O. Sundman was born in Vaxholm and spent much of his youth in Stockholm; at school he was a contemporary and friend of Stig Dagerman. Although he began writing at an early age, his debut with the collection of stories *Jägarna* (The Hunters, 1957), came only after years of preparation and experimentation. Stockholm provided little inspiration, but a year spent in the mountains of Härjedalen in 1945/46 proved a significant experience. In 1949 Sundman and his wife took over Jormliens fjällgård, a tourist hotel in remote Frostviken in N.W. Jämtland, close to the Norwegian border. Sundman soon became involved in local affairs, joining Bondeförbundet (now Centerpartiet), and was elected to the local council at a time when the power companies were moving into the highland valleys to exploit their hydro-electric potential, and when the local inhabitants were hard-pressed to defend their rights against the powerful national interest. In 1959 he became Chairman of the Council in Frostviken, and in 1963 he returned to live in Vaxholm, which he represented as Member of Parliament for some years. He was also involved in Scandinavian cultural politics on the Nordic Council.

Many of Sundman's books are set among the mountains of Jämtland, and incidents and characters are often drawn from his experiences of people he met as a hotelier and local councillor. Yet Sundman is not a provincialist in the same sense as the proletarian writers of the 1930s. The isolated rural community serves him as a convenient microcosm in which to pursue his sociological research, rather than as a focus of interest in itself.

Two important themes in Sundman's work are present in *Jägarna*. The first is the hunt, search or expedition, either a physical hunt or a search for understanding about an individual or sequence of events. The second is the impossibility of our ever fully understanding our fellow human beings. The first four of the fourteen stories all deal with missing persons, people who have opted out of the social group: a member of an elk hunt is sought by his fellow huntsmen; a young criminal is tracked down and captured in the snow-covered fells by a policeman and an unnamed narrator; a young foreign girl, a guest at a mountain hotel, runs off into the mountain wilderness. The central novella, 'Anakoreten' (The Anchorite) most clearly depicts the individual dropping out of society. This partly autobiographical tale follows a car salesman who leaves the big city for a solitary existence in the North, and tells how he survives the winter. 'Trumslagaren' (The Drummer) is the only tale without a contemporary setting and deals with a group of lads from a northern valley who all march off together to do their military service. Where the other stories show a laconic, calculated and closely defined use of language, in this story Sundman's style is warmer and more expansive — the storyteller practises his art for its own sake. Sundman has written that, in its analysis of the small group, this story is an introduction to his later work. It depicts young men who must undertake a journey towards a goal set for them by society, the differences between individuals in the group and the loyalties forced upon them. He regards the story as a depressing allegory.[13] Sundman is a behaviourist who describes what he sees and hears — dialogue, facial expressions, gestures — but leaves the reader to draw his own conclusions. In the motto to the story 'Observatören' (The Observer) he writes: 'In reality it is always a matter of sticking to observations and nothing else. Avoid drawing conclusions, avoid value judgements, avoid venturing opinions', and in an important commentary on his own narrative method, 'Kommentarer kring en teknik' (Commentary on a Technique) he writes: 'I restrict the narration to external events; I do not go in for psychological constructions of the inner workings of my fictional characters' minds. This restrictive approach comes naturally to me.'[14] Sundman claims that this method has developed out of his own storytelling, but some critics have suggested literary influences as diverse as the Icelandic family saga, Hemingway and the French New Novel.[15] Sundman is constantly absorbed by the problem of the individual's situation in relation to the people around him and to society in general. He is disturbed by the restrictions which the efficient running of the welfare state places upon individual liberty, the trend towards a diminished personal integrity.

The novel *Undersökningen* (The Investigation, 1958), works out a number of these ideas in dramatic form. The documentary basis for the story is Paragraph 12 of the Temperance Law, which stipulates that an investigation should be carried out into any person whom the local temperance committee has reason to believe is misusing alcohol in a manner detrimental to the well-being of others. The law makes no distinction between people. The investigator, Erik Olofsson, is a timber surveyor and Chairman of the local council in Jämtland. The citizen under investigation is Arne Lundgren, an engineer from the city who is in charge of a giant power-station project which is transforming the landscape and the lives of the local community. How, we ask ourselves, can such an investigator possibly discover anything about a man who is socially and culturally so different from himself? Olofsson talks with his sister, interviews Lundgren's wife and listens to a long rambling tale from one of Lundgren's colleagues, the enigmatic Lage. Interspersed with the account of the investigation itself are a number of 'true' details

Chapter X

about the building of a power-station, the work of a local councillor and of a timber surveyor, some of which are relevant to the case while others merely support the very strong illusion of reality. The evidence to be sifted is conflicting and inconclusive, and some of the testimony is downright gossip or deliberately intended to mislead. Olofsson tries hard to be dispassionate: 'An investigation should not have any specific aim. It must result in what it results in. It should be without prejudice.' (52)[16] Perhaps it is possible to regard Olofsson's situation as a projection of the artist's/writer's dilemma: both as timber surveyor and investigator Olofsson is a go-between linking two parties, a purveyor of reality who is assumed to be impartial. And the reader must not demand solutions of him; he must make up his own mind. As Lage remarks: 'Sometimes people say one thing, sometimes another. The two don't add up. You will have noticed this, of course? It is the listener's business to put them together, see that they agree — if he feels inclined to' (117).

Sundman has called the novel *Skytten* (The Marksman, 1960), 'a story about details'[17] for he notes that 'true' details, far from merely supporting the fiction, also possess a value in themselves. The details given here form a picture of a small community, Hovdebyn in Jämtland, while the plot centres on a hunting accident.

Sundman's breakthrough came with *Expeditionen* (The Expedition, 1962), a work which also won acclaim outside Sweden. It deals neither with the North nor his own experiences but does share with earlier books the fascination with the collective, the group with a common goal. The novel is based on the first volume of H.M. Stanley's *In Darkest Africa* (1890), an account of his expedition from Zanzibar by ship to the Congo and then on foot into the interior of the Congo basin. But Sundman's book is not really about Stanley, nor even necessarily about Africa. It is about men like Stanley, strong men who often determine the lives of the rest of us, and about a continent like Africa. Sundman himself sees its theme as the decline and fall of Western imperialism, 'images of a society heading for disaster',[18] and towards the end of the novel two natives are 'tried' and hanged for desertion, a symbol of approaching catastrophe for the expedition. Even before this, things have begun to go wrong. The expedition leader, Sir John, fails to keep his word to the native bearers and discontent among the bearers increases when the expedition enters the jungle and encounters sickness, savage beasts and hostile pigmies who bombard them with poisoned arrows and place razor-sharp sticks in the long grass in their path. As a result the Africans desert in large numbers and Sir John decides to make an example of some deserters who have been recaptured to induce loyalty in the others.

The narrative technique in the book is unusual: Sundman employs two first-person narrators. Laronne is a European officer, a violent man whose watchwords are authority, loyalty, order. Jaffar Topan is an Asian scribe with a poetic bent who inhabits both the native and European worlds. Their alternating accounts differ, yet sometimes overlap. Gradually the focus of the story shifts from the character of Sir John to the expedition itself, the way in which it functions and its progress towards failure. No other work by Sundman has aroused so much interest or prompted so many interpretations.[19] The debate between the author and his critics centres upon the character of Sir John, the Nietzschean figure who stands above law or conventional morality. Some critics see a correspondence between Sundman's own views and those of Sir John, whilst Sundman sees the work as a warning that the world must change; his aim is 'to subject western colonialism to an angry and critical scrutiny'.[20]

In his next two books Sundman returns briefly to his adopted province. The first three stories in *Sökarna* (The Searchers, 1963) appear to be directly from personal experience and the narrator has similarities with Sundman himself. The last story, however, 'Främlingarna' (The Strangers), is told by a man skilled in the art of manipulating others. He describes how he arrives at a ski-hotel and becomes the life and soul of a rather dull party, but his approach to the task is unpleasantly calculating. The restricted viewpoint provides the reader with a distorted view of the real relationships involved. The novel *Två dagar, två nätter* (Two Days, Two Nights, 1965) is based on a film script written for the film *Jakten* (The Hunt), in its turn based on a story in *Jägarna* about a man-hunt. The rights of the individual and those of society are again explored in a story narrated by an individual of suspect views.

Sundman's acknowledged masterpiece is the prize-winning novel *Ingenjör Andrées luftfärd* (The Flight of the Eagle, 1967). Like *Expeditionen* it is based firmly upon documentary evidence and deals with an expedition which is lent allegorical overtones. The adventure described took place at the same period as Stanley's trek. On Sunday 11 July 1897, three Swedes — S.A. Andrée, senior engineer at the Royal

Chapter X

Patent Office and two young companions, Nils Strindberg, amanuensis at the Technical High School, and engineer Knut Fraenkel — took off in a balloon named 'Örnen' (The Eagle) from Spitsbergen. Their intention was to fly over the North Pole and thus become the first men to reach either Pole. The balloon and its crew disappeared northwards, and it was not until the year 1930 that the men's last camp was found at Vitön, east of Spitsbergen. On their bodies were found Andrée's diary, Strindberg's notes and letters, Fraenkel's meteorological log and a number of rolls of unexposed film. It has, therefore, been possible to reconstruct the explorers' three month trek across the Arctic pack-ice. The journey in the air and across the ice forms the centrepiece of Sundman's work, but this is preceded by a no less fascinating account of the events leading up to the ill-fated expedition. He paints a broad panorama of Oscarian Sweden with its chauvinism and hero-worship. This is the era of the great Scandinavian explorers, of Nordenskiöld who forced the North-East passage, of Sven Hedin who travelled widely in central Asia, and especially of Nansen, whose triumphant return from a marathon journey on foot with Lieutenant Johansen across the Arctic ice coincides unfortunately with Andrée's first abortive attempt, for Andrée makes fine speeches about the Pole being essentially a Swedish concern, and aims to drop the Swedish flag over it from his balloon, and the rumblings of Norwegian separatism form an important undercurrent. The crew, and in particular Fraenkel, are obsessed with fame and a place in the history books, an obsession emphasized by the repeated motif of waxwork effigies. This is also a period when technology is king, and there is an unprecedented faith in science. Andrée himself works with invention. Alfred Nobel, who invented (among many other things) dynamite in 1866, is a major sponsor of the expedition. The great Stockholm Exhibition coincides with its preparations. The three men seem blinded by the technology of their undertaking, and Sundman provides a welter of detail about the balloon and its equipment. The plan is to steer the craft by means of a sail and drag-lines stretched across the surface of the ice.

In Paris for flight-trials Strindberg and Fraenkel are the toast of the town — in fact champagne and patriotic speeches abound before the final take-off — and they practise ballooning in calm, fair weather and warm sunshine. The whole affair is a merry jaunt. But the reality of polar aeronautics is very different: once in the Arctic they are bedevilled by cold, fog and damp.

On take-off, amid some panic and confusion, the drag-lines are lost and with them any possibility of steering the craft; they are left at the mercy of the prevailing winds. After sixty hours aloft the weight of the ice condensing on the canopy forces them down onto the pack-ice, and they set off southwards towards Spitsbergen, battling against appalling conditions with ice ridges and open water channels. Andrée who is initially seen as the strong leader (like Sir John) is soon replaced by the physically fitter Fraenkel, whose antipathy towards his leader grows with each discovery of shortcomings in the equipment. Fraenkel gradually comes to realize that the undertaking was doomed to failure from the outset. After a fearful journey Andrée and Strindberg die and Fraenkel kills himself out of a feeling of loyalty to his companions.

Sundman is fascinated by two major questions concerning Andrée's expedition. Firstly, how could a group of sane, rational men deceive themselves into attempting a feat which would have made a fine plot for a Jules Verne novel, but which lacked any sound basis in reality? This problem is hinted at in the title of the novel, in which 'Ingenjör' (Engineer) represents a factual, down-to-earth approach to life while 'luftfärd' ('air journey' rather than the more prosaic 'ballongfärd', balloon journey) evokes the unreal, the fantastic.[21] Secondly, how would the relationship between these men have developed under the extreme pressures of their long struggle across the ice? This section of the novel is reconstructed on the basis of what is known of the men's characters.

Sundman chooses Fraenkel to tell the story. He is the least known of the men and the only one not to keep a diary, and this lack of character definition allows the author considerable leeway. In an admirable companion volume to the novel, called *Ingen fruktan, intet hopp* (Without Fear, Without Hope, 1968), Sundman provides the factual background in the form of a collage of annotated documents. The probable cause of death of the men is now thought to be trichinosis, heart failure induced by the eating of polar bear meat infected with a parasite. A comparison of these two books reveals the other freedoms the author has allowed himself in the novel, and which scenes and details find no support in the documentation. For *Ingenjör Andrées luftfärd* is a work of literature, a carefully constructed pattern of repeated motifs, contrasts, hints, contradictions and riddles.[22] Beyond the measurable, the describable, there is in the final analysis something immeasurable and inexplicable about the events, and it is possible for the reader ignorant of Andrée and his expedition to ask: did all this ever really take place?

In *Expeditionen* Sundman uses the technique of 'submerged form', and the same narrative method is employed in his last novel *Berättelsen om Såm* (The Story of Såm, 1977) whose underlying plot is that of the thirteenth-century *Hrafnkels Saga*.[23] This short saga, set in the pastoral society of eastern Iceland in the early tenth century, traces the dramatic conflict between Hrafnkel and Såm, in which Hrafnkel loses and then regains the farm at Adalbol. Sundman retains the main lines of the beautifully structured tale in his retelling, but he develops with great subtlety the contrasting personalities of the two protagonists. Both Hrafnkel and Såm are outstanding farmers, but Hrafnkel has a vitality and determination which is lacking in Såm. This vitality is symbolized by the 'gillestuga' (45ff, 159ff, 188, 247) where he holds his orgies, and which is burned down by Såm's supporters for the good of his soul when Såm takes over the farmstead. Hrafnkel is a strong man and natural leader (again like Sir John) whilst Såm finds himself somewhat unwillingly leader of the little men. The minor characters of the saga are given more prominence in Sundman's story, and some new characters, notably women, are introduced; in fact in Sundman's story it is the women who are largely instrumental in causing the tragedy. This story is set in modern times; whereas the saga-men ride on horseback and carry swords, Sundman's characters drive jeeps and carry rifles. Landscape and nature are pictured in the saga with unusual clarity and Sundman presents in effective detail the topography and present-day society of a land vaguely resembling Iceland.

Sven Delblanc (1931-92)

by Karin Petherick

Delblanc's autobiographical works *Livets ax* (The Sweetcorn of Life, 1991), and *Agnar* (Chaff, 1993), make harrowing and illuminating reading, covering the formative conditions and experiences in the period between infancy and his entry into adulthood. His childhood was traumatic due to a psychopathically violent father, and the child created for himself an all-powerful and merciless God cast in the image of father Delblanc, and he saw the world as peopled either by tormentors or victims. In many ways, this deeply pessimistic view haunted him throughout his life. Later, Manichean Gnosticism, with its dualistic world view and belief in a supreme God of light in a remote heaven, who has no dealing with and did not create our fallen world, and on the other hand the evil Demiurge, creator and ruler of our brutal and chaotic planet, provided Delblanc with a mythology around which to structure his imaginary universe. He did not 'believe in' Gnosticism theologically speaking — in the here-and-now he was a materialist and positivist, but artists need metaphors. His bleak view was only relieved by the knowledge that women's sustaining love, though unable to eradicate cruelty, nevertheless exists. A flowering cherry tree became its symbol. Another central element in Delblanc's personal life was his experience of involuntary episodes of escape into 'another order', of blessed peace and moments of heightened awareness and timelessness. He calls this mystical state of being 'avlägset land' (*distant land*).[24] The episodes did not feel 'religious', there was no vision of God, but they felt essentially more 'real' than the real world. Delblanc speaks of 'namnlöshet' (*namelessness*) in this land, of shedding the labels and attributes of everyday life in a state of perfect unity with all things. Lovers in his novels at best come together in this namelessness. The concept is not unlike Lars Ahlin's ideology of human meetings shorn of all social and moral status on a bedrock of absolute equality.

It is impossible in a short presentation to mention all Delblanc's novels, but his first one, the allegorical *Eremitkräftan* (The Hermit Crab, 1962), is symptomatically important, for it explores a conflict which he regards as central to human existence, that between Order and Freedom. A young man living under the iron rule of a totalitarian regime escapes to freedom (the White City) only to discover the horrors of a place where licence leads to total depravity. He returns whence he fled, crying out in anguish that there must a third alternative, to which the prison governor replies: 'The freedom you dream of is false ... The ship without a crew is free of a navigator, but it isn't free from the power of currents and winds. Free? Yes, free as a dog, a pig, a snake. But not free as a human being.'[25] Delblanc finds many and varied ways of posing the question which occupied him, as it had Dostoyevsky before him: Does man's nature demand *imposed* order?[26]

In Delblanc's second novel, the picaresque *Prästkappan* (The Cassock, 1963), set in Prussia in 1784, we follow the amazing adventures of the penniless and embattled curate Hermann, who speaks of the land of eternal darkness, which he has read of and and is tempted by, where comforting hopelessness rules. As in many of Delblanc's novels with a 'trial' structure, Hermann fails the test, but not without scenes of love and mysticism. He proves to be the son and heir of his erstwhile aristocratic patron, and once having entered into his new role, he becomes as cruel and despotic as his forbears.

In his third novel Delblanc attempted to formulate a 'positive alternative' to the corruption of the hero in *Prästkappan*. Its title, *Nattresa* (Night Journey, 1967), alludes to L.-F. Céline's shocking masterpiece *Voyage au bout de la nuit* (1932) with its demonstration of anarchic nihilism in response to the slaughter of the First World War, the metaphor being that to go into the night is to shed one's last illusion. The 'trial' in *Nattresa* is that faced by a young man intent on writing a radical political pamphlet. He is pursued by two emissaries of the Demiurge, here the obscenely cruel Lord of Unadulterated Capitalism, name of Minski, straight out of Marquis de Sade's novel *Juliette*, and indeed the Marquis himself is one of the emissaries, for who has spoken more eloquently of the longing for freedom than he, pursuing libertinism *in absurdum*? Minski, with headquarters in New York, offers the hero a retreat into a restful oasis of total detachment from the 'many too many' who hunger and suffer out there in the world. But this time the hero chooses to join the victims, and thereby vanquishes his tempters. Later, Delblanc had misgivings about *Nattresa*; he feared he had been false to his own aesthetic and had got too close to *agitprop* in the wave of political correctness and anti-Americanism then current in Sweden. He felt great respect for the pioneers of Social Democracy, but increasingly disliked fashionable Marxists and band-wagoners.

The reading public at large know and admire Sven Delblanc for his tetralogy chronicling in alternately tragic, burlesque and realistic mode the life and times of Hedeby (in reality Vagnhärad in Sörmland) just before, during and after the Second World War. This is his childhood territory in fictionalized form, *Åminne (*Memories, 1970), *Stenfågel* (The Stone Bird, 1973), *Vinteride* (Winter Lair, 1974), and *Stadsporten* (The Town Gate, 1975). The 'Hedeby cycle' was transformed into successful TV entertainment by the simple expedient of focusing on the comic and slapstick episodes, for Delblanc can be riotously amusing. His second tetralogy *Samuels bok (*Samuel's Book, 1981), *Samuels döttrar,* (Samuel's Daughters, 1982), *Kanaans land* (Land of Canaan, 1984), and *Maria ensam* (Maria Alone, 1985), also widely admired, recreates fictionally the remorseless fate which dogged Delblanc's maternal grandfather (a preacher who becomes mentally ill) and his family. Both chronicles present a world of social inequalities and inexorable pressures, before the serious advent of the Swedish welfare state.

The dreams and visions of Emanuel Swedenborg (1688-1772), scientist-turned-mystic, have inspired many writers, including Blake, Balzac, Emerson, Strindberg, and Delblanc. His spirit hovers over at least two of the latter's novels. Firstly, *Grottmannen* (The Caveman, 1977), which describes a passionate relationship in which the protagonist strains to achieve a state of paradisal, mystical unity with his beloved (say, like the hermaphrodite state described by Plato in *Timaeus*), and who also dreams about his struggles in a corrupt media world (much as Swedenborg dreamt allegorically about his own concerns in his *Dreambook*). Secondly, *Gunnar Emmanuel* (1978), the story of an innocent idealist studying in Uppsala, disillusioned by the cynicism of his peers and lecturers. His girl-friend Vera (a good Swedenborgian allegory for *Truth* or *Art*) disappears. Gunnar Emmanuel visits Nationalmuseum and a magical potion enables him to enter into a number of paintings from various epochs in his desperate search for her. But Vera has gone for good, and shortly, so has our young Candide, who often voiced a longing that 'the pendulum of time might cease' and he escape into eternity.[27] With nice irony, only his teacher 'Sven Delblanc' is left behind, who in his self-centred middle age has failed to recognize this portrait of himself as a young man.

Delblanc cared greatly about his 'idéromaner' and spoke of the following as a trilogy. *Kastrater* (The Castrati, 1975) concerns the role of the artist. Rome of 1783 is conjured up with the Young Pretender Charles Edward and King Gustaf III surrounded by aristocratic debauchees and libertines, all indifferent to the sufferings and humiliations of the lower orders (to which artists also belong). The immortal *castrato* Farinelli and his young colleague Marchesi sing for the grandees like angels, but Farinelli has no illusions that art has ever fed the hungry or provided warmth for the freezing: 'What has our art to do with reality and truth? Beware of harbouring pretentions which merely confer on art a responsibility it cannot shoulder ... Artificiality and playfulness are what we should strive for, for when our masters wish to confer on us the more exalted roles of citizens and social reformers, they only do it to cover up their own vile crimes, so that we shall gild their vices and glorify their base villanies.... Seek artificiality,

Chapter X

Marchesi, be the monkey of power — whatever happens don't become its accomplice and executioner's assistant ... be a nightingale, be a monkey, and you will exercise the only virtue we can hope for — that of being victims instead of hangmen' (98 f.). Naturally, this is directed against those regimes where the artist/writer is forced to follow the party line and viciously punished for disobedience, but Delblanc also detested the milder, but irksome, left-wing orthodoxy of the Swedish literary and political establishment in the 1960s and 1970s, with its preferred social realism and its collectivist claim to be sole arbiter of values. [28]

Freedom versus order, already familiar to us from *Eremitkräftan*, is also the theme of *Speranza* (1980), significantly subtitled *en samtida berättelse* (a contemporary tale). It is the diary of a young aristocrat who fails abjectly when his ideals are put to the test. In 1794, attended by tutor and manservant upon the good ship *Speranza*, he discovers that the hold is full of slaves being transported in unspeakable conditions to toil in a Jesuit rum distillery in Porto Rico. His protests to those in command are ineffectual; a Catholic Abbé on board proclaims that the end justifies the means, that these black heathen souls are being saved for heaven from a life of animality, possibly cannibalism; what is earthly suffering compared to eternal bliss? The Abbé rails against the French revolutionaries: 'You want to depose God in order to grant mankind liberty, liberty to wallow in vices and crimes ... you speak of welfare, of society as a home for the people, but the populace will feel only despair, rootlessness and an insane desire to seek intoxication and death, rather than to live without God, without myths, without obedience and without hope'. (84)

Like *Kastrater*, *Jerusalems natt* (Jerusalem's Night, 1983) is essentially dialogic, since Delblanc's predilection for stylized drama was at odds with Sweden's prevailing socio-realist theatrical mode, so that what he *conceived* as plays, he felt impelled to transform into short novels.[29] *Jerusalems natt* shows how an originally sublime ideal — in this case, Christianity — becomes rigid and inhuman when Order is imposed on it (the exclusion of women, the setting up of hierarchies). It features a meeting c.70 AD between Titus, Roman governor of Palestine, the slavish Jewish defector and historian Josephus, Filemon (a sceptical Greek, the novel's narrator), and Eleasar, an elderly Jew who is arrested when trying to escape from beleaguered Jerusalem. Eleasar, one of Jesus' disciples, is now mortally disillusioned by the way the women, with whom he had stood next to the cross, have lost all influence in the congregation, 'everything became order and obedience, while faith and love increasingly faded away' (102), whereas Jesus had seen in these faithful sisters a cornerstone of his teaching. Eleasar quotes from an apocryphical Gnostic gospel: 'When you transform that which is two into one, and when you transform the masculine and the feminine into a whole ... then you shall enter the Kingdom of Heaven.'[30]

The action of *Moria land* (Mount Moriah, 1987), is played out early in the twenty-first century in a Sweden which has been incorporated into a mighty neighbouring totalitarian state, a chilling but conceivable scenario before the collapse of the Soviet Union in 1990. The diarist-protagonist is an old man who several years past betrayed his son to the secret police, and Delblanc's text shows us the pathological workings of a mind demented by guilt feelings. Counterpointed with the old man's shabby evasions and repressions of the truth, the text offers unattributed chunks from Kierkegaard's *Frygt og Bæven* (Fear and Trembling), in which Kierkegaard envisages Abraham's and Isaac's journey to the land of Moriah (as told in *Genesis,* Chapter 22), where Abraham is called upon by God to sacrifice his son. In Kierkegaard's terms defeat is miraculously transformed into victory 'by the power of the absurd', for Abraham complies in the absurd belief that somehow God will save them, and pending that salvation, Abraham lets his son think that it is his father who wills his death, for he will not deprive Isaac of his belief in God's mercy. How different the situation of the old man, who is aware that his son not only knew he had been betrayed by his father, he had no God to turn to in his agony. The hideous truth the old man ultimately cannot suppress is that he sacrificed his son to save his own skin, and that in his materialistic universe 'THERE IS NO FORGIVENESS'. Where would it come from? His victim is dead. The rational side of him cannot deal with the situation, and since he lacks an 'irrational' religious side, the only thing left is for him to intoxicate himself with a blind, destructive, Schopenhauerian Will, overruling morality and self-knowledge, and to live by violence and vampirism. The old man used, when young, to admire Hobbes's *Leviathan*, the absolutism of which is a forerunner to the totalitarian Swedish state, in theory a sort of Utopia realized. In practice, the Sweden in question has grown into a tyranny, and the old man has come to hate it. It is hard now in 1997

Chapter X

to recollect the warning signs of incipient corporativism, legislation by decree, and intolerance of dissidents which were faintly discernible in the years leading up to the end of the era of state expansion and state capitalism. Because the novel's envisaged state of the twenty-first century claims to be founded on the highest ideals, it brooks no criticism, and it offers no future since its aims have already been fulfilled. There is nothing for artists and thinkers to *do* any longer, since paradise on earth has already been achieved. Delblanc is savagely satirical in his treatment of fellow-travellers and opportunists, and he is no less ruthless in the narrator's self-exposure. In narrative terms the book is intricately devised and reads like a thriller, requiring a good deal of hermeneutic skill on the reader's part. *Moria land* drew critical flak because it was regarded as overtly political and inopportune just a year after the murder of Olof Palme, whereas in fact its central issue is essentially existential.

The final line of *Moria land* is identical to that of *Änkan* (The Widow, 1988), with both narrators proclaiming 'I shall live a long time yet'. Hideous lust for life and disregard of morality is what fuels them. Otherwise the novels are unalike, for *Änkan* subverts the Shirley Conran *Lace* genre (assertive women, money and sex).[31] It is a 55-year-old widow's account of her unexpected release from the tutelage of her rich, Nobel-laureate husband. She laments that freedom has come too late, but a youth-drug transforms her gloriously, and she then relentlessly avenges every patriarchal injustice and exults in the 'male' prerogatives of wealth, power and sexual dominance, leaving behind her a trail of murder, suicides, incest and infanticide. The scene of the shocking thriller-like action is Stockholm and Uppsala, and Delblanc inimitably conjures up the manners, clothes and speech of the jet-set. But underneath the glittering surface, the widow of the novel is not only a woman released from her husband's shadow and unable to cope with the consequences, she allegorically represents all of us in a world where God is dead and no holds are barred. Some critics were deluded enough to equate *Änkan* with pulp fiction, a ludicrous idea and one which deeply wounded its author. Delblanc admired Hjalmar Bergman's aesthetic, to which he also adhered; their mode is implicit as opposed to explicit; shunning explanation of their intentions, they choose instead to let their fictions *embody (gestalta)* them, which means of course that they, with their complex vision, in a sense are 'difficult' writers, laying themselves open to misunderstanding.[32]

Ifigenia (1990) is based on the harrowing tale of how King Agamemnon feels impelled to sacrifice his daughter Iphigenia to the goddess Artemis for the sake of wind for his fleet which is setting out to reclaim his brother's wife Helen from Troy. In Euripides' play *Iphigenia in Aulis*, Iphigenia has been miraculously saved by the substitution of a sacrificial hind and transported thence to a place of safety, but the suspicion is voiced already in the play by her mother that this is a poetic fiction to mask hideous reality. The novel's concern is thus both the appalling betrayal of an innocent for the sake of a supposed greater good (the necessity to punish the Trojans), and above all the way poets, for the greater good of their audiences, transform chaos and cruelty into the workings of a benevolent providence ruled over by gods. (The novel's premise is that Iphigenia *was* slaughtered.) The book's second half focusses on the role in this particular story of one Demodokos (here the author of 'Homer's' works and commanded to accompany the expedition to Troy in order to immortalize its exploits). As participant in the action and partly its narrator, he agonizes over his own frailties and the euphemisms and distortions of the truth which his patron demands of him. *Ifigenia* demythologizes an ancient story. Stylized and elliptical narration creates a *Verfremdung*, or distancing effect, which requires readers to grapple with the central issues of 1) a tormented Agamemnon who submits to the belief that 'all human and divine order demands sacrifice', and 2) asking if it is poetry's function, by means of idealized presentations of events, to help humanity take heart in a world subject to cruelty and violence. Delblanc, like Dagerman, believed in unflinchingly facing the night.

P. C. Jersild (born 1935)

by Gavin Orton

P(er) C(hristian) Jersild is a writer who engages directly with the problems of modern Sweden (often in satirical form) but who is also given to extravagant flights of fancy and excursions into world history. In contrast to some of his contemporaries, he is a straightforward storyteller, a rationalist with little time for metaphysics. He qualified as a doctor and worked for many years in the Civil Service Welfare Department. He reveals a keen insight into the functioning of bureaucratic institutions, which is one of the major themes of his

Chapter X

works.³³

A common device in Jersild's works is the juxtaposition of the everyday and the fantastic. His first novel, *Till varmare länder* (To Warmer Climes, 1961), is set both on a Stockholm housing estate and in the warmer lands of Purgatory. In *Prins Valiant och Konsum* (Prince Valiant and the Co-op, 1966), the contrast is between the fantasy world of the hero of a strip-cartoon and the prosaic world of the local supermarket. Fantasy is employed to satirical effect in Jersild's first big success, *Calvinols resa genom världen* (Calvinol's Journey Through the World, 1965). Dr Calvinol, a Rabelaisian character, has a number of adventures in different centuries and countries. He meets Baron von Münchausen, the hero of a book of similarly absurd stories, who greets him as a fellow idealist, claiming that absurdity is an effective weapon against reactionaries: 'Don't you see that it forces us to reflect, to determine our own position, to take sides?' But Calvinol rejects Münchausen as an escapist, who has 'floated over the battlefields in a balloon, regarding suffering through the wrong end of a telescope' (119).³⁴ Satire always runs the risk of being taken at face value as just an amusing story. In the novel there are several stories that reduce great battles (and suffering) to a joke. The story 'El Alamein' is not about Montgomery's victory over Rommel but about a battle in a school playground for access to the boys' urinals. The trench warfare of the First World War is described innocently as an archaeological excavation like that at Troy, in a story called 'Schliemann's Labours'. The great Swedish king Gustavus Adolphus, tragically shot at the Battle of Lützen was, it seems, in fact killed a year earlier, but from political expediency his corpse was disembowelled and blown up like a balloon and placed on his horse to be paraded when necessary. At Lützen, unfortunately, the king sails off like a kite. There is satire of religion, of Jersild's own medical profession, and of international politics. Calvinol is called to the Soviet Union to treat the Party Secretary, who is suffering from elephantiasis (like the Party bureaucracy) and sprawling all over the country. By contrast, on Taiwan (the island with pretensions to represent all China) the inhabitants are shrinking. Calvinol solves the problem by removing Taiwan to Disneyland.

The exuberance of *Calvinols resa* is followed by sober depictions of archetypal bureaucrats. *Grisjakten* (The Pighunt, 1968), is in the form of a diary kept by Lennart Siljeberg, a civil servant who has been assigned the task of eradicating all pigs from the island of Gotland. He does not ask why the pigs should be exterminated — he merely obeys orders. Siljeberg himself is tender towards individual animals, nursing an injured cat at the beginning of the novel, but against pigs as an anonymous mass he considers all possible technical methods of destruction, including gas chambers. His superior, Gård, argues that one of the essential elements of a stable organizational structure is 'dehumanization': 'the psychological process which makes possible the transformation of emotionally charged factors into neutral symbols' (125) — for example, quoting the number of victims of a catastrophe rather than giving individual biographies of them. In fact, Siljeberg fails to achieve this detachment and suffers a breakdown. The novel is clearly an allegory of the Holocaust, and Jersild no doubt had in mind the case of Adolf Eichmann, executed in Israel in 1962 for organizing the Nazis' extermination of the Jews. At his trial Eichmann appeared not as a figure of evil but as a grey bureaucrat.

Vi ses i Song My (See You at My Lai, 1970), takes the argument a stage further, with a bureaucrat who is very aware of what he is doing. Rolf Nylander is a psychologist who sets himself the task of introducing industrial democracy into the feudal institutions of the Swedish army. A test case arises when conscripts refuse to clear forest land that has been treated with defoliants. The soldiers cannot be convinced that the defoliants are harmless ('an unacceptable truth') so Nylander substitutes 'an acceptable truth' — that they might be harmful. The soldiers can then be persuaded, rather than ordered, to clear the forest to protect the environment (a popular cause), so democratic procedures have prevailed. However, Nylander himself is quietly absorbed into the army bureaucracy and rendered harmless: he resigns himself to being a 'manipulator and fellow-traveller' (130). The novel is highly amusing in its presentation of Nylander's manipulative and manipulated democracy, but the title refers to a massacre by the US Army of Vietnamese civilians, and Nylander refers to the Pentagon as one of the world's most advanced and efficient bureaucracies.

In *Vi ses i Song My* Nylander describes the application to the Civil Service of 'programme-budgeting', in which sectors of the administration are to be judged on their ability to achieve 'productivity' (measured in economic terms) and 'efficiency' (measured by the degree to which they achieve their goals). In the novel *Djurdoktorn* (The Animal Doctor, 1973), Jersild sets his story in the Sweden of the near future, a trick that allows him to show trends in contemporary Sweden

Chapter X

in a more highly developed but still perfectly recognizable form — to show in particular where demands for productivity and efficiency lead. The scene is set in the Alfred Nobel Institute, a prestigious medical research establishment. The Institute decides to appoint a vet, worried not about the well-being of the animals used in research but by the economic wastage caused by their untimely deaths: 'It is good economics to love your neighbour,' the Co-op's neon-sign proclaims (259). The job of vet goes to Evy Beck as part of a middle-aged-unemployed-women-quota, and, warm-hearted and naive, she sets about caring for the animals in the Institute. She becomes increasingly appalled by the meaningless cruelty the animals are subjected to and threatens to report the Institute for breaking the law, but she is no match for administrators and manipulators and is sent off to an Ethics Centre to help her adopt a more acceptable attitude. The Institute's goals are improved medical techniques, but these techniques become an end in themselves, as Evy Beck's cantankerous father points out. His liver has failed and he is kept alive on a liver machine, but he sees himself as the victim, not the beneficiary, of medical science: 'To get those bloody machines to work they have to find suitable people for the machines to parasitize' (66). Productivity and efficiency, man's servants, become his masters. Jersild's disgust at man's cruelty to animals is also shown in *Den elektriska kaninen* (The Electric Hare, 1974), which describes the annual congress of Sweden's animals in Stockholm Zoo and their accounts of their treatment by human beings.

Jersild reveals a tender, less satirical side in *Stumpen* (1973) and *Barnens ö* (Children's Island, 1976). 'Stumpen' is an alcoholic and vagrant. He finds that increasingly society treats him not with hostility but with detached tolerance — and even the police give him a lift. But Stumpen regards himself with the greatest self-contempt. He cannot follow the arguments of the radical social worker who assures him he is a victim of the mixed economy, and he cannot accept the security offered him by a group of young people in a commune. The only help that gets through to him is the hell-fire preaching of the Pentacostalists, for they appeal to his sense of sin and shame. Jersild turns from the unprotected world of animals and alcoholics to the equally unprotected world of children in *Barnens ö*. The hero, Reine Larsson, not quite 11, has been sent by his mother to a summer camp for children in the archipelago, but he has absconded on the way. He is determined to spend the summer on his own in Stockholm, in what may be his last chance to think about life and God, before puberty strikes and 'he would be in thrall to sex and other disgusting things, his thoughts would never be pure again' (22). Reine keeps a fearful lookout for pubic hair as, armed with his Bible, *The Guinness Book of Records*, he ponders life's mysteries. In fact he is as obsessed with food (particularly hamburgers) as any adult with sex, and he never finds the solutions to his metaphysical problems. Instead he is the helpless and passive victim of others' violence: of his contemporaries, of a teenage gang, of his mother's boyfriend. Reine seeks escape in a world of purity, of sexless angels: 'Man is a pig. I think there's something else that's — well, pure. Beautiful, pure. That doesn't smell or look disgusting' (253). His only pleasant moments are with an understanding (and hairless) young woman, Nora, who tries to break down his self-absorption and his hatred of the animal workings of the human body. This perceptive portrait of a young child has proved to be one of Jersild's most popular works.

In *Babels hus* (The House of Babel, 1978), Jersild returns to the medical world: the House of Babel is a large Stockholm hospital. Like the Tower of the Bible, the hospital has grown too big for its own good. The different medical specialities speak different languages on different floors, and patients and staff talk past one another. It is another case where the pursuit of efficiency and productivity has led to its opposite. In *En levande själ* (A Living Soul, 1980), medical research and bio-engineering are the targets. The first-person narrative, a kind of inner monologue, expresses the thoughts of Ypsilon, a human brain in a laboratory run by Biochine. Although only a detached organ imprisoned in a tank, Ypsilon appears as a 'living soul', recording love, fear, a desire for freedom, for a past and for information on his future. He is articulate and often amusingly ironic in his comments on those experimenting on him. Some of his longings are expressed in very lyrical passages, while in his mounting despair and plotting to escape he becomes more human than most of those around him. The book ends abruptly. Biochine is taken over by another company. Ypsilon is no longer of interest, and his source of power is cut off.

Efter Floden (After the Flood, 1982), is a bleak picture of the world after a nuclear catastrophe has destroyed our civilization. *Den femtionde frälsaren* (The Fiftieth Saviour, 1984), on the other hand, is about a civilization about to be destroyed: the decadent Venetian Republic, shortly to fall to Napoleon. The young Ciacco Capiello is employed to record in his unique shorthand secret interviews with a prisoner called Magdalenus, who claims to be the forty-ninth saviour in a direct line from Jesus. In a series of trance-like interviews which embrace visions of the future as well as the past Magdalenus describes different generations' reactions to the Saviour. But superficiality and evil threaten: 'Suddenly it was clear that he who called himself my Father would within the not-too-distant future shrink and disappear completely. Why? Lack of nourishment. God needs Man's goodness to be able to grow' (208).

Geniernas återkomst (The Return of the Geniuses, 1987), is a series of episodes from mankind's history, from the earliest hominids to a future of resurrected geniuses cloned from their originals' DNA. History here is especially the history of ideas and intellect — the development of problem-solving, of language, of writing systems, of religions and political ideas. Jersild's geniuses are often not the famous geniuses of history but those who work in their shadow and fail because of circumstances: a Chinese scholar who proposes replacing characters by an alphabet, or a Hellenist philosopher who suggests King Herod should deal with the threat of a Messiah not by massacring baby boys but by setting up his own Messiah instead. The cloned geniuses — the Einsteins and Beethovens in their Jurassic Park — also fail because they are outside their original environment. Genius, Jersild seems to suggest, is not a question of genes alone but of nurture and contingency as well.

Jersild returns to the theme of the all-too-rational bureaucrat in *En lysande marknad* (A Splendid Market, 1992). The novel is set in a Sweden in the near future in which market forces are triumphant and the welfare state is confined to a museum, Folkhemsmuseet. The narrator is incarcerated in a special hospital, found guilty of instigating murder but insane. His problems arise from an excessive rationality and a failure to understand how more muddled human beings behave, and from a strong sense of justice. He has worked for the energetic Majbritt, who runs a company devoted to ensuring that justice is done when the state is incapable of doing it. They plant evidence on known criminals to secure convictions and even murder a serial rapist against whom there is insufficient evidence for a trial. Majbritt is driven by the belief that markets require rules for their proper functioning, and those who ignore the rules (criminals) are a threat to healthy competition. The narrator is also impressed by a lecture course on anarcho-capitalism, in which the state is attacked for its role as oppressor but also as an incompetent organizer of such things as health-care and justice. The narrator has a vision of how out of the anarchy of market forces confronting one another a pattern will emerge: 'the dream of the purity that emerges when natural unregulated cooperation has settled like a calm pattern over chaos. A harmonious equilibrium in freedom without compulsion or authority' (136). The narrator sets about trying to make Swedish justice more efficient. A plan to hold prisoners in cheaper prisons in the low-wage Baltic States comes to nothing, as does a plan for electronic tagging (too much for the sensitive Swedes). His downfall, though, is his scheme for persuading ten top criminals to emigrate, by appealing to their rationality and by signing contracts with them. Unfortunately, reason and respect for contracts prove insufficient and the criminals begin murdering one another, leading to the narrator's arrest.

Like many satirists Jersild seems disenchanted with the world he lives in. Suffering and cruelty haunt his works: the Holocaust, the Vietnam War, nuclear disaster, and man's ill-treatment of animals. Even a tolerant and rational society like Sweden can lose its way in its pursuit of progress, of management techniques and market forces. His is a cold vision of the future.

Per Olov Enquist (born 1934)

by Phil Holmes

P.O. Enquist was born in Hjoggböle, Västerbotten and took his degree at Uppsala in 1960. He made his debut with the novel *Kristallögat* (The Crystal Eye, 1961) and has subsequently established a considerable reputation as a novelist and literary critic. Enquist's breakthrough came in 1965 with a historical novel full of colour and fantasy, set in eighteenth-century Germany.

Magnetisörens femte vinter (The Magnetist's Fifth Winter, 1965) depicts the winter of 1793-94 in the life of Friedrich Meisner who achieves miraculous cures by means of animal magnetism, a mixture of hypnotism and faith healing. Meisner is based on Anton Mesmer (1734-1815). The story is presented partly from Meisner's viewpoint and partly in the form of (fictitious) documents, pages from the diary of Claus Selinger, a physician practising in the town of Seefond. Selinger's daughter is blind and Meisner is able to restore her sight, thereby

Chapter X

convincing the doctor of his extraordinary powers. Selinger subsequently helps the miracle worker to establish a tremendous reputation, and people flock to his seances. Eventually Meisner succeeds in enthralling the whole town, but then Selinger finds the master out in a crude piece of charlatanry and exposes his fraud at a public meeting. The townsfolk turn upon Meisner, and he is thrown in jail pending trial, but the cure of Selinger's daughter remains unexplained.

Erik Henningsen has isolated a number of 'historical layers (periods)' in the novel:[35] the gospel (Meisner has similarities to Christ, not least his ability to bring about miraculous cures); mysticism, magnetism and science (Meisner's method resembles Freud's psychoanalysis); and fascism (Meisner expresses views on the relationship between the individual and the state which are similar to Hitler's). Like Eyvind Johnson before him, Enquist regards history as a continuous cyclical process: what happens at Seefond in 1794 may happen again in, say, 1932.

The collage of pseudo-documents and commentary is also found in *Hess* (1966), Enquist's most obscure work. The title recalls Rudolf Hess, Hitler's deputy who was imprisoned for war crimes, and the book may be seen as an attempt to present the mass of documents which would ultimately face a biographer after Hess's death. It is left to the reader to fashion a novel out of this material.

Legionärerna (The Legionnaires, 1968) is similarly less concerned with presenting a result than with demonstrating the process of investigation which leads to that result. The book departs little from a verifiable historical reality — 'baltutlämningen', the deportation of the Baltic soldiers from Sweden in 1946 — so little in fact that Enquist is moved to write:

This is a novel about the extradition of the Balts, but if the word 'novel' gives offence, then it may be replaced by 'documentary report' or 'book'. I have tried to keep to reality even down to small and insignificant details: if I have failed, then it is because of my inability rather than my intention. The events described have occurred; the persons in the book do exist or have existed.(5)[36]

In May 1945, as the war in Europe came to a close, a large number of soldiers of the German army fled to Sweden. Among these were 167 men from the formerly independent Baltic states of Latvia, Lithuania and Estonia. They were all interned in camps in Sweden. In

November 1945 the Swedish government announced its intention of returning these Baltic soldiers to their homelands, now of course part of the Soviet Union. The internees, fearing Russian reprisals, protested at this decision by means of hunger strikes, self-mutilation and even suicide. On 26 January 1946, 146 of these men were taken aboard the Soviet vessel *Beloostrov* at Trelleborg. 21 others were either dead or too ill to be moved. One man, Peteris Vabulis, stabbed himself in the throat and bled to death on the quayside.

Enquist's researches over a period of four years enabled him to reconstruct in great detail the events of the eight months when the legionnaires were in Sweden, and to discover what fate befell them on arrival in their homelands. Some of this is new, as are his revelations about the political side of the affair, the debate within the Swedish cabinet which resulted in the deportations and which so compromised the much-respected Prime Minister Per Albin Hansson, who was to die suddenly just a few months later. Enquist is interested in the role of Swedish public opinion, and the way in which opinion was manipulated by the press. The Government found itself in a difficult situation in 1945 *vis à vis* the Russians, and tried hard to treat the Soviet Union as it would any other civilized state. Enquist writes: 'My purpose has not primarily been to erect a monument to a Baltic tragedy. Instead, I have tried to describe, as accurately as possible, a Swedish dilemma.' (5)

Another facet of Enquist's approach is the way in which he sees the extradition of the Balts as 'a parable for our time' (397); he delineates the problems for the narrator of attempting to depict one complex political situation whilst in the midst of another. Is it possible, he asks, to provide a truly objective picture of the affair? For, to place ourselves in the same position as the Swedes of 1945 we must, for example, ignore what we have since learned of conditions in Stalinist Russia from Khruschev's speeches and Solzhenitsyn's Gulag novels.[37] Throughout his search for the truth Enquist is at pains to demonstrate his own preconceived opinions, the temperament through which he views the events, in order that the reader may discount these, the narrator's prejudices. He warns the reader: 'Be suspicious. Do not accept everything. Do not accept a version; think for yourself; be suspicious. There is no saintly objectivity, no ultimate truth, freed from political bias. Test, be suspicious, call into question.' (217)

In form the novel approaches the biography or confession insofar as the narrator himself dominates the story: it is *his* experience of the

Chapter X

investigation and of the world of the 1960s which the book describes. He establishes its starting point in Jackson, Mississippi during a civil rights march, and at one point in desperation he writes a letter to Chairman Mao (315-22) to ask his advice on how to evaluate conflicting evidence, advice not to be found in Mao's writings. It also expresses his personal dilemma in an image recurring throughout his works: 'To be able to rest in the fluid of the womb and at the same time to be able to watch the process' (41), to be able to observe objectively the historical process and yet to belong, to participate in the struggle, this is the problem for the writer.

Another device used in the book is the creation of synthetic portraits of witnesses, fictional composites constructed from a number of people whom Enquist interviewed: a typical camp-guard or onlooker at a demonstration (124, 127, 209). This technique departs radically from the usual historical method, but who is to say whether a fictitious portrait is not more truthful than a historical one?

Sekonden (The Second, 1971) is a more clearly fictional work, a more traditional novel, yet it shares with *Legionärerna* a 'documentary' base and the narrator's clear concern to achieve a true and objective picture of a sequence of events, and to understand Swedish society and political life. *Sekonden* is about the relation of sport to society and also about the history of the Swedish Labour movement. The documentary element in this work lies in the precise details of social and political background, the expert knowledge of various sports and, most important, the central event — the revelation in 1947 that a top Swedish hammer-thrower was using an underweight hammer to set records. The narrator is the hammer-thrower's son, literally his 'second', who tries to understand why his father cheated and how his earlier life may throw light on his actions. The narrator — here a fictional character — is once more active and visible in the work: through his personal relationships with his father and with an East German sportswoman, and through his love of sport. The second (pocket) edition of the novel from 1972 emphasizes this personal story rather more than the original in that it contains a new opening chapter describing the death of the narrator's brother.

There are three main characters: the narrator Christian Lindner, his father Matts Jonsson (Engnestam Lindner) and grandfather, Erik Valfrid Jonsson. The story of each traces a period in the history of Swedish socialism, and for each phase there is an important central event, a turning point. In 1917 Sweden comes near to revolution, and in Västervik there are hunger riots. The narrator's grandfather, a quarry worker, speaks out against strike action and averts an unpleasant confrontation between workers and police. But he betrays his comrades: in 1917 and again in 1968, when the narrator begins his search, the choice lies between revolutionary socialism and reformist social-democracy.

The narrator's father describes a typical progression for the Swedish worker. In the 1920s he helps found AIF, the Socialist Workers' Sports Movement. In 1934 he goes to the Stadion in Stockholm to demonstrate against the (Nazi) German-Swedish athletics match but becomes engrossed in the athletics and forgets why he is there, discovering only after the match is over his unused bundle of protest leaflets. Sport now becomes more important to him than politics, and in 1942 he takes up hammer-throwing and joins the police force as a driver. At the internment camp at Långmora he meets an old Communist Party comrade who reviles him for betraying the cause by joining the fascist police. In 1947 he lends his doctored hammer to a fellow athlete who sets a world record, but when the hammer is weighed he is exposed as a cheat and banned from all athletic competition. Yet he has cheated from a sense of solidarity: people expect improved results and he feels he cannot let them down.

The victory of revisionism in Sweden is demonstrated, then, in terms of three generations of this representative family:

And over the years this grandfather's remarkable sociable wisdom would drip down through the generations, his sensible and honourable benevolence would soak into us and finally it would be impossible to say where grandfather ended and father began, or what the limits were to my own personality. And out of everything father's hammer would rise through the air and hover onwards like a balloon, a work of art and a riddle for us all, hover from the 1920s and straight into the 1970s, and grandfather's anti-extremist conscience would expand and triumph and be decorated and become a part of history. (38)

Sekonden not only examines the history of socialism in Sweden but also the failure of the Socialist sports movement in the 1930s and the technology, ideology and political implications of sport today, particularly the way in which sport became an extension of politics in East Germany.

Politics in sport is also a major theme in *Katedralen i München*

Chapter X

(The Cathedral in Munich, 1972), 28 pieces about the Munich Olympic Games which Enquist covered for the newspaper *Expressen*. This collection of essays, which is given a firm composition, deals with the events and personalities which E (the narrator) encountered, but frequently a specific event is only a starting point for more general reflections on political and social problems.[38] Sport is viewed in a much wider social perspective than is usually the case.

Apart from these essays Enquist also produced short stories and dramas in the mid-1970s, all blending fact and fiction, history and literature. After a period teaching Strindberg at university in California, he produced the collection of stories *Berättelser från de inställda upprorens tid* (Stories from the Age of Cancelled Revolutions, 1974), again based partly on pieces for *Expressen*. The title refers to the disillusionment Enquist felt with the failure of the social revolutions begun in the late 1960s. The stories are set mostly in California and each deals with an alienated individual, a victim of the social system whose life is needlessly wasted. The long opening novella 'De trofasta själarnas oro' (The Anxiety of the Loyal Souls) is, however, set in Germany. It describes the unlikely friendship between prisoner Joseph Backmann, would-be assassin of the 1960s revolutionary student leader Rudi Dutschke, and Hildegard Mecke, an old Berlin cleaning lady. Both are victims of politics who have been driven to feel that life is futile. Hildegard withdraws into dreams of the only happy period in her life, when she was pregnant. Josef, after many suicide attempts, finally kills himself by placing a plastic bag over his head, a repetition of the frequent womb-imagery.

Tribadernas natt (The Night of the Tribades, 1975), Enquist's Strindberg play, was an immediate and resounding popular success in both Sweden and the USA. The play introduces some new themes into his work, namely marriage, feminism and sexuality, whilst continuing some of the familiar ones. It is set in 1889 and deals with a rehearsal of Strindberg's two-hander *Den starkare* (The Stronger) in which the playwright's ex-wife Siri produces and plays the lead against a close friend of hers, the Danish actress Marie Caroline David. Strindberg's play focusses on a man (who does not appear) fought over by two women, but Enquist sees this as wish-fulfilment on Strindberg's part, distorting the true circumstances, namely that Marie and Strindberg were struggling over Siri. In the climactic scene Marie and Siri turn the meaning of Strindberg's text on its head: instead of hatred they demonstrate their love and affection for each other. Strindberg begins by vilifying Marie, labelling her an alcoholic and lesbian, but is finally humbled into accepting her strength and personality. In *Tribadernas natt* Enquist demonstrates the stereotyped sex-roles to be devastatingly limiting on the personality and uses Strindberg's metaphor of the battle of the sexes representing a struggle for power to his own ends.

The novel *Musikanternas uttåg* (The March of the Musicians, 1978) marks a departure in Enquist's narrative method. Here he abandons the self-conscious narrator, closely related to himself, and at the same time returns to his own roots in Västerbotten (as had, for example, Sven Delblanc in his Hedeby series and Sara Lidman in her recent tetralogy from Västerbotten), albeit to the period of the General Strike around 1909. The novel is again about politics, yet approached from an obtuse angle — the fate of the Markström family in Bureå — and the author seeks an answer to a puzzle — why did Swedes from this area emigrate to Brazil? Whereas in *Sekonden* the author examines sport and politics, here he looks at religion and politics; he himself was brought up in a pious household and young Nicanor Markström might be seen as a projection of the author as a young man.

The socialist agitator Johan Elmblad arrives in Bureå in 1903 on a kind of descent into Hell. The downtrodden and unenlightened workers capture him in the forest and humiliate him and he is lucky to escape with his life. In 1909 there is a small local industrial conflict at Bure sawmills. Spontaneously and without any prior agitation the workers walk off the job in response to a series of pay cuts. Earlier they had set up the Bure Independent Workers' Association — not Socialist, of course, or affiliated to LO (Sweden's TUC). Ineffectual (they want Sunday evenings off!) it is soon disbanded, but is an indication that men's attitudes are undergoing a gradual change.

The conflict soon peters out, but it has tragic consequences for the Markströms, representatives of the pious, long-suffering and loyal Swedish working class. Nicanor is enthralled by the agitator Elmblad (a magician like Meisner) and after the previous disastrous mission he writes to Elmblad about the strike and implores his help. Nicanor rebels against the passivity and piety of his parents and resorts to sabotage during the strike. Elmblad cannot help the men, but takes his disciple into the wilderness of Bureträsk where the prophet is found wanting and Nicanor suffers a kind of martyrdom, biting through his tongue in a fight with the local peasants.

Uncle Aron meanwhile has become a company spy, reporting on the meetings of the Workers' Association to his employers, and is rewarded for his services with packs of butter. When his treachery is discovered his fellow workers beat him up and solemnly present him with a butter tub. Like the narrator's grandfather in *Sekonden* he betrays his class. When the management finally sack Aron, he rapes young Eva-Liisa, the Markströms' adopted daughter and then commits suicide by laboriously hacking a hole in the sea ice and jumping through with a weighted rucksack. The pregnant Eva-Liisa summarizes the effects of the strike on the family: 'You they have cut up. This is what has happened to me. Uncle Aron is dead. People who want to work are not allowed to. I don't want to stay here any longer.' (368) The novel ends with the family emigrating to Brazil; like the old animals in the folktale who, when they discover they are no longer any use, go off to become town musicians in Bremen, they had nothing to lose but their lives, and 'There is always something better than death' (371).

In *Sekonden* Social Democracy is seen to have betrayed the people, but in *Musikanternas uttåg* it is shown to have been always more radical than the people, and its spirit of cooperation is seen to have grown from the piety and obedience of the Swedish working class. The technique of this novel is similar to that found in *Sekonden*, with a mixture of documents and fiction and a complex time scheme involving alternations both back and forth in time and between in-depth portrayal of no less than six characters and the depiction of action. The result is a rich and satisfying mesh of cross references and allusions.

Enquist has co-authored several works with Anders Ehnmark and published two further plays which together with *Tribadernas natt* form a triptych, namely *Till Fedra* (To Phaedra, 1980) a free-verse play following in the footsteps of Euripides and Jean Racine, and *Från regnormarnas liv — En familjetavla från 1856* (Rain Snakes — a Family Portrait from 1856, 1981) which focuses once more on a Scandinavian author, this time Hans Christian Andersen and his relationship with the Heibergs. He has also written the script of a TV biography, *Strindberg: Ett liv* (Strindberg: A Life, 1984).

Both *Nedstörtad ängel* (Fallen Angel, 1985) and *Kapten Nemos bibliotek* (Captain Nemo's Library, 1991) are dark but rich postmodernist novels relying on montage and juxtaposition, in which the reader must actively participate in creating meaning from fragments, glimpses and dreams. Each uses a documentary or pseudo-documentary background. In the short novel *Nedstörtad ängel* Enquist explores the nature of love (agape) and the nature of humanity partly through the case of an extreme form of humankind, a monster, a freak in an American circus in the 1920s, who has a woman's head growing out from his own head. The monster Pasqual Pinchon regards this head as his wife, Maria, whom he loves deeply, and the metaphor represents marriage. Enquist interweaves this story with the tale of a friend, K., whose wife is a patient in a psychiatric hospital in Uppsala and who befriends a young child murderer, also a kind of monster. This boy subsequently strangles the couple's daughter, but is forgiven by K., and when the boy finally kills himself they mourn his death.

The documentary background to the more complex and baffling *Kapten Nemos bibliotek* was a true headline-hitting case — in Bureå cottage hospital in the 1930s two infants (in the novel the first-person narrator and Johannes) are inadvertently exchanged at birth. Finally, when they are six years old, they are returned to their rightful parents. The narrator has to leave his home with Josefina Marklund and his beloved foster-sister Eeva-Liisa and move in with Alfhild and Sven Hedman, and this move is to prove very traumatic. Alfhild soon grows increasingly mad and dies. Helped by the narrator Eeva-Liisa gives birth to a still-born child and bleeds to death. The child is put in the river and, in an attempt to find it later, Johannes drowns. When found and incarcerated, the narrator then refuses to speak for some years, and the story represents his search some forty years later for some kind of understanding about his childhood. The truth is hidden behind the layers of documentary and the metaphor of Captain Nemo's library aboard the submarine Nautilus, taken from a Jules Verne novel. In this library the narrator discovers pages written by Johannes about these events. Gradually we become suspicious that Johannes only exists in the narrator's imagination, and that he himself is guilty of some great tragedy.

Torgny Lindgren (born 1938)

by Tom Geddes

Torgny Lindgren is generally regarded as having achieved his real literary breakthrough in 1982 with *Ormens väg på hälleberget* (The

Way of a Serpent Upon a Rock). It marked a change of direction which has been seen as representative of a generation of writers, away from socio-political criticism to a kind of neo-provincialism; but the increasing particularity of both language and setting in his work was paradoxically to provide a vehicle for his concern with the most fundamental existential questions.

Lindgren was born near Norsjö, a small lakeside town in Västerbotten, northern Sweden. After an initial career as a schoolteacher, he became a full-time writer in 1974, living in Vimmerby, south-east Sweden. His position in contemporary Swedish literature was recognized by his election to the Swedish Academy in 1991. He published his first book in 1965, a volume of poetry entitled *Plåtsax, hjärtats instrument* (Plate Shears, the Instrument of the Heart), following it in 1970 with *Dikter från Vimmerby* (Poems from Vimmerby), and in 1971 *Hur skulle det vara om man vore Olof Palme? Fragment ur en anarkists dagbok* (What Would It Be Like To Be Olof Palme? Fragments from an Anarchist's Diary), before turning to prose with *Skolbagateller* (School Trivia) in 1972. His poetry embodies a social-democrat's criticism, often satirically expressed, of how the good intentions of communal solidarity can appear to the individual. He has also written plays for radio.

Skolbagateller is a collection of pieces on school life, best described as socio-political satire on the education system and on the attempts of state bureaucracy to control and mould it. The main theme is the lack of personal responsibility inherent in uncritical adherence to any system. Language itself is seen as part of the problem: the power of words to shape our understanding of reality, and our propensity to conceal reality behind words, not least in the use of prevailing educational or political terminology. This volume clearly goes beyond any specific satirical critique, but is not of great literary merit.

The latter judgement could also be applied to Lindgren's first novel, *Övriga frågor* (Any Other Business, 1973). Described as 'a little novel about alienation and inaction', it consists of Aron's experience of the local council meetings in which he participates (or rather, fails to participate), and the ironically contrasting direct action taken by his paraplegic friend Evan. The concept is entertaining, as often is the detail, but the self-imposed limitation of plot and setting does not make for a very successful whole. Meetings are depicted as symbolic of the lack of personal responsibility in political activity: only under 'Any other business' is there a possibility of freely exploring new ideas rather than stating prepared positions. The rudimentary and fragmentary plot, primarily a vehicle for Aron's musings, picks up in the third section, when Evan travels through Sweden in a motorized wheelchair, eventually achieving political action and recognition. The novel contains a few comic scenes of farce incongruously analogous to its subject, but it does not come to life in the way one might expect of political satire, even at this level of generality, remaining too sketchy, unleavened by sufficient incident or character interest and too infrequently allowed to erupt into more overt humour. It provides, however, a clear indication of the humour — visual, linguistic, even earthy — that is to underlie Lindgren's subsequent work; and it is a serious attempt to come to terms with, as well as to mock, the role of the individual in the communal political purpose.

Hallen (The Hall, 1975) has a similarly restricted narrative focus. Local youths build a sports hall in a small village. On losing their leader they feel unable to summon the communal enthusiasm to continue the project. When the hall is almost completed, it is burnt down, leaving its framework still standing — open to all possibilities, as the narrator puts it. He is himself one of the youths, but also acts as local correspondent for a newspaper, fulfilling the role of writer trying to interpret the events in which he participates. The village is a microcosm of society; he describes it as a bubble of glass. The building of the hall is an attempt to break out of the bubble, and an attempt to give meaning to their lives. Language is part of their reality, even determines it. 'In the beginning was the word'(21):[39] the youths gave themselves a name (a theatre and sports club) and this decided what they would build, as well as bringing order and method into their lives. This fascination with meaning, order and purpose within a hermetically enclosed microcosm of society adumbrates the much more ambitious treatment of the theme in *Ljuset* (Light). Despite the overly serious narrator in *Hallen*, the tone is gently ironical, and Lindgren achieves a surprisingly diverting yet thought-provoking composition on the nature of the individual and society with what might seem unpromising material.

1979 marked the publication of a much fuller and more discursive narrative in *Brännvinsfursten* (The Brandy King), based on the historical figure of L. O. Smith. Far from being an attempt at a documentary novel, it is the imaginative quasi-autobiography of a nineteenth-century millionaire who made his fortune from aquavit; and it can be no coincidence that Lindgren chose to mock something so quintessentially Swedish in the hypocrisy of the man who profited from so morally dubious a commodity. The narrative is sophisticated, partly first-person, partly third, as it slips in and out of his attempt to draft his memoirs, with an explicit awareness of the biographical process of transforming memory into memoir: 'Perhaps it was all unattainable, his whole life and what he had done ... perhaps it was beyond language, out of reach of words' (31). The dual perspective of the contrast between the style of his earlier memoirs and the reappraisal in the narrative present forms part of Lindgren's examination of the ability of language to convey experience.

Smith finds ways of justifying his life: 'Life is a kind of thirst, and for the workers there is nothing but aquavit to quench it with' (9); for him aquavit has become a symbol, an abstraction, a word for dreams and illusions. In broader terms his life has been seen as embodying Sweden's rapid progress from agrarian society to a country of multinational companies, with Smith a caricature of liberal ideology. The account of his life is full of interest as it charts his inexorable rise in fortune — almost picaresque at times — through the vicissitudes and expansion of his business, including the irony of his being aided by the temperance movement which brought about the introduction of new regulatory laws to his advantage. Smith accredits himself with the creation of the Swedish workers' movement, achieved by introducing 'order and method' (148), the virtue which had enabled him to build his own fortune. Yet at the end of his life his success leaves him with a feeling of existential vacuum: 'I had overestimated the possibilities of steering and controlling my reality' (175). Some of the richness of this novel depends on a passing acquaintance with Swedish history and society to appreciate the sustained jokes, but Lindgren's more general theme is well developed: the role of language itself in our attempt to come to terms with our lives, the creation of order to overcome our sense of meaninglessness.

Lindgren moved on in 1981 to a contemporary marital farce to explore the ambiguities and uncertainties inherent in individual personal relationships. This is not the farce of exaggeration, but rather of low-key improbability, and the rather slight plot is little more than a momentary glimpse of a few weeks in the marriage of Folke and Viveka as they seek counselling. Folke's self-absorption is expressed in his identification with the Swedish neo-romantic poet Heidenstam, from whose verse the novel's title is taken: *Skrämmer dig minuten?* (Does the Minute Frighten You?). Although humorous and perceptive, this novel remains on the level of a rather long-winded spoof with an arbitrariness of narrative which never quite grips the reader.

Ormens väg på hälleberget (1982) has a narrative composition and linguistic style which far surpasses its predecessors. It takes the form of an address to the Lord by Jani, whose mother, sister and wife are in turn forced to repay the family debts by sexual services to the local shopkeeper, Ol Karlsa, and then to his son, Karl Orsa. Set in a remote village in northern Sweden in the mid-nineteenth century, it is cast in a seamless language of dialect and Biblical quotation that flows through both narrative and dialogue, perfectly attuned to the concepts of sin, grace, acceptance and defiance which it explores. The language of economics — debt, credit and repayment — provides a metaphor for the human condition in terms of the religious concepts of original sin and divine grace. The book's title, an allusion to our inability to comprehend, is taken from Proverbs; the novel is permeated with references to both Old and New Testament, including the repeated refrain 'Lord, to whom shall we go?'; and it ends on a quotation from Job: 'And though after my skin worms destroy this body, yet in my flesh shall I see God' (104). Jani is a powerless Job, appealing through his narrative to the Lord to explain His ways, eventually wreaking vengeance with a knife on Karl Orsa's genitals and finally about to exact more drastic revenge when his intention is thwarted by an act of God which punishes good and evil alike.

An implicit theme of *Ormens väg* is that although we can never comprehend the nature of God or the meaning of human existence, we must continue to question. Evil exists, and is part of the God-given order. Karl Orsa sees himself in this way, in his responsibility to preserve the wealth given him and thus to sustain the prevailing order. His incestuous relationship with Jani's sister Eva, who is also his own, leads to a deformed stillbirth, symbolic in itself, and the death of the mother. 'She was the daughter of Ol Karlsa who was Karl Orsa's father, so she was half-sister to both Tilda and her father and also an aunt to her own sister and almost like a sister-in-law to her own mother. That's how things were' (35). The quasi-inversion of the names of father and son and the intricacy of the incest as described embody the relentless pattern of the human predicament, the final refrain an expression of acceptance which even defiance cannot entirely overcome.

Chapter X

One is left with the unforgettable image of Jani, the narrator, having lost everything, still — like Job — uncomprehending, defiant and questioning. The language of Lindgren's roots in northern Sweden, a natural mix of dialect and Biblical quotation and allusion blending in with idiomatic expression and standard language, serves him well as a literary vehicle here and was to do so through much of his subsequent fiction.

Both the Biblical language and the questioning of the nature of God were to be given even more ambitious literary form in *Bat Seba* (Bathsheba) in 1984. Lindgren expands on the story of King David and Bathsheba, so laconically recounted in the Old Testament. Without over-archaicizing, the novel's prose fluently absorbs a Biblical flavour through judicious quotation, allusion and phraseology. The basic events of the Bible are dramatically embellished by incident, characterization and dialogue, giving expression to human lusts but also acting as catalysts for human speculation. There is an omniscient narrative voice, but both David and Bathsheba at times dictate their own thoughts to a tongueless scribe, a device that provides an opportunity again to comment on the nature of writing: 'Every word had to be the result of a decision; and that perhaps was the scribe's true role — to check and restrain the flow of thoughts, to open the words one by one so that the speaker was forced to look into them ... The object and significance of writing was the act of writing itself' (23). Ironically the last sentence is not quite true as stated, of course. Writing in itself constitutes the struggle to understand existence, and both David and Bathsheba use the scribe to communicate with their God and to express their inner thoughts and feelings.

Bat Seba examines mankind's relationship to God, and in so doing posits God as both incomprehensible and made in man's image — or, more pertinently, describes the possibilities of a God made in the image of man or of woman, a God of violence or a God of love, the God of the Old Testament or the God of the New. The novel depicts the gradual reversal of the roles of David and Bathsheba as the latter tries to ensure the succession of her son, Solomon. At the beginning she is the victim of David's lust: 'the King ... embraced her so hard that she felt the bones bending and almost cracking within her body ... She strove to submit and bear it ... she was merely the object of his unbridled love' (6). After the rape she asks: 'What is the nature of the Lord?', to which King David replies 'He is like me' (6). By the end of the novel, and nearing the end of David's life, his strength and power have ebbed away and he asks Bathsheba the same question, to which she, in their reversal of roles, gives the same answer: 'He is exactly like me' (248).

The question 'What is the nature of the Lord?' has echoed throughout the novel, with a multiplicity of replies reflecting human uncertainty. Bathsheba now feels able to instruct David: 'The incomprehensible and the uncertain are all that is holy' (248). Their relationship has come full circle, her influence and power increasing as his strength has diminished, and the last scene, in which she climbs into his bed to try to thaw the frost that has entered his body, is reminiscent of the first rape, except that now it is *his* bones that are fragile and she exudes warmth and love where he had perpetrated violence in the name of love. David has earlier in life tried to explain the evil in God's creation, and by extension the evil in his own deeds, as a necessary imperfection: a creator cannot be good; by creating, he abandons his own perfection. His enigmatic final words express a more open ambiguity: 'You are perfection, Bathsheba. Your perfection is your greatest flaw' (249).

On one level, *Bat Seba* can be read as a feminist retelling of the Old Testament story, but it is much more than this. Bathsheba rejects the all-powerful God of violence in favour of her own wooden idol, from which symbolically she cuts off the phallus. Yet she herself adopts the more 'masculine' actions of plots, vengeance and murder to achieve her ends and rise to power, ruling for seven years after David's death before Solomon's maturity. David and Bathsheba, as God's representatives on earth, are not simply two diametric opposites. The picture presented, our image of God, our understanding of the human condition, is far more complex. The prophet Mephibosheth expresses the conundrum thus: 'The questions 'does he exist?' and 'what is His nature' can never be divorced. He has in his unfathomability moulded these two questions into one. By His very inscrutability He shows us that He exists. He is as He is because we do not know what His nature is. And so that we shall know that He is' (79).

Ljuset (1987) is set in the fourteenth century at the time of the Black Death, in a remote village in northern Sweden named Kadis, a name perhaps with associative overtones (Paradise/Hades, the Biblical Kades, the Arabic word for judge). A villager introduces a rabbit whose fleas spread plague, wiping out all but seven of the inhabitants. The two

Chapter X

main characters are Könik and Önde, the former the principal mouthpiece of anxiety at the breakdown of traditional values and norms, the loss of any spiritual, legal or practical framework for their lives; the latter the self-seeking pragmatist, appropriating to himself all the ownerless property in the village.

Much of the plot depicts the small incidents of daily life which exemplify a gradual coming to terms with the dissolution of the fixed order. The narrative has a medieval simplicity, with a perspective restricted to the understanding of the characters themselves, without authorial comment; a slightly oblique style which moves fluently from straightforward narrative through stream of consciousness to reported and direct speech. Yet there is an implicit irony precisely because the reader is so much more sophisticated than the characters. We know what has brought the plague; and we can see through their self-justification and self-deception.

When a representative of the outside world arrives in the form of Nils, a royal tax inspector, Könik begs him to act as judge upon them, to punish them and restore a system of order. This should be the light in their darkness, but Nils is, as it were, a false god. The narrative humour develops into the grotesque as Nils, who turns out to be a charlatan, sits in judgement reciting back to them the crimes of theft and incest that they have confided to him, and finally convicts their pig, which has killed a child, and Könik, as its owner. Both are subjected to a symbolic hanging. The villagers are by now in a state of mental torpor and passive acceptance, but Könik, suspended above his world, sees the real light: the beauty of nature, the struggles of the pig, which has come to represent for him their community and the whole of creation — and he himself struggles out of his spiritual darkness into the realization that there is after all order and meaning in the world.

Rabbits also have a symbolic function, representing in their copulation and fecundity the disorder and chaos of a life without social or moral constraints. The pig has further symbolic significance in its unnaturally gigantic proportions, which seem to embody the general dissolution of normal life. *Ljuset* is a comic allegory, a fine example of Lindgren's ability to develop a realistic plot into the absurd for serious purpose. The medieval life and outlook are convincingly evoked, but this microcosm of society, suddenly bereft of norms and values, is more akin (as was *Bat Seba*) to our twentieth-century loss of spiritual certainties.

In 1983 and 1986 respectively Lindgren published two volumes of short stories: *Merabs skönhet* (Merab's Beauty) and *Legender* (Legends). *Merab* is in many ways the more satisfying and homogeneous collection: rural tales of love and pathos, suffering and uncertainty, amusing not least in their blend of simple realism and the surreal. The two major themes are the power of words and the power and ambiguous nature of love. The language and style are again a mixture of dialectal and Biblical simplicity. The stories in *Legender* tend even more towards the absurd, ranging from pagan myth to modern urban backgrounds. Nathan, a prophet in *Bat Seba*, says: 'A good parable contains an infinite number of pieces of clear instruction ... even ... that contradict and exclude one another' (58). Lindgren's stories in these two volumes are parables that lend themselves to many interpretations. They grow from and develop the oral tradition, as indeed do *Ormens väg*, *Bat Seba* and *Ljuset*. But above all else they demonstrate the fertility of his imagination, an imagination which flows effortlessly from the realistic into the fantastic.

In 1991 the publication of *Till sanningens lov* (In Praise of Truth) was seen as another change of direction, but of course publication dates indicate nothing of possible gestation periods, nor was it really such a marked divergence from the novels prior to *Ormens väg*. However, since Lindgren was adjudged by the critics to have found his true voice in the Biblically flavoured regional dialects and period settings of his 1980s output, his new book about a pop singer and an unworldly picture-framer in contemporary Sweden was felt by some to be an aberration and a less serious contribution to literature. Yet despite the immediate accessibility of its language and plot, its themes are equally profound, though they veer more towards the contemporary social concerns of his earlier books than the philosophico-religious sphere. The deeper human dilemma is still there: the preservation of identity and integrity in a world of false values.

The subject is the conflict between truth and falsehood, the genuine and the spurious, integral worth and monetary value, essence and superficiality, as epitomized by the world of art, pop music and the media. The novel is imbued with a humour that ranges from the wry to the slapstick, and an irony which derives from the narrative voice, that of Theodor Marklund, whose naive yet principled attitude provides a contrast to the exploitative milieu that he is sucked into. The two strands of the plot focus on Marklund himself and his former neighbour and childhood love Paula, now a pop star. As events progress the strands intertwine and bring them together again from their disparate spheres, with matters turning increasingly to farce as Marklund is drawn out of his self-contained and anti-social bachelor life into the world whose values he so despises. He has intellectual interests, enjoying classical music and reading, primarily art history and Schopenhauer, a philosopher to whom he likes to refer, thus providing a minor refrain to his own pessimistic fatalism and critique of appearance and reality.

The acquisition of an unknown painting, 'Madonna with the Dagger', transforms his life. His indifference to money is viewed with disbelief and he is not taken at face value as the simple man he is. The provision of a copy of the painting by a forger allows for an exploration of the concepts of real and false as a dichotomy which impinges not only on aesthetics but on human happiness. In parallel to this, Paula has been launched twice on a pop-singing career, the relaunch assisted by plastic surgery which causes the surgeon to fall in love with his false creation. Inspired by this idea, Theodor and Paula themselves enlist the aid of the plastic surgeon to adopt new identities. The ultimate irony is that only by changing their superficial individual identity can they re-establish a social identity — and only after the falsification of his appearance does Paula see Theodor as he really is.

Marklund's picture-framing is a profession which alludes again to order and method. In stepping outside it, his exaggerated, single-minded devotion to the Madonna painting brings about his downfall. Paula is worshipped both by him and her public, in the latter case a form of idolatry based on a false, artificially constructed idea of what she is, an idolatry taken to absurd lengths even when her slaughter of rabbits on stage is enthusiastically condoned. Both excesses may be part of our search for values and meaning in a post-religious world, and such an analogy is hinted at by Lindgren at the end of the novel, when Marklund wonders whether instead of writing his story he could have contented himself with his great-grandfather's words carved on the family chest: 'Praised be the Lord'. The inscription is reminiscent of the title, *In Praise of Truth*, an appellation which puts this novel firmly in the corpus of the author's attempt to come to terms with mankind's need to understand the human condition.

Torgny Lindgren's most recent novel at the time of writing is *Hummelhonung* (Bumblebee Honey, 1995). It marks a return to the rural environment of northern Sweden, to the isolated existence of two brothers living in mutual enmity in cottages within sight of each other, never communicating, both ailing, but each kept alive by a resolve to outlive the other. A woman who comes to the village hall to give a lecture on holy fools stays overnight with one of them and is trapped there by snow for several weeks, during which time she cares for them both and alternates between them, listening to their stories, while writing a book on St Christopher. Although she is rather a negative portrait of a writer, it is she who, in a manner of speaking, redeems the two brothers — she becomes the saint, serving others; they in a sense are holy fools, imprisoned within the confines of their imaginations. It is she too, the writer, who in the end manipulates reality to bring about their deaths.

This story can be read metaphorically in many ways. It shows the destructiveness of any obsession carried to fanatical lengths; the absurdity of hatred; as a political allegory it could represent countries divided by mutual enmity. There is a scene of grotesque black humour recounted by one of the brothers showing how even the innocent suffer from such divisive hatred: in digging a ditch and embankment to separate them their son becomes caught in a stone-hoisting contraption, flailing in the air while they battle for the right to cut him down. The skirmish over, they find him dead. Each brother self-righteously believes the son and wife they share to be his own. The wife had increasingly left Olof for Hadar, tiring of the over-sweet food the former indulged in, and she was the source of their antagonism. Hadar is emaciated, living on an ascetic diet of salt meat; Olof is grossly overweight, having acquired a taste for sweet food from the bumblebee honey of the novel's title, collected by their grandfather, sniffed out by his dog, until the day both he and the dog fell into a deep well and died there, one having eaten the other. Hadar interprets this as exemplifying his grandfather's view that however close they become, people still remain ultimately alone, strangers to one another.

The compression of this short novel, its naive simplistic dialogue, its spare and concentrated style, yet its richness of potential interpretation, mark it out as a further progression in Torgny Lindgren's writing. Here and elsewhere his irony and black humour, the tall-story element as the realistic crosses over into the absurd, the engagement with ultimate questions, but above all his imaginative narrative gifts and linguistic formulation, ensure that his writing remains long in the reader's memory. His all-embracing theme is the power of literature, of words, to interpret our reality and express its ambiguities.

Kerstin Ekman (born 1933)

by Sarah Death

'As a Swedish writer, I come from a singularly unassuming setting. From a fir-forest culture. Lonely glimmerings of tallow candles. A host of cut-glass chandeliers in the natural darkness. I feel tender towards this language and grateful to this little culture, so improbable up here.'[40]

In her own words and her inimitably poetic prose, Kerstin Ekman here succinctly expresses how it feels to be a Swedish writer. She is one of Sweden's leading and most versatile late twentieth-century authors, now also gaining international acclaim. Born in Östergötland in 1933, she grew up in the small town of Katrineholm, studied at Uppsala University and then worked in film-making and as a teacher. She began her writing career in 1959, producing a series of crime novels and earning herself the title of 'Deckardrottning' (Queen of the Thrillers). She has made strenuous efforts to live this down, but in her most recent novels *Händelser vid vatten,* (1993, translated as *Blackwater,* 1995), and *Gör mig levande igen* (Make Me Live Again, 1996), appears to have reached a synthesis of her various earlier approaches, combining the best elements of her crime fiction — zest for storytelling, narrative pace, suspense, fascination with mystery and psychology — with the illusion and symbolism, social conscience, historical awareness and deep-rooted identification with other women, familiar from her novels of the 1970s and 1980s. She now lives in Jämtland and has made herself very much part of the local rural community, a perspective which is also apparent in the increasing importance in her writing of environmental concerns.

Kerstin Ekman's eye for landscape and her concern for the survival of traditional values surface even in her early thrillers, notably *De tre små mästarna* (1961, translated as *Under the Snow,* 1997), set in remote Lapland, and above all *Dödsklockan* (Death Knell, 1963), where the close-knit hunting community of the forest is thrown out of balance by the intrusion of an urban outsider. Stylistically too, these later thrillers show the emergence of narrative skills refined in her subsequent books.

Kerstin Ekman gradually pushes out the boundaries of the thriller genre. The watershed in this respect is her innovatory *Pukehornet* (The Devil's Horn, 1967), mischievously subtitled 'Om konsten att dö på rätt ställe' (The Art of Dying in the Right Place). The first part of the book, like *Dödsklockan*, is not so much a whodunnit but a study of the fear of discovery. In his confusion the dim and lonely character Per (Päron) leaves an old lady to die in the snow, and covers up the 'crime' by pretending to neighbours that he is still caring for her at home as usual. In the second part, conventional chronology is abandoned in favour of metafiction, concentrating on a woman writer in the flat upstairs, who turns out to have 'created' the characters of Päron and the old lady, and their story. Ekman explores the problematic relationship between reality and fiction, and the idea that we need to narrate in order to understand, introducing for the first time the concept of the importance of 'berättelse' (narrative) which becomes so central in her later work.

Because it defied genre boundaries, *Pukehornet* unsettled critics and readers at the time, and Ekman's next two novels proved equally hard to categorize. *Menedarna* (The Perjurers, 1910), set in the USA, is the story of the Swedish-born trade union activist Joe Hill, executed in 1919, and its narrator is a man who had never met Hill. It is perhaps a detective novel of sorts, but its conclusion is that we can never know the whole truth about anything.

Mörker och blåbärsris (Darkness and Bilberry Sprigs, 1972) deals with rural poverty and the hopelessness of life in a small, remote community with high unemployment. The setting, and the outlook of the local people, resemble those which Ekman later explores in *Händelser vid vatten*. While the men can occasionally escape in search of work, or drown their sorrows in alcohol from their illicit still, the women often fail to avoid the descent into jealousy, despair, and even mental illness. The denouement occurs in the half-light of midsummer night, as the drunken protagonists roam the countryside and vent their inarticulate feelings before lapsing into resignation once more.

Kerstin Ekman's next project involved many months of preparatory research in municipal files, newspaper archives and family history. The so-called Katrineholm tetralogy is made up of the novels *Häxringarna* (1974, translated as *Witches' Rings*, 1997), *Springkällan* (The Spring, 1976), *Änglahuset* (House of Angels, 1979) and *En stad av ljus* (A City of Light, 1983). It is an epic, panoramic account of the impact of industrialization on the lives of people in a small Swedish town. The earlier parts of the series have been seen as examples of documentary realism, but these are multi-layered novels with a highly individual point of view, focussing on the feelings and experiences of several generations of women, mostly working-class, from the 1870s to the latter part of the twentieth century. Their lives, often spent in grinding poverty and subservient roles, are dominated by the cyclical nature of women's time: the biological clock of childbearing, the recurring patterns of childrearing and domestic work.

These cycles are contrasted to men's time, to boardroom meetings, factory whistles and train timetables, as the coming of the railway and the construction of grandiose municipal buildings transforms the landscape. But although it is men who wield the power in the town and outwardly regulate their women's lives, the women find strategies for survival, and Ekman punctures male pomposity whenever it appears. Idle men — lazy, rich or unemployed — are contrasted with purposeful women for whom leisure is unknown. Accounts of women at work provide a coherent structural framework for the first three novels of the series. There are thankless, ill-paid, backbreaking tasks like Frida doing other people's laundry. There is other heavy and repetitive work, such as the women volunteers' catering for troops in transit, where at least the women's sense of camaraderie sustains them. There are desperate jobs, like Tekla and Linnea struggling to protect Tora's home-made sweets from the rain when the market stall blows over. And there are the more personally satisfying but exhausting and lonely jobs, like Tora's all-night baking of her first batch of loaves to sell.[41]

Ekman shows how social changes gradually relieve women's burden, and the emphasis in the series slowly shifts 'from mere physical survival to the search for meaning and purpose in life'.[42] In the last novel, *En stad av ljus*, the spotlight moves from external events to the psychology of the central character, and the narrative becomes disjointed, overtly symbolic with deep mythological resonance. In her quest for identity and meaning in a modern, secularized society, Ann-Marie is disorientated, until she eventually realizes that the source of any meaning that is to be found in life lies within herself.[43] The proposition running through the whole tetralogy, that lives attain meaning and even a kind of immortality by being remembered and narrated, is central in *En stad av ljus*, where Ann-Marie is herself a writer, and she and her world are ultimately a distorted and fragmentary product of her own writing.[44]

An interesting parenthesis in this stage of Kerstin Ekman's life was provided by her election in 1978 to the prestigious Swedish Academy, as only the third female member in Swedish history, following in the footsteps of Selma Lagerlöf and Elin Wägner. Despite initial misgivings,[45] she discharged her duties as an Academy member enthusiastically, sitting on the Nobel Prize committee, and producing a witty and learned study of the evolving ritual of members' inaugural speeches, *Mine Herrar...* (Gentlemen...,1986). In 1989, however, incensed by the Academy's unwillingness to take a moral stand on the death threat issued by Iran to the writer Salman Rushdie, she resigned, an unprecedented step which gave rise to much acrimonious debate in the academic establishment. She subsequently worked energetically for the Rushdie campaign.[46]

After the Katrineholm series, Ekman's constant evolution of form and genre continued with her next three titles. *Hunden* (The Dog, 1986), is a timeless adventure story, just over a hundred pages long. A puppy, born in a comfortable human household, gets lost in the snow when its mother tries to follow her master out hunting. The little dog survives the winter in a cruelly beautiful landscape by instinctive skill and sheer luck, and is eventually found and redomesticated. Ekman sets herself the challenge of exploring the limitations and possibilities inherent in writing from the inarticulate dog's point of view, and shows human language faced with its inadequacy for expressing the animal's experience. The minutely observed descriptions of the forest landscape, and the attempt to see both nature and culture through non-human eyes, resurface in Ekman's next book, the epic *Rövarna i Skuleskogen* (The Robbers of Skule Forest, 1988). It is the story of the troll Skord, who lives in various incarnations through 500 years of history, from the Middle Ages to the nineteenth century. His name, a combination of the words *skog* (forest) and *ord* (word), encapsulates the novel's central tension, between nature and art, body and soul, wilderness and civilization. Skord emerges from the forest, and returns to become an organic part of it on his death. He evolves from wordless troll into human being through phases as alchemist's assistant, barber surgeon, prisoner, outlaw, scholar and doctor, finally becoming mortal through his love for a girl called Xenia. He is both observer and rebel, fascinated by human culture but also repelled by it. The behaviour of human beings, Ekman shows, is often more sub-human than anything of which Skord might be capable.

Again, this is a novel about identity and its creation through narration. History is merely a selective representation of reality: the novel plays on the fact that the Swedish word *historia* means both 'history' and 'story'. Human concepts of change and time are made to seem purely relative by Skord's transformations and imperceptible ageing. His progress towards a human state is parallelled by the alchemist's attempts to turn base metal into gold; the mysterious atmosphere of the alchemist's workshop permeates the novel.

After the free fantasies of *Rövarna i Skuleskogen*, Kerstin Ekman's next published work, *Knivkastarens kvinna* (The Knife-Thrower's Woman, 1990, completed in 1984), abruptly deposits the reader into the consciousness of one individual trapped in a malfunctioning body and mind. It is written in free verse with prose interludes, and relates the experiences of an ordinary woman, variously referred to as 'she', 'you' and finally an autobiographical 'I'. The woman undergoes an operation to terminate an ectopic pregnancy, which ends in a complete hysterectomy; she suffers severe depression, spends some time in a mental hospital, and returns home to a joyless everyday existence and a suicide attempt before finally coming to terms with her situation.

It is a story both private and universal, and told in richly allusive language which echoes many other kinds of text, from medieval ballads to well-known hymns, from the Bible to classics of Swedish literature. There is a conscious mythological dimension: the woman is identified with the goddess forced to descend into the underworld in search of a lost daughter before she can return to life once more.[47] Uniquely in Ekman's works, this book is bitterly anti-men: the doctor who performs the woman's operation and the partner from whom she separates are perceived as enemies, violators, in league with the circus knife-thrower of the title, whose female assistant stands vulnerable and assailed. Consequently, the way out of her degradation is a female one, when she finds a haven of calm in women's territory, in the hospital's linen store.[48] Nurses have come here through the years to do mending, whenever they had time. Their accumulated store of precious minutes, 'measured only by the progress of the needle through fabric' (40) provides solace for the woman, and enables her to begin the long journey back to self-acceptance.

From the sparse prose-poetry of *Knivkastarens kvinna*, Kerstin Ekman has moved back to long novels in *Händelser vid vatten* (1993) and *Gör mig levande igen* (1996). These are panoramic commentaries on two faces of modern Sweden, one with a rural, northern setting, the other an urban Stockholm one.

Händelser vid vatten has won many prizes and become an international bestseller. It is set in a landscape of water, in wild, unspoilt places which are rendered sinister by violence erupting there. The action takes place partly in the early 1970s, when Annie Raft arrives with her young girl to join her unreliable boyfriend in a hippie commune out in the wilds, only to discover two people brutally murdered in a tent by the river; and partly in the 1990s, when the mature Annie herself disappears and is found dead in the same river. In between, the earlier deaths have had far-reaching consequences for the inward-looking rural community. Annie has eventually won uneasy acceptance from the local people, and found some security and happiness in her long-term relationship with the humane but deeply disillusioned district doctor. She is killed because of her continuing urge to unearth the past and understand her experience.

The novel is full of Biblical and mythological allusion, with deliberate echoes of the brutality of Norse sagas. For all its length, nothing is incidental; there is a Chekhovian precision about the positioning on the first page of the shotgun which Annie keeps by her bed: that shotgun must eventually be fired.[49] To those who asked why she had written another 'crime novel' she would probably answer, as she did in one interview, that she is fascinated by the darkness lurking beneath the surface of our lives: 'I do have a dark event, a criminal act or something like that, at the hub of a story.... I certainly find that extremely productive. It's what makes the wheel turn, that dark point.'[50] As a thriller, this novel is a gripping page-turner. As social commentary it is astute and saddening, showing rural communities at their lowest ebb, before the attempts at regeneration of recent years. As a depiction of nature, it is eerily beautiful and intimate, but also outspoken in its criticism of the devastating result of clear-felling the forests.

The country people of *Händelser vid vatten* are united, albeit grudgingly, by their common predicament. The city dwellers of *Gör mig levande igen* find that the possibility of communality is being eroded by the pace and brutality of modern society. At the centre is an all-female discussion group, comprising seven very different women, old and young. They meet, separate, and meet again, like the strange and colourful flock of birds of many species on the valuable silken fragment Blenda is vainly trying to restore. Indeed, it has been noted

Chapter X

that many of the women have bird names.[51]

At the core of the novel is a fast-moving adventure story, developing on many fronts simultaneously. The action takes place in the present, in a world of rock music, cyberspace and multinational computer empires, in a graffiti-daubed Stockholm where (as in real life) violent motorbike gangs and racist, neo-Nazi groups create a climate of fear. Once again, there is a dark point at the hub, in the mysterious disappearance of a young woman, murdered for stumbling across high-powered criminal dealings, and her little sister's increasingly desperate attempts to find her.

In counterpoint to the hostile urban environment are the daily lives and conversation of the women. Their group begins to disintegrate, pulled in all directions by the emotional demands of families and friends. They find themselves unwittingly caught up in the violent action of the plot on the level of realism, and also playing parts in fantastic, dream-like sequences: Ulla's ghostly carriage ride, Blenda's journey on a raft through the reed beds, and Sigge's metamorphosis into an eighteenth-century performing ape.

In addition, the whole novel is a conscious dialogue with Eyvind Johnson's *Krilon* novels, written in the 1940s about the members of a male discussion club. Elin Wägner's ecofeminist book *Tusen år i Småland* (A Thousand Years in Småland, 1939), is also an important intertext, and there are a myriad other literary allusions, probably too many for the average reader to recognize. Ekman cheerfully admits that this literary correspondence is partly for her own satisfaction.[52] *Gör mig levande igen* also has a metafictional dimension, integrating into its plot discussions of the function of narrative in general, and literature in particular — and of course it is no accident that Sigge, the main character, is herself working on a doctoral thesis about Eyvind Johnson.

By the end of the novel, one of the women has been driven to suicide and all their lives have been irreparably changed. Ekman asks whether they were naive to go on for so long believing that talk is any solution to the evils of modern life. Are talkers (and novelists) ultimately, as Sylvia says, mere 'linguistic confectioners', who 'pipe a decorative icing of words onto the unspeakable' (508)?

Kerstin Ekman's career is proof that words can make a difference to our lives. There is no way of predicting what, if anything, this all-Swedish Renaissance woman will publish next, but it will without doubt be a product of conscience, curiosity, imagination and craftsmanship.

Göran Tunström (born 1937)

by Charlotte Whittingham

Göran Tunström, born in Värmland, is keenly aware of the literary heritage of his home province. He even treats us to a cameo-appearance by Selma Lagerlöf in one of his novels.[53] Brought up in the parsonage of Sunne, Tunström's childhood was a happy one until the death of his father, the traumatic turning-point in the life of the twelve-year-old boy. The early loss of his father has had a major impact on Tunström's life and literary career. In his frequently autobiographical novels he tries to continue an aborted conversation with him and the theme of loss also permeates Tunström's works. In *Prästungen* (The Priest's Son, 1976), the young Göran wants to be like his father, and the positive influences of his father — the hospitality, interest in stories and Christian faith — can be glimpsed in the son's pageant of characters, his delight in storytelling and interest in spirituality.

Tunström made his literary debut in the late 1950s with the first of several poetry collections. His first novels were *Karantän* (Quarantine, 1961) and *Maskrosbollen* (The Dandelion Clock, 1962). These early works about growing up give hints of the more rounded and enriching authorship to come, and deal with some of the themes which are to become central to Tunström's oeuvre. The youths narrating these novels respectively, Henrik Synge and Bernard Ottosson known as Bastiano, lose their fathers. Whilst the former, at the age of thirteen, discovers his father's suicide amongst the blood-stained books of his library, Bastiano's outlook on life is more relaxed. *Maskrosbollen* is the story of Bastiano's erotic encounters and his struggles to get away from his parochial hometown. As so often in Tunström's works, men desert their women: Bastiano leaves Rita Karin to pursue his dream of becoming an architect, and on his return he finds her in a dead-end job, engaged to a solid but dull older man. Bastiano reawakens in her old dreams of escape and fulfilment but it is too late and she marries. Yet in this largely light-hearted novel the hero is not overpowered by his feelings of guilt and failed responsibility. He is like a dandelion clock, 'You're blown away, when it comes to the crunch,' Rita Karin tells him (202).

Tunström's prose works during the 60s were out of tune with the radical documentarism favoured at that time, but he began to make a name for himself in the 70s with the first changes in the literary tide.[54] In *De heliga geograferna* (The Holy Geographers, 1973) and *Guddöttrarna* (The Goddaughters, 1975) Tunström continues to focus upon the time and scene of his childhood. It is the autumn of 1939; war has been declared. On the home front the 'holy family', the new parson Hans-Cristian Wermelin and his pregnant wife Paula, arrive in Sunne. The men — the idealists — of Sunne with Hans-Cristian as their chairman form a Geographical Society in an attempt to educate and unite people. Tunström knows that danger, sadness and trauma are part of human experience but he is interested in how people deal with crises, and the novel explores human relationships, guilt and mental illness. Paula suffers a post-natal breakdown, but her psychotic experiences are painted in a far from negative light: they are enlightening, holy encounters, which Hans-Cristian wants to share with her. Paula has no language for her visionary experiences and although Hans-Cristian draws close to her, they remain a private affair. Tunström's men sometimes betray or fail their women, and experience punishment through the women's emotional or psychological withdrawal. Women can seem superior, as they do in *Guddöttrarna*, where the women of the town decide to grow carrots as their war-effort: the physical setting in which the women work in the fields, elevated above and visible from the town and their men folk, is clearly symbolic.

Even more obviously autobiographical is *Prästungen* (1976), which follows first-person narrator Göran from earliest childhood to his early twenties. The narrative is basically chronological and the perspective largely that of a young Tunström. The young narrator experiences women as a threat as well as a magnet but in *Prästungen* guilt is focussed, not upon Göran's unconsummated relationships with girls, but upon his father. The young Göran feels he has a responsibility to look after the family after his father's death. Although the mother survives the father, the narrative is restricted to her actions and words whilst Göran tries to capture and share with the reader the essence of his lost father. The loss of the cherished father is keen: 'It was like going out onto thin ice which you knew wouldn't hold' (107). As he flounders, setting off for Uppsala and later for a year in Greece, two events — Göran's literary encounter with Lorca[55] and his admittance to a psychiatric unit — prove decisive. The themes are gloomy — death, loss, guilt, mental illness, failure — but *Prästungen* is a readable book written in an informal style, an episodic book interspersed with dialogue in fresh Värmland dialect.

In *Stormunnens bön* (Big Mouth's Prayer, 1974) Tunström had already turned to pastures new in a cautionary tale set in Latin America about temporal and spiritual power, embodied in the personages of the ludicrous dictator Big Belly and his sacked archbishop Big Mouth. Big Mouth — who takes the President and his army into the wilderness in order to give the Indians a respite from their bondage — can be seen as a Christ-figure[56] and in his next novel *Ökenbrevet* (Letter from the Wilderness, 1978) Tunström goes further as he writes a first-person narrative by Jesus. In the wilderness for his forty days and forty nights Tunström's very human Jesus looks back at his early life in flashback. Jesus's love of God is evident but what is special about him is his overwhelming love and compassion for his fellow human beings. One of his earliest memories is of his neighbours being driven out of their homes by the Romans; the child Jesus is saved from discovery by an old friend, Hamal, who is shot in the back. Empathy and guilt are the legacies to Jesus. Later he goes to live with aunt Elisabeth, uncle Zacharias and cousin Johannes (John the Baptist) where he is impressed by the closeness of the family. This nearness is not to last: after a successful fishing-trip the young Johannes gives his sleeping mother a fish; waking suddenly the old woman sees the fish jerking on her chest and is shocked into petrifaction. Johannes is left with guilt and a sense of exclusion from a woman he loves, and it is Jesus, driven by sympathy for his cousin, who manages to get close to her and who can share a moment of love with her.

It is these unique gifts which suggest to Johannes that Jesus is the Messiah. 'Messiah! He was someone else ... as if a Messiah could grow from within. Grow inside what was already there. Like an embryo ...' (41) Thus Jesus dismisses Johannes's suspicions, enrolling at the Temple as a novice, where he meets those whose religion is just a set of rules. Jesus makes his way to the wilderness, tending a dying zealot and nursing a sick baby on a personal journey of self-discovery and active love. Bravely, Tunström has chosen to write about Jesus, but the novel is for anyone who has pondered the meaning of life, thought about good and evil, about suffering and most of all, about love. *Ökenbrevet* is a focussed, lyrical, absorbing and moving novel, which has a consistent air of mysticism which does not detract from its core of realism and credibility.

Perhaps the greatest of Tunström's works to date are his novels of the 1980s, set in his Värmland hometown. Reading Tunström's next novel, *Juloratoriet* (The Christmas Oratorio, 1983) is an adventure. This is a multi-layered narrative, full of imaginatively-created and lovingly-presented characters. Victor Udde is the narrator of this three-generational story. Like a musical composition the novel is made up of leitmotifs — references to the Bach family, allusions to angels, mythological patterns — and a variety of texts-within-texts, including American ditties, letters and a diary.

Sidner is twelve years old as Victor's story begins. His Swedish-American mother Solveig sets off for a rehearsal of Bach's *Christmas Oratorio*. The musical Solveig, who glistens with love and vitality, has been the inspiration behind the performance. In a matter of minutes, however, Solveig crashes off her bicycle into her husband Aron's herd of cows and is trampled to death. 'We're short of love,' (219) are Jesus's final words in *Ökenbrevet*. It is love which will overcome the barriers of suffering and loss in *Juloratoriet*, but it is a slow and hazardous process. Fanny Udde, sophisticated but eccentric spinster, believes she is in telepathic communication with Swedish explorer Sven Hedin, but it is Sidner she seduces. After their only night of passion Fanny gives birth to their child, Victor. Sidner may still come and play Schumann to her, but she makes herself emotionally and sexually inaccessible to him. Meanwhile Aron, in his grief, has tantalisingly brief visits from his dead wife. Thus when he gains a correspondent through Sunne's Radio Hams Club, he thinks it must be Solveig in disguise. The woman is in fact Tessa Schneidermann, lonely sister of a New Zealand sheep farmer. She falls in love with Aron through their letters and pins her hopes on his coming to New Zealand to marry her, but on the journey Aron sees that Tessa is not Solveig and throws himself overboard. Aron's failure to arrive leads Tessa into madness. The diary section *Om Smekningar* (On Caresses) describes Sidner's own breakdown, caused by guilt,[57] grief and sexual frustration. Sidner later finds Tessa in New Zealand, where they both face the past and unite in love to face the future.

Throughout *Juloratoriet* music and love are parallel themes which bring light to the lives of hard-pressed individuals. Sidner's priest-friend links the two in his image of a lover dancing: 'Love is a positive action: it's giving life to another ... so that you see the soles of her feet dancing, even if it means they dance away from you ...' (284). *Juloratoriet* is also a novel about homecoming.[58] In the first chapter

Victor comes home to Sunne to conduct Bach's *Christmas Oratorio*, abandoned after Solveig's death. Now those remaining have worked through their grief and guilt and are ready for jubilation, the celebration of love and life through music. The last chapter continues the theme of homecoming. Sidner is on a visit from New Zealand, and as father and son get acquainted they share an experience: they pass Sidner's uncle Torin and his gold-toothed companion Härliga Birgitta, relaxed and naked. 'They need this loving space for themselves. Let it be enough that you know. That you and I know. Let it be enough that you have seen it, just once. That you know this can happen on earth' (329).

Such optimism is harder to find in the 'dark sister'[59] of *Juloratoriet*, *Tjuven* (The Thief, 1986). Tunström leaves Fanny Udde's elegant drawing-room for the slums of Torvnäs: 'Plates on the table, a greasy dish of fried pork and cold potatoes and a half-empty glass of pilsner were all waiting for her. The door to the slop-pail cupboard was open ...' (21)[60] Ida Pripp, daughter of the kindly local cobbler, falls for Fredrik Jonson Lök. Fredrik is a drunken lay-about but she hopes married bliss will change him. It does not and Ida is left to bring up their twelve children in squalor.

Tjuven is really the story of Fredrik's nephew Johan. The book starts as a third-person narrative but halfway through Johan, who is writing down this history whilst in prison, removes his mask and continues his tale in the first person. Johan's life changes when he meets retired school-master Hägern who shows him a letter telling of his ancestor's theft of the Gothic Silver Bible. Now housed in Uppsala it is the only known text of note in the Gothic language. Johan resolves to steal back the Book as a means of making a better life for himself and Hedvig, the cousin he loves. Hedvig has by now become mentally disturbed, a damaged being, who withdraws from Johan. In order to get access to the Silver Bible Johan reads Gothic at Uppsala where he makes a breakthrough discovery which leads him to Ravenna. With the help of a vegetable-growing priest Johan finds a secret Gothic manuscript by the Silver Bible's scribe Wiljarith. Like Johan, Wiljarith was obsessed with the Silver Bible. During the war-time siege of Ravenna, Wiljarith stole the purple dye, gold and silver he needed and, despite the shortage of food, made his parchment from young calves and aborted calf-foetuses. The final piece he used is the skin from his own dead wife. The betrayal of a beloved woman in pursuit of one's life's work is a theme common to the manuscript section and the main plot. Johan smuggles the manuscript into Sweden for which he is eventually sent to prison. First, however, comes academic success, a doctorate and the keys to the vault where the Silver Bible is kept. At last the Book could be his, but Johan is not the thief of the title: Wiljarith blamed the Silver Bible for stealing his life, forcing him to sacrifice his nearest and dearest; Johan sees how he himself has used the Book as an excuse not to help Hedvig. Tunström points to the myth of Orpheus: as Orpheus fails to rescue Eurydice from the Underworld, so Johan fails Hedvig as he hides behind his elaborate plans to steal the Book. He fails her and her retreat into mental breakdown is irreversible: on the last page of the novel Hedvig perishes in a fire she has started.

Despite the sombre and tragic theme of *Tjuven*, Tunström's delight in story-telling, in comedy and poetry are very much in evidence, with the captivating farces at wedding, christening and funeral and the colourful parade of minor characters. And a message of hope shines through: before Hedvig dies she gives birth to Johan's son, cared for by Ida who has found love with the so-called Grey Reminiscence. 'You're alive and have already smiled your first smile, Ida writes ... She writes that you bring such joy that it makes up for most of life's troubles.' (356) *Tjuven* is a warning against putting other considerations before human ones: the consequences are seen in Hedvig; the alternative is the new life, the child to whom Johan addresses his story. Thus by the 80s Tunström's writing had reached new heights in these elaborate yet unified volumes in which he has given full expression to his poetic talents and his humanitarianism.

After *Tjuven* Tunström left his literary Sunne and took a break from the novel.[61] In 1996 he returned with *Skimmer* (Shimmer, 1996). The central plot is imaginative, interwoven with comic and poignant stories, memories and episodes. The Icelandic setting may be unfamiliar to Tunström readers but he revisits many of the themes of his earlier authorship. In the story of Halldór and Pétur, Tunström continues to explore the relationship between father and son. Halldór — himself brought up by his father — is both mother and father to Pétur. Like other Tunström heroes before him Pétur makes a new life for himself in Paris, advancing in his career and falling in love. And as Pétur's life is moving forwards, Halldór's sun is setting. Once so full of life, loyalty and love he suffers a breakdown during a radio broadcast — reciting one of his own erotic poems during the fishing report — and later suffers a heart attack and a stroke. Like *Juloratoriet*, *Skimmer* is a novel about homecoming. Pétur is the first-person narrator of *Skimmer*, piecing together his family saga after his father's death. He revisits his home country and his family's past with a new perspective, a new perception. In the pathos of Tunström's story, father and son come to a degree of acceptance and of peace. And behind Pétur's voice is Tunström, doing what he does best: showing people as they are in the comedies and tragedies of human life, suffering, growing, yearning, loving, trusting, living, dying and making music.

Göran Tunström is amongst the very best of the writers associated with the 1980s, thanks to the unique blend of rich entertainment, poignant meditations, distinctive provincial flavour and particularly Swedish kind of magical realism[62] of his novels. Entertaining as his novels are, Tunström has a serious purpose:[63] in *Juloratoriet* Splendid suggests that Sidner should become a locksmith in order 't' open doors for folk who's locked theirselves out. There's a right many tha' doz ...' (63);[64] by means of his literary production Tunström is able to release those locked in.

Carina Burman (born 1960)

by Sarah Death

Carina Burman lives in Uppsala and has a dual career as a literary scholar and a successful writer of fiction. She has made an art of using the results of her academic research to recreate historical periods in her novels, with playful pastiche as her favoured technique.

Burman wrote her doctoral thesis in comparative literature on the eighteenth-century poet J. H. Kellgren: *Vältalaren J. H. Kellgren* (The Orator J. H. Kellgren, 1988). She made her debut in fiction with an imaginative retelling of Kellgren's adventures in love and literature: *Min salig bror Jean Hendrich* (My Dear Departed Brother Jean Hendrich, 1993). Realizing the impossibility of 'faking' (Burman's own word) Kellgren's own rhetorical style, she rejected the option of a first-person narrator in favour of viewing the poet through the eyes of other people, specifically his mistress, and his disapproving yet envious clergyman brother. As an expert on Kellgren's life and times, Burman found that gaps in factual biography are goldmines for the creative writer. The novel won critical acclaim for its evocation of the eighteenth century

Chapter X

and the bravura with which the pastiche is carried through. Carina Burman herself has described pastiche as 'stylistic bungee-jumping', in which her personal technique is to write initially in a neutral twentieth-century prose, stripped of contemporary references, and then launch herself into embellishment of the text with idioms, archaisms, French and Latin phrases, thus creating the 'feel' of older language.[65]

In 1996, after a decade or more of research, Burman published two volumes of previously uncollected (and in many cases, unknown) correspondence of the prolific nineteenth-century writer and early feminist Fredrika Bremer: *Fredrika Bremer. Brev. Ny följd* I-II, 1821-52, 1853-65 (1996).[66] These consist of over a thousand pages of letters and commentaries, and complement the four volumes published by two earlier women scholars, Klara Johanson and Ellen Kleman, between 1915 and 1920.

Collection of the Bremer letters took Carina Burman to numerous archives and several foreign countries, and publication of the letters was complicated by the fact that new ones continued to come to light. This experience provided her with inspiration for her next novel, *Den tionde sånggudinnan* (The Tenth Muse, 1996), which features a group of women researchers from the university town of Uppsala in the early years of the twentieth century, working at the same time and in the same adventurous spirit as Johanson and Kleman. They are not on the trail of the letters of Bremer, however, but those of the famous authoress of the baroque period, Sophia Elisabeth Brenner (1659-1730), called in her day 'the Swedish Sappho'. She was the mother of fifteen children, and the first Swedish woman to devote herself publicly to poetry. In Burman's novel, young Dr Elisabet Grahn (one of few women in the predominantly male academic world of that time) makes a Faustian wager with her professor: if she can collect enough original material for an edition of Brenner's letters, her academic future will be assured; otherwise she is likely to face an anonymous future as a small-town schoolmistress.

The subsequent plot is a marriage of detective fiction and literary history. Elisabet's quest takes her, with her friends and collaborators Choice and Thea, to a Swedish manor house and on to Denmark, Germany and Italy, where they seek entry to the shadowy Secret Archive of the Vatican Library — where Burman also went in search of material. They witness the outbreak of the Great War in Berlin, and the heat of the Russian Revolution in St Petersburg in the winter of 1917.

In Brenner's letters and other manuscripts the researchers find tantalising traces of a long-forgotten association of women or muses, with its roots in ancient Greece, and members including the Mexican poetess Sor Juana de la Cruz and Queen Christina of Sweden. That circle of women debated the merits of chastity, but men lend an important dimension to Elisabet's life: her relationships with her professor, the young student Månson (the novel is full of imagery of the moon and stars) and a Russian prince she keeps meeting on her travels are fruitful sources of narrative tension. Thea, however, sees herself as a rational New Woman and views such diversions with contempt.

The novel's structure permits the author to shift between modern prose and pastiches of period letters, in both the baroque style and the cultivated academic jargon of the years around 1910. The book's stylistic versatility was one of the features which won it critical praise, and it has now been translated into German and Polish; Burman relishes active cooperation with her translators.

Carina Burman spent the academic year 1996-97 as a Visiting Fellow at Clare Hall, University of Cambridge. She continues her dual career, currently working on the period 1730-1809 for a new history of Finland-Swedish literature, and nearing completion of her third novel.

Jonas Gardell (born 1963)

by Neil Smith

Since making his literary debut in 1985 with the novel *Passionsspelet* (The Passion Play), Jonas Gardell has become not only one of Sweden's most respected and successful writers, but also one its most popular media personalities. He has worked within a bewildering variety of cultural forms, as author, playwright, essayist, chat-show host, artist, librettist, and most notably as a stand-up performer and comedian, but, in contrast to many of the multi-media performers in the English-speaking world, it was as a writer that he first made his name.

Gardell was born in 1963, and grew up in a middle-class home in the northern suburbs of Stockholm. His experience of childhood is reflected in the semi-autobiographical Bildungsroman *En komikers uppväxt* (Growing up a Comedian, 1992), in which the sense of loss that pervades much of his work is most closely identifiable with Gardell himself. The novel depicts the loss of childhood innocence by Juha, the twelve-year-old protagonist, as he learns to conceal his feelings of inadequacy behind a mask of humour. The adult Juha, now a professional comedian, periodically interrupts the narrative to emphasize the child's development, and in particular his use of humour as a defence against his isolation: 'Humour is an invocation against sorrow. When I tell jokes about childhood we laugh, relieved, because in spite of everything, we survived. As long as we keep laughing we haven't been defeated'(47).[67] The novel can also be read as a nostalgic record of a lost world, with its evocative descriptions of the minutiae of 1970s pop-culture seen from a child's perspective. The changes in Swedish society over recent decades, in particular the erosion of social cohesion and the trivialization of individual tragedy in a media-driven world, form a recurrent theme in Gardell's work.

As might be expected from someone who has often joked about his popular image as 'Sweden's national queen', there is a strong gay theme in much of his writing, most noticeable in his early work: taking homophobia and problems of sexual identity as his starting point, Gardell has progressed to highlight other instances of social exclusion in his work. The critically acclaimed *Passionsspelet* tells the story of a young man's first homosexual affair, and parallels his betrayal by his lover with that of Jesus by Judas, the roles they are enacting in the play of the title. After the less well-received *Odjurets tid* (The Time of the Beast, 1986), which depicted the tragic effects of one harsh Stockholm winter on four characters (two of them gay), Gardell's breakthrough in terms of public awareness and mass sales came in 1987 with *Präriehundarna* (The Prairie Dogs).

Set mainly in Stockholm, like all Gardell's novels, *Präriehundarna* was described by one reviewer as 'a novel which succeeds in filling the much discussed vacuum of life in the 1980s'.[68] It introduces a group of characters who are the human equivalents of the rodents of the title: cuddly, cute, yet 'cannibalistic'. Lena and Percy live in a loveless marriage, casually inflicting damage on each other in bitter resignation at their unfulfilled dreams. Reine, their teenage son, embarks on a homosexual affair, which comes to a tragic, rather melodramatic conclusion when his lover is killed in a road accident. Told in the extremely short chapters that are characteristic of Gardell's writing, the narrative is often highly amusing, the humour arising largely from the characters' inability to communicate their emotions because they cannot rid themselves of the detritus of consumer society: Lena, for example, seems able to express herself only by selecting the appropriate Abba song, both vocally and in stream of consciousness reflections of her thoughts. A philosophical note is provided by short lyrical passages ascribed to a melancholic figure identified as 'the accuser', who stands beyond the narrative like Eliot's Tiresias in *The Waste Land*, providing an indication of the darker perspective of Gardell's more recent work.

In 1990 Gardell published *Fru Björks öden och äventyr* (The Wonderful Adventures of Mrs Björk), an avenger's tragedy in which Vivian Björk escapes the mundanity of her life by fleeing to Rome. Her dream of *la dolce vita* proves to be an illusion, though, and she returns to Stockholm to take revenge on the men she has allowed to cheat her — principally the first husband who left her for a younger woman. The black humour and subject matter of the novel led to comparisons with Fay Weldon's *The Life and Loves of a She-Devil*, although Gardell's treatment of the subject is ultimately darker and more tragic in tone: the novel closes with Vivian's suicide.

Frestelsernas berg (The Mountain of Temptation, 1995) also focuses upon the tragedy of a woman who has lost control of her life. Maria is a seventy-year-old living out her life in a small caretaker's apartment surrounded by cardboard boxes containing the remnants of her earlier betrayals and disappointments. Her son, Johan (a gay character, although here this is almost incidental), in attempting to come to terms with the losses that characterized his childhood, ends up piecing together his mother's past. Partly as a result of her own frustrated passivity, Maria has lost her husband, her home, her eldest son and her childhood home, but she has a quite different memory of events (a device reminiscent of Hjalmar Bergman's *Farmor och Vår Herre*), and cannot accept the story of a woman complicit in her own suffering that Johan has uncovered. Gardell draws explicit parallels with the suffering of Job, as the catalogue of Maria's countless losses and disappointments adds up — to a point where she and they have become inextricable. Unlike Vivian Björk, Maria has no means of regaining control of her life. Her situation is compared with that of the monks living on the mountain outside Jericho where Jesus was tempted: they are both living (in one case quite literally) 'on the edge'. Although the novel has elements of the comedy that was so much a part of Gardell's earlier work, it is dominated by a darker, more reflective tone.

The Biblical allusions that abound in *Frestelsernas berg*, and which

Chapter X

are present in all of Gardell's novels to a greater or lesser extent, also colour his theatrical work, particularly his 1997 black comedy *Människor i solen* (People in the Sun), in which the mysterious character Fru Sörensson repeatedly backs up her preparedness for the Second Coming with Biblical quotations. This, and the earlier plays *Isbjörnarna* (The Polar Bears, 1990) and *Cheek to Cheek* (1992), deal with themes familiar from Gardell's novels: the problems caused by a lack of communication and self-delusion, and the alienation that Gardell sees as inherent in modern society. The most mundane incidents and trivial remarks become signifiers of intense irony in Gardell's work, simultaneously revealing the tragedy and the humour of the human condition.

Notes and Bibliographies

Select General Bibliography
Standard works on modern Swedish literature.

Algulin, I., *Contemporary Swedish Prose*. Stockholm, 1983.
Algulin, I., *A History of Swedish Literature*. Stockholm, 1989.
Ardelius, L. & Rydström, G. (eds), *Författarnas litteraturhistoria*. 3 vols, Stockholm, 1977-78. (Vols 2 & 3 cover Swedish writers from mid-19th century to the present day).
Alving, Hj. & Hasselberg, G., *Svensk litteraturhistoria*. Stockholm, 1965.
Ahnlund, K., *Diktarliv i Norden. Litterära essäer*. Stockholm, 1981. (Includes Strindberg, Sven Lidman and Harry Martinson).
Björck, S., Sallnäs, H. & Palmqvist, B., *Litteraturhistoria i fickformat. Svensk diktning från 80-tal till 70-tal*. Stockholm, 1975.
Brandell, G., *Svensk litteratur 1900-1950*. Stockholm, 1967.
Brandell, G. & Stenkvist, J., *Svensk litteratur 1870-1970*. 3 vols. Vol. I *1870 till 1:sta världskriget;*. Vol.II *Från 1:sta världskriget till 1950*; Vol.III *Den nyaste litteraturen*. (Vol.III contains bibliography by H. Attius).
Bredsdorff, E., Mortensen, B., & Popperwell, R. G., *An Introduction to Scandinavian Literature*. Cambridge, 1951. (repr. 1970).
Brostrøm, T., *Modern svensk litteratur 1940-1972*. Stockholm, 1974.
Death, S. & Forsås-Scott, H. eds., *A Century of Swedish Narrative: Essays in Honour of Karin Petherick*. Norwich, 1994.
Florin, M., Steinsaphir, M. & Sörenson, M., *Literature in Sweden*. Stockholm, 1997. (A brief survey of contemporary Swedish prose, poetry and drama).
Forsås-Scott, H., *Swedish Women's Writing 1850-1995*. London, 1997. (Women in Context Series, 4).
Gustafson, A., *A History of Swedish Literature*. Minneapolis, 1961. (Contains comprehensive list of English translations).
Henriques, A., *Svensk litteratur efter 1900*. Stockholm, 1951.
Hägg, G., *Den svenska litteraturhistorien*. Stockholm, 1996.
Linder, E. Hj., *Fem decennier av 1900-talet*. 2 vols. Stockholm, 1965-66. (Comprises vol. 5 of *Ny illustrerad svensk litteraturhistoria*.)
Lönnroth, L. et al., *Den svenska litteraturen*. 7 vols. Stockholm, 1987-1990 (Vols III onwards cover literature from mid-19th century to present day).

Mazzarella, M., *Från Fredrika Runeberg till Märta Tikkanen. Frihet och beroende i Finlandsvensk kvinnolitteratur.* Helsinki, 1985.

Møller Jensen, E. (ed.-in-chief) & Witt-Brattström, E. (Swedish ed.), *Nordisk kvinnolitteratur.* 4 vols. Höganäs, 1993-97. (Vols II-IV cover 19th century to present day.)

Olsson, B., & Algulin, I., *Litteraturens historia i Sverige.* Stockholm. 4th ed., Stockholm, 1995.

Ramnefalk, M. L. & Westberg, A. (eds), *Kvinnornas litteratur.* 2 vols. Lund, 1981-83.

Rossel, S. H., *A History of Scandinavian Literature 1870-1980.* Minneapolis, 1982.

Schück, H. & Warburg, K., *Ilustrerad svensk litteraturhistoria.* 8 vols. Stockholm, 1926-1949.

Svenskt litteraturlexikon. Lund, 1970.

Tigerstedt, E. N., *Svensk litteraturhistoria.* Stockholm, 1969.

Tigerstedt, E. N. (ed.), *Ny illustrerad svensk litteraturhistoria.* 5 vols. Stockholm, 1955-66.

Zuck, V. (ed.), *Dictionary of Scandinavian Literature.* New York, Westport and London, 1990.

CHAPTER 1 *Åttitalister (Writers of the 1880s)*

1. Schück & Warburg, *Illustrerad svensk litteraturhistoria*, vol. VII, p. 155.
2. Brandell, G., *Svensk litteratur 1870-1970*, vol. I, p. 125.
3. *Nordisk kvinnolitteraturhistoria*, 2, p. 513. (See General bibliography).
4. Sylvan, M., *Anne Charlotte Leffler*, p.170.
5. Ahlström, G., *Det moderna genombrottet*, p. 287.

SELECT BIBLIOGRAPHY

General

Ahlström, G., *Det moderna genombrottet i Nordens litteratur.* 2nd rev. ed. Stockholm, 1974.

Brandell, G., *Vid seklets källor.* Stockholm, 1961.

Bredsdorff, E., *Den store nordiske krig om seksualmoralen.* Copenhagen, 1973.

Dahlerup, P., *Det moderne gennembruds kvinder* I-II. Copenhagen, 1984.

Forsås-Scott, H., *Swedish Women's Writing 1850-1995.* London, 1997.

Furst, L. R. & Skrine, P. N., *Naturalism* (in the series The Critical Idiom). London, 1971.

Lundevall, K.-E., *Från åttital till nittital. Om åttitalslitteratur och Heidenstams debut och program.* Stockholm, 1953.

Mortensen, J., *Från Röda rummet till sekelskiftet* I-II. Stockholm, 1918-19.

Nolin, B. & Forsgren, P. (eds), *The Modern Breakthrough in Scandinavian Literature 1870-1905.* Gothenburg, 1988.

Nordisk kvinnolitteratur (ed. E. Møller Jensen), vol. II *Fadershuset, 1800-talet.* Höganäs, 1993.

Stenström, T., *Den ensamme. En motivstudie i det moderna genombrottets litteratur.* Stockholm, 1961.

Tjäder, P. A., *Det unga Sverige. Åttitalsrörelse och genombrottsepok.* Lund, 1982.

Individual authors
(See Chapter 2 for a comprehensive Strindberg bibliography.)

Ahlenius, H., *Georg Brandes i svensk litteratur till och med 1890.* Stockholm, 1932.

Ahlenius, H., *Tor Hedberg.* Stockholm, 1935.

Ahlström, G., *Georg Brandes' Hovedstrømninger.* Lund, 1937.

Ahlström, S., *Ola Hansson.* Stockholm, 1958.

Benedictsson, Victoria (ed. C. Sjöblad), *Stora boken* I-III. Lund, 1978-1985.(Frequent references to Axel Lundegård).

Boëthius, U., *Strindberg och kvinnofrågan till och med Giftas I.* Stockholm, 1969.

Böök, F., *Victoria Benedictsson.* Stockholm, 1950.

Hertel, H. & Møller Kristensen, S. (eds), *The Activist Critic. A symposium on the political ideas, literary methods and international reception of Georg Brandes.* Copenhagen, 1980.

Holm, I., *Ola Hansson. En studie i åttiotalsromantik.* Lund, 1957.

Johnsson, M., *En åttitalist. Gustaf af Geijerstam 1858-1895.* Gothenburg, 1934.

Jørgensen, C., *Ernst og Victoria: Et dobbeltportræt af Victoria Benedictsson.* Copenhagen, 1995.

Knudsen, J., *Georg Brandes: Symbolet og manden 1883-1895* I-II. Copenhagen, 1994.

Linder, S., *Ibsen, Strindberg och andra.* Stockholm, 1936.

Linder, S., *Ernst Ahlgren i hennes romaner — ett bidrag till det litterära åttitalets karakeristik.* Stockholm, 1930.

Lundbo Levy, J., *Den dubbla blicken. Om att beskriva kvinnor: ideologi och estetik i Victoria Benedictssons författarskap.* Stockholm, 1982.

Møller Kristensen, S., *Georg Brandes. Kritikeren, liberalisten, humanisten.* Copenhagen, 1980.

Nolin, B., *Georg Brandes.* (Twayne's World Authors series). New York, 1976.

Nordin Hennel, I., *Dömd och glömd. En studie i Alfhild Agrells liv och dikt.* Umeå, 1981.

Rosengren, K.-E., *Victoria Benedictsson.* Stockholm, 1965.

Sandström, T., *En psykoanalytisk kvinnostudie — Ernst Ahlgren — Victoria Benedictsson*. Stockholm, 1935.

Schultén, I. af, *Ernst Ahlgren. En litterär studie*. Helsinki, 1925.

Sylvan, M., *Anne Charlotte Leffler. En kvinna finner sin väg*. Stockholm, 1984.

Enquist, P.O., Gustaf af Geijerstam. Författaren anträder återtåget in *Författarnas litteraturhistoria* 2, (eds L. Ardelius & G. Rydström), Stockholm, 1978, pp. 148-156.

Thompson, B., 'Victoria Benedictssons novell *Den bergtagna*'. *Fenix* X (1993) Nos 3-4, pp. 6-107.

Werkmäster, B., I livet. Om Anne Charlotte Leffler och Alfhild Agrell in *Författarnas litteraturhistoria* 2, (eds L. Ardelius & G. Rydström), Stockholm, 1978, pp. 109-120.

CHAPTER 2 August Strindberg

1. The first collected edition, *Samlade skrifter av August Strindberg*, ed. John Landquist, 55 vols. (Stockholm, 1912-1920), is now being superseded by *August Strindbergs Samlade Verk: Nationalupplaga*, general ed. Lars Dahlbäck (Stockholm, in progress). References in my text are, if in Roman numerals, to *Samlade skrifter*; if in Arabic numerals, to published volumes of the *Nationalupplaga*. Translations from the Swedish are my own, except in the case of Strindberg's letters, which are quoted from *Strindberg's Letters*, selected, ed. and trans. by Michael Robinson, 2 vols. (London and Chicago, 1992), referred to in my text as *Letters*.
2. Robert Brustein, *The Theater of Revolt: An Approach to the Modern Drama* (London, 1965), p.99.
3. T. S. Eliot, 'Tradition and the Individual Talent' (1919), in *Selected Essays*, new ed. (New York, 1950), p.7.
4. Quoted in Martin Lamm, *August Strindberg*, 2nd rev. ed. (Stockholm, 1948), p. 270. Cf. also Strindberg's letter to his German translator, Emil Schering, 2 April 1907 (*Letters* II, 757).
5. See the pamphlet on *Hamlet*, published as a '*Minnesblad*' on the first anniversary of the opening of the Intimate Theatre, on 26 November 1908, which reprints a number of the Shakespeare essays from *En blå bok* (notably 'Characterization' (*Karaktärsteckning*), 'Shakespeare's World View' (*Shakespeares världsåskådning*) and 'King Lear's Wife' (*Kung Lears hustru*), as well as providing a scene-by-scene analysis of *Hamlet*. The 1909 pamphlet's title, *Shakespeares 'Macbeth', 'Othello', 'Romeo och Julia', 'Stormen', 'Kung Lear', 'Henrik VIII' och 'En midsommarnattsdröm'*, speaks for itself; but the essay on *A Midsummer Night's Dream* has particularly interesting comments on that play's structure.
6. Though Strindberg, in common with a whole generation of Scandinavians,

was to be deeply affected by Brandes's *Hovedstrømninger*, especially the first part, *Emigrantlitteraturen*, which he read in 1872, the Brandes work which he is here commenting on is *Kritiker og Portraiter*, 2 vols. (Copenhagen, 1870). It was the analysis of Shakespeare's *Henry IV* in the essay called 'Det uendeligt Smaa og det uendeligt Store i Poesin' (II, 279-297) which particularly impressed Strindberg.

7. T. S. Eliot, essay on 'John Ford' (1932), in *Selected Essays*, p.179.
8. Martin Lamm, *August Strindberg*, passim.
9. Quoted in Lamm, *August Strindberg*, p. 281. (The letter was never sent).
10. There are different English translations of Strindberg's ambiguous title; I prefer Evert Sprinchorn's. His translation (London, 1961) is based on Ellie Schleussner's version, *The Confession of a Fool* (London, 1915). There is also A. Swerling's *A Madman's Manifesto* (Cambridge, 1968).
11. Frederick J. Marker and Lise-Lone Marker, *The Scandinavian Theatre, A Short History* (Oxford, 1975), p.188.
12. See August Falck, *Fem år med Strindberg* (Stockholm, 1935); and G. M. Bergman, 'Strindberg and the Intima Teatern' *Theatre Research* IX (1967), 14-47. See also the present writer's section on 'Scandinavia 1849-1912' in Claude Schumacher, ed., *Naturalism and Symbolism in European Theatre 1850-1918* (Cambridge, 1996), especially pp. 311-15.
13. Strindberg's characteristically accurate use of scientific terminology may need expounding: the verb 'polymerize' brings in an analogy from either chemistry or biology and means 'to render multiform' or 'to pass through successive variations'.
14. In Chapter 10 of *Författaren* (The Author) Strindberg, without referring to the idea of generally exploring 'the concept of character', also speaks of *'sin själs uppkomst- och utvecklingshistoria'*. In the context, as often in Strindberg (cf. the *Vivisections* essay 'Om själamord'), *själ* seems to me best translated by the English word 'mind', or 'consciousness' (cf. Rousseau's use of *'l'âme'*), rather than 'soul'. Often he uses *själ* as the equivalent of 'self'.
15. I am referring to Strindberg's *theoretical* rejection, in the first half of the 1880s, both of fiction (*konstruktionslitteratur*: see, e.g. XVIII, 457) and of imaginative language, metaphors, etc. The story 'Above the Clouds', one of the four published in 1884 as *Utopier i verkligheten* (Utopias in Reality) has two moribund poets, patients at an Alpine sanatorium (an early Magic Mountain), discuss poetry and agree in condemning it for coming between the individual and his experience of reality. Poetry 'lulls our faculties into a kind of semi-paralysis where reality and dreams are intermingled' (XV, 169-170); in the future people won't be playing with thoughts and words; they will silently contemplate the real thing (170). Even in this story there is an ironic contrast, however unintentional, between the point made and the inventiveness and eloquence with which it is made. In *practice,* fortunately,

Strindberg's urge to write - to invent fictions and 'play' with language - got the better of his theoretical position.
16. Lionel Trilling, in *Sincerity and Authenticity* (London, 1972), pp. 58 ff., has a brilliant discussion of Rousseau and sincerity.
17. Trilling, *op.cit.* pp. 59ff., maintains that Rousseau's description of himself as *une âme dechirée* corresponds to Hegel's analysis of *der sich entfremdete Geist* (in *Phänomenologie des Geistes*); and that the 'disintegrated consciousness' is the equivalent of both. My point is that Strindberg was uniquely able to prove the disintegration on his own pulse, and on the reader's, or audience's.
18. I am referring to Frank Kermode's seminal study of the theory of fiction, *The Sense of an Ending* (London, 1970).
19. See, for example, in Chapter V, the section called 'Research': 'There was no conceivable trick or absurdity it would not have pleased nature to commit by way of variation upon this fixed procedure (i.e. of conception). In some animals, the male was a parasite in the intestine of the female. In others, the male parent reached with his arm down the gullet of the female to deposit the semen within her; after which, bitten off and spat out, it ran away by itself upon its fingers, to the confusion of scientists who for long had given it Greek and Latin names as an independent form of life'. (*The Magic Mountain*, translated by H. T. Lowe-Porter, Penguin Books, 1960, pp. 278-9).
20. Gunnar Ollén, *Strindbergs dramatik* (4th rev. ed., Stockholm, 1982), p. 245.
21. Egil Törnqvist has a useful detailed analysis of the structure of *Till Damaskus* I: 'Strindberg and the drama of half-reality' in *Strindberg and Modern Theatre* (Stockholm, Strindbergsällskapet, 1975), pp. 119-150. The Eliot reference is mine.
22. Quoted from F. J. and L. L. Marker, *The Scandinavian Theatre*, p.193.
23. Karl-Åke Kärnell, *Strindbergs bildspråk. En studie i prosastil* (Stockholm, 1962), p. 19.
24. Quoted from William K. Wimsatt Jr. and Cleanth Brooks, *Modern Criticism* (vol. 4 of *Literary Criticism. A Short History*; paperback ed., London, 1970), p. 591. Wimsatt and Brooks also point to Baudelaire's indebtedness to Swedenborg.

SELECT BIBLIOGRAPHY

An exhaustive Strindberg bibliography would be extremely long and far beyond the scope of this book. Further information will be found in A. Gustafson's *A History of Swedish Literature* (Minneapolis, 1961) and in G. Lindström's 'Strindberg Studies 1915-1962' in *Scandinavica* 1963. *Strindbergssällskapets* (The Strindberg Society's) *Meddelanden*, which carry reviews of books on

Strindberg, have been appearing since 1945. See also Jan Stenkvist's *Den nyaste litteraturen*, Vol. 3 of *Svensk litteratur 1870-1970* ed. G. Brandell (Stockholm, 1975), pp. 248-251, and S. H. Rossel's *A History of Scandinavian Literature 1870-1980* (Minneapolis, 1982), pp. 444-447.

Primary Sources (place of publication Stockholm unless otherwise stated). John Landquist's *Strindbergs Samlade Skrifter* in 55 vols, supplemented by V. Carlheim-Gyllensköld's *Strindbergs Samlade otryckta skrifter* I & II (1918-1919). *August Strindbergs Samlade Verk. Nationalupplaga* (in progress. See Note 1 above). G. Brandell's *Skrifter av August Strindberg* (1945-46) in 12 vols is a selection based on the Landquist ed.

C. R. Smedmark's scholarly *Kommentarer till August Strindbergs dramer* 1 - 4 (Stockholm, 1962-70) was planned to cover the major plays but only 4 vols appeared.

En dåres försvarstal (Le plaidoyer d'un fou) (1976) transl. from the original French by H. Levander.

Klostret (1966) ed. C. G. Bjurström, a novel previously unpublished in its entirety.

Ockulta dagboken (1977). Facsimile with appendix by Harry Järv. Strindberg had insisted that his 'diary' covering the period 1896-1908 should remain unpublished.

August Strindbergs brev I - (1947 -), ed. (vols I — XV) Torsten Eklund and (vols XVI —) Björn Meidal. Exemplary annotated edition, still in progress.

Secondary Sources
Biographical
Several books appeared shortly after Strindberg's death in 1912 by people with personal memories of him: Fanny Falkner, *Strindberg i Blå tornet* (1921); B. Mörner, *Den Strindberg jag känt* (1924); Karin Smirnoff, *Strindbergs första hustru* (1925) where Strindberg's daughter puts forward her mother's point of view; she tries again to put the record straight in *Så var det i verkligheten* (1956); Anna von Philp & Nora Hartzell, *Strindbergs systrar berätta om bror August* (1926); J. Mortensen, *Strindberg som jag minnes honom* (1931); Frida Uhl, *Strindberg och hans andra hustru* I & II (1933-34); *Marriage with a Genius* (London, 1937); A. Falck, *Fem år med Strindberg* (1935); J. Landquist, *Som jag minns dem* (1949); and *John Landquist om Strindberg personen och diktaren* (ed. and commentary by Solveig Landquist, 1984); S. Ahlström and T. Eklund have included extracts from several of the above in *Ögonvittnen om August Strindberg* I & II (1956-61). Other works covering different aspects of Strindberg's life include E. Hedén, *Strindberg. En ledtråd vid studiet av hans verk* (1926); A. Herrlin, *Från sekelskiftets Lund* (1936); H. Jacobsen, *Digteren og Fantasten* (Copenhagen, 1945); ibid, *Strindberg og hans første hustru*

(Copenhagen, 1946); ibid, *Strindberg i firsernes København* (Copenhagen, 1948); G. Brandell, *Strindbergs Infernokris* (1950. *Strindberg in Inferno*, Cambridge, Mass., 1970); A. Hagsten, *Den unge Strindberg* (1951); D. Norrman, *Strindbergs skilsmässa från Siri von Essen* (1953); N. Norrman, *Den unge Strindberg och väckelserörelsen* (1953); S. Ahlström, *Strindbergs erövring av Paris* (1956); S. A. Edqvist, *Samhällets fiende. En studie i Strindbergs anarkism t.o.m. Tjänstekvinnans son.* (1961); H. Järv, *Strindbergsfejden. 465 debattinlägg och kommentarer.* I & II (1968); U. Boethius, *Strindberg och kvinnofrågan t.o.m. Giftas* I (Halmstad, 1969); G. Stockenström, *Ismael i öknen. Strindberg som mystiker* (1972); H. G. Carlson, *Strindberg och myterna* (1979. *Strindberg and the Poetry of Myth*, Berkeley, 1982). Martin Lamm's study *August Strindberg* appeared in 1940-42 (trans. *August Strindberg*, New York, 1971). Subsequent monographs include B. Mortensen & B. W. Downs, *Strindberg. An Introduction to his Life and Works* (Cambridge, 1948; repr. 1965); E. Sprigge, *The Strange Life of August Strindberg* (London, 1949; repr. 1972); O. Lagercrantz, *August Strindberg* (1973, transl. London, 1984); W. Johnson, *August Strindberg* (Boston, 1976); B. Steene, *August Strindberg: an Introduction to his Major Works* (Carbondale, 1982); G. Brandell, *August Strindberg: ett författarliv.* 4 vols (Stockholm, 1983-89); M. Meyer, *August Strindberg. A Biography.* (London, 1985); M. Robinson, *Strindberg and Autobiography* (Norwich, 1986).

Drama

Martin Lamm's seminal work *Strindbergsdramer* I & II (1924-25); A. Jolivet, *Le théâtre de Strindberg* (Paris, 1931); J. Bulman, *Strindberg and Shakespeare* (London, 1933); C. E. W. Dahström, *Strindberg's Dramatic Expressionism* (Ann Arbor, 1930; 2nd ed. 1965); V. Børge, *Strindbergs mystiske Teater* (Copenhagen, 1942), G. Ollén, *Strindbergs dramatik* (1948, 4th rev ed. 1982. English version via German, New York, 1974); C. R. Smedmark, *Mäster Olof och Röda rummet* (1952); B. G. Madsen, *Strindberg's Naturalistic Theatre. Its relation to French Naturalism* (Seattle, 1963; repr. New York, 1973); W. Johnson, *Strindberg and the Historical Drama* (Seattle, 1963); L. Josephson, *Strindbergs drama Fröken Julie* (1965); C. R. Smedmark (ed.), *Essays on Strindberg* (1966), including *inter al.* R. Williams's 'Strindberg and Modern Tragedy', B. Rothwell's 'The Chamber Plays' and J. R. Northam's 'Strindberg's Spook Sonata'; O. Reinert (ed.), *Strindberg. A Collection of Critical Essays* (Englewood Cliffs, 1971). Included are R. Brustein's 'August Strindberg' and E. Sprinchorn's 'The Logic of A Dream Play'; U.-B. Lagerroth and G. Lindström (eds), *Perspektiv på Fröken Julie* (1972); *Strindberg and Modern Theatre* (The Strindberg Society, 1975. Papers read at the 1973 Strindberg Symposium); E. Sprinchorn, *Strindberg as Dramatist* (New Haven, 1982); E. Törnqvist, *Strindbergian drama: themes and structure* (1982); E. Törnqvist & B. Jacobs, *Strindberg's 'Miss Julie': A Play and its Transpositions*

(Norwich, 1988); M. Wirmark, *Den kluvna scenen: kvinnor i Strindbergs dramatik* (Värnamo, 1988); M. Robinson (ed.), *Strindberg and Genre* (Norwich, 1991); B. Steene (ed.), *Strindberg and History* (1992); H.-G. Ekman, *Villornas värld: Studier i Strindbergs kammarspel* (Uppsala, 1997).

Prose Works

G. Lindblad, *Strindberg som berättare* (1924); C. R. Smedmark, *Mäster Olof och Röda rummet* (1952); K.-Å. Kärnell, *Strindbergs bildspråk. En studie i prosastil* (1962); E. O. Johannesson, *The Novels of August Strindberg. A Study in Theme and Structure* (Berkeley, 1968); E. & U.-B. Lagerroth (eds), *Perspektiv på Röda rummet* (1971); L. Dahlbäck, *Strindbergs Hemsöborna* (1974); C. Fisher, *August Strindberg: Hemsöborna* (Studies in Swedish Literature 14. Hull, 1982); B. Ståhle Sjönell, *Strindbergs 'Taklagsöl' — ett prosaexperiment* (1986).

Poetry

G. Ollén, *Strindbergs 1900-talslyrik* (1941); J. E. Bellqvist, *Strindberg as a Modern Poet: A Critical and Comparative Study* (Berkeley, 1986); M. Robinson (ed.), *Strindberg and Genre* (Norwich, 1991).

Strindberg's psychology has been studied, sometimes by writers with no other sources than his autobiographies in translation as, for instance, K. Jasper's *Strindberg und Van Gogh* (Berlin, 1922, trans, *Strindberg and Van Gogh*, Tucson, 1977). More medically sound is H. Hedenberg's *Strindberg i skärselden* (1961). Two good literary psychological studies, T. Eklund: *Tjänstekvinnans son: en psykologisk Strindbergsstudie* (1948) and H. Lindström, *Hjärnornas kamp* (1952).

Influences

S. Linder, *Ibsen, Strindberg och andra litteraturhistoriska essäer* (1936); H. Borland, *Nietzsche's Influence on Swedish Literature, with special reference to Strindberg, Ola Hansson, Heidenstam and Fröding* (Gothenburg, 1956); A. Swerling, *Strindberg's Impact in France 1920-1960* (Cambridge, 1970); M. J. Blackwell (ed.), *Structures of Influence. A Comparative Approach to August Strindberg. Festschrift to Walter Johnson.* (Chapel Hill, 1981). (B. Steene's contribution, 'August Strindberg in America, 1963-1979: A Bibliographical Assessment' is very useful.); I.-S. Ewbank, 'Shakespeare and Strindberg: Influence as Insemination' in J. Batchelor, T. Cain & C. Lamont (eds), *Shakespearean Continuities* (London, 1997).

Fine Arts

V. Hellström, *Strindberg och musiken* (1917); G. Söderström, *August Strindberg och bildkonsten* (1972); M. Schmidt (ed.), *Strindbergs måleri* (1972).

Notes and Bibliographies

Note also K.-Å. Kärnell's *Strindbergslexikon. Figurer, titlar, bevingade ord m.m. i Strindbergs verk* (1972); M. Robinson, *Strindberg and Genre* (Norwich, 1991).

CHAPTER 3 *Nittitalister (Writers of the 1890s)*

1. *Pepitas bröllop.* En litteraturanmälan tills. med O. Levertin, 1890, p. 10.
2. Gustaf Fröding, *Samlade dikter,* Stockholm: Wahlström & Widstrand, 1984. All page references are to this edition.
3. Verner von Heidenstam, *Samlade dikter,* Stockholm: Wahlström & Widstrand, 1985. This is the edition used throughout my essay for all quotations from Heidenstam's works.
4. Quotations from Selma Lagerlöf's works are all taken from *Skrifter av Selma Lagerlöf,* Stockholm: Bonniers, 1964.
5. Levertin in a letter to Verner von Heidenstam quoted by Alrik Gustafson in *Six Scandinavian Novelists,* p. 186.
6. Harry Martinson in his poem 'Vildgåsresan' (The Voyage of the Wild Goose) from Vivi Edström's 'En gång om våren', *Allt om böcker,* p. 20.
7. Vivi Edström, *ibid.* p. 20.
8. Maja Petré, *Selma Lagerlöf and her home at Mårbacka,* p. 37; quotation from Algot Werin on Downie.
9. The letters to Sophie Elkan (*Du lär mig att bli fri. Selma Lagerlöf skriver till Sophie Elkan,* Stockholm, 1992) and Lagerlöf's diary are of special interest in ascertaining what lay hidden behind a mask of reluctance. What is very obvious is the duality: the public image of Selma Lagerlöf and the private, fragile one.
10. Erik Axel Karlfeldt, *Samlade dikter,* Stockholm: Wahlström & Widstrand, 1981. This is the edition used throughout my essay for all quotations from Karlfeldt's poems.
11. Gunnar Brandell, *Svensk litteratur 1870-1970,* p. 245.
12. For an analysis of the theme of love see Hildeman, *En löskerkarl.*
13. From Karlfeldt's *Tankar och tal* (Thoughts and Speeches) p. 29.
14. For a more extensive treatment of Karlfeldt's belief see Hildeman, *Sub luna,* pp. 87-113.

SELECT BIBLIOGRAPHY

Björck, Staffan, *Lyriska läsövningar.* Lund, 1961.
Brandell, Gunnar, Verner von Heidenstam; Fröding och Karlfeldt; Nittiotalets berättare in *Ny illustrerad svensk litteraturhistoria* IV, Stockholm, 1957, pp. 258-354.

Brandell, Gunnar, Nittiotalets berättare in *Svensk litteratur 1870-1970*. Stockholm, 1974, pp. 257-283.
Geijerstam, C. E. af *et al.* (eds), *Lyrisk tidsspegel*. Lund, 1956.
Platen, M. von (ed.), *Svenska diktanalyser*. Stockholm, 1965.

Bibliography
Annual bibliographies in *Samlaren*.
Svensk litteraturhistorisk bibliografi1900-1935. Stockholm, 1939-50.

Verner von Heidenstam

Primary material
Verner von Heidenstam, *Samlade verk* 1-23 (eds K. Bang & F. Böök). Stockholm, 1943-44.

Critical works
Axberger, Gunnar, *Diktaren och elden. En Heidenstamstudie*. Stockholm, 1959.
Björck, Staffan, *Heidenstam och sekelskiftets Sverige*. Stockholm, 1946.
Böök, Fredrik, *Verner von Heidenstam*. Stockholm, 1945-1946. 2 vols.
Mårbacka och Övralid. Minnen av Selma Lagerlöf och Verner von Heidenstam av 40 författare (ed. Sven Thulin), Uppsala, 1940.
Stenkvist, Jan, *Nationalskalden. Heidenstam och politiken från och med 1909*. Stockholm, 1982.
Svanberg, Victor, *Diktaren i samhället. Litteratursociologiska studier*. Stockholm, 1968.

Holmberg, Olle, Folke Filbyter in *Lovtal över svenska romaner*. Stockholm 1957.
Lagerroth, Erland, Karolinerna in *Svensk berättarkonst. Röda rummet, Karolinerna, Onda sagor och Sibyllan*. Lund, 1968.

Individual poem: 'Jairi Dotter' in *Lyriska läsövningar*.

Selma Lagerlöf

Bibliography
Afzelius, Nils & Anderson, Eva, *Selma Lagerlöfs bibliografi. Originalskrifter*. Stockholm, 1975. (Acta Bibliothecae Regiae Stockholmiensis XXIII).
Primary material
Selma Lagerlöf, *Samlade skrifter* 1-12. Stockholm, 1933.
Brev I 1871-1902. *Brev* II 1903-40. I urval av Ying Toijer-Nilsson. *Selma Lagerlöf-sällskapet Skrifter* 7 & 8. Lund, 1967 & 1969.
Dagbok: Mårbacka I. Stockholm, 1924; *Mårbacka II*. Stockholm, 1930;

Mårbacka III. Stockholm, 1932 (new ed. *Dagbok: Mårbacka III*, 1997).
Critical works
Ahlström, Gunnar, *Den underbara resan. En bok om Selma Lagerlöfs Nils Holgersson*. Lund, 1942.
Ahlström, Gunnar, *Kring Gösta Berlings saga*. Stockholm, 1959.
Arvidsson, Stellan, *Selma Lagerlöf*. Stockholm, 1933.
Berendsohn, Walter, *Selma Lagerlöf. Her Life and Work*. London, 1931.
Böök, Fredrik, *Stridsmän och sångare*. Stockholm, 1910.
Edström, Vivi, *Livets stigar*. Stockholm, 1960.
Edström, Vivi, *Selma Lagerlöfs litterära profil*. Stockholm, 1986.
Ek, Bengt, *Selma Lagerlöf efter Gösta Berlings saga. En studie över genombrottsåren 1891-1897*. Stockholm, 1951.
Green, Brita, *Selma Lagerlöf: Herr Arnes penningar. (Studies in Swedish Literature* no. 9). University of Hull, 1977 (reissued 1986).
Holm, Birgitta, *Selma Lagerlöf och ursprungets roman*. Stockholm, 1984.
Lagerroth, E, *Landskap och natur i Gösta Berlings saga och Nils Holgersson*. Stockholm, 1958.
Lagerroth, E., *Selma Lagerlöf och Bohuslän. En studie i hennes 90-talsdiktning*. Lund, 1963.
Lagerroth, E., *Selma Lagerlöfs Jerusalem. Revolutionär sekterism mot fäderneärvd bondeordning*. Lund, 1966.
Lagerroth, Ulla Britta, *Körkarlen och Bannlyst. Motiv och idéstudier i Selma Lagerlöfs 10-talsdiktning*. Stockholm, 1963.
Olsson-Buckner, E., *The Epic Tradition in Gösta Berlings saga*. Brooklyn, NY, 1978.
Selma Lagerlöf och kärleken (ed. K. E. Lagerlöf). Selma Lagerlöf-sällskapet, Sunne, 1997.
Selma Lagerlöf and her home at Mårbacka (ed. Maja Petré). Ystad, 1980.
Toijer-Nilsson, Y. (ed.), *Du lär mig att bli fri. Selma Lagerlöf skriver till Sophie Elkan*. Stockholm, 1992.
Ulvenstam, L., *Den åldrade Selma Lagerlöf. En studie i hennes Löwensköldscykel*. Stockholm, 1955.
Weidel, Gunnel, *Helgon och gengångare. Gestaltningen av kärlek och rättvisa i Selma Lagerlöfs diktning*. Lund, 1964.
Wägner, Elin, *Selma Lagerlöf* I-II. Stockholm, 1942-43.
Återkommande mönster i Selma Lagerlöfs författarskap (ed. Maria Kikolajeva). Sunne: Selma Lagerlöf-sällskapet, 1995.

Afzelius, Nils, 'Selma Lagerlöf — den förargelseväckande'. *Selma Lagerlöf-sällskapet. Skrifter 10*. Lund, 1973.
Edström, Vivi, 'Att finna stilen. En studie i Jerusalems framväxt'. *Lagerlöfstudier 4*. Lund, 1971.
Edström, Vivi, 'En gång om våren'. *Allt om böcker*. Stockholm, 1984.

Ekman, Kerstin, 'Undret på Malmskillnadsgatan. Om Selma Lagerlöf'. *Kvinnornas litteraturhistoria* 1. Stockholm, 1981.
Gustafson, Alrik, Saga and Legend of a Province. Selma Lagerlöf in *Six Scandinavian Novelists*, pp. 177-225. London, 1940.
Holmberg, Olle, 'En herrgårdssägen', pp. 55-61; 'Charlotte Löwensköld', pp. 115-122. *Lovtal över svenska romaner*. Stockholm, 1957.
Lagercrantz, Olof, 'Gösta Berlings saga', pp. 18-23, *Från Aeneas till Ahlin. Kritik 1951-1975*. Stockholm, 1978.
Lagerroth, E, 'Gösta Berlings saga', *Romanen i din hand*. Ystad, 1976, pp. 203-238.
Levertin, O, *Svenska gestalter*. Stockholm, 1903.
Lindqvist, Sigvard A., 'Om stoff och psykologi i En herrgårdssägen'. *Lagerlöfsstudier 3*. Lund, 1966.
Nordström, Ludvig, 'Mårbacka och Övralid. Ett par personliga minnen' (ed. Sven Thulin). Uppsala, 1940.
Toijer-Nilsson, Y., 'Att gyckla sig fri'. *Allt om böcker* no.1. Stockholm, 1984.
Torpe, U., 'Den vedervärdiga kvinnan från korskyrka. Om en romanfigur hos Selma Lagerlöf'. *Kvinnornas litteraturhistoria* 2. Stockholm, 1983.
Tournier, Michel, 'Från gåskarlens rygg'. *Allt om böcker*. Stockholm, 1984.
Tunström, Göran, 'Selma Lagerlöf'. *Författarnas litteraturhistoria* 2. Stockholm, 1978.

Gustaf Fröding

Bibliography
Szczepanski, Jan, *Litteratur om Gustaf Fröding. En bibliografi*. Gothenburg, 1984.
Primary material
Fröding, Gustaf, *Skrifter*. Stockholm, 1935. 6 vols.
Fröding, Gustaf, *Brev*. Utgivna och kommenterade av Germund Michanek och Ingvald Rosenblad. Stockholm, 1981-82. 2 vols.
Critical works
Böök, Fredrik, *Analys och Porträtt*. Lund, 1962.
Fröding, Cecilia, *Och minns du Ali Baba*. Stockholm, 1960.
Landquist, John, *Gustaf Fröding. En levnadsteckning*. Stockholm, 1964.
Olsson, Henry, *Fröding. Ett diktarporträtt*. Stockholm, 1950.
Olsson, Henry, *Vinlövsranka och hagtornskrans. En bok om Fröding*. Stockholm, 1970.

Beckman, Erik, Gustaf Fröding in *Författarnas litteraturhistoria* 2. Stockholm, 1978.
Hagliden, Sten, Fröding i mitt sinne in *Författarnas litteraturhistoria* 2. Stockholm, 1978.

Notes and Bibliographies

Individual poems: 'Aningar' in *Lyriska läsövningar*; 'Fylgia' in *Svenska diktanalyser*.

Erik Axel Karlfeldt

Bibliography
Afzelius, Nils & Bergstrand, Arne, *Erik Axel Karlfeldts bibliografi*. Stockholm, 1974.
Primary material
Sundgren, Nils P. (ed.), *Dikter* Stockholm, 1962.
Critical works
Banck, Majt (ed.), *Karlfeldt. Synpunkter och värderingar*. Stockholm, 1971.
Fogelqvist, Torsten, *Erik Axel Karlfeldt*. Stockholm, 1941.
Hallberg, Peter, *Natursymboler i svensk lyrik från nyromantiken till Karlfeldt*. 1-3. Gothenburg, 1951.
Hildeman, Karl-Ivar, *Sub Luna och andra Karlfeldt essäer*. Stockholm, 1966.
Hildeman, Karl-Ivar, *En löskerkarl. En Karlfeldtsbok*. Stockholm, 1977.
Lagercrantz, Olof, *Jungfrun och demonerna. En Karlfeldtstudie*. Stockholm, 1938.
Mjöberg, Göran, *Det folkliga och det förgångna i Karlfeldts lyrik*. Stockholm, 1945.
Tideström, Gunnar *et al.* (eds), *Karlfeldtdikter*. Stockholm, 1972.

Individual poems: 'Sång efter skördeanden' and 'Jag är en sjungandes röst' in *Lyrisk tidsspegel*; 'Hjärtstilla' in *Lyriska läsövningar*; 'Vinterorgel' in *Svenska diktanalyser*.

CHAPTER 4 Swedish Fin-de-Siècle: Hjalmar Söderberg

1. The most important influences on Söderberg were from Denmark and Norway. There was also a *fin-de-siècle* tendency in Finland, which is of less relevance in the present context. See Koskimies, *Der nordische Dekadent*.
2. For a much fuller presentation of Decadence in Swedish literature at the turn of the century, see Sjöblad, *Baudelaires väg till Sverige*.
3. The first unfavourable review was by Harald Molander, in *Aftonbladet*, 9 November 1895.
4. Quotations are given in English translation, but page references are to Swedish editions: for the four novels and *Historietter* to the Delfin paperback editions; otherwise to the original edition. In all cases Stockholm, Bonniers Förlag.
5. See Per Gunnar Kyle, 'Martin Bircks ungdom. En belysning av dess tillkomsthistoria', in *Göteborgsstudier i litteraturhistoria tillägnade Sverker Ek,* Gothenburg, 1954, p.299ff.

6. A novel by Gun-Britt Sundström, *För Lydia*, Stockholm, 1973, retells Söderberg's story from Lydia's viewpoint, against an updated background and with the emphasis on women's emancipation and sexual equality.
7. Bure Holmbäck, *Det lekfulla allvaret*, pp. 122-123.
8. Cassirer, *Stilen i Hjalmar Söderbergs 'Historietter'*, p.106.
9. Knut Jaensson, 'Hjalmar Söderberg', in Jaensson, *Essayer*, Stockholm, 1946, pp. 45-78.
10. Two further stories were added to this group later; first published together in *Skrifter*, vol. 4, 1921.

SELECT BIBLIOGRAPHY

Hjalmar Söderberg

Bibliography
Friedländer, Herbert, *En Hjalmar Söderberg bibliografi*. Stockholm, 1944.

General
Koskimies, Rafael, *Der nordische Dekadent. Eine vergleichende Literaturstudie*. Helsinki, 1968.
Sjöblad, Christina, *Baudelaires väg till Sverige. Presentation, mottagande och litterära miljöer 1855-1917*. Lund, 1975.

Primary sources
Söderberg, Hjalmar, *Skrifter*. 10 vols. Stockholm, 1919-21.
Söderberg, Hjalmar, *Samlade verk*. 10 vols. Stockholm, 1943.
Söderberg, Hjalmar, *Skrifter*. 9 vols. Stockholm, 1978.

Critical works
Bergman, Bo, *Hjalmar Söderberg. Minnesteckning*. Stockholm, 1951.
Butt, Wolfgang, *Hj. Söderberg: Martin Bircks ungdom*. Hull, 1976. (Studies in Swedish Literature, no.7).
Cassirer, Peter, *Stilen i Hjalmar Söderbergs 'Historietter'*. Gothenburg, 1970.
Ciaravolo, Massimo, *Den insiktsfulle läsaren: några drag i Hjalmar Söderbergs litteraturkritik*. Stockholm, 1994. (Söderbergsällskapets skriftserie, no. 8).
Geddes, Tom, *Hj. Söderberg: Doktor Glas*. Hull, 1975. Third edition 1993. (Studies in Swedish Literature, no. 3).
Holmbäck, Bure, *Det lekfulla allvaret. Studier över erotiska och polemiska motiv i Hjalmar Söderbergs roman Den allvarsamma leken mot bakgrund av hans tidigare författarskap*. Stockholm, 1969.
Holmbäck, Bure, *Hjalmar Söderberg: ett författarliv*. Stockholm, 1988.
Holmbäck, Bure, *Hjalmar Söderberg och passionerna*. Stockholm, 1991.

Holmbäck, Bure (ed.), *Den mångsidige Stockholmsflanören: perspektiv på Hjalmar Söderbergs debutroman Förvillelser*. Stockholm, 1995. Söderbergsällskapets skriftserie, no. 9).

Kjellberg, Lennart, *Stildrag i Hjalmar Söderbergs 'Förvillelser' och 'Martin Bircks ungdom'*. Uppsala, 1937.

Lagerstedt, Sven, *Hjalmar Söderberg och religionen*. Stockholm, 1982. (Stockholm Studies in History of Literature, no. 24).

Ljungberg, Lars, *Alltför mänskligt: om Hjalmar Söderbergs kristendoms kritik*. Lund, 1982. (Livsåskådningsforskning, no. 3).

Lofmark, Carl, *Hj. Söderberg: Historietter*. Hull, 1977. Reprint 1984. (Studies in Swedish Literature, no. 10).

Lundgren, Lars, *Liv, jag förstår dig inte. Hjalmar Söderbergs Doktor Glas*. Stockholm, 1987.

Olofsson, Tommy, *Frigörelse eller sammanbrott? Stephen Dedalus, Martin Birck och psykologin*. Stockholm, 1981.

Sundberg, Björn, *Sanningen, myterna och intressenas spel. En studie i Hjalmar Söderbergs författarskap från och med Hjärtats oro*. Uppsala, 1981. (Skrifter utgivna av Litteraturvetenskapliga institutionen vid Uppsala universitet, no.15).

Ahlund, Claes, 'Doktor Glas och den fria viljan'. *Horisont* XXXII (1985), no.1, pp. 12-21.

Ekner, Reidar, 'Hjalmar Söderbergs Historietter'. *Nordisk tidskrift* XXXVII (1961), pp. 279-300.

Friedlander, Herbert, 'Hjalmar Söderberg som stockholmsskildrare'. *Svensk litteraturtidskrift* XV (1952), pp. 158-184.

Holmbäck, Bure, 'Den röda stjärnan. Några anteckningar om slutkapitlet i Martin Bircks ungdom'. *Samlaren* CIII (1982).

Leth, Göran, 'Känslan som figurer och bilder — en studie av Hjalmar Söderbergs författarskap till och med Doktor Glas'. *Samlaren* CVIII (1987), pp. 39-53.

Lofmark, Carl, 'Hjalmar Söderberg (1869-1941): a Swedish freethinker'. *Question*, 11, 1978, pp. 3-14.

Merrill, Reed, 'Ethical Murder and Doctor Glas'. *Mosaic* XII (1979), no. 4, pp. 47-59.

Schoolfield, George C., 'Music in Hjalmar Söderberg's "Doktor Glas"', in *Grenzerfahrung — Grenzüberschreitung. Festschrift für P. M. Mitchell*. Heidelberg, 1989.

Törnqvist, Egil, 'Mordet på pastor Gregorius: ett bidrag till tolkningen av Doktor Glas'. *Tijdschrift voor Skandinavistiek*, IX, 1988, pp. 144-155.

CHAPTER 5 *Tiotalister and Hjalmar Bergman*

1. For a full bibliography of Elin Wägner, see H. Forsås-Scott, *Swedish Women's Writing 1850-1995*. London, 1997, pp. 303-304.
2. E. Hj. Linder, nestor of Bergman research, provides a full account of Bergman's childhood, early manhood and works up to 1918 in *Sju världars herre*, 1962. The quotation comes from p. 45.
3. Ibid., p. 45.
4. Hjalmar Bergman, *Brev*, ed. by J. Edfelt, 1964, p. 109; letter to Ellen Key 29 November 1915.
5. K. Petherick, *Stilimitation i tre av Hjalmar Bergmans romaner*. Uppsala, 1971.
6. Page references to Bergman's work are to *Samlade skrifter*.
7. *Brev*, p. 42 to Ellen Key 22 November 1904.
8. Cf. E. Hj. Linder, *Sju världars herre*, p. 474.
9. Published in 'Kåserier och kritiker', *Samlade skrifter* XXVII, pp. 264-287.
10. *Brev*, p.109 to Ellen Key 29 November 1915.
11. *Brev*, p.173 to Hans Larsson 9 May 1923.
12. Bergman discusses the complex problem of the will in a letter to Algot Ruhe, 6 December [1918] in *Brev*, p. 144-146.
13. G. Axberger, *Den brinnande skogen*, 1960, p. 39.
14. *Brev*, p. 160 to Hans Larsson 21 February 1922.
15. *Brev*, p. 161 to Algot Ruhe 21 February 1922.
16. *Brev*, p. 160 to Hans Larsson 21 February 1922.
17. For a detailed study of *Markurells* see Ö. Lindberger, 'Herr Markurell och livslögnen' in *Studier tillägnade Henry Olsson,* Stockholm, 1956; G. Qvarnström, *I lejonets tecken* (chapters 6 & 7), Lund, 1959; G. Tidestöm, 'Katt och råtta i några av Hjalmar Bergmans romaner. Ett bidrag till tolkningen av Markurells i Wadköping' in both *Samlaren,* 1954, and *Kring Hjalmar Bergman*, ed. by S. R. Ek, Stockholm, 1965; K. Petherick, *Markurells i Wadköping* (Studies in Swedish Literature, 4), University of Hull, 1975.
18. For a discussion of archaisms and Cederborgh-affinities, see K. Petherick, *Stilimitation i tre av Hjalmar Bergmans romaner*, 1971. For all-round coverage see M. Bergom-Larsson, *Diktarens demaskering. En monografi över Hjalmar Bergmans roman Herr von Hancken*, 1970.
19. Cf. B. Ahlmo-Nilsson, '"Och till på köpet är det far dins pengar." En studie i Hjalmar Bergmans roman Farmor och Vår Herre', *Perspektiv på prosa*, ed. by B. Ahlmo-Nilsson *et al.*, Gothenburg, 1981, pp. 105-127. Cf. also Staffan Björck, 'Farmor hos Hjalmar Bergman', *Svensk litteraturtidskrift*, no. 1, 1982, pp. 3-15.

Notes and Bibliographies

SELECT BIBLIOGRAPHY

Bibliographies
Brandell, Gunnar & Stenkvist, Jan, *Svensk litteratur 1870-1970*, vol. 3, pp.187f.
Hjalmar Bergman Samfundets årsbok, starting with its first volume 1959, has included bibliographies every few years up to 1987 when the publication was re-named *Skrifter utgivna av Hjalmar Bergman Samfundet*, but it continues to include bibliographies from time to time.
Lund, Edgar, 'Hjalmar Bergman', *Korta bibliografier* II, Stockholm, 1939.

Primary material
The standard edition of Bergman's work is *Samlade skrifter* comprising 30 volumes, each with a valuable commentary by J. Edfelt, including extracts from early reviews of the works in question. Edfelt has also edited a wide selection of Bergman's letters under the title *Brev*, Stockholm 1964. *Hjalmar Bergman Samfundets årsbok* has over the years included previously unpublished works and letters by Bergman. A complete, annotated edition of letters under the title *Hjalmar Bergmans brev* is under preparation by its editors Kerstin Dahlbäck and Sverker R. Ek; estimated publication date at the earliest 2000.

Critical works on Bergman
For works on *Markurells i Wadköping*, *Herr von Hancken*, and *Farmor och Vår Herre*, please consult notes 17, 18, and 19 above. Please also note that *Hjalmar Bergman Samfundets årsbok* 1959-87 has a host of articles on various aspects of Bergman's work, too numerous be listed here, but it is hoped readers can consult the yearbooks in a library, ditto the annual *Skrifter utgivna av Hjalmar Bergman Samfundet* which replaced the yearbook from 1987 onwards (an oddity is that the last *årsbok* 1987 and vol.1 of *Skrifter* 1987 are identical). A modest annual membership subscription to Hjalmar Bergman Samfundet provides current publications free of charge (contact Hjalmar Bergman Samfundet, c/o Litteraturvetenskapliga institutionen, Stockholms universitet, S-106 92 Stockholm, for information, membership application details, etc.).
Axberger, Gunnar, *Den brinnande skogen. En studie i Hjalmar Bergmans diktning.* Stockholm, 1960.
Ek, Sverker R., *Verklighet och vision. En studie i Hjalmar Bergmans romankonst,* Stockholm, 1964. Dissertation with a chapter on Bergman and the problematics of "the will", and in-depth treatment of *Solivro, En döds memoarer,* and *Clownen Jac.*
Ek, Sverker R. (ed.), *Kring Hjalmar Bergman* (Essays by seven Bergman scholars, including Gunnar Tideström's 'Katt och råtta i några av Hjalmar

Bergmans romaner. Ett bidrag till tolkningen av Markurells i Wadköping'). Stockholm, 1965.

Hästbacka, Elisabeth, *Det mångstämmiga rummet. Hjalmar Bergmans romankonst 1913-1918*. (Skrifter utg. av Hjalmar Bergman Samfundet, 4), Stockholm, 1990. Dissertation applying Michael Bachtin's theory of polyphony to *Loewenhistorier* and *En döds memoarer*.

Levander, Hans, *Hjalmar Bergman*. Stockholm, 1962. Excellent little monograph.

Linder, Erik Hjalmar, *Sju världars herre. Hjalmar Bergmans liv och diktning till och med En döds memoarer*. Stockholm, 1962.

Linder, Erik Hjalmar, *Kärlek och fadershus farväl. Hjalmar Bergmans liv och diktning från Markurells i Wadköping till Farmor och Vår Herre*, Stockholm, 1973.

Linder, Erik Hjalmar, *Se fantasten. Hjalmar Bergmans liv och diktning från Eros begravning till Clownen Jac*, Stockholm, 1983. (These three volumes by the nestor of Bergman scholarship covering his life and works, represent a gold mine of information).

Linder, Erik Hjalmar, *Hjalmar Bergman*. Transl. from the Swedish by Catherine Djurklou. Boston: Twayne's World Authors Series, 1975. (Recommended for anyone requiring an English-language authoritative chronological survey, including Bergman's plays).

Qvarnström, Gunnar, *I lejonets tecken. En studie i Hjalmar Bergmans symbolkonst*. Lund, 1958.

Bonnier, Tor, 'Hjalmar Bergman' in *Längesen*, Stockholm, 1973, pp. 130-198. (A gripping chapter by Bergman's brother-in-law).

Dahlbäck, Kerstin, 'Den moderne Hjalmar Bergman' in *Den moderne Hjalmar Bergman*. (Skrifter utg. av Hjalmar Bergman Samfundet, 4). Stockholm, 1988, pp. 32-54.

Dahlbäck, Kerstin, 'Döden i Mellanspelet. En studie i En döds memoarer' in *Hjalmar Bergman Samfundets årsbok 1979*, pp. 35-69.

CHAPTER 6 *Pär Lagerkvist*

1. *Ordkonst och bildkonst*, p. 32.
2. The original volume *Ångest* (Stockholm, 1916) contains lyric poetry and short prose poems interspersed, and it is this I have in mind when mentioning the order in which the poems appear. For ease of access, however, my page references are to Lagerkvist's collected poems, *Dikter*, Stockholm, 1952 and *Prosa* (*Prosastycken ur Ångest, Den fordringsfulla gästen, Det eviga leendet, Morgonen* and *onda sagor*), Stockholm, 1955.
3. *Lyrisk tidspegel*, p. 60.
4. From 'Stinkande avskrädeshög'.

5. From 'Runt omkring mig ligger evigheten'.
6. Page references are to *Prosa* as above.
7. Linnér, *Pär Lagerkvists livstro*, p. 9.
8. Page references to *Prosa*.
9. Oberholzer, *Pär Lagerkvist*, p. 60.
10. A sequel to *Gäst hos verkligheten* dating from about 1925 but first published in 1985 with the title *Den svåra resan* (The Difficult Journey) depicts some rather corpulent Danish matrons whom Lagerkvist encountered in Denmark in 1916. They would seem to be the model for the miller's wife.
11. Blomberg, *Stadens fångar*, p. 178.
12. Linnér, *Livsförsoning och idyll*, p. 31.
13. Page references are to the Delfin edition.
14. See my article 'The Significance of Lagerkvist's Dwarf', *Scandinavica* Lagerkvist Supplement, 1971.
15. Page references are to *Aftonland*, Stockholm, 1953.
16. Page references are to the Delfin edition.
17. See my articles 'Contrasting characters in *Barabbas*' and 'The Origins and Development of Lagerkvist's *Barabbas*' in *Scandinavian Studies*, 1960 and 1983.
18. Page references are to *Sibyllan*, Stockholm, 1956.
19. Page references are to the Delfin edition.
20. Page references are to *Pilgrim på havet*, Stockholm, 1962.
21. Page references are to *Det heliga landet*, Stockholm, 1964.
22. Page references are to *Mariamne*, Stockholm, 1967.
23. See my article 'An Interpretation of Lagerkvist's *Mariamne*', *Scandinavian Studies*, 1973.
24. Manuscript dated 4 November 1945 in Gothenburg University Library.

SELECT BIBLIOGRAPHY

Bibliographies
Ryberg, A., *Pär Lagerkvist in Translation. A Bibliography*. Stockholm, 1964.
Yrlid, R., *Pär Lagerkvists kritiker. En recensionsbibliografi*. Stockholm, 1970.
Willers, U., *Pär Lagerkvists bibliografi*. Stockholm, 1951.

Primary material
Most of Lagerkvist's work is available in *Dikter, Dramatik* I — III and *Prosa* I — VI, all published by Bonniers, Stockholm. *Onda sagor, Gäst hos verkligheten, Själarnas maskerad, Bödeln, Dvärgen, Barabbas, Sibyllan, Ahasverus död, Pilgrim på havet, Det heliga landet* and *Mariamne* have all appeared in the Delfin paperback series. His daughter Elin Lagerkvist has edited *Antecknat. Ur efterlämnade dagböcker och anteckningar*, Stockholm,

1977, comprising hitherto unpublished fragments, and *Den svåra resan* (The Difficult Journey), the sequel to *Gäst hos verkligheten,* was published in Stockholm in 1985. *Pär Lagerkvist. Brev.* (Stockholm, 1991) contains a selection of Lagerkvist's letters from 1908 to 1971 ed. by Ingrid Schöier.

Bergman, G. M., *Pär Lagerkvists dramatik.* Stockholm, 1928. (Lagerkvist's development as a dramatist up to *Han som fick leva om sitt liv*).

Fearnley, R., *Pär Lagerkvist.* Oslo, 1950.

Fredén, G., *Pär Lagerkvist. Från Gudstanken till Barabbas.* (Verdandis småskrifter). Stockholm, 1954.

Fredén, G., *Uppbrott till verkligheten.* Stockholm, 1961.

Granlid, H., *Det medvetna barnet. Stil och innebörd i Pär Lagerkvists Gäst hos verkligheten.* Gothenburg, 1961.

Henmark, K., *Främlingen Lagerkvist.* Stockholm, 1966.

Hörnström, E., *Pär Lagerkvist. Från den röda tiden till Det eviga leendet.* Stockholm, 1946. (Lagerkvist's literary development up to 1920).

Karahka, U. — L., *Jaget och ismerna. Studier i Pär Lagerkvists estetiska teori och lyriska praktik t.o.m. 1916.* Stockholm, 1978. (Uses unpublished material available at the Royal Library, Stockholm after Lagerkvist's death in 1974).

Jönsson, W., *Gud, matos och kärlek. Om Pär Lagerkvists fädernemiljö och barndomsvärld.* Växjö, 1978.

Lagerkvist, Ulf, *Den bortvändes ansikte. En minnesbok.* Stockholm, 1991. (Lagerkvist's son records memories of his father).

Lagerkvist, Ulf, *Denna långt försvunna stund.* Stockholm, 1992.

Linnér, S., *Pär Lagerkvists livstro.* Stockholm, 1961. (Concentrates on Lagerkvist's works around 1920).

Malmström, G., *Menneskehjertets verden. Hovedmotiv i Pär Lagerkvists diktning.* Oslo, 1970. (Excellent survey in Norwegian).

Mjöberg, J., *Livsproblemet hos Lagerkvist.* Stockholm, 1951.

Oberholzer, O., *Pär Lagerkvist. Studien zu seiner Prosa und seinen Dramen.* Heidelberg, 1958.

Schöier, I., *Som i Aftonland. Studier kring temata, motiv och metod i Pär Lagerkvists sista diktsamling.* Stockholm, 1981.

Schöier, I., *Pär Lagerkvist. En biografi.* Stockholm, 1987.

Schönström, R., *Dikten som besvärjelse. Begärets dialektik i Pär Lagerkvists författarskap.* Stockholm, 1987.

Scobbie, I., *Pär Lagerkvist's Gäst hos verkligheten.* (Studies in Swedish Literature, no. 2). Hull, 1979.

Sjöberg, L., *Pär Lagerkvist.* (Columbia Essays on Modern Writers, 74). New York, 1976.

Skartveit, A., *Gud skapt i menneskets bilete. Ein Lagerkviststudie.* Oslo, 1966. (Religious problems in the later novels; in nynorsk).

Spector, R. D., *Pär Lagerkvist*. (Twayne World Author Series). New York, 1973.
Svanberg, V., *Heidenstam och Lagerkvist: en studie i diktens sociologi*. Stockholm, 1941.
Tideström. G. (ed), *Synpunkter på Pär Lagerkvist*. Stockholm, 1966.
Yrlid, R., *Litteraturrecensionens anatomi. Dagskritikens utformning och dagskritikernas värdekriterier vid bedömningen av Pär Lagerkvist*. Lund, 1973.

Abenius, M., 'Innestängd — utestängd. Reflexioner kring Dvärgen', *BLM* XIV (1945).
Abenius, M., 'Mörkret som symbol i Barabbas', *BLM* XX (1951).
Barck, P. O., Essay in *Dikt och förkunnelse*. Helsinki, 1936.
Blomberg, E., Det besegrade livet. En studie i Pär Lagerkvists författerskap in *Stadens fånger*. Stockholm, 1933.
Brantly, S., 'The Stylistic Legacy of Religious Literature in Pär Lagerkvist's Poetry', *Scandinavica* XX (1983), pp. 47-68.
Brunius, T., 'Det kubistiska experimentet', *BLM* XXIII (1954) pp. 805-14.
Gustafson, W., '*Sibyllan* and the Patterns of Lagerkvist's Works', *Scandinavian Studies* XXX (1958), pp. 131-136.
Hallberg, P., 'Stjärnsymboliken i Pär Lagerkvists lyrik' in *Göteborgsstudier i litteraturhistoria tillägnade Sverker Ek*. Gothenburg, 1954.
Heggelund, K., 'Det onde og virkeligheten' in *Fiksjon og virkelighet*. Oslo, 1966. (On *Dvärgen*).
Herrlin, O., Essay in *Den yttersta gränsen*. Stockholm, 1955.
Hörnström, E., 'Pär Lagerkvist om sin ungdoms diktning', *Svensk Litteraturtidskrift* XXXVIII (1975), no. 2, pp. 3-8.
Johannesson, E. O., 'Pär Lagerkvist and the Art of Rebellion', *Scandinavian Studies* XXX (1958), pp. 19-29.
Karahka, U. — L., 'Pär Lagerkvists aktualisering av historieromangenren: en studie i "Bödeln "och "Dvärgen"', *Fenix* VI (1988), nos 3 & 4, pp. 90-175.
Lagerroth, E., 'Det onda livet' (on *Onda sagor*) and 'Guden och gudsupplevelsen' (on *Sibyllan*) in *Svensk berättarkonst*. Lund, 1968.
Linnér, S., 'Pär Lagerkvists barndomsmiljö', *Samlaren* XXVIII (1947), pp. 53-90.
Linnér, S., Från Kaos till Den osynlige in *Livsförsoning och idyll. En studie i rikssvensk litteratur 1915-1925*. Stockholm, 1954.
Linnér, S. (ed.), Pär Lagerkvist Supplement. *Scandinavica*. May, 1971.
Mjöberg, J., 'Det förnekade mörkret', *Samlaren* XXXV (1954) pp.78-112.
Schwab, G. B., 'Herod and Barabbas. Lagerkvist and the Long Search', *Scandinavica* XX (1981), pp. 75-85.
Scobbie, I., 'Contrasting characters in *Barabbas*', *Scandinavian Studies* XXXII (1960), pp. 212-220.

Scobbie, I., 'An Interpretation of Lagerkvist's *Mariamne*', *Scandinavian Studies* XLV (1973), pp. 128-134.

Scobbie, I., 'The Further Development of Anders in Pär Lagerkvist's *Gäst hos verkligheten*', *Scandinavica* XIX (1980), pp. 31-37.

Scobbie, I., 'The Origins and Development of Lagerkvist's *Barabbas*', *Scandinavian Studies* LXV (1983), pp. 55-66.

Scobbie, I., 'Lagerkvist's Difficult Journey', Swedish Book Review III (1985), no.1, pp. 2-7.

Spector, R. D., 'Lagerkvist and Existentialism', *Scandinavian Studies* XXXII (1960), pp. 203-210.

Stenström, T., Pär Lagerkvists Dvärgen — en jagroman in *Berättartekniska studier*. Stockholm, 1964.

Svanberg, V., Lagerkvists livstro in *Dikt och studie*. Stockholm, 1922.

Swanson, R. A., 'Evil and Love in Lagerkvist's Crucifixion Cycle', *Scandinavian Studies* XXXVIII (1966), pp. 302-317.

Tideström, G., 'Den unge Pär Lagerkvist och hans prosakonst', *Proceedings of First International Conference on Scandinavian Studies*. Cambridge, 1956.

Individual poems: 'Ångest, ångest är min arvedel'; 'Lyft dig på blodiga vingar'; 'Nu löser solen sitt blonda hår'; 'I själens gränder' in *Lyrisk tidsspegel*, Lund, 1967; 'Torso' in *Lyriska läsövningar*, Lund, 1961; 'Det är vackrast när det skymmer' in *Svenska diktanalyser*, Stockholm, 1965.

Pär Lagerkvist-Samfundet (The Pär Lagerkvist Society), Samfundets förlag, Box 424, 351 06 Växjö, now publishes regularly a series of articles on Lagerkvist.

CHAPTER 7 *Swedish Poetry of the Twentieth Century.*

1. For a detailed treatment of this theme see Kjell Espmark, *Själen i bild* (1977).
2. See Ingemar Algulin, *Tradition och modernism* (1969), pp.14-21.
3. See Staffan Bergsten, *Östen Sjöstrand*. (Twayne's World Authors Series). New York, 1974.
4. See Johan Wrede, 'The Birth of Finland-Swedish Modernism: A Study in the Social Dynamics of Ideas', *Scandinavica* XV, May 1976. Supplement on Modernism in Finland-Swedish Literature, pp.73-103.
5. See Jocelyne Fernandez, 'La Poési Finlandaise d'Expression Suédoise', *Scandinavica* XII, May 1973, Supplement on Contemporary Scandinavian Poetry, pp. 41-64.
6. Most easily available editions are: *Samlade dikter* in the series *Vår tids lyrik* (1963), including *Fridas bok, Fridas andra bok, Kriser och kransar, Minnen från jorden; Kvartetten som sprängdes* in Delfin edition (1968); *Kriser och*

Notes and Bibliographies

kransar in Delfin edition (1966).
7. *Birger Sjöberg Sällskapet*, 1970, pp. 143-184.
8. See Gunnar Tideström, 'Det dagsaktuella i Konferensman' in *Synpunkter på Birger Sjöberg*.
9. *Birger Sjöberg Sällskapet*, 1968, pp. 99-192.
10. Gullberg's complete poems were published for the first time in 1985 by Norstedts, Stockholm, under the title *Dikter*, with a full and useful introduction by Anders Palm.
11. *Gentleman, Single, Refined and Selected Poems*, 1937-1959, transl. by Judith Moffett. Stockholm, 1979. Page references are prefaced by JM.
12. Page references are given to the anthologies *Hundra dikter* (1939) and *Femtio dikter* (1961) in the abbreviated form *100* and *50* immediately followed by colon and page number. Quotations from *Ögon, läppar* are indicated by ÖL followed by page number.
13. See Carl Fehrman, *Hjalmar Gullberg* (1967), pp. 114f.
14. For similarities with Christian Morgenstern's *Galgenlieder*, see Fehrman, *op. cit.*, pp. 82ff.
15. See Anders Palm, *Kristet, indiskt och antikt i Hjalmar Gullbergs diktning* (1976), p. 193.
16. Palm, *op.cit.*, pp. 192-211.
17. Quotations from 'Insnöad' (Snowed In), 50:77; JM:57.
18. Karin Boye, *Kris*, 1934, p. 181. *Kris* has also been published in the anthology Karin Boye, *Kris, Kallocain, Dikter* in *Svalans svenska klassiker* series, Bonniers, Stockholm, 1977. All the verse quotations in my essay are page-referenced to Boye, *Dikter* in Bonnier's series *Vår tids lyrik*, and as a *Bonnier Pocket* 1985, with reprints. After the bracketed page-number follows an abbreviation indicating which collection the poem is taken from, i.e. *Moln* = M, *Härdarna* = H, *För trädets skull* = FTS, *De sju dödssynderna* = DSD.
19. Karin Boye, *Samlade skrifter*, vol. 9, p. 40.
20. For a detailed account of Martinson's childhood and a comparison with the two novels, see Sonja Erfurth, *Harry Martinsons barndomsvärld* and *Harry Martinson och vägen ut*.
21. Peter Hallberg, 'Om bildspråket i Harry Martinsons Nässlorna blomma', p.108.
22. Lars Ulvenstam, p. 219, suggests that Sandemar may be a compound of *Sand*gren (Gustav Sandgren, one of the *fem unga*) and *Mar*tinson.
23. Lars Ulvenstam, p. 210.
24. Interview in *Dagens Nyheter*, 16 December 1953, quoted by Johan Wrede in *Aniara*, (1997), p. 207.
25. Wrede, *Aniara*, (1997), p. 223.
26. Wrede, *Aniara*, (1997), p. 202.
27. Wrede, *Sången om Aniara*, p. 29.

28. Wordlists in Wrede, *Sången om Aniara,* and Tideström, *Ombord på Aniara,* are helpful for interpretations of the innovative vocabulary.
29. Wrede, *Aniara,* (1997), p. 232.
30. Kjell Espmark, *Harry Martinson erövrar sitt språk,* p. 123.
31. Lindegren, Erik, 'Gunnar Ekelöf, en modern mystiker' in Karl Vennberg and Werner Aspenström, *Kritiskt 40-tal* (1948).
32. Gunnar Ekelöf, 'En outsiders väg', most easily accessible in *Promenader och utflykter* (1963) (*Delfinböcker*), p. 166.
33. *ibid.* p. 175.
34. *ibid.* p. 174.
35. Ekelöf's views are also expressed in 'Jag tror på den ensamma människan', a poem which, being shorter than the one quoted here, is often included in anthologies.
36. An excellent analysis of 'Samothrake' by Gunnar Tideström appears in Geijerstam *et al., Lyrisk tidsspegel* (1947) (new edition 1967). Some aspects of the analysis are challenged by Gunnar Brandell in his 'Samothrake än en gång' in *Konsten att citera* (1966) (*Aldus*), pp. 114ff.
37. Leif Sjöberg provides an indispensable aid, aimed at English-speaking readers, with his illuminating book *A Reader's Guide to Gunnar Ekelöf's 'A Mölna Elegy'*, New York, 1973. A translation of the poem, by Muriel Rukeyser and Leif Sjöberg, was published by Unicorn Press in 1958.
38. The opening line, which appears as a motif in *Vägvisaren till underjorden,* is in fact a selfquotation from a poem in *Strountes.* Two informative sources regarding the background and meaning of the Diwan trilogy are the later essays in Reidar Ekner's book *I den havandes liv* and Bengt Landgren's study 'Jungfrun, döden och drömmarna' (see Bibliography). Of special interest to English-speaking readers are the foreword (by W. H. Auden and Leif Sjöberg) and the introduction (by Göran Printz-Påhlson) to the Penguin edition of Gunnar Ekelöf, *Selected Poems,* also Leif Sjöberg's essay 'The Later Poems of Gunnar Ekelöf: Diwan and Fatumeh' in *Mosaic,* IV, no. 2 (Winter 1970), pp. 101-115.
39. Letter from Lindegren to Bertil Örnberg, 24 January 1933, quoted by Bäckström on p. 36 of his book on Lindegren.
40. The main attack on obscurity in modern poetry was by Sten Selander in *Svenska Dagbladet,* 23 April 1946; Lindegren's reply, 'Tal i egen sak', appeared in *Stockholms-Tidningen,* 20 May 1946, and is reprinted in the collection of his articles, *Tangenter,* published in 1974, and in Karl Vennberg and Werner Aspenström, *Kritiskt 40-tal* (1948).
41. *40-tal,* 1946, no. 1. A summary of the subsequent debate can be found in Lennart Göthberg, 'Marginalanteckningar till en debatt', *40-tal,* 1946, no.5.
42. See Vennberg's articles 'Franz Kafka' in *Horisont,* Spring 1944, and 'Inledning till Kafka' in *40-tal,* 1945, no. 2. Vennberg was also concerned with several translations of Kafka's works published around this time (e.g.

Der *Prozess* and *Die Verwandlung*).
43. Vennberg edited a booklet, *Tredje ståndpunkten* (1951), containing the most important essays advocating this view. See also Thomas Forser and Per Arne Tjäder, *Tredje ståndpunkten* (1972).
44. Interview in *Lyrikvännen*, 1973, no. 6, p. 58.
45. Tomas Tranströmer, *New Collected Poems*, translated by Robin Fulton, Bloodaxe Books, Newcastle upon Tyne, 1997. Translations of poems quoted here are taken from this book. Page references are prefaced by F.
46. Page references for Palm's poems are to his collection *Själens furir och andra dikter* (1967).
47. From 'Experiment i enkelhet?' in *Expressen*, 8 September 1961.
48. See Lars Bäckström, 'Friheten i träden och trafiken' in his *Klippbok* (1965), pp. 120-128, (p. 125).
49. Björn Håkanson and Leif Nylén, *Nya linjer* (1966), p. 8.
50. Torben Broström, *Modern svensk litteratur* (1974), p. 180.
51. From 'Socialisten som konstnär', *Dagens Nyheter*, 14 April 1969. Reprinted in Sven Nilsson and Rolf Yrlid, *Svensk litteratur i kritik och debatt* 1957-1970 (1972), pp. 235-238 (p. 235).
52. Page references for Sonja Åkesson's poems are to her collection *Man får vara glad och tacka Gud* (1967).
53. *Svensk litteratur i kritik och debatt*, p. 112.
54. Page references for Göran Sonnevi's poems are to his collection *Dikter 1959-1973* (1974).
55. Mona Sandquist, review of Sonnevi's *Framför ordens väggar*, *BLM* LXII (1993), no. 3, p. 73.
56. See Arne Johnsson, 'Trösten i att inte vara skild från oändligheten', *BLM* LXV (1996), no. 6, pp. 44-45.
57. Göran Sonnevi, *Mozarts tredje hjärta*, 1996, p. 234.
58. A particularly useful study of the major tendencies and some of the less well-known inclinations in contemporary Swedish poetry is Nina Burton's *Den hundrade poeten: tendenser i fem decenniers poesi* (Stockholm, 1988).
59. The motif of a more humane world derives in part from the United Nations conference on environmental protection held in Stockholm in 1972.
60. Though specifically addressing the issue in response to Palm's poem, the general concern was of taking an engaged and committed stance *vis-à-vis* the environment as opposed to the dispassionate contemplation of nature.
61. The title is a play on words. 'Lugn' means 'calm' and the title of these collected poems can mean 'Lugn Just Lugn' or 'Just Keep Calm'.
62. *Samlat Lugn* can mean 'Collected Lugn' or 'Calm and Collected'.
63. 'Trying to understand a poem that doesn't want to be understood', *BLM* LXIII (1994), pp. 39-41.
64. The introduction of Bob Dylan to the Swedish reading public played a significant role in promoting popularized poetry. Although the major and

traditional publications such as *Ord och Bild* and *BLM* responded to the rising tide of interest in popular poetry, the significance of mimeographed quasi-underground publications like *Inferi* and the *Guru Papers* was notable.
65. Espmark's election to the Swedish Academy in 1981 and his gradually more prominent role in its various activities has contributed to his visibility and importance in contemporary Swedish culture.

SELECT BIBLIOGRAPHY

General

Borum, Poul, *Poetisk modernism*. Stockholm, 1968. (A general introduction to Modernism in Europe and America).

Burton, Nina, *Den hundrade poeten. Tendenser i fem decenniers poesi*. Stockholm, 1988.

Espmark, Kjell, *Själen i bild. En huvudlinje i modern svensk poesi*. Stockholm, 1977. (A study of how spiritual states are expressed in concrete images in modern Swedish poetry).

Fehrman, Carl & Palmlund, Evald, (eds), *Svenska litteraturstudier. Ny samling*. Stockholm, 1968. Includes essays on Birger Sjöberg, Edith Södergran, Hjalmar Gullberg, Gunnar Ekelöf, Harry Martinson, *Fem unga*, among others.

Hedlund, Tom, *Den svenska lyriken från Ekelund till Sonnevi*. Stockholm, 1978. Two volumes, one an anthology, the other a commentary.

Printz-Påhlson, Göran, *Solen i spegeln. Essäer om lyrisk modernism*. Stockholm, 1958. Includes essays on Birger Sjöberg, Elmer Diktonius, Rabbe Enckell, Gunnar Ekelöf, Erik Lindegren, Karl Vennberg among others.

Analysis of Individual Poems

Björck, Staffan, *Lyriska läsövningar*. Lund, 1961.
Cederroth, Sigvard, *et al.*, *Elva diktanalyser*. Stockholm, 1958.
af Geijerstam, Carl-Erik, *et al.*, *Lyrisk tidsspegel*. Lund, 1967.
Julén, Björn, *Tjugo diktanalyser från Södergran till Tranströmer*. Stockholm, 1962.
Lindberger, Örjan and Ekner, Reidar, *Att läsa poesi*. Stockholm, 1965.
Platen, Magnus von, *et al.*, *Svenska diktanalyser*. Stockholm, 1965.

Birger Sjöberg

Birger Sjöberg Sällskapet. The yearbooks, from 1962, contain a variety of essays, interviews and unpublished or little known works by Sjöberg.

Notes and Bibliographies

Axberger, Gunnar, *Lilla Paris' undergång. En bok om Birger Sjöberg.* Stockholm, 1960.

Delblanc, Sven, *Treklöver.* Stockholm, 1980.

Lawton, C. J., *Birger Sjöberg's Kriser och kransar.* Hull University, 1975 (Doctoral thesis). Translated into Swedish with commentary, published as Birger Sjöberg Sällskapet Yearbook, 1977.

Olafsson, E. Haettner, *Fridas visor och folkets visor.* Stockholm, 1985.

Peterson, August, *Birger Sjöberg den okände.* Stockholm, 1944.

Tunving, L. H., (ed.), *Synpunkter på Birger Sjöberg.* Stockholm, 1966.

Edstam, Gunvor, 'Fridastilens egenart', *Birger Sjöberg Sällskapet*, 1972, pp. 161-202.

Ohlsson, Barbro, 'Rörelse och samtalston. Några drag i Birger Sjöbergs estetik', *Birger Sjöberg Sällskapet*, 1968, pp. 92-192.

Wizelius, Ingemar, 'Birger Sjöberg — autodidakten', *Birger Sjöberg Sällskapet*, 1969, pp.189-202.

Hjalmar Gullberg

Hjalmar Gullberg. En bibliografi 1952-1979, compiled by Lennart Karlström. Stockholm, 1981.

Algulin, Ingemar, *Tradition och modernism. Bertil Malmbergs och Hjalmar Gullbergs lyriska förnyelse efter 1940-talets mitt.* Stockholm, 1969.

Fehrman, Carl, *Hjalmar Gullberg.* Stockholm, 1967. An excellent introduction.

Palm, Anders, *Kristet, indiskt och antikt i Hjalmar Gullbergs diktning.* Stockholm, 1976.

Fehrman, Carl, 'Spex och parodi i Hjalmar Gullbergs tidiga diktning' in *Poesi och parodi. Essayer,* Stockholm, 1957, pp. 143-169.

Fehrman, Carl, 'Det orfiska i Hjalmar Gullbergs diktning', *ibid.*, pp. 290-313.

Lugn, Kristina, 'Avgrundens staket. Kring Hjalmar Gullbergs dikter', *BLM* LIV (1985), pp. 283-286.

Individual poems: 'Dock finnas' analysed in *Lyriska läsövningar;* 'Aftonsång', 'Hänryckning' and 'Död amazon' in *Lyrisk tidsspegel*, 'Kärlekens stad' in *Elva diktanalyser* and 'Vid Cap Sunion' in *Svenska diktanalyser* (see above).

Sveriges Radios förlag, S-105 10, Stockholm, market an audio-cassette with Hjalmar Gullberg reading a selection of his own poems.

Karin Boye

Abenius, Margit, *Karin Boye*. Stockholm, 1965. (Original edition entitled *Drabbad av renhet*, Stockholm, 1950.) (Invaluable monograph).
Abenius, M. and Lagercrantz, O., (eds), *Minnen och studier*. Stockholm, 1942. (Collection of informative essays).
Boye, Karin, *Det hungriga ögat. Journalistik 1930-1936. Recensioner och essäer*. Urval och redigering av Gunnar Ståhl. Stockholm, 1979.
Boye, Karin, *Månsång*, ed. Barbro Gustafsson. Gothenburg, 1979.
Boye, Karin, *Det stora undret*, ed. Barbro Gustafsson. Gothenburg, 1981.
Boye, Karin, *Soldrottningens gudson*, ed. Barbro Gustafsson. Gothenburg, 1982. (These three volumes contain previously unpublished poems, plays and stories written by the young Boye before her first collection, *Moln*).
Det moderna genombrottets andra fas, ed. Bertil Nolin. Stockholm, 1993, pp. 171-201.
Domellöf, Gunilla, *I oss är en mångfald levande. Karin Boye som kritiker och prosamodernist*. Umeå, 1986.

Abramson, Ingeborg, 'Karin Boye. Några minnesanteckningar'. *Svensk litteratur tidskrift* XIV (1982), no.1, pp. 16-31.
Domellöf, Gunilla, 'Karin Boye och den revolutionära humanismen' in *Kulturradikalismen*.
Forsås-Scott, Helena, Chapter on Karin Boye in *Swedish Women's Writing 1850-1995*. London, 1997.

Individual poems: 'Unga viljor viner' analysed in *Lyriska läsövningar*; 'Min hud är full av fjärilar' and 'Bön till solen' in *Lyrisk tidsspegel* (see above).

Sveriges Radios förlag, S-105 10 Stockholm, market an audio-cassette with Karin Boye reading a selection of her own poems.

Harry Martinson

Several of Harry Martinson's prose books are in print, some in paperback, e.g. the travel books and the autobiographical novels. There is a paperback edition of his poetry, *Dikter* (Delfin, 1991). Bonniers, in cooperation with the Harry Martinson Society, are planning a ten-volume series of new editions of his works to appear before 2001. The first volume, *Aniara*, was published in 1997.
Erfurth, Sonja, *Harry Martinsons barndomsvärld*. Stockholm, 1980.
Erfurth, Sonja, *Harry Martinson och vägen ut*. Stockholm, 1981.
Erfurth, Sonja, *Harry Martinson och Moa 1920-31*. Stockholm, 1987.
Erfurth, Sonja, *Harry Martinsons 30-tal*. Stockholm, 1987.

Espmark, Kjell, *Harry Martinson erövrar sitt språk. En studie i hans lyriska metod 1927-1934.* Stockholm, 1970.

Hall, Sonja Glimstedt, *Aniara. Studiehandledning för gymnasier, folkhögskolor m.fl.* Södra Sandby, 1991.

Hall, Tord, *Vår tids stjärnsång. En naturvetenskaplig studie omkring Harry Martinsons Aniara.* Stockholm, 1961.

Hallberg, Peter, *Studier i Harry Martinsons språk.* (Skrifter utgivna av samfundet för stilforskning, IX). Uppsala, 1941.

Holm, Ingvar, *Harry Martinson. Myter, målningar, motiv.* Stockholm, 1960.

Lagerroth, Erland, *Aniara — en dikt av sin tid eller i tingens natur har människan sin lag. Harry Martinsons dikt läst 1990.* Harry Martinson-sällskapets skriftserie 1, 1991.

Lundberg, Johan, *Den andra enkelheten. Studier i Harry Martinsons lyrik.* Harry Martinson-sällskapets skriftserie 2, 1992.

Sandelin, Staffan, *Nässlorna blomma.* (Studies in Swedish Literature No. 15). Hull, 1987.

Söderblom, Staffan, *Harry Martinson.* Stockholm, 1994.

Tideström, Gunnar, *Ombord på Aniara. En studie i Harry Martinsons rymdepos.* Stockholm, 1975.

Ulvenstam, Lars, *Harry Martinson. Ett utkast.* Stockholm, 1950.

Wrede, Johan, *Sången om Aniara. Studier i Harry Martinsons tankevärld.* Stockholm, 1965.

Wrede, Johan, *"Efterord" in Harry Martinson's Aniara.* Stockholm, 1997.

Green, Brita, 'Foregrounding and prominence. Finding patterns in Harry Martinson's poetry', *Scandinavica*, XXXVI (1997), pp. 43-57.

Hallberg, Peter, 'Om bildspråket i Harry Martinsons Nässlorna blomma', *Nordisk Tidskrift,* LI (1975), pp. 81-109.

Holm, Ingvar, 'Tankar och tendenser i Harry Martinsons diktning', *Svensk litteraturtidskrift* XI (1948), pp. 97-127.

Holmberg, Olle, 'Vägen till Klockrike' in his *Lovtal över svenska romaner.* Stockholm, 1957.

Håkansson, B., 'Men bara ord det är och bara vind'. *Lyrikvännen XXXIX* (1992), pp. 46-53.

Jaensson, Knut, 'Återblick på Harry Martinson' in his *Sanning och särprägel.* Stockholm, 1960, pp. 97-123.

Ström, Eva, 'Saklighet och extas', *Lyrikvännen* XXXIX (1992), pp. 11-15.

Tideström, Gunnar, 'Harry Martinson's "Aniara"', *Scandinavica* XIII (1974), pp. 1-17.

Lyrikvännen, 1992, Nos 1/2, special Martinson issue.

Parnass 1994, No.3, special Martinson issue.

Gunnar Ekelöf

Ekner, Reidar, *I den havandes liv*. Stockholm, 1967. (Essays on Ekelöf).
Ekner, Reidar, *Gunnar Ekelöf. En bibliografi*. Stockholm, 1970.
Landgren, Bengt, *Ensamheten, döden och drömmarna*. Uppsala, 1971.
Olsson, Anders, *Ekelöfs nej*. Stockholm, 1983. (A difficult but rewarding study of themes in Ekelöf's poetry).
Shideler, Ross, *Voices under the Ground: Themes and Images in the Early Poetry of Gunnar Ekelöf*. Berkeley, 1973.
Sjöberg, Leif, *A Reader's Guide to Gunnar Ekelöf's 'A Mölna Elegy'*. New York, 1973.
Wigforss, Brita, *Konstnärens hand*. Gothenburg, 1983. (The hand symbol in Ekelöf's poetry).

Enckell, Rabbe, 'Gunnar Ekelöfs lyrik' in *En bok om Gunnar Ekelöf*, ed. Stig Carlson and Axel Liffner. Stockholm, 1956.
Landgren, Bengt, 'Jungfrun, döden och drömmarna. En studie i Ekelöfs Diwantrilogi', *Samlaren* XC (1969), pp. 52-110.

Individual poems: 'Helvetes-Brueghel' and 'Panthoidens sång' in *Att läsa poesi*; 'En verklighet (drömd)' in *Lyriska läsövningar*; 'blommorna sover i fönstret' in *Elva diktanalyser*; 'Höstsejd' and 'Absentia animi' in *Svenska diktanalyser*.

40-talet: Erik Lindegren, Karl Vennberg.

40-talsförfattare, (ed. Lars-Olof Franzén). Stockholm, 1965. (Contains several articles on Lindegren and Vennberg. Especially useful is K-G. Wall, 'Mannen utan väg. Kommentarer av en oinvigd').
Algulin, Ingemar, *Den orfiska reträtten*. Stockholm, 1977.
Bäckström, Lars, *Erik Lindegren*. 2nd ed. Stockholm, 1979.
Cullhed, Anders, *'Tiden söker sin röst'. Studier kring Erik Lindegrens 'mannen utan väg'*. Stockholm, 1982. (Deals mainly with the background to the cycle).
Hermelin, Carola, *Vinteroffer och Sisyfos. En studie i Erik Lindgrens senare diktning*. Uppsala, 1976.
Lagerlöf, Karl Erik, *Den unge Karl Vennberg*. Stockholm, 1967.

Individual poems. Lindegren: 'Scherzando' in *Att läsa poesi*; 'Ikaros' in *Lyriska läsövningar;* 'Vid Shelleys hav' in *Tjugo diktanalyser*; 'Hamlets himmelsfärd' in *Elva diktanalyser* (reprinted in *Svenska diktanalyser*). Vennberg: 'Du måste värja ditt liv' in *Lyriska läsövningar*; 'Traktat' in *Tjugo diktanalyser*; 'Mitt på ljusa dagen ser du' in *Elva diktanalyser*;

Notes and Bibliographies

'Gatukorsning' in Svenska diktanalyser.

Tomas Tranströmer

Karlström, Lennart, *Tomas Tranströmer. En bibliografi*. Stockholm, 1990.
Bergsten, Staffan, *Den trösterika gåtan. Tio essäer om Tomas Tranströmers lyrik*. Stockholm, 1989.
Espmark, Kjell, *Resans formler. En studie i Tomas Tranströmers poesi*. Stockholm, 1983.

Fulton, Robin, 'The Poetry of Tomas Tranströmer'. *Scandinavica* XII, May 1973, Supplement on Contemporary Scandinavian Poetry, pp.107-123.
Hallberg, Peter, '"Distansernas makt har sammanströmmat". Om bildspråket i Tomas Tranströmers "Sång" och "Elegi"', *Edda* LXXV (1975), pp. 111-131.
Steene, Birgitta, 'Vision and Reality in the Poetry of Tomas Tranströmer', *Scandinavian Studies* XXXVII (1965), pp. 236-244.

Individual poem: 'Hemligheter på vägen' in *Tjugo diktanalyser*.

Poetry of the 1960s

Bäckström, Lars, *Klippbok*. Stockholm, 1965.
Forsås-Scott, Helena, *Swedish Women's Writing 1850 — 1995*. London, 1997.
Gustafsson, Lars and Rasmusson, Torkel, *Dikterna från 60-talet*. Stockholm, 1970.
Håkanson, Björn and Nylén, Leif, *Nya linjer*. Stockholm, 1966.
Lagerlöf, Karl Erik, *Strömkantringens år*. Stockholm, 1975.
Lilja, Eva, *Den dubbla tungan. En studie i Sonja Åkessons poesi*. Gothenburg, 1991.
Rydén, Per, *Till de folkhemske: om den verkliga vitterheten under efterkrigstiden*. Stockholm, 1994. (Deals with Åkesson, Palm and Povel Ramel.)
Ullén, Jan Olov, *Det skrivna är partitur*. Stockholm, 1979.

Everling, Bo, 'Aldrig på taktslaget: Petter Bergman och Göran Sonnevi', in his *Blå toner och svarta motiv*, Stockholm, 1993, pp. 245-64.
William-Olsson, Magnus, 'Det vi kallar allvar. Om Göran Sonnevis poesi', in his *Livets skrift*, Stockholm, 1992, pp. 95-110.

CHAPTER 8 Three Novelists of the 1930s

1. See Lennart Thorsell, 'Den svenska parnassens demokratisering och de folkliga bildningsvägarna'.
2. See Lars Furuland, *Folkhögskolan — en bildningsväg för svenska författare*.
3. See also H. O. Granlid, *Martin Koch och arbetarskildringen*. Stockholm, 1957, pp. 55-56.
4. See Peter Graves, 'The Collective Novel in Sweden'.
5. A useful introduction to Primitivism is to be found in Kjell Espmark, *Livsdyrkaren Artur Lundkvist*. Stockholm, 1964, pp. 132-161.
6. See Helena Forsås-Scott, *Swedish Women's Writing 1850-1995*, pp. 131-33.
7. See Ebba Witt-Brattström, *Moa Martinson. Skrift och drift i trettiotalet*, pp. 267-70.
8. For a detailed account of Moberg's background, childhood and youth, see Magnus von Platen, *Den unge Vilhelm Moberg*.
9. See also Sigvard Mårtensson, 'Krönikan och dramat'.
10. See also Maj Danelius, 'Vilhelm Mobergs *Mans kvinna* — från roman till drama'.
11. Page references are to the Delfin editions of the novels.
12. For a more detailed account of the novel see G. K. Orton & P. A. Holmes, 'Memoirs of an Idealist' Vilhelm Moberg's *Soldat med brutet gevär*, Scandinavian Studies, XXXXVIII (1976), pp. 29-51.
13. 'For a critical introduction to this novel, see Philip Holmes, *Vilhelm Moberg: Utvandrarna*.
14. See particularly the section 'Källorna' in *Perspektiv på Utvandrarromanen* and Chapter II of Eidevall's *Vilhelm Mobergs emigrantepos*. A fascinating study of Moberg's documentary method is to be found in Ingrid Wennberg's 'Bönder på havet' i Vilhelm Mobergs Utvandrarna. En studie i författarens material', *Svensk litteraturtidskrift* XXV (1962), pp. 160-74.
15. For an account of Lo-Johansson's background see Lars Furuland, *Statarnas ombudsman i dikten*, pp. 23-43.
16. Furuland, p. 13.
17. Ivar Lo-Johansson, *Godnatt, jord*. Stockholm, 1962.
18. See also Knut Jaensson, *Nio moderna svenska prosaförfattare*. Stockholm (Verdandis småskrifter nr. 439), 1943, p. 29.
19. Ivar Lo-Johansson, 'Kommentar till statarböckerna' in *Statarskolan i litteraturen*, p. 71. The article first appeared in *BLM* XIV (1945).
20. Ivar Lo-Johansson, 'Statarskolan i litteraturen' in *Statarskolan i litteraturen*, p. 25. An earlier version of the article appeared in *BLM* VII (1938).
21. For a discussion of *Traktorn* as a collective novel see Peter Graves, 'The Collective Novel in Sweden'.
22. Ivar Lo-Johansson, *Passionerna*. Stockholm, 1968.
23. *Passionerna*, p. 10.

24. Knut Ahnlund in *Svensk litteraturtidskrift* XXXV (1972), no. 4, p. 44.
25. Ivar Lo-Johansson, *Pubertet*. Stockholm, 1978.
26. For a good description of the influences on Eyvind Johnson see Gavin Orton, *Eyvind Johnson*, pp. 32-37.
27. Page reference is to the Bonniers Folkbibliotek edition of 1947.
28. Page reference is to the Bonnier edition of 1943.
29. Erik Hjalmar Linder, *Fem decennier av 1900-talet,* vol. II, p. 623.
30. Page reference is to the First Edition, Bonnier, 1930.
31. Page reference is to the Bonnier edition of 1950.
32. Orton, *op. cit.*, p. 64.
33. Page reference is to the Bonnier single volume edition of 1948.
34. Stig Bäckman, *Den tidlösa historien*, p. 193.
35. Page references are to the Delfin edition of 1960.
36. Page references are to the Delfin edition of 1962.
37. Bäckman, p.194.
38. All further page references are to the First Editions.

SELECT BIBLIOGRAPHY

General

Adolfsson, Eva et al., *Vardagsslit och drömmars språk. Svenska proletärförfattarinnor från Maria Sandel till Mary Andersson.* Enskede, 1981.

Bouquet, Philippe, *Spaden och pennan: den svenska proletärromanen*, Stockholm, 1990.

Forsås-Scott, Helena, *Swedish Women's Writing 1850-1995.* London, 1997.

Furuland, Lars, *Folkhögskolan — en bildningsväg för svenska författare.* Uppsala, 1968.

Granlid, H. O., *Martin Koch och arbetarskildringen.* Stockholm, 1957.

Runnquist, Åke, *Arbetarskildrare från Hedenvind till Fridell.* Stockholm, 1952.

Strindberg, Axel, *Människor mellan krig.* Stockholm, 1941.

Witt-Brattström, Ebba, *Moa Martinson: skrift och drift i trettiotalet.* Stockholm, 1988.

Furuland, Lars, 'Agrarian Society and Industrialism in Scandinavian Literature' in *Literature and Western Civilisation. The Modern World III Reactions,* ed. David Daiches and Anthony Thorlby, London, 1976, pp. 275-294.

Ord och Bild LXXXV (1976) is devoted to 'Proletärlitteratur i Sverige'.

Thorsell, Lennart, 'Den svenska parnassens demokratisering och de folkliga bildningsvägarna', *Samlaren* LXVIII (1957), pp. 53-135.

Vilhelm Moberg

Eidevall, Gunnar, *Berättaren Vilhelm Moberg*. Stockholm, 1976.
Eidevall, Gunnar (ed.), *Vilhelm Moberg läst på nytt*. Stockholm, 1994.
Holmes, P. A., *Vilhelm Moberg*. New York, 1980.
Moberg, Vilhelm, *Berättelser ur min levnad*. Stockholm, 1968.
Mårtensson, Sigvard, *Vilhelm Moberg. En biografi*. Stockholm, 1956.
Mårtensson, Sigvard, *Vilhelm Moberg och teatern*. Stockholm, 1992.
von Platen, Magnus, *Den unge Vilhelm Moberg*. Stockholm, 1978.

Danelius, Maj, 'Vilhelm Mobergs *Mans kvinna* — från roman till drama', *SLÅ* 1975, pp. 114-44.
Holmes, Phil, 'Leitmotifs in Vilhelm Moberg's *Rid i natt!*', in Death, Sarah and Forsås-Scott, Helena (eds), *A Century of Swedish Narrative*, Norwich, 1994, pp. 167-80.
Lundkvist, Artur, 'Epikern Vilhelm Moberg', in *Vilhelm Moberg — en vänbok*. Stockholm, 1973, pp. 110-46.
Moberg, Vilhelm, 'Betraktelse om romanskrivning', in *Avsikter, Aderton författare om sina verk,* Stockholm, 1945, pp. 157-67.
Mårtensson, Sigvard, 'Krönikan och dramat. En återblick på *Raskens,* Vilhelm Mobergs store soldatroman', *BLM* XXIV (1955), pp. 528-32.
Parnass 1996, no.1, special Moberg issue.

Ivar Lo-Johansson

Edstrom, Mauritz, *Äran, kärleken och klassen*. Stockholm, 1976.
Furuland, Lars, *Statarnas ombudsman i dikten*. Stockholm, 1976.
Furuland, Lars, & Oldberg, Ragnar, *Ivar Lo-Johansson i trycksvärtans ljus. En bibliografi*. Stockholm, 1961.
Holmgren, Ola, *Kärlek och ära. En studie i Ivar Lo-Johanssons Måna-romaner*. Stockholm, 1978.
Lo-Johansson, Ivar, *Stridskrifter* I-II. Lund, 1971.
Lo-Johansson, Ivar, *Statarskolan i litteraturen*. Gothenburg, 1972.
Lo-Johansson, Ivar, *Dagar och dagsverken*. Stockholm, 1975.
Lo-Johansson, Ivar, *Till en författare*. Stockholm, 1988.
Oldberg, Ragnar, *Ivar Lo-Johansson. En monografi*. Stockholm, 1957.

Adolfsson, Eva, 'Ivar Johanssons *Författaren*', *Tidskrift för litteraturvetenskap* III (1973-74), pp. 21-14.
Bouquet, Philippe, 'Ivar Lo and Swedish Working Class Literature', *Swedish Book Review (Supplement)*, 1991, pp. 10-15.
Edstrom, Mauritz, 'Ivar Lo-Johanssons samhällskritik', *BLM* XXII (1953), pp. 436-42.

Graves, Peter, 'The Collective Novel in Sweden', *Scandinavica* XII (1973), pp. 113-27.
Graves, Peter, 'Ivar Lo-Johansson: Community and Isolation', *Swedish Book Review*, 1 (1983) pp. 6-9.
Graves, Peter, 'Ivar Lo and the Short Story', *Swedish Book Review (Supplement)*, 1991, pp. 20-25.
Holmgren, Ola, 'Resan till Eklandet', *BLM* XLII (1973), pp. 13-20.
Käll, Per-Olov, 'Statarnas historia. Ivar Lo-Johansson och jordproletärerna', *OoB* LXXIX (1970), pp. 356-61.
Munkhammar, Birgit, 'Det svåra vägvalet', *BLM* XXXXIX (1980), pp. 146-51.
Nerman, Bengt, 'Ivar Lo-Johanssons mystik', *BLM* XXXXIX (1980), pp. 36-41.
Oldberg, Ragnar, 'Bild och idé. En sida av Ivar Lo-Johanssons konstnärskap', *BLM* XVIII (1949), pp. 537-43.
Swedish Book Review (Supplement), 1991, is devoted to articles on and translations of Lo-Johansson.
Wright, Rochelle, 'Ivar Lo-Johansson and the Autobiographical Narrative', *Swedish Book Review (Supplement)*, 1991, pp. 15-20.
Wright, Rochelle, 'Dream and Dream Imagery in Ivar Lo-Johansson's *Godnatt, jord*', *Scandinavian Studies* LXIV (1992), pp. 53-67.

Eyvind Johnson

Bäckman, Stig, *Den tidlösa historien. En studie i tre romaner av Eyvind Johnson*. Stockholm, 1975.
Jansson, Bo, *Självironi, självbespegling och självreflexion. Den metafiktiva tendensen i Eyvind Johnsons diktning*. Uppsala, 1990.
Lindberger, Örjan, *Norrbottningen som blev europé. Eyvind Johnsons liv och författarskap till och med Romanen om Olof*. Stockholm, 1986.
Lindberger, Örjan, *Människan i tiden. Eyvind Johnsons liv och författarskap 1938-76*. Stockholm, 1990.
Mazzarella, Merete, *Myt och verklighet. Berättandets problem i Eyvind Johnsons roman Strändernas svall*. Helsinki, 1981.
Meyer, Ole, *Eyvind Johnsons historiska romaner. Analyser av språksyn och världsyn i fem romaner*. Copenhagen, 1976.
Orton, Gavin, *Eyvind Johnson*. New York, 1972.
Orton, Gavin, *Eyvind Johnson: Nu var det 1914*. (Studies in Swedish Literature 1). Hull, 1974.
Petterson, Torsten, *Att söka sanningen: en grundprincip i Eyvind Johnsons författarskap*. Åbo, 1986.
Schwartz, Nils, *Hamlet i klasskampen. En ideologikritisk studie i Eyvind Johnsons 30-talsromaner*. Lund, 1979.
Stenström, Thure, *Romantikern Eyvind Johnson*. Uppsala, 1978.

Söderberg, Barbro, *Flykten mot stjärnorna. Struktur och symbol i Eyvind Johnsons Hans nådes tid*. Stockholm, 1980.

Blackwell, Marilyn Johns, 'The redemption of the past. Narrative as moral imperative in *Strändernas svall*', *Scandinavica* XXV (1986), pp.153-76.

Göransson, Sverker, 'Berättartekniken i Eyvind Johnsons roman *Molnen over Metapontion*', *Samlaren* LXXXIII (1962), pp. 67-91.

Hallberg, Peter, 'Eyvind Johnson, ordet och verkligheten', *BLM* XXVII (1958), pp. 538-48.

Johnson, Eyvind, 'Romanfunderingar', in *Avsikter*, Stockholm, 1945, pp.73-90.

Johnson, Eyvind, '"En forfattare i sin tid ... "(Ett kåseri)'. *MLFÅ*, 1962, pp. 112-23.

Lindberger, Örjan, 'Eyvind Johnsons möte med Proust och Joyce', *BLM* XXIX (1960), pp. 554-63.

Munkhammar, Birgit, 'Det svåra vägvalet', *BLM* XLIX (1980), pp. 146-151.

Munkhammar, Birgit, 'Tiotusendens återtåg. Om Eyvind Johnsons *Romanen om Olof*'. *OoB* LXXXVII (1978), pp. 39-52.

Svensk litteraturtidskrift XL (1977), no. 3-4, is devoted to Eyvind Johnson and contains eight articles by or on him.

Wiman, Gunnar, 'Den inre monologen i Eyvind Johnsons roman *Kommentar till ett stjärnfall*', *MLFÅ*, 1956, pp. 59-73.

Öberg, Ingrid, 'Upprepning och variation i Eyvind Johnsons roman *Hans nådes tid*', *SLÅ*, 1972, pp. 122-43.

CHAPTER 9 Stig Dagerman and fyrtiotalismen

1. Rådström, Pär & Vennberg, Karl, 'Samtal om 40-talet', *Folket i bild*, Xmas issue, 1962, pp. 16-20, 75.
2. It is reasonable to regard 1946 as the breakthrough year for Sartre and Camus in Sweden. Camus' novel *L'Etranger* was published in Swedish translation, and his play *Caligula* was performed; Sartre's novel *Le Mur* was published, and several of his plays produced on the Swedish stage, including *Huit clos*, *Les Mouches*, and the world première of *Morts sans Sépulture*. Moreover, part of Camus' *Le Mythe de Sisyphe* was published in Swedish (*40-tal*, October, 1946), and the same year saw the publication of Sartre's *L'Existentialisme est un Humanisme*.
3. The person chiefly responsible for introducing Kafka to the Swedish reading public was Karl Vennberg, with his essays 'Franz Kafka', *Horisont*, 1944, no. 4, pp. 39-55, and 'Inledning till Kafka', *40-tal*, 1945 no.2, pp. 1-13.
4. Runnquist, Åke, 'Romantiker mot sin vilja', *40-tal*, 1945, no.1, pp. 10-12.
5. The attempt by Vennberg and his colleagues to launch *Votum* is described briefly in Linder's *Fem decennier av nittonhundratalet*, vol. II, p. 801 (see

bibliography).
6. The reconciliation is described generously by Vennberg in the article referred to in Footnote 1.
7. A booklet entitled *Tredje ståndpunkten* was published by Bonniers in 1951. Karl Vennberg supplied an introductory foreword, and the booklet reprinted 10 polemical newspaper articles in favour of the socialistic but neutral point of view by authors such as Arnér, Aspenström, Carlson, Lundkvist and Vennberg himself.
8. The page references here and in subsequent quotations from *Ormen* are to vol.1 in Stig Dagerman, *Samlade skrifter*, edited by Hans Sandström and published by Norstedts in 1981 (and subsequently in paperback); the figure after the oblique stroke refers to the English translation, *The Snake*, published by Quartet Books in 1995.
9. Carlson, Stig, 'Till fruktans psykologi', *Arbetaren,* 29 November 1945.
10. Dagerman, Stig, 'Min synpunkt på anarkismen', *40-tal*, 1946, no.2, pp. 56-59.
11. Sandberg, Hans, 'De dömdas ö — en politisk idéroman', *Samlaren,* 1972, pp. 62-90.
12. The page references are to vol.2 in Stig Dagerman, *Samlade skrifter* (see note 8) and, after the oblique stroke, to the English translation, *Island of the Doomed*, published by Quartet Books in 1991.
13. For a comparison of *Bränt barn* and *Ingen går fri* by the present writer, see Death, S. & Forsås-Scott, H. (eds.), *A Century of Swedish Narrative*, 1994, pp. 181-94. Ranelid wrote and was featured in many newspaper and magazine articles, as well as radio and television programmes, prior to the appearance of his novel; but the best way of becoming acquainted with his revelations about Dagerman's private life is to read *Mitt namn skall vara Stig Dagerman*.
14. Dagerman wrote well over a thousand satirical poems for *Arbetaren*, and a selection of some 200 was published shortly after his death in 1954 under the title *Dagsedlar*, which is a pun referring both to pages in a calendar, and boxes on the ear; a slightly extended version is volume 9 in the *Samlade skrifter* referred to in note 8. At the time of writing, negotiations are taking place regarding the publication of another selection; but it is unclear if and when it will appear. Relevant back copies of *Arbetaren* are held by several Swedish libraries, notably Kungliga Biblioteket in Stockholm.

SELECT BIBLIOGRAPHY

General on writing in the 1940s
40-tal, Stockholm, 1944-1947. This journal contains prose, poetry, drama and critical essays by all the *fyriotalister*. There is no better way of becoming

acquainted with the spirit of the age than reading through *40-tal*.
Franzén, Lars-Olof, (ed.), *40-talsförfattare*. Stockholm, 1965. Contains short reviews of works by the most important *fyrtiotalister*. See especially Franzén's introductory essay, '40-talets prosa'.
Henmark, Kai, *En fågel av eld*. Stockholm, 1962, pp. 98-188. Articles on the prose of the 1940s, especially Dagerman and Ahlin.
Häggqvist, Arne, (ed.), *Fyrtiotalisterna*. Stockholm, 1954. Anthology of creative and critical writings by *fyrtiotalister*, with a useful brief introduction by the editor.
Linder, Erik Hj., *Ny illustrerad litteraturhistoria. Fem decennier av nittonhundratalet*, II. Stockholm, 1966, pp. 787-818; 912-986.
Rådström, Pär & Vennberg, Karl, 'Samtal om 40-talet', *Folket i bild*, Xmas issue, Stockholm, 1962, pp.16-20; 75. Vennberg is prompted by Rådström to reminisce knowledgeably on the Swedish literary scene in the 1940s.
Vennberg, Karl & Aspenström, Werner, (eds), *Kritiskt 40-tal*. Stockholm, 1948. Anthology of critical writings by *fyrtiotalister*.

Stig Dagerman

Cullberg, Johan, *Skaparkriser. Strindbergs inferno och Dagermans*. Stockholm, 1992. (An examination of Dagerman's personality and creative crisis by a professional psychiatrist).
Lagercrantz, Olof, *Stig Dagerman*. Stockholm, 1958 and later (revised). (Strong on biographical detail and psychology, but contains little analysis of Dagerman's works — only *De dömdes ö* is examined in detail).
Laitinen, Kerstin, *Begärets irrvägar*. Stockholm, 1986. (A study of Existential themes in Dagerman's works, including anxiety, eroticism, maternal symbiosis and suicide).
Ljung, Per Erik, (ed.), *Ångestens hemliga förgreningar*. Stockholm, 1984. (Essays on *Nattens lekar*).
Périlleux, Georges, *Stig Dagerman et l'existentialisme*. Paris, 1982. (Places Dagerman's early novels in the context of French Existentialism).
Périlleux, Georges, *Stig Dagerman. Le mythe et l'oeuvre*. Brussels, 1993. (Attempts to ignore biographical circumstances and examines Dagerman's works in the context of French Existentialism).
Sandberg, Hans, *Stig Dagerman — författare och journalist*. Stockholm, 1975. (Comprehensive bibliography of Dagerman's work, containing several extracts and pictures. Lists reviews of all Dagerman's books).
Sandberg, Hans, *Den politiske Stig Dagerman*. Stockholm, 1979. (This stimulating book discusses Dagerman's links with Anarcho-Syndicalism and contains analyses of *Ormen* and *De dömdes ö*).
Thompson, Laurie, *Stig Dagerman: Nattens lekar*. (Studies in Swedish Literature 5). Hull, 1975. (A critical introduction to the work with

Notes and Bibliographies

vocabulary notes for English-speaking sudents).
Thompson, Laurie, *Stig Dagerman*. Boston, 1983. (Analyses all Dagerman's main works).
Ueberschlag, Georges, *Stig Dagerman ou l'innocence préservée: une biographie*. Nantes, 1996.
Werner, Gösta, *De grymma skuggorna*. Stockholm, 1986. (A study of Dagerman's works with special reference to film techniques).

Bergmann, S. A., 'Blinded by Darkness. A Study of the novels and plays of Stig Dagerman', *Delta* no.11, Spring, 1957, pp. 16-31. (A useful short survey of Dagerman's work).
Gran, Ulf, 'Stig Dagermans Bröllopsbesvär', *Perspektiv*, XIII (1962), pp. 158-61. (A brief introduction to serve as a starting point of discussions).
Losløkk, Ola, 'Billedspråk og symbolikk i Dagermans roman *De dömdes ö'*, *Edda*, 1970, no.5, pp. 289-310. (Stimulating discussion of images and symbols which facilitates interpretation of the novel considerably).
Pleijel, Agneta, 'Djuret och skräcken', *Samlaren* LXXXVI (1965), pp. 96-114. (Discussion of Dagerman's animal imagery in *De dömdas ö*, with references also to *Ormen*).
Törnqvist, Egil, 'Berättartekniken i Stig Dagermans roman *Bränt barn'*, *Svensk litteraturtidskrift*, 1969, no. 4, pp. 25-37. (A useful starting point for discussion on this novel).
Törnqvist, Egil, 'Heroes and Hero-Worship: On Stig Dagerman's *The Shadow of Mart'*, *Scandinavica*, 1993, no.1. (An analysis of Dagerman's dramatic methods).
The Stig Dagerman Supplement, *Swedish Book Review*, Lampeter, 1984 contains general essays on Dagerman and translations of his work. Two other issues of journals with special sections on Stig Dagerman are *Tidskrift för litteraturvetenskap*, 1990, no. 3, and *Ariel*, 1994, no. 2-3.

CHAPTER 10 *Twelve Modern Novelists*

1. Trotzig, Pleijel, and Kandre are dealt with in Helena Forsås-Scott, *Swedish Women's Writing 1850-1995*, London, 1997. For Evander, see the previous edition of *Aspects of Modern Swedish Literature* (1988). See also Karin Petherick, *Per Gunnar Evander*, Boston (Mass), 1982.
2. See Morten Henriksen and Jan Sand Sørenssen, 'Att omskapa en genre', *BLM* XLVI (1977), pp.14-27.
3. Page references to Gyllensten's works are to the Bonnierbiblioteket edition of *Moderna myter*, the Delfin editions of *Senatorn* and *Sokrates död*, and to First Editions of all other works.
4. In the article 'Ordning och provokation', printed in his interesting collection of essays, *Nihilistiskt credo* (1964), pp.7-16.

5. In the selection from his notebooks published as *Lapptäcken Livstecken* (Patchworks, Signs of Life, 1976), p.114.
6. Page references to *Fromma mord* are to the 1968 edition and to *Natt i marknadstältet* to the Delfin edition.
7. Page references to Sara Lidman's works are to the Delfin editions of the novels.
8. Karl Hampus Dahlstedt has provided a useful guide to the dialect employed in several novels. See his 'Folkmål i rikssvensk prosadiktning'.
9. 'Sara Lidman's progress', pp.98-99.
10. Gunnar Thorell, 'Samtal med Sara', p.39.
11. See H. H. Borland, 'Sara Lidman, novelist and moralist', p.28.
12. Gunnar Thorell, 'Samtal med Sara', p.39.
13. 'Om att övertolka', p.416.
14. 'Kommentarer kring en teknik', p.231.
15. See Rolf E. Stern, 'Per Olof Sundmans roman Expeditionen', p.32 and Hans Peterson, 'Rapport från en observatör', *OoB* LXX (1961), p.51.
16. Page references to Sundman's works are to the PAN editions except in the case of *Berättelsen om Såm* (Bonniers, 1977).
17. 'Kommentarer kring en teknik', p.232.
18. 'Om att övertolka', p.417.
19. See particularly P.O. Enquist, 'Den svåra lojaliteten', *BLM* XXXII (1963), pp.25-31; Michel Butor, 'Vid minsta tecken', *BLM* XXXIV (1965), pp. 441-48; Tobias Berggren, 'Expeditionskårens hemligheter', *BLM* XXXIX (1970), pp. 172-82; P.O. Sundman, 'Om att övertolka'.
20. 'Om att övertolka', p.416.
21. See Erland Lagerroth, *Romanen i din hand*. Stockholm, 1976, p.273.
22. The literary techniques of the novel are treated to a careful analysis by Gunnar Tideström in 'Ingenjör Andrées luftfärd som dokumentärskildring och litterärt konstverk'.
23. See *Hrafnkel's Saga and Other Icelandic Stories*, translated with Introduction by Herman Pálson. Harmondsworth, 1971.
24. For fuller treatment of these mystical episodes, see K. Petherick, 'The Farewell of a Secular Mystic: Sven Delblanc's *Livets ax* and *Slutord*', in *Scandinavica* XXXI (1992), pp.73-82.
25. *Eremitkräftan*, 'En bok för alla', 1980, p. 182. Except in the case of *Eremitkräftan* quotations from Delblanc's works are followed by a bracketed page number referring to the First Edition.
26. In Dostoyevsky's *Notes from the Underground* and *The Brothers Karamazov* (chapter 'The Grand Inquisitor'), the central question is of man's nature and the limits of freedom.
27. In his 'Sermon on Fire', Buddha speaks of the fire of desire which burns in all mankind's senses, bringing in its train suffering and evil; he speaks, too, of the freedom to be attained by learning to abhor the products of the

senses, at which point the endless cycle of rebirth is at an end and the liberated one is no longer of this world. In a letter to me (7 September 1990) Delblanc speaks of a Buddhist longing in *Gunnar Emmanuel* for liberation from sentient existence, linking this with his own personal experiences of mysticism.
28. Other writers, e.g. P.C. Jersild, Per Gunnar Evander and Göran Tunström also felt unease at the prescriptive literary climate.
29. *Kastrater* was successfully dramatized and had its première at Dramaten 26 March 1977.
30. Delblanc had studied apocryphical New Testament gospels as well as Elaine Pagel's book *The Gnostic Gospels* (1979, Penguin Books, 1990) about the Dead Sea scrolls. Note that Gnostic mythology about the Demiurge is used by Delblanc to speak of the suffering of the world under a cruel creator, but that the Gnostic Gospels are altogether different in their presentation of love.
31. Shirley Conran, *Lace* (1982, Penguin Books, 1983); the genre is colloquially known as 'tantsnusk' in Sweden.
32. For Delblanc's reaction to the critical reception of *Änkan* and for his admiration for Hjalmar Bergman, see K. Petherick, 'Diktverket enbart ska tala! Kring några brev från Sven Delblanc', *Artes*, 1993 no.4, pp. 90 and 95.
33. Excellent guides to Jersild's life are his autobiographical works *Uppror bland marsvinen* (Revolt Among the Guinea Pigs, 1972), *Professionella bekännelser* (Professional Confessions, 1981). and *Fem hjärtan i en tändsticksask* (Five Hearts in a Matchbox, 1989).
34. Page references to Jersild's works are to the Delfin edition of *Calvinols resa* and *Grisjakten* and to the First Edition of other works.
35. *Per Olov Enquist*, pp. 48ff.
36. References to Enquist's works are to the PAN editions.
37. See Sven Linnér, 'Per Olov Enquists "Legionärerna"', p. 84.
38. See Erik Henningsen, *Per Olov Enquist*, pp. 127-50.
39. Page references to Torgny Lindgren's works are to the original Swedish editions except where a published English translation exists, in which case they are to the latter in the first British edition.
40. 'Kerstin Ekman om sin romantradition', *Röster om Kerstin Ekman*, p. 104. Also published as 'En roligare romantradition än den strindbergskt modernistiskt enpipiga', *BLM*, LXII (1993) pp. 22-28.
41. See Anna Williams, 'Arbete och liv. Kvinnors verk i Kerstin Ekmans romaner', *Röster om Kerstin Ekman*, pp. 50-61.
42. Rochelle Wright, 'Approaches to History in the Works of Kerstin Ekman', *Scandinavian Studies*, LXIII (1991), p.298.
43. See Maria Schottenius, *Den kvinnliga hemligheten*, p.19.
44. See Helena Forsås-Scott, *Swedish Women's Writing*, p.228.

45. See Kerstin Ekman, 'Why I said yes to the Swedish Academy', *Swedish Book Review Supplement*, pp. 42-46.
46. See, for example, Kerstin Ekman, 'What can we learn from the Rushdie affair?' in Frid-Nielsen, Niels (ed.), *Freedom of Expression: The Acid Test*. Nordic Council, 1995, pp. 89-94.
47. See Anders Palm, 'Om konsten att förvandla — reflexion över Knivkastarens kvinna', *Röster om Kerstin Ekman*, pp. 30-43.
48. See Ingrid Elam, 'Linneförrådet och andra rum i Knivkastarens kvinna', *Röster om Kerstin Ekman*, pp. 44-49. Also Ekman's own commentary, 'Försoningen', *Kvinnovetenskaplig tidskrift*, XVI (1995), p.6.
49. Conversation with the author, 12 February 1997.
50. Örnkloo, Ulf, 'Man måste sitta vid!', *Jury. Tidskrift för deckarvänner*, XIX, (1990), no.2, p.9.
51. Stenholm, Olle, 'Kerstin blinkar till Selma', *Dagens Nyheter*, 24 September 1996.
52. Letter from the author, 12 October 1996.
53. An aged Lagerlöf gets Sidner, for the sake of appearances, to cut the pages of unread books she has received over the years. (*Juloratoriet*, 205).
54. Tunström refers to the dilemma he faced, in the preface to *Hallonfallet* (The Raspberry Slope, originally 1967, reprinted in 1985), 'Telling stories was a sin and telling stories was what I wanted to do'.
55. Tunström's copy includes a prologue by Artur Lundkvist. Lundkvist's words about Lorca might also aptly describe what Tunström appears to want for himself and his fictional characters: 'He wanted to meet death with his hands full, as a worthy opponent. Life against death everywhere!' (*Prästungen*, p.153).
56. For a theological discussion of *Stormunnens bön* and other works see Bo Larsson's *Närvarande frånvaro*. Stockholm, 1987.
57. It was Sidner who gave his mother's bicycle the initial push down the hill on her brief but fatal final journey.
58. Tunström himself returns time and again to Sunne as the centre of his own fictional world. 'It's not a real Sunne... It's nice to have a place where you know your way around, where you can place all the people and problems. I know it like the back of my hand and it gives me the security I need in terms of narrative technique. Sunne is a limitation which gives me freedom'. Margareta Garpe, 'Våra kroppar är märkliga katedraler: En intervju med Göran Tunström', *OoB XCII* (1983), no. 2, p.8.
59. '*The Thief* is to be the dark sister of *The Christmas Oratorio*'. 'Ögonblickets tid, gemenskapens rum: Göran Tunström i samtal med Arne Melberg', *Norsk Litterær Årbok* XXIV (1989), p.38.
60. This translation from *Tjuven* is by Joan Tate, from an extract translated for *Swedish Book Review*: Supplement, 1988.
61. In the decade after *Tjuven*, Tunström published *Chang Eng*, premiered at

Klarateatern in 1987, the prose book *Under tiden* (Meanwhile, 1993) and a collection of short stories, *Det sanna livet* (The True Life, 1991).
62. Similarities with the magical realism of Latin-American fiction have often been noted. See for example Olsson & Algulin, *Litteraturens historia i Sverige*, Stockholm, 1987. Tunström seems to have nothing against such comparisons (see 'Nu drar jag mig undan ett par år', *Dagens Nyheter*, 29 May 1986).
63. Tunström's need to instruct and to nurture others would seem to be a legacy from his ordained father. He admits as much in conversation with Arne Melberg, *Norsk Litterær Årbok* XXIV (1989) p. 37.
64. The orthography of the original Swedish captures the quality of Splendid's broad Värmland dialect.
65. 'Faking the Eighteenth Century', a lecture given on 4 March 1997 at University College, London. Burman also describes her stylistic techniques in the article 'Dikt och sanning: Om författarskap och forskning'.
66. Another publication arising from the project was Carina Burman, *Mamsellen och förlagarna: Fredrika Bremers förlagskontakter 1828-65*. (The Spinster and her Publishers: Fredrika Bremer's Contacts with her Publishing Companies, 1828-65). Uppsala, 1995.
67. Page references are to the First Edition.
68. Jörgen Hammenskog, *Göteborgs-Posten*, 7 September 1987.

SELECT BIBLIOGRAPHY

General

Algulin, Ingemar, *Contemporary Swedish Prose*. Stockholm, 1983.
Broström, Torben, *Moderne svensk litteratur 1948-1972*. Copenhagen, 1973. (Swedish translation, Stockholm, 1974).
Forsås-Scott, Helena, *Swedish Women's Writing 1850-1995*. London, 1997. (Includes Trotzig, Lidman, Ekman, Pleijel and Kandre).
Lagerlöf, Karl Erik (ed.), *Femtitalet i backspegeln*. Stockholm, 1968. (Articles on authors of 1950s).
Larsson, Bo, *Närvarande frånvaro. Frågor kring liv och tro i modern svensk skönlitteratur*. Stockholm, 1987. (Includes Lars Andersson, Delblanc, Gyllensten, Jersild, Sara Lidman, Astrid Lindgren, Torgny Lindgren and Tunström).
Lundqvist, Åke, *Från sextital till åttital. Färdvägar i svensk prosa*. Stockholm, 1981. (Essays on *inter al.* Delblanc, Enquist and Jersild).
Mawby, Janet, *Writers and Politics in Modern Scandinavia*. London, 1978.
Nilsson, Sven & Yrlid, Rolf (eds), *Svensk litteratur i kritik och debatt 1957-1970*. Stockholm, 1972. (Anthology of reviews, articles, etc.).
Norén, Kjerstin (ed.), *Linjer i nordisk prosa 1965-1975*. Lund, 1977.

Rossel, Sven H., *A History of Scandinavian Literature 1870-1980*. Minneapolis, 1982.
Stenkvist, Jan, *Den nyaste litteraturen, 1870-1970*. III. Stockholm, 1975. (On period 1950-1970).

Bisztray, George, 'Documentarism and the Modern Scandinavian Novel', *Scandinavian Studies* XLVIII (1976), pp.71-83.
Hallberg, Peter, 'Dokument — Engagemang — Fiktion', *Nordisk tidskrift* XL (1970), pp.77-98. (On contemporary Swedish fiction).

Lars Gyllensten

Isaksson, Hans, *Hängivenhet och distans. En studie i Lars Gyllenstens romankonst*. Stockholm, 1974.
Isaksson, Hans, *Lars Gyllensten*. Boston (Mass.), 1978.
Lilliestam, Åke, *Lars Gyllenstens bibliografi:1946-92*. Stockholm, 1993.
Munck, Kerstin, *Gyllenstens roller. En studie över tematik och gestaltning i Lars Gyllenstens författarskap*. Lund, 1974.

Liedman, Sven-Eric, 'Mänskligt och omänskligt. Operationalism och existentialism i Lars Gyllenstens författarskap', *SLT* XXIX (1966), no.1, pp.24-39.
Orton, Gavin, 'A Swedenborgian Dream-Book: Lars Gyllensten's *Palatset i parken*', *Scandinavica* XXIII (1984), pp. 5-23.
Orton, Gavin, 'St Antony in Värmland: Lars Gyllensten's *Grottan i öknen*', *Scandinavica* XXX (1991), pp. 41-62.
Palmqvist, Bertil, 'Satsa på undret. Lars Gyllenstens dialektiska trilogi', *BLM* XXXII (1963), pp. 262-88. (On *Moderna myter, Det blå skeppet* and *Barnabok*).
Warme, Lars G., 'Lars Gyllensten's *Diarium Spirituale*: The Creative Process as a Novel', *Scandinavica* XIX (1980), pp.165-80.

Lars Ahlin

Ekman, Hans-Göran, *Humor, grotesk och pikaresk. Studier i Lars Ahlins realism*. Staffanstorp, 1975. (Concentrates on *Tåbb med manifestet* and *Min död är min*).
Furulund, Lars (ed.), *Synpunkter på Lars Ahlin*. Stockholm, 1971. (Contains article by Furuland on 'Lars Ahlin — ursprungsmiljö och bildningsgång' and three articles on *Natt i marknadstältet*).
Hansson, Gunnar D., *Nådens oordning: studier i Lars Ahlins roman Fromma mord*. Stockholm, 1988.
Melberg, Arne, *På väg från realismen. En studie i Lars Ahlins författarskap*,

dess sociala och litterära förutsättningar. Uppsala, 1973.

Lundell, Torborg, *Lars Ahlin.* Boston (Mass.), 1977.

Nielsen, Erik A., *Lars Ahlin. Studier i sex romaner.* Stockholm, 1968. (On *Tåbb med manifestet, Min död är min, Om, Fromma mord, Natt i marknadstältet* and *Bark och löv*).

Hansson, Gunnar D., 'Den dubbla tillhörigheten. En tolkning av Lars Ahlins humoruppfattning', *Tidskrift för litteraturvetenskap* I (1971/1972), pp. 97-109 and 234-49.

Lundell, Torborg, 'Lars Ahlin's Concept of Equality', *Scandinavian Studies* XLVII (1975), pp. 339-51.

Lundell, Torborg, 'Lars Ahlin's Concept of the Writer as Identificator and Förbedjare', *Scandinavica* XIV (1975), pp. 27-35.

Sara Lidman

Röster om Sara Lidman. Från ABF:s litteraturseminarium i mars, 1991. Stockholm, 1991.

Adolfsson, Eva, 'I gränslandet. Om språkliga kraftfält i Sara Lidmans jernbaneepos', *BLM* LV (1986), pp. 96-101.

Björck, Nina, 'Ett långsamt lyssnande, ett ständigt vidgande av ord', *BLM* LXV (1996).

Borland, H. H., 'Sara Lidman's Progress', *Scandinavian Studies* XXXIX (1967), pp. 97-114.

Borland, H. H., 'Sara Lidman, Novelist and Moralist', *SLT* XXXVI (1973), pp. 27-34.

Dahlstedt, Karl-Hampus, 'Folkmål i rikssvensk prosadiktning. Några synpunkter med utgångspunkt från Sara Lidmans Västerbottens romaner', *Nysvenska studier* XXXIX (1959), pp. 106-68.

Forsås-Scott, Helena, 'Sara Lidman' in *Swedish Women's Writing 1850-1995.* London, 1997, pp. 197-215.

Holm, Birgitta, 'Det stoff som jernvägar göres av. Några drag i Sara Lidmans prosa', *BLM* XLVIII (1982), pp.51-58.

Holm, Birgitta, 'Fästen lagda över gungfly. Smärtan, skulden och vämjelsen i Lidmans romansvit Jernbanan', *BLM* LXIII (1994), pp.8-18.

Källestål, C. & Sörm, S., 'Vreden som "lifsens rot". Sara Lidman intervjuar'. *BLM* XLIX (1983), pp. 322-29.

Mannheimer, Carin, 'Från angelägenhet till angelägenhet', in *Femtitalet i backspegeln,* pp. 81-86.

Thorell, Gunnar, 'Samtal med Sara (före gruvstrejken)', *OoB* LXXIX (1970), pp.36-39.

Per Olof Sundman

Hinchliffe, Ian, *Per Olof Sundman: Ingenjör Andrées luftfärd*. (Studies in Swedish Literature 13). Hull, 1982.
McGregor, Rick, *Per Olof Sundman and the Icelandic Sagas: A Study of Narrative Method*. Gothenburg, 1994.
Warme, Lars G., *Per Olof Sundman: Writer of the North*. Westport (Conn.), 1984.

Bäckström, Lars G., 'Sanningen och Sundman', *TLM* (1996), pp. 35-66.
Lindberger, Örjan, 'Den svåråtkomliga kunskapen om människan. Om författaren Per Olof Sundman', *Nordisk tidskrift* LXIX (1993), pp. 205-15.
Sjöberg, Leif, 'Per Olof Sundman and the Uses of Reality', *The American Scandinavian Review* LIX (1971), pp. 145-54.
Stern, Rolf E., 'Per Olof Sundmans roman Expeditionen', *SLÅ* (1974), pp. 30-53.
Sundman, P. O., 'Stenen i vägskälet', *BLM* XXX (1961), pp. 529-32.
Sundman, P. O., 'Kommentarer kring en teknik', *BLM* XXXII (1963), pp. 231-34.
Sundman, P. O., 'Om att övertolka', *BLM* XXXIX (1970), pp. 414-18.
Tideström, Gunnar, 'Ingenjör Andrées luftfärd som dokumentärskildring och litterärt konstverk', in *Från Snoilsky till Sonnevi. Litteraturvetenskapliga studier tillägnade Gunnar Brandell*. Stockholm, 1976, pp.182-202.

Sven Delblanc

Agrell, Beata, *Frihet och facticitet. En resa genom Sven Delblancs textvärld*. Gothenburg, 1982. (Dissertation).
Ahlbom, Lars, *Sven Delblanc*. Stockholm, 1996. (An invaluable monograph which deals with the works chronologically and provides a full bibliography of books and articles about Delblanc).
Robinson, Michael, *Sven Delblanc: Åminne*. (Studies in Swedish Literature 12). Hull, 1981.

Lundqvist, Åke, 'Det mörka landets lockelse' in *Från sextital till åttital. Färdvägar i svensk prosa*. Stockholm, 1981.
Nilsson, Björn, 'Delblancs presens historicum', *BLM* LV (1986), pp. 88-93.
Petherick, Karin, '"Att dikta in en mening i vårt kaos." Some thoughts on the fiction of Sven Delblanc', *Proceedings of the Eighth Biennial Conference of Teachers of Scandinavian Studies in G.B. and N. Ireland*, Edinburgh University 2-7 April 1989, ed. by I. Scobbie, pp.249-60.
Petherick, Karin, 'Skuldbördans plåga. Sven Delblancs Moria land', *Samlaren* CXI (1990), pp. 77-84.

Petherick, Karin, 'Diktverket enbart ska tala! Kring några brev från Sven Delblanc', *Artes* 1993, no.4, pp. 87-97. (Delblanc throws light on his own aesthetic principles and practice).

Whittingham, Charlotte, 'Expressing the Inexpressible: Sven Delblanc and the Role of the Artist', *Scandinavica* XXXVI (1997) no.1, pp. 59-75.

Wästberg, Per, 'Sven Delblanc' in *Lovtal*. Stockholm, 1996.

P. C. Jersild

Anshelm, Jonas, *Förnuftets brytpunkt: om teknikkritiken i P. C. Jersilds författarskap*. Stockholm, 1990.

Nordwall-Ehrlow, Rut, *Människan som djur: en studie i P. C. Jersilds författarskap*. Lund, 1983.

Nordwell-Ehrlow, Rut, *Bibliografi över P. C. Jersilds författarskap* [1960-1984]. Lund, 1989.

Scobbie, Irene, 'P. C. Jersild's novel *Djurdoktorn* and Modern Swedish Society', *Northern Studies* XXII (1985), pp. 40-51.

Shideler, Ross, 'Dehumanization and the Bureaucracy in Novels by P. C. Jersild', *Scandinavica* XXIII (1985), pp. 25-38.

Shideler, Ross, 'P.C. Jersild's *Efter floden* and Human Value(s)', *Scandinavica* XXVII (1988), pp. 31-43.

Swedish Book Review Supplement on Jersild, 1984.

Per Olov Enquist

Bredsdorff, Thomas, *De svarta hålen. Om tillkomsten av ett språk i Per Olov Enquists författarskap*. Stockholm, 1991.

Ekselius, Eva, *Andas fram mitt ansikte: om den mystiska och djuppsykologiska strukturen hos Per Olov Enquist*. Stehag, 1996.

Henningsen, Erik H., *Per Olov Enquist. En undersøgelse af en venstreintellektuel forfatters forsøg på at omfunktionere den litterære institution*. Copenhagen, 1975.

Jansson, Henrik, *Per Olov Enquist och det inställda upproret: ett författarskap i relation till svensk debatt 1981-86*. Åbo, 1987.

Schideler, Ross, *Per Olov Enquist: A Critical Study*. Connecticut and London, 1984.

Adolfsson, Eva, et al. 'Det liberala medvetandets gränser. Texter om P. O. Enquists författarskap', *BLM* XL (1971), pp. 273-87.

Enander, Crister, 'Mannen på stranden', *BLM* LX (1991), pp. 24-35.

Gunnarsson, Björn, 'När planen går om intet. Om Per Olov Enquist', *BLM* LXII (1993), pp. 46-49.

Linnér, Sven, 'Per Olov Enquists Legionärerna', in *Den moderne roman og*

romanforskning i Norden. Oslo, 1971, pp. 68-89.
Myhren, Dagne Groven, 'Selvoversettelsens tragikk. En studie i Per Olov Enquists Från regnormarnas liv', *Nordisk tidskrift* LXV (1989), pp.147-57.
Zetterström, Margareta, '"Det finns ingen helgonlik objectivitet". En studie i Per Olov Enquists *Legionärerna*', *BLM* XXXIX (1970), pp. 524-32.
Öhman, Anders, 'Att få det hoplagt om Per Olov Enquists roman Kapten Nemos bibliotek', *Horisont* XL (1993), pp. 31-37.

Torgny Lindgren

Pehrson, Ingela, *Livsmodet i skrönans värld: en studie i Torgny Lindgrens romaner Ormens väg på hälleberget, Bat Seba och Ljuset*. Uppsala, 1993.

Hedlund, Tom, 'Torgny Lindgren', in Hedlund, Tom, *Mitt i 70-talet: 15 yngre svenska författare presenteras*. Stockholm, 1975.
Hinchliffe, Ian, 'Torgny Lindgren', in *Swedish Book Review*, 1985: Supplement, pp. 5-12.
Larsson, Bo, 'Hurudan är Herren? (Torgny Lindgren)', in Larsson, Bo, *Närvarande frånvaro*. Stockholm, 1987, pp. 247-85.
Schueler, Kaj, 'Hurudan är Herren? Ett samtal med Torgny Lindgren', *OoB* XCIII (1984) no. 3, pp. 12-21.
Sjögren, Lennart, '"Och det var som en tröst". Anteckningar runt Torgny Lindgrens roman Ormens väg på hälleberget', *Vår lösen* 1982, no. 6, pp. 402-7.
Söderlund, Mats, '"Orden dem hava stormvindens kraft": att läsa Torgny Lindgren', *Horisont* XXXVII (1990), pp. 71-75.

Kerstin Ekman

Röster om Kerstin Ekman. Stockholm, 1993. (A collection of substantial papers from a seminar held by ABF, Stockholm).
Schottenius, Maria, *Den kvinnliga hemligheten: en studie i Kerstin Ekmans romankonst*. Stockholm, 1992.

Death, Sarah, '"They can't do this to time": Women's and men's time in Kerstin Ekman's *Änglahuset*' in Death, S. & Forsås-Scott, H., (eds), *A Century of Swedish Narrative: Essays in Honour of Karin Petherick*. Norwich, 1994, pp. 267-80.
Forsås-Scott, Helena, *Swedish Women's Writing 1850-1995*. London, 1987, pp. 216-35.
Gruvaeus, Jonas, 'Kerstin Ekman', in *Svenska samtidsförfattare*, 1. Bibliotekstjänst, Lund, 1997, pp. 36-46.

Johnsson, Arne, 'Det som bestämmer en som människa', *BLM* LXV (1996), pp. 39-41.
Schottenius, Maria, 'Så modern och så olycklig!' in *I lärdomens trädgård. Festskrift till Louise Vinge*, ed. Sjöblad, C. *et al.* Lund, 1996, pp. 423-30.
Stenström, Thure, 'Kerstin Ekman, Krilon och vår ondska', *Svenska Dagbladet*, 2 September 1996.
Swedish Book Review. Kerstin Ekman Supplement, eds Death, S. & Forsås-Scott, H., Lampeter, 1995. [Articles on Ekman's writing, translations of articles by her and extracts from her work, and a previously unpublished autobiographical poem 'Barndomen' (Childhood)].
Wästberg, Per, 'Siare och sibylla, reporter och poet', *Dagens Nyheter*, 7 June 1995. Reprinted in *Lovtal*. Stockholm, 1996, pp. 229-51.
Wright, Rochelle, 'Theme, imagery and narrative perspective in Kerstin Ekman's *En stad av ljus*'. *Scandinavian Studies* LIX (1987), pp. 1-27.
Wright, Rochelle. 'Approaches to history in the works of Kerstin Ekman',*Scandinavian Studies* LXIII (1991), pp. 293-304.

Göran Tunström

Bergh, Magnus, 'En bro till Göran Tunström', *BLM* LVIII (1989), pp. 99-107.
Garpe, Margareta, 'Våra kroppar är märkliga katedraler', *OoB* XCII (1983), pp. 4-16.
Larsson, Bo, *Närvarande frånvaro*. Stockholm, 1987, pp. 322-67.
Söderblom, Staffan, 'Fadern, Sonen och den heliga Modern', *BLM* LII (1983), pp. 284-87.
Göran Tunström. Swedish Book Review Supplement. Lampeter, 1988.
Weyler, Svante, 'Hur många älskande ser du?' *OoB* XCII (1983), pp. 25-28.

Carina Burman

Burman, Carina, 'Dikt och sanning: om författarskap och forskning', *Tijdschrift voor Skandinavistiek*, XVIII (1997), pp. 63-70.
Death, Sara, 'Carina Burman', *Swedish Book Review* XVI (1998), no.1, pp. 2f.
Death, Sara, 'An Interview with Carina Burman, March 1998', *Swedish Book Review*, 1998, no.1, pp. 4-6.

Jonas Gardell

Petherick, Karin, 'Three Swedish Voices', *The European Gay Review*, 1988, no. 3.
Smith, Neil, 'Jonas Gardell', *Swedish Book Review* XV (1997), no. 2, pp. 16-17.

Select list of translations

Note: more comprehensive lists will be found in the following:

Geddes, Tom, *Sweden: Books in English 1963-1978*. London: Swedish Embassy, 1979.
Gustafson, Alrik, List of Translations in English in *A History of Swedish Literature*. Minneapolis: University of Minnesota, 1961, pp. 645-60.
Holmbäck, Bure, *About Sweden: A bibliographical outline 1900-1963*. Stockholm: Sweden Illustrated, 1968.
Larson-Fleming, S., *Books on Sweden in English*. New York: Swedish Information Service, 1983.
New Books in the Reference Library of the Swedish Information Service. New York. (Annual).
Ng, M. & Batts, M., *Scandinavian Literature in English Translation 1928-1977*. Vancouver: CAUTG, 1978.
Publications on Sweden. Stockholm: Swedish Institute. (Annual).
'Recent Books Published in Non-Scandinavian Languages'. Compiled by Tom Geddes. *Scandinavica*, Norwich. (Annual).
Suecana extranea. Books on Sweden and Swedish Literature in Foreign Languages. Stockholm: Royal Library. (Annual).
Swedish Book Review (ed. Laurie Thompson). St David's University College, Lampeter, SA48 7ED, Wales. (Published twice annually). Contains translated excerpts from modern Swedish literature and lists of new English translations.

Anthologies, etc.
An Anthology of Modern Swedish Literature, compiled by Per Wästberg. New York: Merrick, 1979. (Extracts from works by 30 authors written after World War II).
Anthology of Swedish Lyrics from 1750 to 1925. Transl. by C. Wharton Stork. New York: Granger, 1979 (Reprint of 1930 edition).
Contemporary Swedish Poetry. Transl. by John Matthias & G. Printz-Påhlson. London: Anvil & Chicago, 1980.
Dimensions, 1994. Special Issue on Contemporary Nordic Literature, (ed. John Weinstock). Austin, Texas: Dimensions, 1994.
Four Swedish Poets — Tranströmer, Ström, Sjögren and Espmark. Transl. by Robin Fulton, Buffalo, N.Y.: White Pine; London: Forest Books, 1990.
Eight Swedish Poets. Transl. by F. Fleisher. Malmö: Cavefors, 1969. (Gunnar Ekelöf, Lars Forssell, Hjalmar Gullberg, Björn Håkanson, Pär Lagerkvist,

Translations

Erik Lindegren, Harry Martinson, Edith Södergran).
Five Swedish Poets. Transl. by Robin Fulton. New Jersey: Spirit, 1972. (Tomas Tranströmer, Östen Sjöstrand, Göran Sonnevi, Gunnar Harding, Eli Hillbäck).
Five Swedish Poets. Trans. by Robin Fulton. Norwich: Norvik Press, 1997. (Kjell Espmark, Lennart Sjögren, Eva Ström, Staffan Söderblom, Werner Aspenström).
Forays into Swedish Poetry, (ed. L. Gustafson). Transl. by R. T. Rovinsky. Austin & London, 1978. (Includes poems by Göran Printz-Påhlson, Vilhelm Ekelund, Erik Blomberg, Edith Södergran and Tomas Tranströmer).
International Portland Review. Portland, Oregon, 1980. (Includes Gunnar Harding, Kjell Espmark, Margareta Ekström, Östen Sjöstrand *et al.*).
Literary Review. Swedish Issue, (guest ed.) R. B. Vowles. Fairleigh Dickinson University, New Jersey, 1965-66.
Modern Scandinavian Poetry 1900-1977, (ed.) M. Allwood. Mullsjö: Anglo-American Center, 1982.
Modern Scandinavian Poetry: The Panorama of Poetry 1900-1980. Transl. by Martin Allwood *et al*. (2nd revised ed). Mullsjö: Persona Press; Walnut Creek, Calif: Eagleye Books, 1986.
Modern Swedish Poetry in Translation, (eds G. Harding & A. Hollo). Minneapolis: University of Minnesota Press, 1979.
Modern Swedish Prose in Translation, (ed. Karl Erik Lagerlöf). Minneapolis: Minnesota Press, 1979.
'New Swedish Poetry from the 1990s', *Swedish Book Review*, 1998, no.1. (Poems by Bengt Emil Johnson, Johanna Ekstrom, Bruno K.Öijer, Gunnar Harding, Birgitta Trotzig, Werner Aspenström, Johannes Edfelt *et al*. intro. and transl. by Anne Born).
New Swedish Plays, ed. & intro. by Gunilla Anderman. Norwich: Norvik Press, 1992. (Ingmar Bergman, *A Matter of the Soul*. Stig Larsson, *Red Light*. Lars Norén, *Munich — Athens*. Agneta Pleijel, *Summer Nights*).
Preparations for Flight and Other Swedish Stories. Transl. Robin Fulton. London: Forest Books, 1990. (Includes Lars Gustafsson, Kristian Petri, Werner Aspenström, Mare Kandre, Ola Larson, Torgny Lindgren, Niklas Rådström and Erland Josephson).
Scandinavian Review. *Literary Issue*. Vol. 69, New York, 1981. (Includes Birger Sjöberg, Lars Andersson, Kjell Sundberg, Kjell Espmark, Edith Södergran, *et al.*).
Scandinavian Women Writers. Anthology from the 1880s to the 1980s (ed. Ingrid Claréus). New York and London: Greenwood Press, 1989.
Swedish Poets in Translation, (guest ed. G. Tunström). Transl. by D. Harry. Australia: South Head Press, 1985. (Includes Werner Aspenström, Göran Tunström, Göran Sonnevi, Gunnar Harding, Tomas Tranströmer, *et al.*).
Writ. Translation Issue. Writ, Toronto, 1983. (Includes Harry Martinson,

Werner Aspenström, Jacques Werup, *et al.*).

Individual Authors

Ahlin, Lars, *Cinnamoncandy*. (Kanelbiten) Transl. by Hanna Kalter Weiss. New York: Garland, 1990 (The Garland Library of World Literature in Translation, 1).

Aspenström. Werner, *Thirty-seven Poems from Four Books*. Transl. by Robin Fulton. London: Oasis Books, 1977.

Aspenström, Werner, *You and I and the World*. Transl. Siv Cedering. Merrick, N.J.: Cross-Cultural Communications, 1980. (Swedish-English parallel text).

Aspenström, Werner, *The Blue Whale and Other Pieces*. Transl. by Robin Fulton. London: Oasis Books, 1981.

Aspenström, Werner, *Selected Poems*. Transl. by Robin Fulton in *Quarterly Review of Literature*. Poetry Series, vol. 34. Princeton, N.J: QRL, 1995.

Bergman, Hjalmar, *God's Orchid* (*Markurells i Wadköping*). Transl. by E. Classen, New York: Knopf, 1924.

Bergman, Hjalmar, *The Head of the Firm* (*Chefen fru Ingeborg*). Transl. by E. Sprigge & C. Napier. London: Allen & Unwin, 1936.

Bergman, Hjalmar, *Thy Rod and Thy Staff*. (*Farmor och Vår Herre*). Transl. by C. Napier. London: J. Cape, 1937.

Bergman, Hjalmar, *Four plays*, (ed. Walter Johnson). Transl. by Henry Person *et al.* Seattle and London: University of Washington Press, 1968. (*Markurells of Wadköping, The Baron's Will, Swedenhielms* and *Mr Sleeman is Coming*).

Boye, Karin, *Kallocain*. Transl. by Gustaf Lannestock. Madison & London: Wisconsin University Press, 1966.

Boye, Karin, *Complete Poems*. Transl. by David McDuff. Newcastle-upon-Tyne: Bloodaxe Books, 1994.

Carpelan, Bo, *Voices at the Late Hour* (*Rösterna i den sena timmen*). Transl. by Irma Margareta Martin. Athens, Georgia: University of Georgia Press, 1988.

Carpelan, Bo, *Axel*. Transl. by David McDuff. Manchester: Carcanet, 1989; London: Paladin, 1991.

Carpelan, Bo, *The Wristwatch*. Transl. by Joan Tate. Lampeter: St David's University College, 1991. (Lampeter Translation Series, 3).

Dagerman, Stig, *The Condemned* (*Den dödsdömde*). Transl. by H. Alexander & Llewellyn Jones. Princeton: Princeton University Press, 1951. (In *Scandinavian plays of the 20th century*).

Dagerman, Stig, *The Games of the Night* (*Nattens lekar* and *Vårt behov av tröst*). Transl. by Naomi Walford. London: Bodley Head, 1959; Philadelphia, 1961.

Dagerman, Stig, *Swedish Book Review: Stig Dagerman Supplement*, (ed. Laurie

Thompson). Lampeter, 1984. (Selected passages in translation).
Dagerman, Stig, *A Burnt Child* (*Bränt barn*) Transl. by Alan Blair. Intro. by Laurie Thompson. London: Quartet, 1990. (Reissue)
Dagerman, Stig, *Pithy Poems* (*Dagsedlar*). Transl. by Laurie Thompson. Lampeter: St David's University College, 1990. (The Lampeter Translation Series, 4) (Parallel Swedish-English text).
Dagerman, Stig, *Island of the Doomed* (*De dömdes ö*). Transl. by Laurie Thompson. London: Quartet, 1992.
Dagerman, Stig, *The Snake* (*Ormen*). Transl & intro. by Laurie Thompson. London: Quartet, 1995.
Delblanc, Sven, *The Castrati* (*Kastrater*). Transl. by C. W. Williams. Ann Arbor, (Mich): Karoma, 1979.
Delblanc, Sven, *Speranza*. Transl. by Paul Britten Austin. London: Secker & Warburg, 1983.
Edfelt, Johannes, *Family Tree: Thirteen Prose Poems*. Transl. by Robin Fulton. London: Oasis Books, 1981.
Ekelund, Vilhelm, *Agenda*. Transl. by Lennart Bruce. Berkeley, California: Cloud Marauder, 1976. (Selected aphorisms).
Ekelöf, Gunnar, *Late Arrival on Earth: Selected Poems* (*Sent på jorden*). Transl. by Robert Bly & Christina Paulston. London: Rapp & Carroll, 1967. (Poetry Europe series).
Ekelöf, Gunnar, *Selected poems*. Transl by W. H. Auden & Leif Sjöberg, with an introduction by G. Printz-Påhlson. Harmondsworth: Penguin, 1971 & New York: Pantheon, 1972. (Penguin modern European poets).
Ekelöf, Gunnar, *Guide to the Underworld* (*Vägvisare till underjorden*).Transl. by Rika Lesser. Amherst: University of Massachusetts Press, 1980.
Ekelöf, Gunnar, *Songs of Something Else. Selected Poems*. Transl. by Nathan & James Larson. Princeton: Princeton University Press, 1982. (English and Swedish parallel text).
Ekelöf, Gunnar, *A Mölna Elegy*. Transl by Muriel Ruleyser & Leif Sjöberg. Greensboro, N.C.: Unicorn Press, 1985. 2 vols, Swedish and English.
Ekelöf, Gunnar, *Modus Vivendi: Selected Prose of Gunnar Ekelöf* . Ed. & transl. by Erik Thygesen. Norwich: Norvik Press, 1995.
Ekman, Kerstin, *Blackwater* (*Händelser vid vatten*). Transl. by Joan Tate. London: Chatto & Windus, 1995.
Ekman, Kerstin, Ekman Supplement, *Swedish Book Review*, 1995. (Poems and extracts from novels. Various translators).
Ekman, Kerstin, *Under the Snow* (*De tre små mästarna*).Transl. by Joan Tate. London: Chatto & Windus, 1997.
Ekman, Kerstin, *Witches' Rings* (*Häxringarna*). Transl. by Linda Schenck. Norwich: Norvik Press, 1997.
Enquist, Per Olov, *The Legionnaires: a Documentary Novel* (*Legionärerna*). Transl. by Alan Blair. London: Cape, 1974.

Enquist, Per Olof, *The Night of the Tribades* (*Tribadernas natt*). Transl. by Ross Shideler. New York: Dramatists Play Service, 1978.

Enquist, Per-Olov, *The Magnetist's Fifth Winter* (*Magnetisörens femte vinter*). Transl. by Paul Britten Austin. London: Quartet, 1989.

Enquist, Per-Olov, *The Hour of the Lynx* (*I lodjurets timma*). Transl. by Ross Shideler. London: Forest Books, 1990; Chester Springs, Pa: Dufour Editions, 1991.

Enquist, Per-Olov, *Captain Nemo's Library* (*Kapten Nemos bibliotek*). Transl. by Anna Paterson. London: Quartet, 1992.

Enquist, Per Olof, *The March of the Musicians*. (*Musikanternas uttåg*).Transl. by Joan Tate. Intro. by Kathryn Mead. London: Quartet, 1993.

Espmark, Kjell, *Route Tournante: Poems*. Transl. by Joan Tate. London: Forest Books, 1993.

Fridegård, Jan, *I, Lars Hård*. Transl. by Robert E. Björk. Lincoln, Nebraska, 1983.

Fridegård, Jan, *Land of the Wooden Gods* (*Trägudarnas land*). Transl. by Robert E. Bjork. Lincoln & London: University of Nebraska Press, 1989.

Fridegård, Jan, *People of the Dawn* (*Gryningsfolket*). Transl. by Robert E. Bjork. Lincoln & London: University of Nebraska Press, 1990.

Fridegård, Jan, *Sacrificial Smoke* (*Offerrök*). Transl. by Robert E. Bjork. Lincoln & London: University of Nebraska Press, 1990.

Frostenson, Katerina, *Jan Håfström* (A suite of poems to Jan Håfström). Transl. by Joan Tate *et al.* Malmö: Rooseum, 1994. (Rooseums utställningskatalog, 17). (Parallel Swedish-English text.)

Fröding, Gustaf, *The Selected Poems of Gustaf Fröding*. Transl. by Henrik Aspan, in collaboration with Martin Allwood. Walnut Creek, Ca.: Eagleye Books; Mullsjö: Persona Press, 1993.

Gullberg, Hjalmar, *Gentleman, Single, Refined* (*Ensamstående bildad herre*). Transl. with an introduction by Judy Moffett. Stockholm: Norstedts, 1979.

Gustafsson, Lars, *The Death of a Beekeeper* (*En biodlares död*). Transl by Janet K. Swaffar & Guntram H. Weber. New York: New Direction, 1981; London: Collins Harvill, 1990; London: Collins Harvill, 1991.

Gustafsson, Lars, *The Tennis Players* (*Tennisspelarna*). Transl. by Yvonne L. Sandstroem. New York: New Directions, 1983.

Gustafsson, Lars, *Funeral Music for Freemasons* (*Sorgemusik för frimurare*). Transl. by Yvonne L. Sandstroem. New York: Grove Press, 1987.

Gustafsson, Lars, *Bernard Foy's Third Castling* (*Bernard Foys tredje rockad*). Transl. by Yvonne L Sandstroem. New York: New Directions, 1988.

Gustafsson, Lars, *The Stillness of the World Before Bach: New Selected Poems,* (ed. Christopher Middleton). Transl. by Robin Fulton, Philip Martin, Yvonne L. Sandstroem, Harriet Watts, and Christopher Middleton, in collaboration with Lars Gustafsson. New York: New Directions, 1988.

Gustafsson, Lars, *A Tiler's Afternoon* (*En kakelsättares eftermiddag*). Transl. by

Tom Geddes. London: Harvill; New York: New Directions, 1993.

Gyllensten, Lars, *The Testament of Cain (Cains memoarer)*. Transl. by Keith Bradfield. London: Calder & Boyars, 1967.

Hammarskjöld, Dag, *Markings (Vägmärken)*. Transl. by Leif Sjöberg & W. H. Auden. London: Faber, 1964. (Reissue London: Faber & Faber, 1988).

Harding, Gunnar, *They Killed Sitting Bull and Other Poems*. Transl. by Robin Fulton. London: London Magazine, 1973. (Poems from *Blommor till James Dean, Örnen har landat*).

Harding, Gunnar, *Starnberger See*. Transl. by Robin Fulton. London: Oasis Books, 1983. (Selection from *Starnberger See*).

Heidenstam, Verner von, *Sweden's Laureate. Selected poems*. Transl. by C. W. Stork. New Haven: Yale University, 1919.

Heidenstam, Verner von, *The Swedes and Their Chieftains (Svenskarna och deras hövdingar)*. Transl. by C. W. Stork. New York: American Scandinavian Foundation's Scandinavian Classics, 1925.

Heidenstam, Verner von, *The Charles Men (Karolinerna)*. Transl. by C. W. Stork. New York: American Scandinavian Foundation's Scandinavian Classics 15-16, 1930.

Hellström, Gustaf, *Lacemaker Lekholm Has an Idea (Snörmakare Lekholm får en idé)*. Transl. by F. H. Lyon. London: Allen & Unwin, 1930; New York: The Dial Press, 1931.

Jansson, Tove, *Comet in Moominland*. Transl. by Elizabeth Portch. London: Penguin, 1967.

Jansson, Tove, *The Summer Book (Sommarboken)*. Transl. by Thos Teal. London: Hutchinson, 1975.

Jansson, Tove, *Sun City (Solstaden)*. Transl. by Thos Teal. London: Hutchinson, 1977.

Jersild, P.C., *The Animal Doctor (Djurdoktorn)*. Transl. by David Mel Paul & Margareta Paul. New York: Pantheon, 1975.

Jersild, P. C., *Jersild Supplement*. Swedish Book Review, Lampeter, 1983. (Extracts from four novels in English translation).

Jersild, P. C., *The House of Babel (Babels hus)*. Transl. by Joan Tate. Lincoln: University of Nebraska Press, 1987. (Modern Scandinavian Literature in Translation).

Jersild, P. C., *A Living Soul (En levande själ)*. Transl. by Rika Lesser. Norwich: Norvik Press, 1989.

Johnson, Eyvind, *Return to Ithica. (Strändernas svall)*. Transl. by Maurice Michael. London & New York: Thames & Hudson, 1952.

Johnson, Eyvind, *1914 (Nu var det 1914)*. Transl. by Mary Sandbach. London: Adam, 1970.

Johnson, Eyvind, *Dreams of Roses and Fire (Drömmar om rosor och eld)*. Transl. by Erik J. Friis. New York: Hippocrene Books, 1984. (Library of Nordic Literature 2).

Kallifatides, Theodar, *Masters and Peasants* (*Bönder och herrar*). Transl. by Thos Teal. New York: Doubleday, 1977.

Kallifatides, Theodor, *The Plow and the Sword* (*Plogen och svärdet*). Transl. by Paul Norlen. Seattle: Fjord Press, 1992.

Key-Åberg, Sandro, *O and An Empty Room*. (*O: Scenprator*). Transl. by Brian Rothwell & Ruth Link. London: Calder & Boyars, 1970.

Lagerkvist, Pär, *The Man Without a Soul* (*Mannen utan själ*) in *Scandinavian Plays of the 20th Century*, ed. by A. Gustafson. New York, 1944.

Lagerkvist, Pär, *Barabbas*. Transl. by Alan Blair. New York, 1951; London; 1952; York: Vintage Books, 1989 (reissue).

Lagerkvist, Pär, *The Death of Ahasuerus* (*Ahasverus död*). Transl. by Naomi Walford. New York, 1962.

Lagerkvist, Pär, *The Dwarf* (*Dvärgen*). Transl. by Alexandra Dick. London, 1967.

Lagerkvist, Pär, *The Eternal Smile* Transl. by Erik Mesterton & Denys W. Harding. New York, 1971. (Contains translation of *Det eviga leendet, Gäst hos verkligheten* and *Bödeln*).

Lagerkvist, Pär, *The Man who Lived his Life Over* (*Mannen som fick leva om sitt liv*) in *Five Modern Scandinavian Plays*. New York, 1971. (Twayne's Library of Scandinavian Literature, vol. II).

Lagerkvist, Pär, *The Difficult Hour* (*Den svåra stunden*) in *Masterpieces of the Modern Scandinavian Theatre* (ed. Robt W. Corrigan). New York, 1976.

Lagerkvist, Pär, *Evening Land = Aftonland*. Transl. by W. H. Auden & Leif Sjöberg. London, 1977. (English — Swedish parallel text).

Lagerkvist, Pär, *The Holy Land* (*Det heliga landet*). Transl. by Naomi Walford. New York, 1982.

Lagerkvist, Pär, *Pilgrim at Sea* (*Pilgrim på havet*). Transl. by Naomi Walford. New York, 1982.

Lagerkvist, Pär, *Herod and Mariamne* (*Mariamne*). Transl. by Naomi Walford. New York: Vintage Books, 1982.

Lagerkvist, Pär, *Five Early Works. Iron and Men* (*Järn och människor*), *The Last Man* (*Sista mänskan*), *The Expectant Guest* (*Den fordringsfulle gästen*), *The Morning* (*Morgonen*), *The Clenched Fist* (*Den knutna näven*). Transl. by Roy Arthur Swanson. Lewiston, N.Y.: Edwin Mellen Press, 1988. (Scandinavian Studies, 1).

Lagerkvist, Pär, *Guest of Reality* (*Gäst hos verkligheten*).Transl. by Robin Fulton. London: Quartet Books, 1989. (Quartet Encounters).

Lagerlöf, Selma, *The Wonderful Adventure of Nils* (*Nils Holgerssons underbara resa*). Transl. by Velma Swanston Howard. New York: Doubleday, 1907.

Lagerlöf, Selma, *Jerusalem* I-II. Transl. by Velma Swanston Howard. New York: Doubleday, 1915 and 1918.

Lagerlöf, Selma, *Thy Soul Shall Bear Witness* (*Körkarlen*). Transl. by W. F. Harvey. London: Odhams Press, 1921.

Lagerlöf, Selma, *The Treasure (Herr Arnes penningar)*. Transl. by Arthur G. Chater. New York: Doubleday, 1925.

Lagerlöf, Selma, *Charlotte Löwensköld*. Transl. by Velma Swanston Howard. New York: Doubleday, 1927.

Lagerlöf, Selma, *From a Swedish Homestead (En herrgårdssägen* and short stories from *Drottningar i Kungahälla, Legender* and *Osynliga länkar)*. Transl. by Jessie Brochner. New York: Books for Libraries Press, 1970.

Lagerlöf, Selma, *The Diary of Selma Lagerlöf (Mårbacka, 3. Dagbok)*. Transl. by Velma Swanston Howard. New York: Kraus Repro Co., 1975.

Lagerlöf, Selma, *The Story of Gösta Berling (Gösta Berlings saga)*. Transl. by Robert Bly. Karlstad: Press Förlag, 1982.

Lagerlöf, Selma, *Christ Legends and other stories (Kristuslegender)*. Transl. Velma Swanston Howard and Pauline Flach. Edinburgh: Floris, 1984.

Lagerlöf, Selma, *The Löwensköld Ring (Löwenskölds ringen)*. Transl. by Linda Schenck. Norwich: Norvik Press, 1991.

Lagerlöf, Selma, *The Changeling (Bortbytingen)*. Transl. by Susana Stevens. New York: Knopf, 1992.

Lagerlöf, Selma, *Christ Legends and Other Stories*. Transl. by Velma Swanston Howard. Edinburgh: Floris Books, 1993.

Lidman, Sara, *The Rain Bird (Regnspiran)*. Transl. by E. Harley Schubert. London: Hutchinson, 1962.

Lidman, Sara, *Naboth's Stone (Nabots sten)*. Transl. by Joan Tate. Norwich: Norvik Press, 1989.

Lindegren, Erik, *The man without a way (Mannen utan väg)*. Transl. by Leif Sjöberg & Ronald Bates, in *New Directions in Prose and Poetry* (ed. J. Laughlin). New York, 1969.

Lindgren, Torgny, *Bathsheba (Bat Seba)*. Transl. by Tom Geddes. London: Collins Harvill, 1988; New York: Harper & Row, 1989.

Lindgren, Torgny, *Merab's Beauty and Other Stories (Merabs skönhet; Legender)*. Transl. by Mary Sandbach. London: Collins Harvill, 1989.

Lindgren, Torgny, *The Way of a Serpent (Ormens väg på hälleberget)*. Transl. by Tom Geddes. London: Collins Harvill, 1990.

Lindgren, Torgny, *Ljuset (Light)*. Transl. by Tom Geddes. London: Harvill, 1992. Pbk 1994.

Lindgren, Torgny, *In Praise of Truth (Till sanningens lov)*. Transl. by Tom Geddes. London: Harvill, 1994.

Lo-Johansson, Ivar, *Bodies of Love (Lyckan)*. Transl. by Allan Tapsell. London: Souvenir Press, 1971; Sphere, 1973.

Lo-Johansson, Ivar, *Breaking Free (Godnatt jord)*. Transl. by Rochelle Wright. Lincoln: University of Nebraska Press, 1990.

Lo-Johansson, Ivar, *Only a Mother (Bara en mor)*. Transl. by Robt E. Bjork. Lincoln: University of Nebraka Press, 1991.

Lundkvist, Artur, *Agadir*. Transl. by William Jay Smith and Leif Sjöberg.

Chicago: Ohio University Press, 1980.

Lundkvist, Artur, *The Talking Tree* (prose poems from 7 different collections). Trans. by Diana Wormuth and Steven P. Sondrup. Utah: Brigham Young University Press, 1982.

Lundkvist, Artur, *Journeys in Dream and Imagination* (*Färdas i drömmen och föreställningen*). Transl. by Ann B. Weissman & Annika Planck. Intro. by Carlos Fuentes. New York: Four Walls Eight Windows; London: Turnabout, 1991.

Martinson, Harry, *Cape Farewell* (*Kap farväl*). Transl. by Naomi Walford. London: Cresset, 1934.

Martinson, Harry, *Flowering Nettle* (*Nässlorna blomma*). Transl. by Naomi Walford. London: Cresset, 1936.

Martinson, Harry, *The Road* (*Vägen till Klockrike*). Transl. by Maurice Michael. London: J. Cape, 1955; New York: Reynal, 1956.

Martinson, Harry, *Aniara*. Transl. by Hugh MacDiarmid and E. Harley Schubert. London: Hutchinson, 1963.

Martinson, Harry, *Wild Bouquet: Nature Poems*. Transl. and intro. by William Jay Smith and Leif Sjöberg. Kansas City: BkMk Press, 1985.

Martinson, Harry, *Aniara: A Review of Man in Time and Space*. Transl. by Stephen Klass & Leif Sjöberg. Södra Sandby: Vekerum, 1991.

Martinson, Moa, *Women and Apple Trees* (*Kvinnor och äppleträd*). Transl. by Margaret S. Lacy. London: Women's Press, 1987.

Martinson, Moa, *My Mother Gets Married* (*Mor gifter sig*). Transl. by Margaret S. Lacy. New York: Feminist Press, 1988.

Moberg, Vilhelm, *The Emigrants* (*Romanen om utvandrarna*). Transl. by Gustaf Lannstock. Vol. 1, *The Emigrants*, 1971; Vol. 2, *Unto a Good Land*, 1971; Vol. 3, *The Settlers*, 1978; Vol. 4, *Last Letter Home*, 1978. New York: Fawcett Popular Library.

Moberg, Vilhelm, *A Time on Earth* (*Din stund på jorden*). Transl. by Naomi Walford. London: Heinemann, 1965.

Myrdal, Jan, *Confessions of a Disloyal European* (*Samtida bekännelser av en europeisk intellektuell*). London: Chatto & Windus, 1968. Chicago: Lake View Press, 1990.

Myrdal, Jan, *Childhood* (*Barndom*). Trans. by Christine Swanson. Chicago: Lake View Press, 1991.

Myrdal, Jan, *Another World: An Autobiographical Novel* (*En annan värld*). Transl. by Alan Bernstein. Chicago: Ravenswood, 1994.

Pleijel, Agneta, *Eyes from a Dream. Poems* (*Ögon ur en dröm*). Transl. by Anne Born. London: Forest Books, 1991.

Pleijel, Agneta, *The Dog Star* (*Hundstjärnan*). Transl. by Joan Tate. London: Peter Owen, 1991.

Siwertz, Sigfrid, *Downstream* (*Selambs* I-II). Transl. by E. Classen. London: Gyldendal, 1922; New York: Knopf, 1929.

Translations

Siwertz, Sigfrid, *Goldman's* (*Det stora varuhuset*). Transl. by E. Gee Nash. London: Allen & Unwin, 1929; New York: Knopf, 1923.

Sjöstrand, Östen, *Toward the Solitary Star: Selected Poetry and Prose*. Transl. by Robin Fulton, Yvonne Sandstroem, Steven P. Sondrup, Diana W. Wormuth. Provo, Utah: Brigham Young University, 1988. (Values in Literature Monographs, 3).

Sonnevi, Göran, *The Economy Spinning Faster and Faster*. Poems chosen and transl. by Robert Bly. New York: SUN, 1982.

Sonnevi, Göran, *A Child is not a Knife: Selected Poems*. Transl. & ed. by Rika Lesser. Princeton, N.J.: Princeton University Press, 1993. (English & Swedish text).

Strindberg, August. The following is a small selection. See bibliographies listed above for more comprehensive coverage.

Strindberg, August, *Queen Christina, Charles XII, Gustav III*. Transl. by Walter Johnson. Seattle and London: University of Washington Press, 1955.

Strindberg, August, *The People of Hemsö* (*Hemsöborna*). Transl. by E. Harley Schubert. London: Cape, 1959.

Strindberg, August, *The Vasa Trilogy. Master Olof, Gustav Vasa. Erik XIV*. Transl. by Walter Johnson. Seattle: University of Washington Press, 1959.

Strindberg, August, *Letters to the Intimate Theatre* (*Öppna brev till Intima teatern*). Transl. by Walter Johnson. Seattle: University of Washington Press, 1959; London: Owen, 1967.

Strindberg, August, *The Red Room* (*Röda rummet*). Transl. by Elizabeth Sprigge. London: Dent, 1967. (Everyman's Library).

Strindberg, August, *The Scapegoat* (*Syndabocken*). Transl. by Arvid Paulson. London: Allen & Unwin, 1967.

Strindberg, August, *The Son of a Servant* (*Tjänstekvinnans son*). Transl. by Evert Sprinchorn. London: Cape, 1967.

Strindberg, August, *A Madman's Defense* (*Le plaidoyer d'un fou*). Transl. by Evert Sprinchorn. London: Cape, 1968.

Strindberg, August, *Inferno and other writings*. Transl. by Evert Sprinchorn. New York: Doubleday, 1968.

Strindberg, August, *The Cloister* (*Klostret*). Transl. by Mary Sandbach. London: Secker & Warburg, 1969.

Strindberg, August, *World Historical Plays. The Nightingale of Wittenberg. Through Deserts to Ancestral Lands. Hellas. The Lamb and the Beast* (*Näktergalen i Wittemburg. Genom öknar till arvland. Hellas. Lammet och odjuret*). Transl. by Arvid Paulson. New York: Twayne, 1970. (The Library of Scandinavian Literature).

Strindberg, August, *Getting Married* (*Giftas* I-II). Transl. by Mary Sandbach. London: Gollancz, 1972.

Strindberg, August, *Dramas of Testimony. The Dance of Death I-II. Advent. Easter. There are Crimes and Crimes.* (*Dödsdansen* I-II. *Advent. Påsk. Brott* och brott).Transl. by Walter Johnson. Seattle and London: University of Washington Press, 1975.

Strindberg, August, *The Plays*. Vol.1. *The Father. Miss Julie. Creditors. The Stronger. Playing with Fire. Erik XIV. The Storm. Ghost Sonata.* Vol. 2. *To Damascus* I-III. *Easter. Dance of Death* I-II. *Crown Bride* (*Fadren. Fröken Julie. Fordringsägare. Den starkare. Leka med elden. Erik XIV. Oväder. Spökssonaten. Till Damaskus* I-III. *Påsk. Dödsdansen* I-II. *Kronbruden*). Transl. by Michael Meyer. London: Secker & Warburg, 1975.

Strindberg, August, *Sleepwalking Nights on Wide-Awake Days* (*Sömngångarnätter*). Transl. by Arvid Paulson. New York: Law-arts publ., 1978.

Strindberg, August, *Inferno* and *From an Occult Diary* (selected by Torsten Eklund) (*Inferno;* ur *Ockulta dagboken*). Transl. by Mary Sandbach. Harmondsworth: Penguin, 1979. (Penguin Classics).

Strindberg, August, *Apologia* and *Two Folk Plays* (*The Great Highway, The Crownbride* and *Swanwhite*). Transl. by Walter Johnson. Seattle and London: University of Washington Press, 1981.

Strindberg, August, *The Chamber Plays. Storm Weather. The Burned House. The Ghost Sonata. The Pelican.* (*Oväder. Brända tomten. Spöksonaten. Pelikanen*).Transl. by Evert Sprinchorn, Seabury Quinn, Jr, and Kenneth Peterson. Minneapolis: Minnsota University Press, 1981.

Strindberg, August, *Five Plays. The Father. Miss Julie. The Dance of Death. A Dream Play. The Ghost Sonata.* (*Fadren. Fröken Julie. Dödsdansen. Ett drömspel. Spöksonaten*). Transl. by Harry G. Carlson. Berkeley and London: University of California Press, 1983.

Strindberg, August, *Plays from the Cynical Life. Playing with Fire. Debit and Credit. Mother Love. The First Warning. Facing Death. Pariah. Simoon.* (*Leka med elden. Debet och Kredit. Moderkärlek. Första varningen. Inför döden. Paria. Samum*). Transl. by Walter Johnson. Seattle and London: University of Washington Press, 1983.

Strindberg, August, *By the Open Sea* (*I havsbandet*). Transl. by Mary Sandbach. London: Secker & Warburg, 1984.

Strindberg, August, *Selected Plays.* Vol. 1. *Miss Julie. Creditors. The Father. The Stronger. Master Olof. Playing with Fire.* (*Fröken Julie. Fordringsägare. Fadren. Den starkare. Mäster Olof. Leka med elden*) Vol. 2. *The Dance of Death* I. *Crimes and Crimes. A Dream Play. The Ghost Sonata. To Damascus* I. *The Pelican* (*Dödsdansen* I. *Brott och brott. Ett drömspel. Spöksonaten. Till Damaskus* I. *Pelikanen.*) Transl. and intro. by Evert Sprinchorn. Minneapolis: University of Minnesota Press, 1986.

Strindberg, August, *Strindberg's The Father and Ibsen's Hedda Gabler.* Adapted by John Osborne. London: Faber and Faber, 1989.

Strindberg, August, *Thunder in the Air* (*Oväder*). Transl. by Eivor Martinus. Bath: Absolute Classics, 1989.

Translations

Strindberg, August, *The Chamber Plays*: *Thunder in the Air. After the Fire. The Ghost Sonata. The Pelican. The Black Glove.* (*Oväder. Brända tomten. Spöksonaten. Pelikanen. Svarta Handsken*). Transl. by Eivor Martinus. Bath: Absolute Press, 1991.

Strindberg, August, *Miss Julie: A Naturalistic Tragedy* (*Fröken Julie*). Transl. & intro. by Helen Cooper from a literal translation by Peter Hogg. London: Methuen Drama, 1992.

Strindberg, August, *The Father* (*Fadren*). New adaptation by Robert Brustein. Chicago: Ivan R. Dee, 1992.

Strindberg, August, *The Pelican & The Isle of the Dead* (*Pelikanen & Toten-Insel*), ed., transl. & intro. by Michael Robinson. Birmingham: University, 1994. (Studies in Drama and Dance).

Strindberg, August, *Miss Julie and Other Plays* (Fröken Julie. Fadren. Dödsdansen. Ett drömspel. Spöksonaten.) Transl. and intro. by Michael Robinson. Oxford University Press, 1998.

Sundman, Per Olof, *The Expedition* (*Expeditionen*). Transl. by Mary Sandbach. London: Secker & Warburg, 1967.

Sundman, Per Olof, *Two Days. Two Nights* (*Två dagar, två nätter*). Transl. by Alan Blair. New York: Pantheon, 1969.

Sundman, Per Olof, *The Flight of the Eagle* (*Ingenjör Andrées luftfärd*). Transl. by Mary Sandbach. London: Secker & Warburg, 1970.

Söderberg, Hjalmar, *Martin Bircks Youth* (*Martin Bircks ungdom*). Transl. by C. W. Stork. London and New York: Harper, 1930.

Söderberg, Hjalmar, *Doctor Glas* (*Doktor Glas*). Transl. by Paul Britten Austin. London: Tandem, 1970.

Söderberg, Hjalmar, *Short stories* (*Historietter*). Selected and transl. by Carl Lofmark. Norwich: Norvik Press, 1987.

Södergran, Edith, *Love and Solitude. Selected Poems 1916-1923*. Transl. by Stina Katchadourian. San Francisco: Fjord Press, 1981. (Bilingual ed).

Södergran, Edith, *Complete Poems*. Transl. by David McDuff. Newcastle-upon-Tyne: Bloodaxe Books, 1984. (Revised ed. 1992).

Södergran, Edith, *Poems*. Transl. by Gounil Brown. Eastbourne: Ixcon Press, 1994. (2nd, enlarged ed).

Södergran, Edith, *Violet Twilights* (Poems). Transl. by Daisy Aldan & Leif Sjöberg. Merrick, N.J.: Cross-Cultural Communications, 1994.

Tranströmer, Tomas, *Night Vision*. Selected and transl. by Robert Bly. London: London Magazine Eds, 1972.

Tranströmer, Tomas, Selected poems in *Paavo Haavikko, Tomas Tranströmer*. Transl. by Anselm Hollo and Robin Fulton. Harmondsworth: Penguin, 1974.

Tranströmer, Tomas, *Citoyens*. Transl. by Robin Fulton. Knotting: Sceptre Press, 1974.

Tranströmer, Tomas, *Baltics* (*Östersjöar*). Transl. by Samuel Charters.

Berkeley: Oyez, 1975.

Tranströmer, Tomas, *How the Late Autumn Night Novel Begins*. Transl. by Robin Fulton. Knotting: Sceptre Press, 1980.

Tranströmer, Tomas, *Baltics* (*Östersjöar*). Transl. by Robin Fulton. London: Oasis Books, 1980.

Tranströmer, Tomas, *Truth Barriers* (*Sanningsbarriären*). Transl. by Robert Bly. San Francisco: Sierra Club Books, 1980.

Tranströmer, Tomas, *The Truth Barrier* (*Sanningsbarriären*). Transl. by Robin Fulton. London: Oasis, 1984.

Tranströmer, Tomas, *Collected Poems*. Transl. by Robin Fulton. Newcastle-upon-Tyne: Bloodaxe Books, 1988.

Tranströmer, Tomas, *For the Living and the Dead* (*För levande och döda*). Transl. by John F. Deane. Dublin: Dedalus, 1994. (Icarus series, 2).

Tranströmer, Tomas, *New Collected Poems*. Transl. by Robin Fulton. Newcastle-upon-Tyne: Bloodaxe Books, 1997.

Trotzig, Birgitta, 'Diary' (excerpt from *Ett landskap* (*A Landscape*, 1959). Transl. by Roland Hindmarsh in Lars Bäckström and Göran Palm (eds), *Sweden Writes: Contemporary Swedish Poetry and Prose*. Stockholm: Prisma/Swedish Institute, 1965.

Trotzig, Birgitta, 'The Story of Søved Fischer' (excerpt from *De utsatta* (*The Exposed*), 1957). Transl. by Roland Hindmarsh. In *An Anthology of Modern Swedish Literature* (ed. Per Wästberg). New York: Merrick, 1979.

Trotzig, Birgitta, 'Anima'; 'Malady'; 'Brigid of Sweden' (excerpts from *Utkast och förslag*); 'Poetry and Ideology' (from *Jaget och världen*) in *Crosscurrents*, XXXV (1985).

Wahlöö, Per, *The Assignment* (*Updraget*). Transl. by Joan Tate. London: Joseph, 1965.

Wahlöö, Per, *Murder on the 31st Floor* (*Mord på 31:a våningen*). Transl. by Joan Tate. London: Joseph, 1966; Sphere, 1970.

Wahlöö, Per, *The Lorry* (*Lastbilen*). Transl. by Joan Tate. London: Joseph, 1968.

Wahlöö, Per, *The Steel Spring* (*Stålsprånget*). Transl. by Joan Tate. London: Joseph, 1970.

Wahlöö, Per, *The Generals* (*Generalerna*). Transl. by Joan Tate. London: Joseph, 1974.

For translations of Maj Sjöwall's and Per Wahlöö's numerous Martin Beck police stories see Tom Geddes' *Books in English* above.

Werup, Jacques, *The Time in Malmö on the Earth* (*Tiden i Malmö, på jorden*). Transl. by Roger Greenwald. Toronto: Exile Editions, 1989.

Wästberg, Per, *The Air Cage* (*Luftburen*). Transl. by Thomas Teal. London: Souvenir Press, 1977.

Wästberg, Per, *Love's Gravity* (*Jordmånen*). Transl. by Ann Henning. London: Souvenir Press, 1978.

INDEX

(The letters å, ä and ö are taken in Swedish sequence)

Agrell, Alfhild, 22-4
Ahlgren, Ernst, see V. Benedictsson
Ahlin, Lars, 304, 309, 312, 325, 336-40, 357
Alfons, Sven, 190, 304
Almqvist C. J. L., 230
Andersen, Hans Christian, 377
Andersson, Dan, 193
Andersson, Lars, 325
Andrée, Salomon August, 354-6
Anouilh, Jean, 240
Anzengruber, Ludwig, 13
Arnér, Sivar, 309
Aspenström, Werner, 190, 304, 308-9, 312

Babs, Alice, 252
Bach, Johann Sebastian, 236, 398
Balzac, Honoré de, 12, 37, 144, 359
Bang, Herman, 15
Baudelaire, Charles P., 70, 77, 108, 111, 187
Beckett, Samuel, 60
Bellman, Carl Michael, 101, 193-5, 232, 323
Benedictsson, Victoria, 15-16, 21-2, 25-9
9
Berggren, Tobias, 257
Bergman, Bo, 111-2, 116, 187
Bergman, Hjalmar, 137-61, 240, 363
Bergman, Ingmar, 39
Bergström, Sven, 308
Bergwall, Sonja, 304
Bernard, Claude, 10, 13, 395
Björling, Gunnar, 191-2, 236
Bjørnson, Bjørnstjerne, 15, 18, 41
Blake, William, 33, 359
Blomberg, Erik, 174

Blomdahl, Karl-Birger, 222, 240
Bly, Robert, 244, 284
Boccaccio, Giovanni, 317
Bogart, Humphrey, 307
Bosse, Harriet, 39
Boye, Karin, 187, 207-12
Brandes, Georg, 9, 14-6, 19, 21, 26, 28-9, 35, 74, 84
Branting, Hjalmar, 14, 16
Bremer, Fredrika, 402
Brenner, Sophia E., 402
Breton, André, 189, 226
Brezhnev, Leonid I., 327
Browne, Sir Thomas, 64
Brustein, Robert, 33
Buckle, Henry T., 10-1, 16-7, 37
Burman, Carina, 325, 328, 401-03
Burns, Robert, 77
Byron, George Gordon, Lord, 77
Bäckman, Stig, 295
Böök, Fredrik, 122

Caldwell, Erskine P., 306
Camus, Albert, 305, 322
Capone, Al, 221
Carlson, Stig, 256, 275, 308, 312, 316
Carlyle, Thomas, 80, 84
Cederborgh, Fredrik, 151, 156
Charlemagne, 300
Chekhov, Anton, 13
Chopin, Fréderic, 257
Chomsky, Noam, 254-5
Christensén, John, 194
Churchill, Sir Winston, 295
Claudel, Paul, 240
Comte, Auguste, 10-11

Dagerman, Stig, 303-24, 350, 363
Dali, Salvador, 189, 226

Index

Dante, Alighieri, 63, 204
Darwin, Charles, 9, 16-7, 37, 49, 168
Delblanc, Sven, 107, 325-9, 356-63, 375
Dickens, Charles, 12, 33, 37, 39, 40
Diktonius, Elmer, 191-2, 214, 236
Dostoyevsky, Fydor, 358
Drachmann, Holger, 15
Dreyfus, Alfred, 122, 246
Dumas, Alexandre, 293

Edfelt, Johannes, 190
Edgren, Gustaf, 24
Edlund, Mårten, 307-8
Edstam, Gunvor, 195
Ehnmark, Anders, 376
Eichmann, Adolf, 365
Ekelund, Vilhelm, 187-8
Ekelöf, Gunnar, 187, 189, 225-35, 256
Ekman, Gösta, 144
Ekman, Kerstin, 107, 325, 328-9, 388-95
Eliot, T. S., 35, 36, 39, 226, 240, 261
Ellerström, Lars, 260
Elster, Kristian, 15
Emerson, Ralph Waldo, 359
Enckell, Rabbe, 191-2, 236
Eriks, Gustaf Rune, 307, 312
Espmark, Kjell, 223, 261
Essen, Siri von, 24, 41
Euripides, 363, 376
Evander, Per Gunnar, 325

Falck, August, 42
Farrell, James T., 306
Faulkner, William, 236
Ferlin, Nils, 193, 195
Ferlinghetti, Lawerence, 252-3
Fersen, Axel von, 251
Forssell Lars, 190-91
Fraenkel, Knut, 354-5
Freud, Sigmund, 46, 208, 233, 314
Fridegård, Jan, 282
Frostenson, Kristina, 259-61

Fröding, Gustaf, 74, 77, 91-9, 107, 111, 193
Furuland, Lars, 277

Garborg, Arne, 15
Gardell, Jonas, 225, 403-6
Gaulle, C. de, 327
Geijerstam, Gustaf af, 16, 19
Gide, André, 246, 288-9
Gjellerup, Karl, 15
Goebbels, Joseph, 295
Goering, Hermann, 295
Goethe, J. W. von, 36, 77-8, 82-4, 135, 144, 246
Gogol, Nikolay V., 244
Goldwyn, Samuel, 142
Goncourt, Edmond de and Jules de, 12
Gozzoli, B., 144
Grandinson, Emil, 42
Greene, Graham, 236
Gullberg, Hjalmar, 187, 190, 199-205, 209
Gyllensten, Lars, 325, 329-37, 340
Göthberg, Lennart, 304, 308-10

Hammarskjöld, Dag, 326
Hamsun, Knut, 77, 288
Hansson, Ola, 16, 20-21
Hansson, Per Albin, 272, 371
Hardy, Thomas, 77
Hartmann, Eduard v., 11
Hauptmann, Gerhart, 13
Haydn, Joseph, 247
Hazelius, Artur, 76
Hedberg, Tor, 16, 19-20
Hedenvind-Ericsson, Gustav, 137
Hedin, Sven, 354, 398
Hegel, G. W. F., 37
Heiberg, J. L., 377
Heidenstam, Verner von, 22, 74-83, 105-6, 111, 282, 381
Heine, Heinrich, 97
Hellström, Gustav, 138
Hemingway, Ernest, 306, 323, 351
Hess, Rudolf, 370

Index

Hill, Joe, 279, 389
Himmler, Heinrich, 295
Hitler, Adolf, 177, 305, 331
Hobbes, Thomas, 362
Homer, 291-2, 296, 363
Hoogland, Claes, 308
Huxley, Aldous, 297
Huysmans, Joris-Karl, 13, 110
Håkanson, Björn, 250
Hörnström, Erik, 167

Ibsen, Henrik, 14-18, 22-3, 29, 38-54

Jacobsen, J. P., 15, 20
Jansson, Tove, 125-6, 329
Jersild, P.C., 325, 363-9
Jonason, Olov, 304, 308
Johnson, Eyvind, 137, 225, 263-6, 287-302, 304, 312, 326, 345, 370, 394
Jonsson, Thorsten, 306, 373
Joyce, James, 72, 229, 232, 288-9
Jæger, Hans, 15
Jørgensen, Johannes, 29, 77

Kafka, Franz, 109, 242, 306, 310, 3-6-22
Kallifatides, Theodor, 328
Kant, Immanuel, 78, 203
Karlfeldt, Erik Axel, 75, 77, 100-06, 111, 167, 193
Keats, John, 239
Kellgren, Johan Henrik, 402
Key, Ellen, 139, 145
Kielland, Alexander, 15
Kierkegaard, Søren, 37, 66, 336, 361
Kipling, Rudyard, 86
Kjellgren, Josef, 264
Kléen, Emil, 111, 117
Koch, Martin, 137, 264
Koestler, Arthur, 310
Krohg, Christian, 111
Kämpe, Alfred, 264
Kärnell, Karl-Åke, 70

Lagerkvist, Pär, 129, 162-88, 264
Lagerlöf, Selma, 74-7, 80, 83-92, 97, 106, 111, 391, 395
Lagerström, Bertil, 307
Lamm, Martin, 37
Larsson, Carl, 76
Larsson, Hans, 145, 148, 160
Larsson, Leon, 264
Larsson, Staffan, 195, 199
Lassalle, Ferdinand, 12
Leffler-Edgren, Anne Charlotte, 16, 22, 23-25
Levertin, Oscar, 16, 74, 78, 83, 105, 111, 122
Lidman, Sara, 107, 325-9, 341-9, 375
Lidman, Sven, 138
Lie, Jonas, 15
Liffner, Axel, 304, 308, 311
Lindberg, August, 139
Lindberg, Stina, 139
Lindcrantz, Ingrid, 217
Lindegren, Erik, 187-90, 222, 225, 236-41, 256, 304, 309, 311-12
Lindgren, Astrid, 329
Lindgren, Torgny, 107, 325, 378-88
Lindqvist, Sven,326
Linnér, Sven, 171
Lo-Johansson, Ivar, 137, 263-5, 276-87, 302
Lucidor (Johansson, Lars), 193
Lugn, Kristina, 259-60
Lundegård, Axel, 16, 21-22, 25
Lundkvist, Artur, 137, 189-90, 236, 257, 261, 306-08
Lustine, Karin, 194-5

Maeterlinck, Maurice, 37, 39, 42, 140
Malmberg, Bertil, 190
Mann, Thomas, 64
Mao Tse-Tung, 326
Marcus, C. D., 137
Martinson, Harry, 137, 187, 189, 212-225, 240, 263, 265
Martinson, Moa, 265, 282
Marx, Karl, 12, 19, 337

Maupassant, Guy de, 13
Mendelssohn, Felix, 69
Mesmer, Anton, 370
Mesterton, Erik, 207
Mill, John Stuart, 12, 14, 18, 44
Moberg, Vilhelm, 263, 265-76, 294, 302, 312
Mozart, Wolfgang Amadeus, 255
Myrdal, Jan, 326

Nabokov, Vladimir, 44
Nansen, Fridtjof, 354
Nietzsche, Friedrich, 11, 22, 29, 37, 49, 60, 74, 80, 291
Nijinsky, Vaslav, 191
Nisser, Peter, 308
Nobel, Alfred, 87, 89, 144, 180, 223, 225, 302, 328, 354, 362, 366, 291
Nordenskiöld, N.A.E., 354
Nordström, Ludvig, 138
Norlind, Ernst, 194
Nyblom, Carl Rupert, 14

O'Casey, Sean, 236
Oehlenschläger, Adam, 37
Ohlson, Barbro, 199
Ollén, Gunnar, 65-6

Palm, Göran, 191, 249-51, 258
Perse, St. John, 240
Peterson, August, 195
Peterson-Berger, Wilhelm, 76
Petri, Olaus, 17
Pirandello, Luigi, 42
Plath, Sylvia, 258
Plato, 359
Pleijel, Agneta, 243, 325
Poe, Edgar Alan, 77, 97, 267
Pontoppidan, Henrik, 15, 20
Proust, Marcel 288

Racine, Jean, 376
Ranelid, Björn, 323
Renan, Ernest, 10

Richards, I. A., 35
Richelieu, Cardinal, 297-8
Rilke, Rainer Maria, 240
Rimbaud, Jean Arthur, 227, 232
Rogberg, Martin, 307
Rousseau, Jean-Jacques, 18, 20, 37, 46, 76
Ruhe, Algot, 148
Runeberg, Johan Ludvig, 80-4
Rydberg, Viktor, 10
Rådström, Per, 304

Sachs, Nelly, 240
St John of the Cross, 201
Saint-John Perse, 240
Sandberg, Hans, 321
Sandel, Maria, 264
Sansom, William, 310
Saroyan, William, 306
Sartre, Jean Paul, 305, 310, 322
Schandorph, Sophus, 15
Schnitzler, Arthur, 110
Schopenhauer, Arthur, 11, 37, 76-7, 272, 386
Scott, Sir Walter, 77, 80
Sexton, Anne, 74, 258
Shakespeare, William, 33-9, 49, 59, 66
Siwertz, Sigrid, 108, 111, 138
Sjöberg, Birger, 187-8, 193-9, 202, 206
Sjögren, Lennart, 258
Sjöstrand, Östen, 190
Sjöwall, Maj, 329
Skram, Amalie, 15
Smith, Lars Olsson, 380
Sonnevi, Göran, 187, 253-5
Spencer, Herbert, 37
Spender, Stephen, 240
Stagnelius, Erik J., 228
Stalin, Josef, 326, 331
Steinbeck, John, 306
Sten, John, 65
Stenhammar, Wilhelm, 76
Stravinsky, Igor, 227, 236, 239

Index

Strindberg, Johan August, 9-24, 29, 31-82, 135, 139, 163, 168-9, 264, 268, 282, 359, 374-5
Ström, Eva. 259, 347
Sudermann, Hermann, 13
Sundman, Per Olof, 325, 349-56
Swedenborg, Emanuel, 29, 37, 60, 62, 70-1, 232, 359
Swinburne, Algernon, 77
Söderberg, Hjalmar, 29, 108-36
Södergran, Edith, 191-2, 232

Taine, Hippolyte, 10-17
Taube, Evert, 193, 195
Tegnér, Esaias, 80, 84
Thomas, Dylan, 240
Thomas à Kempis, 201
Thoursie, Ragnar, 190, 304
Tideström, Gunnar, 198
Trilling, Lionel, 49
Tolstoy, Alexey K., 13
Topelius, Zachris, 80
Tranströmer, Tomas, 187-8, 244-8
Troell, Jan, 275
Trotzig, Birgitta,
Tunström, Göran, 95, 243, 325
Turgenev, Ivan S., 12

Ulvenstam, Lars, 219

Valéry, Paul, 236
Vennberg, Karl, 187, 190, 240-3, 260, 304, 308-12
Verne, Jules, 355, 377

Wagner, Richard, 22
Wahlöö, Per, 329
Wilde, Oscar, 110
Wirsén, Carl David af, 14
Witt-Brattström, Ebba, 265
Wordsworth, William, 46-7
Wrede, Johan, 220-2
Wägner, Elin, 138, 391, 394
Wästberg, Per, 326

Xenophon, 293, 299

Yeats, William Butler, 33

Zola, Emile, 13, 29, 37, 45, 51, 54, 60
Zorn, Anders, 76, 101

Åkesson, Sonja, 253